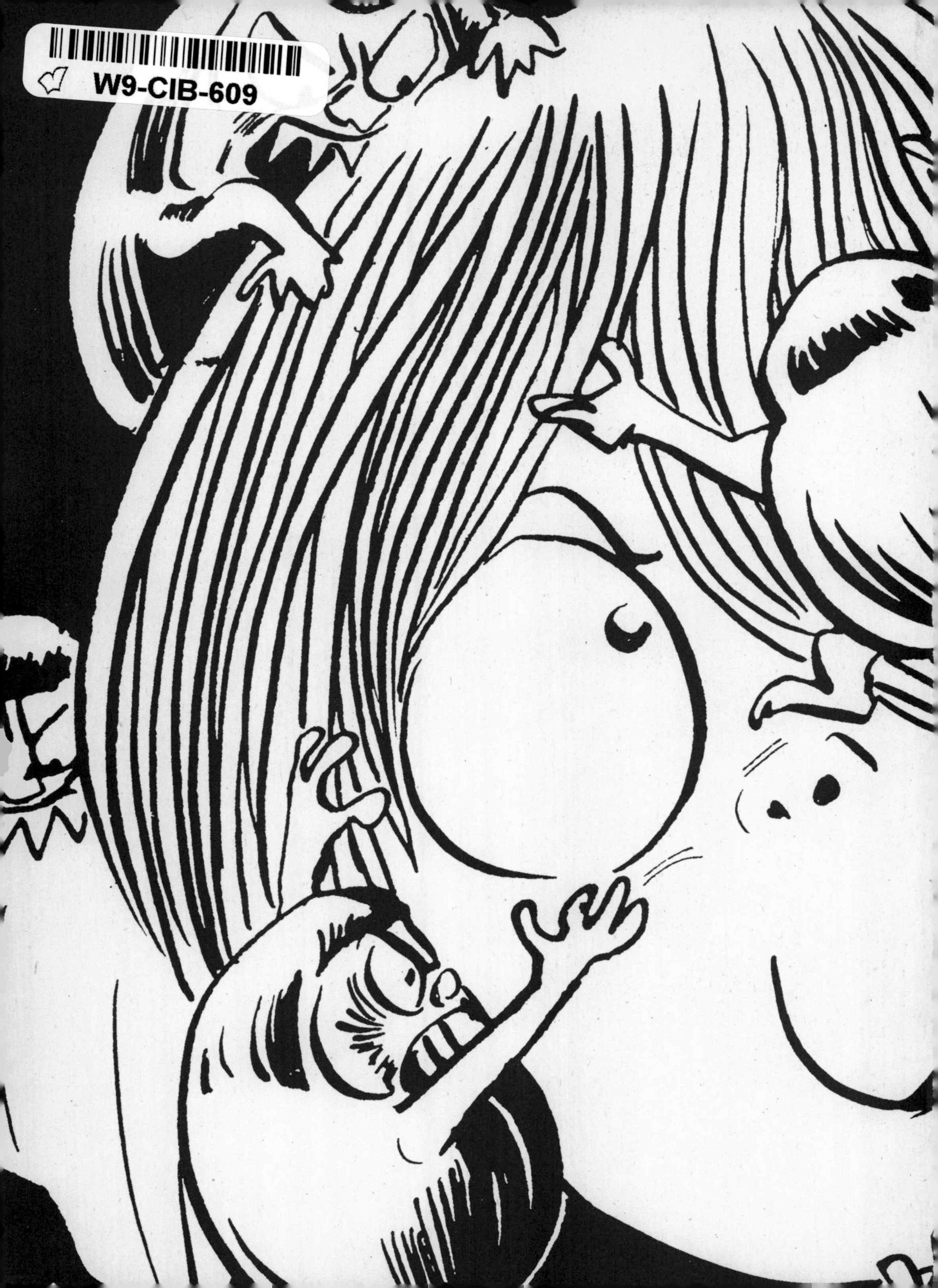

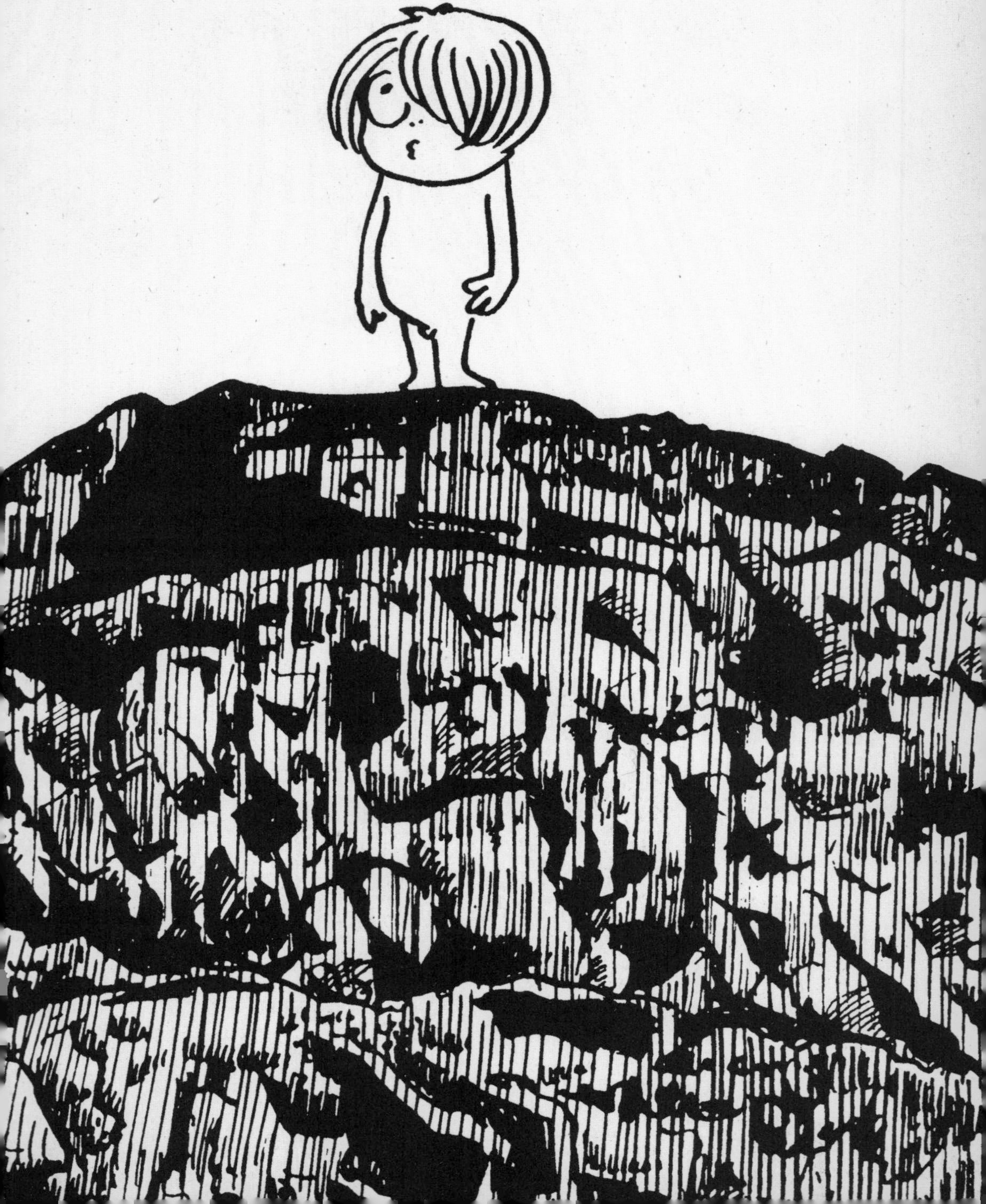

KiTARO

SHIGERU MIZUKI

Drawn & Quarterly

ALSO BY SHIGERU MIZUKI
Onward Towards Our Noble Deaths (2011)
Nonnonba (2012)

Story and art copyright © 2013 Shigeru Mizuki/Mizuki Productions. Foreword copyright © 2013 Matt Alt. Yokai Glossary copyright © 2013 Zack Davisson. Translation copyright © 2013 Jocelyne Allen. This edition copyright © 2013 Drawn & Quarterly. Edited by Malcolm Macrae-Gibson and Tom Devlin. Story selection by Maki Hakui. All rights reserved. No part of this book (except small portions for review purposes) may be reproduced in any form without written permission from Shigeru Mizuki/Mizuki Productions or Drawn & Quarterly. Font design: Kevin Huizenga. Drawn & Quarterly acknowledges the financial contribution of the Government of Canada through the Canada Book Fund for our publishing activities and for support of this edition. Drawn & Quarterly also gratefully acknowledges Presspop Inc. and Maki Hakui for their invaluable assistance with the publication of this book.

www.drawnandquarterly.com.

First softcover edition: July 2013. Printed in Canada.

Library and Archives Canada Cataloguing in Publication. Mizuki, Shigeru, 1922-. *Kitaro* / Shigeru Mizuki; translation by Jocelyne Allen. Translated from the Japanese. ISBN 978-1-77046-110-9 1. Graphic novels. I. Title PN6790.J33M5613 2013. 741.5'952. C2012-905366-X.

Published in the USA by Drawn & Quarterly, a client publisher of Farrar, Straus and Giroux; Orders: 888.330.8477. Published in Canada by Drawn & Quarterly, a client publisher of Raincoast Books; Orders: 800.663.5714. Published in the United Kingdom by Drawn & Quarterly, a client publisher of Publishers Group UK; Orders: info@pguk.co.uk.

INTRODUCTION MATT ALT

Ge Ge Ge no Kitaro is quite possibly the single most famous Japanese manga series you've never heard of, even if you happen to be a manga fan. Which is a shame, because Kitaro's uncanny pulse beats beneath the surface of Japanese pop culture like a tell-tale heart.

Kitaro is heir to a vast cultural tradition that is intimately familiar to Japanese, and all but unknown in the West: the *yokai*, mythological shape-shifters and monsters that have populated Japanese folktales since time immemorial. They are the things that go bump in Japan's night.

Fittingly for such a group of fluidly changing creatures, a strict definition of yokai is maddeningly difficult to pin down. Over the years many translations have been floated: "monster," "ghost," "demon," "goblin" and more, but none of these quite cut it, as they're saddled with their own Western cultural baggage. Yokai are yokai — just like sashimi is sashimi, not "cold raw fish."

So what, then, exactly is a yokai?

Legend says the islands of Japan are home to some eight million gods. These multitudes aren't like the monolithic Capital-G-God of Judeo-Christian tradition. In Japan's traditional animistic, polytheistic beliefs, almost anything can harbor a spirit, not just humans but animals, plants, even inanimate objects. Even the very terrain itself.

Some gods are benevolent creators and protectors; others are angry spirits in need of appeasement. There are greater and lesser, stronger and weaker deities; there's even, as a recent pop song goes, a God of the Toilet.

The yokai fall somewhere along this vast continuum of deities. Unlike holy gods of the high heavens, they actually inhabit our physical world, yet they aren't precisely of it. Some are humanoid or animal-like. Others are the faces behind inexplicable natural phenomena, superstitions personified. More than a few are what we might call "haunted" objects, everyday tools and things taken uncanny sentient form. Some are dangerous, some indifferent, some simply mischievous, a few even benevolent, but to a one they're inherently unpredictable, utterly beyond human control, and thus deserving of respect.

While Mizuki wasn't the first artist to attempt drawing the visual appearances of the various yokai, he is arguably the best and indisputably the most popular. Having dominated the field for close to fifty years, generations of children have been raised on his manga and anime. If you ask the average Japanese to describe a yokai, chances are one of Mizuki's portrayals will spring to mind. And the reason why is simple: Kitaro.

Kitaro is the glue that holds a nation's worth of disassociated folk characters together. Being based in the oral tradition, yokai tales are a mix-and-match patchwork of local legends from across Japan. Mizuki's genius was devising a way to tie all of these unconnected stories together into a single narrative, transforming the yokai from terrors of the night into a force for justice. Without Mizuki's creations of Kitaro, his father, Medama Oyaji, and Nezumi Otoko, we'd be adrift in the world of the yokai.

What separates Mizuki from the average horror manga artist is his long familiarity with his nation's folktales. He was weaned on them in the Japanese countryside in his youth, and continued to collect and study them throughout his life (in addition to his manga, Mizuki has also published numerous illustrated "yokai encyclopedias" that catalog regional folk beliefs.) Mizuki's success was due in no small part to his knowledge of and affection for three key artists that preceded him: Sekien Toriyama, Lafcadio Hearn, and Kunio Yanagita.

Although it seems the yokai have always haunted Japan, their first heyday came at the turn of the 19th century thanks to the artist Sekien Toriyama. In 1776, Toriyama penned and published the first visual guide to the yokai, called *Gazu Hyakki Yako*, (or *The Illustrated Demons' Night-Parade*) which featured profiles of more than fifty yokai. Sekien's portrayals represented the first time many of the yokai described in folklore had ever been illustrated. His tongue-in-cheek approach interwove both traditional monsters and ones he invented as social satire. It proved so popular that it spawned three sequels, making the series one of the proto-blockbusters of early Japanese pop culture — and a direct forerunner of modern manga.

A little over a century later in 1868, Japanese ports opened to the world, ending two hundred years of isolation and ushering in a wave of foreign interest that came to be called "Japonism." Japanese porcelain, scroll paintings, and woodblock prints inspired the likes of Toulouse-Lautrec, Renoir, Degas, and Whistler; Van Gogh even took a stab at copying a Japanese painting with a brush and oils. Along with the art came stories and literature. At the turn of the 20th century, a transplanted American journalist by the name of Lafcadio Hearn toured the Japanese countryside with his wife and interpreter Setsuko Koizumi, compiling superstitions, ghost stories, and folktales from all over Japan. The resulting series of English-language books represented the first time many of these stories had ever been committed to paper in any language. Translated back into Japanese shortly after Hearn's death in 1905, they sparked a renewed interest in tales of the macabre among locals.

Among them was a government bureaucrat turned writer, Kunio Yanagita, who began compiling folktales of his own during business trips to far-flung Japanese locales. His 1910 *Tales of Tono*, which described the supernatural legends of the isolated northern village of the same name, proved a critical hit and almost singlehandedly established the field of *minzoku-gaku*: Japanese folklore studies.

After losing his left arm on the Pacific battlefields of World War II, young Mizuki returned to Japan and found employment as an illustrator for *kashi-bon* rental comics and *kami-shibai* — narrated "paper-card dramas" presented to kids by traveling peddlers in the era before television. In spite of the enjoyment the finished products brought children, it was a brutal industry for the artists who actually created the content. Mizuki spent many years struggling to feed his family on his meager earnings — when he even got paid at all.

In 1954, his publisher asked him to revive a once-popular kami-shibai series called *Hakaba no Kitaro*, or *Graveyard Kitaro*. Taking inspiration from the illustrations of Toriyama and the stories of Hearn and Yanagita, and weaving in the folktales he had heard growing up in the countryside, Mizuki expanded and refined Hakaba no Kitaro into a dark series of horror stories, but failed to find a mainstream audience.

However, major change was afoot. By the late Fifties, kashi-bon and kami-shibai publishers were squeezed out of business by what came to be called manga. These thick compilations of comic serials were sold on newsstands every single week — and unlike their haphazardly managed predecessors, they promised a steady wage for those hardy few able to keep pace with the unrelenting publishing schedule. Mizuki rose to the challenge, getting his foot in the door with a 1961 series called *Kappa no Sanpei* (*Sanpei the Kappa*), followed by the even more successful *Akuma-Kun* (*Devil Boy*). In 1965, the weeklies' insatiable demand for new work finally landed *Graveyard Kitaro* a spot in the popular manga magazine *Weekly Shonen Sunday*.

Even still, Graveyard Kitaro struggled to find its audience. Mizuki unsuccessfully shopped the manga around to various studios in an attempt to land an animation deal. Finally, a producer friend suggested that he change the title. There were already some concerns that yokai were too grotesque of a topic for children. And "graveyard" was too macabre of a word for sponsors, who didn't want to see their products associated with a symbol of death.

Mizuki again turned towards his childhood to solve the problem. At a very young age, a predilection for lisping his given name as "Gegeru" instead of the proper "Shigeru" had earned him the nickname "Ge-ge." The nonsensical phrase also happened to echo the traditional Japanese expression of disgust ("Ge!") and the croaking of toads, a classic familiar of the yokai.

The serendipitous trifecta allowed Mizuki to surreptitiously (and undoubtedly a little mischievously) inject himself directly into the mix. Re-christening the series *Ge Ge Ge no Kitaro* in 1967, he also subtly shifted the concept from horror to superhero, with Kitaro and his "good" yokai family standing between humanity and "bad" yokai.

The new formula clicked. Fan letters, the mark by which manga magazines measured the success of a series, poured in. Mizuki made folktales cool by re-contextualizing them in modern, often urban, settings. While kids grooved to the spectacle of yokai slugging it out with giant robots in downtown Tokyo, a subtle counter-cultural commentary emerged in references to Vietnam, foolish adult authority figures, and perhaps most importantly, the consistent failure of violent solutions to problems — a legacy of his own wartime experience.

In 1968, the animated *Ge Ge Ge no Kitaro* television series debuted to instant success. Whatever the sponsors' misgivings about graveyards and monsters, they certainly didn't seem to be shared by the children of Japan. *Ge Ge Ge no Kitaro* continued to be serialized in various forms for the next half-century, spawning no less than half a dozen animated and live-action television series, well over a dozen video games, two live-action films, and most recently, the popular *Ge Ge Ge Wife*, a 2010 prime-time TV drama chronicling the struggles of Mizuki's long-suffering spouse before his rise to fame. Capping it all off, in 2011 the airport near Mizuki's childhood home renamed itself Yonago Kitaro Airport in his honor.

Mizuki's legacy lives on today not only through his own continuing works but their influence on countless others. Kitaro's family of friendly monsters is an obvious predecessor of the ever-popular Pokémon, for example. And in the wake of environmental disasters like that of the Fukushima Nuclear Power Plant, Kitaro's admonishment of humankind's hubris and over-dependence on technology seems if anything more relevant today than when first put to paper.

It is a testament to Mizuki's skill that his name has become virtually synonymous with yokai in Japan, to the point where even Japanese mistake many yokai for his personal creations. There is no question that the transformation of yokai from terrifying beasts of legend into approachable — and merchandisable — modern characters is almost entirely due to Mizuki's handiwork. Yet in spite of his significant achievements precious few of his manga have ever made it into the English language.

The stories contained in this collection hail from the 1967-1969 timeframe and are revered as classics by Japanese *Ge Ge Ge no Kitaro* fans. It gives me great pleasure to see them — and Japan's yokai -- get the international recognition they have long deserved.

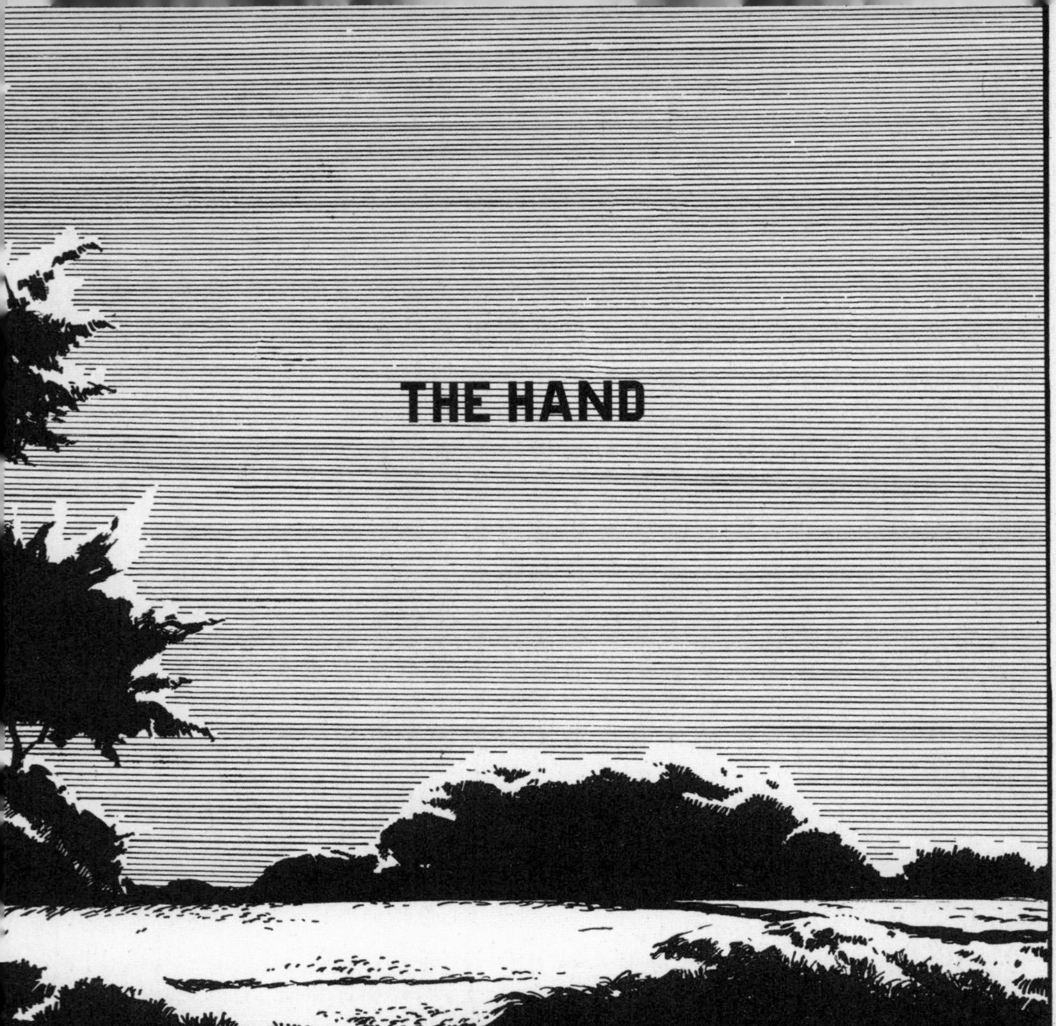
THE HAND

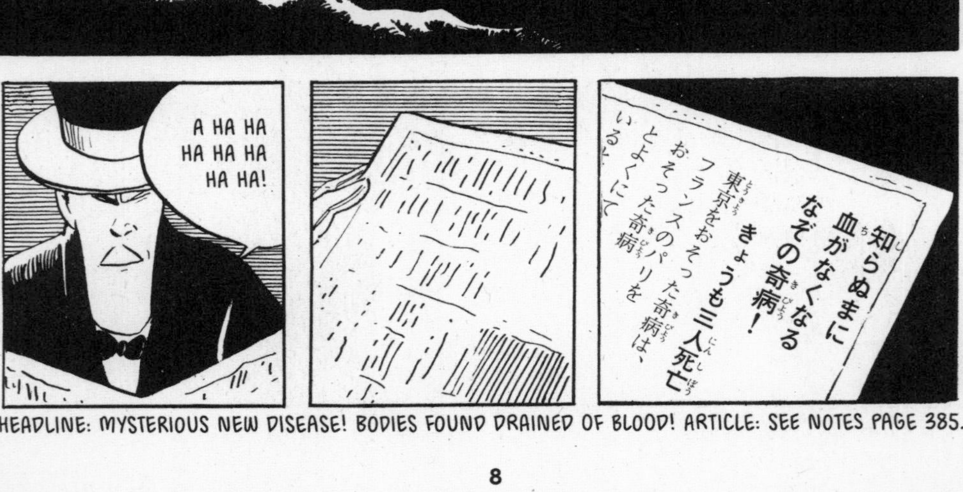
知らぬまに
血がなくなる
なぞの奇病！
きょうも三人死亡
東京をおそった奇病は、
フランスのパリを
おそった奇病
とよくにて
いる
A HA HA
HA HA HA
HA HA!

HEADLINE: MYSTERIOUS NEW DISEASE! BODIES FOUND DRAINED OF BLOOD! ARTICLE: SEE NOTES PAGE 385.

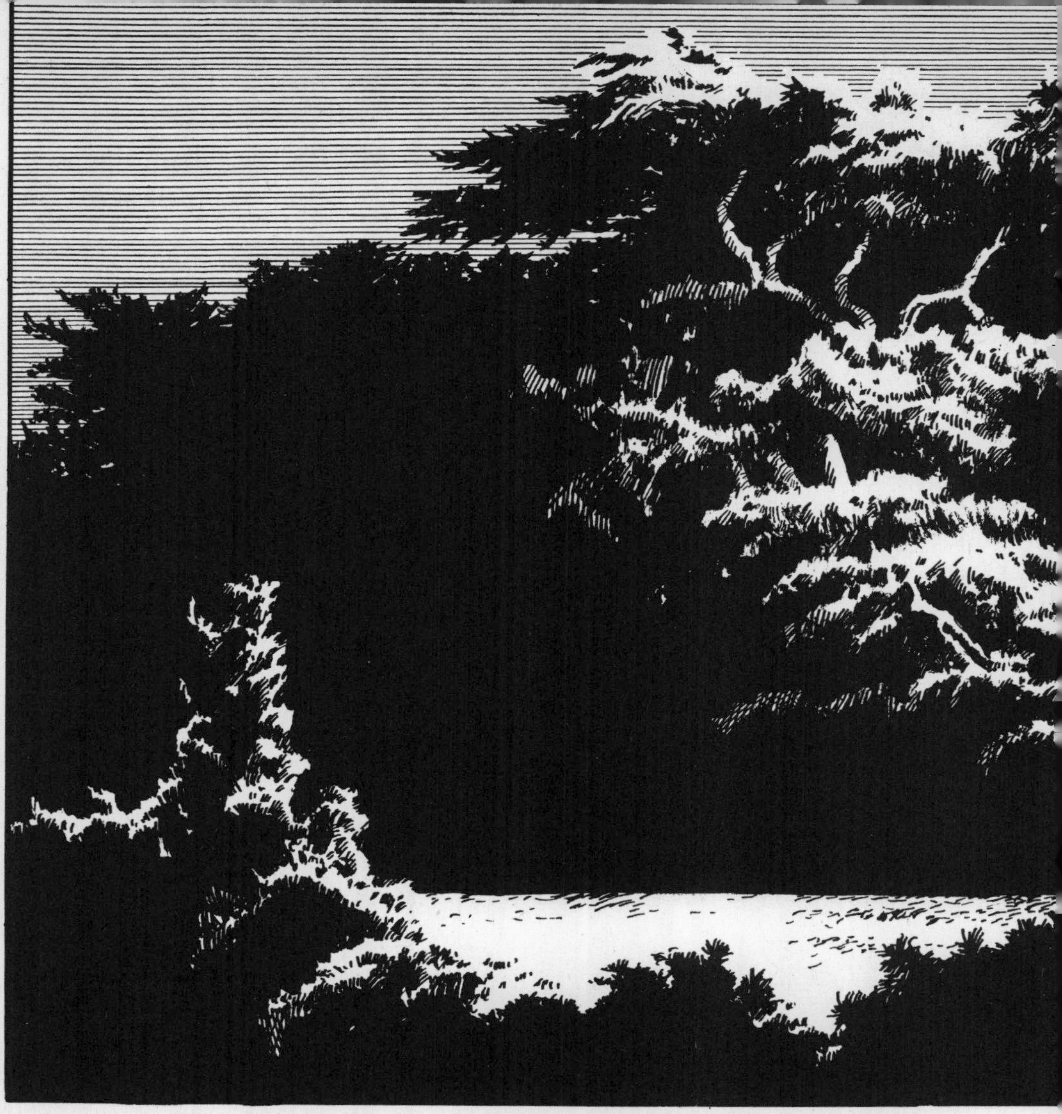

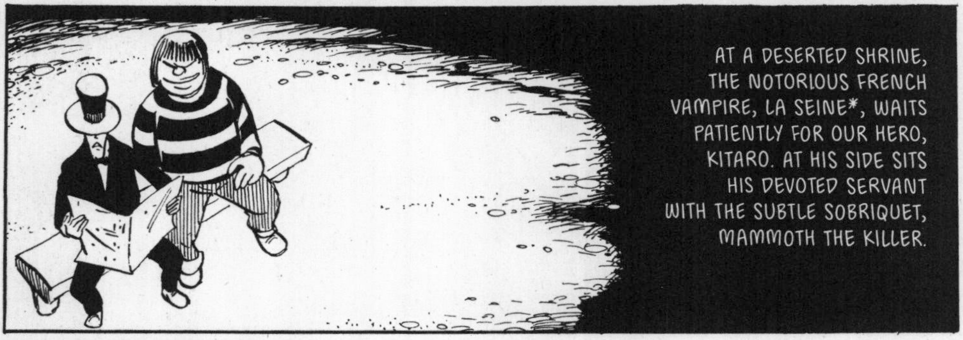
AT A DESERTED SHRINE, THE NOTORIOUS FRENCH VAMPIRE, LA SEINE*, WAITS PATIENTLY FOR OUR HERO, KITARO. AT HIS SIDE SITS HIS DEVOTED SERVANT WITH THE SUBTLE SOBRIQUET, MAMMOTH THE KILLER.

*SEE YOKAI GLOSSARY PAGE 389.

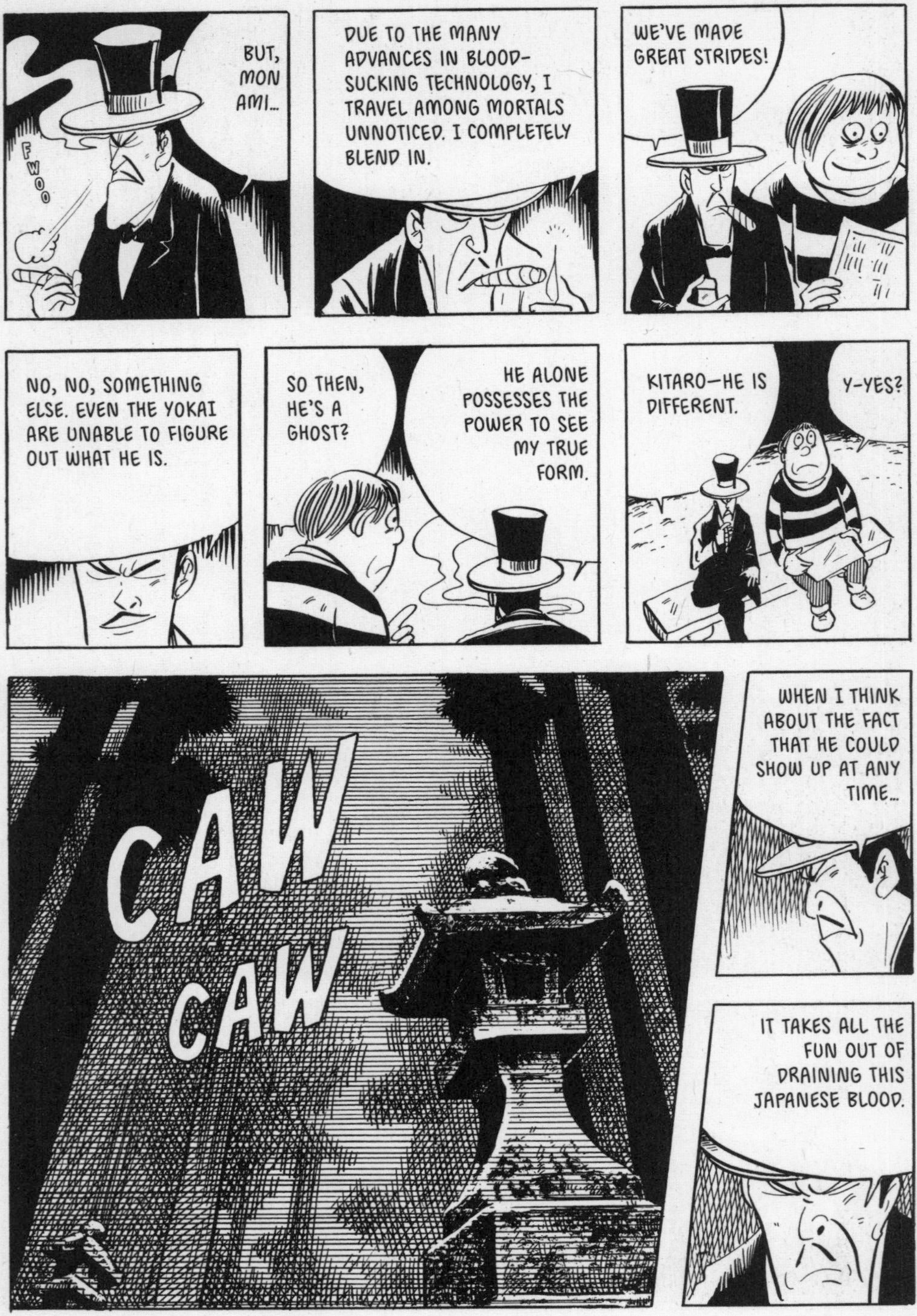
WE'VE MADE GREAT STRIDES!
DUE TO THE MANY ADVANCES IN BLOOD-SUCKING TECHNOLOGY, I TRAVEL AMONG MORTALS UNNOTICED. I COMPLETELY BLEND IN.
BUT, MON AMI...
FWOO
Y-YES?
KITARO—HE IS DIFFERENT.
HE ALONE POSSESSES THE POWER TO SEE MY TRUE FORM.
SO THEN, HE'S A GHOST?
NO, NO, SOMETHING ELSE. EVEN THE YOKAI ARE UNABLE TO FIGURE OUT WHAT HE IS.
WHEN I THINK ABOUT THE FACT THAT HE COULD SHOW UP AT ANY TIME...
IT TAKES ALL THE FUN OUT OF DRAINING THIS JAPANESE BLOOD.
CAW
CAW

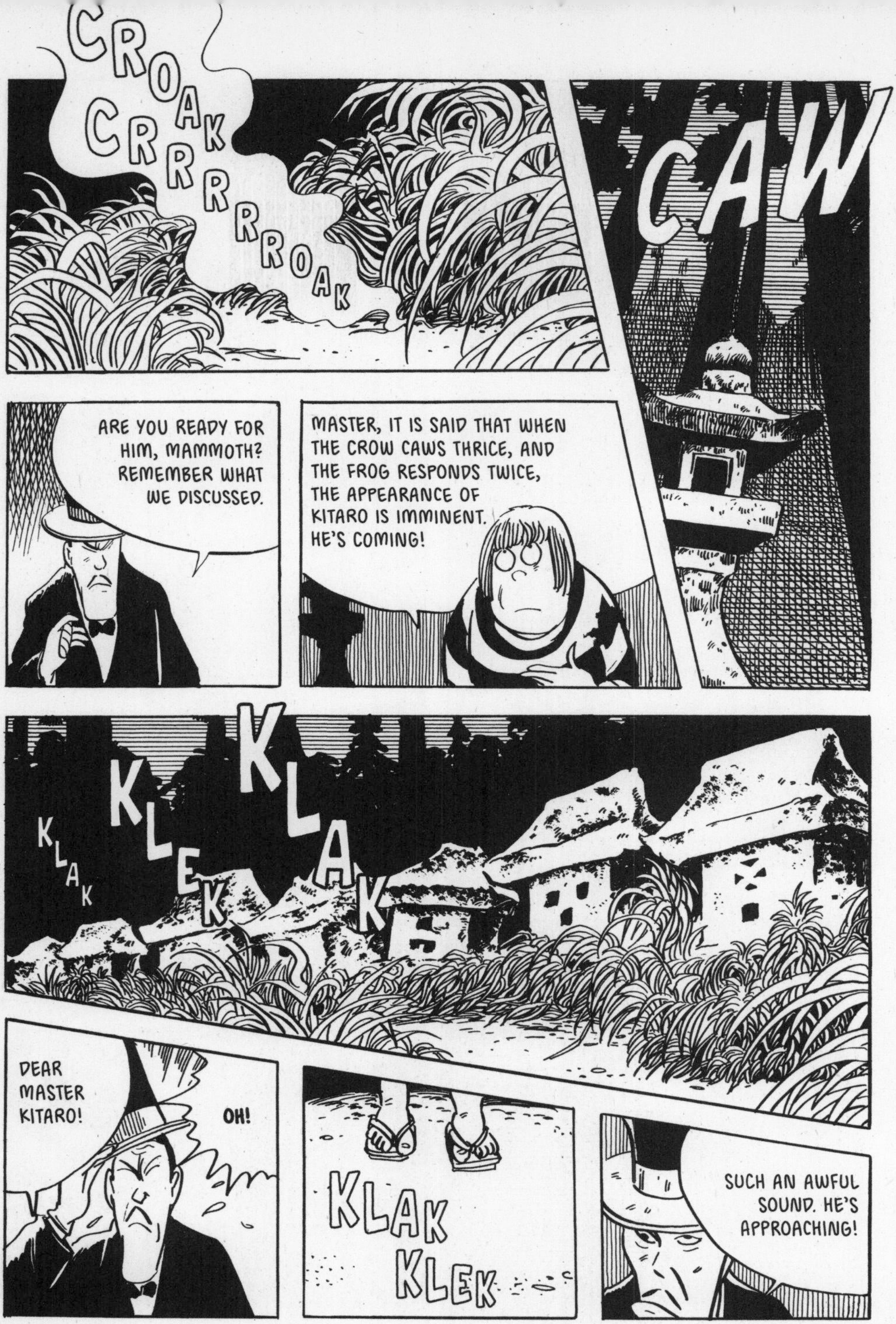
CAW
CROAK
CRRRRROAK
MASTER, IT IS SAID THAT WHEN THE CROW CAWS THRICE, AND THE FROG RESPONDS TWICE, THE APPEARANCE OF KITARO IS IMMINENT. HE'S COMING!
ARE YOU READY FOR HIM, MAMMOTH? REMEMBER WHAT WE DISCUSSED.
KLAK
KLEK
KLAK
SUCH AN AWFUL SOUND. HE'S APPROACHING!
KLAK
KLEK
OH!
DEAR MASTER KITARO!

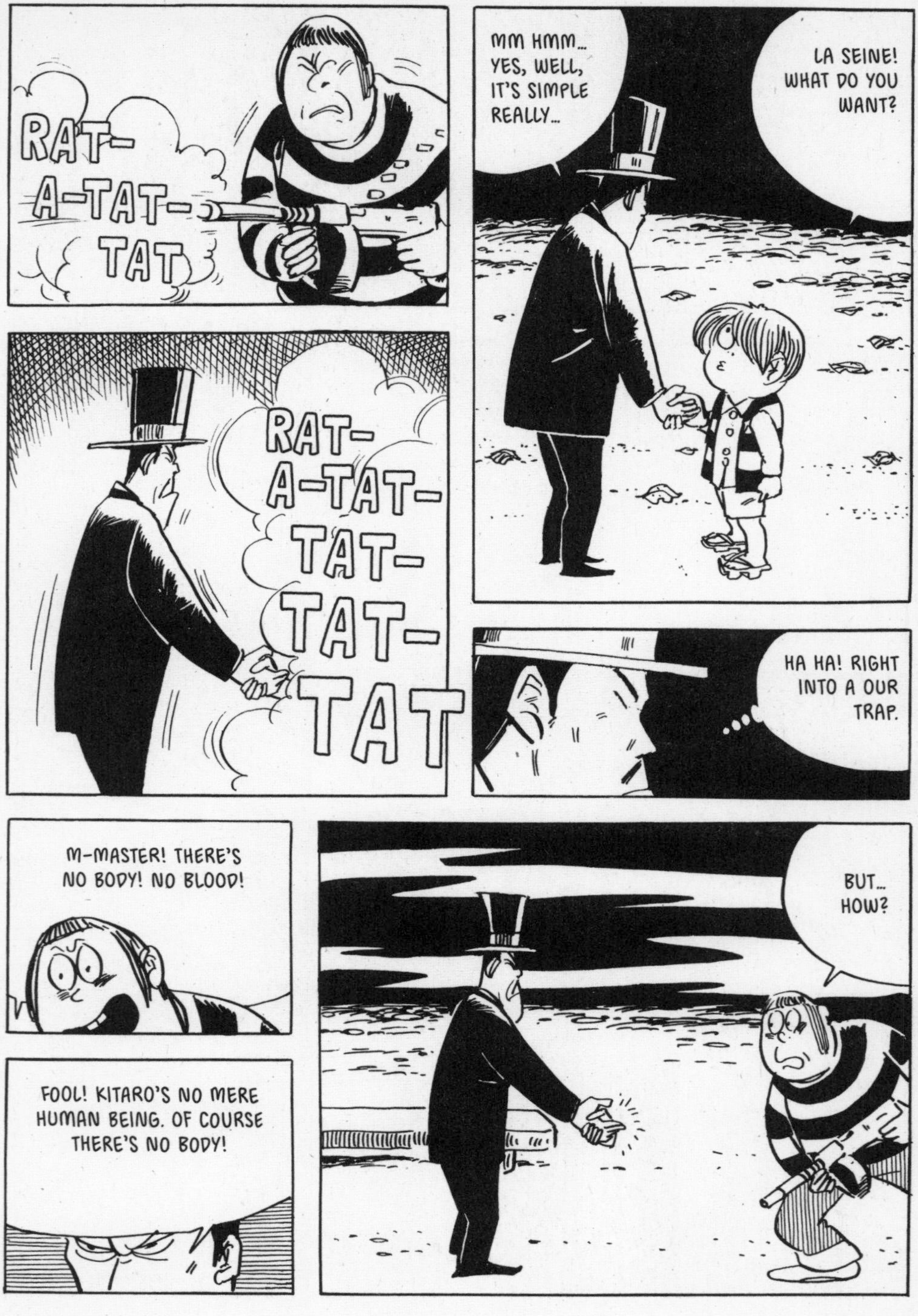
LA SEINE! WHAT DO YOU WANT?
MM HMM... YES, WELL, IT'S SIMPLE REALLY...
HA HA! RIGHT INTO A OUR TRAP.
RAT-A-TAT-TAT
RAT-A-TAT-TAT-TAT-TAT
BUT... HOW?
M-MASTER! THERE'S NO BODY! NO BLOOD!
FOOL! KITARO'S NO MERE HUMAN BEING. OF COURSE THERE'S NO BODY!

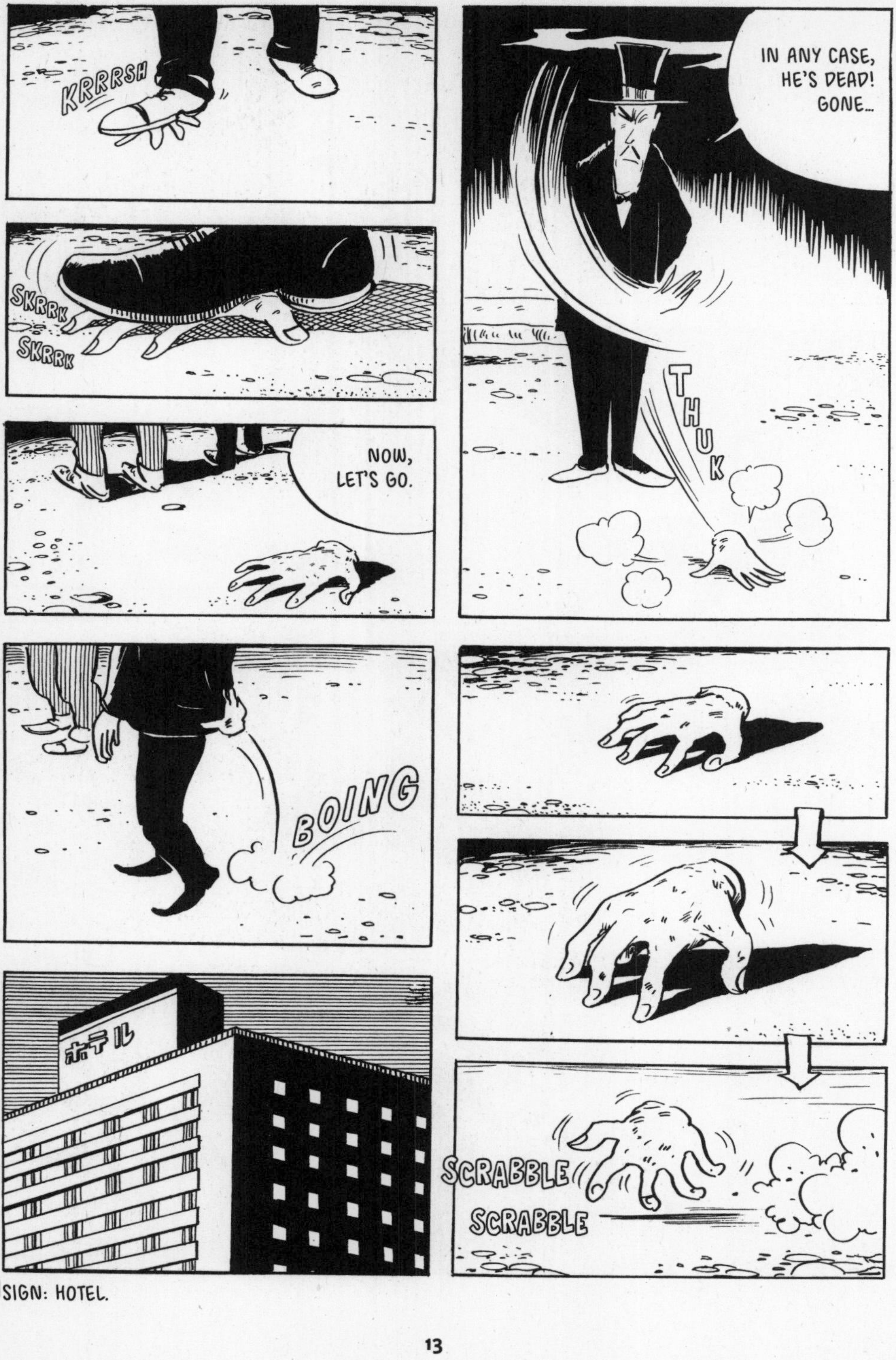
IN ANY CASE, HE'S DEAD! GONE...
THUK
KRRRSH
SKRRK
SKRRK
NOW, LET'S GO.
SCRABBLE
SCRABBLE
BOING
ホテル

SIGN: HOTEL.

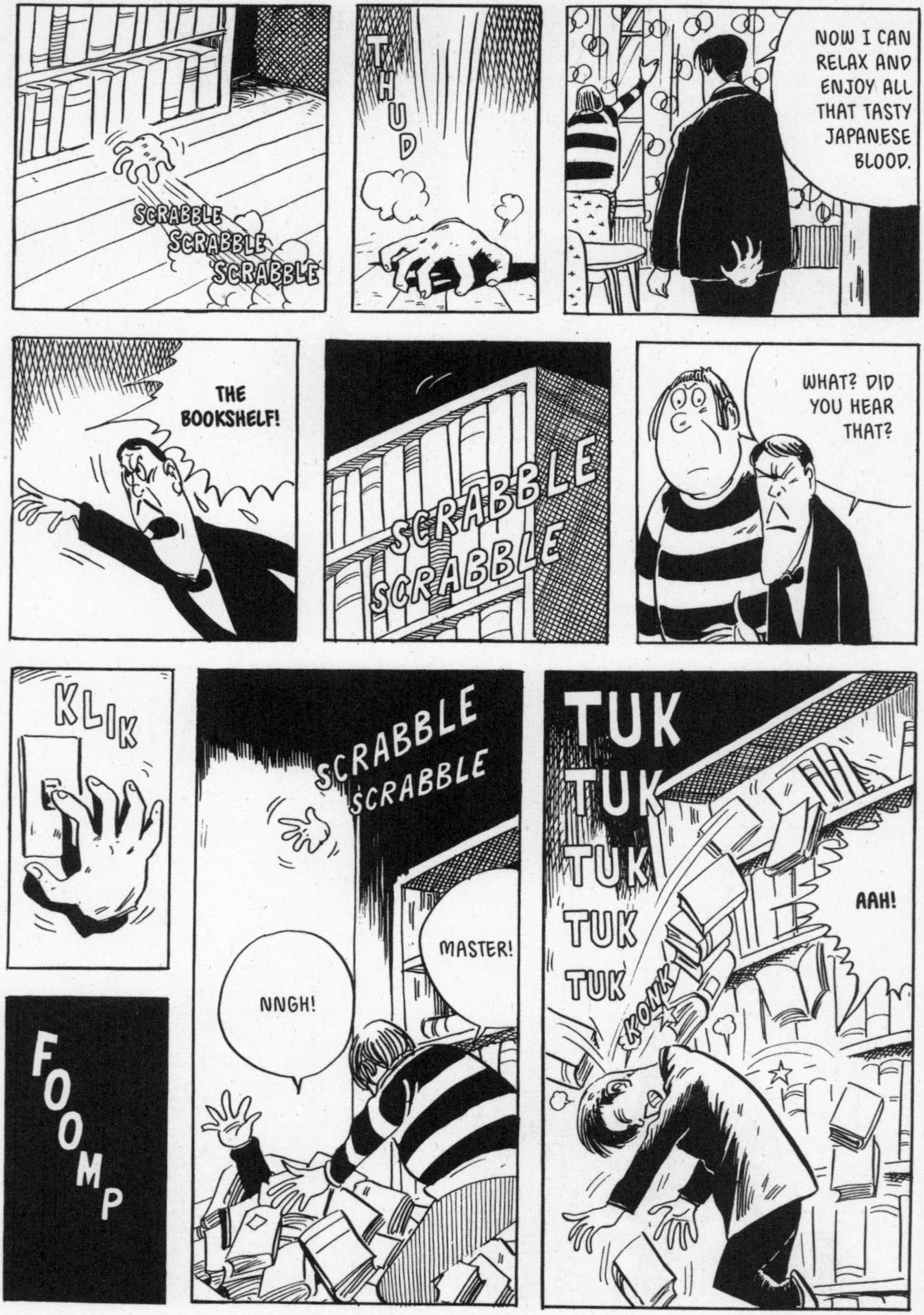
NOW I CAN RELAX AND ENJOY ALL THAT TASTY JAPANESE BLOOD.
THUD
SCRABBLE
SCRABBLE
SCRABBLE
WHAT? DID YOU HEAR THAT?
SCRABBLE
SCRABBLE
THE BOOKSHELF!
TUK
TUK
TUK
TUK
TUK
AAH!
KONK
SCRABBLE
SCRABBLE
MASTER!
NNGH!
KLIK
FOOMP

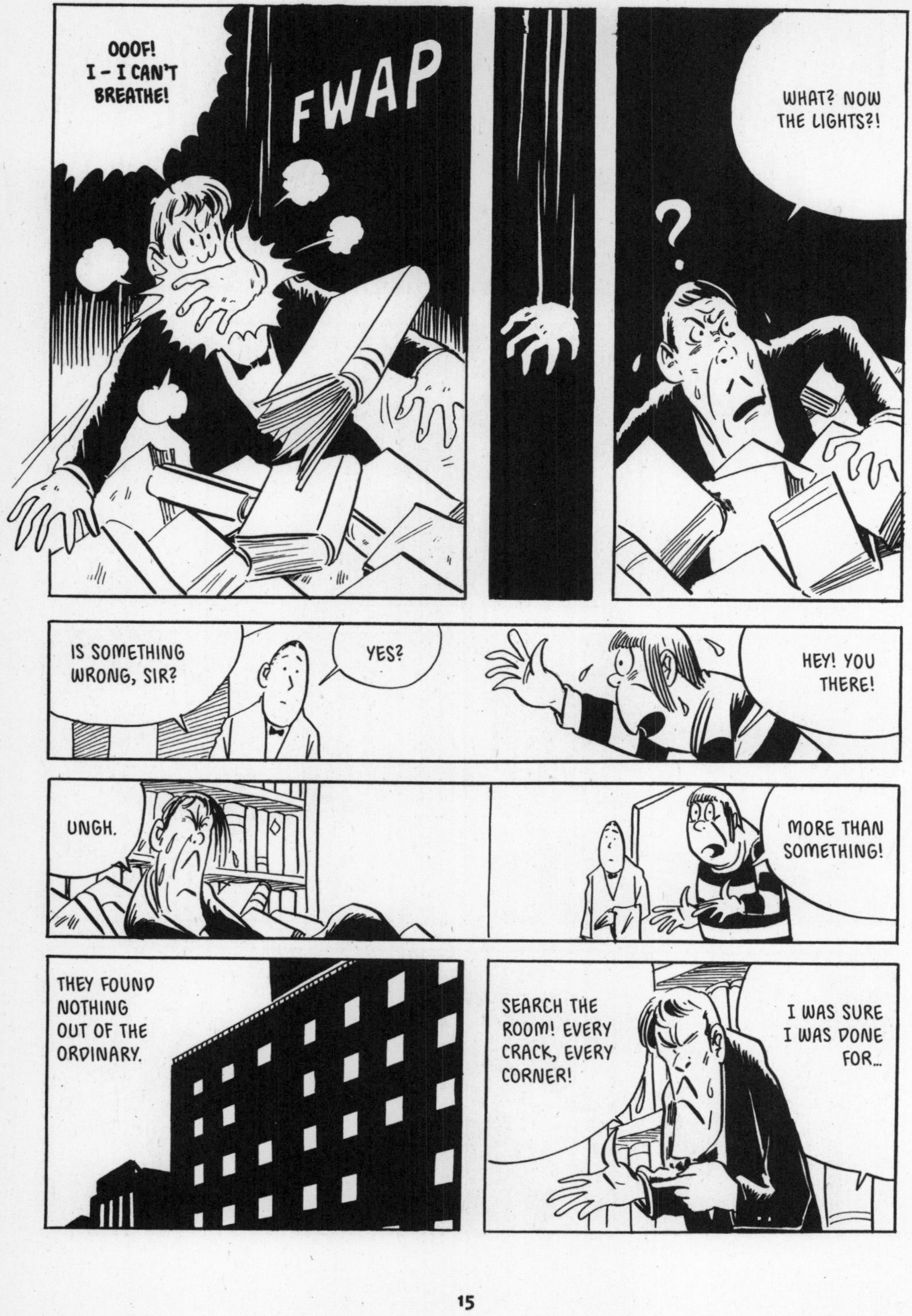
?
WHAT? NOW THE LIGHTS?!
OOOF! I - I CAN'T BREATHE!
FWAP
HEY! YOU THERE!
YES?
IS SOMETHING WRONG, SIR?
MORE THAN SOMETHING!
UNGH.
I WAS SURE I WAS DONE FOR...
SEARCH THE ROOM! EVERY CRACK, EVERY CORNER!
THEY FOUND NOTHING OUT OF THE ORDINARY.

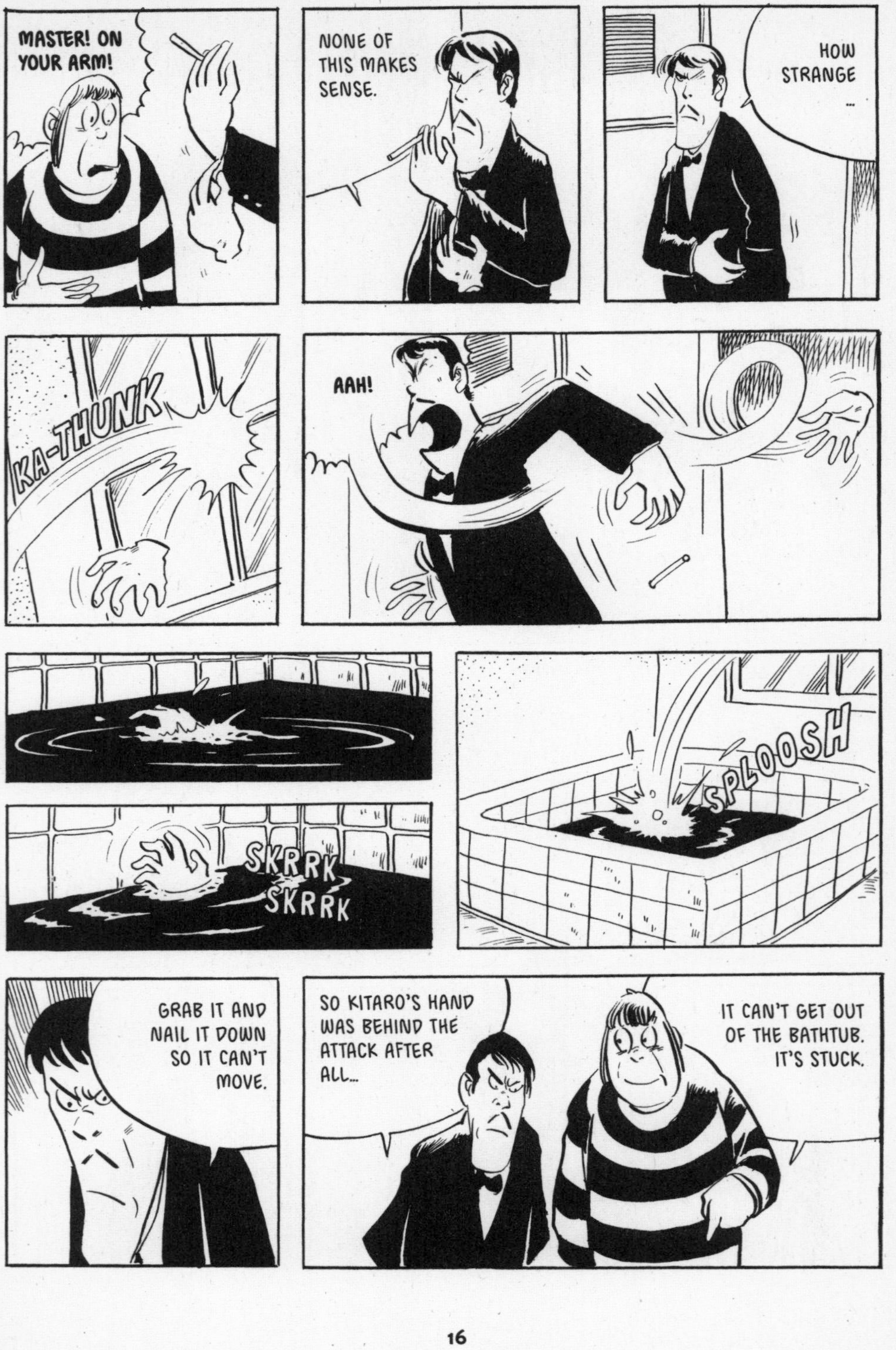
HOW STRANGE ...
NONE OF THIS MAKES SENSE.
MASTER! ON YOUR ARM!
AAH!
KA-THUNK
SPLOOSH
SKRRK SKRRK
IT CAN'T GET OUT OF THE BATHTUB. IT'S STUCK.
SO KITARO'S HAND WAS BEHIND THE ATTACK AFTER ALL...
GRAB IT AND NAIL IT DOWN SO IT CAN'T MOVE.

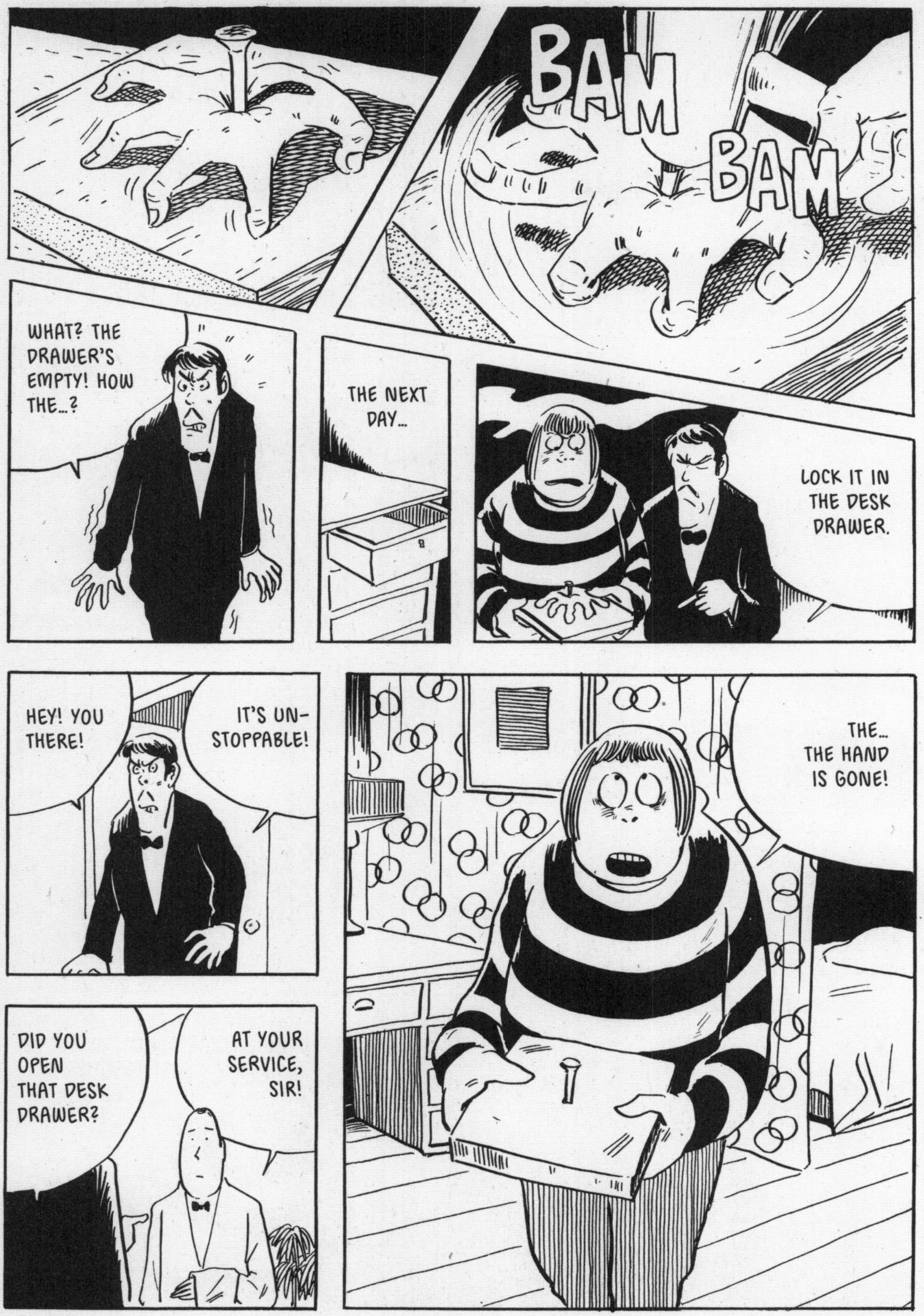
BAM
BAM
LOCK IT IN THE DESK DRAWER.
THE NEXT DAY...
WHAT? THE DRAWER'S EMPTY! HOW THE...?
THE... THE HAND IS GONE!
IT'S UN-STOPPABLE!
HEY! YOU THERE!
AT YOUR SERVICE, SIR!
DID YOU OPEN THAT DESK DRAWER?

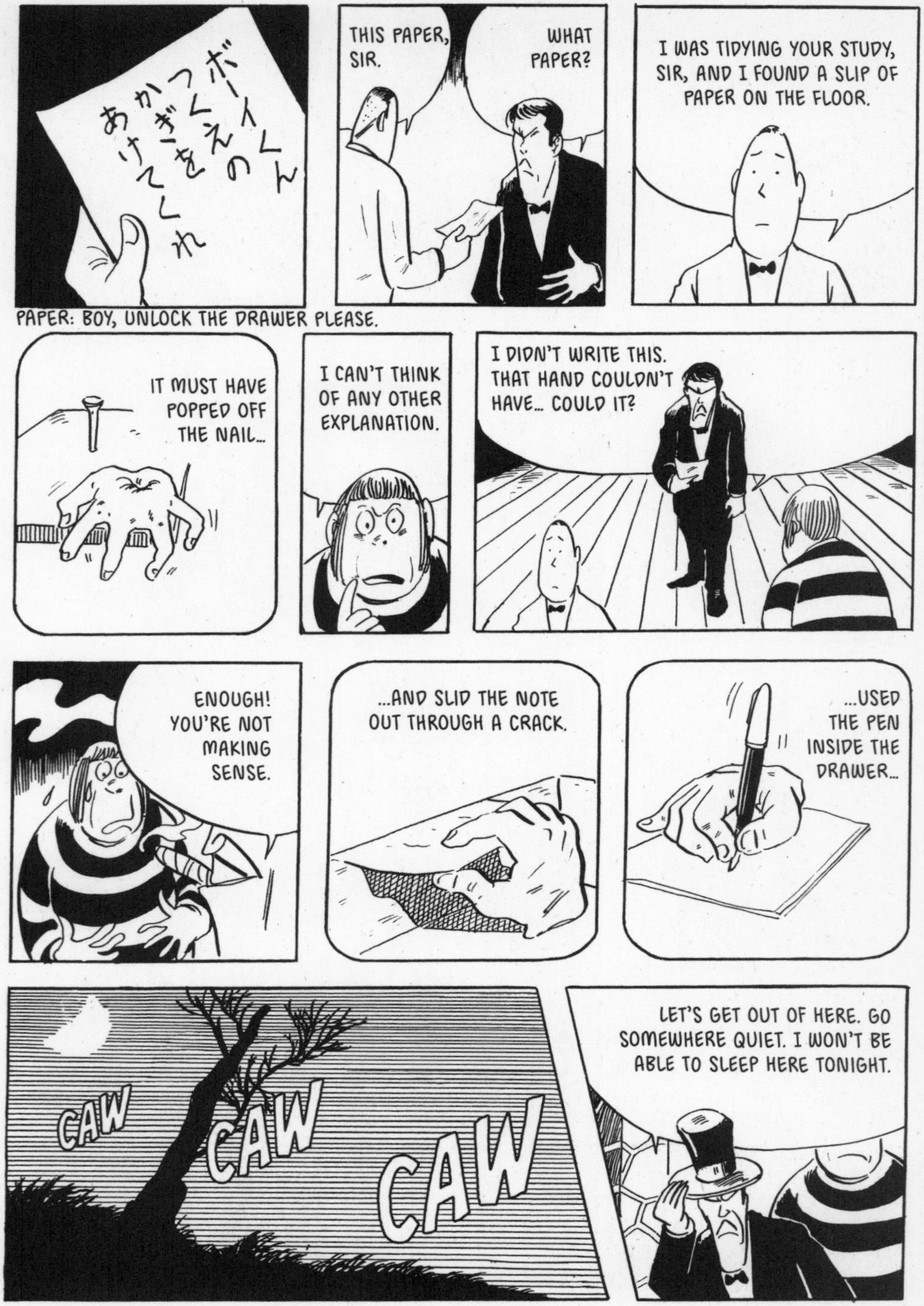
I WAS TIDYING YOUR STUDY, SIR, AND I FOUND A SLIP OF PAPER ON THE FLOOR.
WHAT PAPER?
THIS PAPER, SIR.
ボーイくん つくえの かぎを あけてくれ
PAPER: BOY, UNLOCK THE DRAWER PLEASE.
I DIDN'T WRITE THIS. THAT HAND COULDN'T HAVE... COULD IT?
I CAN'T THINK OF ANY OTHER EXPLANATION.
IT MUST HAVE POPPED OFF THE NAIL...
...USED THE PEN INSIDE THE DRAWER...
...AND SLID THE NOTE OUT THROUGH A CRACK.
ENOUGH! YOU'RE NOT MAKING SENSE.
LET'S GET OUT OF HERE. GO SOMEWHERE QUIET. I WON'T BE ABLE TO SLEEP HERE TONIGHT.
CAW
CAW
CAW

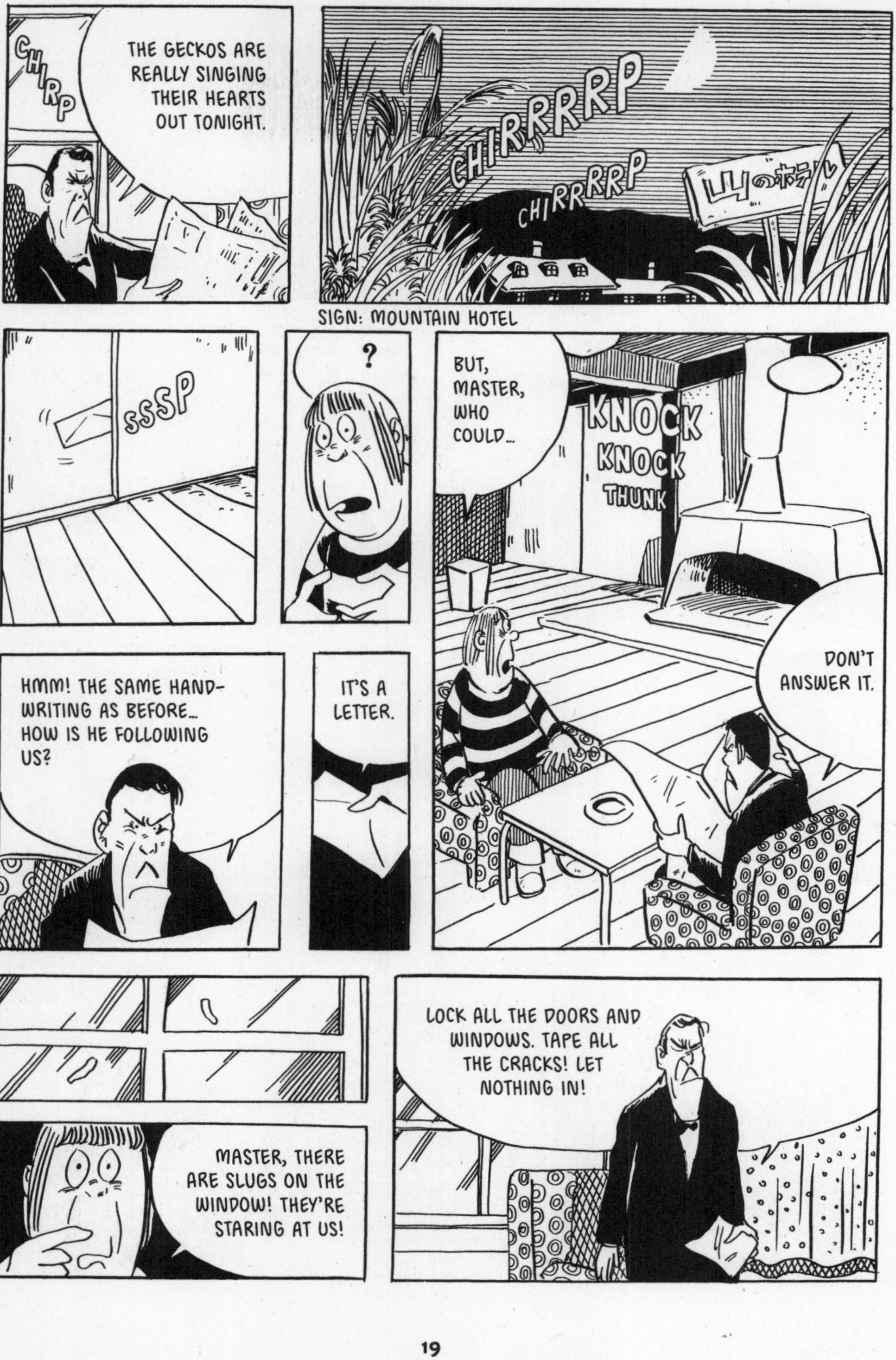
CHIRRRRP
CHIRRRRP
山のホテル
SIGN: MOUNTAIN HOTEL
CHIRP
THE GECKOS ARE REALLY SINGING THEIR HEARTS OUT TONIGHT.
BUT, MASTER, WHO COULD...
KNOCK
KNOCK
THUNK
DON'T ANSWER IT.
?
SSSP
IT'S A LETTER.
HMM! THE SAME HAND-WRITING AS BEFORE... HOW IS HE FOLLOWING US?
LOCK ALL THE DOORS AND WINDOWS. TAPE ALL THE CRACKS! LET NOTHING IN!
MASTER, THERE ARE SLUGS ON THE WINDOW! THEY'RE STARING AT US!

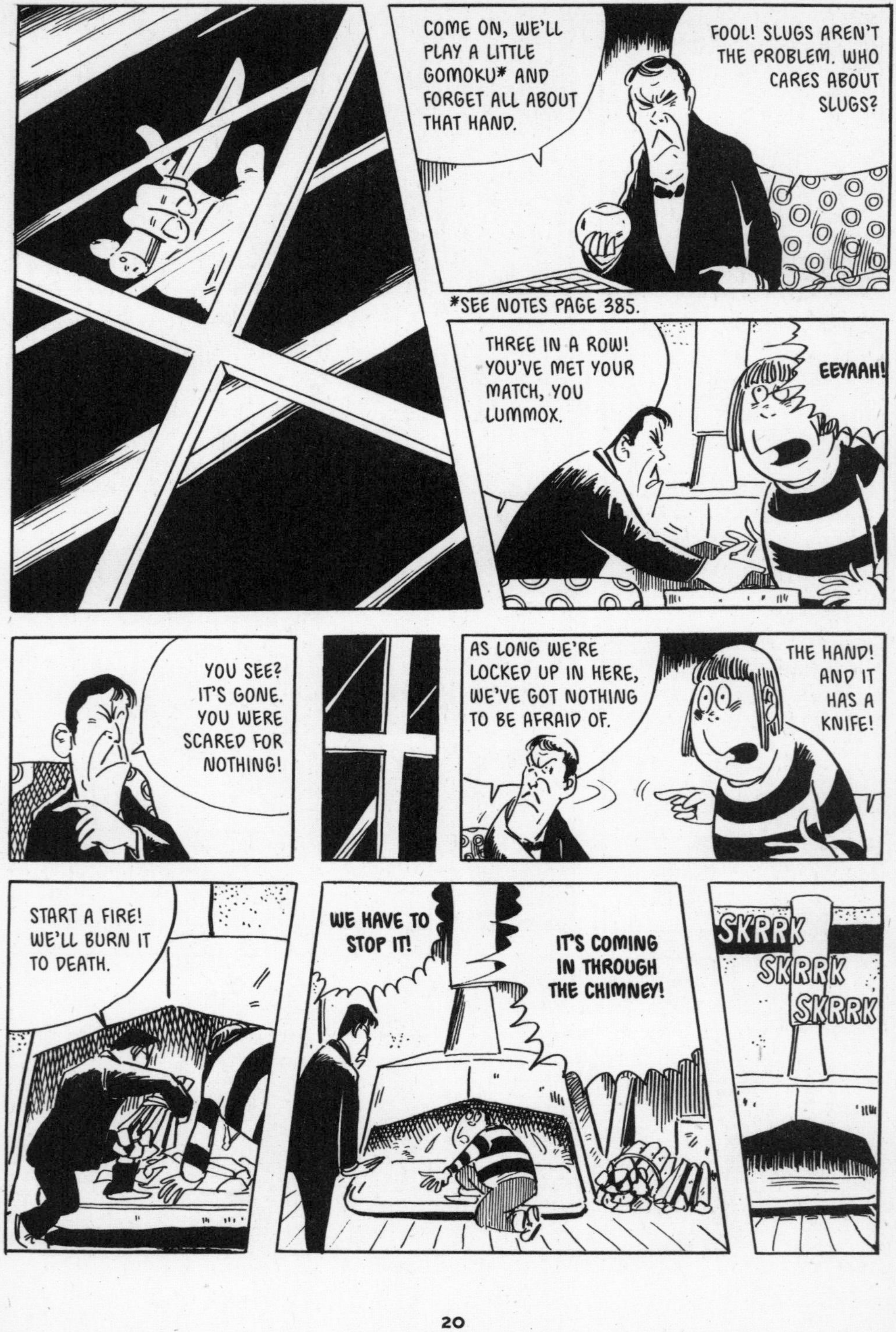
FOOL! SLUGS AREN'T THE PROBLEM. WHO CARES ABOUT SLUGS?
COME ON, WE'LL PLAY A LITTLE GOMOKU* AND FORGET ALL ABOUT THAT HAND.
EEYAAH!
THREE IN A ROW! YOU'VE MET YOUR MATCH, YOU LUMMOX.
THE HAND! AND IT HAS A KNIFE!
AS LONG WE'RE LOCKED UP IN HERE, WE'VE GOT NOTHING TO BE AFRAID OF.
YOU SEE? IT'S GONE. YOU WERE SCARED FOR NOTHING!
SKRRK
SKRRK
SKRRK
IT'S COMING IN THROUGH THE CHIMNEY!
WE HAVE TO STOP IT!
START A FIRE! WE'LL BURN IT TO DEATH.

*SEE NOTES PAGE 385.

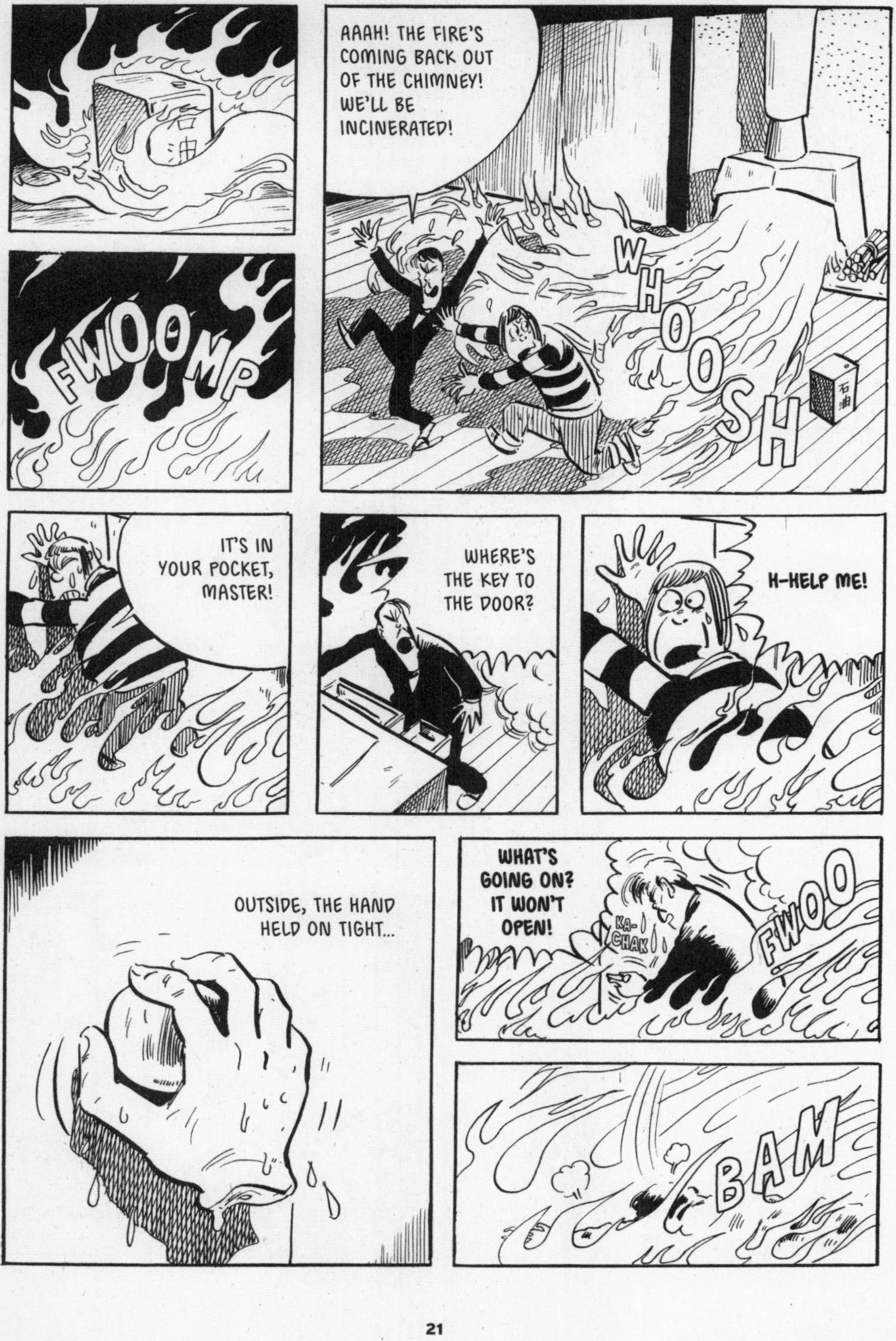
AAAH! THE FIRE'S COMING BACK OUT OF THE CHIMNEY! WE'LL BE INCINERATED!
WHOOSH
石油
石油
FWOOMP
H-HELP ME!
WHERE'S THE KEY TO THE DOOR?
IT'S IN YOUR POCKET, MASTER!
WHAT'S GOING ON? IT WON'T OPEN!
KA-CHAK
FWOO
BAM
OUTSIDE, THE HAND HELD ON TIGHT...

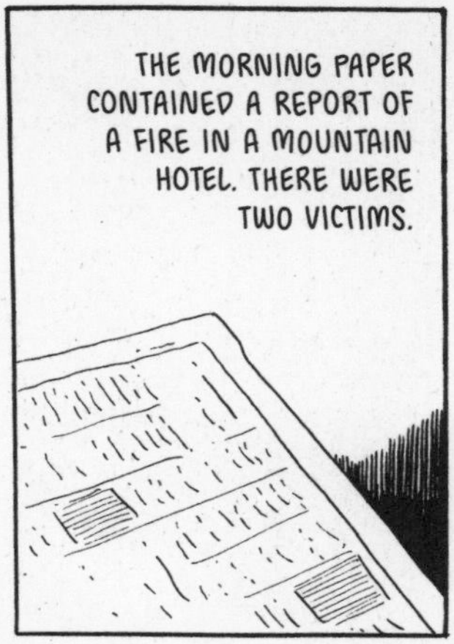
THE MORNING PAPER CONTAINED A REPORT OF A FIRE IN A MOUNTAIN HOTEL. THERE WERE TWO VICTIMS.

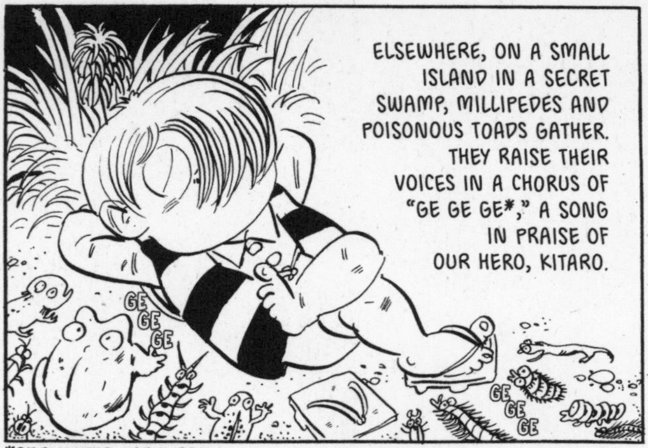
ELSEWHERE, ON A SMALL ISLAND IN A SECRET SWAMP, MILLIPEDES AND POISONOUS TOADS GATHER. THEY RAISE THEIR VOICES IN A CHORUS OF "GE GE GE*," A SONG IN PRAISE OF OUR HERO, KITARO.
GE GE GE
GE GE GE

*SEE NOTES PAGE 385.

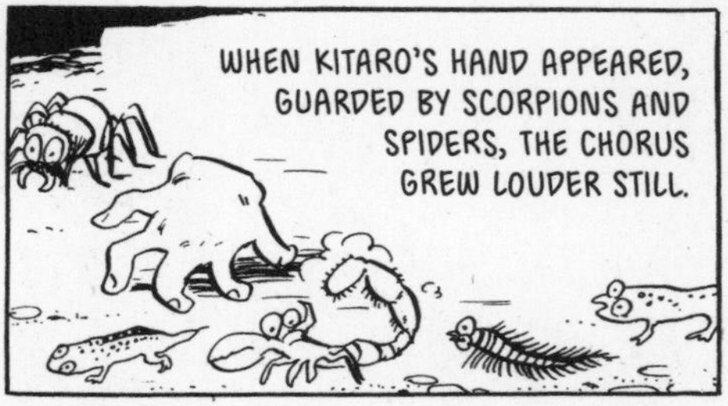
WHEN KITARO'S HAND APPEARED, GUARDED BY SCORPIONS AND SPIDERS, THE CHORUS GREW LOUDER STILL.

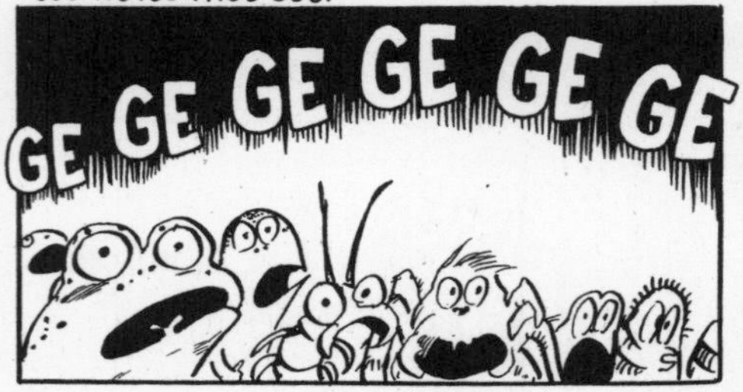
GE GE GE GE GE GE

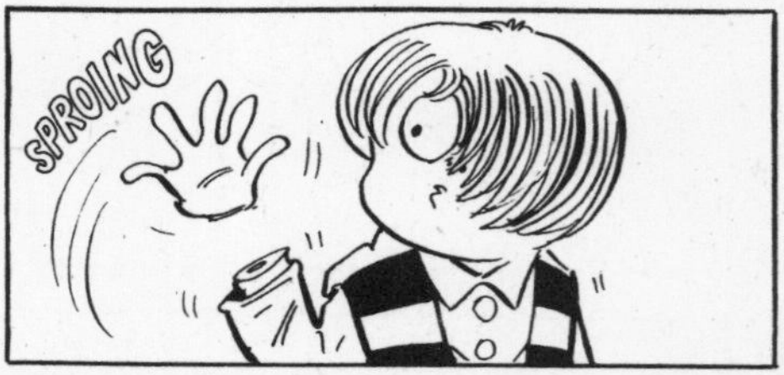
SPROING

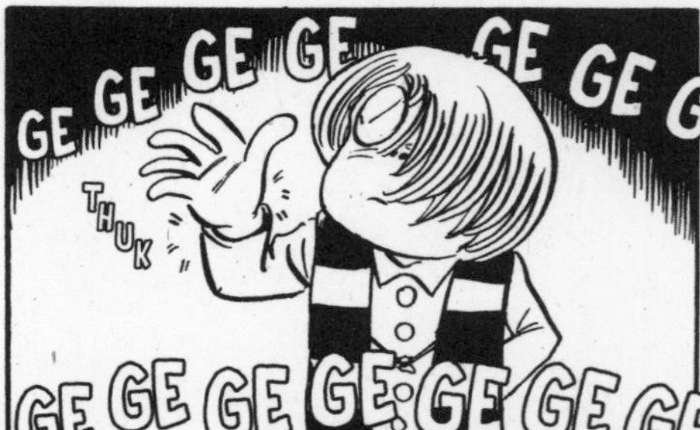
GE GE GE GE
GE GE GE
THUK
GE GE GE GE GE GE GE GE

KITARO'S GREAT POWERS ALLOWED HIS HAND TO LIVE ON WITHOUT HIM LIKE THE TAIL OF A GECKO LEFT BEHIND. UNLIKE, THAT TAIL WHICH WOULD JUST LIE THERE, THIS HAND WAS ABLE TO SEEK REVENGE ON LA SEINE AND HIS HENCHMAN. ALL HAIL KITARO!! GE GE GE!! GE GE GE!!

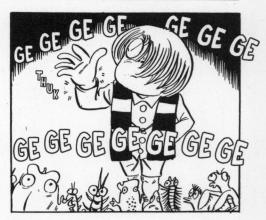

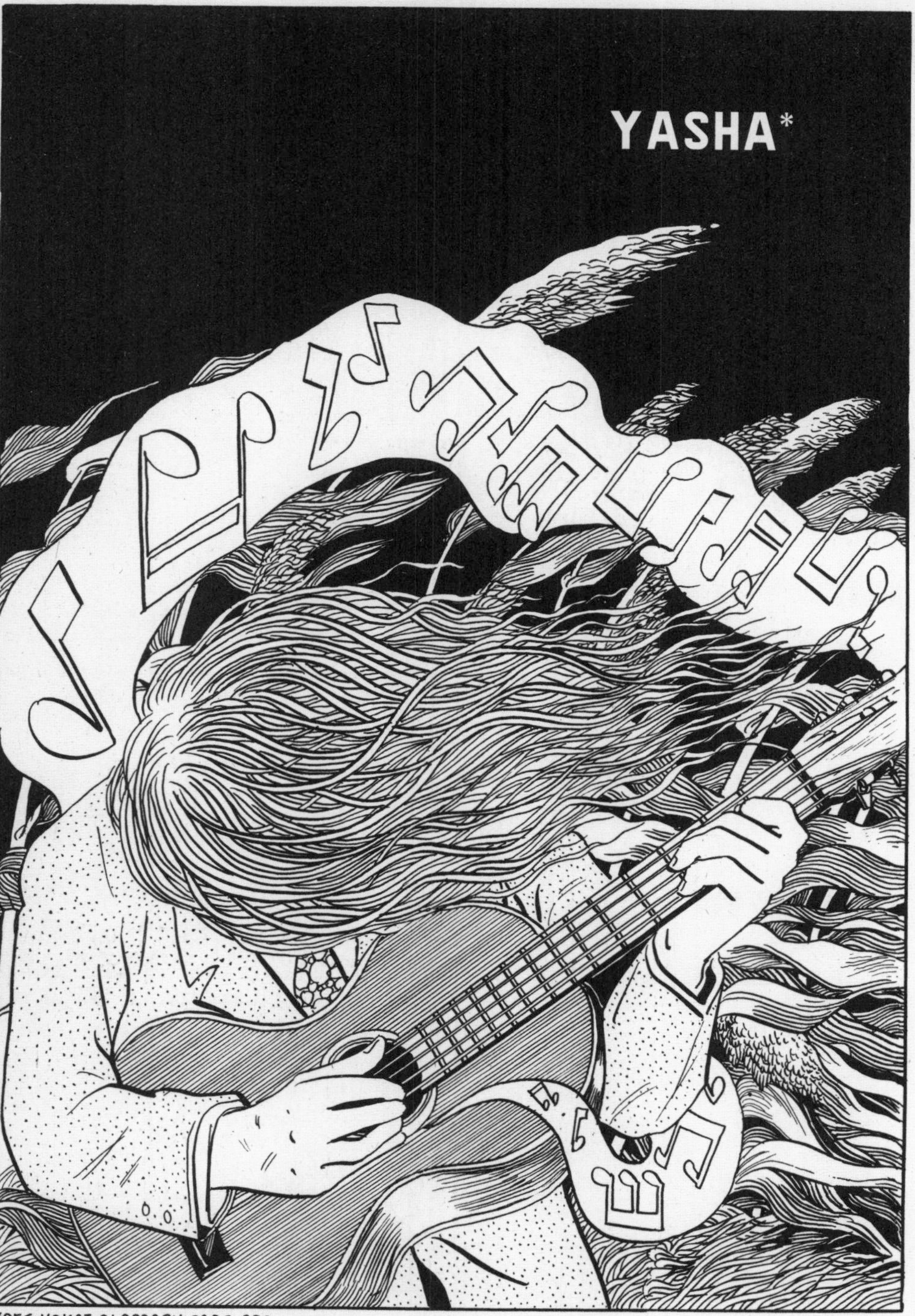
YASHA*

*SEE YOKAI GLOSSARY PAGE 389.

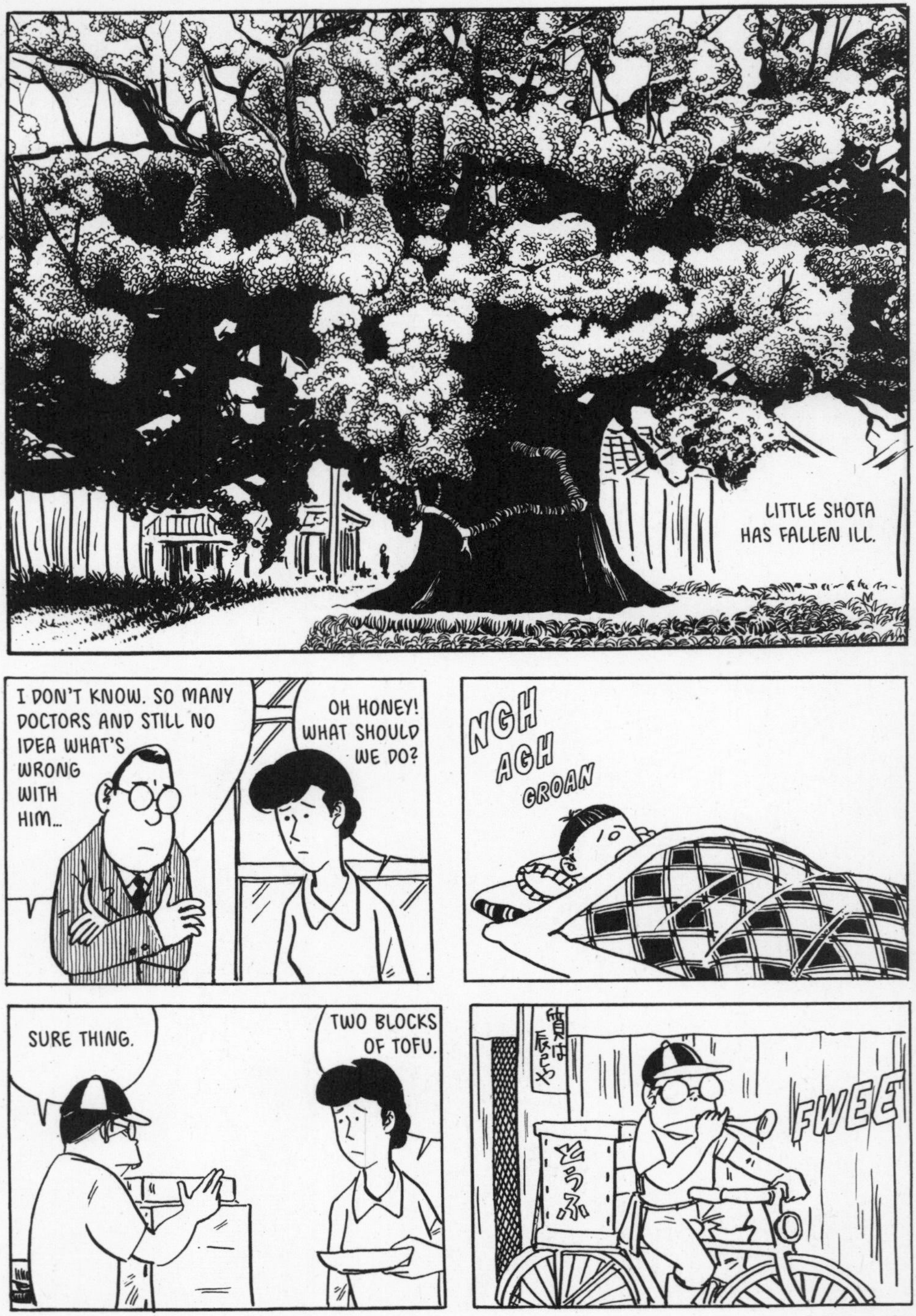
LITTLE SHOTA HAS FALLEN ILL.
NGH
AGH
GROAN
OH HONEY! WHAT SHOULD WE DO?
I DON'T KNOW. SO MANY DOCTORS AND STILL NO IDEA WHAT'S WRONG WITH HIM...
質は辰巳や
とうふ
FWEE
TWO BLOCKS OF TOFU.
SURE THING.

BOX: TOFU

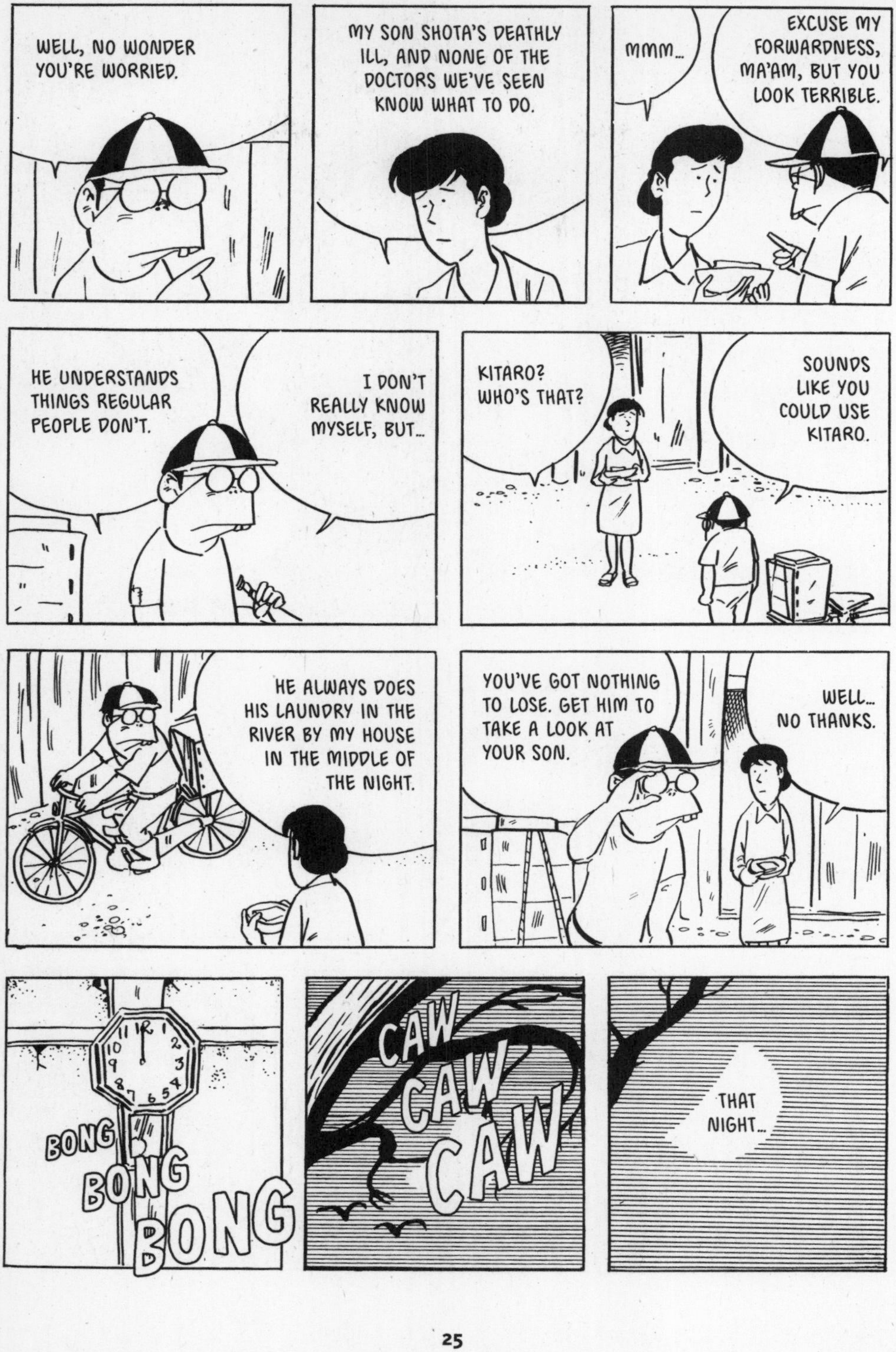
EXCUSE MY FORWARDNESS, MA'AM, BUT YOU LOOK TERRIBLE.
MMM...
MY SON SHOTA'S DEATHLY ILL, AND NONE OF THE DOCTORS WE'VE SEEN KNOW WHAT TO DO.
WELL, NO WONDER YOU'RE WORRIED.
SOUNDS LIKE YOU COULD USE KITARO.
KITARO? WHO'S THAT?
I DON'T REALLY KNOW MYSELF, BUT...
HE UNDERSTANDS THINGS REGULAR PEOPLE DON'T.
WELL... NO THANKS.
YOU'VE GOT NOTHING TO LOSE. GET HIM TO TAKE A LOOK AT YOUR SON.
HE ALWAYS DOES HIS LAUNDRY IN THE RIVER BY MY HOUSE IN THE MIDDLE OF THE NIGHT.
THAT NIGHT...
CAW
CAW
CAW
BONG
BONG
BONG

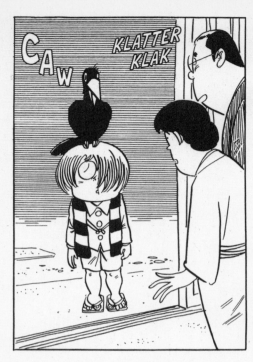

KNOCK KNOCK
WHO ON EARTH COULD IT BE AT THIS HOUR?
WHO'S THERE? SHOW YOURSELF!
THE TOFU SELLER, MATAHACHI, ASKED ME TO COME BY. MY NAME IS KITARO.
KLATTER KLAK
CAW
OH... HONEY, WHAT DO YOU THINK?
I'M AT MY WITS' END. I DON'T KNOW.
I GUESS HE CAN LOOK AT SHOTA IF HE WANTS.
...
NGH AGH
...
IT'S SIMPLE. HIS SOUL HAS BEEN STOLEN.
WHAT? HIS SOUL?

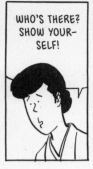

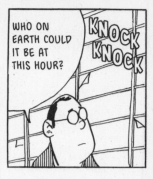

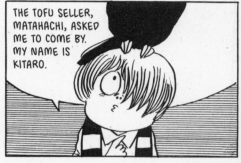

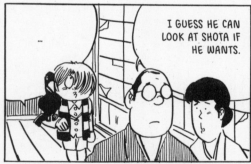

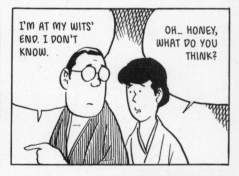

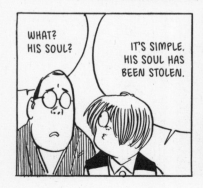

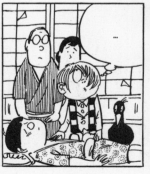

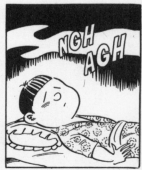

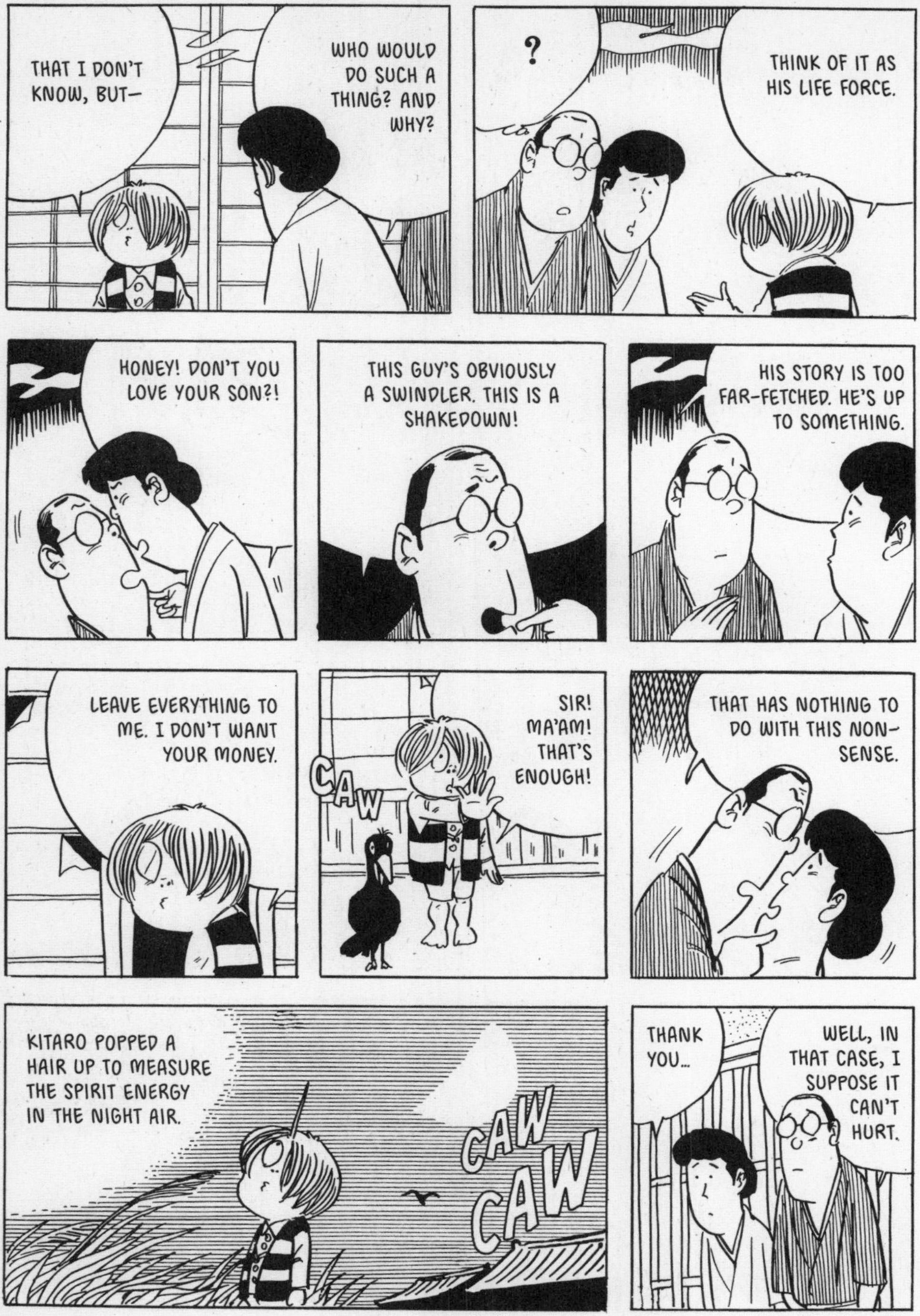
THINK OF IT AS HIS LIFE FORCE.
?
WHO WOULD DO SUCH A THING? AND WHY?
THAT I DON'T KNOW, BUT—
HIS STORY IS TOO FAR-FETCHED. HE'S UP TO SOMETHING.
THIS GUY'S OBVIOUSLY A SWINDLER. THIS IS A SHAKEDOWN!
HONEY! DON'T YOU LOVE YOUR SON?!
THAT HAS NOTHING TO DO WITH THIS NON-SENSE.
SIR! MA'AM! THAT'S ENOUGH!
CAW
LEAVE EVERYTHING TO ME. I DON'T WANT YOUR MONEY.
WELL, IN THAT CASE, I SUPPOSE IT CAN'T HURT.
THANK YOU...
KITARO POPPED A HAIR UP TO MEASURE THE SPIRIT ENERGY IN THE NIGHT AIR.
CAW
CAW

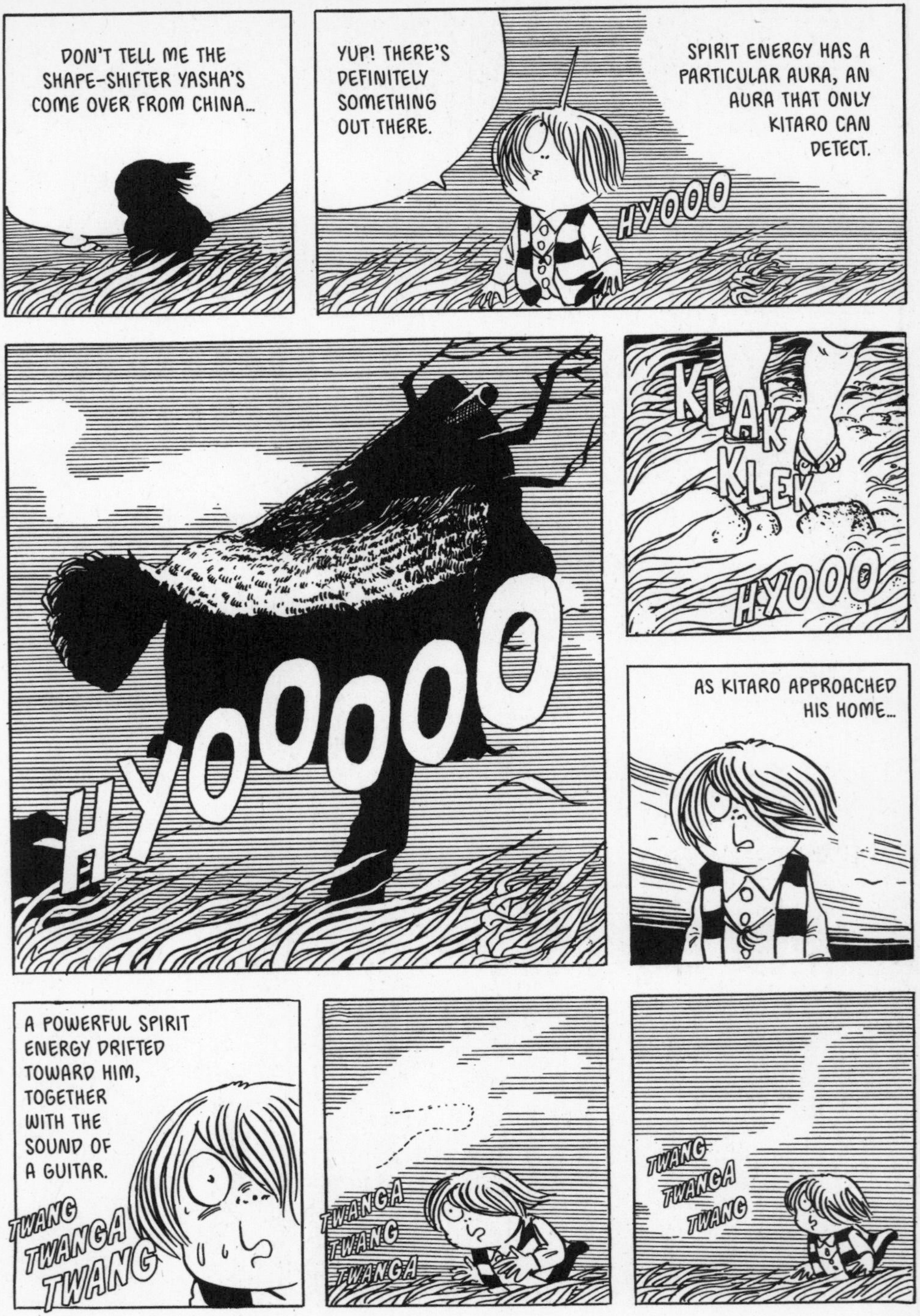
SPIRIT ENERGY HAS A PARTICULAR AURA, AN AURA THAT ONLY KITARO CAN DETECT.
YUP! THERE'S DEFINITELY SOMETHING OUT THERE.
HYOOO
DON'T TELL ME THE SHAPE-SHIFTER YASHA'S COME OVER FROM CHINA...
KLAK KLEK
HYOOO
AS KITARO APPROACHED HIS HOME...
HYOOOOOO
TWANG
TWANGA
TWANG
TWANGA
TWANG
TWANGA
A POWERFUL SPIRIT ENERGY DRIFTED TOWARD HIM, TOGETHER WITH THE SOUND OF A GUITAR.
TWANG
TWANGA
TWANG

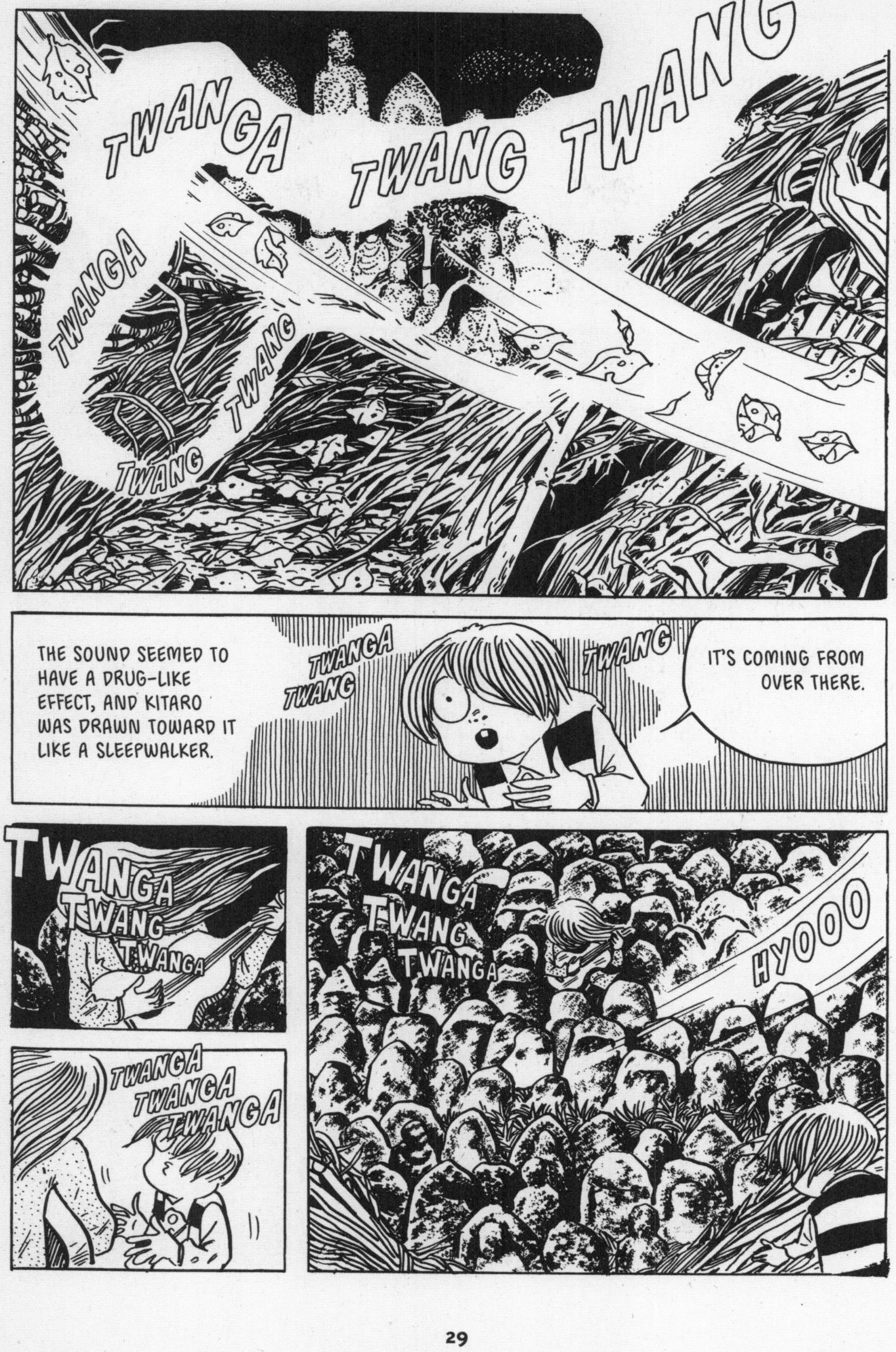
TWANG
TWANG
TWANGA
TWANGA
TWANG
TWANG
IT'S COMING FROM OVER THERE.
TWANG
TWANGA TWANG
THE SOUND SEEMED TO HAVE A DRUG-LIKE EFFECT, AND KITARO WAS DRAWN TOWARD IT LIKE A SLEEPWALKER.
HYOOO
TWANGA TWANG TWANGA
TWANGA TWANG TWANGA
TWANGA TWANGA TWANGA

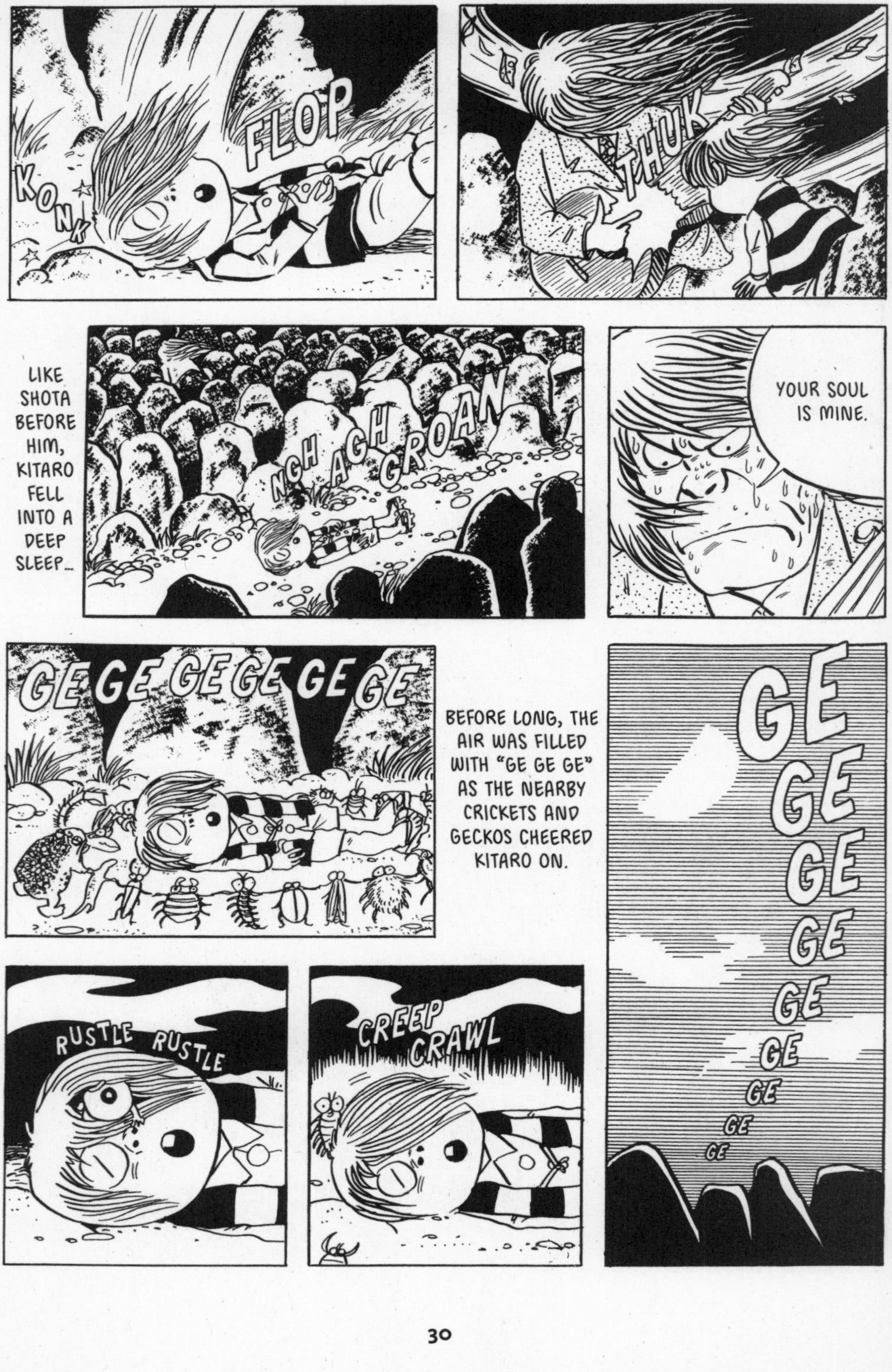
THUK
FLOP
KONK
YOUR SOUL IS MINE.
LIKE SHOTA BEFORE HIM, KITARO FELL INTO A DEEP SLEEP...
NGH AGH GROAN
GE GE GE GE GE GE GE GE GE
GE GE GE GE GE GE GE
BEFORE LONG, THE AIR WAS FILLED WITH "GE GE GE" AS THE NEARBY CRICKETS AND GECKOS CHEERED KITARO ON.
CREEP CRAWL
RUSTLE RUSTLE

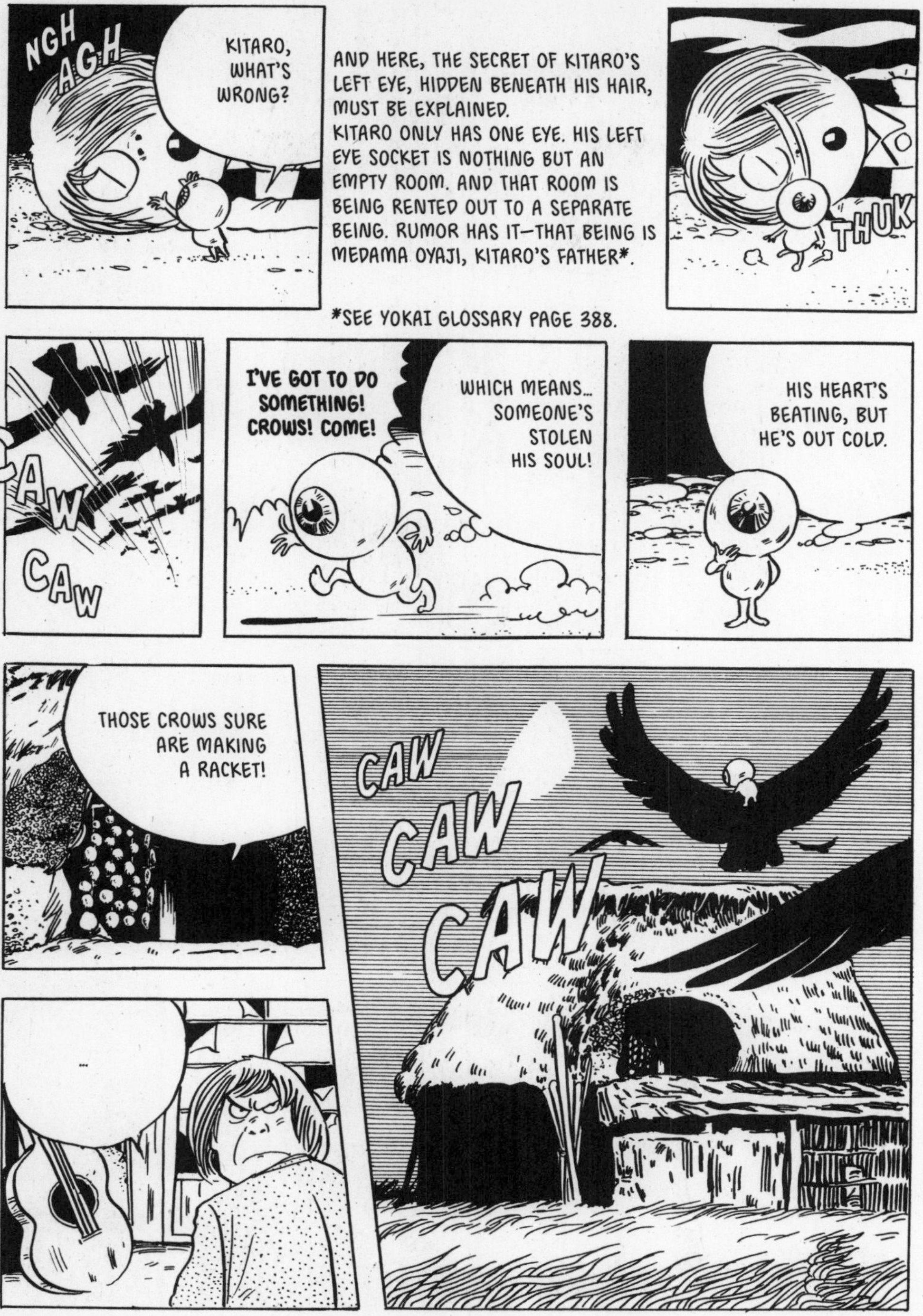
THUK
AND HERE, THE SECRET OF KITARO'S LEFT EYE, HIDDEN BENEATH HIS HAIR, MUST BE EXPLAINED.
KITARO ONLY HAS ONE EYE. HIS LEFT EYE SOCKET IS NOTHING BUT AN EMPTY ROOM. AND THAT ROOM IS BEING RENTED OUT TO A SEPARATE BEING. RUMOR HAS IT—THAT BEING IS MEDAMA OYAJI, KITARO'S FATHER*.
*SEE YOKAI GLOSSARY PAGE 388.
KITARO, WHAT'S WRONG?
NGH AGH
HIS HEART'S BEATING, BUT HE'S OUT COLD.
WHICH MEANS... SOMEONE'S STOLEN HIS SOUL!
I'VE GOT TO DO SOMETHING! CROWS! COME!
CAW CAW
CAW
CAW CAW CAW
THOSE CROWS SURE ARE MAKING A RACKET!
...

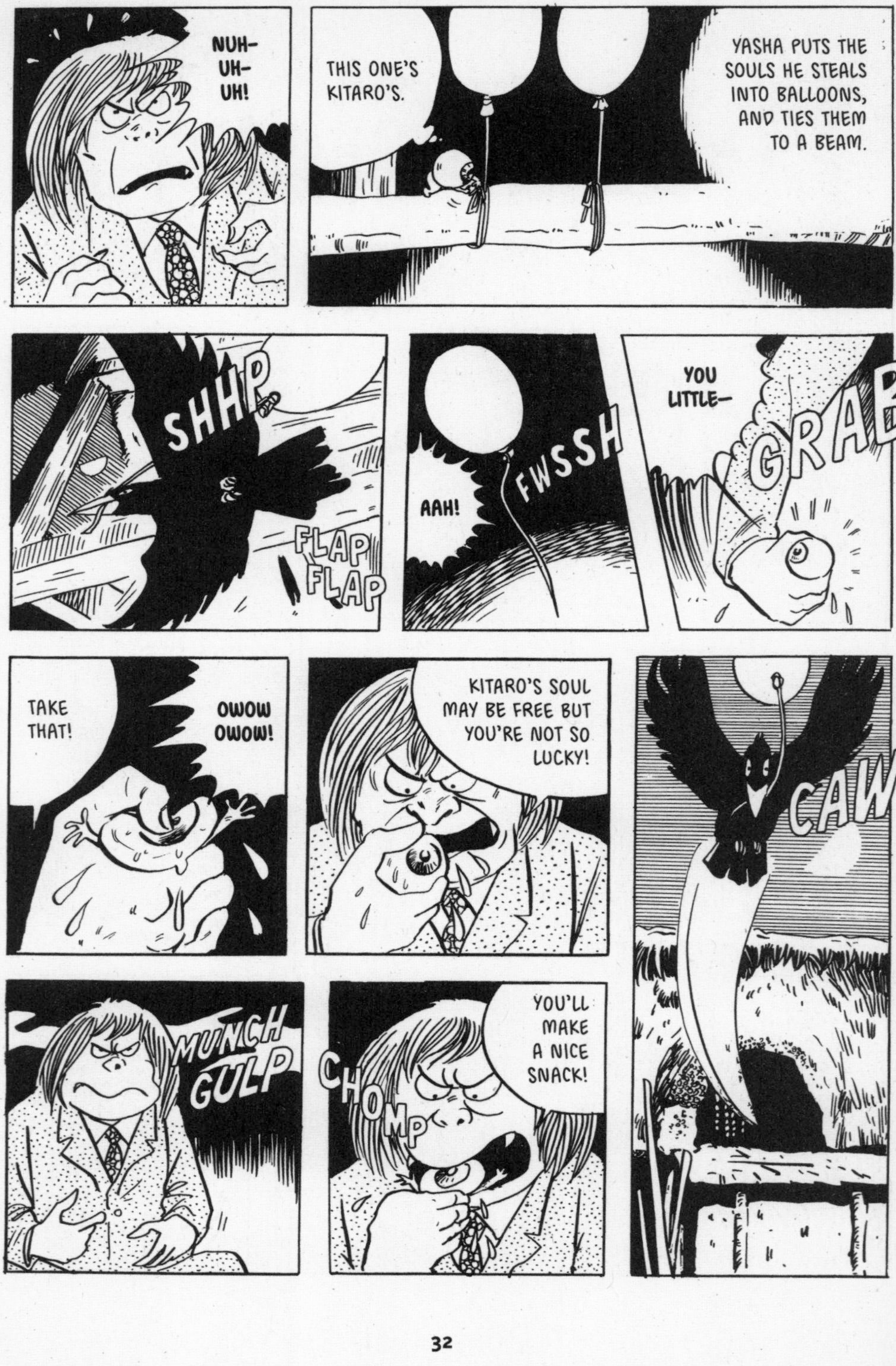

YASHA PUTS THE SOULS HE STEALS INTO BALLOONS, AND TIES THEM TO A BEAM.
THIS ONE'S KITARO'S.
NUH-UH-UH!
YOU LITTLE—
GRAB
FWSSH
AAH!
SHHP
FLAP FLAP
CAW
KITARO'S SOUL MAY BE FREE BUT YOU'RE NOT SO LUCKY!
OWOW OWOW!
TAKE THAT!
YOU'LL MAKE A NICE SNACK!
CHOMP
MUNCH GULP

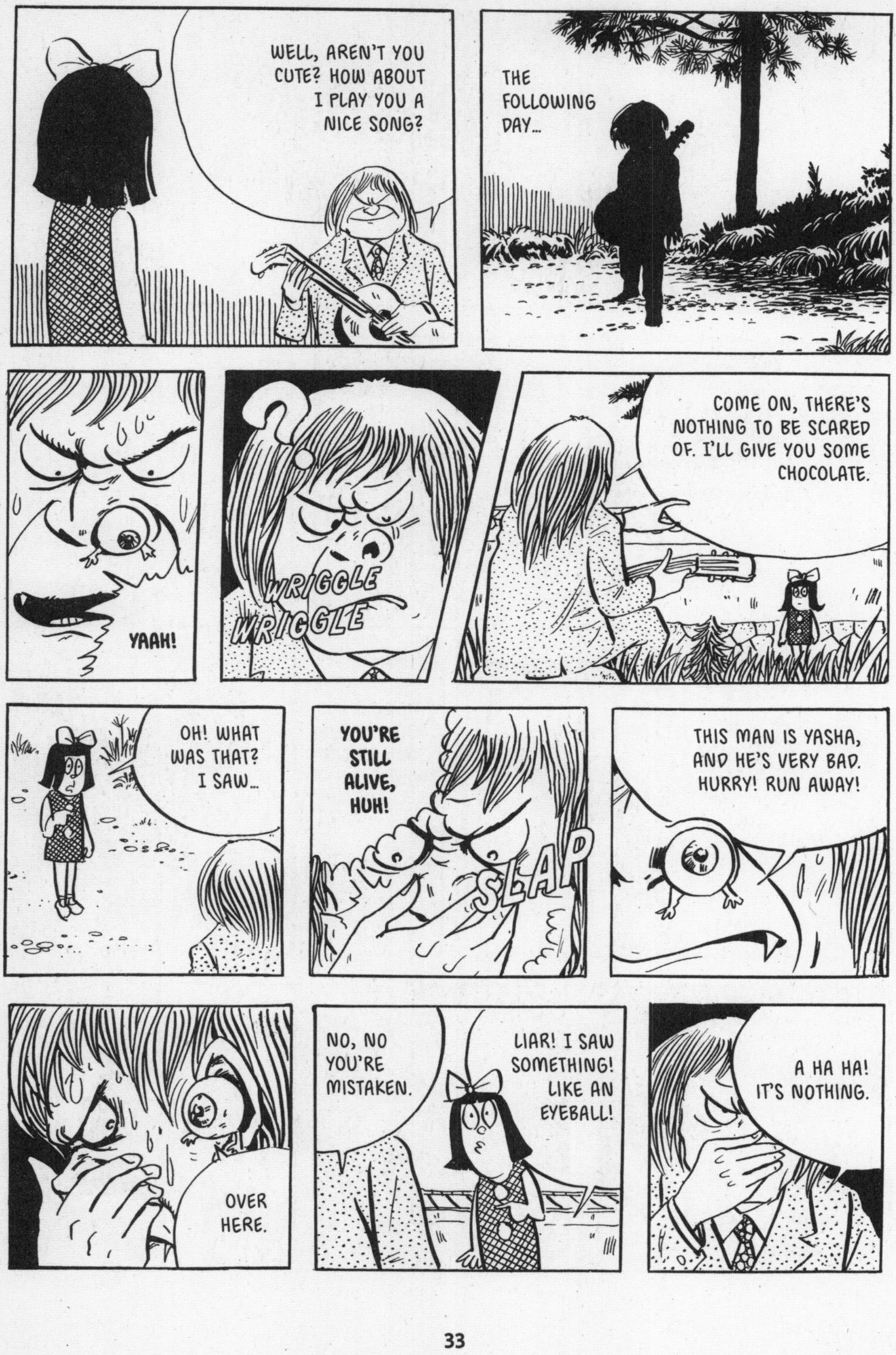
THE FOLLOWING DAY...
WELL, AREN'T YOU CUTE? HOW ABOUT I PLAY YOU A NICE SONG?
COME ON, THERE'S NOTHING TO BE SCARED OF. I'LL GIVE YOU SOME CHOCOLATE.
WRIGGLE WRIGGLE
YAAH!
THIS MAN IS YASHA, AND HE'S VERY BAD. HURRY! RUN AWAY!
YOU'RE STILL ALIVE, HUH!
SLAP
OH! WHAT WAS THAT? I SAW...
A HA HA! IT'S NOTHING.
LIAR! I SAW SOMETHING! LIKE AN EYEBALL!
NO, NO YOU'RE MISTAKEN.
OVER HERE.

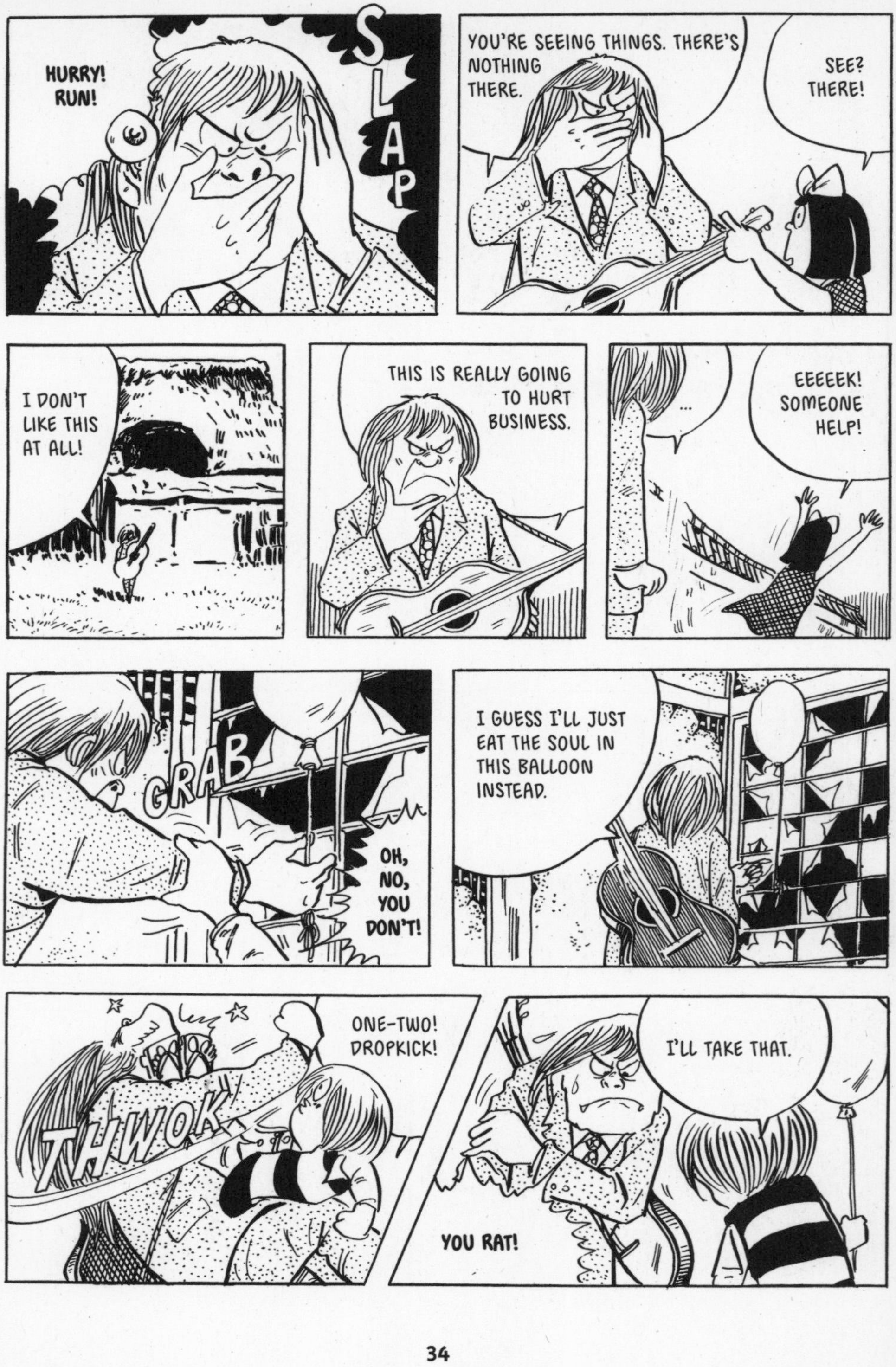
SEE? THERE!
YOU'RE SEEING THINGS. THERE'S NOTHING THERE.
SLAP
HURRY! RUN!
EEEEEK! SOMEONE HELP!
...
THIS IS REALLY GOING TO HURT BUSINESS.
I DON'T LIKE THIS AT ALL!
I GUESS I'LL JUST EAT THE SOUL IN THIS BALLOON INSTEAD.
GRAB
OH, NO, YOU DON'T!
I'LL TAKE THAT.
YOU RAT!
ONE-TWO! DROPKICK!
THWOK

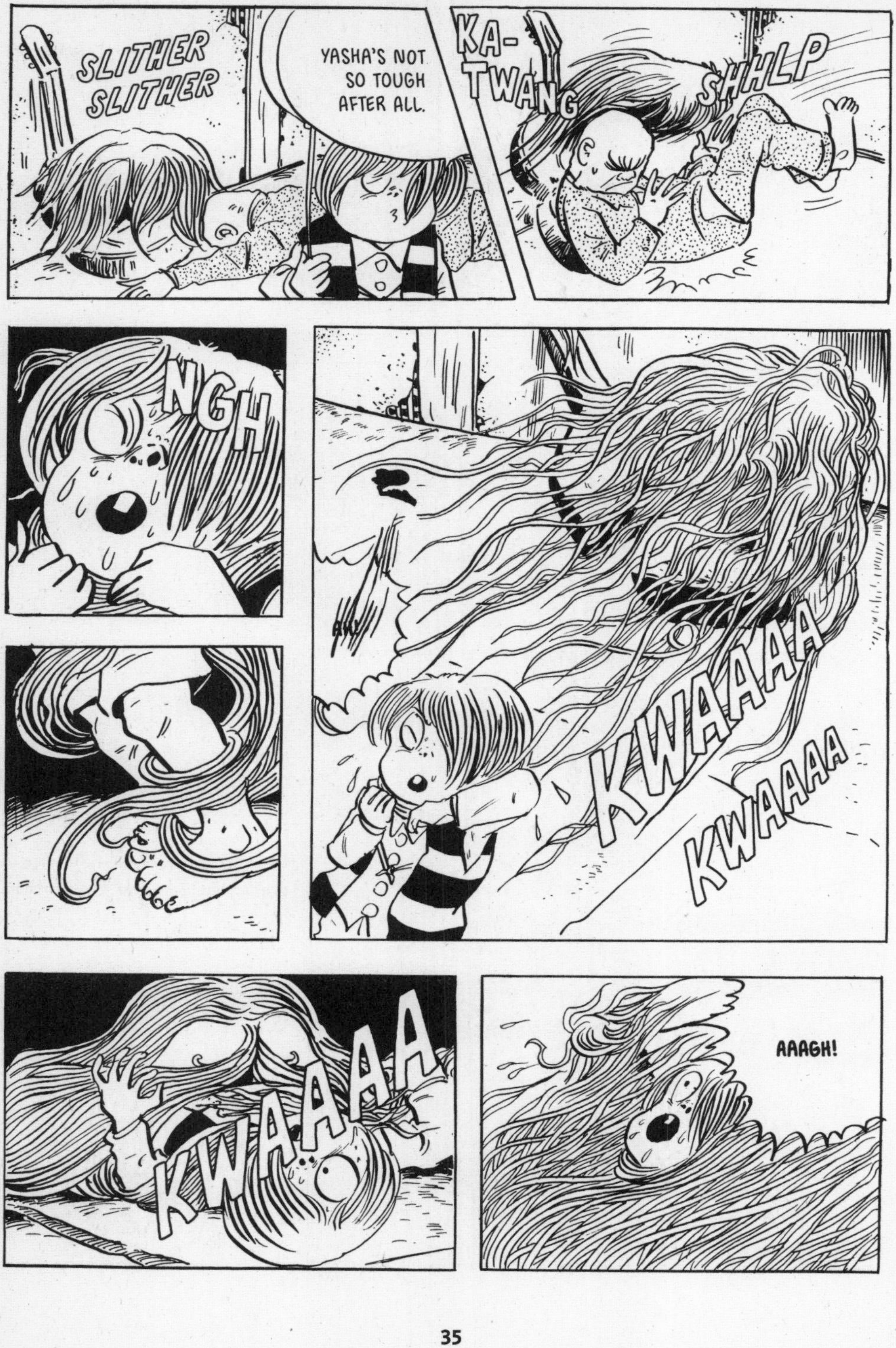
SHHLP
KA-TWANG
YASHA'S NOT SO TOUGH AFTER ALL.
SLITHER SLITHER
KWAAAAA
KWAAAAA
NGH
AAAGH!
KWAAAAA

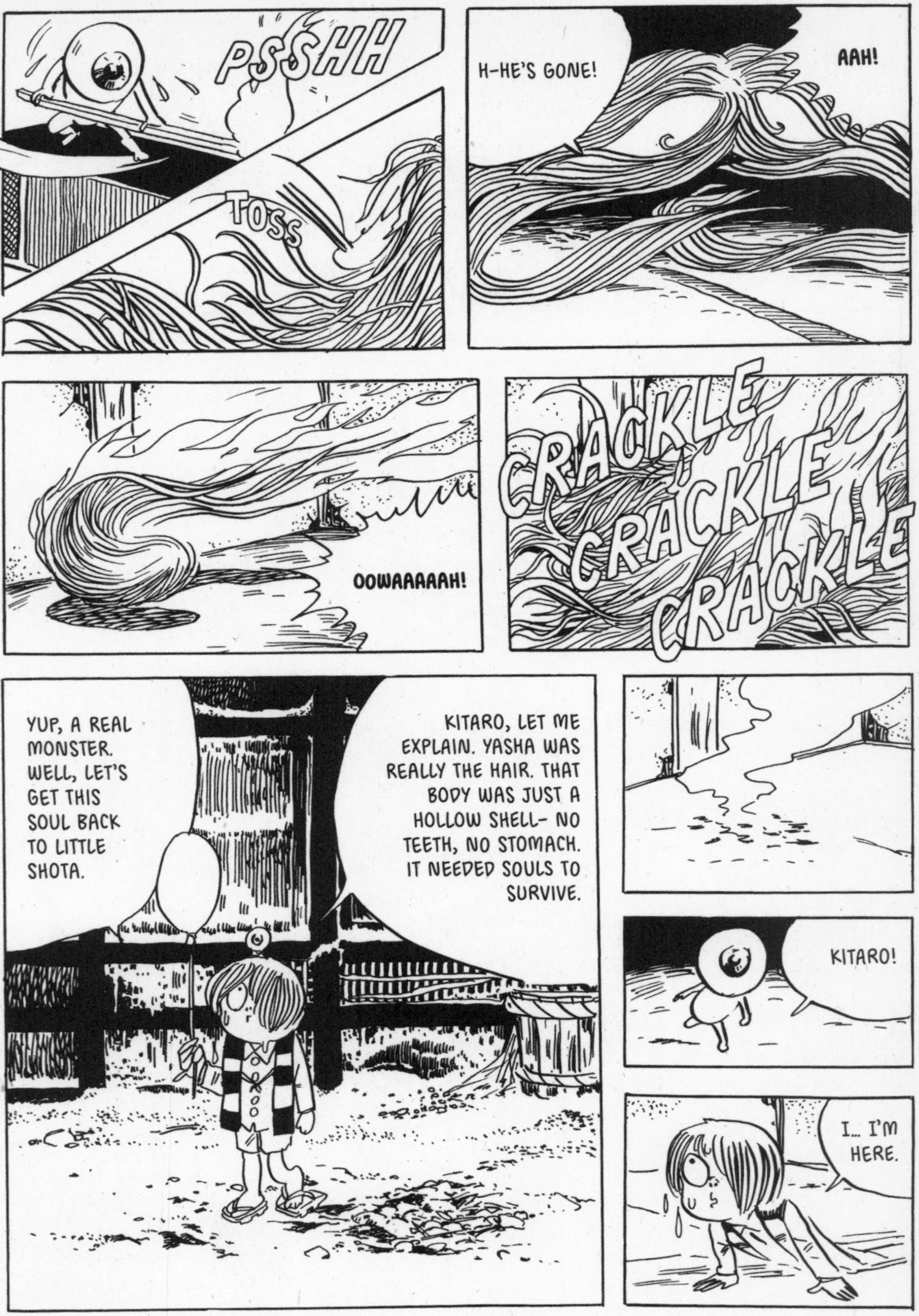
AAH!
H-HE'S GONE!
PSSHH
TOSS
CRACKLE
CRACKLE
CRACKLE
OOWAAAAAH!
KITARO!
I... I'M HERE.
KITARO, LET ME EXPLAIN. YASHA WAS REALLY THE HAIR. THAT BODY WAS JUST A HOLLOW SHELL- NO TEETH, NO STOMACH. IT NEEDED SOULS TO SURVIVE.
YUP, A REAL MONSTER. WELL, LET'S GET THIS SOUL BACK TO LITTLE SHOTA.

KITARO RELEASED THE SOUL INTO SHOTA'S MOUTH AND HIS EYES POPPED OPEN INSTANTLY.

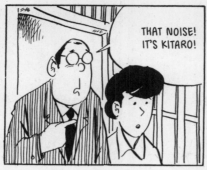

KLAK
KLEK
THAT NOISE! IT'S KITARO!

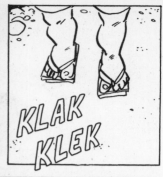

THANK GOODNESS!
MY WORK HERE IS DONE.
THIS IS JUST A TOKEN OF OUR APPRECIATION...

AT THAT MOMENT, THE BUGS IN THE SEWER BEGAN TO SING "GE GE GE" IN PRAISE OF KITARO.

BUT, WAIT, HOW DID KITARO DISAPPEAR DURING THE BATTLE WITH YASHA? WELL, MUCH LIKE A CHAMELEON, KITARO CAN CAMOUFLAGE HIMSELF WHEN HE FEELS HE'S IN DANGER. IN THIS CHASE, HIS SELF-PRESERVATION INSTINCT TOOK OVER AND HE BECAME THE SAME COLOR AS THE STRAW MATS. HE EVEN FLATTENED OUT LIKE A PANCAKE! SUCH A MYSTERY, THIS KITARO!

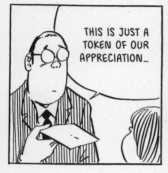

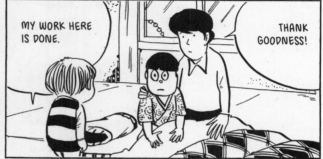

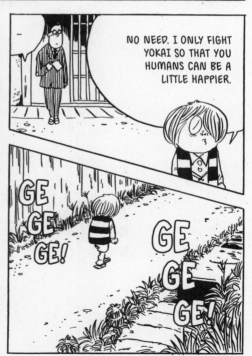

NO NEED. I ONLY FIGHT YOKAI SO THAT YOU HUMANS CAN BE A LITTLE HAPPIER.
...
GE
GE
GE!
GE
GE
GE!

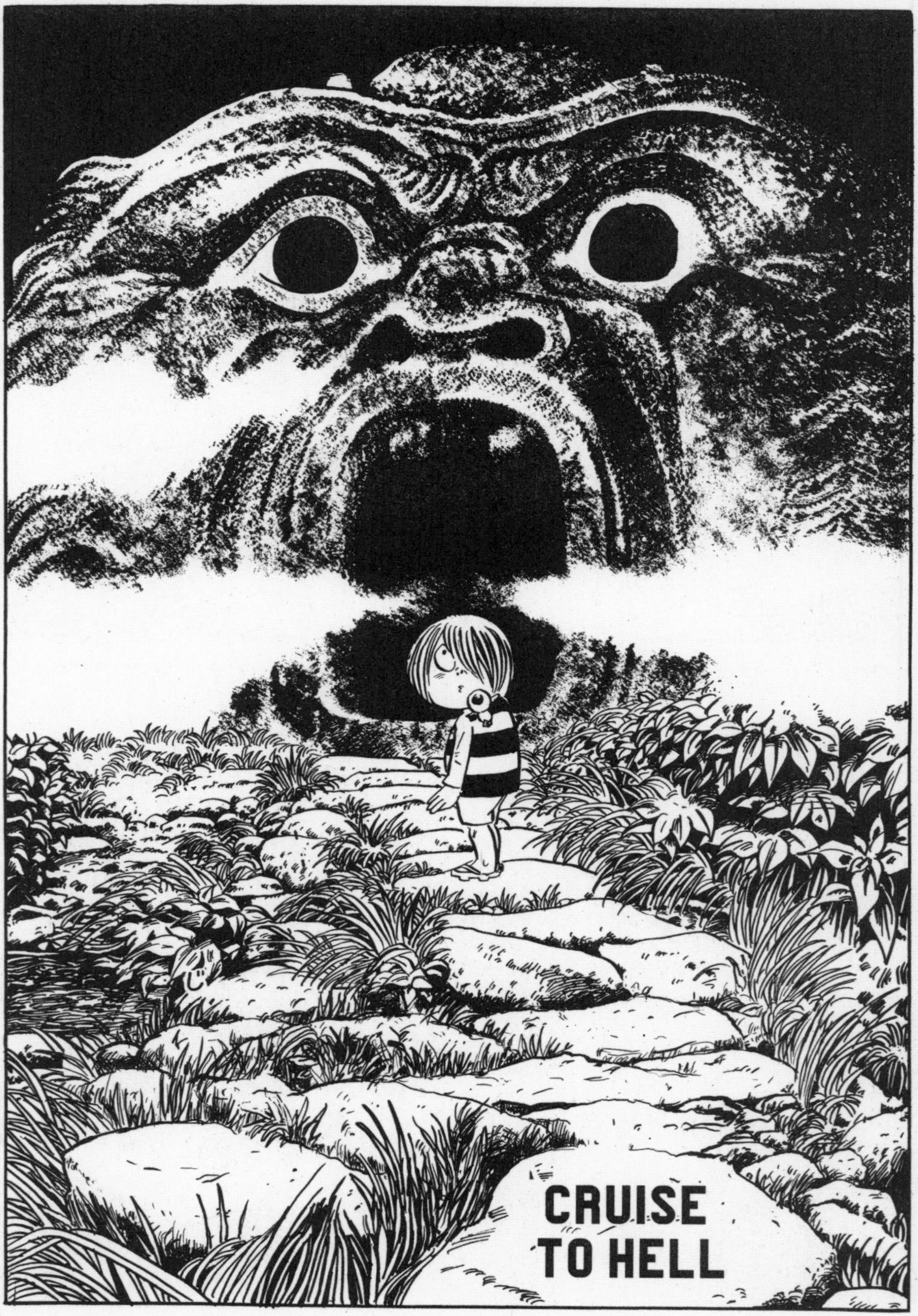
CRUISE
TO HELL

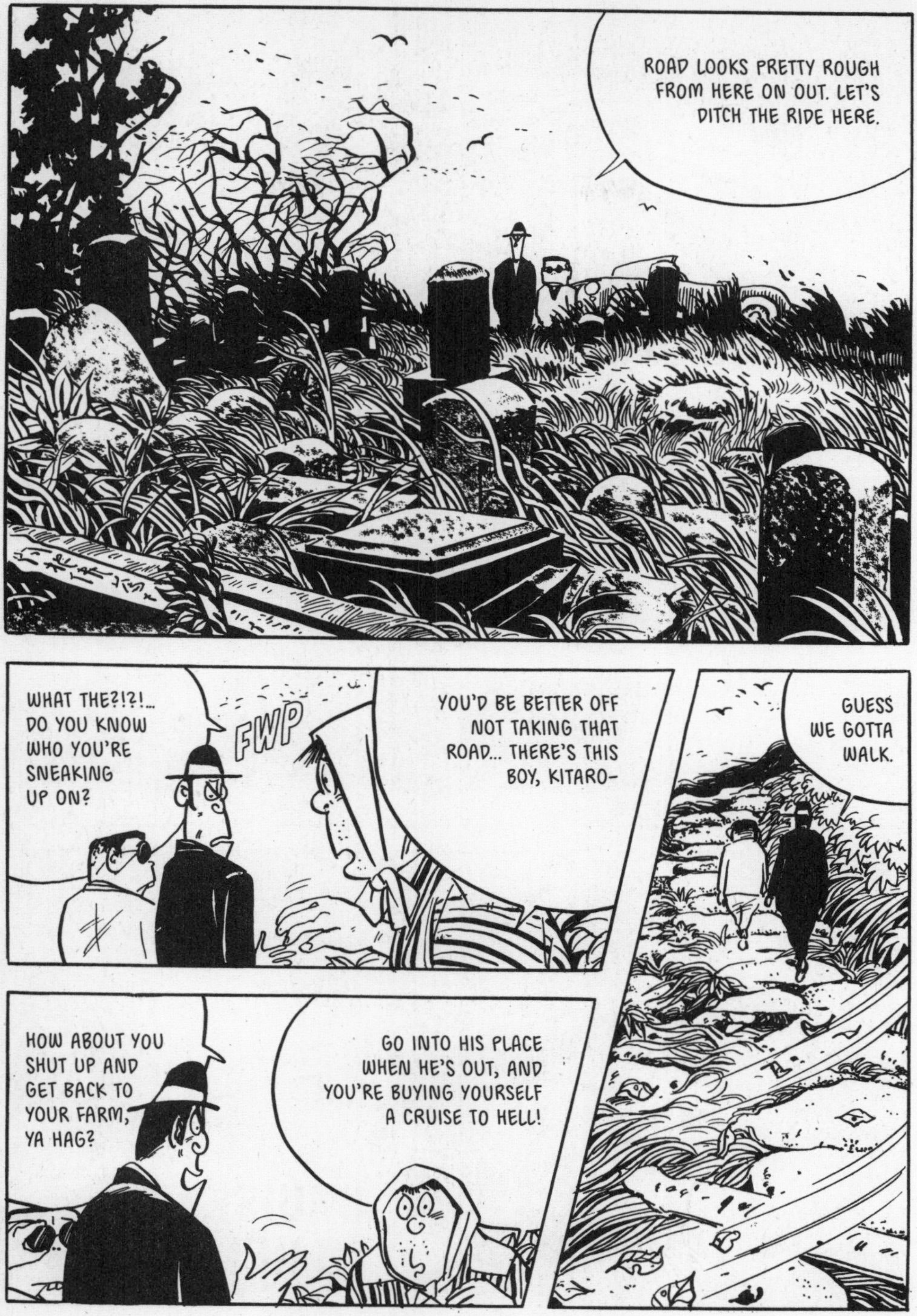
ROAD LOOKS PRETTY ROUGH FROM HERE ON OUT. LET'S DITCH THE RIDE HERE.
GUESS WE GOTTA WALK.
YOU'D BE BETTER OFF NOT TAKING THAT ROAD... THERE'S THIS BOY, KITARO-
FWP
WHAT THE?!?!... DO YOU KNOW WHO YOU'RE SNEAKING UP ON?
GO INTO HIS PLACE WHEN HE'S OUT, AND YOU'RE BUYING YOURSELF A CRUISE TO HELL!
HOW ABOUT YOU SHUT UP AND GET BACK TO YOUR FARM, YA HAG?

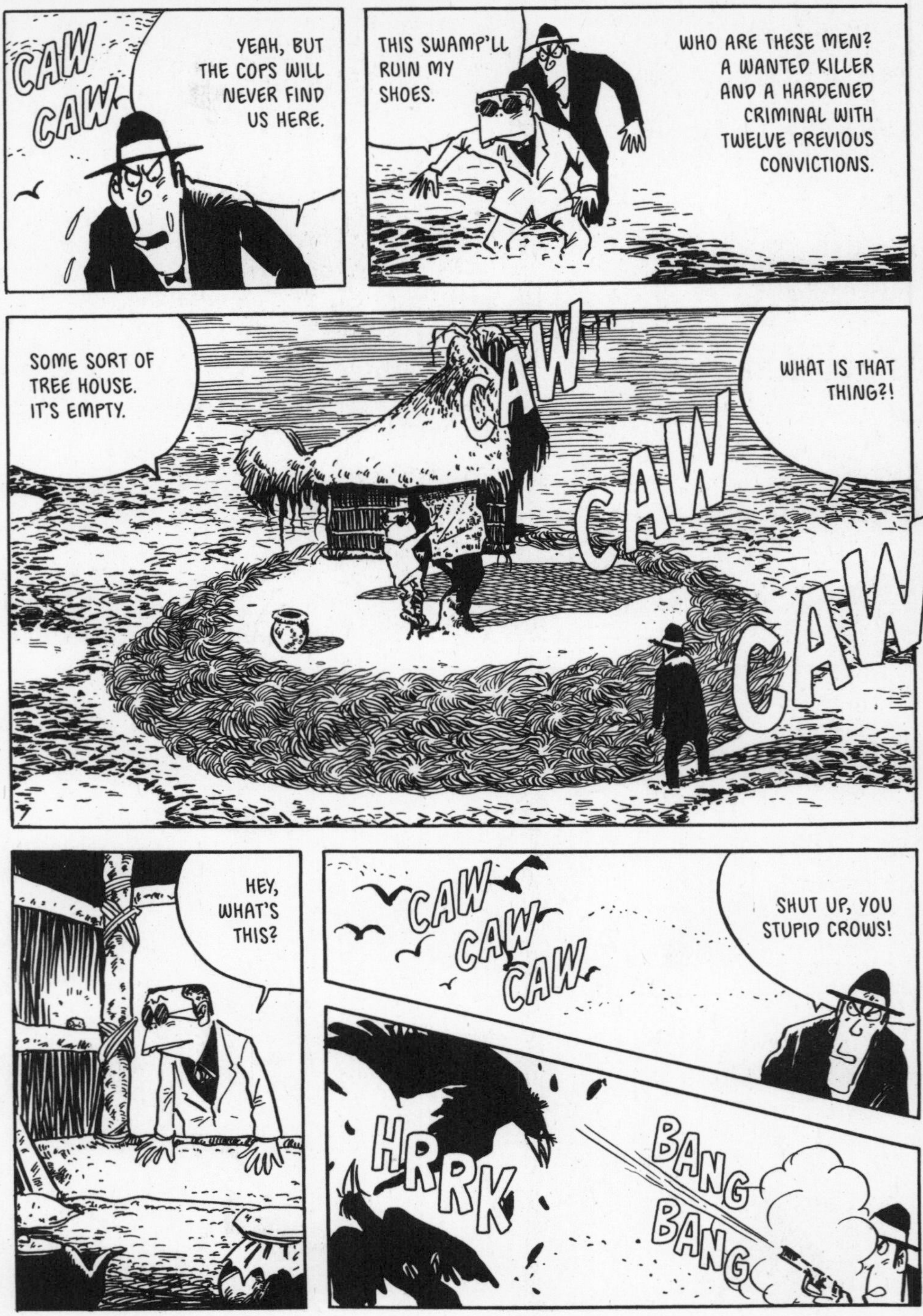
WHO ARE THESE MEN? A WANTED KILLER AND A HARDENED CRIMINAL WITH TWELVE PREVIOUS CONVICTIONS.
THIS SWAMP'LL RUIN MY SHOES.
YEAH, BUT THE COPS WILL NEVER FIND US HERE.
CAW
CAW
WHAT IS THAT THING?!
CAW
CAW
CAW
CAW
SOME SORT OF TREE HOUSE. IT'S EMPTY.
SHUT UP, YOU STUPID CROWS!
CAW
CAW
CAW
BANG
BANG
HRRK
HEY, WHAT'S THIS?

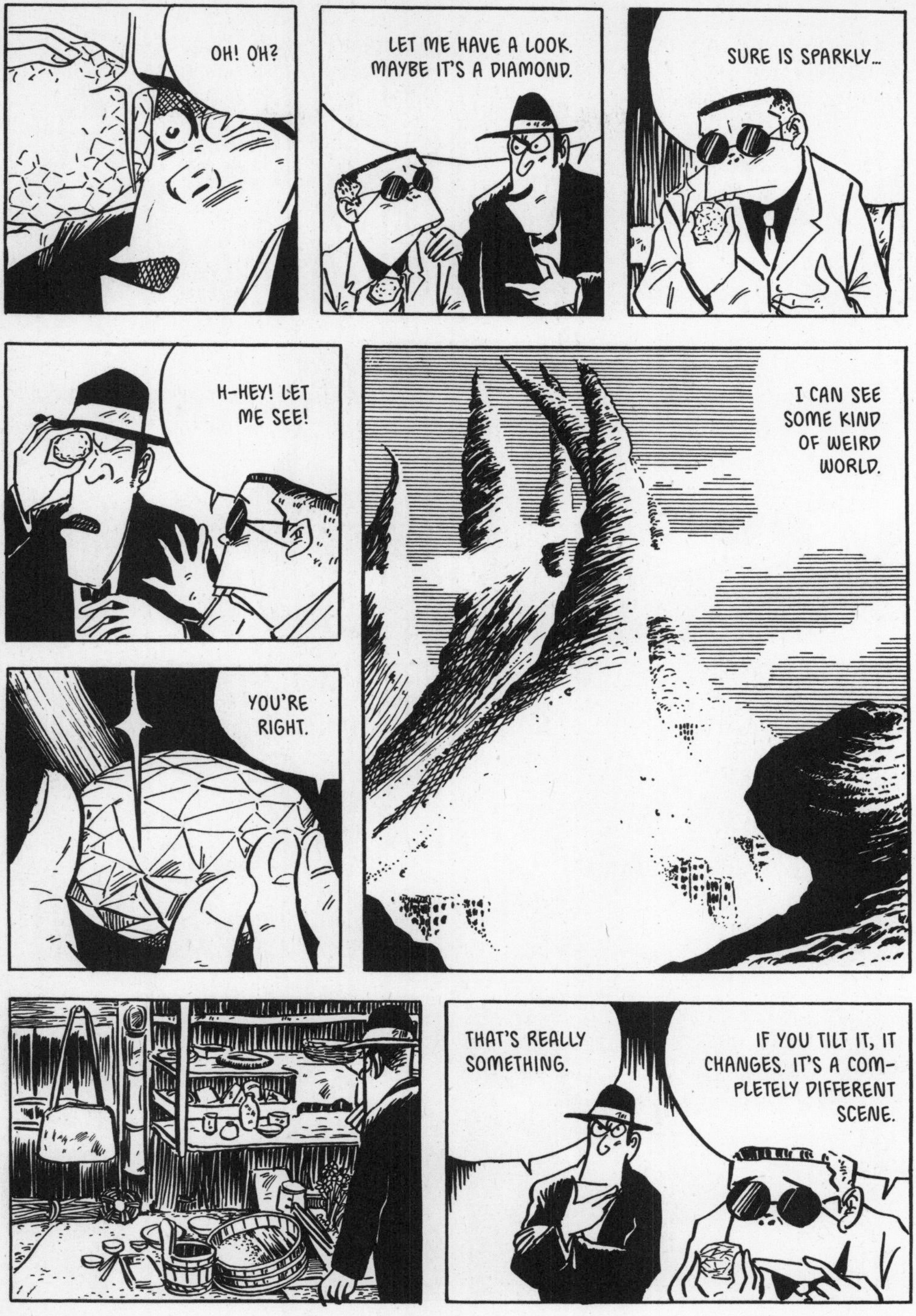
SURE IS SPARKLY...
LET ME HAVE A LOOK. MAYBE IT'S A DIAMOND.
OH! OH?
I CAN SEE SOME KIND OF WEIRD WORLD.
H-HEY! LET ME SEE!
YOU'RE RIGHT.
IF YOU TILT IT, IT CHANGES. IT'S A COMPLETELY DIFFERENT SCENE.
THAT'S REALLY SOMETHING.

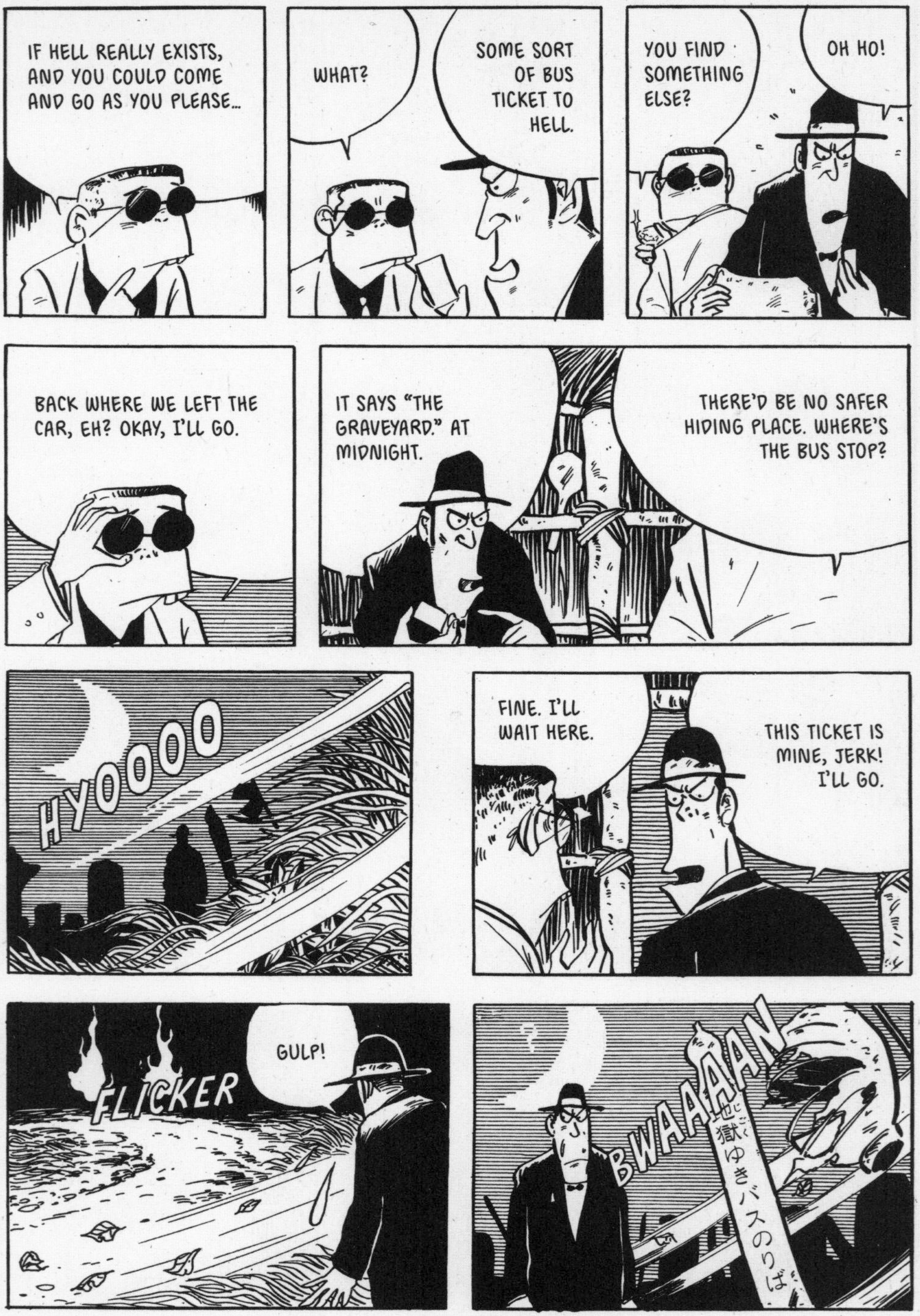
OH HO!
YOU FIND SOMETHING ELSE?
SOME SORT OF BUS TICKET TO HELL.
WHAT?
IF HELL REALLY EXISTS, AND YOU COULD COME AND GO AS YOU PLEASE...
THERE'D BE NO SAFER HIDING PLACE. WHERE'S THE BUS STOP?
IT SAYS "THE GRAVEYARD." AT MIDNIGHT.
BACK WHERE WE LEFT THE CAR, EH? OKAY, I'LL GO.
THIS TICKET IS MINE, JERK! I'LL GO.
FINE. I'LL WAIT HERE.
HYOOOO
BWAAAAAN
地獄ゆきバスのりば
GULP!
FLICKER

SIGN: BUS TO HELL.

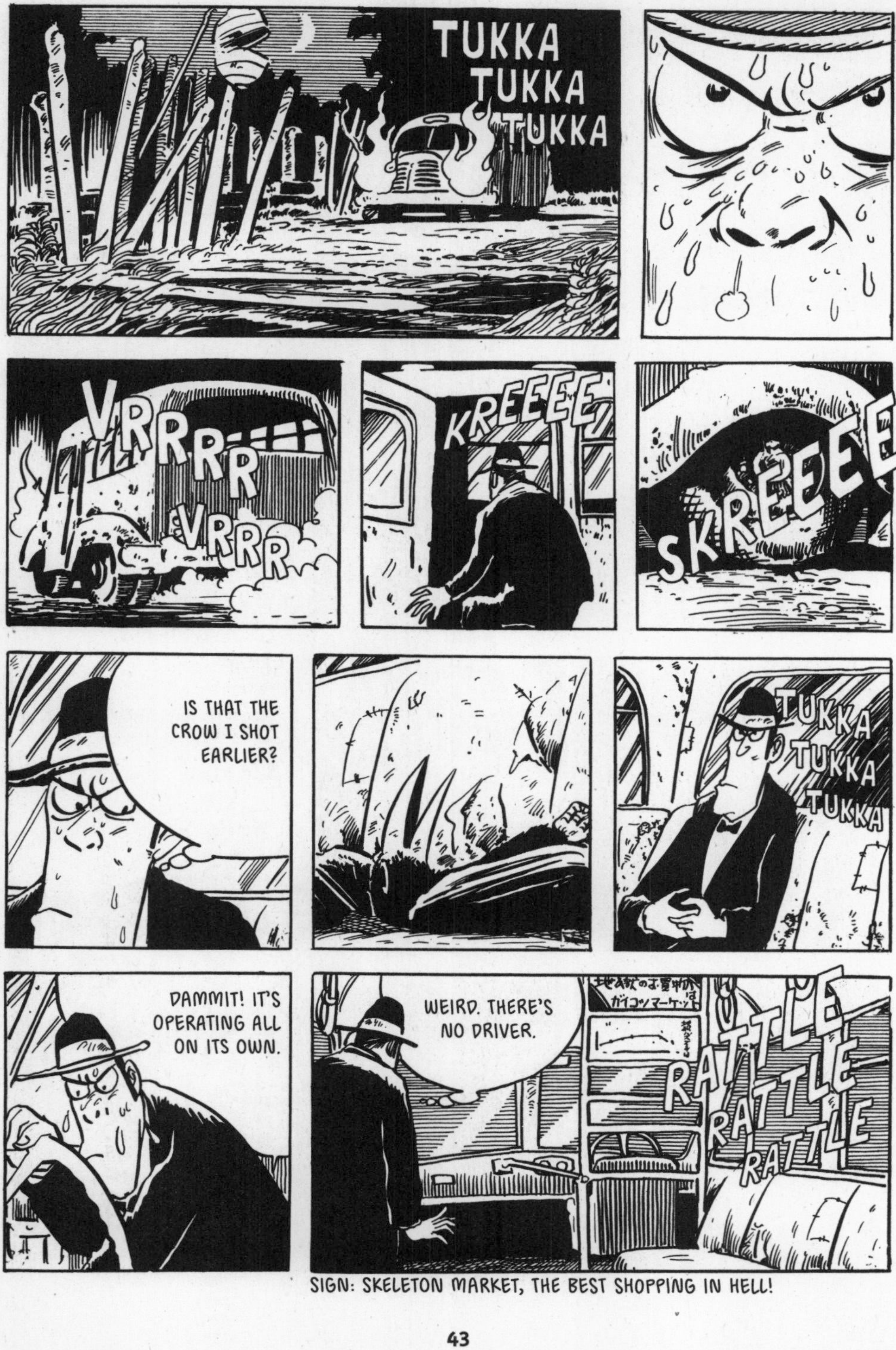
TUKKA
TUKKA
TUKKA
SKREEEE
KREEEE
VRRRR
VRRR
TUKKA
TUKKA
TUKKA
IS THAT THE CROW I SHOT EARLIER?
WEIRD. THERE'S NO DRIVER.
RATTLE
RATTLE
RATTLE
DAMMIT! IT'S OPERATING ALL ON ITS OWN.
SIGN: SKELETON MARKET, THE BEST SHOPPING IN HELL!

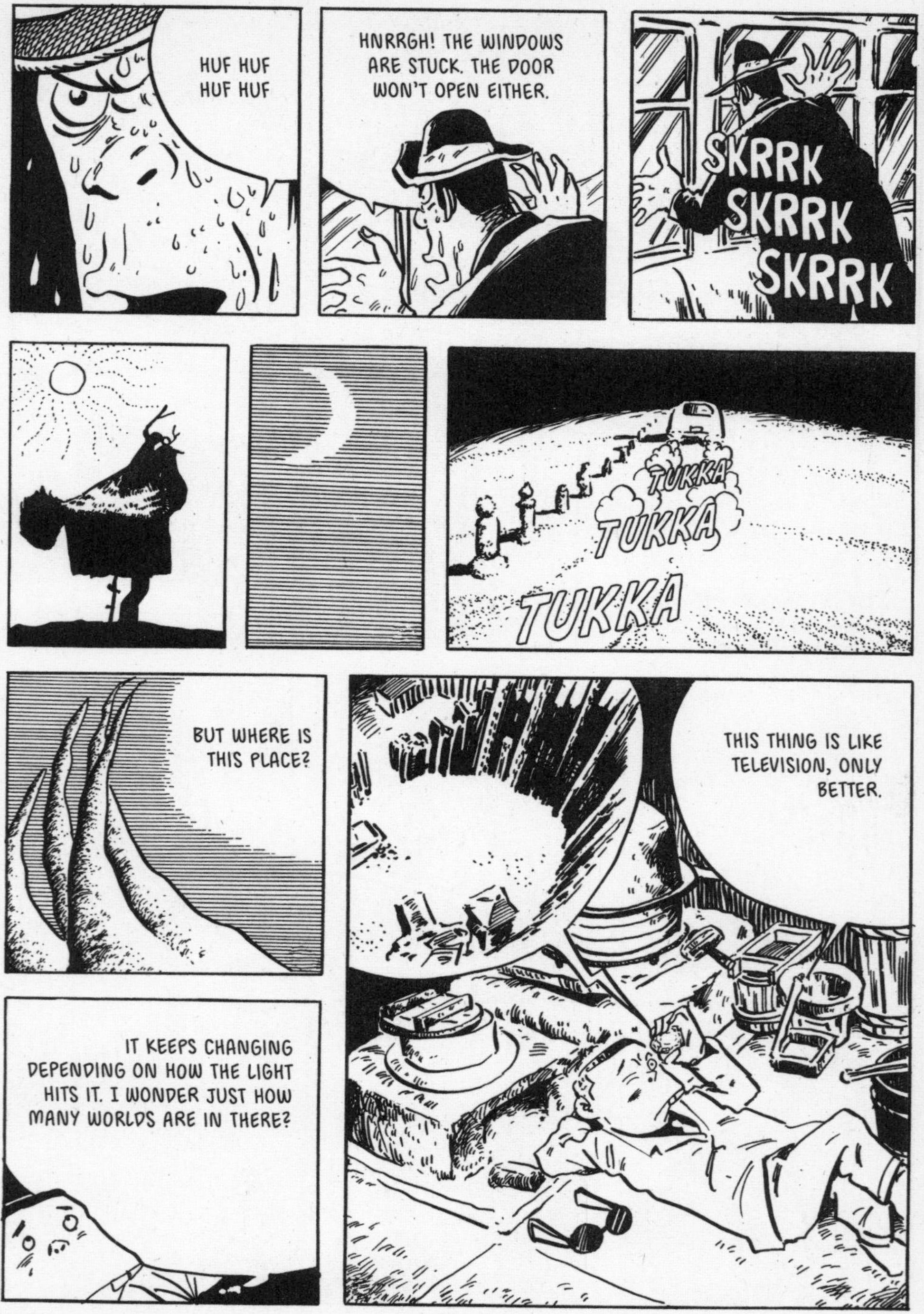
SKRRK
SKRRK
SKRRK
HNRRGH! THE WINDOWS ARE STUCK. THE DOOR WON'T OPEN EITHER.
HUF HUF
HUF HUF
TUKKA
TUKKA
TUKKA
THIS THING IS LIKE TELEVISION, ONLY BETTER.
BUT WHERE IS THIS PLACE?
IT KEEPS CHANGING DEPENDING ON HOW THE LIGHT HITS IT. I WONDER JUST HOW MANY WORLDS ARE IN THERE?

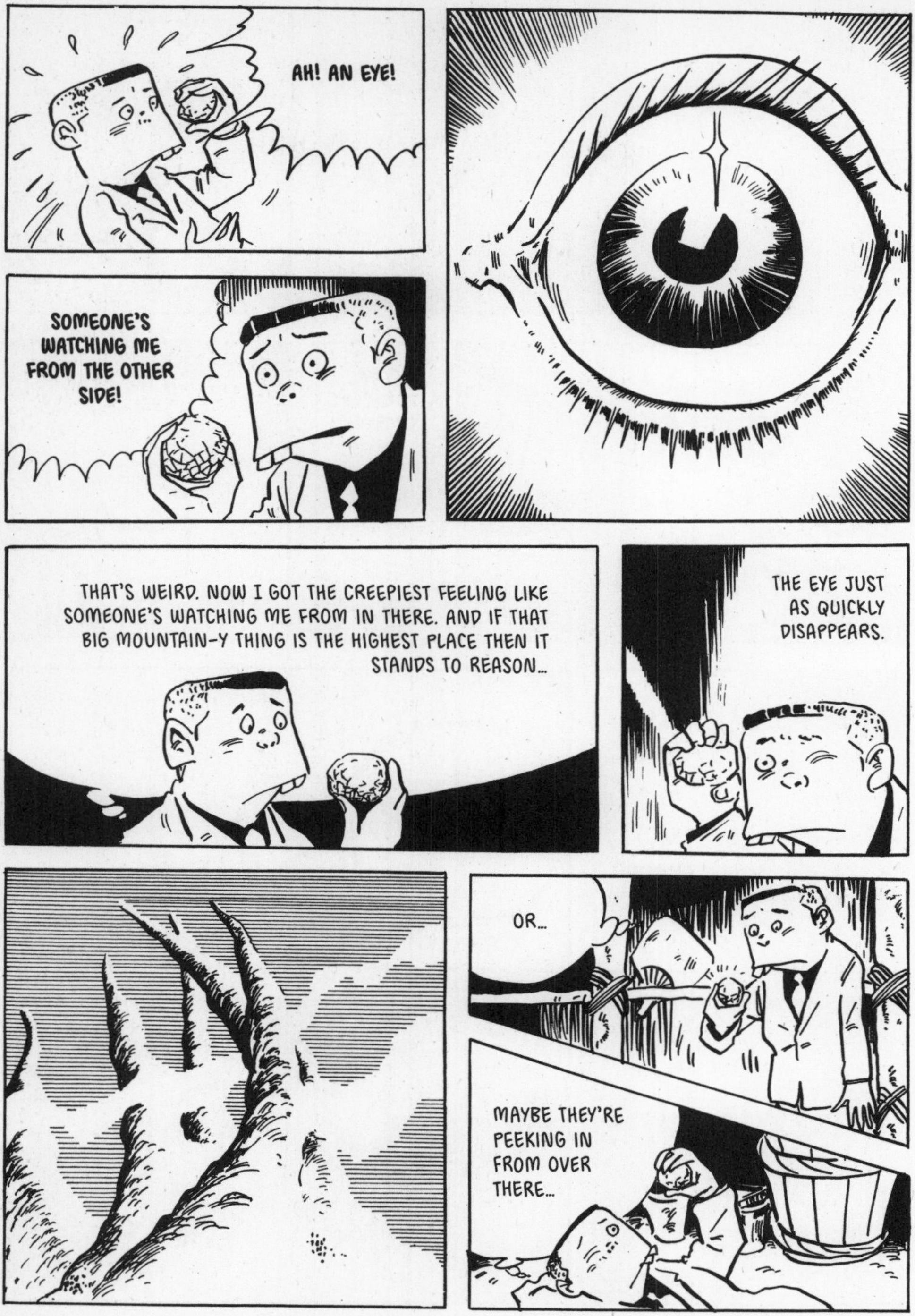
AH! AN EYE!
SOMEONE'S WATCHING ME FROM THE OTHER SIDE!
THE EYE JUST AS QUICKLY DISAPPEARS.
THAT'S WEIRD. NOW I GOT THE CREEPIEST FEELING LIKE SOMEONE'S WATCHING ME FROM IN THERE. AND IF THAT BIG MOUNTAIN-Y THING IS THE HIGHEST PLACE THEN IT STANDS TO REASON...
OR...
MAYBE THEY'RE PEEKING IN FROM OVER THERE...

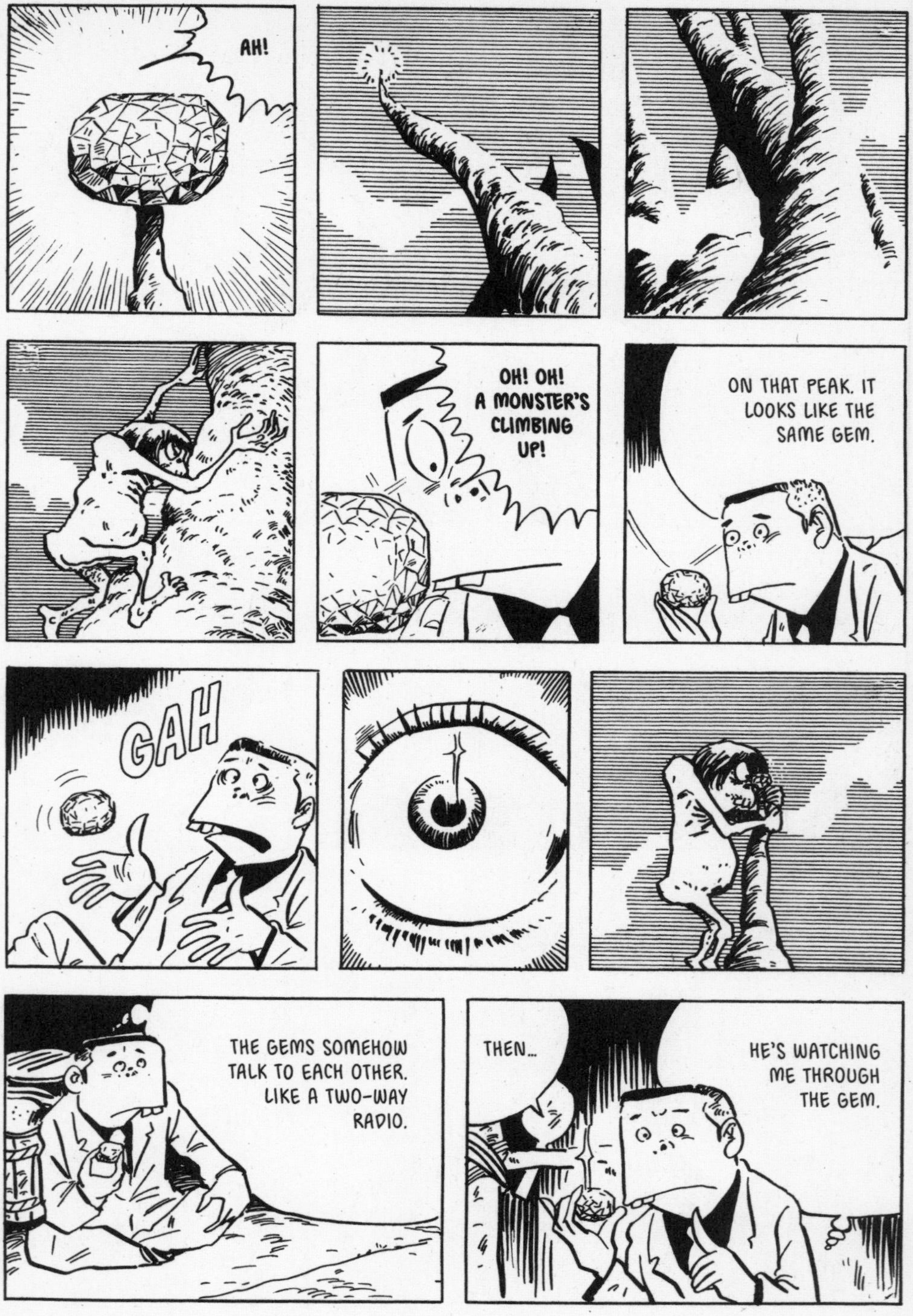
AH!
ON THAT PEAK. IT LOOKS LIKE THE SAME GEM.
OH! OH! A MONSTER'S CLIMBING UP!
GAH
HE'S WATCHING ME THROUGH THE GEM.
THEN...
THE GEMS SOMEHOW TALK TO EACH OTHER. LIKE A TWO-WAY RADIO.

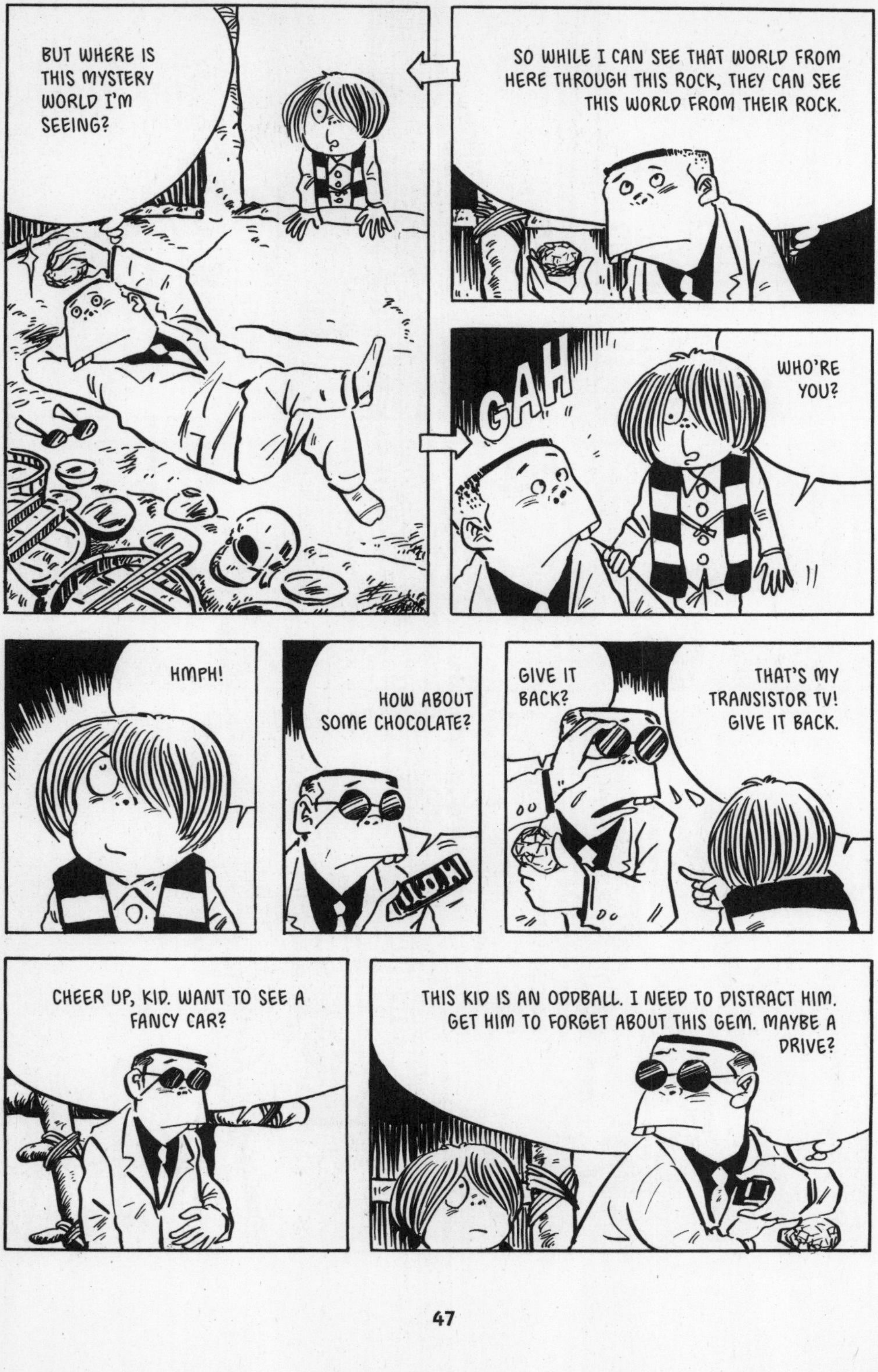
SO WHILE I CAN SEE THAT WORLD FROM HERE THROUGH THIS ROCK, THEY CAN SEE THIS WORLD FROM THEIR ROCK.
BUT WHERE IS THIS MYSTERY WORLD I'M SEEING?
WHO'RE YOU?
GAH
THAT'S MY TRANSISTOR TV! GIVE IT BACK.
GIVE IT BACK?
HOW ABOUT SOME CHOCOLATE?
HMPH!
THIS KID IS AN ODDBALL. I NEED TO DISTRACT HIM. GET HIM TO FORGET ABOUT THIS GEM. MAYBE A DRIVE?
CHEER UP, KID. WANT TO SEE A FANCY CAR?

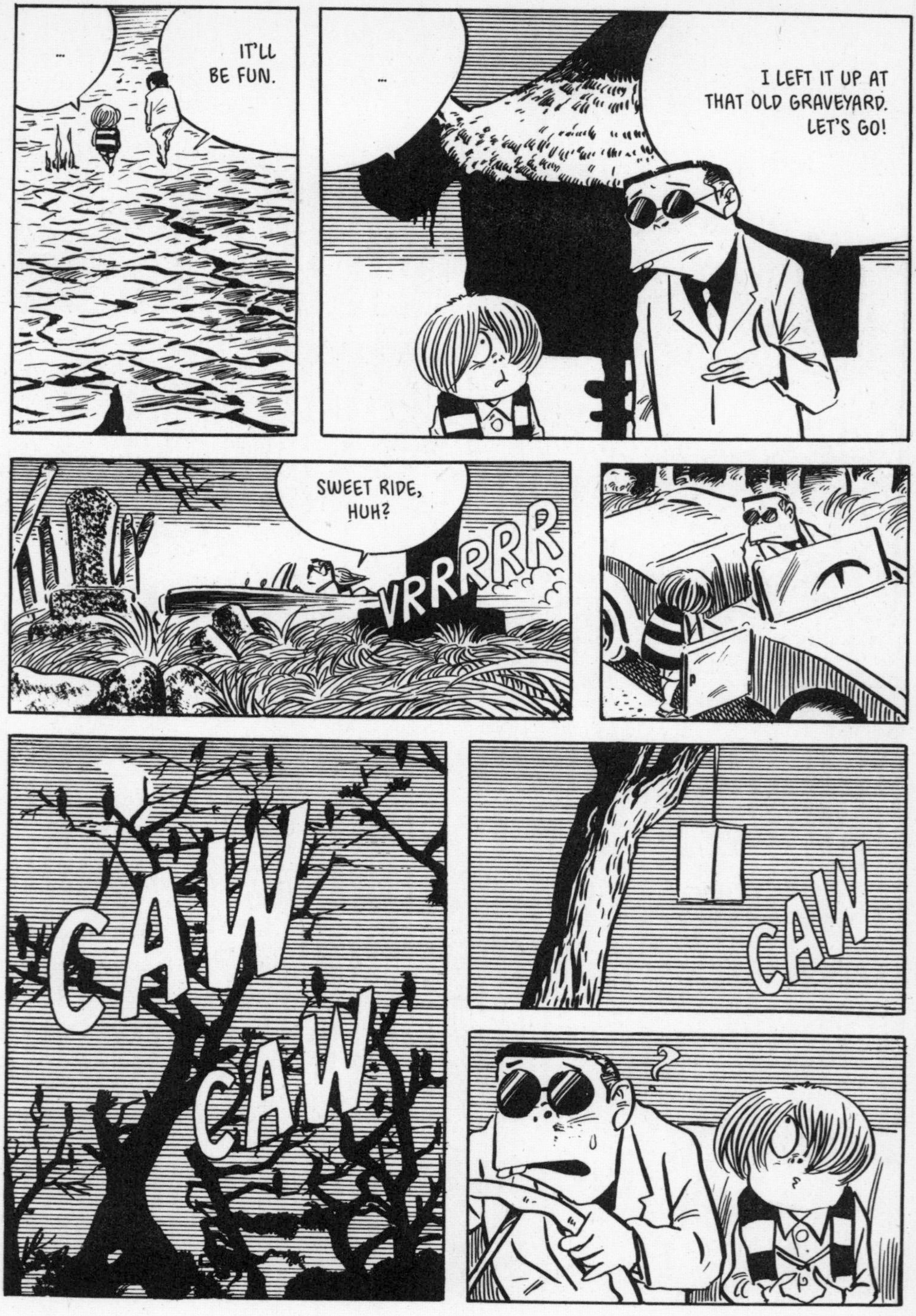
I LEFT IT UP AT THAT OLD GRAVEYARD. LET'S GO!
...
IT'LL BE FUN.
...
SWEET RIDE, HUH?
VRRRRR
CAW
?
CAW
CAW

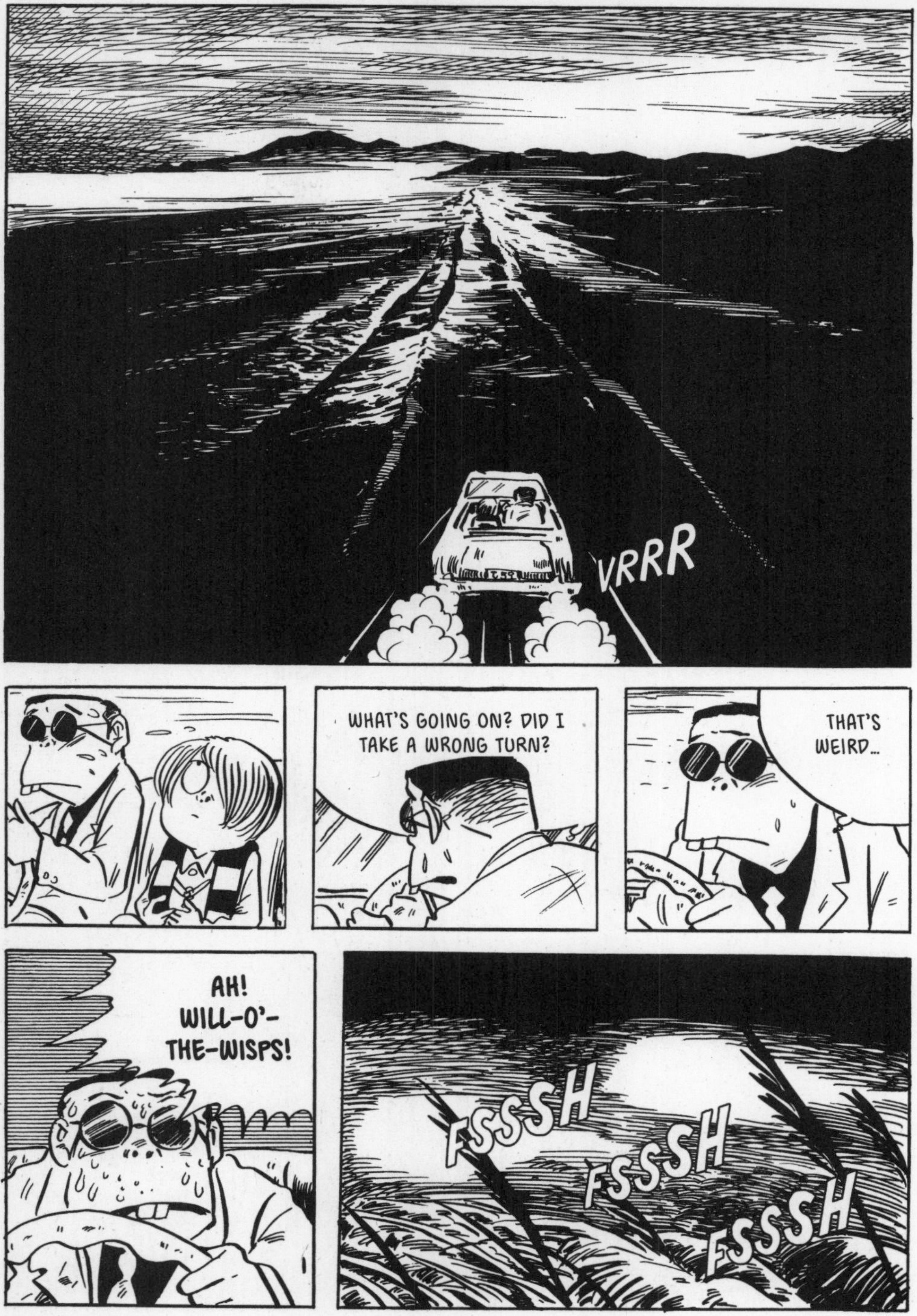
VRRR
THAT'S WEIRD...
WHAT'S GOING ON? DID I TAKE A WRONG TURN?
FSSSH
FSSSH
FSSSH
AH! WILL-O'-THE-WISPS!

AAAAAH!
EEAAGGH!
STOP YOUR HOLLERING. PLEASE GET OUT OF THE CAR.
?
IT'S DESOLATE HERE.
HMM. THAT LOOKS FAMILIAR--LIKE THE PLACE I SAW IN THE GEM.

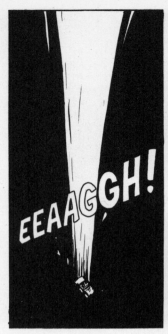

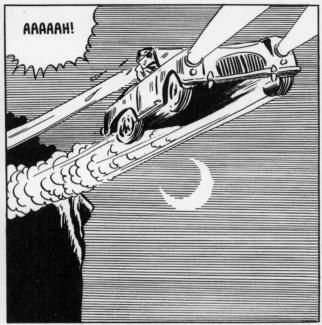

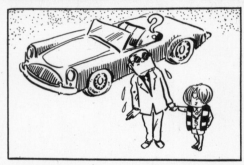

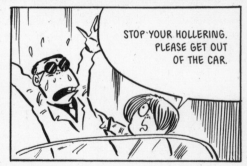

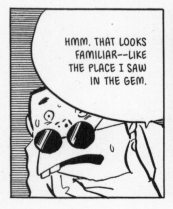

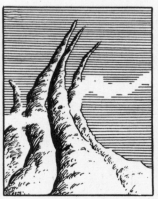

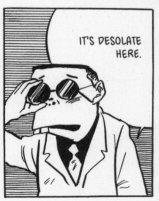

WHERE EXACTLY ARE WE?
THERE'S SOMETHING I WANT TO SHOW YOU.
HEY, WHAT'S THAT OVER THERE?
LOOKS LIKE SOME KIND OF FIGHT'S GOING ON...
CHATTER CHATTER CHATTER

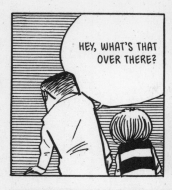

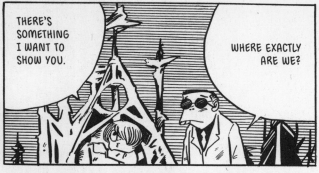

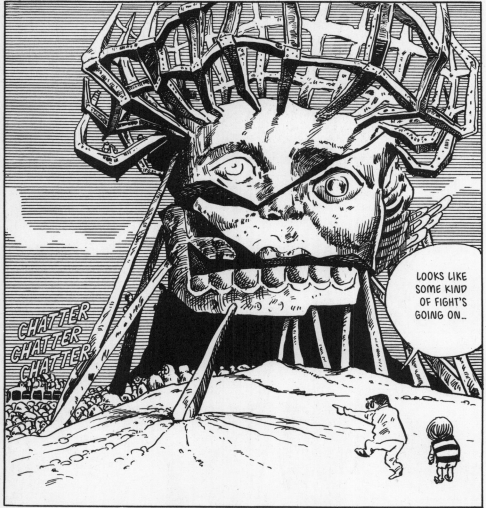

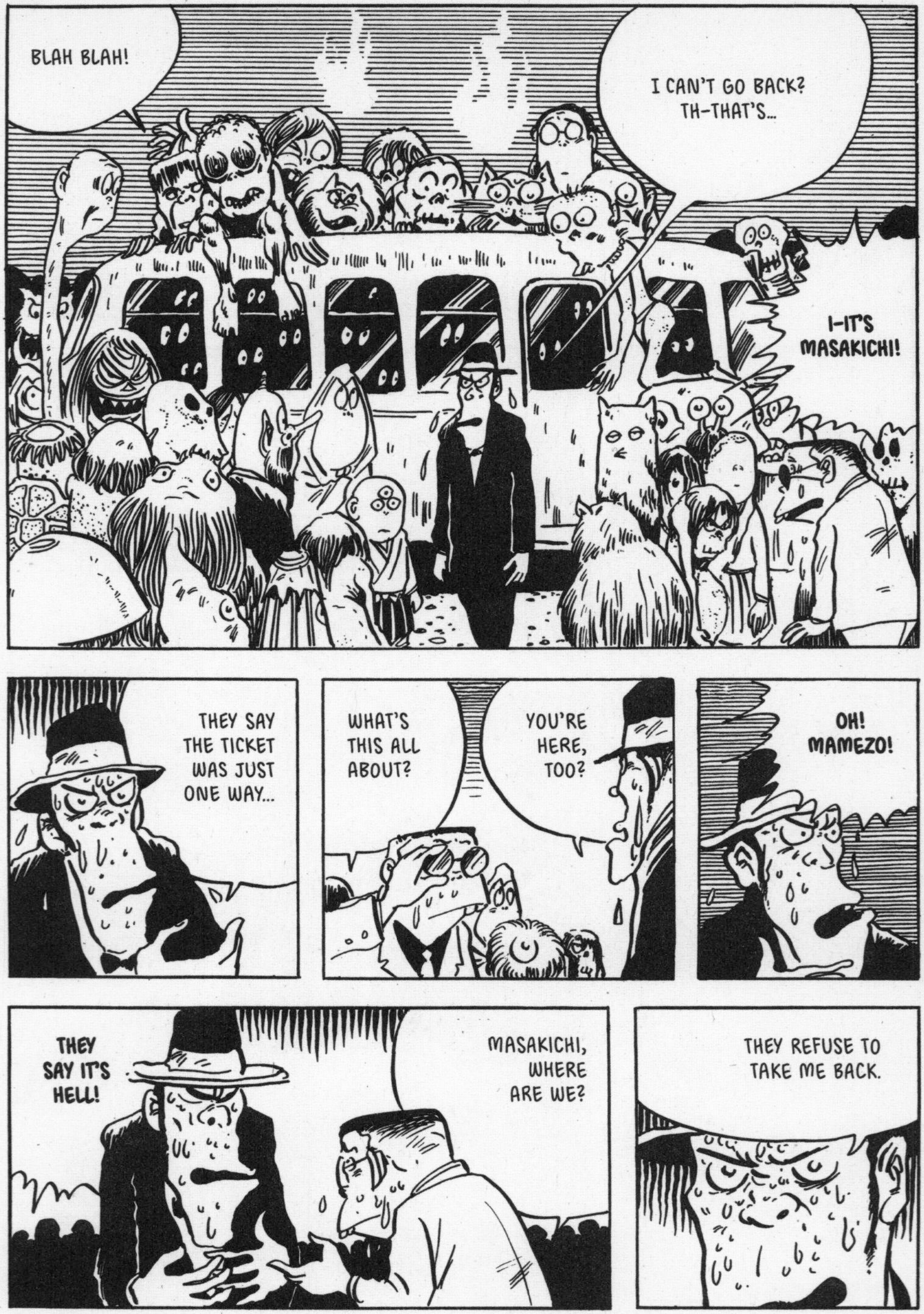
I CAN'T GO BACK? TH-THAT'S...
I-IT'S MASAKICHI!
BLAH BLAH!
OH! MAMEZO!
YOU'RE HERE, TOO?
WHAT'S THIS ALL ABOUT?
THEY SAY THE TICKET WAS JUST ONE WAY...
THEY REFUSE TO TAKE ME BACK.
MASAKICHI, WHERE ARE WE?
THEY SAY IT'S HELL!

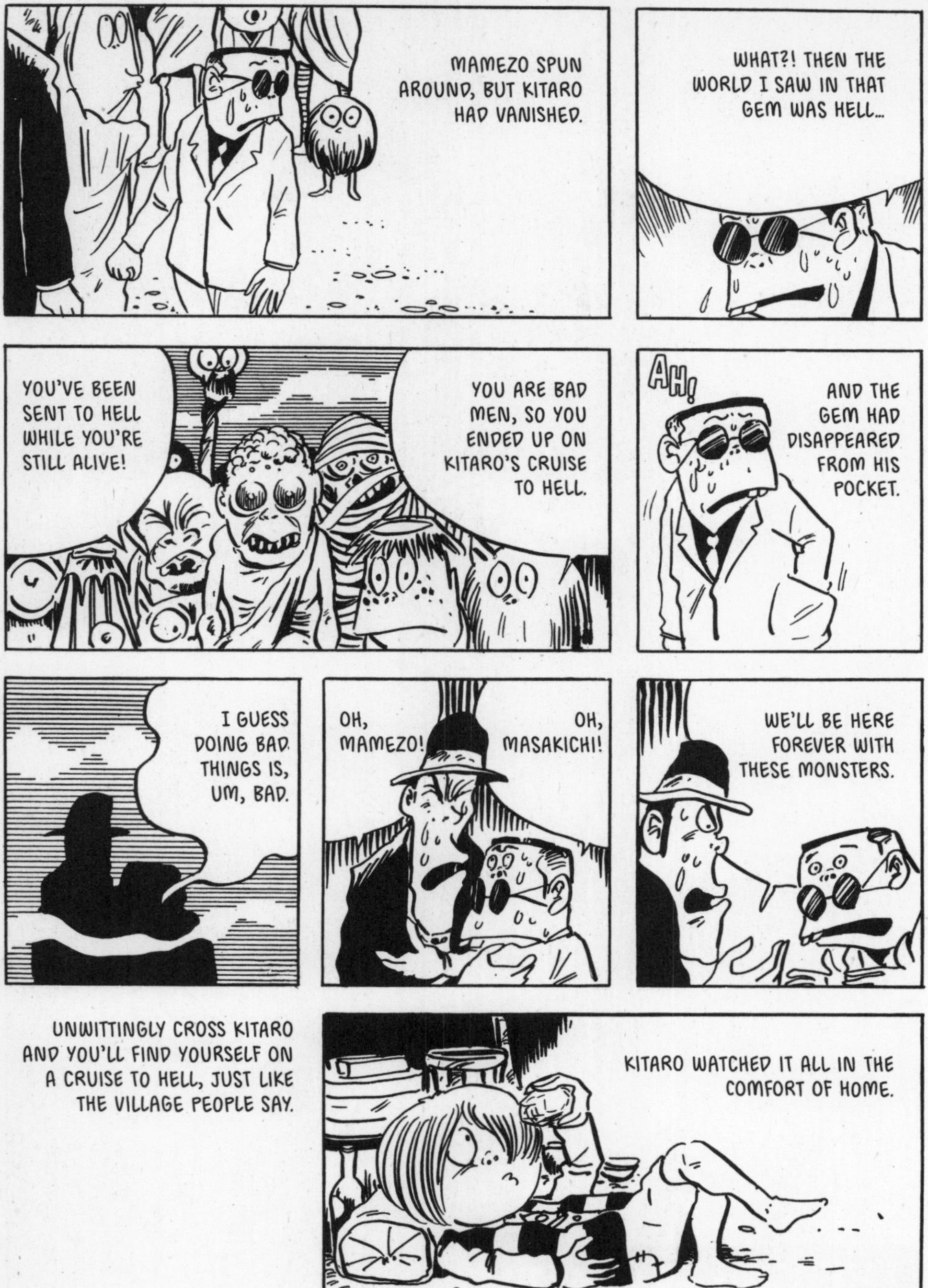
WHAT?! THEN THE WORLD I SAW IN THAT GEM WAS HELL...
MAMEZO SPUN AROUND, BUT KITARO HAD VANISHED.
AH!
AND THE GEM HAD DISAPPEARED FROM HIS POCKET.
YOU ARE BAD MEN, SO YOU ENDED UP ON KITARO'S CRUISE TO HELL.
YOU'VE BEEN SENT TO HELL WHILE YOU'RE STILL ALIVE!
WE'LL BE HERE FOREVER WITH THESE MONSTERS.
OH, MASAKICHI!
OH, MAMEZO!
I GUESS DOING BAD THINGS IS, UM, BAD.
KITARO WATCHED IT ALL IN THE COMFORT OF HOME.
UNWITTINGLY CROSS KITARO AND YOU'LL FIND YOURSELF ON A CRUISE TO HELL, JUST LIKE THE VILLAGE PEOPLE SAY.

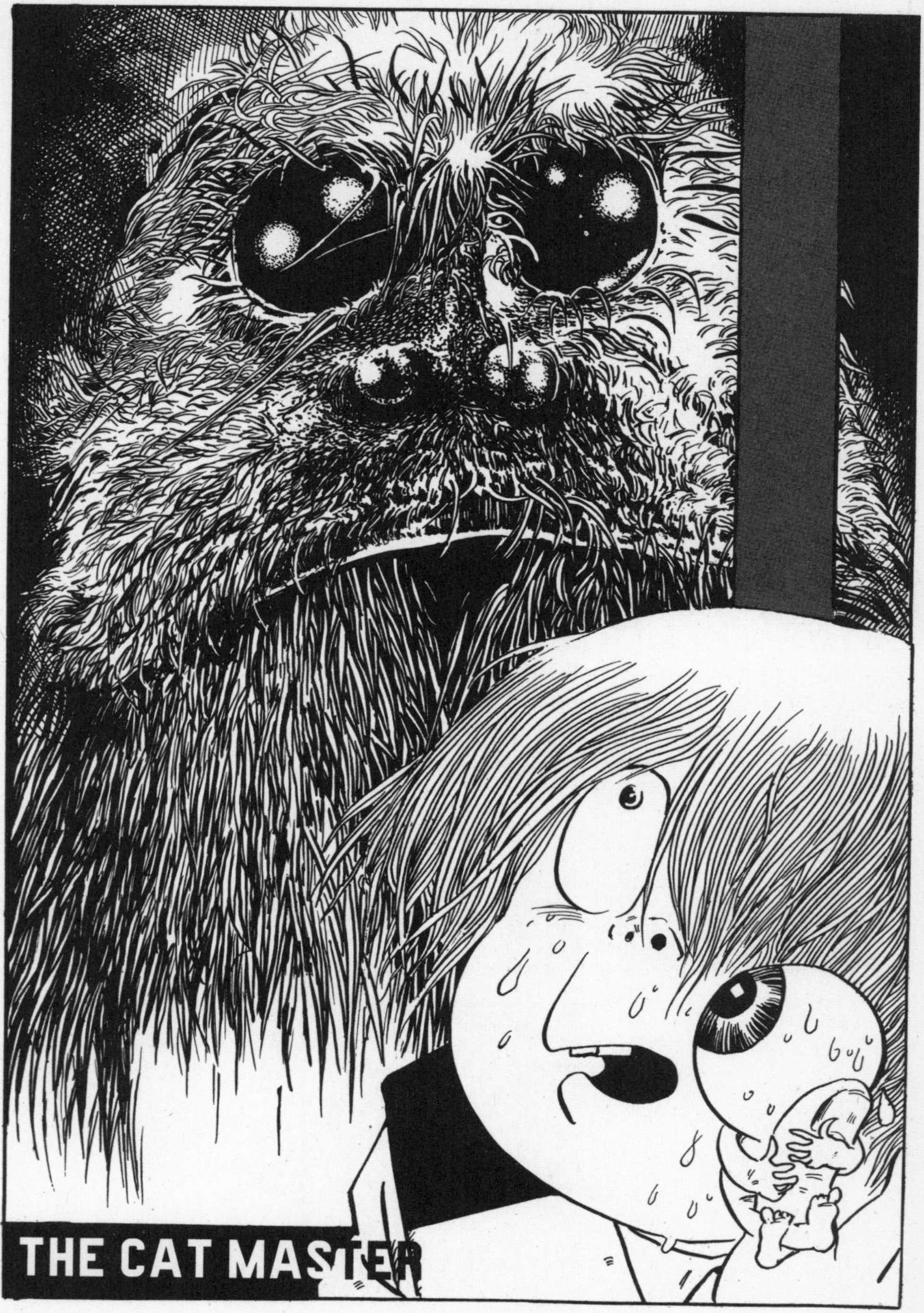
THE CAT MASTER

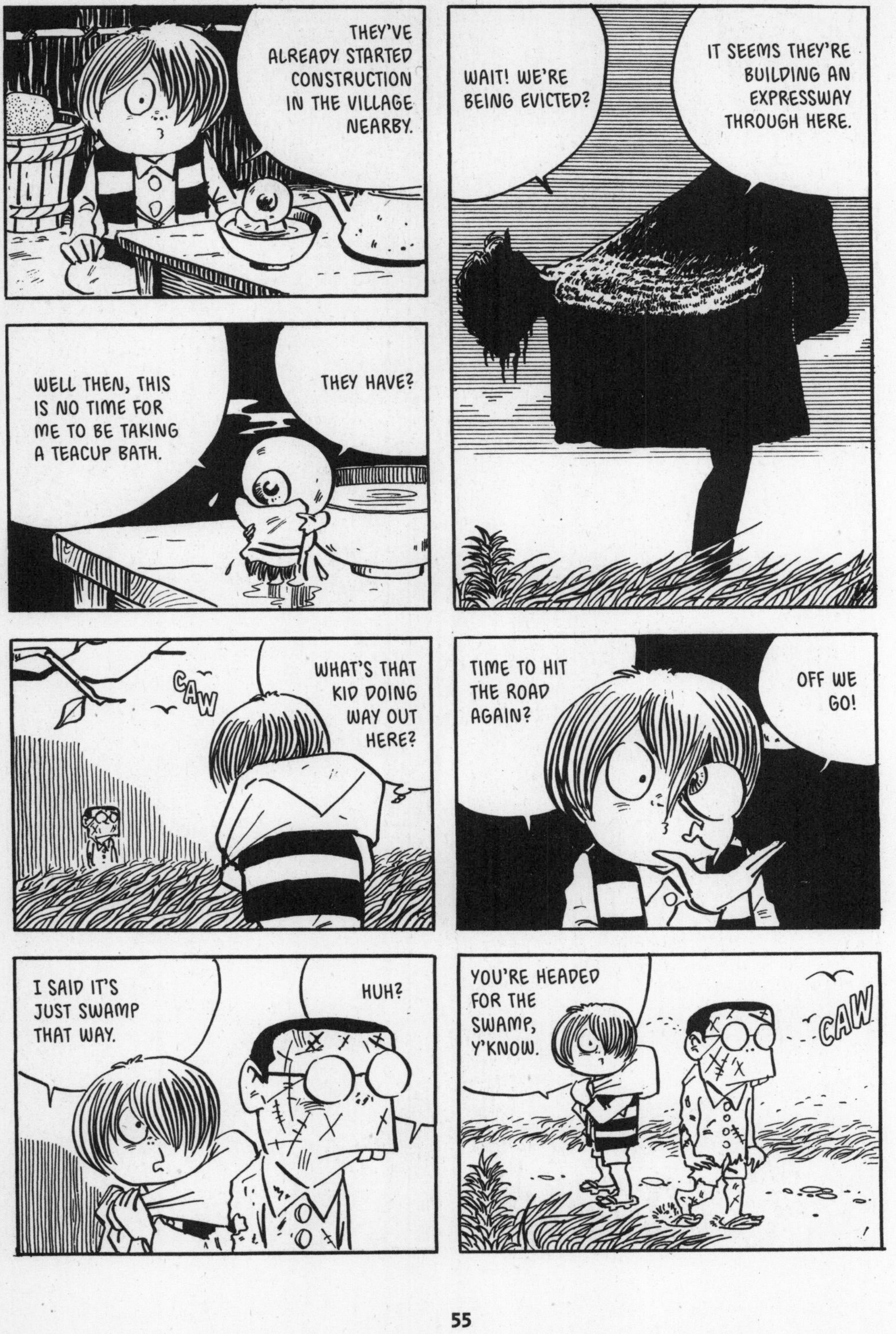
IT SEEMS THEY'RE BUILDING AN EXPRESSWAY THROUGH HERE.
WAIT! WE'RE BEING EVICTED?
THEY'VE ALREADY STARTED CONSTRUCTION IN THE VILLAGE NEARBY.
THEY HAVE?
WELL THEN, THIS IS NO TIME FOR ME TO BE TAKING A TEACUP BATH.
OFF WE GO!
TIME TO HIT THE ROAD AGAIN?
WHAT'S THAT KID DOING WAY OUT HERE?
CAW
YOU'RE HEADED FOR THE SWAMP, Y'KNOW.
CAW
HUH?
I SAID IT'S JUST SWAMP THAT WAY.

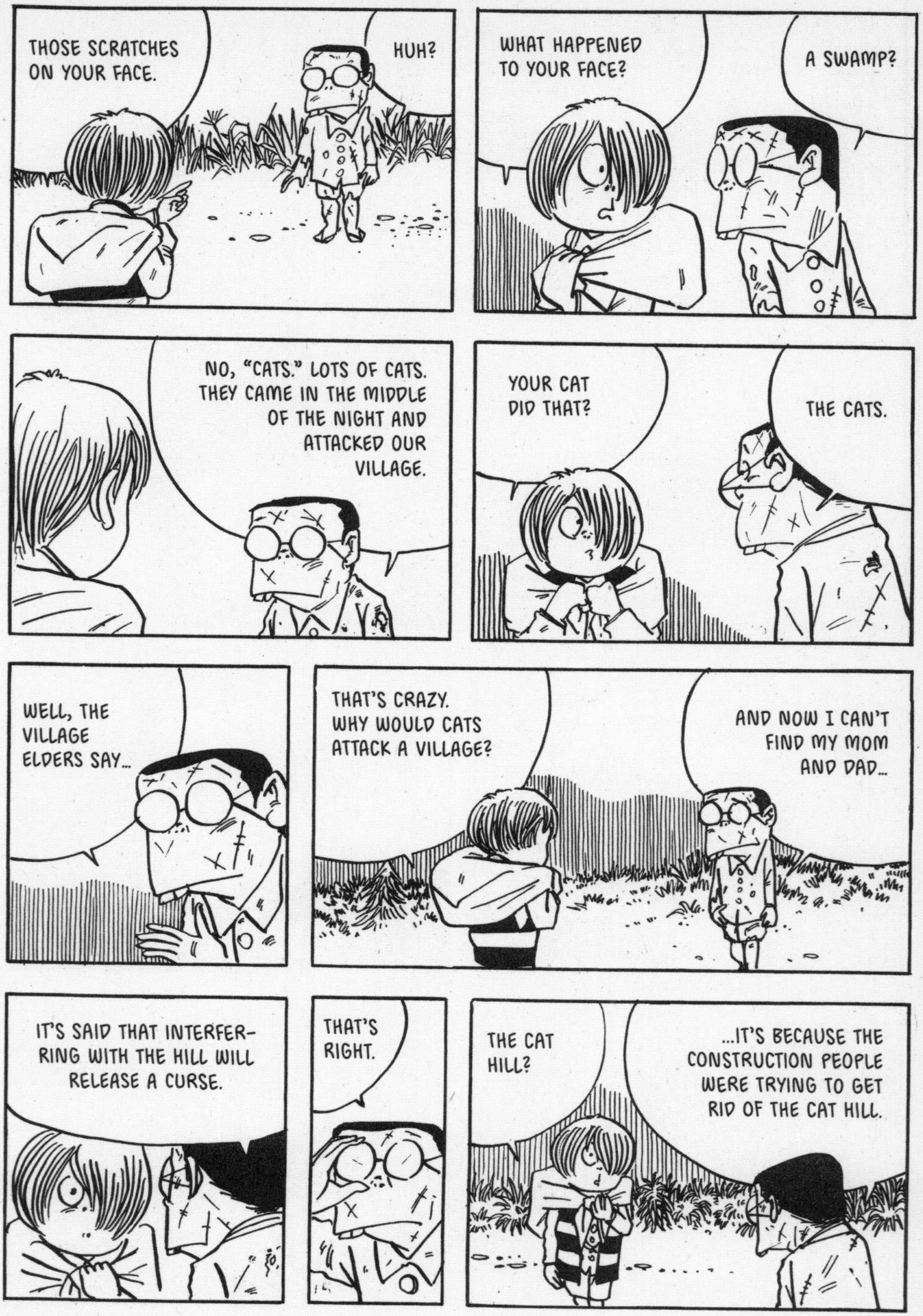
A SWAMP?
WHAT HAPPENED TO YOUR FACE?
HUH?
THOSE SCRATCHES ON YOUR FACE.
THE CATS.
YOUR CAT DID THAT?
NO, "CATS." LOTS OF CATS. THEY CAME IN THE MIDDLE OF THE NIGHT AND ATTACKED OUR VILLAGE.
AND NOW I CAN'T FIND MY MOM AND DAD...
THAT'S CRAZY. WHY WOULD CATS ATTACK A VILLAGE?
WELL, THE VILLAGE ELDERS SAY...
...IT'S BECAUSE THE CONSTRUCTION PEOPLE WERE TRYING TO GET RID OF THE CAT HILL.
THE CAT HILL?
THAT'S RIGHT.
IT'S SAID THAT INTERFER-RING WITH THE HILL WILL RELEASE A CURSE.

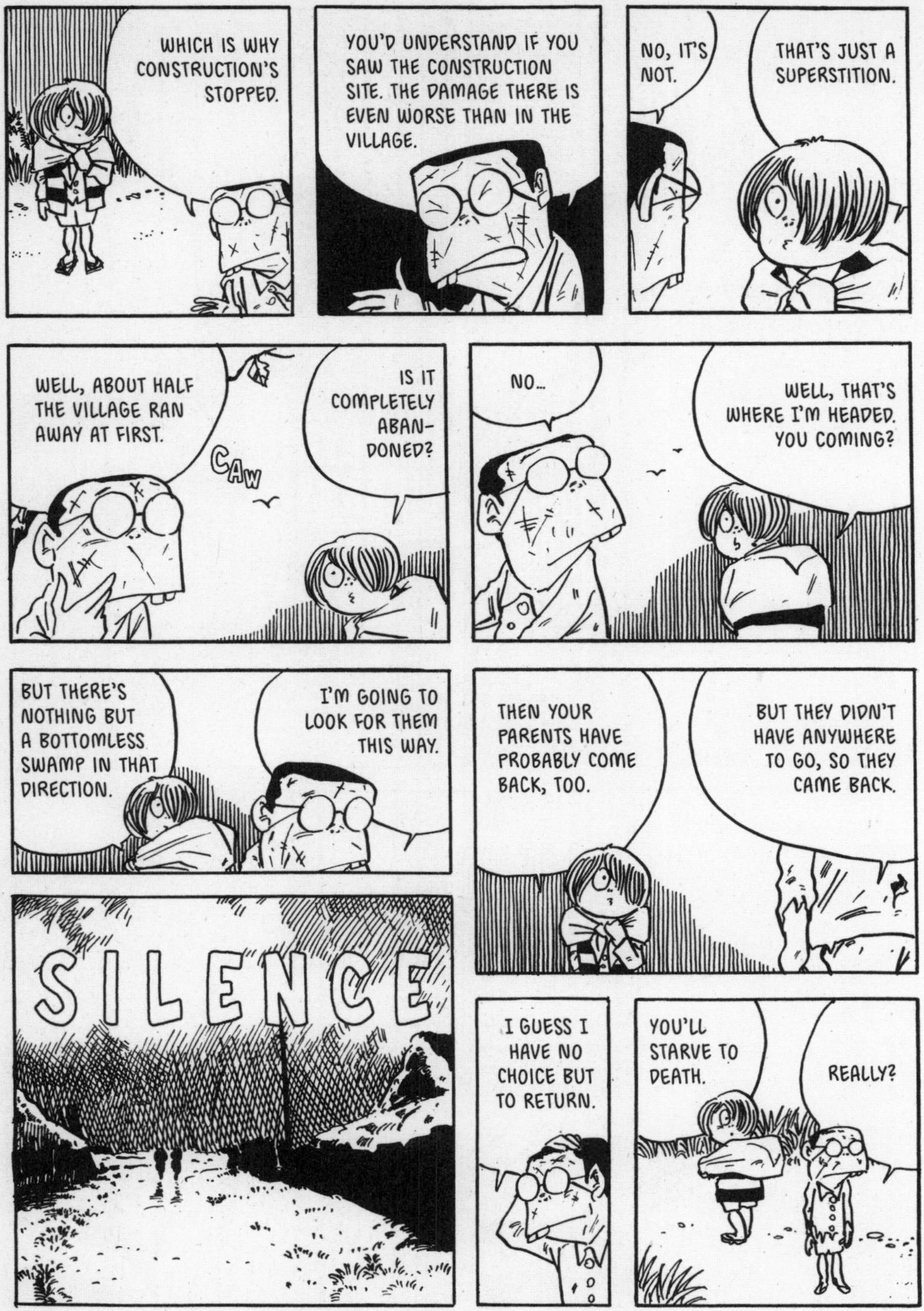
THAT'S JUST A SUPERSTITION.
NO, IT'S NOT.
YOU'D UNDERSTAND IF YOU SAW THE CONSTRUCTION SITE. THE DAMAGE THERE IS EVEN WORSE THAN IN THE VILLAGE.
WHICH IS WHY CONSTRUCTION'S STOPPED.
WELL, THAT'S WHERE I'M HEADED. YOU COMING?
NO...
IS IT COMPLETELY ABAN- DONED?
CAW
WELL, ABOUT HALF THE VILLAGE RAN AWAY AT FIRST.
BUT THEY DIDN'T HAVE ANYWHERE TO GO, SO THEY CAME BACK.
THEN YOUR PARENTS HAVE PROBABLY COME BACK, TOO.
I'M GOING TO LOOK FOR THEM THIS WAY.
BUT THERE'S NOTHING BUT A BOTTOMLESS SWAMP IN THAT DIRECTION.
REALLY?
YOU'LL STARVE TO DEATH.
I GUESS I HAVE NO CHOICE BUT TO RETURN.
SILENCE

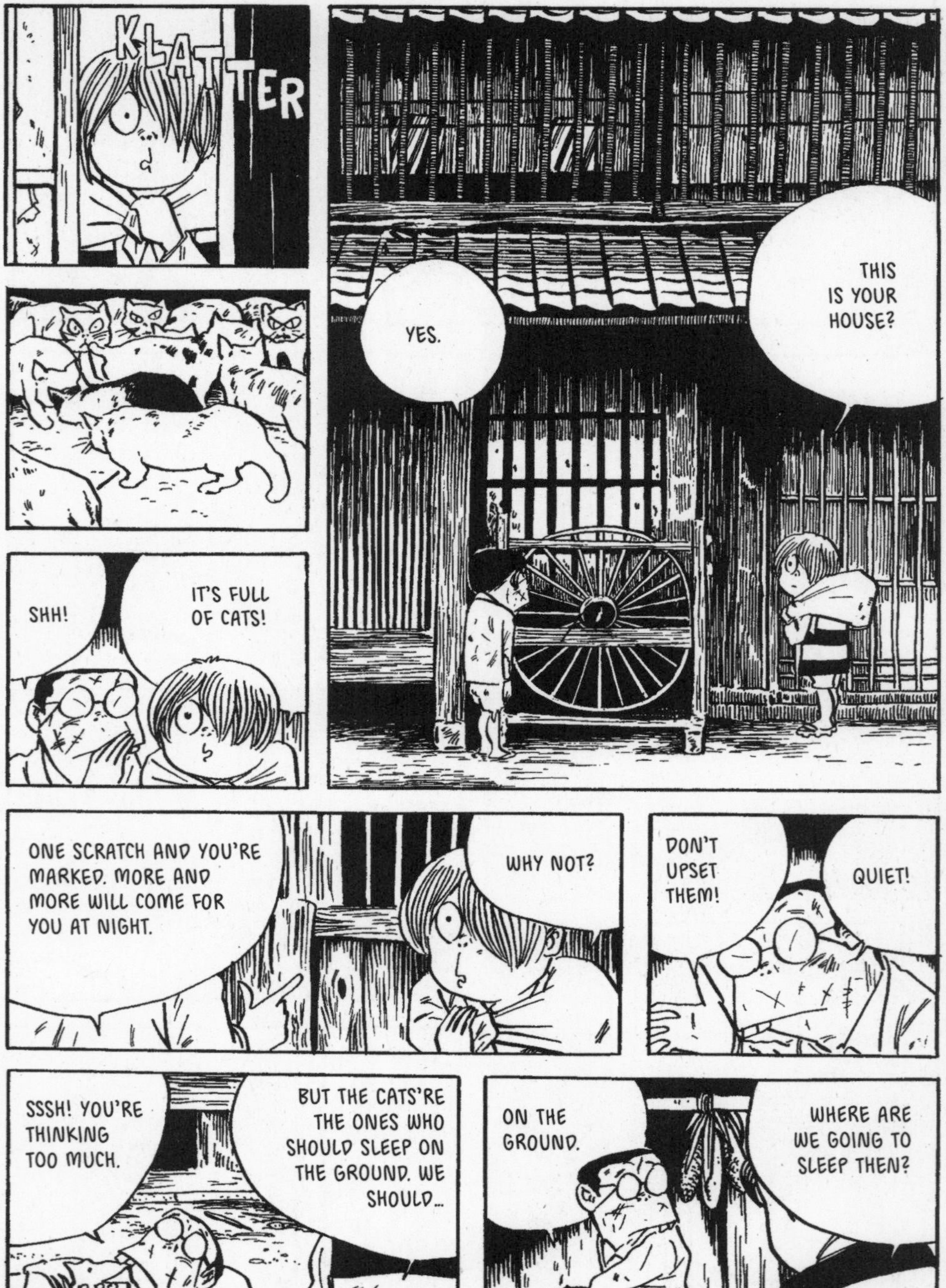
THIS IS YOUR HOUSE?
YES.
KLATTER
IT'S FULL OF CATS!
SHH!
QUIET!
DON'T UPSET THEM!
WHY NOT?
ONE SCRATCH AND YOU'RE MARKED. MORE AND MORE WILL COME FOR YOU AT NIGHT.
WHERE ARE WE GOING TO SLEEP THEN?
ON THE GROUND.
BUT THE CATS'RE THE ONES WHO SHOULD SLEEP ON THE GROUND. WE SHOULD...
SSSH! YOU'RE THINKING TOO MUCH.

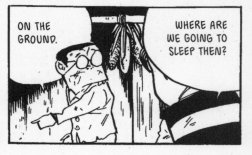

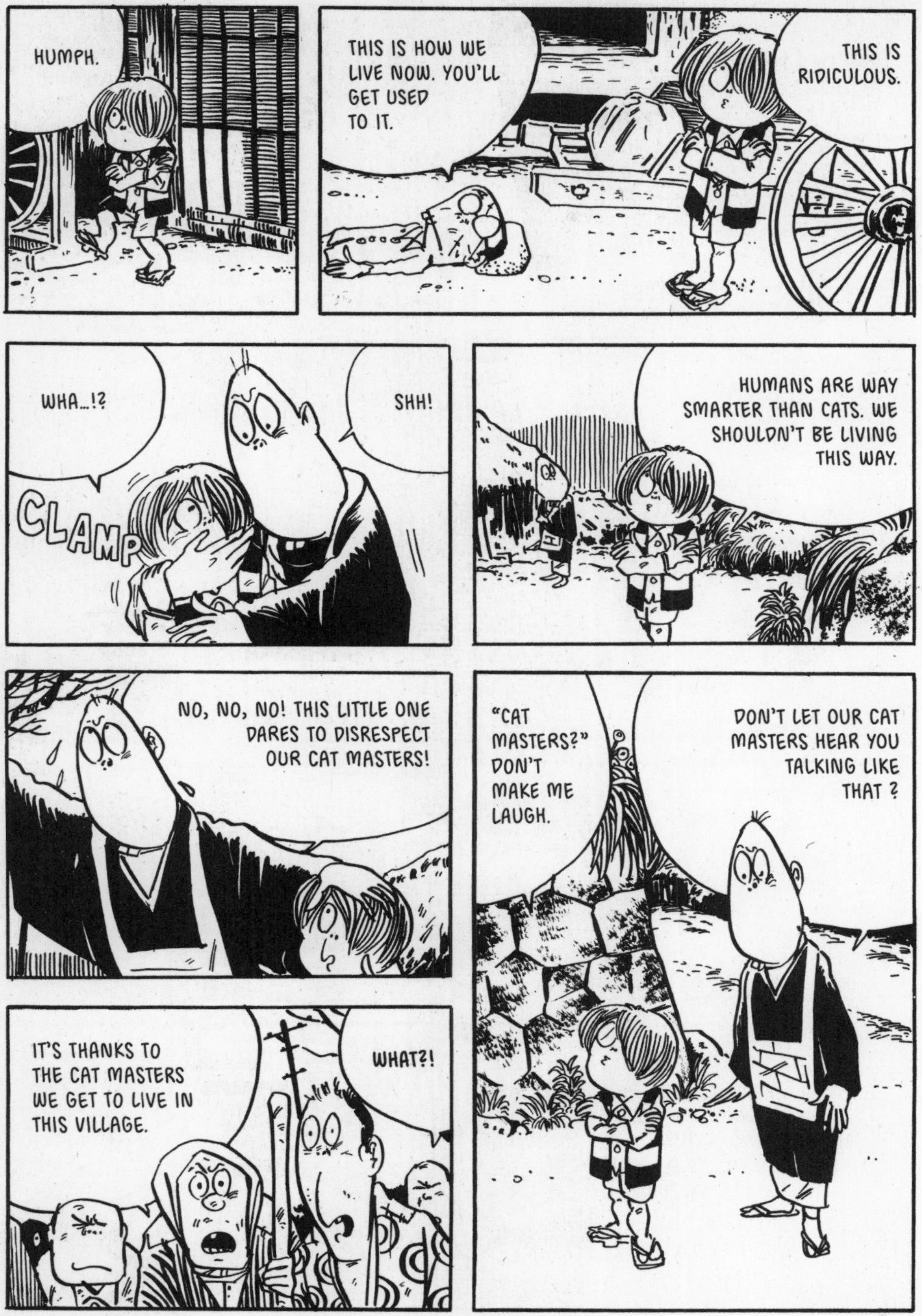
THIS IS RIDICULOUS.
THIS IS HOW WE LIVE NOW. YOU'LL GET USED TO IT.
HUMPH.
HUMANS ARE WAY SMARTER THAN CATS. WE SHOULDN'T BE LIVING THIS WAY.
SHH!
WHA...!?
CLAMP
DON'T LET OUR CAT MASTERS HEAR YOU TALKING LIKE THAT ?
"CAT MASTERS?" DON'T MAKE ME LAUGH.
NO, NO, NO! THIS LITTLE ONE DARES TO DISRESPECT OUR CAT MASTERS!
WHAT?!
IT'S THANKS TO THE CAT MASTERS WE GET TO LIVE IN THIS VILLAGE.

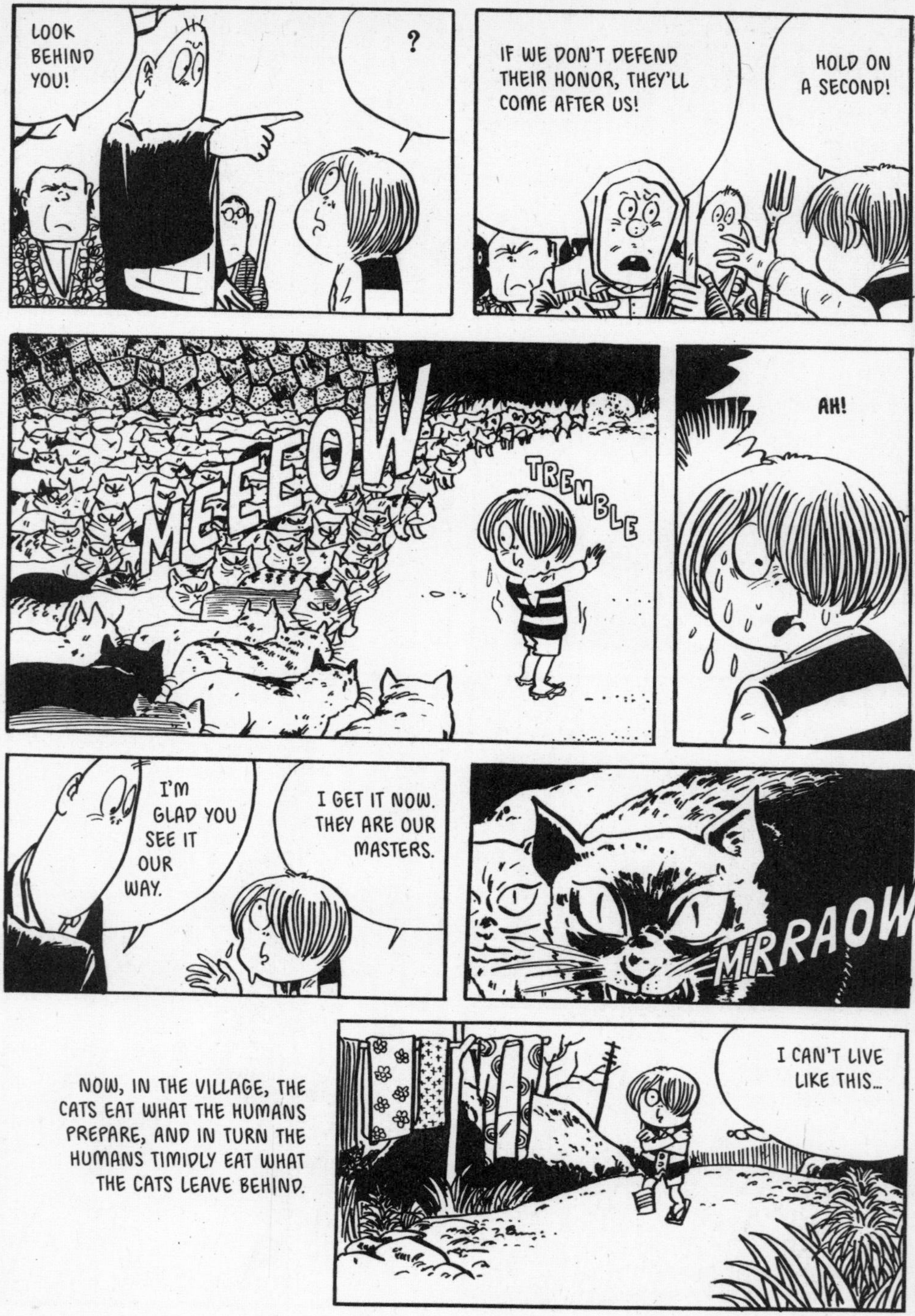
HOLD ON A SECOND!
IF WE DON'T DEFEND THEIR HONOR, THEY'LL COME AFTER US!
?
LOOK BEHIND YOU!
AH!
MEEEOW
TREMBLE
MRRAOW
I GET IT NOW. THEY ARE OUR MASTERS.
I'M GLAD YOU SEE IT OUR WAY.
I CAN'T LIVE LIKE THIS...
NOW, IN THE VILLAGE, THE CATS EAT WHAT THE HUMANS PREPARE, AND IN TURN THE HUMANS TIMIDLY EAT WHAT THE CATS LEAVE BEHIND.

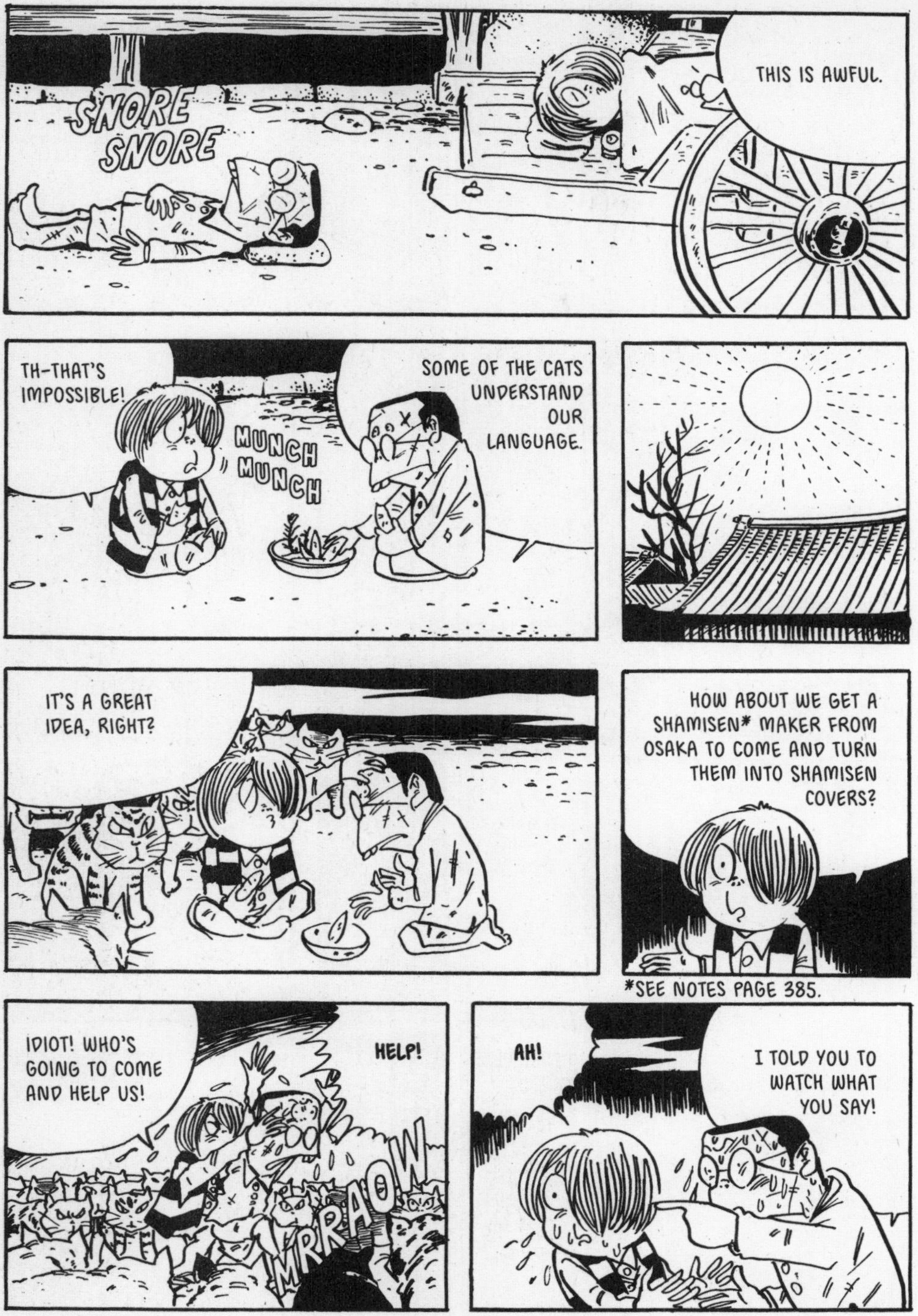
THIS IS AWFUL.
SNORE SNORE
SOME OF THE CATS UNDERSTAND OUR LANGUAGE.
TH-THAT'S IMPOSSIBLE!
MUNCH MUNCH
HOW ABOUT WE GET A SHAMISEN* MAKER FROM OSAKA TO COME AND TURN THEM INTO SHAMISEN COVERS?
IT'S A GREAT IDEA, RIGHT?
I TOLD YOU TO WATCH WHAT YOU SAY!
AH!
HELP!
IDIOT! WHO'S GOING TO COME AND HELP US!
MRRAOW

*SEE NOTES PAGE 385.

WOW! POOR GUY...

GULP. THEY COMPLETELY DE-VOURED HIM.

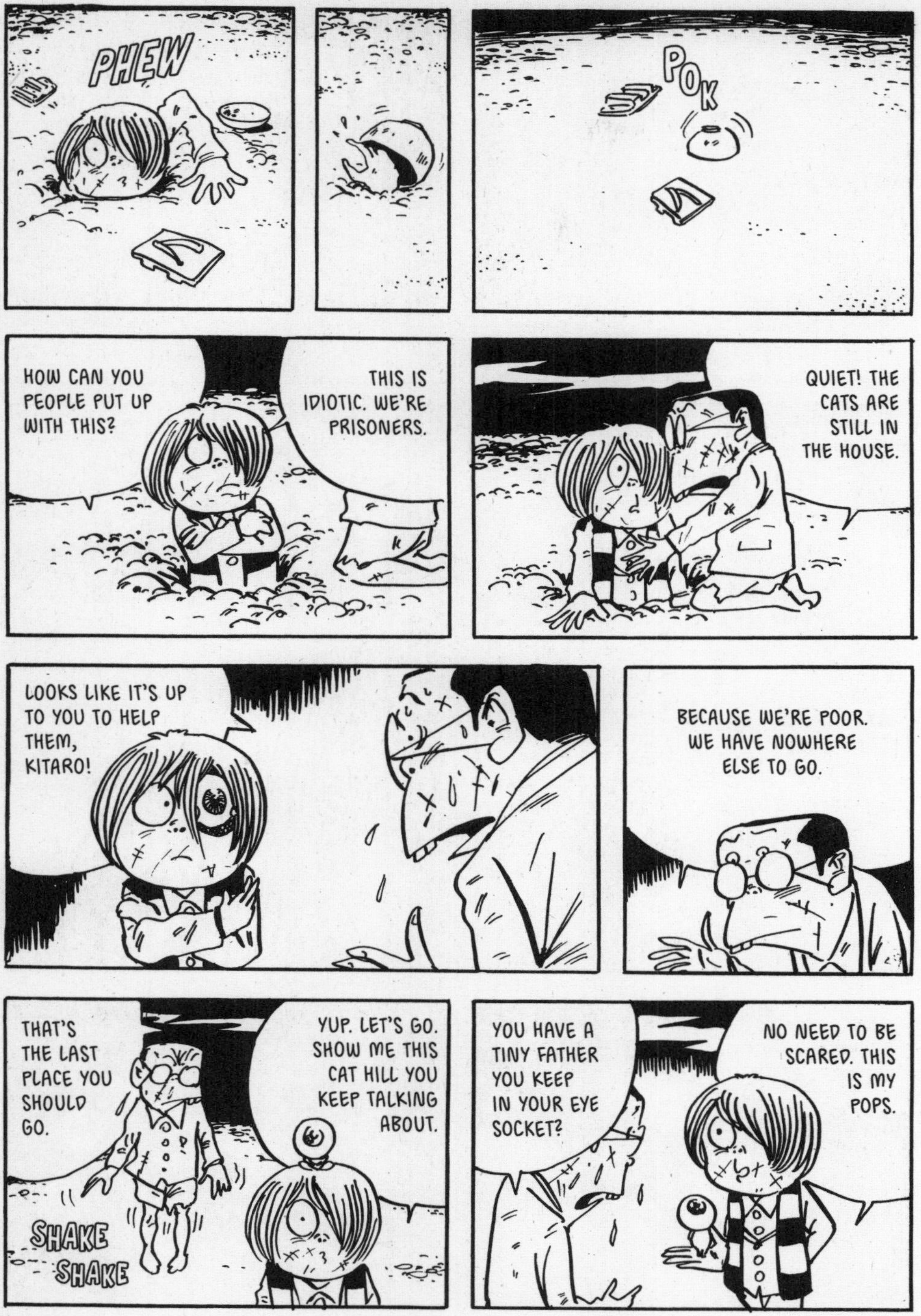
POK
PHEW
QUIET! THE CATS ARE STILL IN THE HOUSE.
THIS IS IDIOTIC. WE'RE PRISONERS.
HOW CAN YOU PEOPLE PUT UP WITH THIS?
BECAUSE WE'RE POOR. WE HAVE NOWHERE ELSE TO GO.
LOOKS LIKE IT'S UP TO YOU TO HELP THEM, KITARO!
NO NEED TO BE SCARED. THIS IS MY POPS.
YOU HAVE A TINY FATHER YOU KEEP IN YOUR EYE SOCKET?
YUP. LET'S GO. SHOW ME THIS CAT HILL YOU KEEP TALKING ABOUT.
THAT'S THE LAST PLACE YOU SHOULD GO.
SHAKE
SHAKE

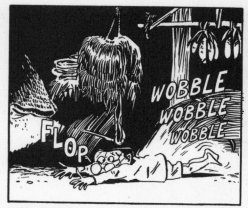

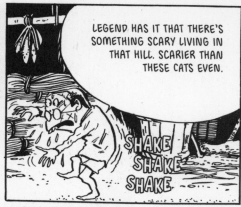

LEGEND HAS IT THAT THERE'S SOMETHING SCARY LIVING IN THAT HILL. SCARIER THAN THESE CATS EVEN.
SHAKE
SHAKE
SHAKE
WOBBLE
WOBBLE
WOBBLE
FLOP
OH, GREAT. NOW HE'S FAINTED.
I'VE GOT NO CHOICE THEN.
IT'LL TAKE A WHILE, BUT I'LL ASK THE FLEAS.
SKRCH
SKRCH
SKRCH
TOING KRUNK, SKRAT SKRAT
KITARO GAVE AN ORDER TO THE THREE FLEAS LIVING ON HIS BODY.
ZZZ
ZZZ
BOING
SKRAT SKRAT, KRUNK KRUNK.
URNK FWOOK, KRUNK.

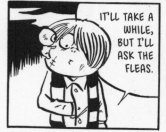

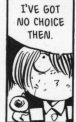

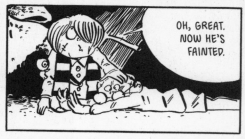

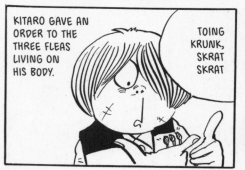

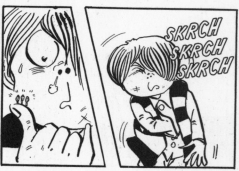

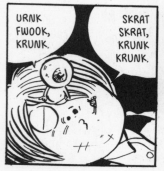

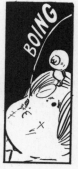

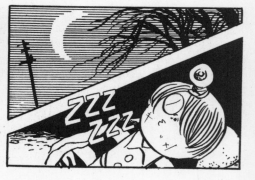

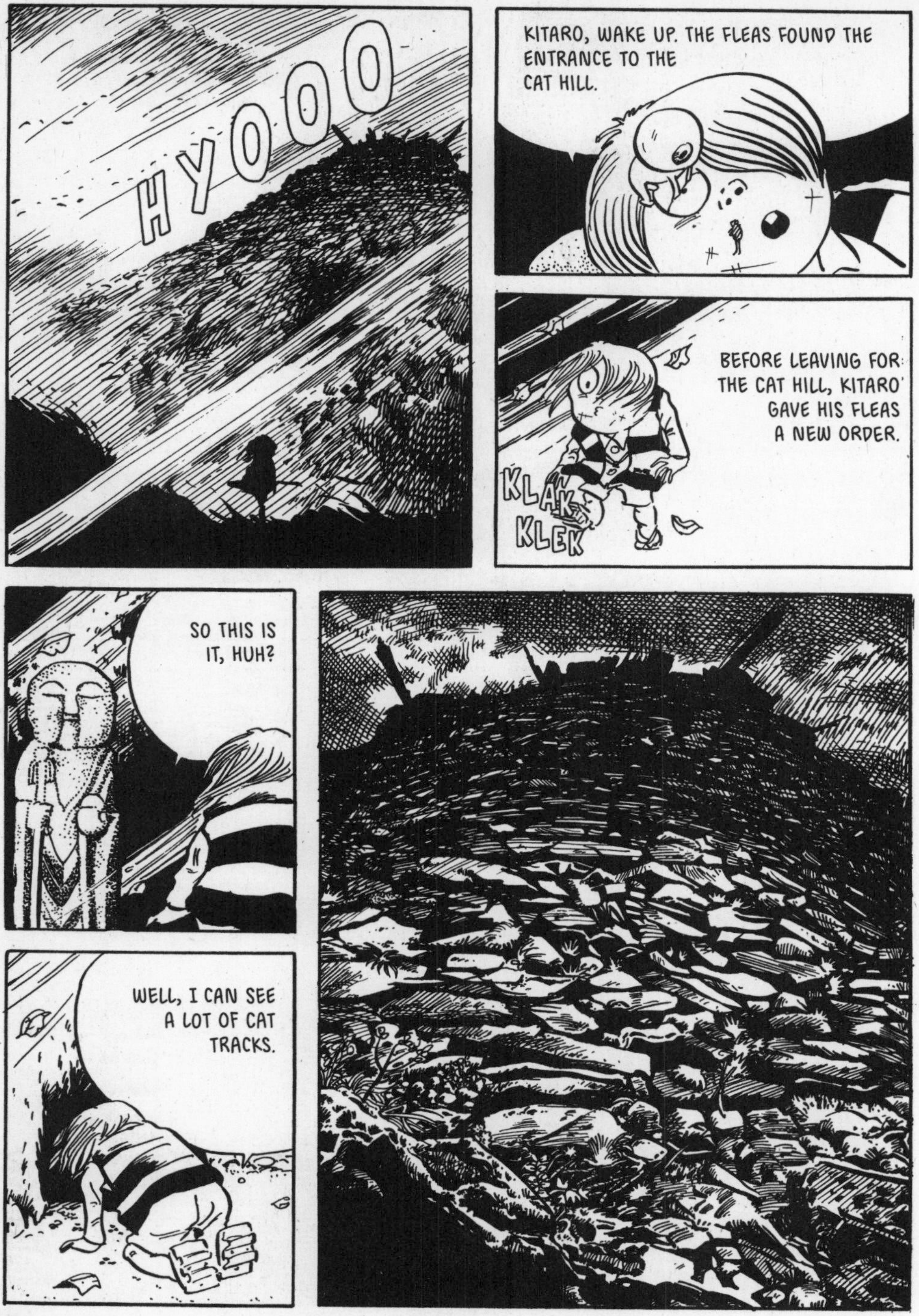
KITARO, WAKE UP. THE FLEAS FOUND THE ENTRANCE TO THE CAT HILL.
BEFORE LEAVING FOR THE CAT HILL, KITARO' GAVE HIS FLEAS A NEW ORDER.
KLAK KLAK KLEK
HYOOO
SO THIS IS IT, HUH?
WELL, I CAN SEE A LOT OF CAT TRACKS.

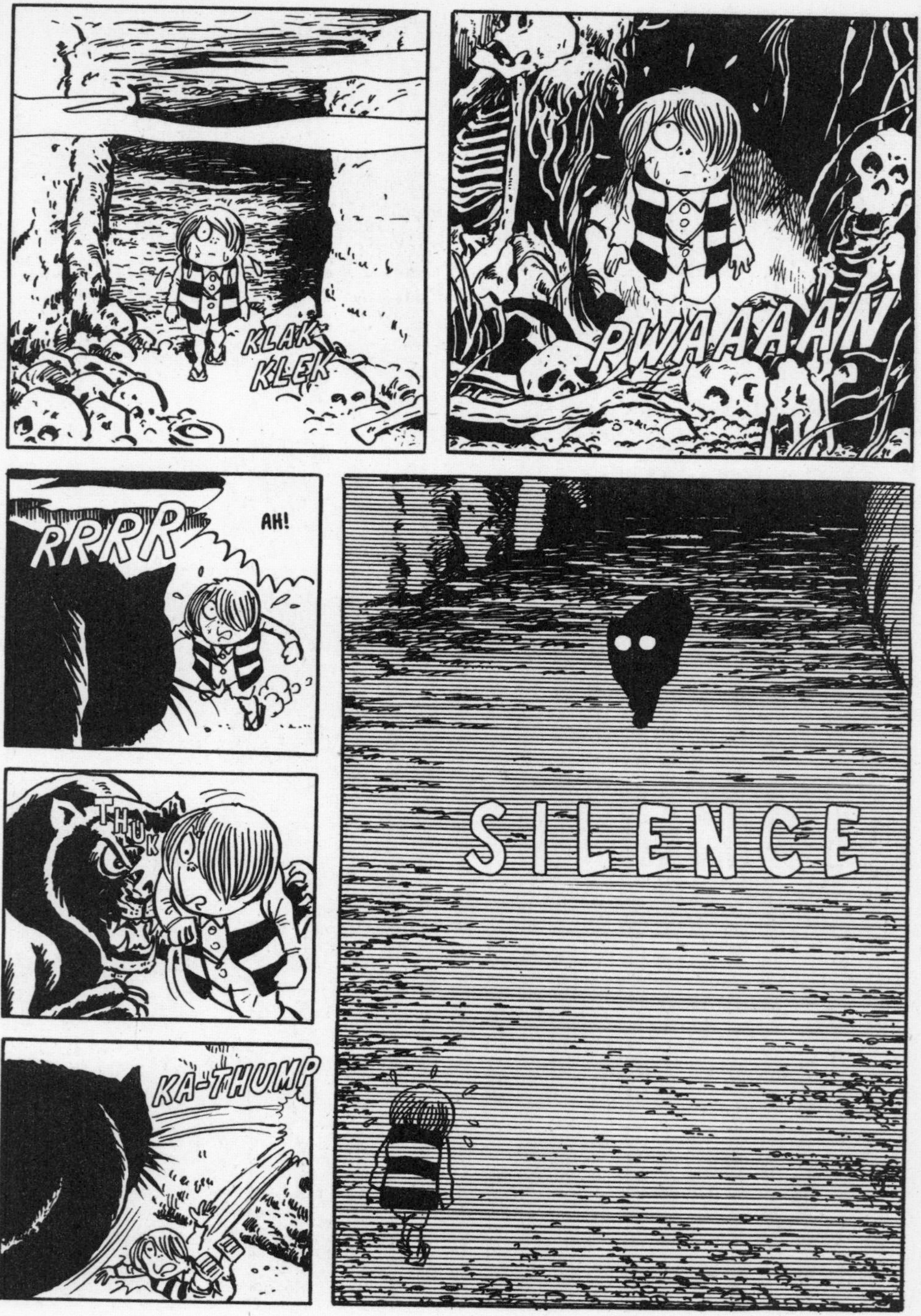
PWAAAAAN
KLAK-KLEK
SILENCE
AH!
RRRR
THUK
KA-THUMP

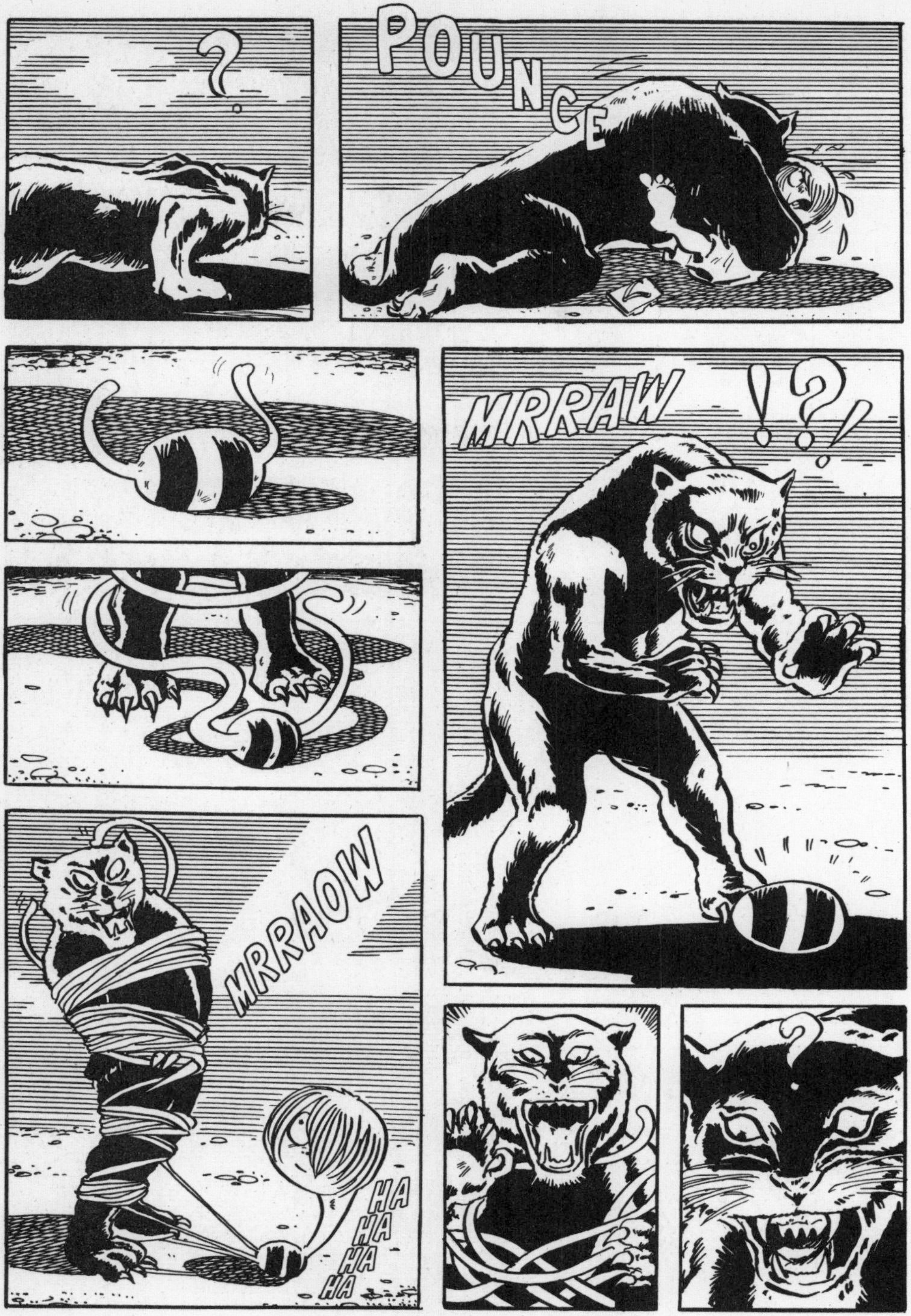
POUNCE
?
MRRAW
!?!
?
MRRAOW
HA HA HA HA

MEEEOW
CHOMP
CHOMP
OWOWOWOW!
SKRCH
SKRCH
SKRCH
RRRRRAW
AH! NOOOO!

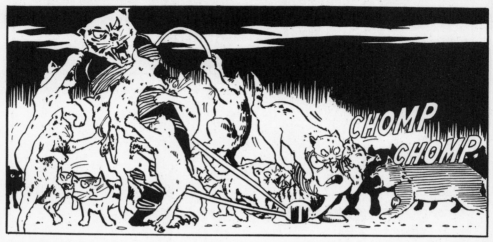

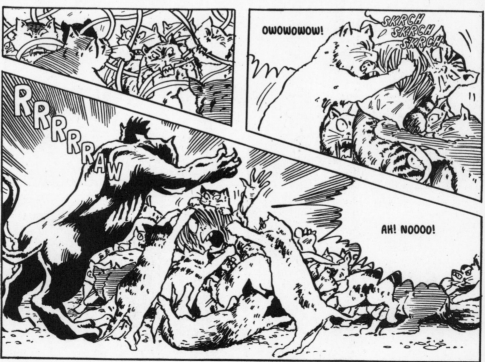

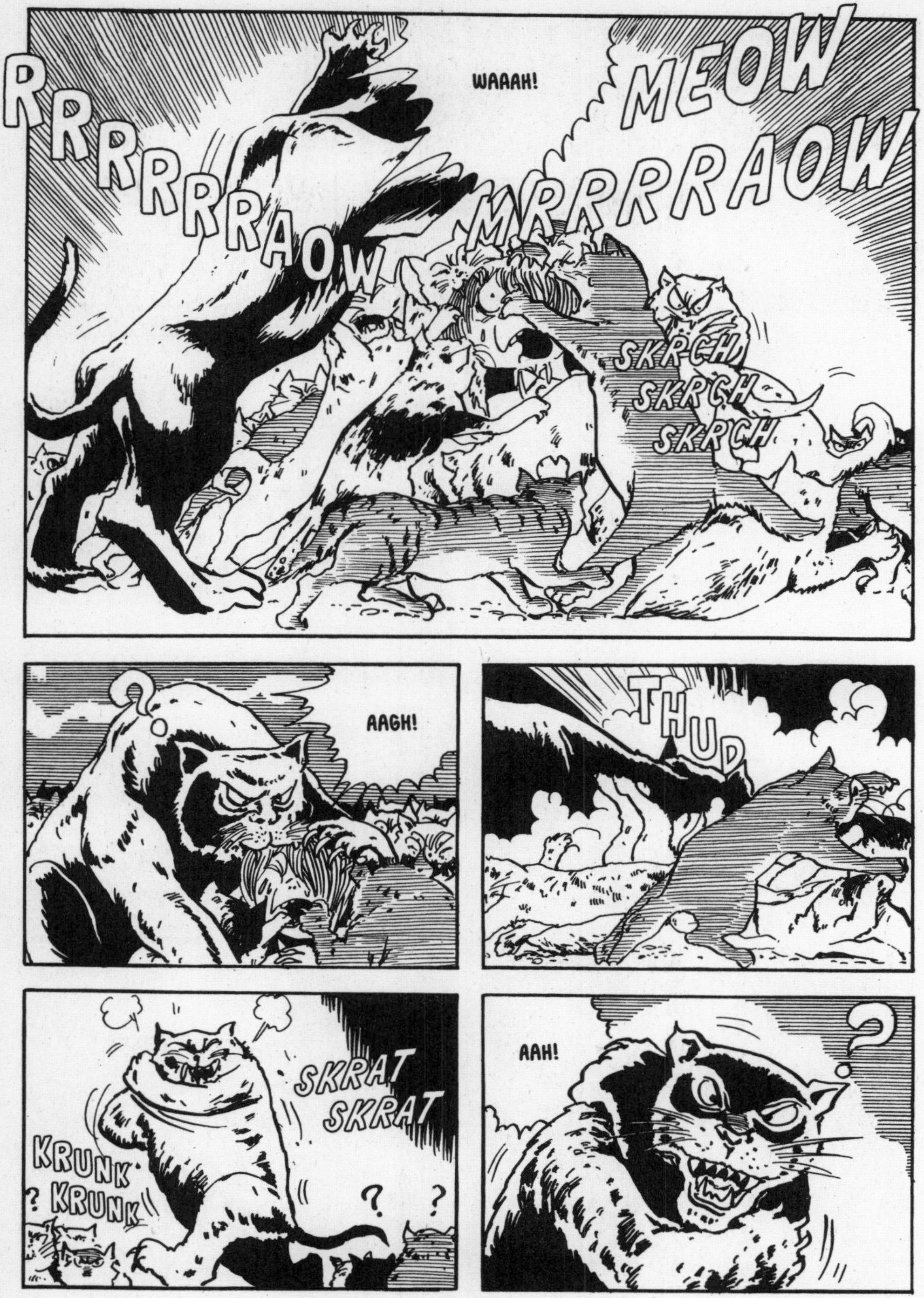
MEOW
MRRRRRAOW
WAAAH!
RRRRRRAOW
SKRCH
SKRCH
SKRCH
THUD
AAGH!
AAH!
SKRAT
SKRAT
KRUNK
KRUNK

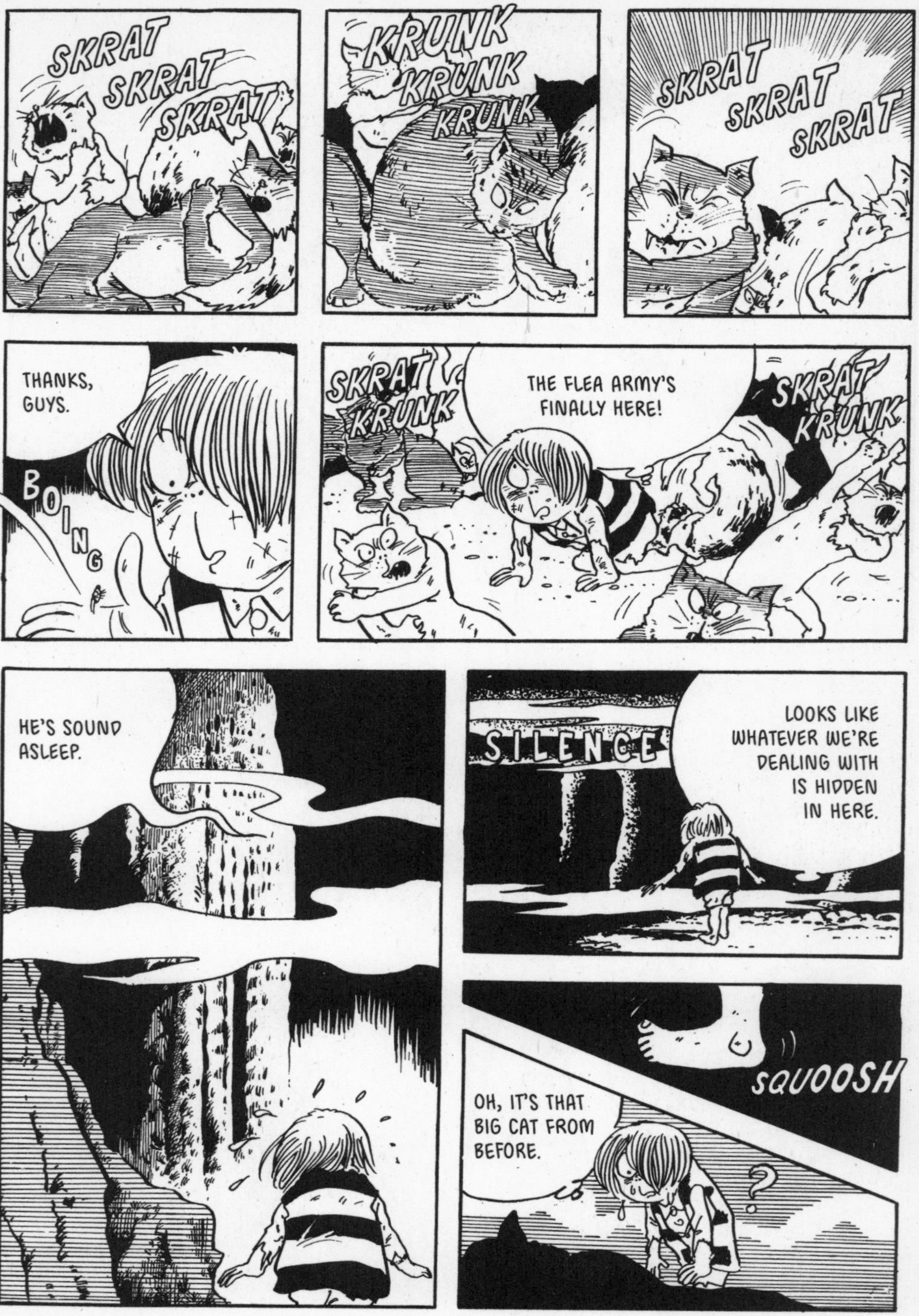
SKRAT SKRAT SKRAT
KRUNK KRUNK KRUNK
SKRAT SKRAT SKRAT
SKRAT KRUNK
THE FLEA ARMY'S FINALLY HERE!
SKRAT KRUNK
THANKS, GUYS.
BOING
LOOKS LIKE WHATEVER WE'RE DEALING WITH IS HIDDEN IN HERE.
SILENCE
SQUOOSH
OH, IT'S THAT BIG CAT FROM BEFORE.
HE'S SOUND ASLEEP.

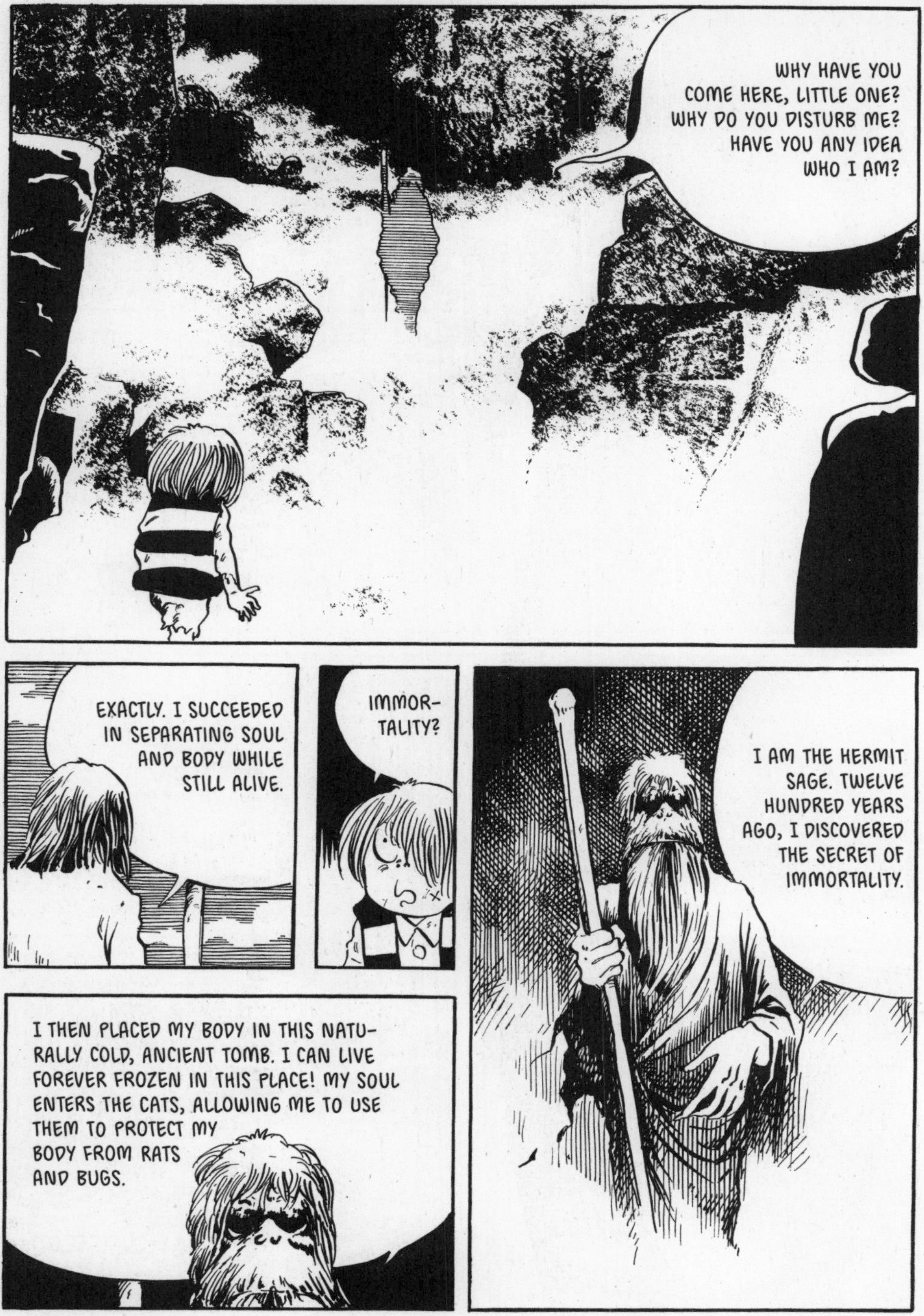
WHY HAVE YOU COME HERE, LITTLE ONE? WHY DO YOU DISTURB ME? HAVE YOU ANY IDEA WHO I AM?
I AM THE HERMIT SAGE. TWELVE HUNDRED YEARS AGO, I DISCOVERED THE SECRET OF IMMORTALITY.
IMMOR-TALITY?
EXACTLY. I SUCCEEDED IN SEPARATING SOUL AND BODY WHILE STILL ALIVE.
I THEN PLACED MY BODY IN THIS NATU-RALLY COLD, ANCIENT TOMB. I CAN LIVE FOREVER FROZEN IN THIS PLACE! MY SOUL ENTERS THE CATS, ALLOWING ME TO USE THEM TO PROTECT MY BODY FROM RATS AND BUGS.

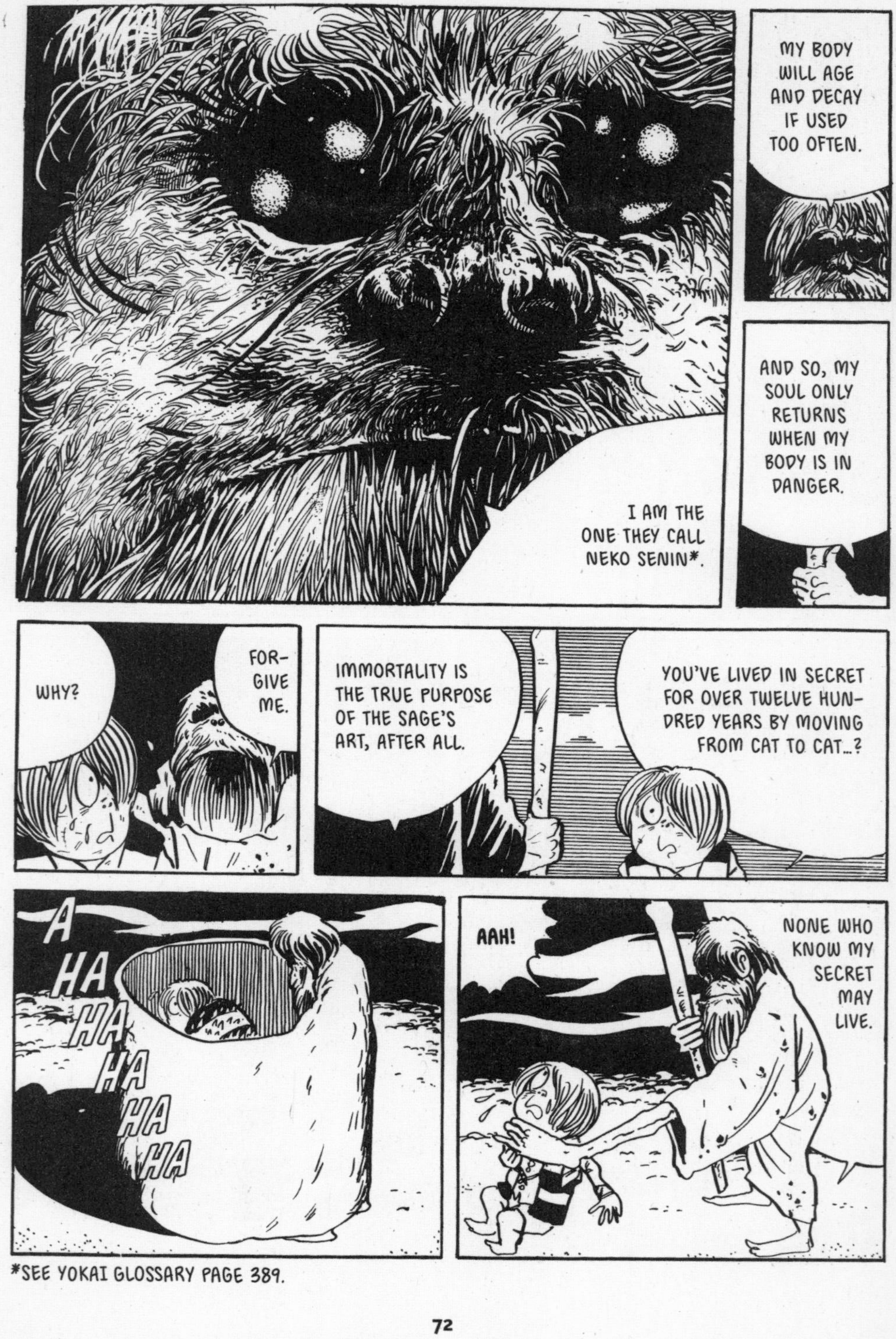
MY BODY WILL AGE AND DECAY IF USED TOO OFTEN.
AND SO, MY SOUL ONLY RETURNS WHEN MY BODY IS IN DANGER.
I AM THE ONE THEY CALL NEKO SENIN*.
YOU'VE LIVED IN SECRET FOR OVER TWELVE HUN-DRED YEARS BY MOVING FROM CAT TO CAT...?
IMMORTALITY IS THE TRUE PURPOSE OF THE SAGE'S ART, AFTER ALL.
FOR-GIVE ME.
WHY?
NONE WHO KNOW MY SECRET MAY LIVE.
AAH!
A HA HA HA HA HA

*SEE YOKAI GLOSSARY PAGE 389.

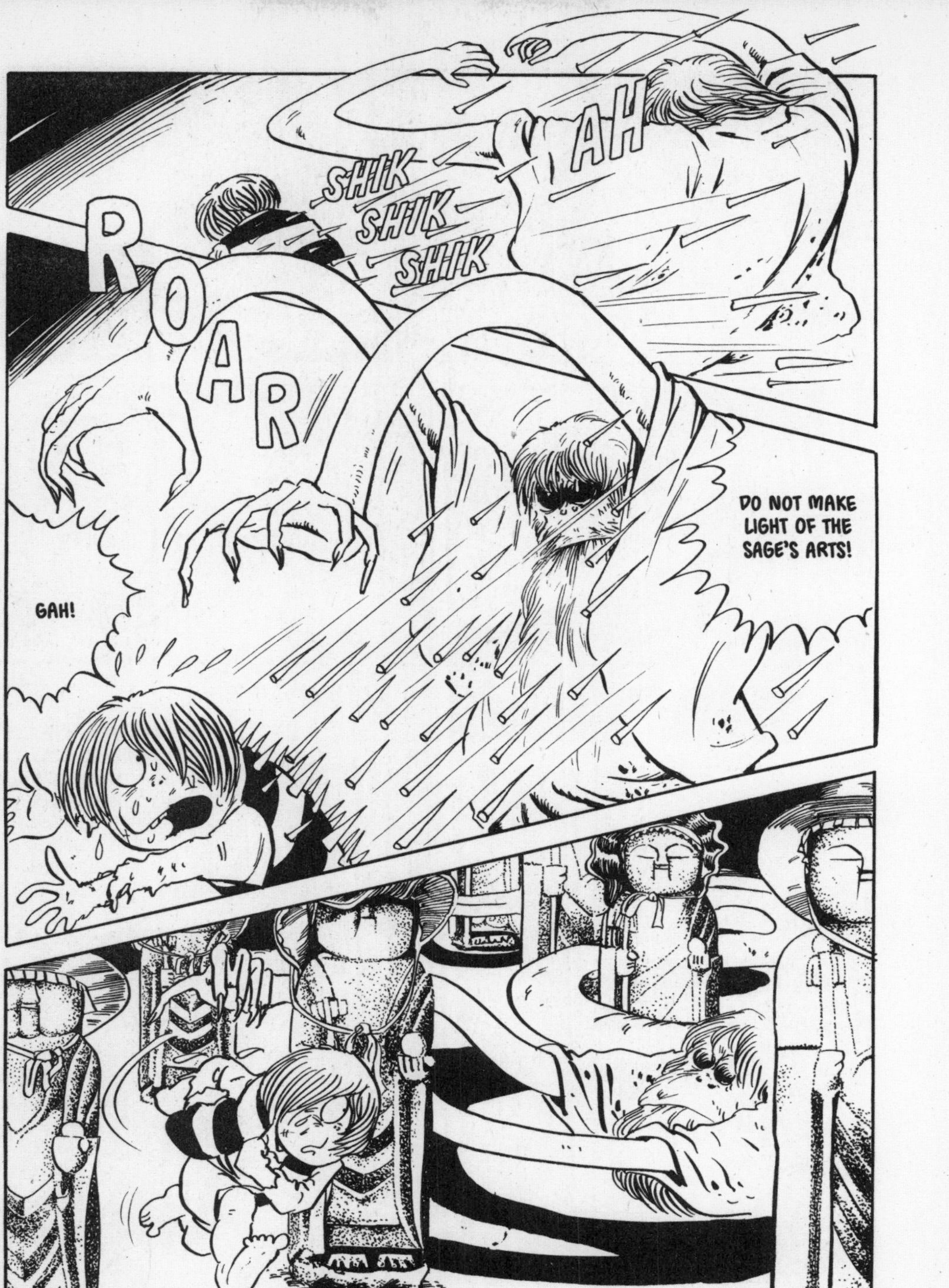
AH
SHIK
SHIK
SHIK
ROAR
DO NOT MAKE LIGHT OF THE SAGE'S ARTS!
GAH!

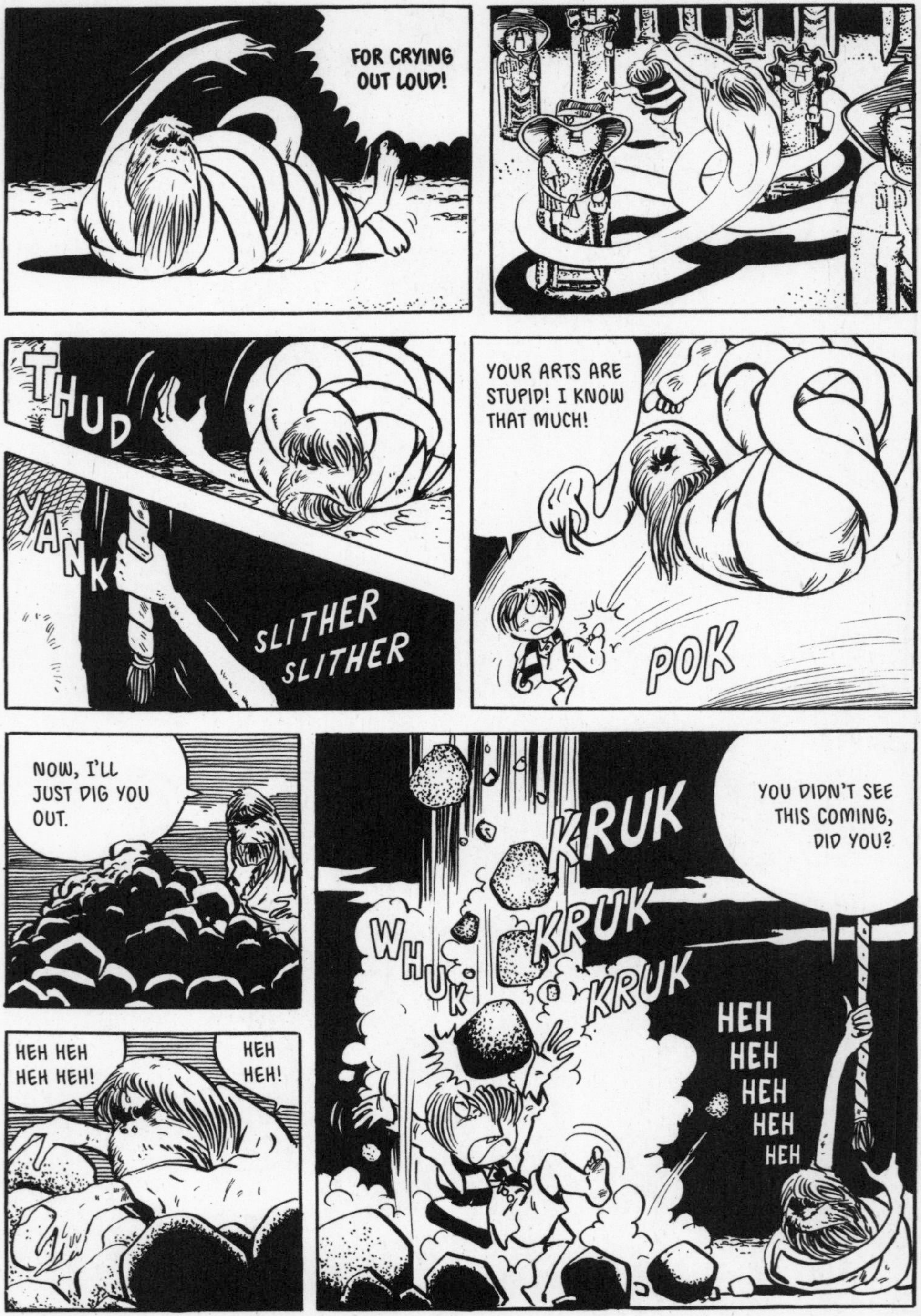
FOR CRYING OUT LOUD!
YOUR ARTS ARE STUPID! I KNOW THAT MUCH!
POK
THUD
YANK
SLITHER SLITHER
YOU DIDN'T SEE THIS COMING, DID YOU?
KRUK
KRUK
WHUK
KRUK
HEH HEH HEH HEH HEH
NOW, I'LL JUST DIG YOU OUT.
HEH HEH!
HEH HEH HEH HEH!

?
THIS MUST BE ONE OF THOSE TRUNKS THAT ARE SO POPULAR THESE DAYS. HEH HEH.
BUT HOW EXACTLY DO I EAT IT?
AAH!
SHHP
TAKE THAT!
THUD
SO, YOU ARE ALSO A MASTER OF THE SAGE'S ARTS!
BAM
OOMPH!

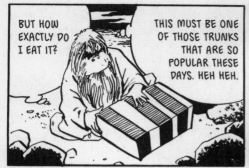

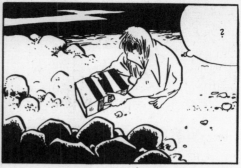

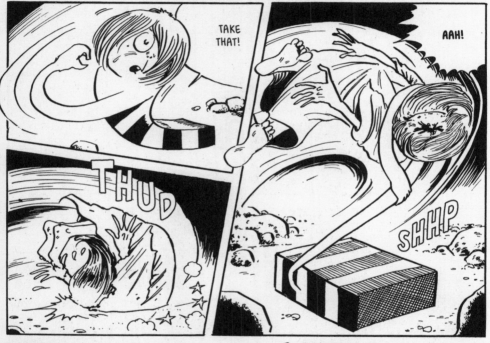

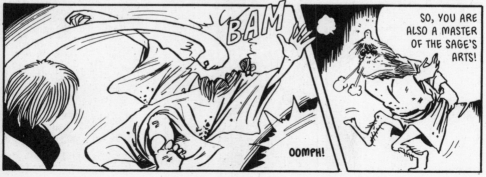

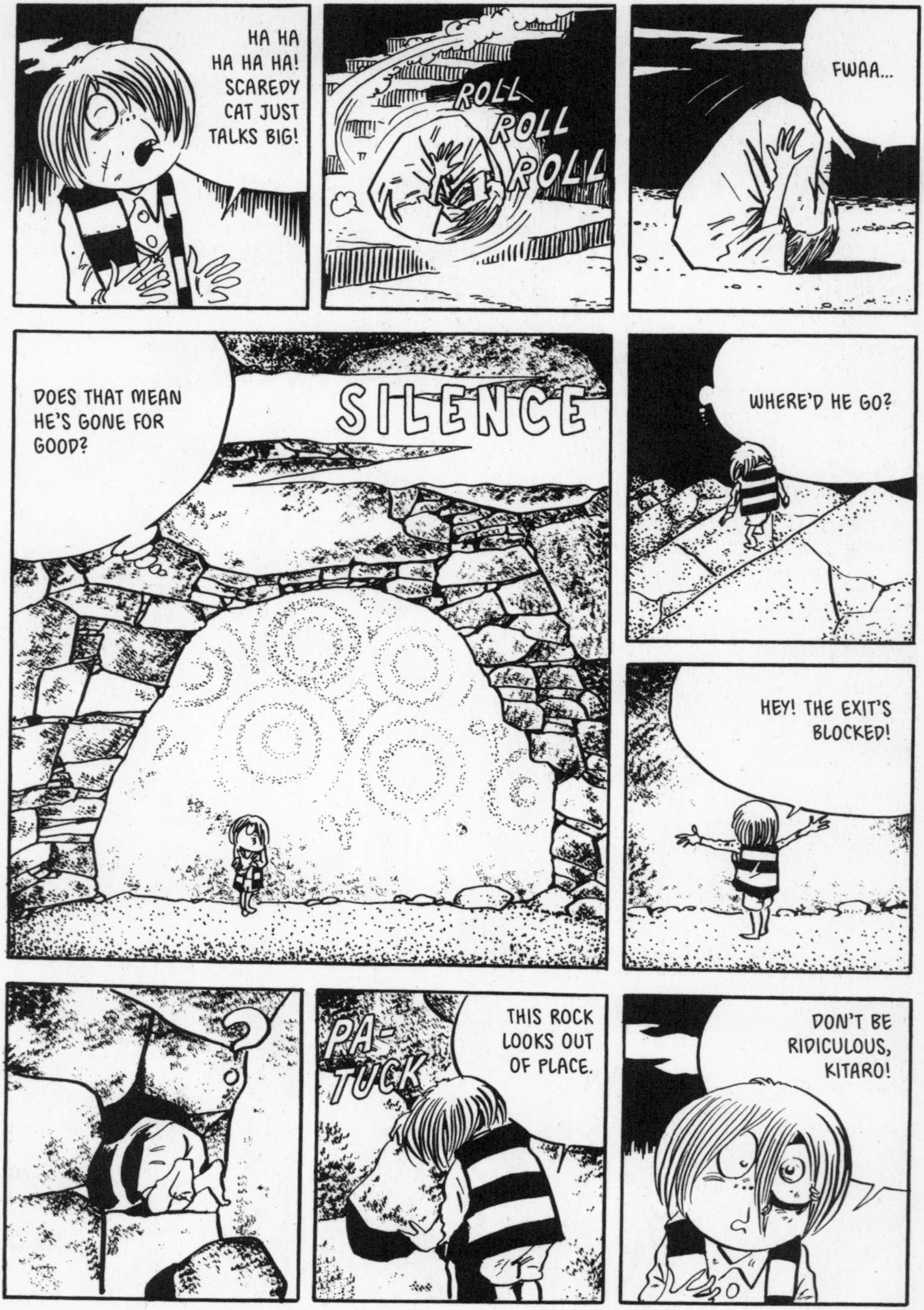
FWAA...
ROLL ROLL ROLL
HA HA HA HA HA! SCAREDY CAT JUST TALKS BIG!
WHERE'D HE GO?
HEY! THE EXIT'S BLOCKED!
SILENCE
DOES THAT MEAN HE'S GONE FOR GOOD?
DON'T BE RIDICULOUS, KITARO!
THIS ROCK LOOKS OUT OF PLACE.
PA-TUCK

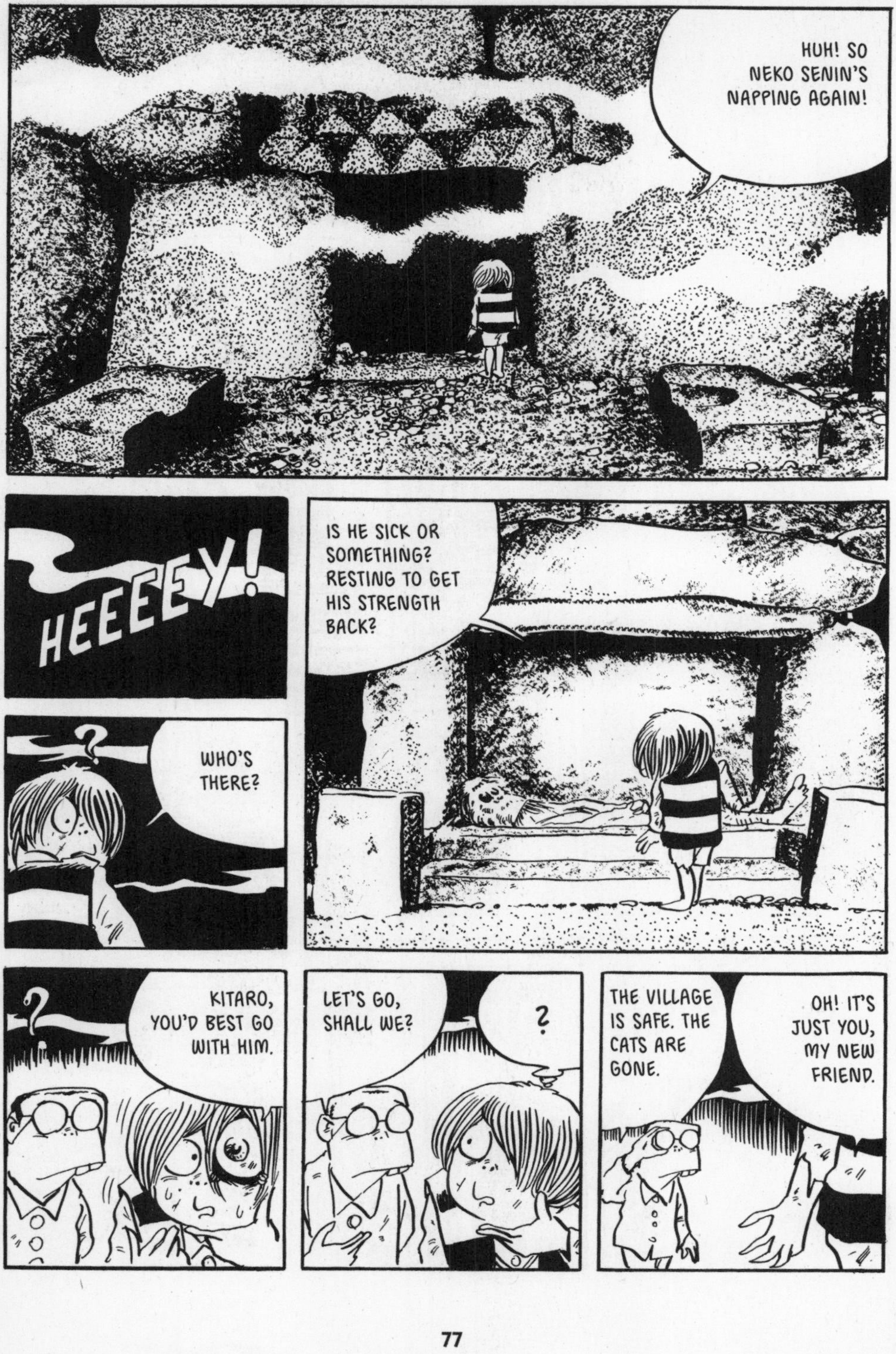
HUH! SO NEKO SENIN'S NAPPING AGAIN!
IS HE SICK OR SOMETHING? RESTING TO GET HIS STRENGTH BACK?
HEEEEY!
WHO'S THERE?
?
OH! IT'S JUST YOU, MY NEW FRIEND.
THE VILLAGE IS SAFE. THE CATS ARE GONE.
?
LET'S GO, SHALL WE?
KITARO, YOU'D BEST GO WITH HIM.
?

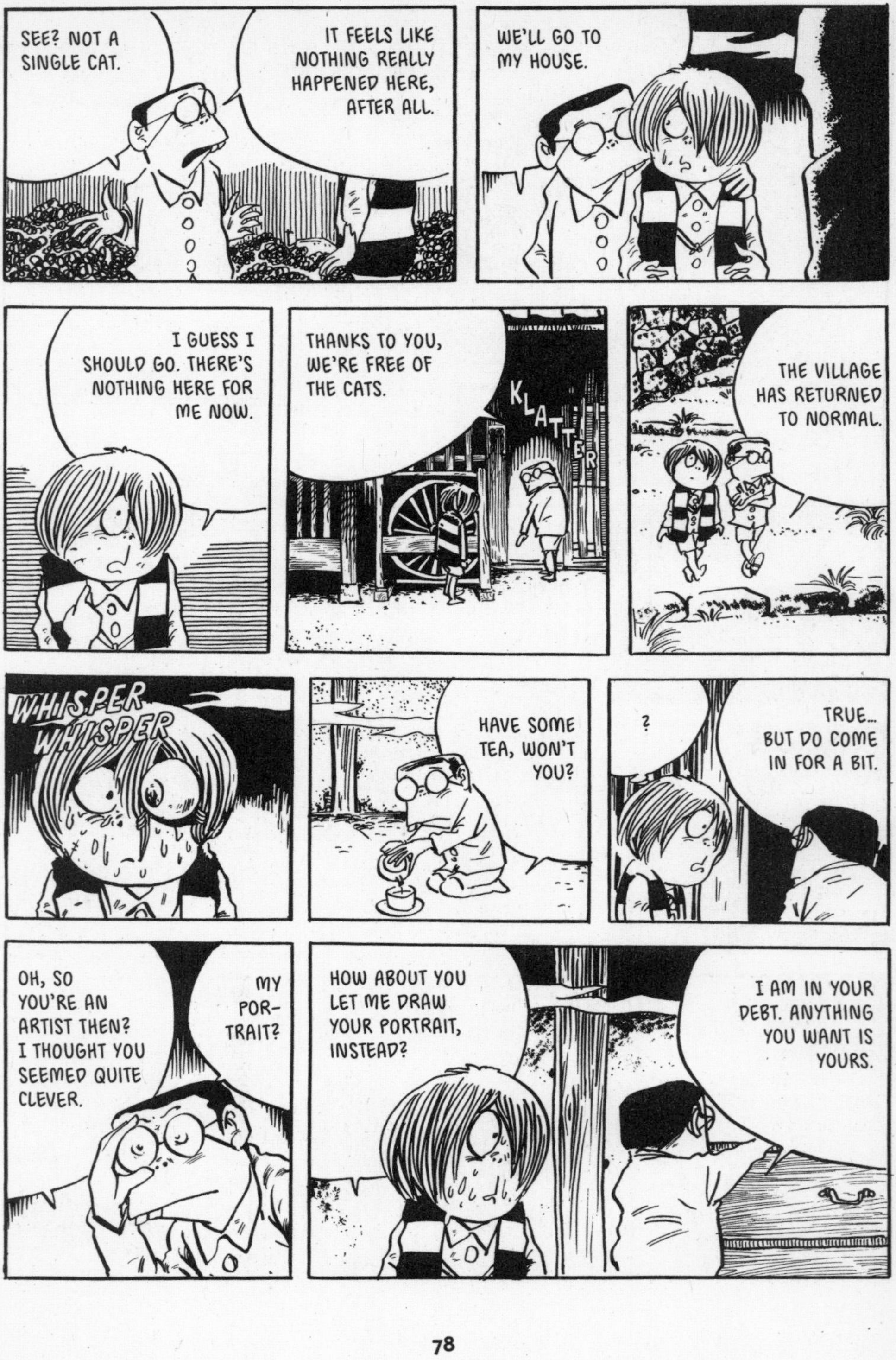
WE'LL GO TO MY HOUSE.
IT FEELS LIKE NOTHING REALLY HAPPENED HERE, AFTER ALL.
SEE? NOT A SINGLE CAT.
THE VILLAGE HAS RETURNED TO NORMAL.
THANKS TO YOU, WE'RE FREE OF THE CATS.
KLATTER
I GUESS I SHOULD GO. THERE'S NOTHING HERE FOR ME NOW.
TRUE... BUT DO COME IN FOR A BIT.
?
HAVE SOME TEA, WON'T YOU?
WHISPER WHISPER
I AM IN YOUR DEBT. ANYTHING YOU WANT IS YOURS.
HOW ABOUT YOU LET ME DRAW YOUR PORTRAIT, INSTEAD?
MY POR-TRAIT?
OH, SO YOU'RE AN ARTIST THEN? I THOUGHT YOU SEEMED QUITE CLEVER.

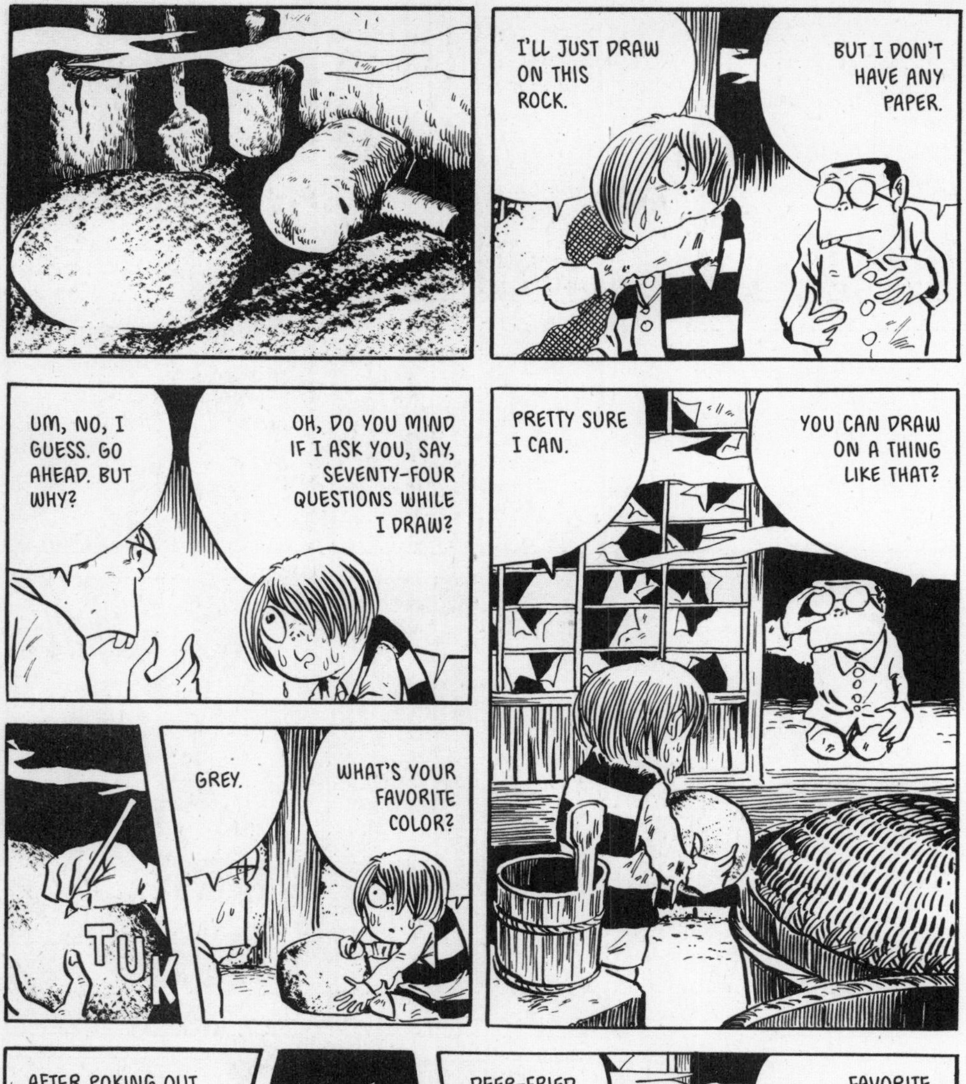
BUT I DON'T HAVE ANY PAPER.
I'LL JUST DRAW ON THIS ROCK.
YOU CAN DRAW ON A THING LIKE THAT?
PRETTY SURE I CAN.
OH, DO YOU MIND IF I ASK YOU, SAY, SEVENTY-FOUR QUESTIONS WHILE I DRAW?
UM, NO, I GUESS. GO AHEAD. BUT WHY?
WHAT'S YOUR FAVORITE COLOR?
GREY.
TUK
FAVORITE MIDDAY SNACK BETWEEN LUNCH AND DINNER?
DEEP-FRIED TOFU.
TUK
AFTER POKING OUT SEVENTY-FOUR POINTS, KITARO CONNECTED THE DOTS WITH A FIERCE INTENSITY.

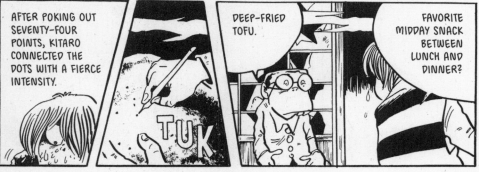

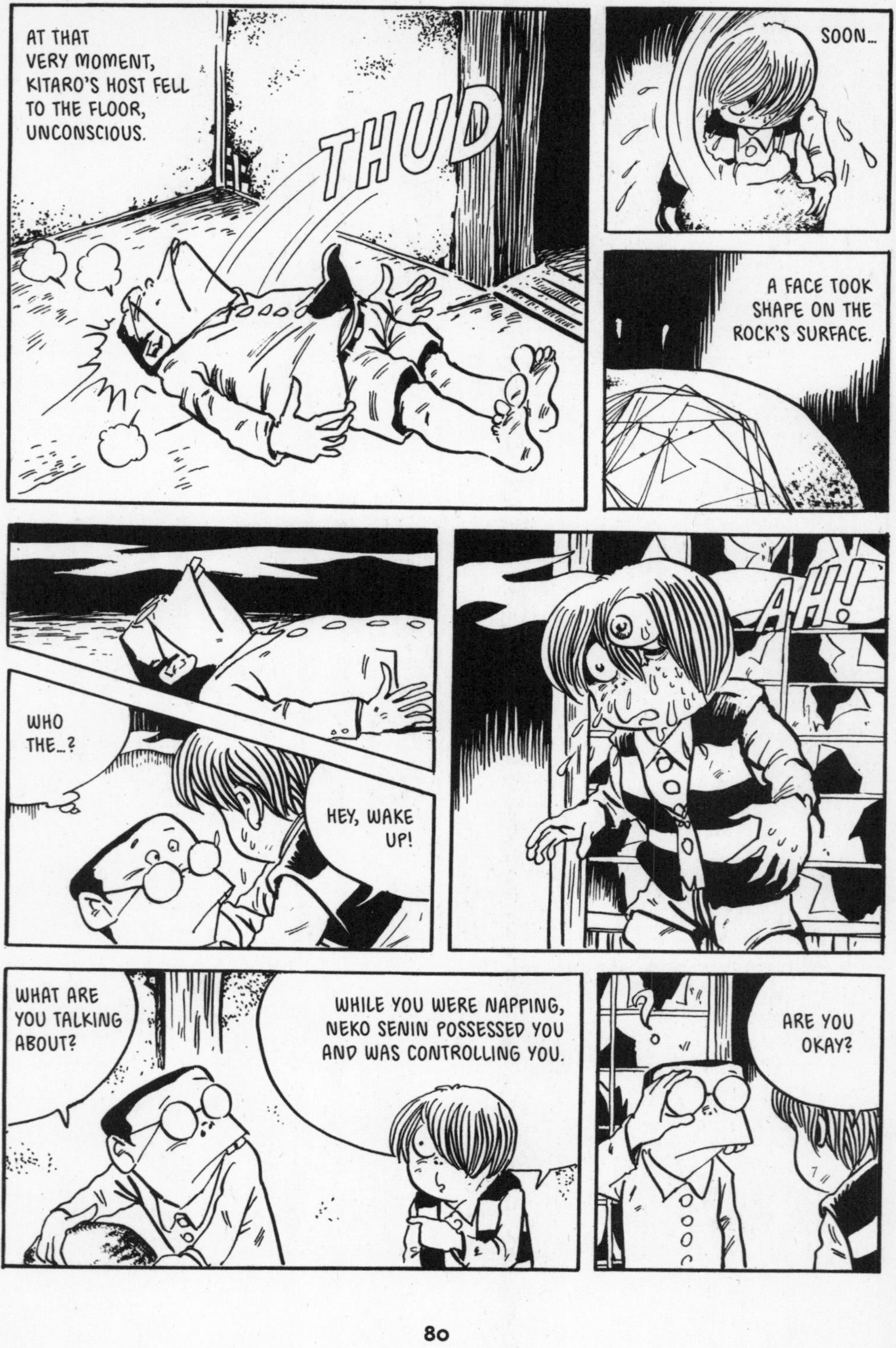
SOON...
A FACE TOOK SHAPE ON THE ROCK'S SURFACE.
AT THAT VERY MOMENT, KITARO'S HOST FELL TO THE FLOOR, UNCONSCIOUS.
THUD
AH!
HEY, WAKE UP!
WHO THE...?
ARE YOU OKAY?
WHAT ARE YOU TALKING ABOUT?
WHILE YOU WERE NAPPING, NEKO SENIN POSSESSED YOU AND WAS CONTROLLING YOU.

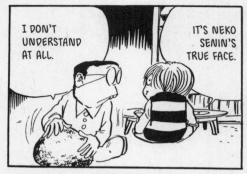

OH HEY! SOMEONE DREW A STRANGE FACE ON THIS ROCK.
WHO IS IT?
IT'S NEKO SENIN'S TRUE FACE.
I DON'T UNDERSTAND AT ALL.
CAREFUL! DON'T HANDLE THE ROCK TOO MUCH. NEKO SENIN'S SOUL IS IN THERE.
HUH?
I SEALED HIM IN THERE WITH MY SOUL-BINDING POWER.
IF I HADN'T, WHO KNOWS WHAT TROUBLE HE'D GET UP TO?
IS THERE AN ABANDONED WELL AROUND HERE?
THERE'S ONE THIS WAY.
SPLASH
NEKO SENIN MIGHT BE ABLE TO MOVE FROM ONE LIVING THING TO ANOTHER, BUT NOW THAT HE'S IN THIS STONE, HE WON'T BE ABLE TO GET OUT AGAIN.

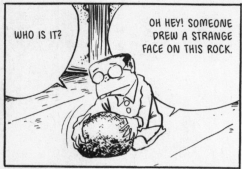

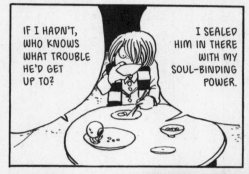

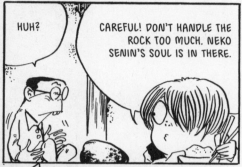

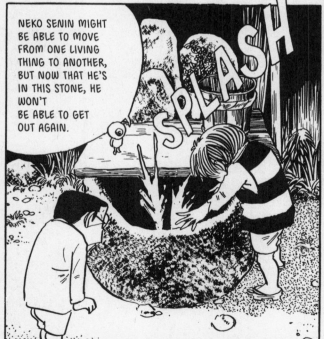

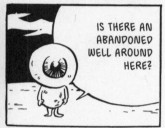

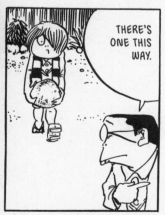

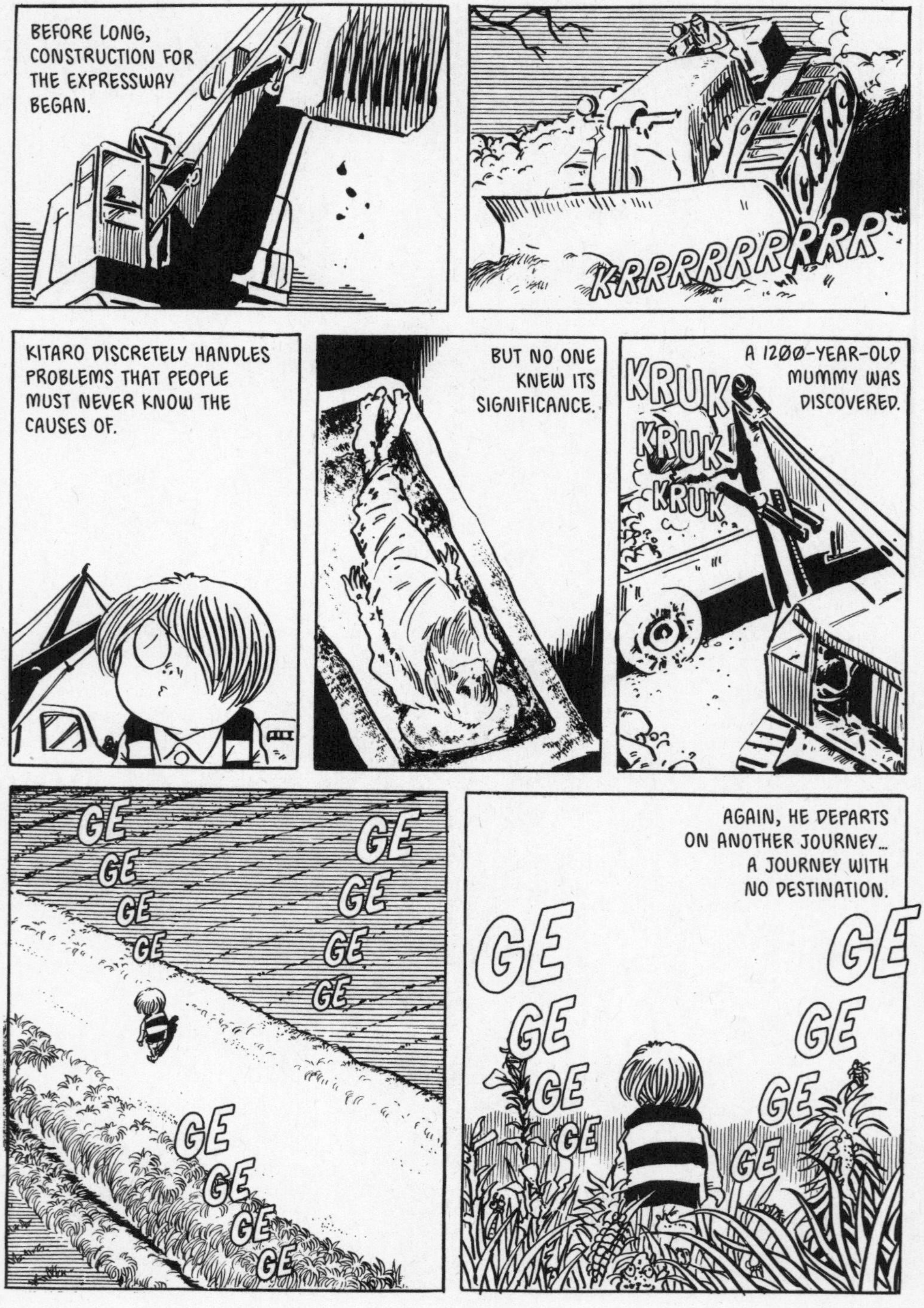
KRRRRRRRRRRR
BEFORE LONG, CONSTRUCTION FOR THE EXPRESSWAY BEGAN.
A 1200-YEAR-OLD MUMMY WAS DISCOVERED.
KRUK
KRUK!
KRUK
BUT NO ONE KNEW ITS SIGNIFICANCE.
KITARO DISCRETELY HANDLES PROBLEMS THAT PEOPLE MUST NEVER KNOW THE CAUSES OF.
AGAIN, HE DEPARTS ON ANOTHER JOURNEY... A JOURNEY WITH NO DESTINATION.
GE GE GE GE
GE GE GE GE
GE GE GE GE
GE GE GE GE
GE GE GE GE

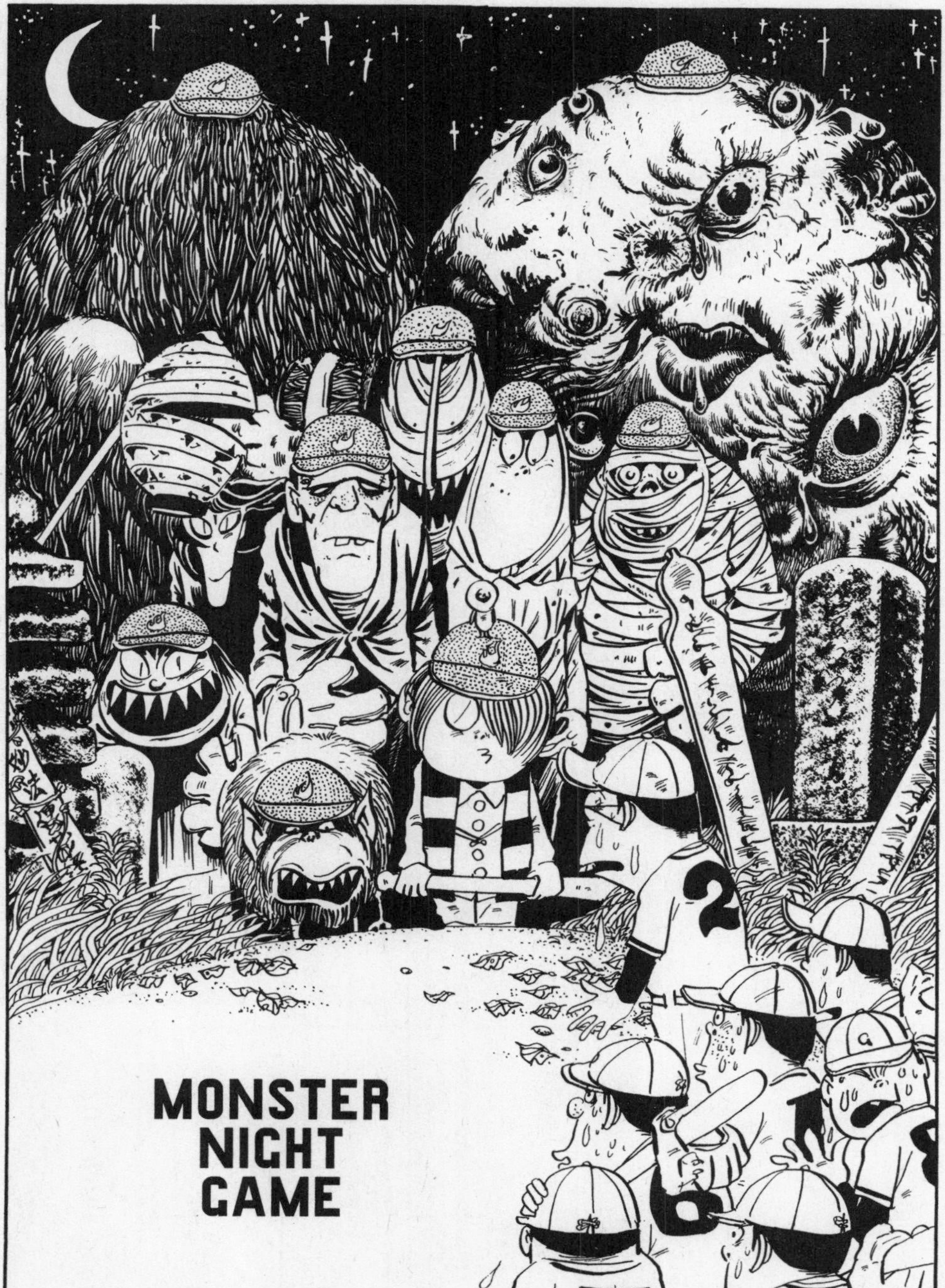
MONSTER
NIGHT
GAME

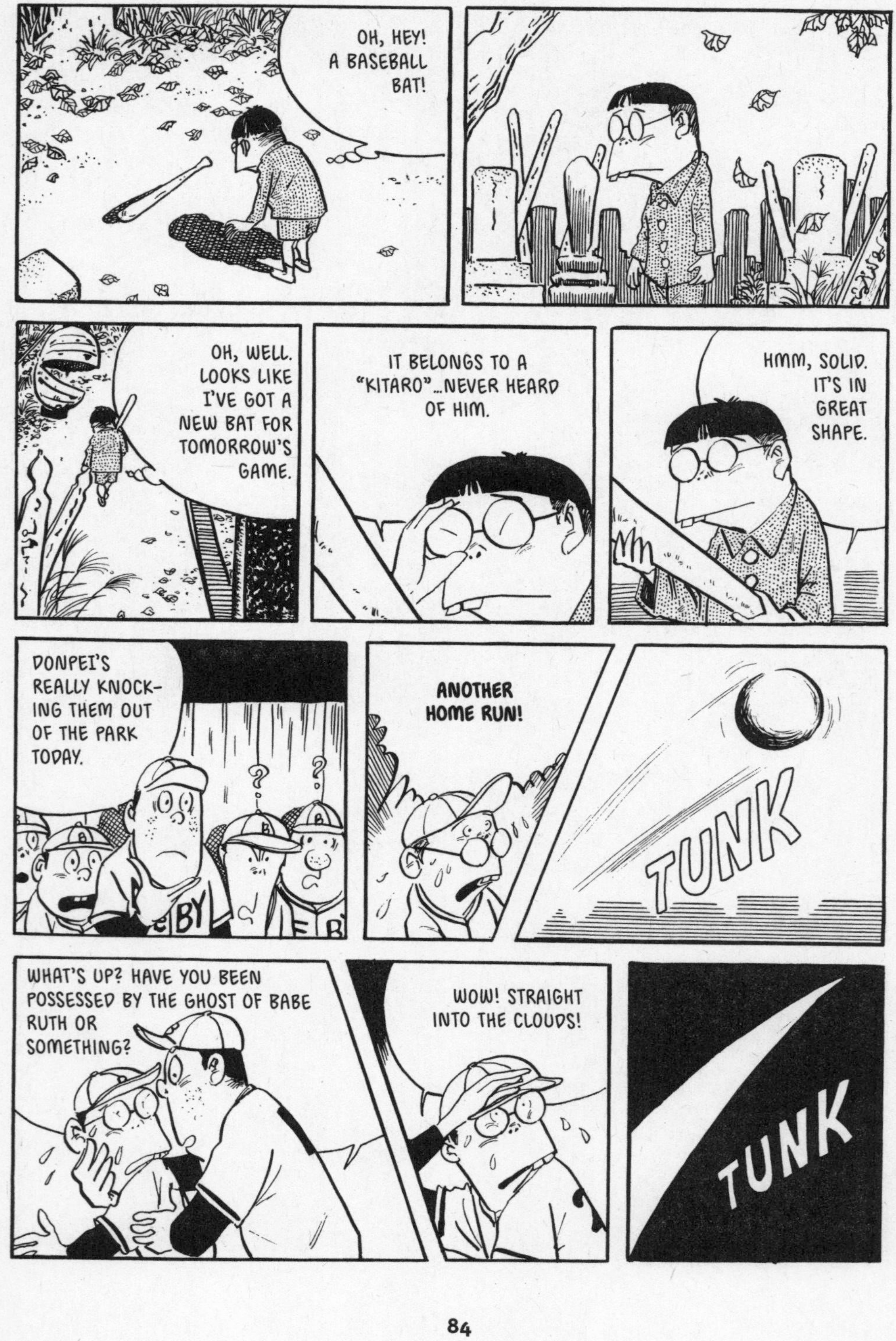
OH, HEY! A BASEBALL BAT!
HMM, SOLID. IT'S IN GREAT SHAPE.
IT BELONGS TO A "KITARO"...NEVER HEARD OF HIM.
OH, WELL. LOOKS LIKE I'VE GOT A NEW BAT FOR TOMORROW'S GAME.
TUNK
ANOTHER HOME RUN!
DONPEI'S REALLY KNOCKING THEM OUT OF THE PARK TODAY.
TUNK
WOW! STRAIGHT INTO THE CLOUDS!
WHAT'S UP? HAVE YOU BEEN POSSESSED BY THE GHOST OF BABE RUTH OR SOMETHING?

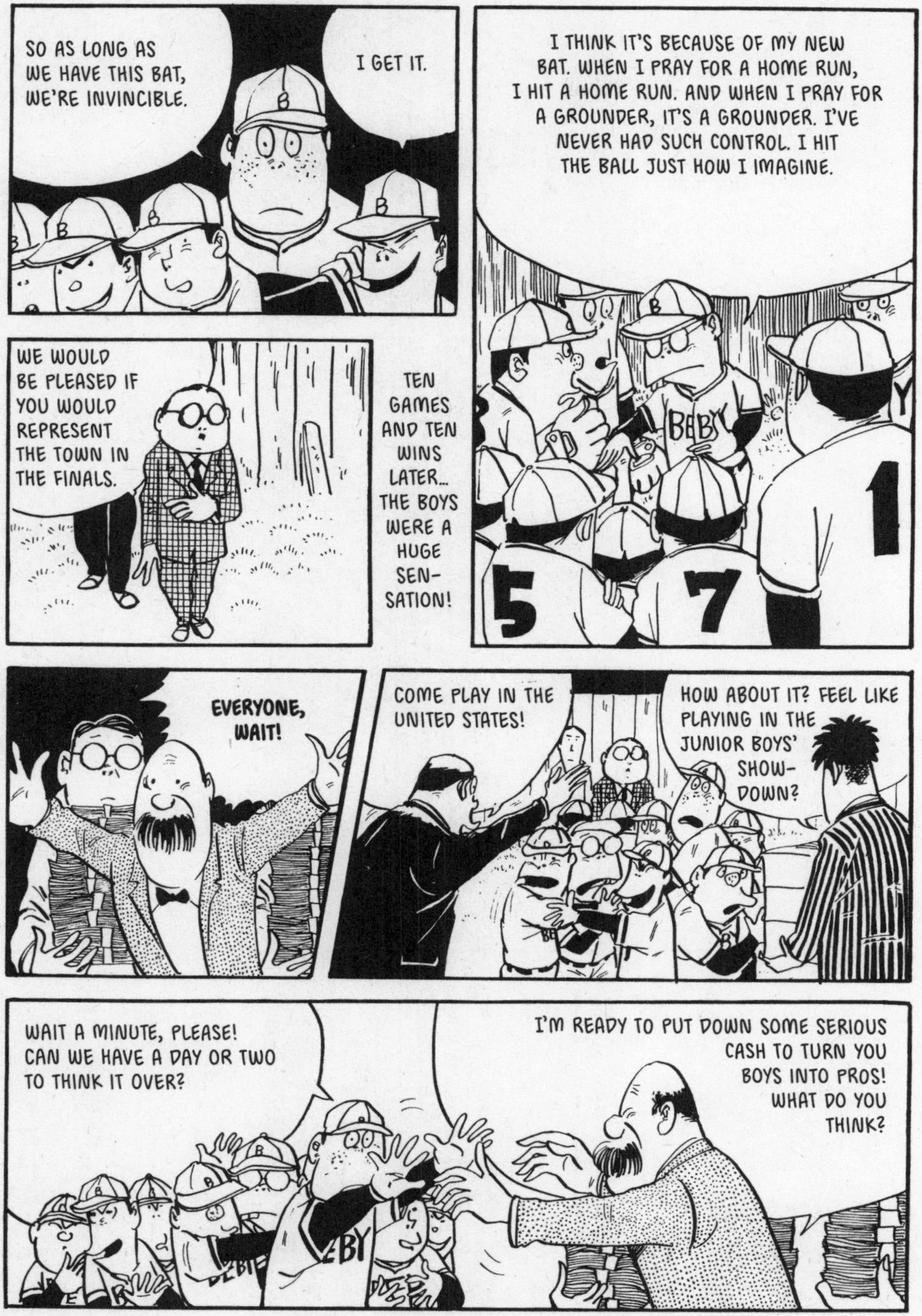
I THINK IT'S BECAUSE OF MY NEW BAT. WHEN I PRAY FOR A HOME RUN, I HIT A HOME RUN. AND WHEN I PRAY FOR A GROUNDER, IT'S A GROUNDER. I'VE NEVER HAD SUCH CONTROL. I HIT THE BALL JUST HOW I IMAGINE.
I GET IT.
SO AS LONG AS WE HAVE THIS BAT, WE'RE INVINCIBLE.
TEN GAMES AND TEN WINS LATER... THE BOYS WERE A HUGE SEN-SATION!
WE WOULD BE PLEASED IF YOU WOULD REPRESENT THE TOWN IN THE FINALS.
HOW ABOUT IT? FEEL LIKE PLAYING IN THE JUNIOR BOYS' SHOW-DOWN?
COME PLAY IN THE UNITED STATES!
EVERYONE, WAIT!
I'M READY TO PUT DOWN SOME SERIOUS CASH TO TURN YOU BOYS INTO PROS! WHAT DO YOU THINK?
WAIT A MINUTE, PLEASE! CAN WE HAVE A DAY OR TWO TO THINK IT OVER?

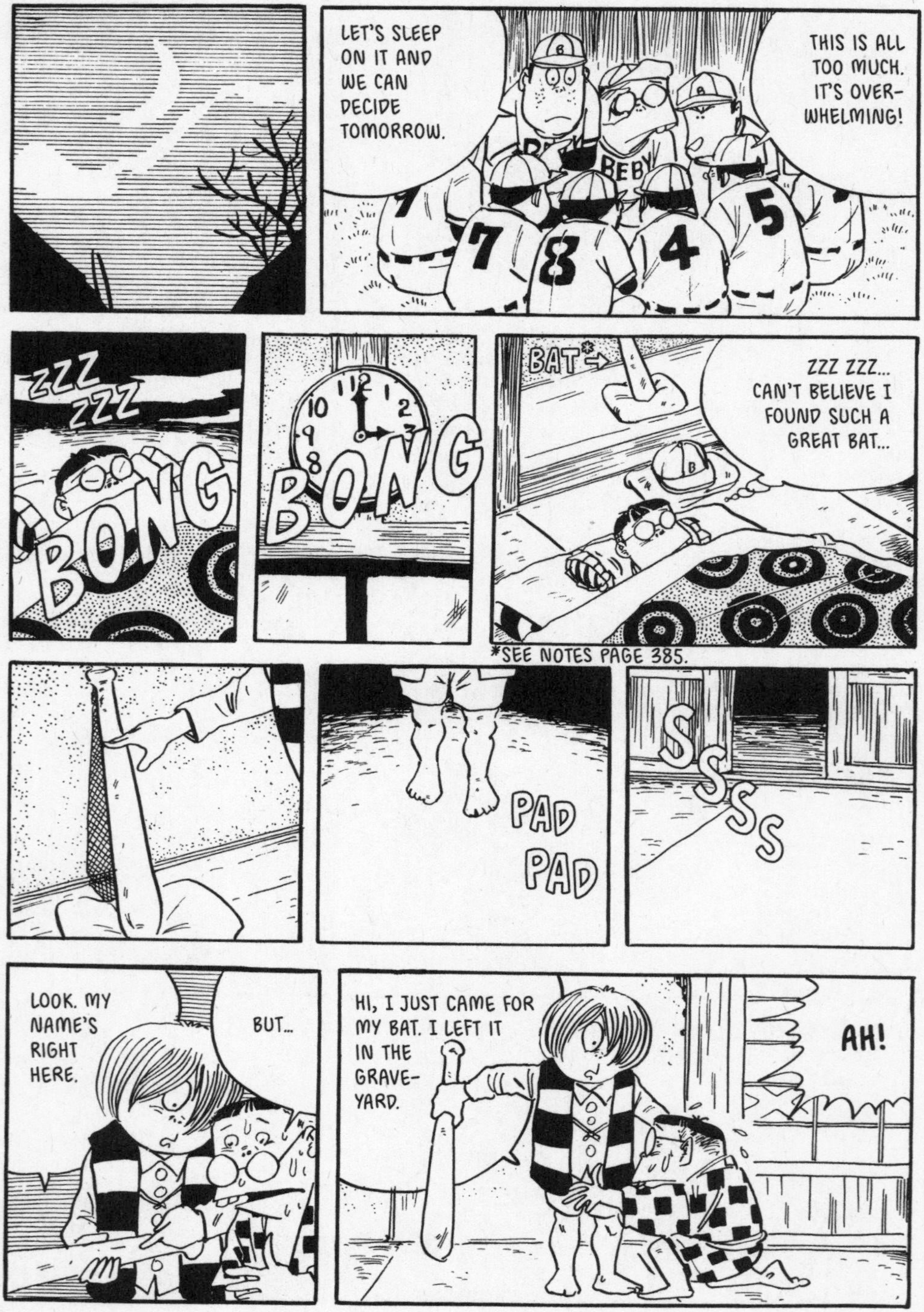
THIS IS ALL TOO MUCH. IT'S OVER-WHELMING!
LET'S SLEEP ON IT AND WE CAN DECIDE TOMORROW.
ZZZ ZZZ... CAN'T BELIEVE I FOUND SUCH A GREAT BAT...
BAT*→
BONG
ZZZ ZZZ
BONG
SSSS
PAD PAD
AH!
HI, I JUST CAME FOR MY BAT. I LEFT IT IN THE GRAVE-YARD.
BUT...
LOOK. MY NAME'S RIGHT HERE.

*SEE NOTES PAGE 385.

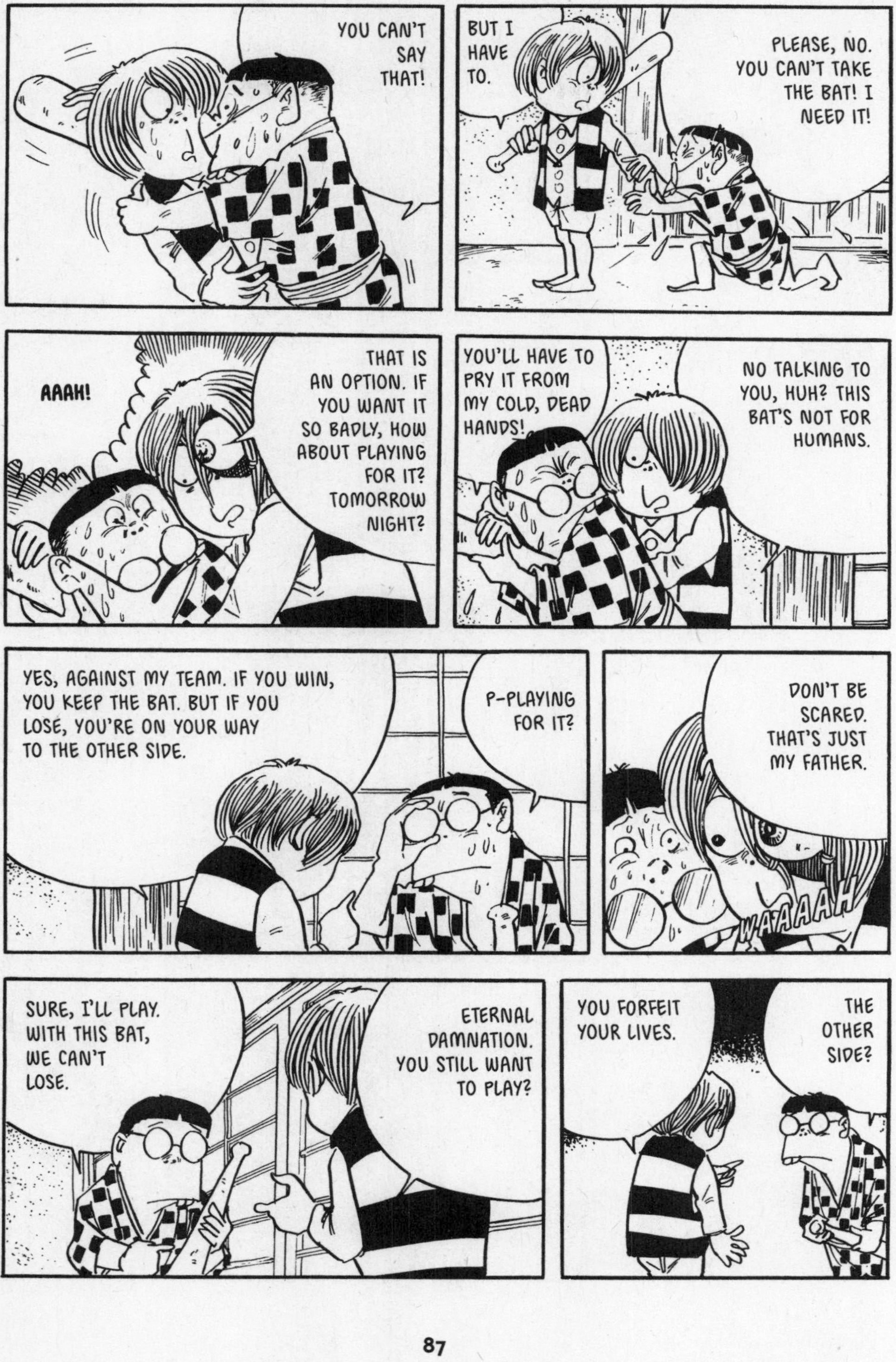
PLEASE, NO. YOU CAN'T TAKE THE BAT! I NEED IT!
BUT I HAVE TO.
YOU CAN'T SAY THAT!
NO TALKING TO YOU, HUH? THIS BAT'S NOT FOR HUMANS.
YOU'LL HAVE TO PRY IT FROM MY COLD, DEAD HANDS!
THAT IS AN OPTION. IF YOU WANT IT SO BADLY, HOW ABOUT PLAYING FOR IT? TOMORROW NIGHT?
AAAH!
DON'T BE SCARED. THAT'S JUST MY FATHER.
WAAAAAH
P-PLAYING FOR IT?
YES, AGAINST MY TEAM. IF YOU WIN, YOU KEEP THE BAT. BUT IF YOU LOSE, YOU'RE ON YOUR WAY TO THE OTHER SIDE.
THE OTHER SIDE?
YOU FORFEIT YOUR LIVES.
ETERNAL DAMNATION. YOU STILL WANT TO PLAY?
SURE, I'LL PLAY. WITH THIS BAT, WE CAN'T LOSE.

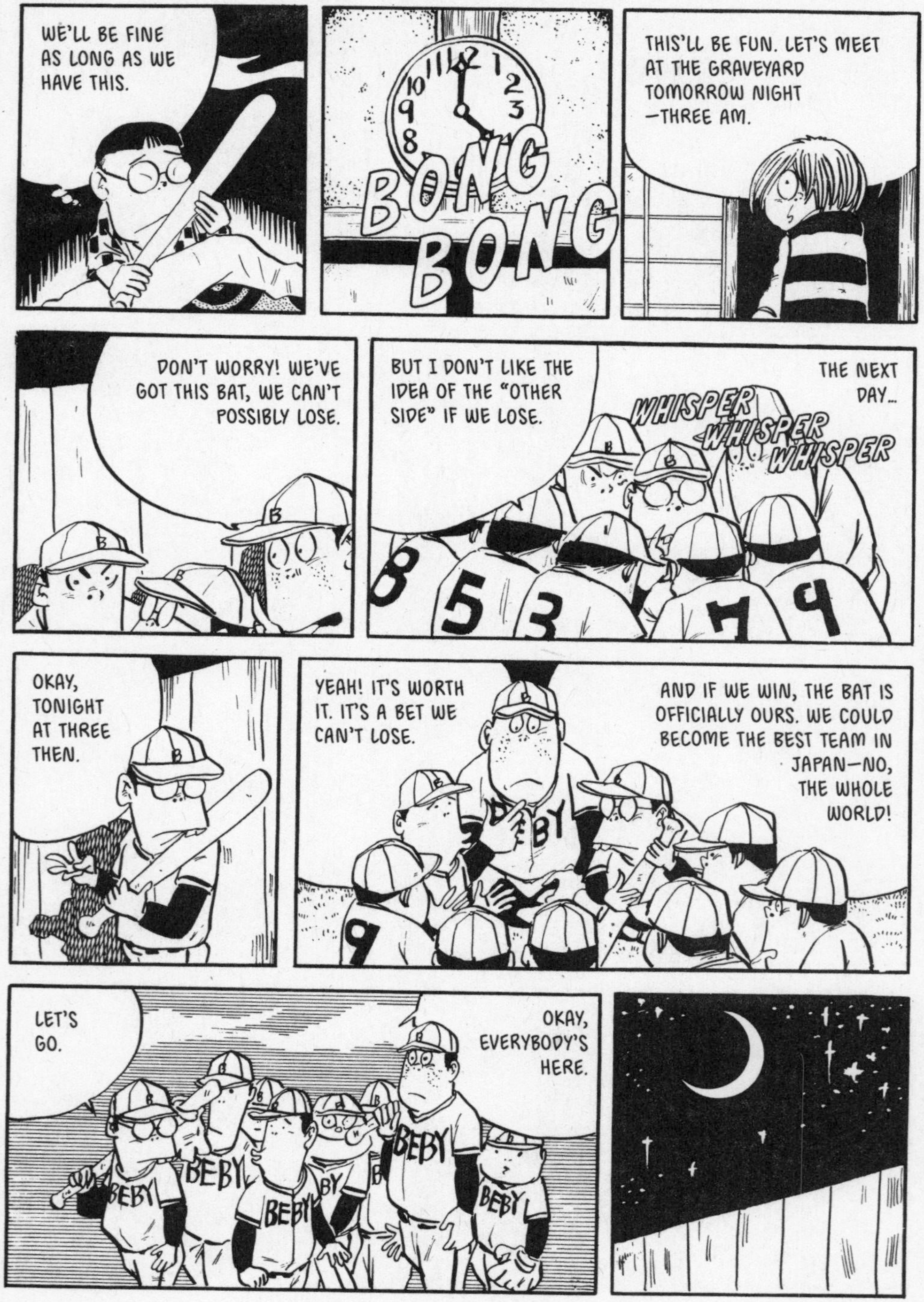
THIS'LL BE FUN. LET'S MEET AT THE GRAVEYARD TOMORROW NIGHT —THREE AM.
BONG BONG
WE'LL BE FINE AS LONG AS WE HAVE THIS.
THE NEXT DAY...
WHISPER WHISPER WHISPER
BUT I DON'T LIKE THE IDEA OF THE "OTHER SIDE" IF WE LOSE.
DON'T WORRY! WE'VE GOT THIS BAT, WE CAN'T POSSIBLY LOSE.
AND IF WE WIN, THE BAT IS OFFICIALLY OURS. WE COULD BECOME THE BEST TEAM IN JAPAN—NO, THE WHOLE WORLD!
YEAH! IT'S WORTH IT. IT'S A BET WE CAN'T LOSE.
OKAY, TONIGHT AT THREE THEN.
OKAY, EVERYBODY'S HERE.
LET'S GO.

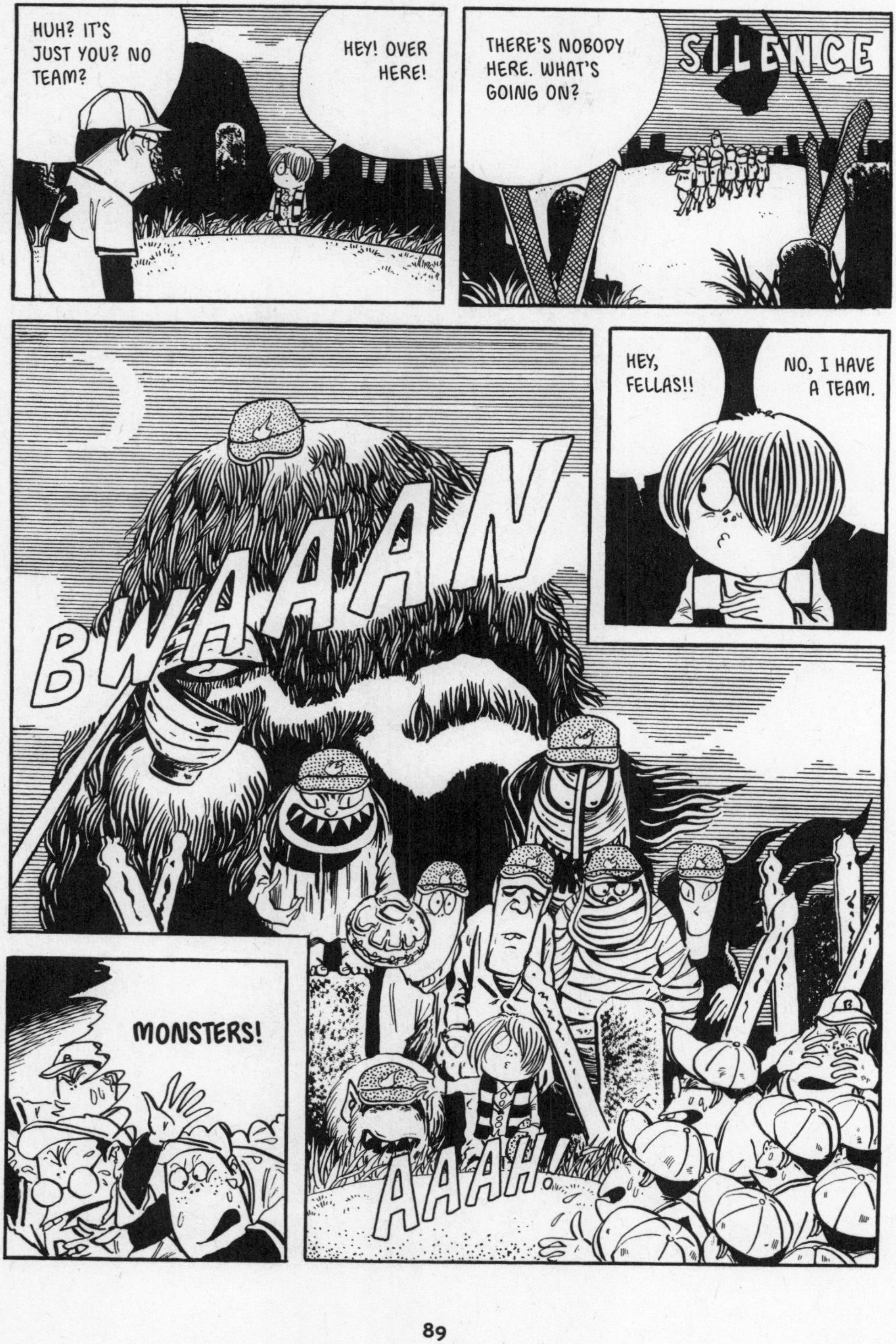
THERE'S NOBODY HERE. WHAT'S GOING ON?
SILENCE
HEY! OVER HERE!
HUH? IT'S JUST YOU? NO TEAM?
NO, I HAVE A TEAM.
HEY, FELLAS!!
BWAAAN
AAAH!
MONSTERS!

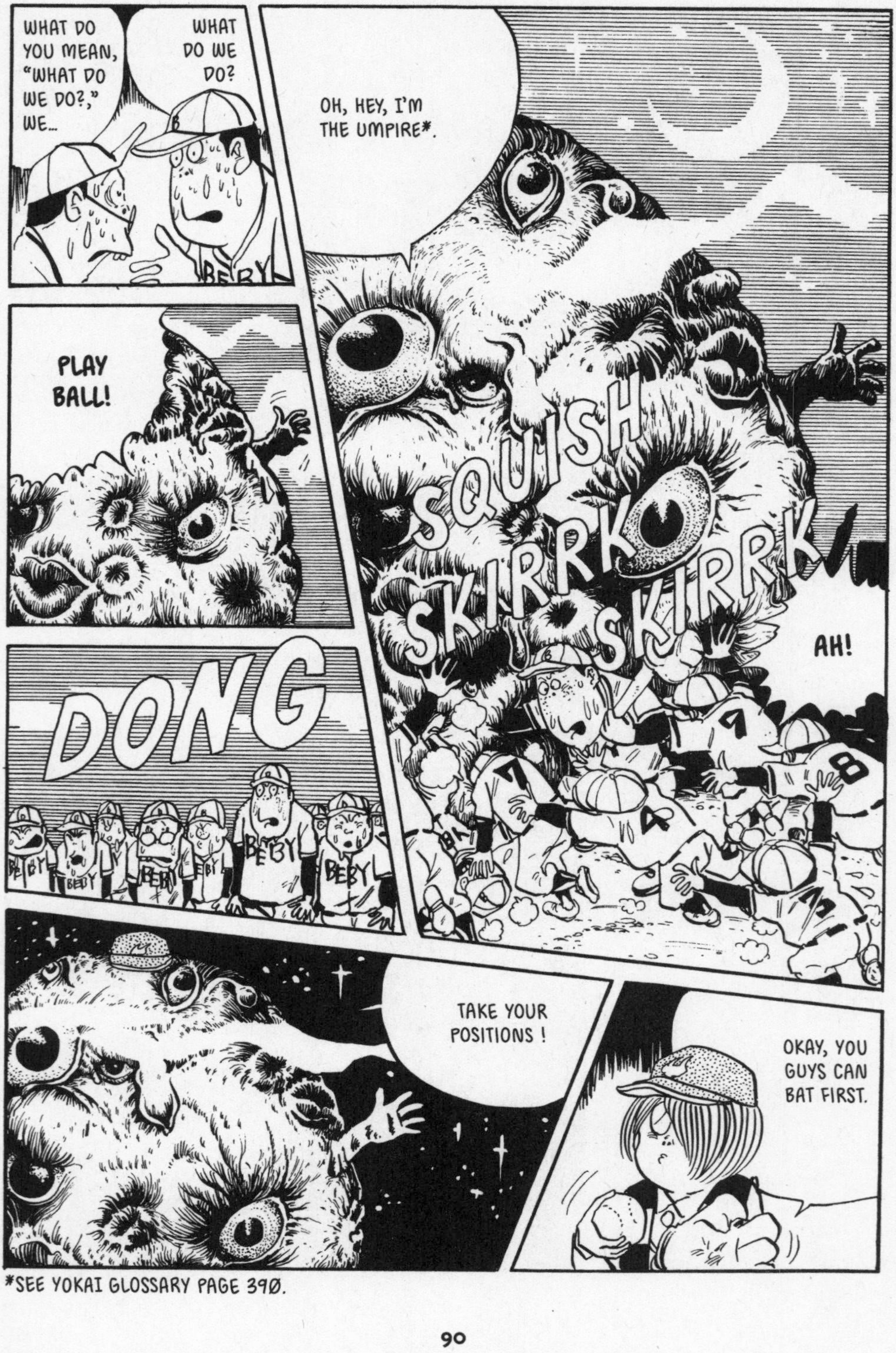
OH, HEY, I'M THE UMPIRE*.
SQUISH
SKIRRK
SKIRRK
AH!
WHAT DO WE DO?
WHAT DO YOU MEAN, "WHAT DO WE DO?," WE...
PLAY BALL!
DONG
OKAY, YOU GUYS CAN BAT FIRST.
TAKE YOUR POSITIONS !

*SEE YOKAI GLOSSARY PAGE 390.

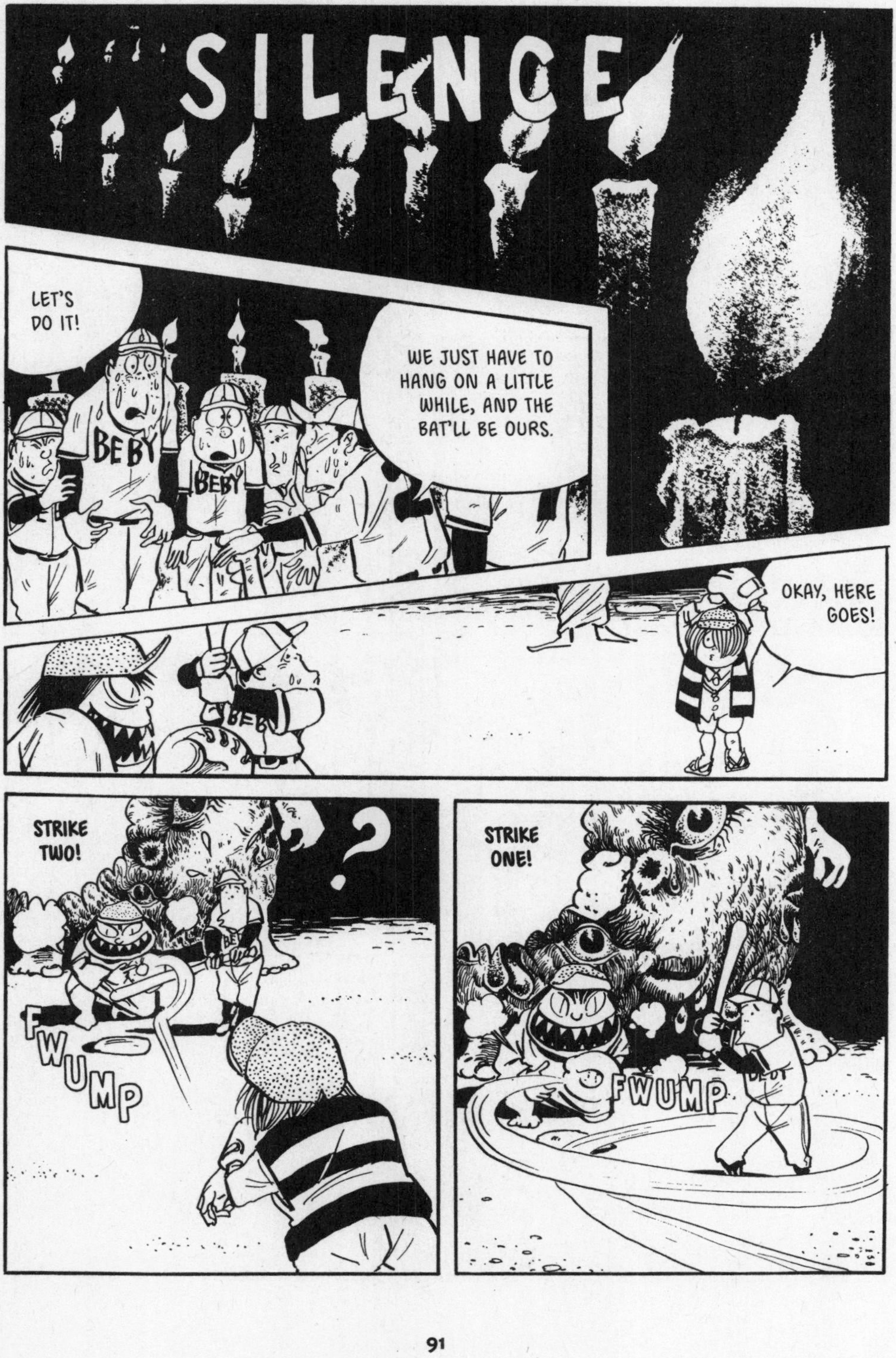
SILENCE
WE JUST HAVE TO HANG ON A LITTLE WHILE, AND THE BAT'LL BE OURS.
LET'S DO IT!
OKAY, HERE GOES!
STRIKE ONE!
FWUMP
STRIKE TWO!
FWUMP

WHEE!

I'LL BE OKAY WITH THIS BAT, THOUGH.

IT LOOKS LIKE THE BALL IS RUNNING AWAY FROM THE BAT!

THAT'S WEIRD, RIGHT?

STRIKE THREE!

FWOOSH

B	0	0	0	0			
	2	3	4	5	6	7
	1	3	0	2			

KEH KEH KEH KEH!

WHAT? YOU'RE QUITTING ALREADY? THAT WAS FAST.

T-TIME OUT!

NATURALLY, KITARO HAD A BALL THAT AVOIDED BATS. WITH THE MONSTER TEAM LEADING AT 6-0, THEY HEADED INTO THE TOP OF THE FIFTH.

92

W-WE'RE NOT QUITTING YET... I MEAN EVER.
YEAH, WE'RE PROTESTING! USING THAT BALL IS CHEATING.
LET'S COMPROMISE. IF YOU GUYS DON'T USE THAT BAT, I WON'T USE THIS BALL.
WE HAVE TO GIVE UP THE BAT.
I AGREE. WE'LL NEVER GET A RUN OTHERWISE.
HUP! I'LL HANG ON TO THAT FOR YOU.
NOW KITARO, YOU HAND OVER THE BALL.
CHOMP
PLAY BALL!
YIKES...
HEE HEE HEE HEE HEE HEE!

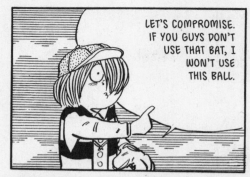

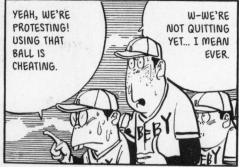

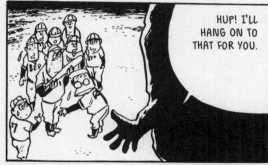

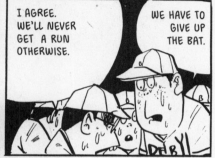

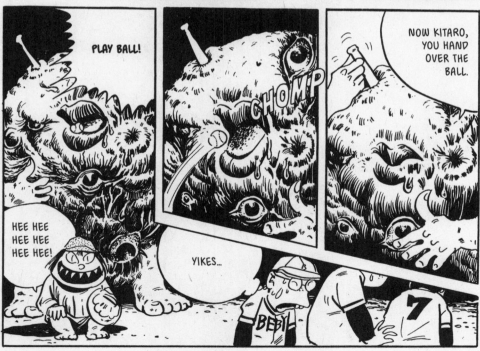

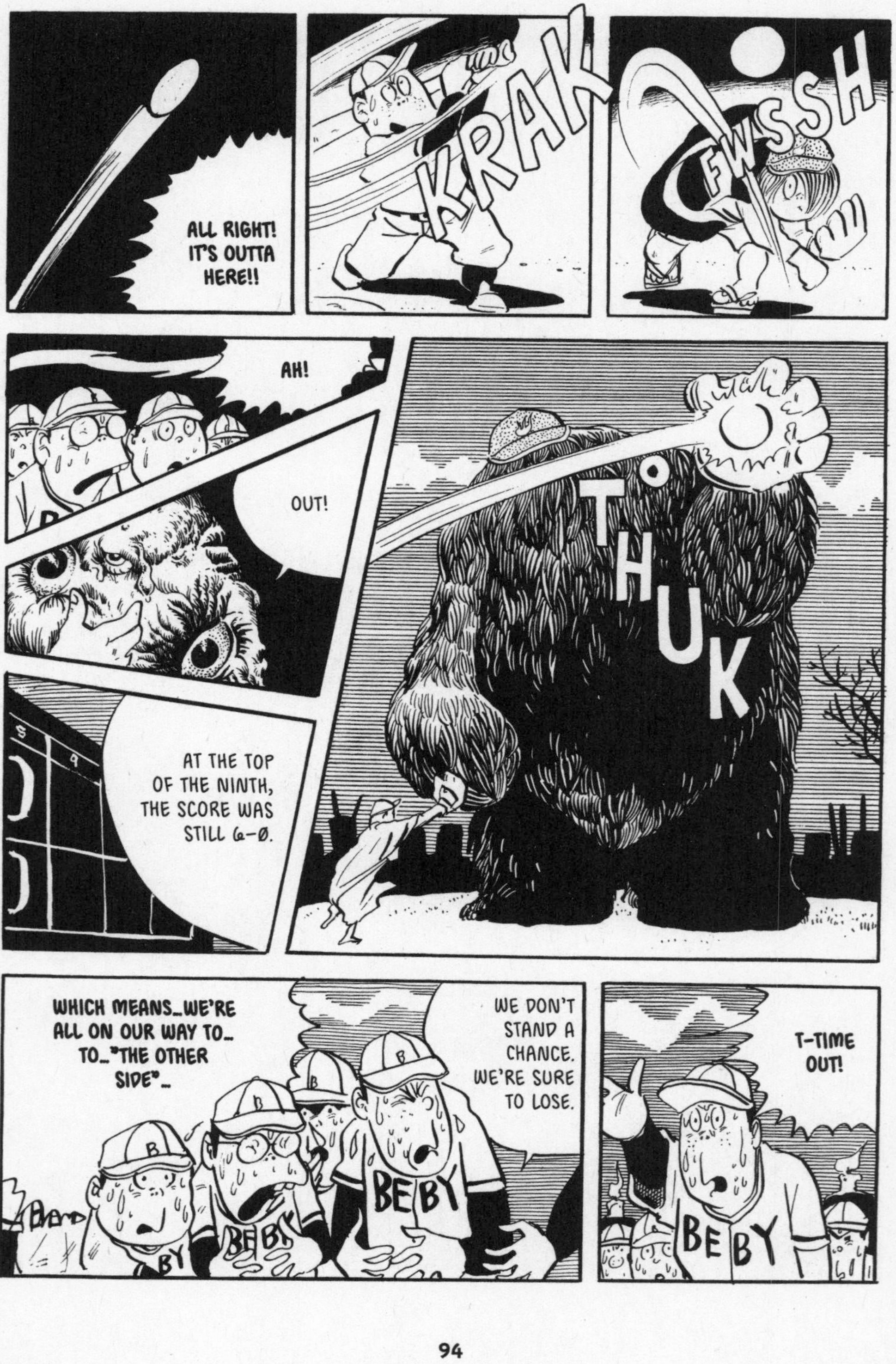
FWSSH
KRAK
ALL RIGHT! IT'S OUTTA HERE!!
THUK
AH!
OUT!
AT THE TOP OF THE NINTH, THE SCORE WAS STILL 6-Ø.
T-TIME OUT!
WE DON'T STAND A CHANCE. WE'RE SURE TO LOSE.
WHICH MEANS...WE'RE ALL ON OUR WAY TO... TO..."THE OTHER SIDE"...

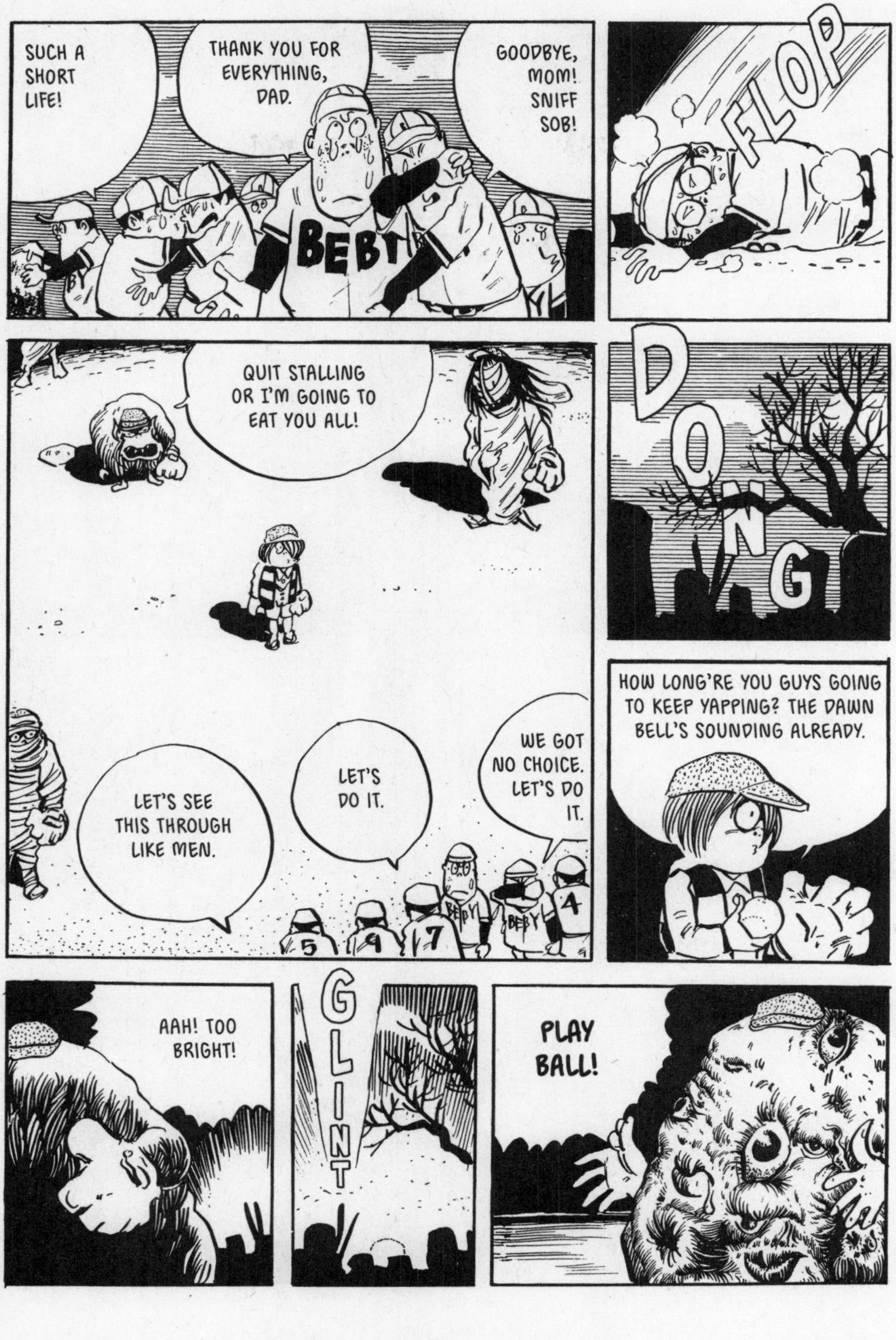
FLOP
GOODBYE, MOM! SNIFF SOB!
THANK YOU FOR EVERYTHING, DAD.
SUCH A SHORT LIFE!
DONG
HOW LONG'RE YOU GUYS GOING TO KEEP YAPPING? THE DAWN BELL'S SOUNDING ALREADY.
QUIT STALLING OR I'M GOING TO EAT YOU ALL!
WE GOT NO CHOICE. LET'S DO IT.
LET'S DO IT.
LET'S SEE THIS THROUGH LIKE MEN.
PLAY BALL!
GLINT
AAH! TOO BRIGHT!

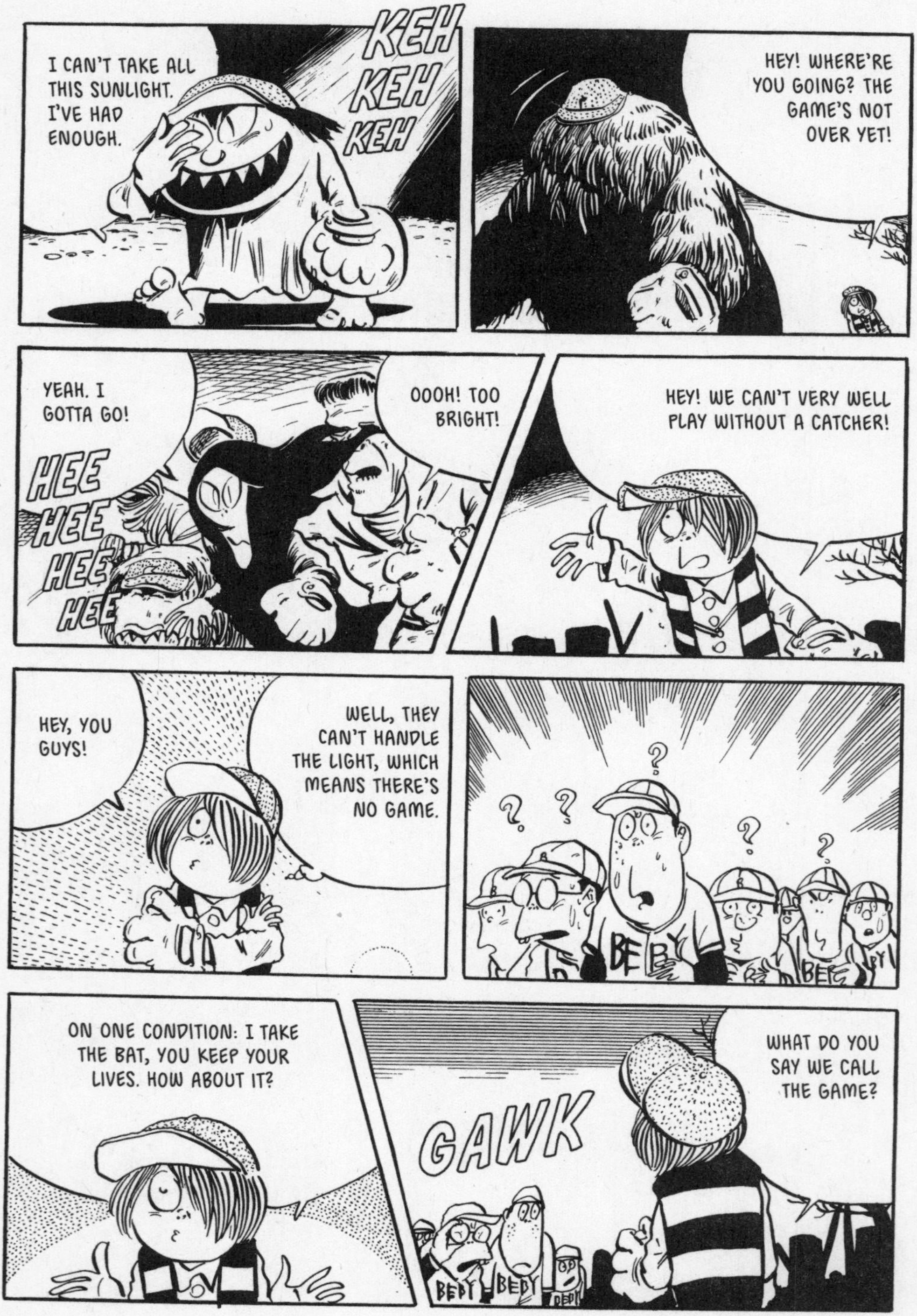
HEY! WHERE'RE YOU GOING? THE GAME'S NOT OVER YET!
KEH KEH KEH
I CAN'T TAKE ALL THIS SUNLIGHT. I'VE HAD ENOUGH.
HEY! WE CAN'T VERY WELL PLAY WITHOUT A CATCHER!
OOOH! TOO BRIGHT!
YEAH. I GOTTA GO!
HEE HEE HEE HEE
WELL, THEY CAN'T HANDLE THE LIGHT, WHICH MEANS THERE'S NO GAME.
HEY, YOU GUYS!
WHAT DO YOU SAY WE CALL THE GAME?
GAWK
ON ONE CONDITION: I TAKE THE BAT, YOU KEEP YOUR LIVES. HOW ABOUT IT?

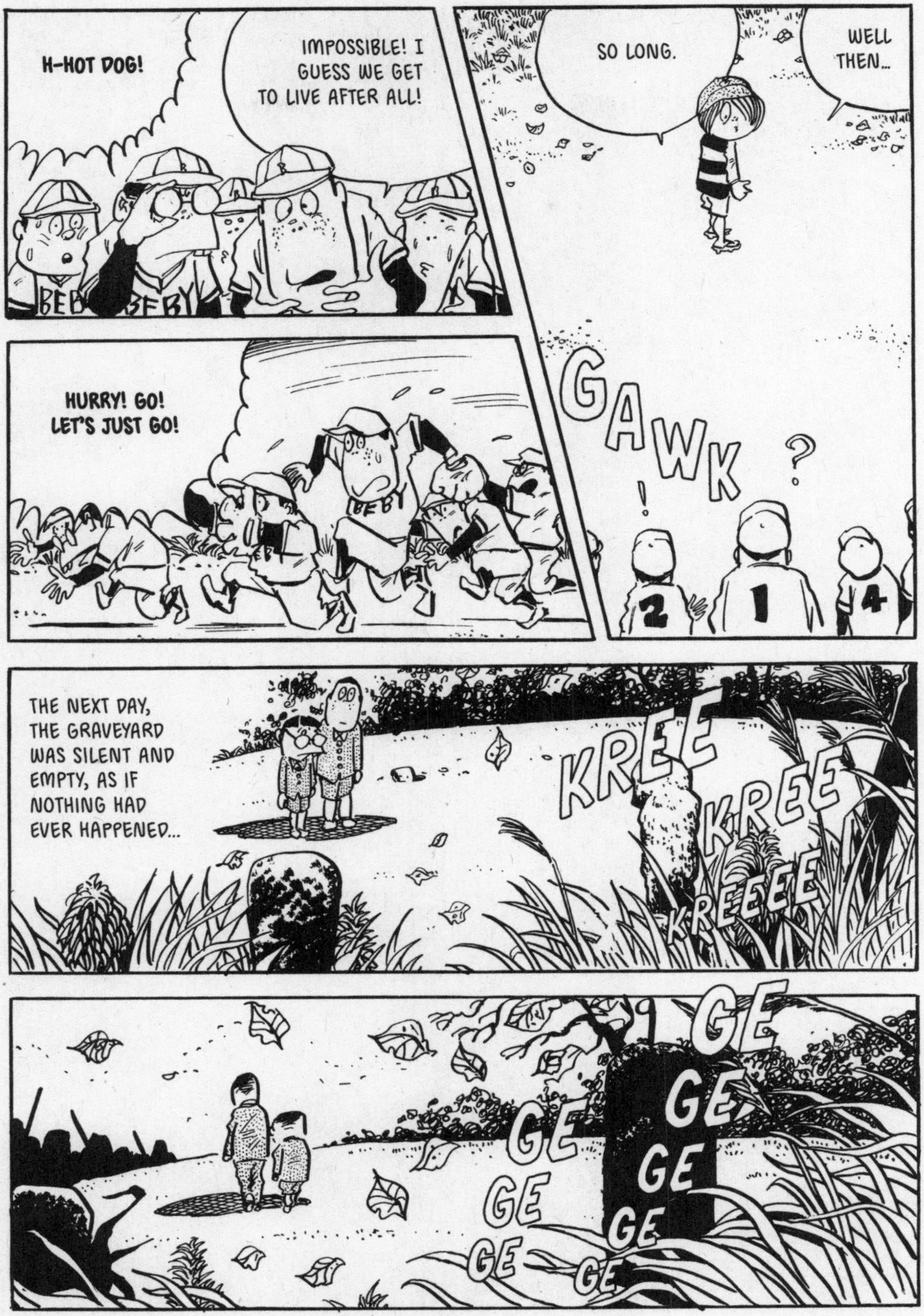
WELL THEN...
SO LONG.
GAWK
IMPOSSIBLE! I GUESS WE GET TO LIVE AFTER ALL!
H-HOT DOG!
HURRY! GO! LET'S JUST GO!
KREE
KREE
KREEEEE
THE NEXT DAY, THE GRAVEYARD WAS SILENT AND EMPTY, AS IF NOTHING HAD EVER HAPPENED...
GE GE GE GE GE GE GE GE

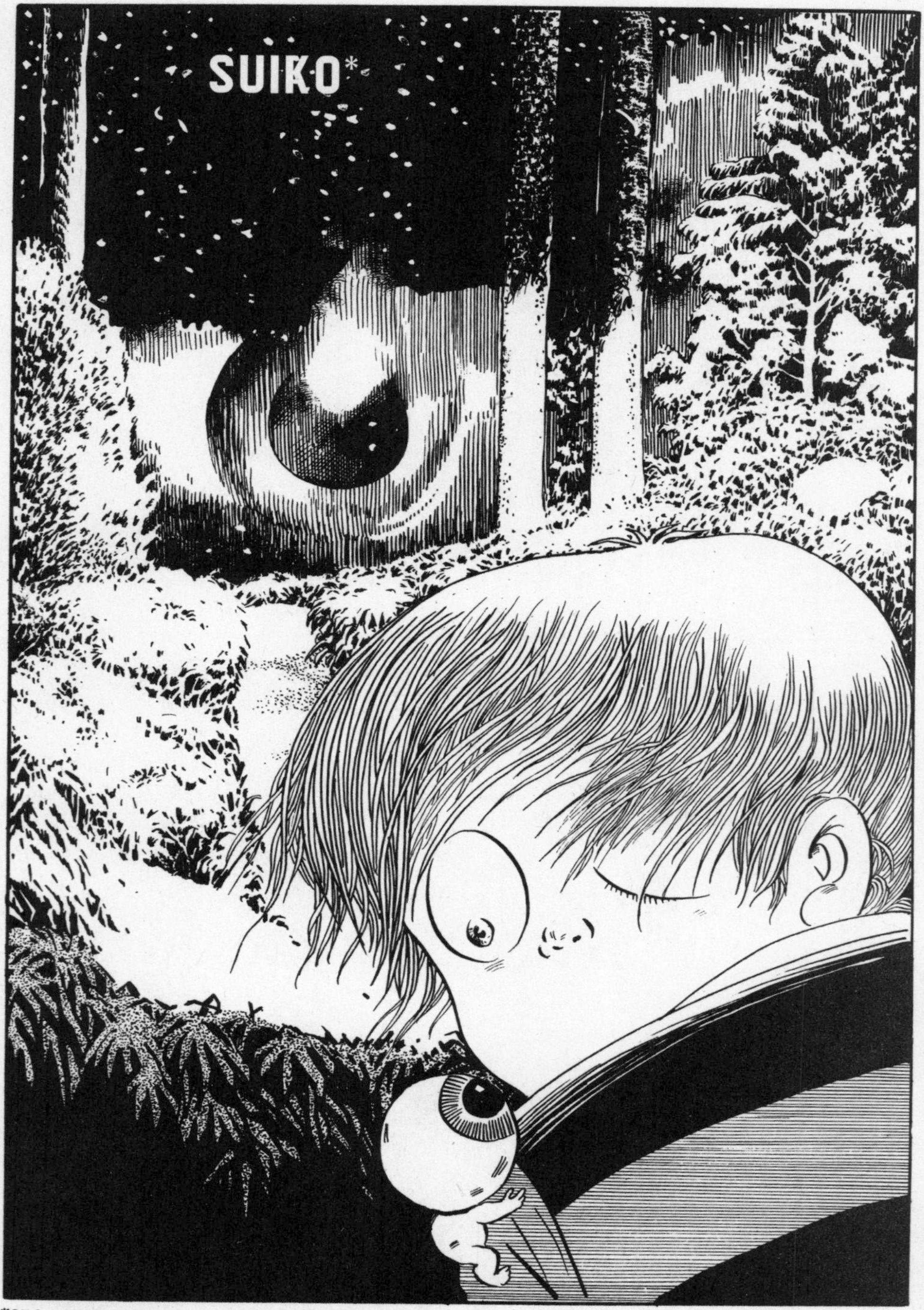
SUIKO*
*SEE NOTES PAGE 385, YOKAI GLOSSARY PAGE 390.

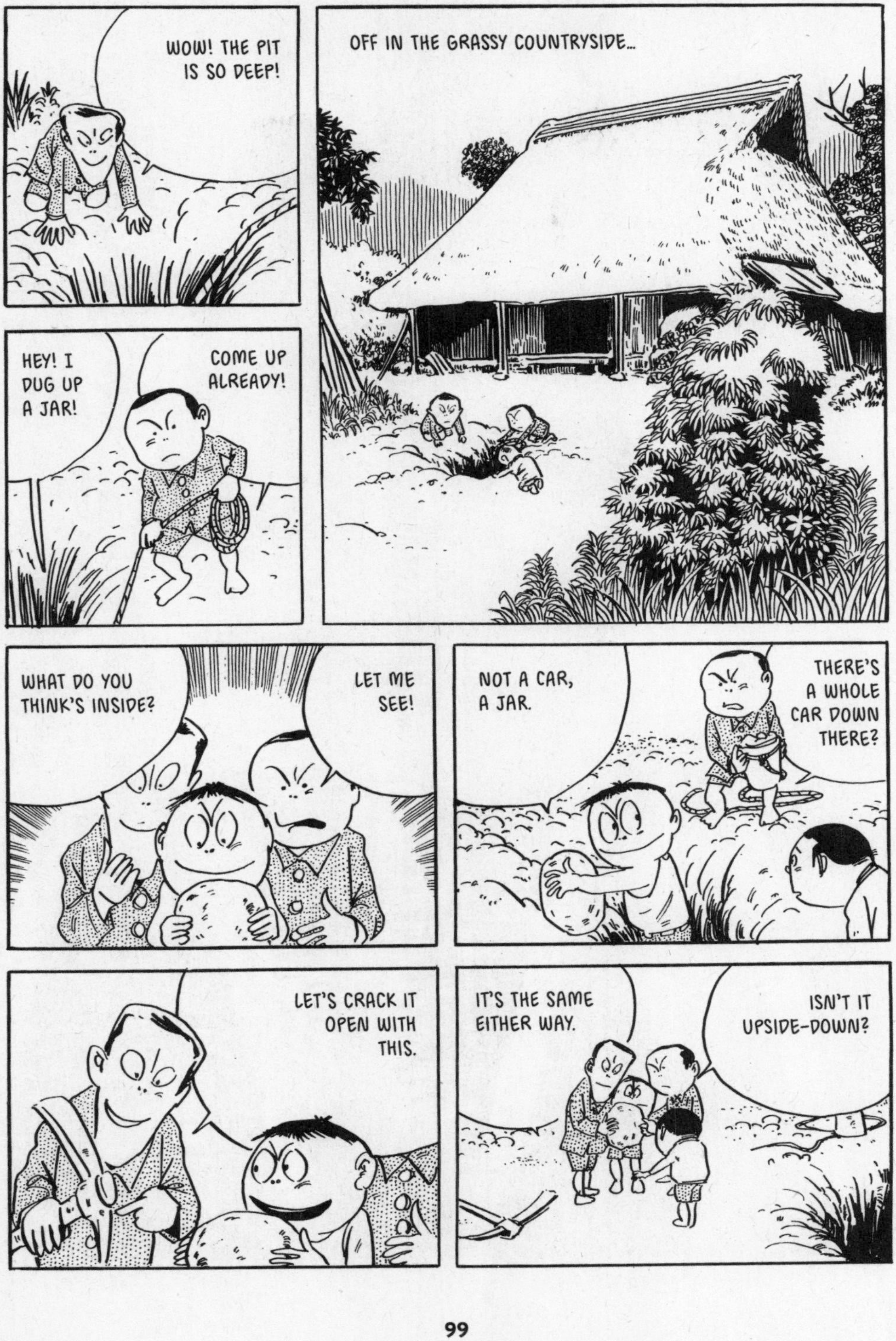
OFF IN THE GRASSY COUNTRYSIDE...
WOW! THE PIT IS SO DEEP!
COME UP ALREADY!
HEY! I DUG UP A JAR!
THERE'S A WHOLE CAR DOWN THERE?
NOT A CAR, A JAR.
LET ME SEE!
WHAT DO YOU THINK'S INSIDE?
ISN'T IT UPSIDE-DOWN?
IT'S THE SAME EITHER WAY.
LET'S CRACK IT OPEN WITH THIS.

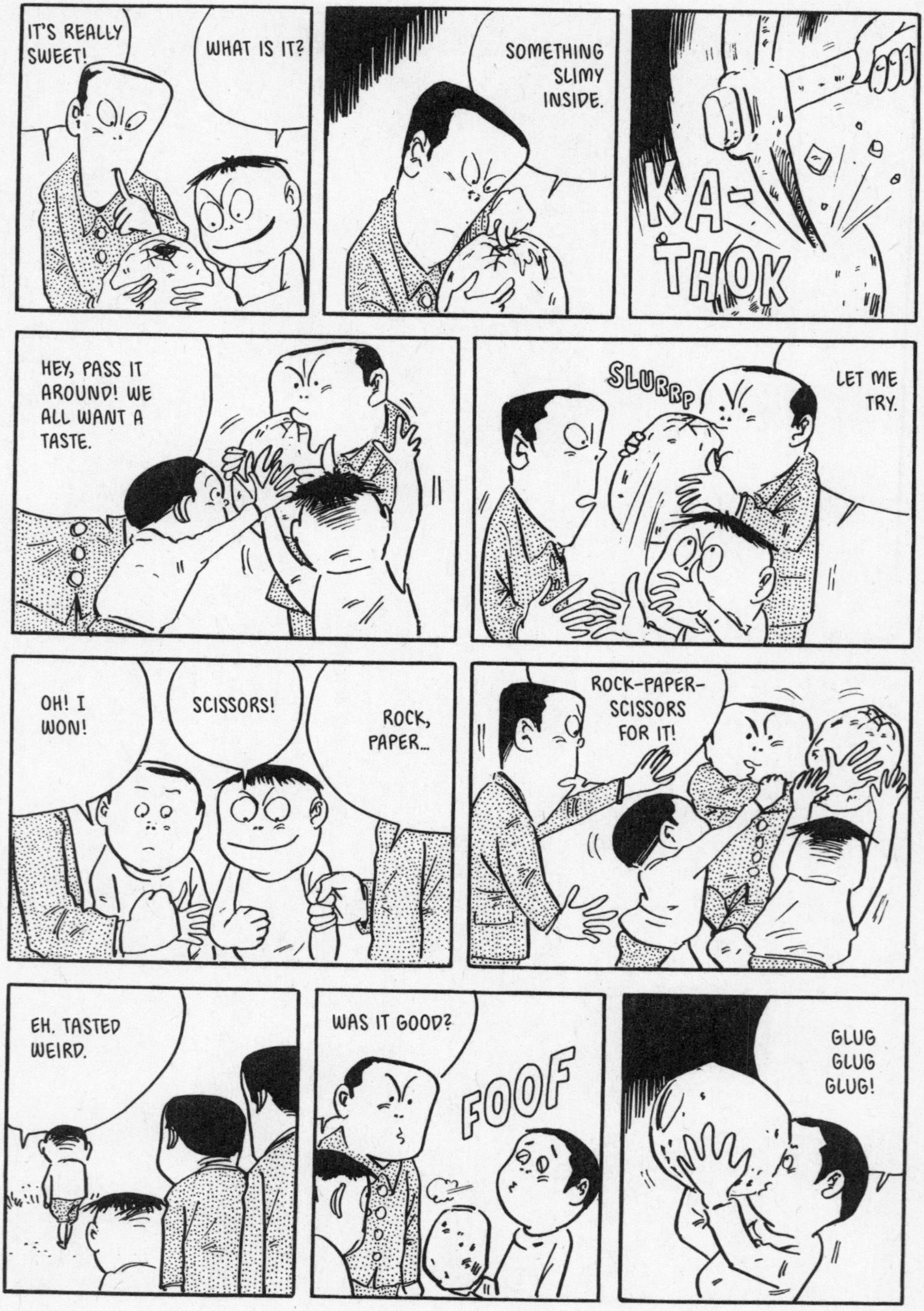
KA-THOK
SOMETHING SLIMY INSIDE.
WHAT IS IT?
IT'S REALLY SWEET!
LET ME TRY.
SLURRP
HEY, PASS IT AROUND! WE ALL WANT A TASTE.
ROCK-PAPER-SCISSORS FOR IT!
ROCK, PAPER...
SCISSORS!
OH! I WON!
GLUG GLUG GLUG!
WAS IT GOOD?
FOOF
EH. TASTED WEIRD.

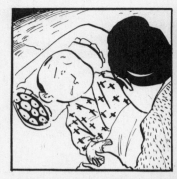

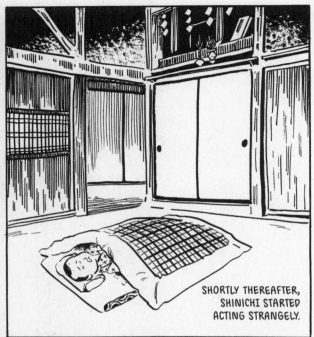

SHORTLY THEREAFTER, SHINICHI STARTED ACTING STRANGELY.
WHAT IS GOING ON WITH HIM?
HE OVERSLEEPS EVERY MORNING AND HIS HANDS ARE ALWAYS FILTHY!
THAT'S ODD. I'LL WATCH HIM TONIGHT AND SEE WHAT HE'S UP TO.
BONG
AH-HA!

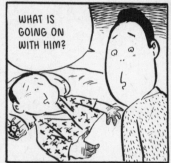

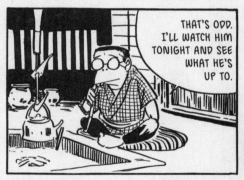

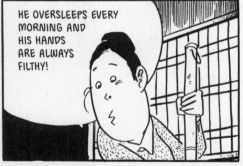

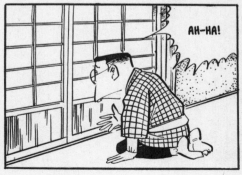

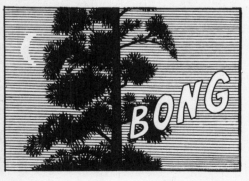

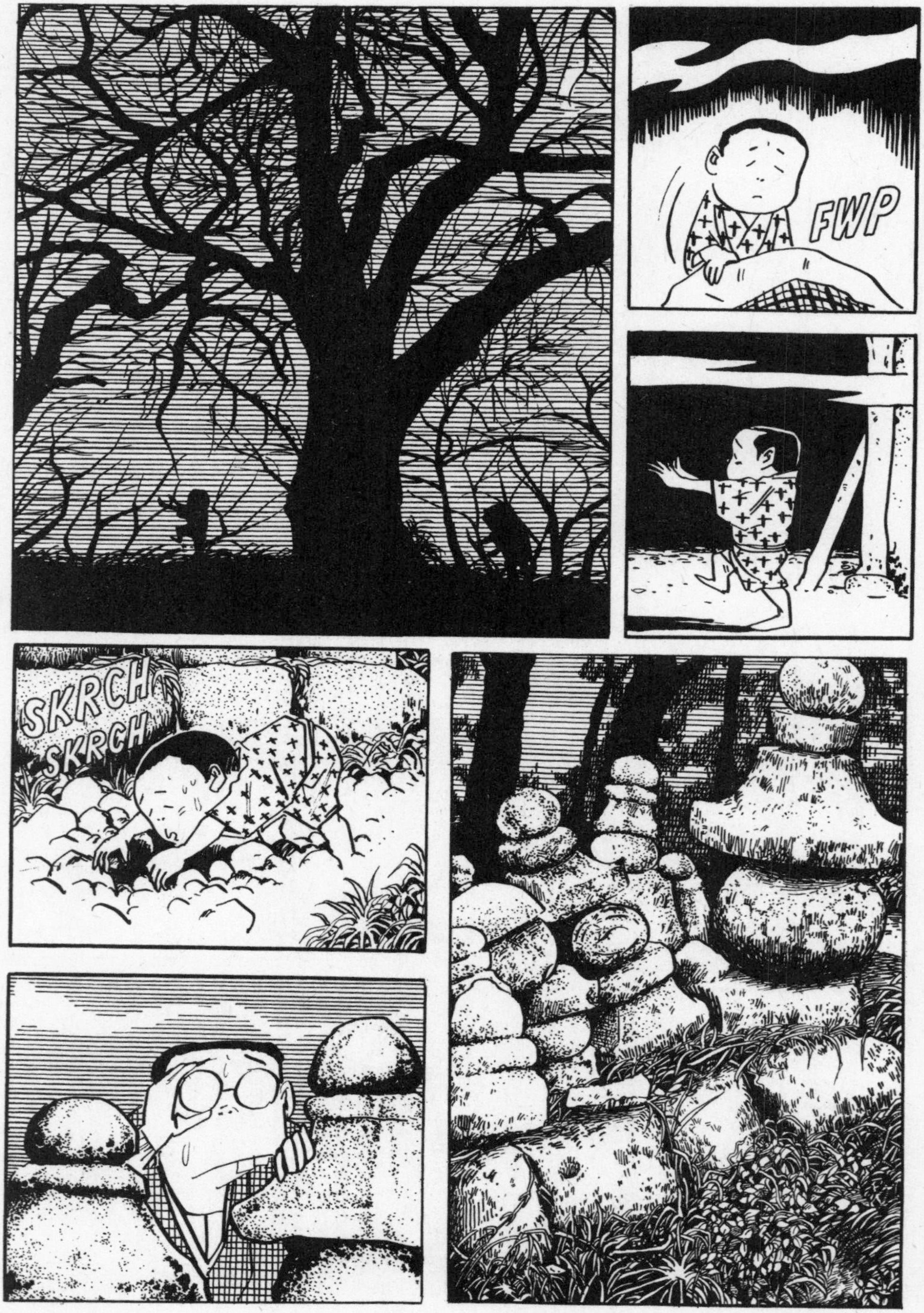
FWP
SKRCH
SKRCH

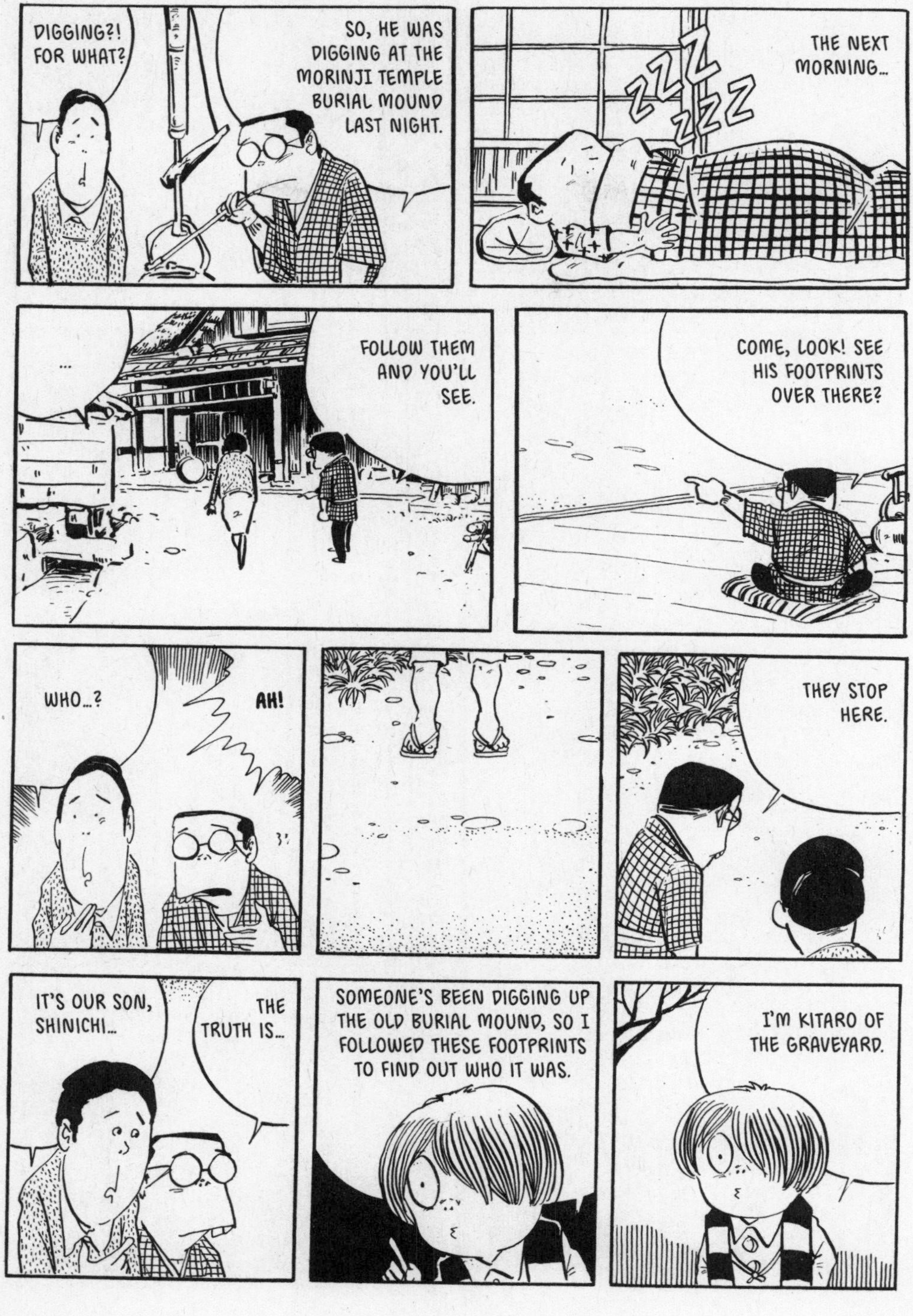
THE NEXT MORNING...
ZZZ ZZZ
SO, HE WAS DIGGING AT THE MORINJI TEMPLE BURIAL MOUND LAST NIGHT.
DIGGING?! FOR WHAT?
COME, LOOK! SEE HIS FOOTPRINTS OVER THERE?
FOLLOW THEM AND YOU'LL SEE.
...
THEY STOP HERE.
AH!
WHO...?
I'M KITARO OF THE GRAVEYARD.
SOMEONE'S BEEN DIGGING UP THE OLD BURIAL MOUND, SO I FOLLOWED THESE FOOTPRINTS TO FIND OUT WHO IT WAS.
THE TRUTH IS...
IT'S OUR SON, SHINICHI...

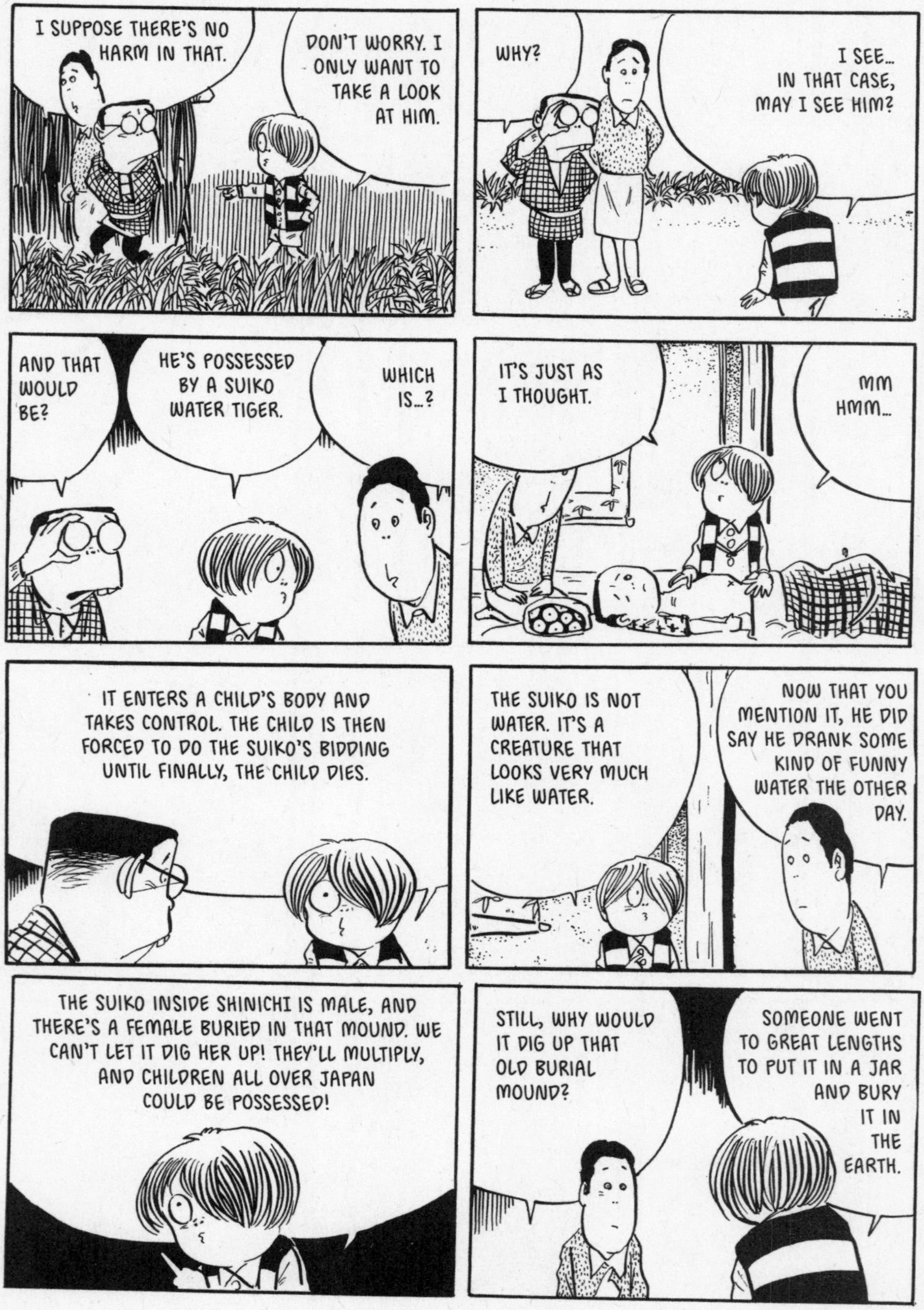
I SEE... IN THAT CASE, MAY I SEE HIM?
WHY?
DON'T WORRY. I ONLY WANT TO TAKE A LOOK AT HIM.
I SUPPOSE THERE'S NO HARM IN THAT.
MM HMM...
IT'S JUST AS I THOUGHT.
WHICH IS...?
HE'S POSSESSED BY A SUIKO WATER TIGER.
AND THAT WOULD BE?
NOW THAT YOU MENTION IT, HE DID SAY HE DRANK SOME KIND OF FUNNY WATER THE OTHER DAY.
THE SUIKO IS NOT WATER. IT'S A CREATURE THAT LOOKS VERY MUCH LIKE WATER.
IT ENTERS A CHILD'S BODY AND TAKES CONTROL. THE CHILD IS THEN FORCED TO DO THE SUIKO'S BIDDING UNTIL FINALLY, THE CHILD DIES.
SOMEONE WENT TO GREAT LENGTHS TO PUT IT IN A JAR AND BURY IT IN THE EARTH.
STILL, WHY WOULD IT DIG UP THAT OLD BURIAL MOUND?
THE SUIKO INSIDE SHINICHI IS MALE, AND THERE'S A FEMALE BURIED IN THAT MOUND. WE CAN'T LET IT DIG HER UP! THEY'LL MULTIPLY, AND CHILDREN ALL OVER JAPAN COULD BE POSSESSED!

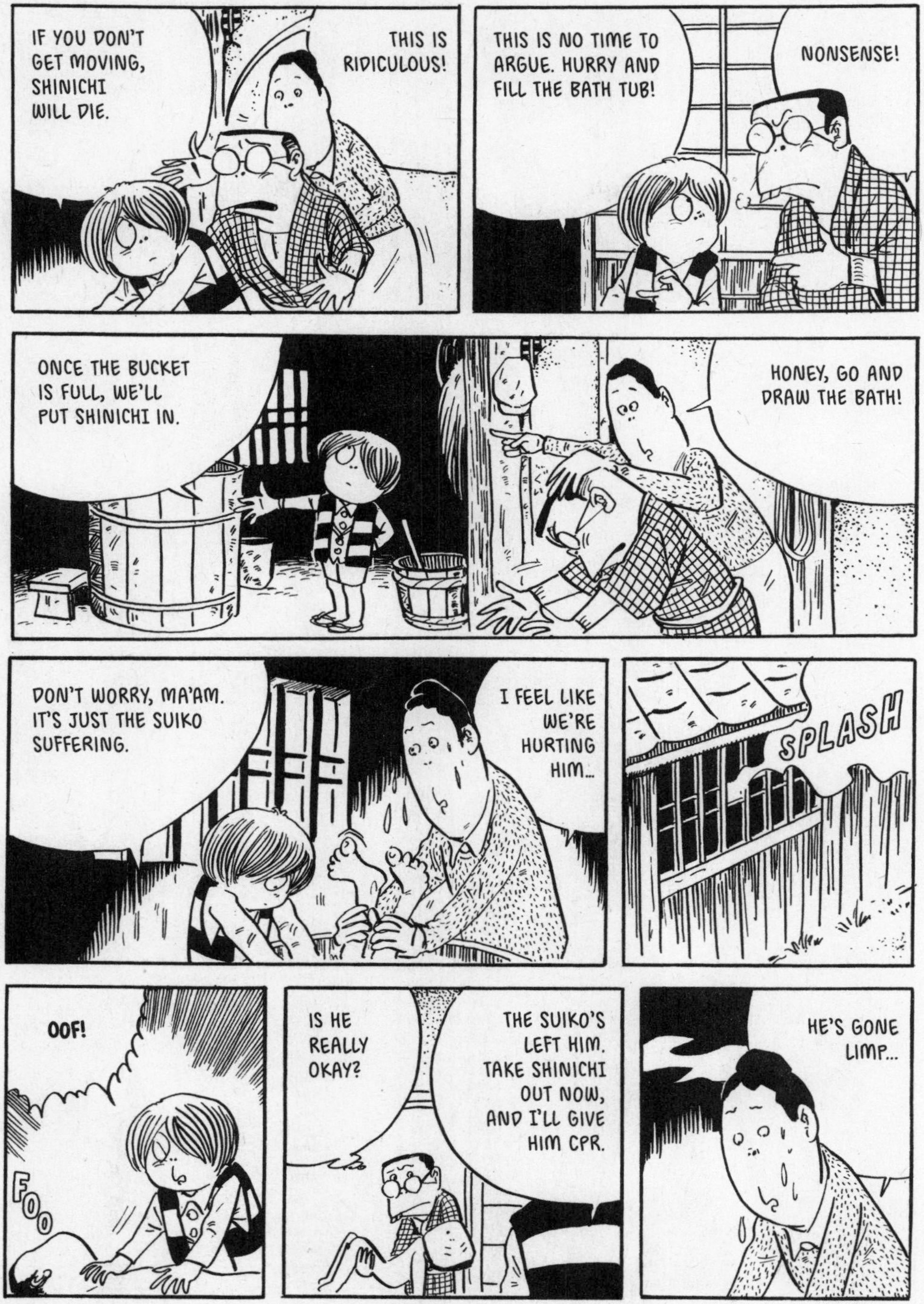
IF YOU DON'T GET MOVING, SHINICHI WILL DIE.
THIS IS RIDICULOUS!
THIS IS NO TIME TO ARGUE. HURRY AND FILL THE BATH TUB!
NONSENSE!
ONCE THE BUCKET IS FULL, WE'LL PUT SHINICHI IN.
HONEY, GO AND DRAW THE BATH!
DON'T WORRY, MA'AM. IT'S JUST THE SUIKO SUFFERING.
I FEEL LIKE WE'RE HURTING HIM...
SPLASH
OOF!
FOO
IS HE REALLY OKAY?
THE SUIKO'S LEFT HIM. TAKE SHINICHI OUT NOW, AND I'LL GIVE HIM CPR.
HE'S GONE LIMP...

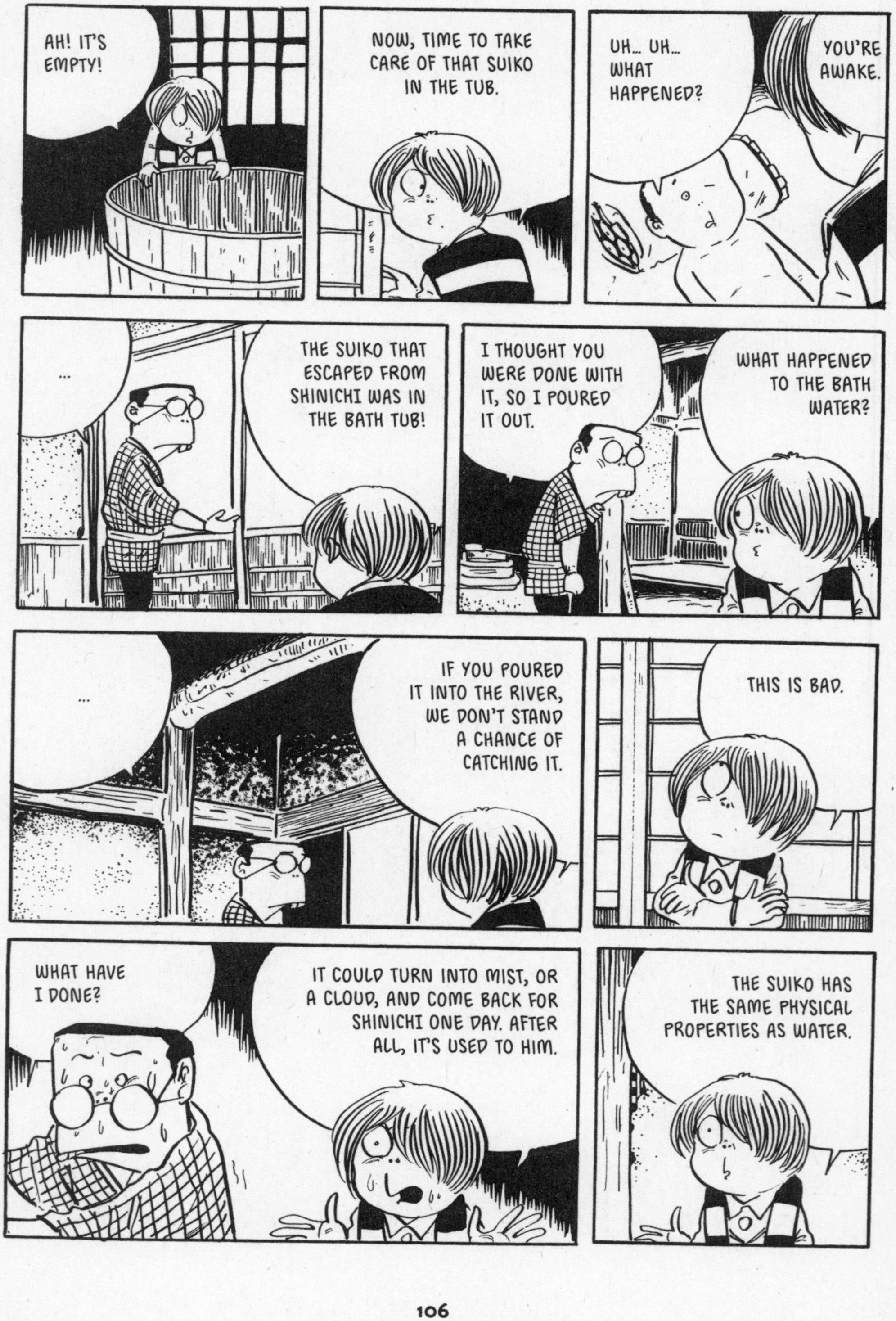

YOU'RE AWAKE.
UH... UH... WHAT HAPPENED?
NOW, TIME TO TAKE CARE OF THAT SUIKO IN THE TUB.
AH! IT'S EMPTY!
WHAT HAPPENED TO THE BATH WATER?
I THOUGHT YOU WERE DONE WITH IT, SO I POURED IT OUT.
THE SUIKO THAT ESCAPED FROM SHINICHI WAS IN THE BATH TUB!
...
THIS IS BAD.
IF YOU POURED IT INTO THE RIVER, WE DON'T STAND A CHANCE OF CATCHING IT.
...
THE SUIKO HAS THE SAME PHYSICAL PROPERTIES AS WATER.
IT COULD TURN INTO MIST, OR A CLOUD, AND COME BACK FOR SHINICHI ONE DAY. AFTER ALL, IT'S USED TO HIM.
WHAT HAVE I DONE?

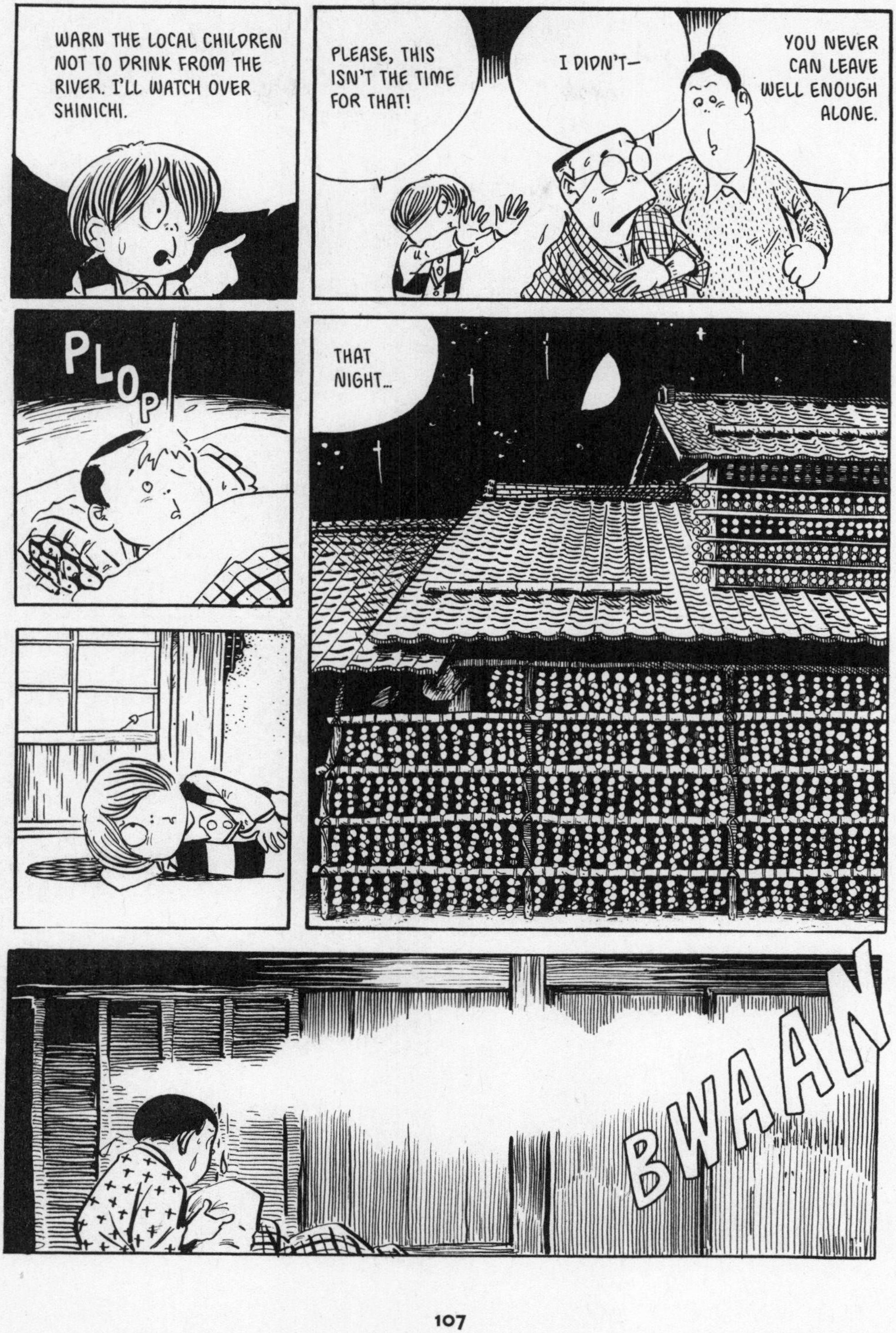
YOU NEVER CAN LEAVE WELL ENOUGH ALONE.
I DIDN'T—
PLEASE, THIS ISN'T THE TIME FOR THAT!
WARN THE LOCAL CHILDREN NOT TO DRINK FROM THE RIVER. I'LL WATCH OVER SHINICHI.
THAT NIGHT...
PLOP
BWAAAN

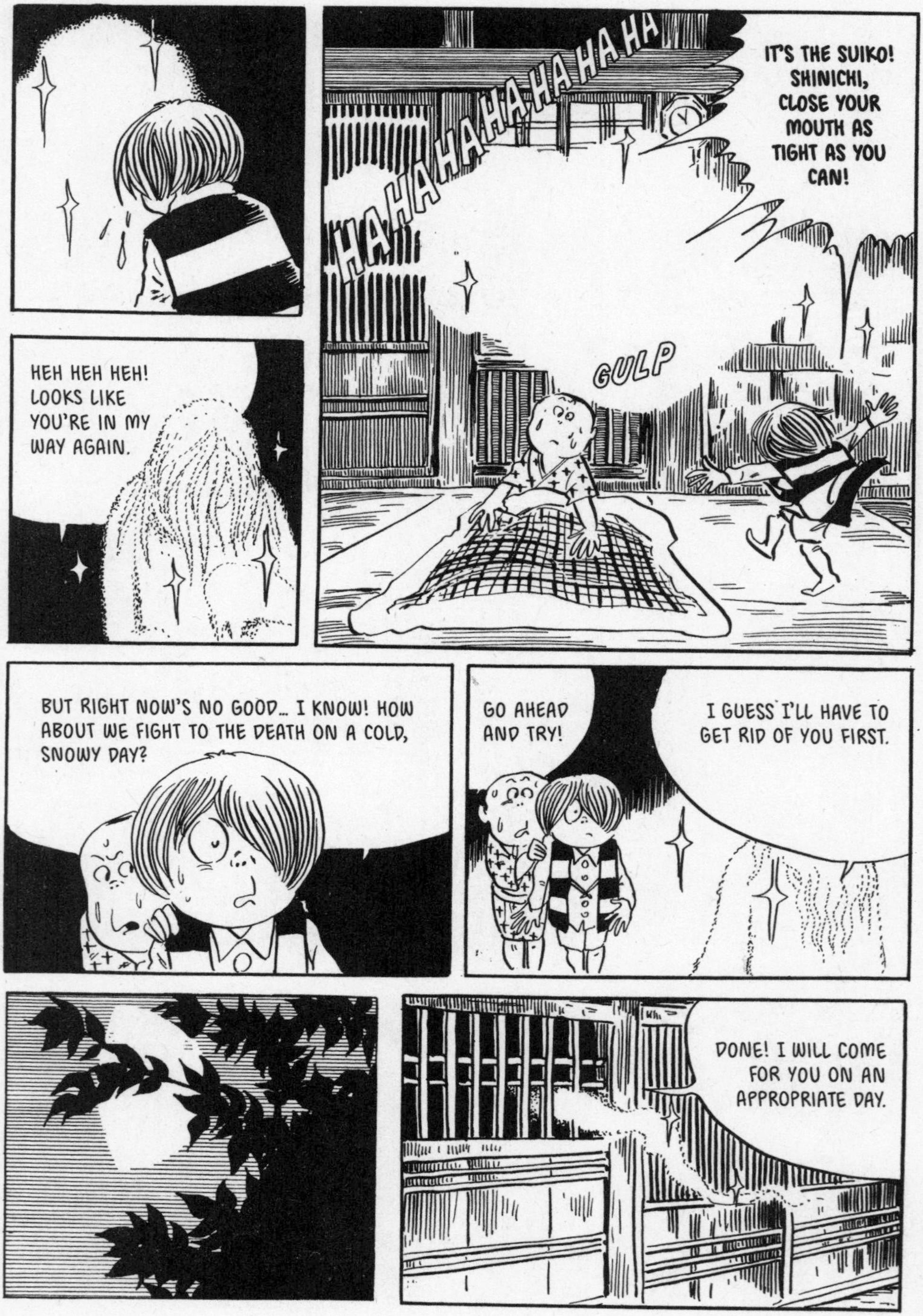
HAHAHAHAHAHAHAHAHA
IT'S THE SUIKO! SHINICHI, CLOSE YOUR MOUTH AS TIGHT AS YOU CAN!
GULP
HEH HEH HEH! LOOKS LIKE YOU'RE IN MY WAY AGAIN.
I GUESS I'LL HAVE TO GET RID OF YOU FIRST.
GO AHEAD AND TRY!
BUT RIGHT NOW'S NO GOOD... I KNOW! HOW ABOUT WE FIGHT TO THE DEATH ON A COLD, SNOWY DAY?
DONE! I WILL COME FOR YOU ON AN APPROPRIATE DAY.

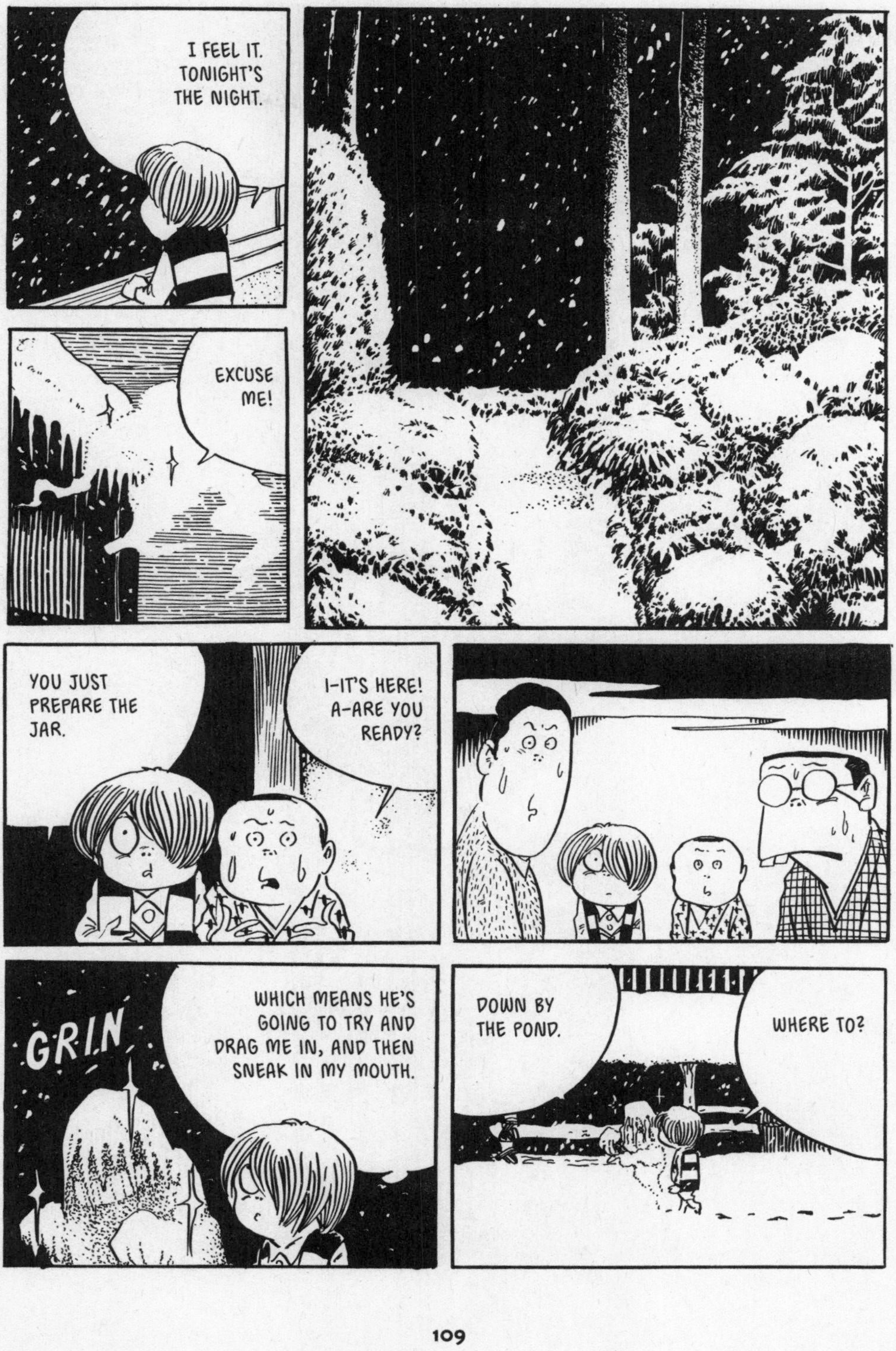
I FEEL IT. TONIGHT'S THE NIGHT.
EXCUSE ME!
I-IT'S HERE! A-ARE YOU READY?
YOU JUST PREPARE THE JAR.
WHERE TO?
DOWN BY THE POND.
WHICH MEANS HE'S GOING TO TRY AND DRAG ME IN, AND THEN SNEAK IN MY MOUTH.
GRIN

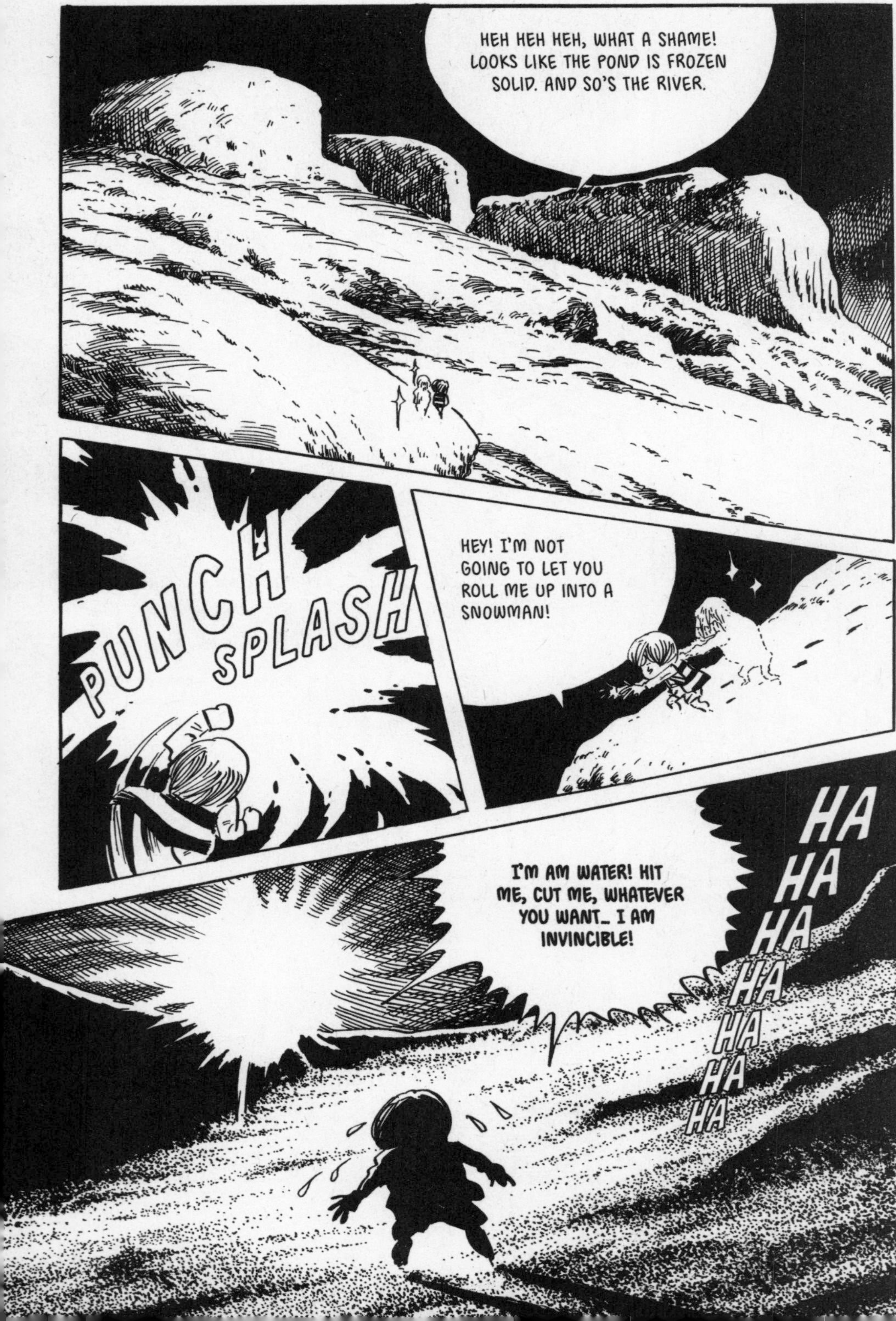
HEH HEH HEH, WHAT A SHAME! LOOKS LIKE THE POND IS FROZEN SOLID. AND SO'S THE RIVER.
HEY! I'M NOT GOING TO LET YOU ROLL ME UP INTO A SNOWMAN!
PUNCH
SPLASH
I'M AM WATER! HIT ME, CUT ME, WHATEVER YOU WANT… I AM INVINCIBLE!
HA HA HA HA HA HA HA HA

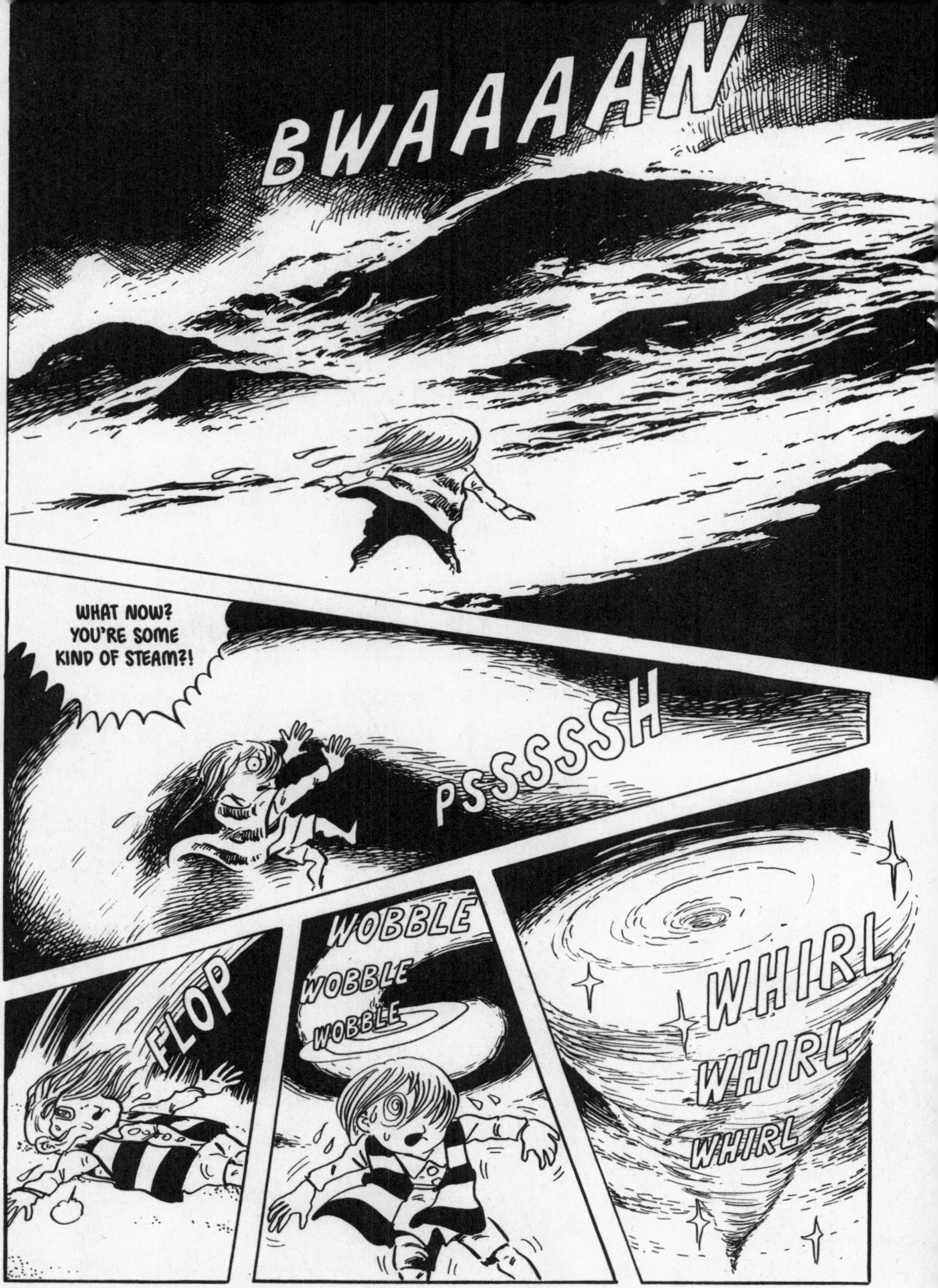
BWAAAAAN
WHAT NOW? YOU'RE SOME KIND OF STEAM?!
PSSSSSH
WHIRL
WHIRL
WHIRL
WOBBLE
WOBBLE
WOBBLE
FLOP

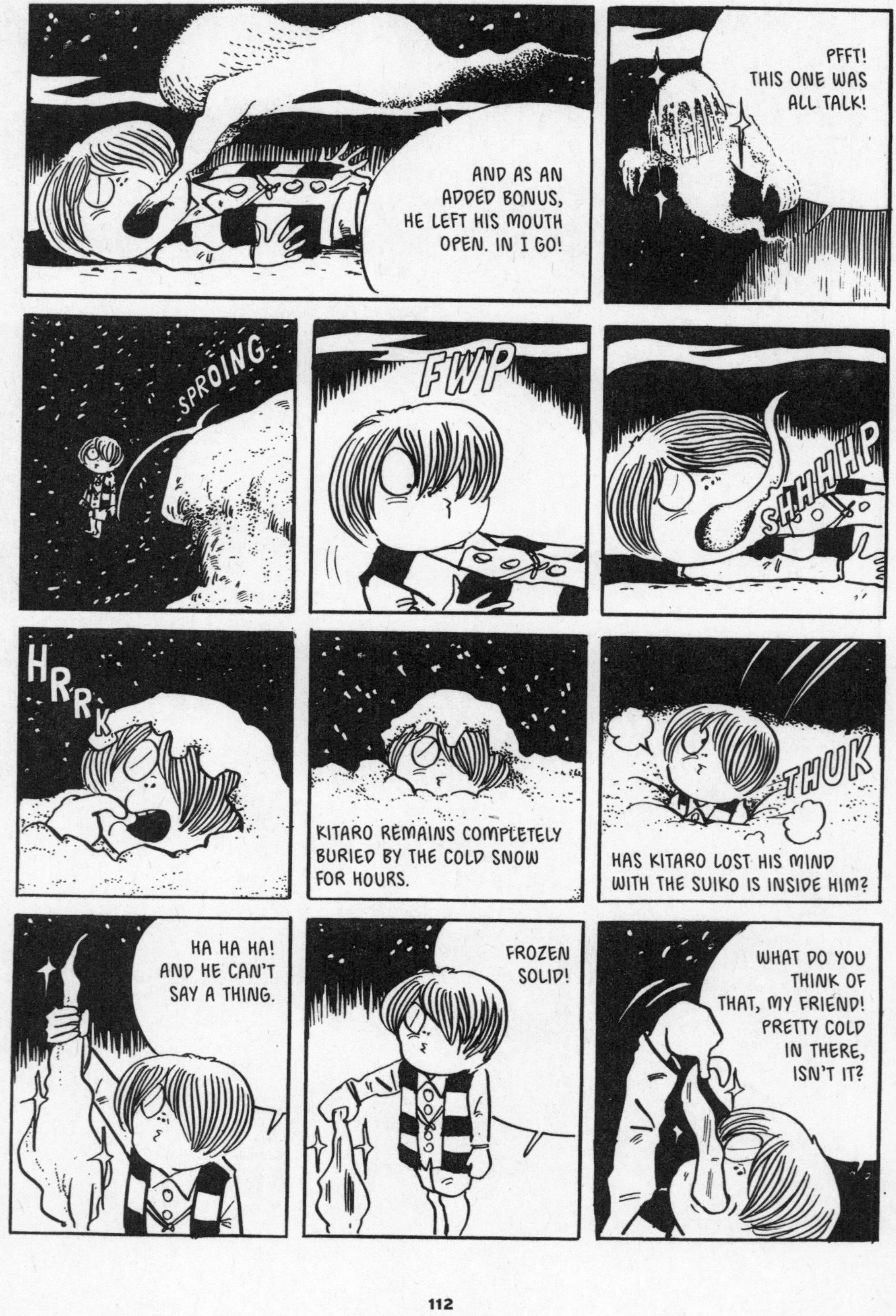
PFFT! THIS ONE WAS ALL TALK!
AND AS AN ADDED BONUS, HE LEFT HIS MOUTH OPEN. IN I GO!
SHHHHP
FWP
SPROING
THUK
HAS KITARO LOST HIS MIND WITH THE SUIKO IS INSIDE HIM?
KITARO REMAINS COMPLETELY BURIED BY THE COLD SNOW FOR HOURS.
HRRK
WHAT DO YOU THINK OF THAT, MY FRIEND! PRETTY COLD IN THERE, ISN'T IT?
FROZEN SOLID!
HA HA HA! AND HE CAN'T SAY A THING.

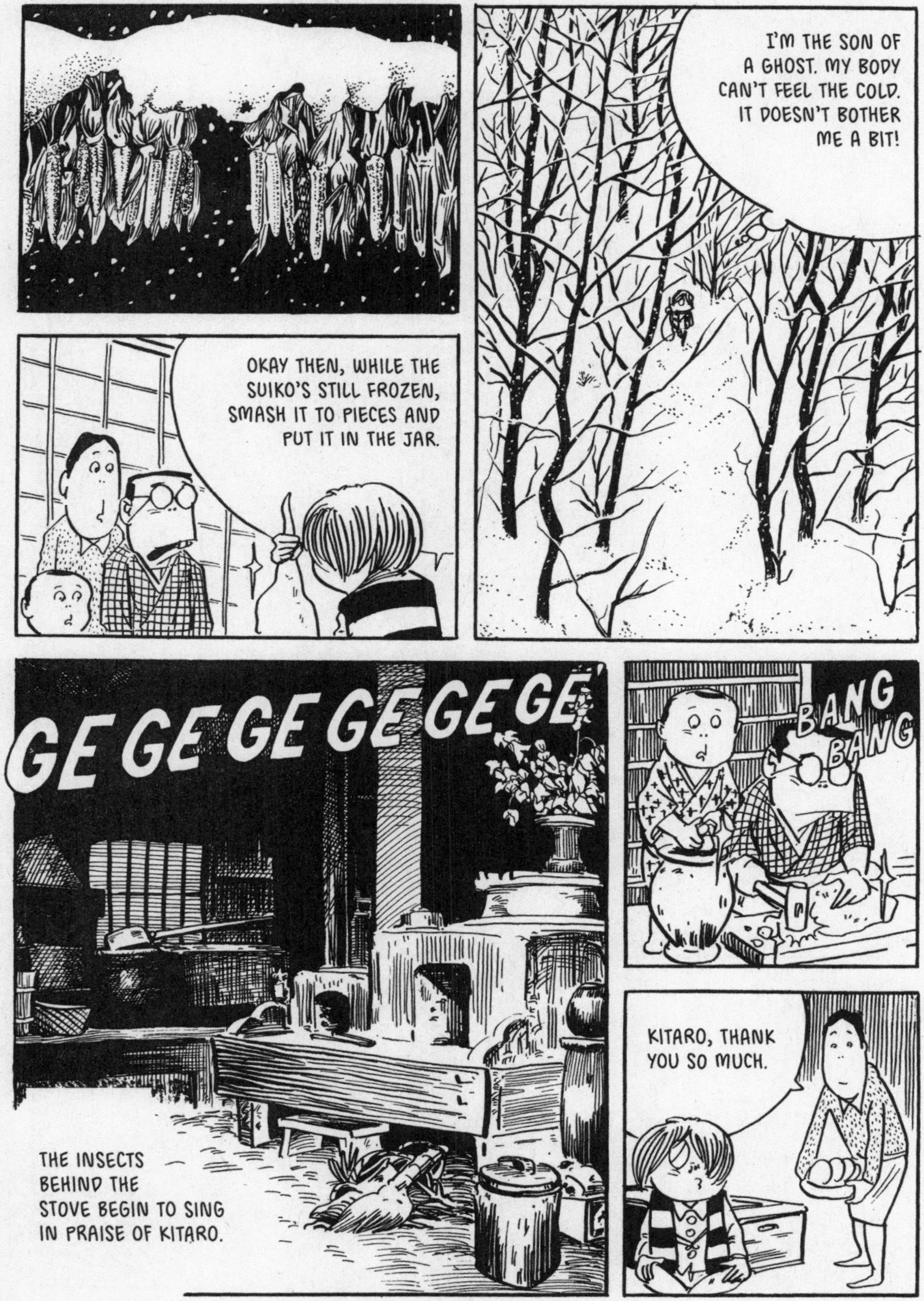
I'M THE SON OF A GHOST. MY BODY CAN'T FEEL THE COLD. IT DOESN'T BOTHER ME A BIT!
OKAY THEN, WHILE THE SUIKO'S STILL FROZEN, SMASH IT TO PIECES AND PUT IT IN THE JAR.
BANG BANG
KITARO, THANK YOU SO MUCH.
GE GE GE GE GE GE
THE INSECTS BEHIND THE STOVE BEGIN TO SING IN PRAISE OF KITARO.

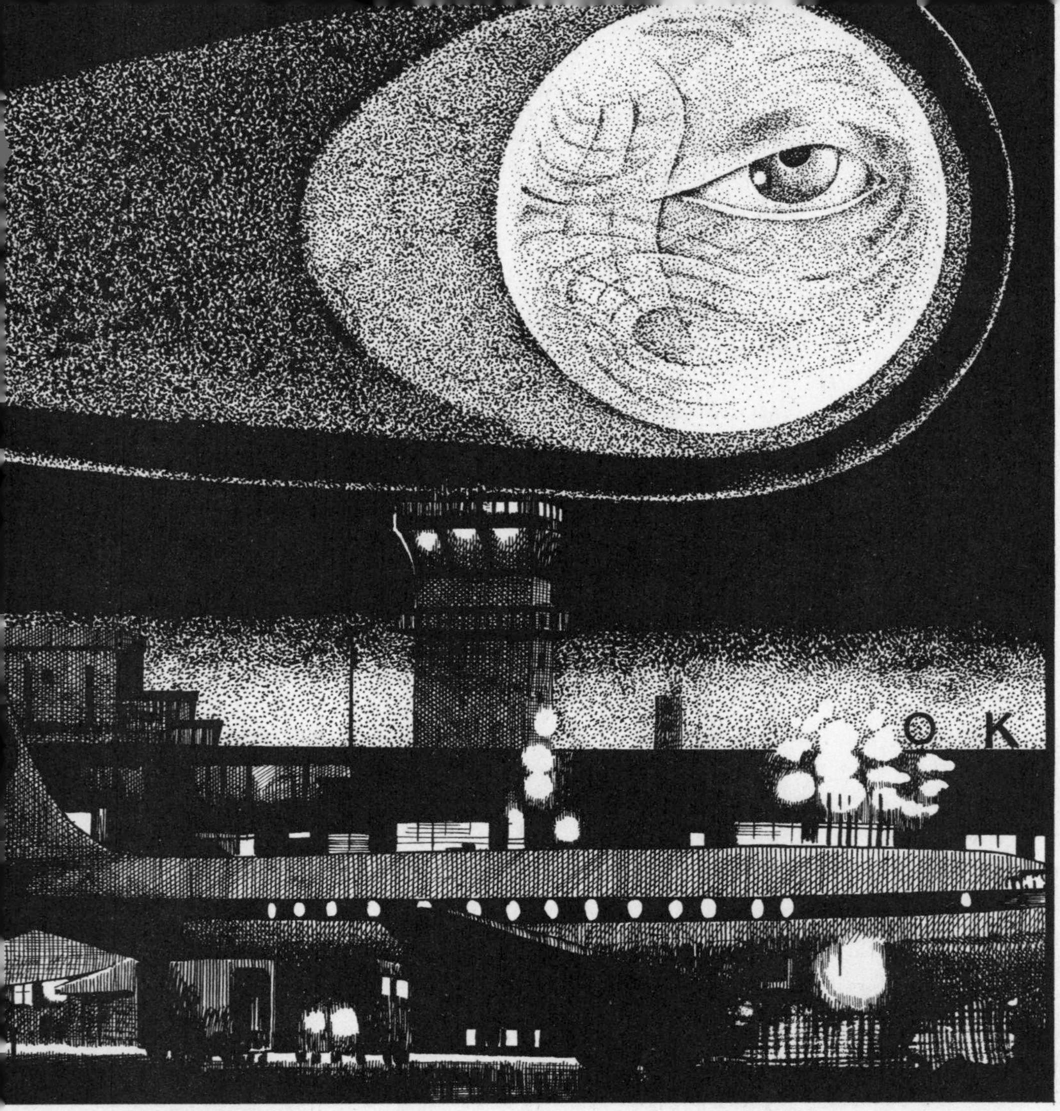
O K

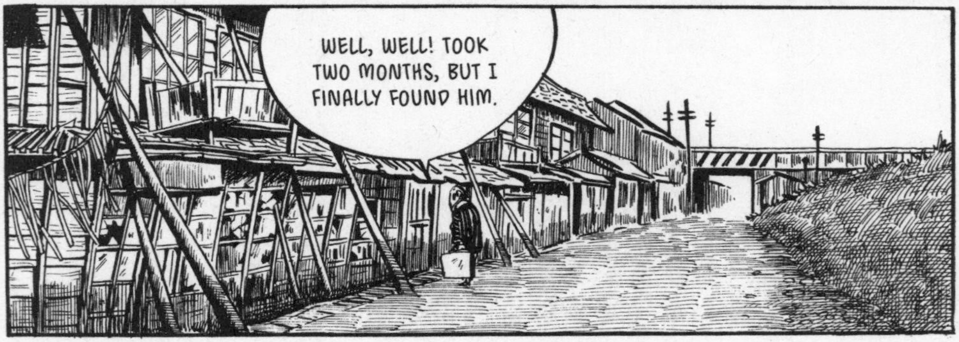
WELL, WELL! TOOK TWO MONTHS, BUT I FINALLY FOUND HIM.

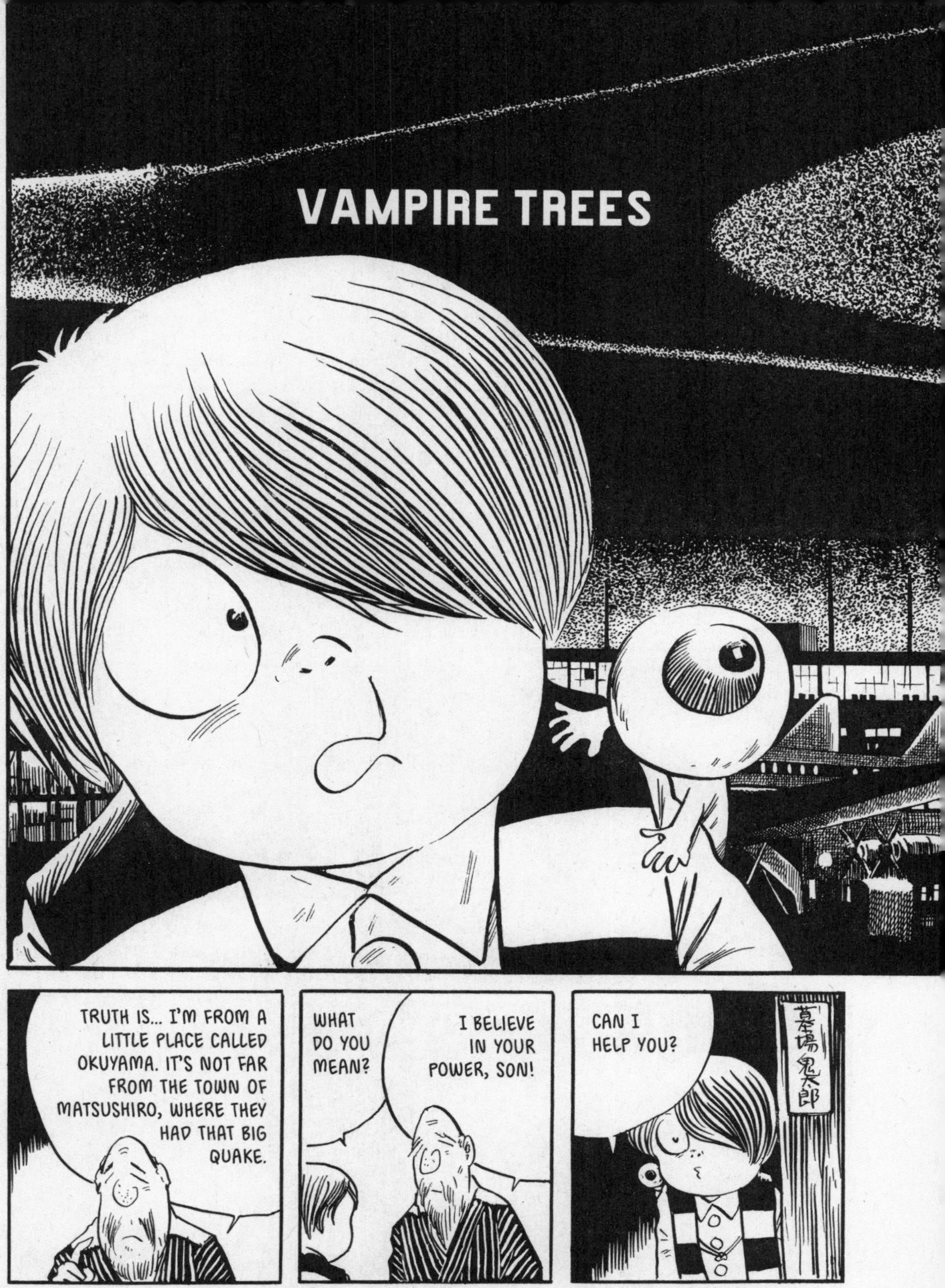
VAMPIRE TREES
墓場鬼太郎
CAN I HELP YOU?
I BELIEVE IN YOUR POWER, SON!
WHAT DO YOU MEAN?
TRUTH IS... I'M FROM A LITTLE PLACE CALLED OKUYAMA. IT'S NOT FAR FROM THE TOWN OF MATSUSHIRO, WHERE THEY HAD THAT BIG QUAKE.

SIGN: KITARO GRAVEYARD.

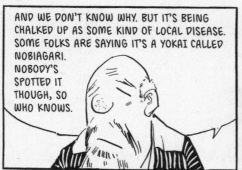

OUR PEOPLE, ONE AFTER ANOTHER, ARE TURNING INTO RED TREES. IT'S PURE CHAOS IN THE VILLAGE NOW.
TURNING INTO TREES?
AND WE DON'T KNOW WHY. BUT IT'S BEING CHALKED UP AS SOME KIND OF LOCAL DISEASE. SOME FOLKS ARE SAYING IT'S A YOKAI CALLED NOBIAGARI. NOBODY'S SPOTTED IT THOUGH, SO WHO KNOWS.
AT THIS RATE, THE VILLAGE IS DOOMED! CAN YOU PLEASE HELP US?
YES, OF COURSE!
THANK GOODNESS! NOW THEN, WE SHOULD GET ON THE BUS RIGHT AWAY. IT'S A THREE-DAY TRIP.
DEEP IN THE COUNTRY, A LAND OVERRUN WITH THICK GRASSES.
TAKKA
TOKKA
OH! WHAT'S THAT?
WHAT'S WHAT?

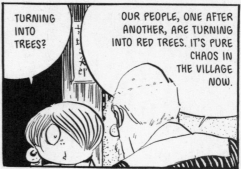

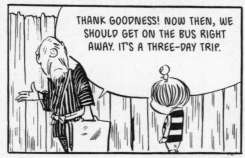

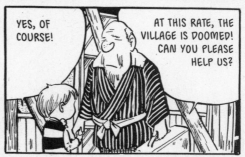

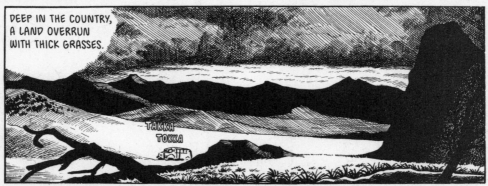

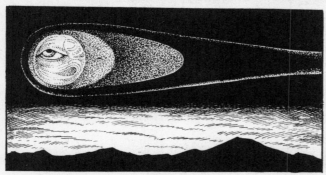

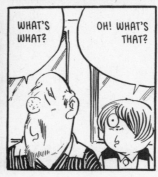

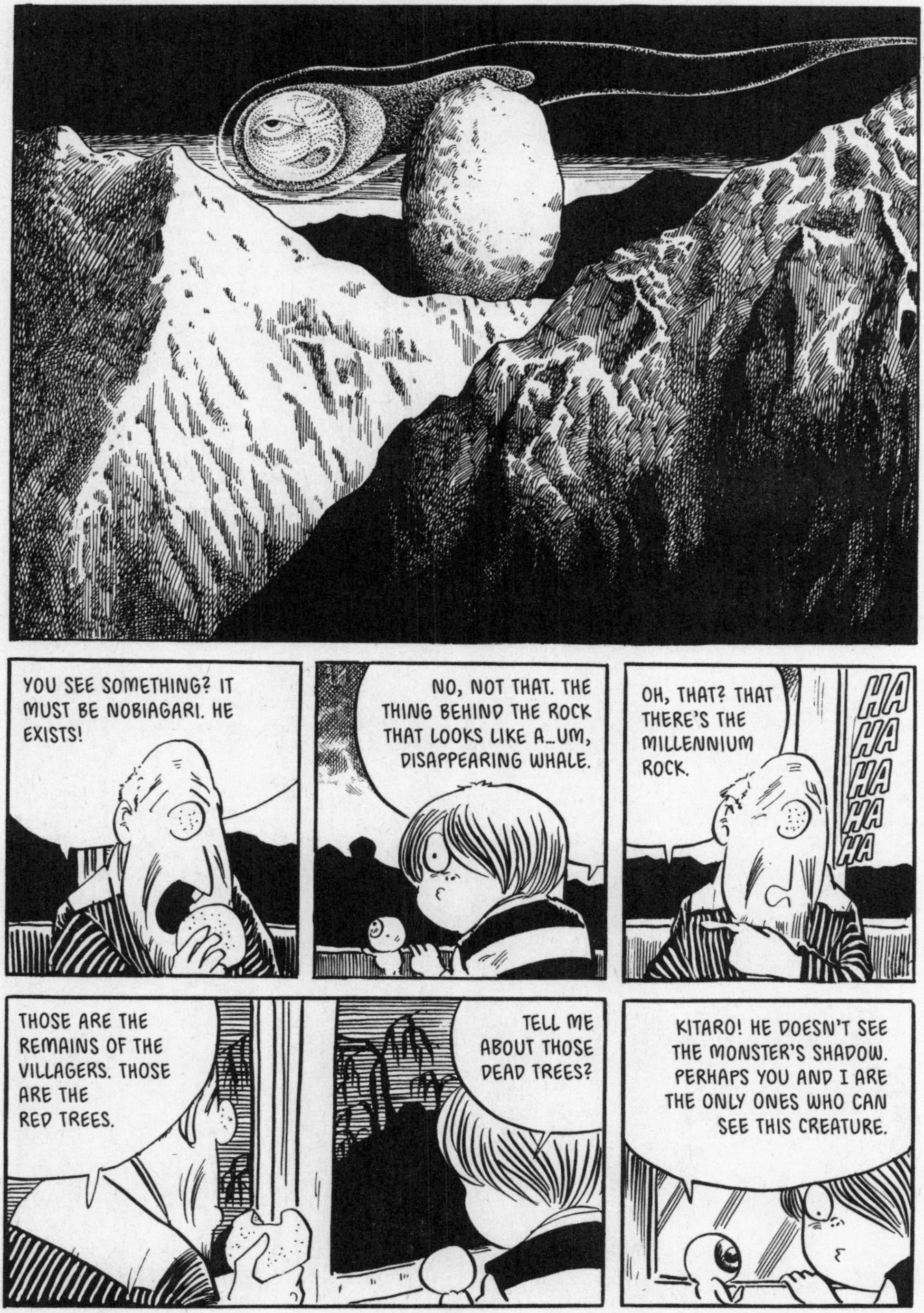
OH, THAT? THAT THERE'S THE MILLENNIUM ROCK.
HA HA HA HA HA HA
NO, NOT THAT. THE THING BEHIND THE ROCK THAT LOOKS LIKE A...UM, DISAPPEARING WHALE.
YOU SEE SOMETHING? IT MUST BE NOBIAGARI. HE EXISTS!
KITARO! HE DOESN'T SEE THE MONSTER'S SHADOW. PERHAPS YOU AND I ARE THE ONLY ONES WHO CAN SEE THIS CREATURE.
TELL ME ABOUT THOSE DEAD TREES?
THOSE ARE THE REMAINS OF THE VILLAGERS. THOSE ARE THE RED TREES.

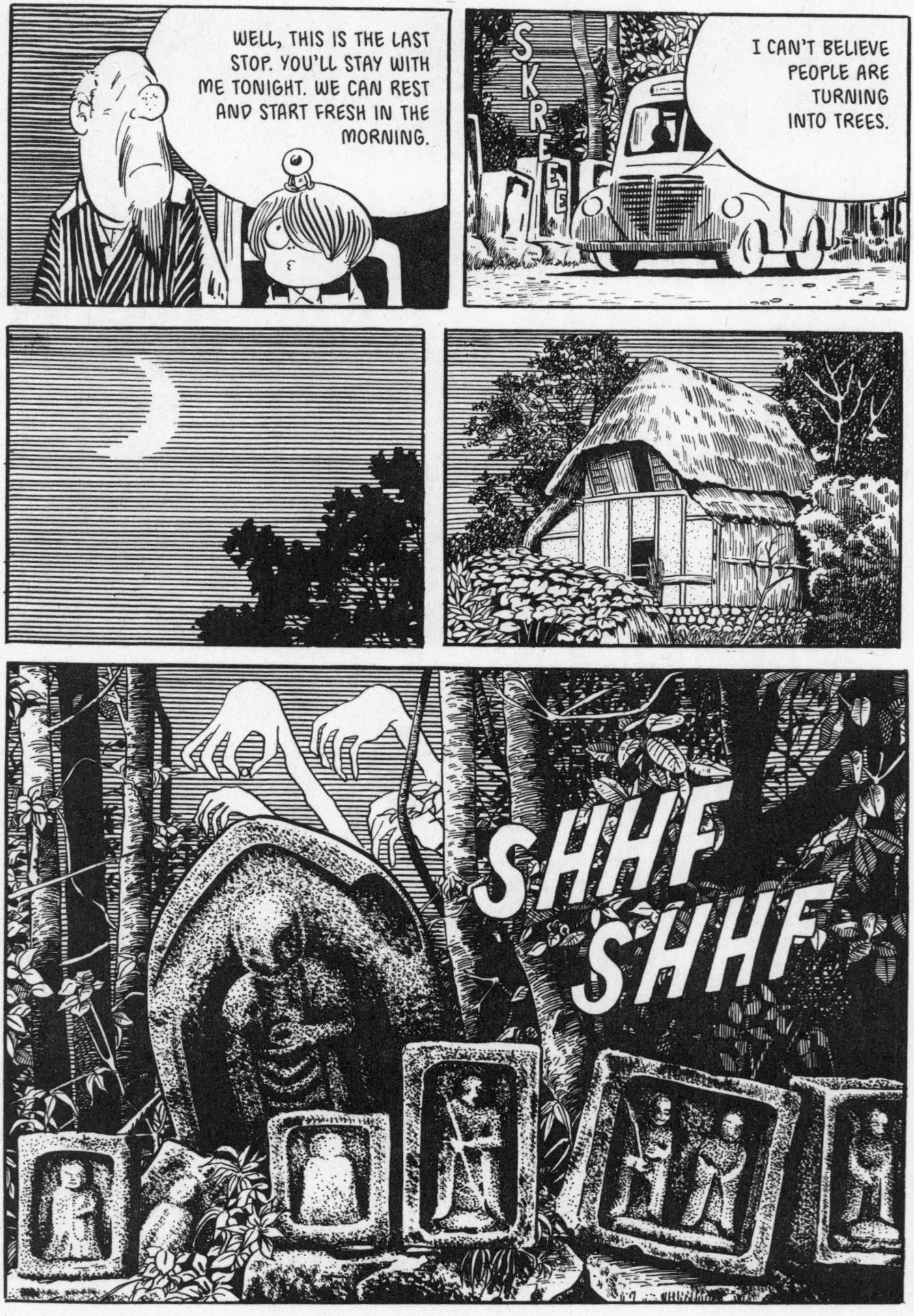
SKREEE
I CAN'T BELIEVE PEOPLE ARE TURNING INTO TREES.
WELL, THIS IS THE LAST STOP. YOU'LL STAY WITH ME TONIGHT. WE CAN REST AND START FRESH IN THE MORNING.
SHHF SHHF

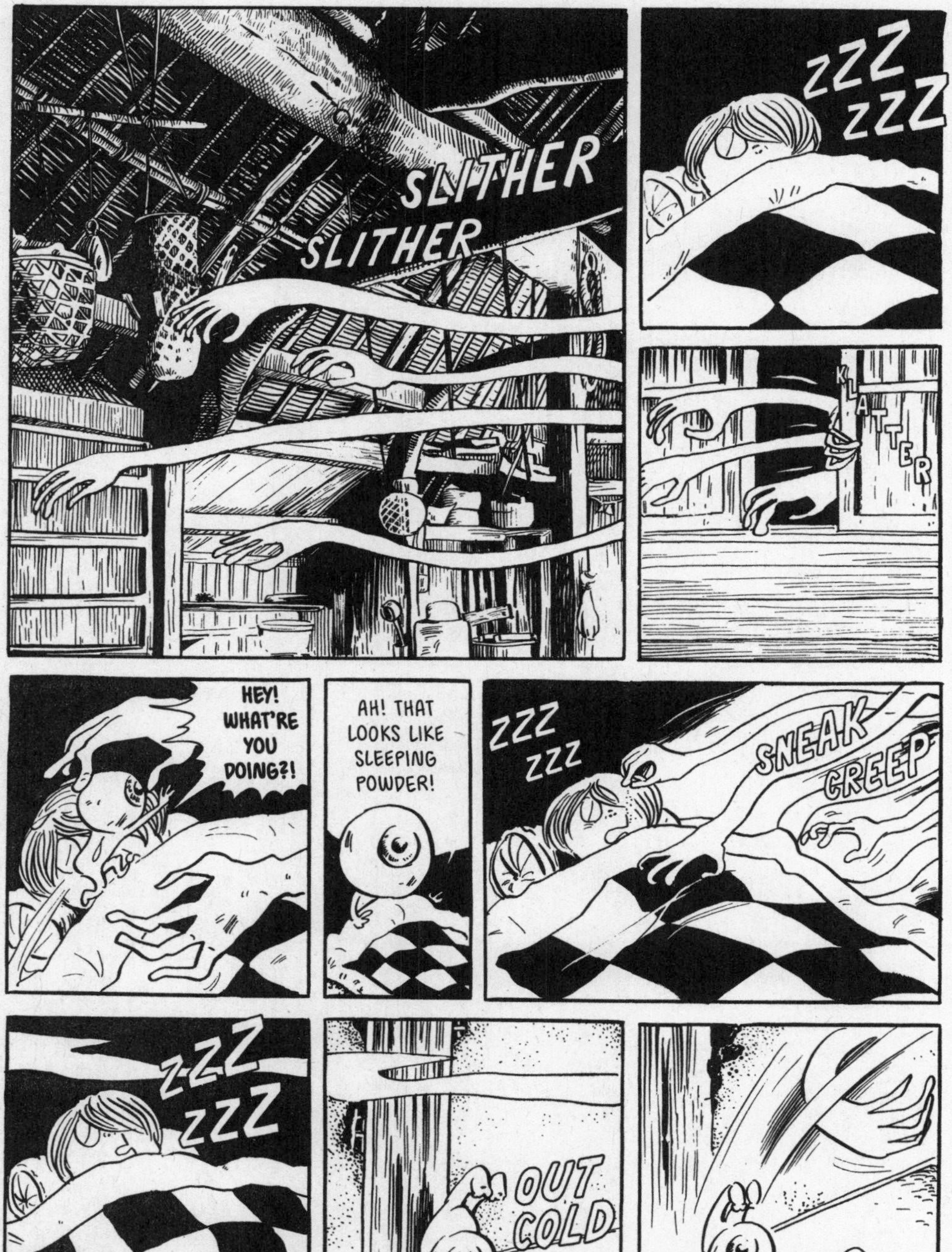
ZZZ
ZZZ
KLATTER
SLITHER
SLITHER
ZZZ
ZZZ
SNEAK
CREEP
AH! THAT LOOKS LIKE SLEEPING POWDER!
HEY! WHAT'RE YOU DOING?!
OUT COLD
Z-ZZ
ZZZ

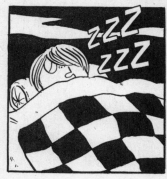

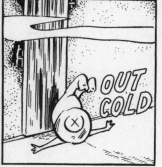

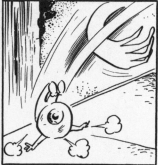

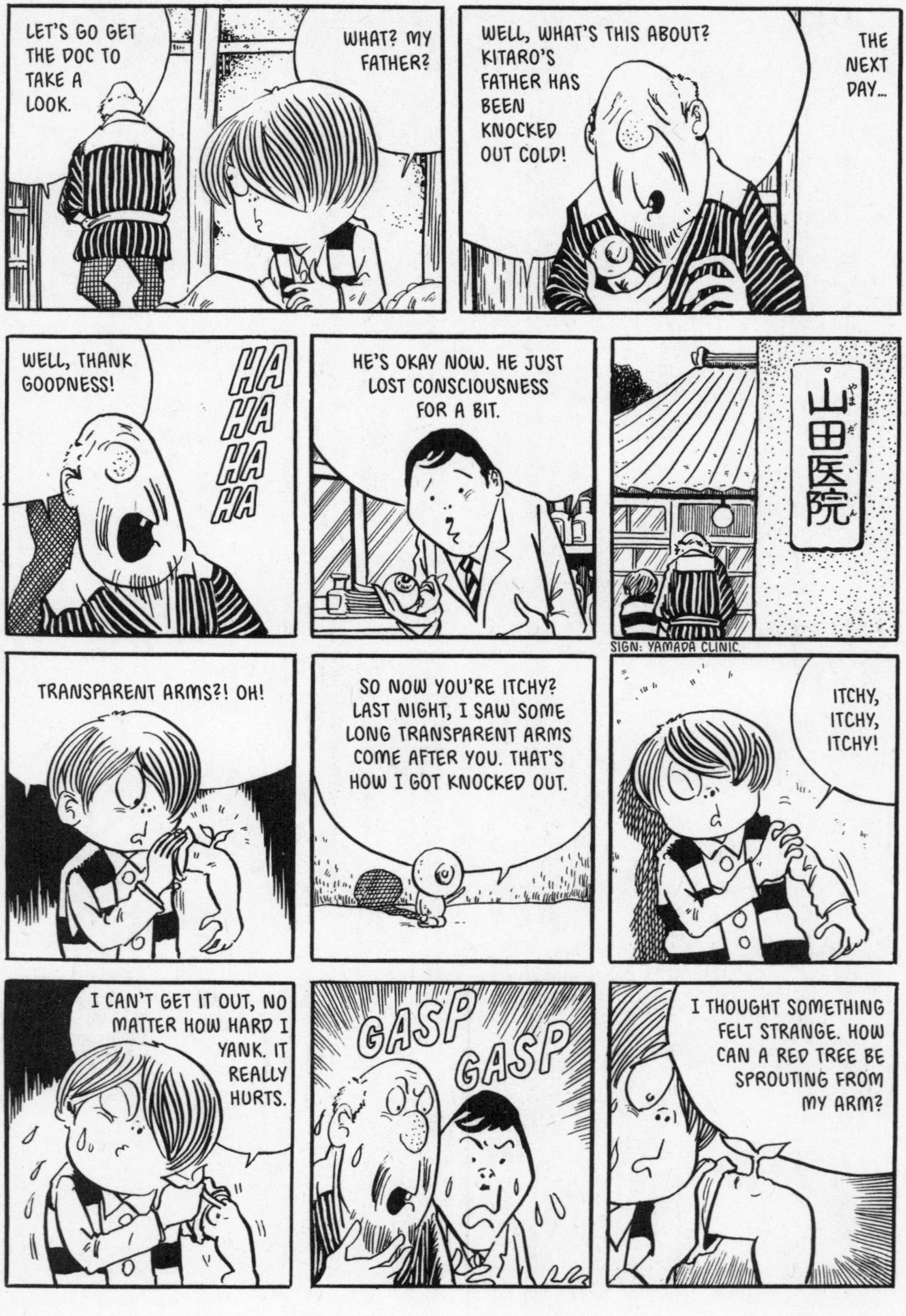
THE NEXT DAY...
WELL, WHAT'S THIS ABOUT? KITARO'S FATHER HAS BEEN KNOCKED OUT COLD!
WHAT? MY FATHER?
LET'S GO GET THE DOC TO TAKE A LOOK.
山田医院
SIGN: YAMADA CLINIC.
HE'S OKAY NOW. HE JUST LOST CONSCIOUSNESS FOR A BIT.
HA HA HA HA HA
WELL, THANK GOODNESS!
ITCHY, ITCHY, ITCHY!
SO NOW YOU'RE ITCHY? LAST NIGHT, I SAW SOME LONG TRANSPARENT ARMS COME AFTER YOU. THAT'S HOW I GOT KNOCKED OUT.
TRANSPARENT ARMS?! OH!
I THOUGHT SOMETHING FELT STRANGE. HOW CAN A RED TREE BE SPROUTING FROM MY ARM?
GASP GASP
I CAN'T GET IT OUT, NO MATTER HOW HARD I YANK. IT REALLY HURTS.

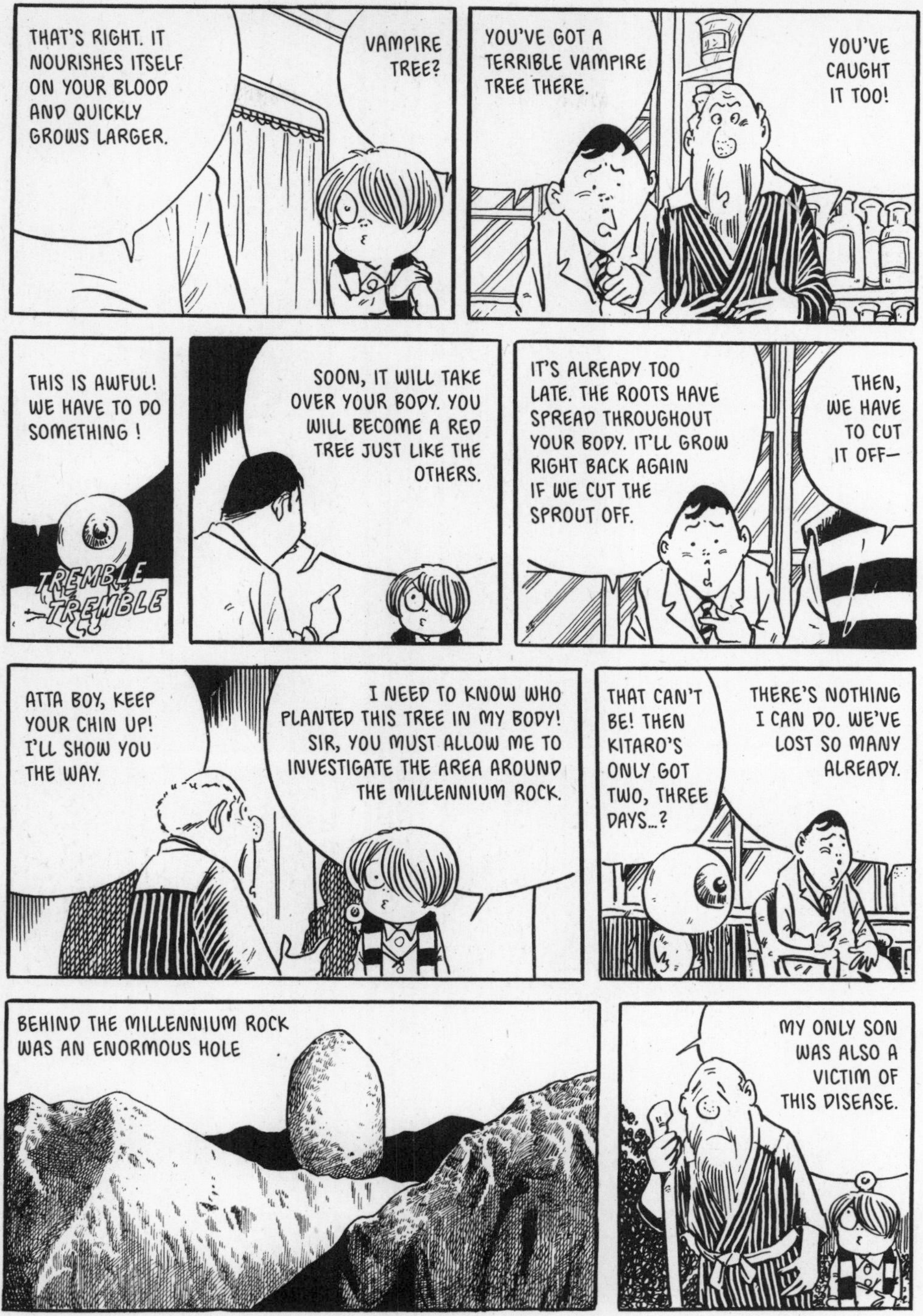
YOU'VE CAUGHT IT TOO!
YOU'VE GOT A TERRIBLE VAMPIRE TREE THERE.
VAMPIRE TREE?
THAT'S RIGHT. IT NOURISHES ITSELF ON YOUR BLOOD AND QUICKLY GROWS LARGER.
THEN, WE HAVE TO CUT IT OFF—
IT'S ALREADY TOO LATE. THE ROOTS HAVE SPREAD THROUGHOUT YOUR BODY. IT'LL GROW RIGHT BACK AGAIN IF WE CUT THE SPROUT OFF.
SOON, IT WILL TAKE OVER YOUR BODY. YOU WILL BECOME A RED TREE JUST LIKE THE OTHERS.
THIS IS AWFUL! WE HAVE TO DO SOMETHING !
TREMBLE TREMBLE
THERE'S NOTHING I CAN DO. WE'VE LOST SO MANY ALREADY.
THAT CAN'T BE! THEN KITARO'S ONLY GOT TWO, THREE DAYS...?
I NEED TO KNOW WHO PLANTED THIS TREE IN MY BODY! SIR, YOU MUST ALLOW ME TO INVESTIGATE THE AREA AROUND THE MILLENNIUM ROCK.
ATTA BOY, KEEP YOUR CHIN UP! I'LL SHOW YOU THE WAY.
MY ONLY SON WAS ALSO A VICTIM OF THIS DISEASE.
BEHIND THE MILLENNIUM ROCK WAS AN ENORMOUS HOLE

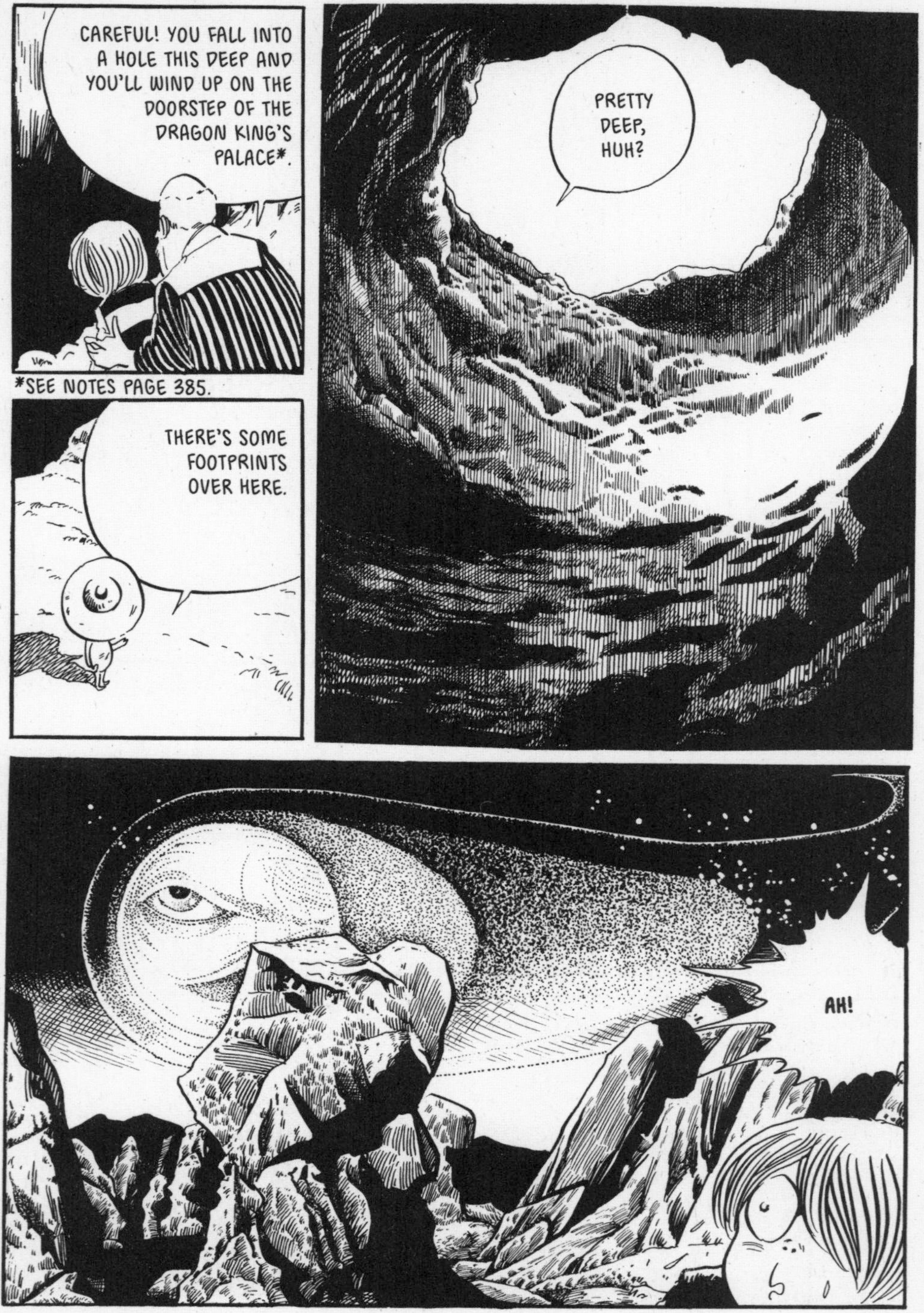
PRETTY DEEP, HUH?
CAREFUL! YOU FALL INTO A HOLE THIS DEEP AND YOU'LL WIND UP ON THE DOORSTEP OF THE DRAGON KING'S PALACE*.
THERE'S SOME FOOTPRINTS OVER HERE.
AH!

*SEE NOTES PAGE 385.

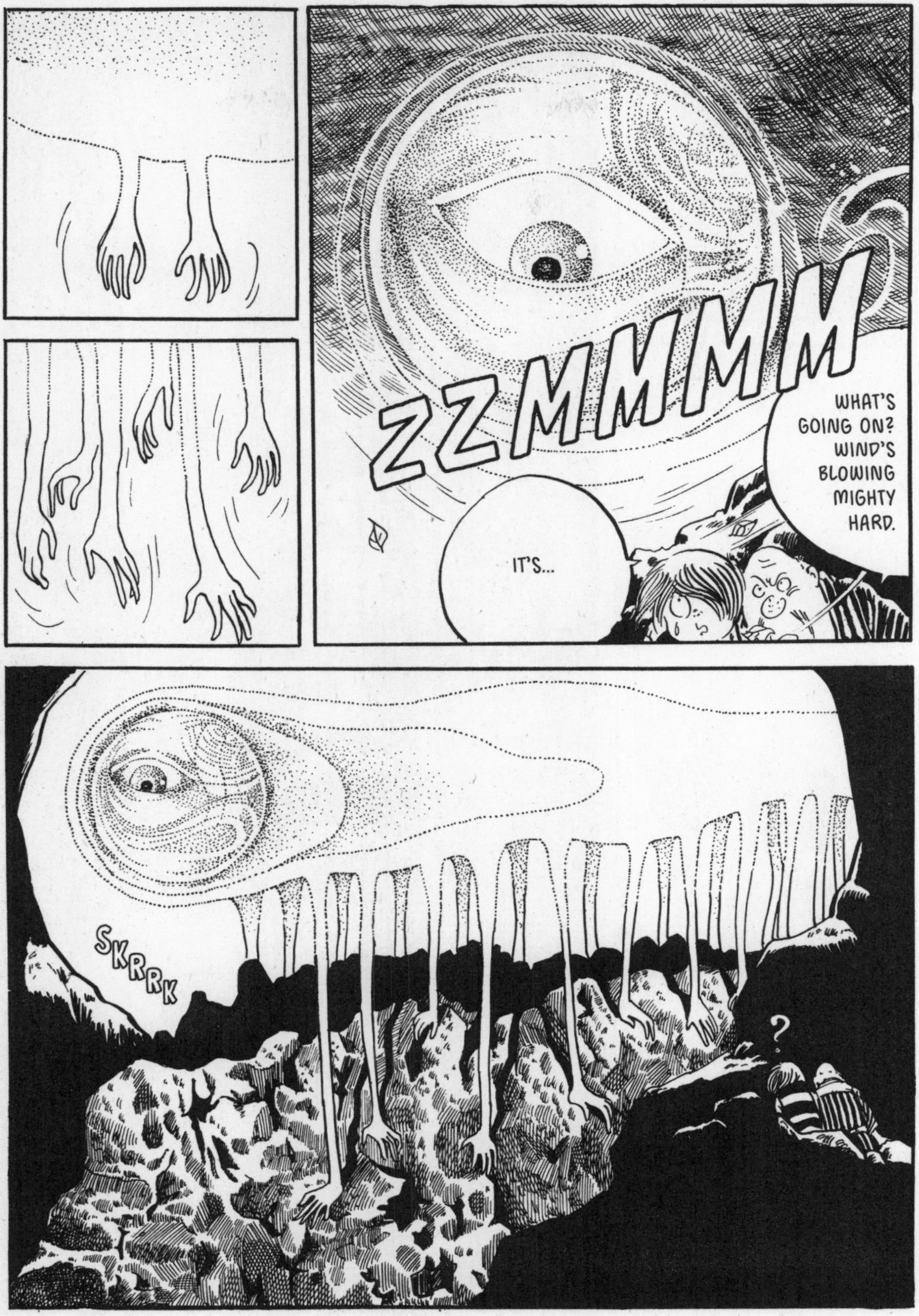
ZZMMMMM
WHAT'S GOING ON? WIND'S BLOWING MIGHTY HARD.
IT'S...
SKRRK
?

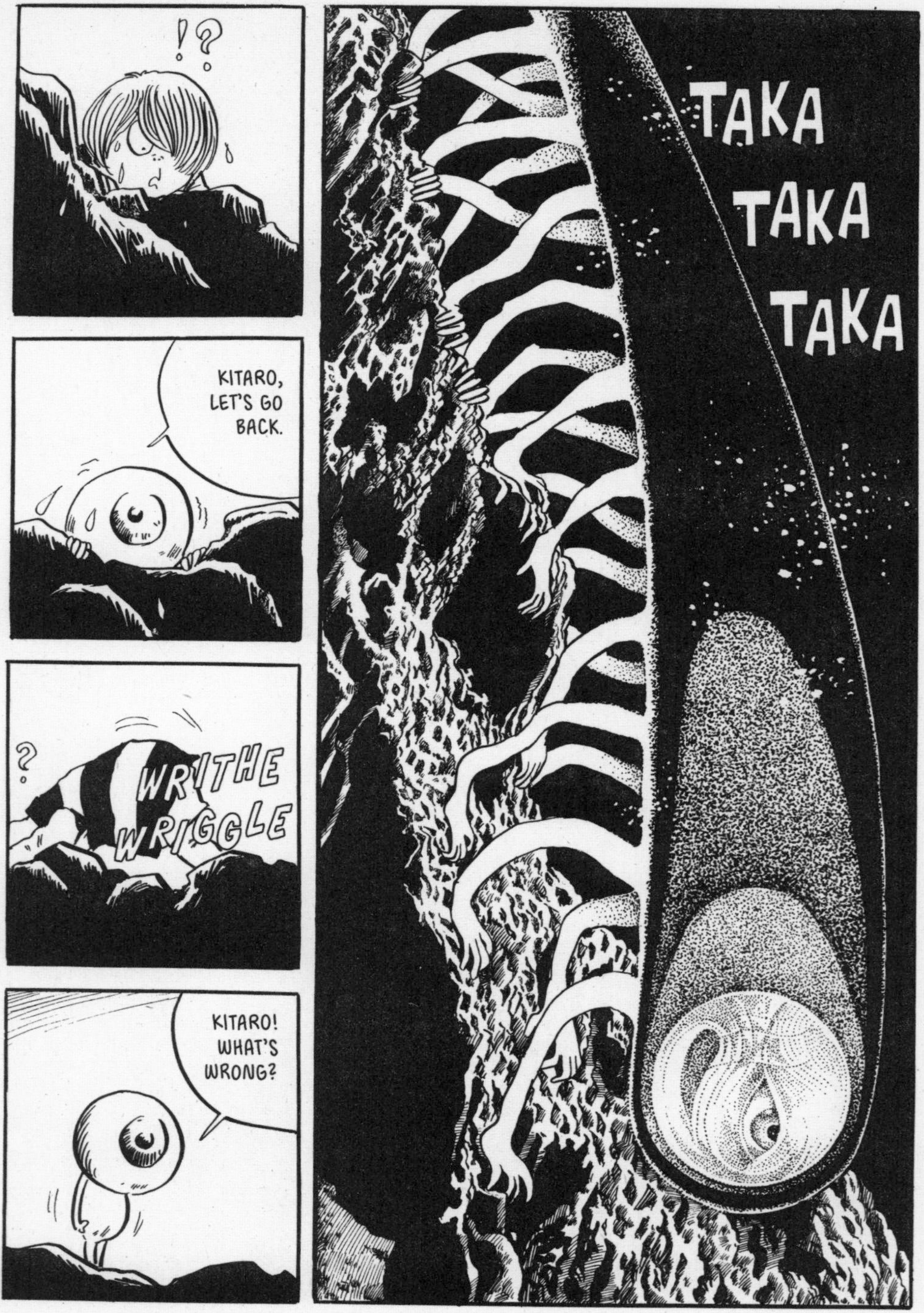
TAKA TAKA TAKA
!?
KITARO, LET'S GO BACK.
?
WRITHE WRIGGLE
KITARO! WHAT'S WRONG?

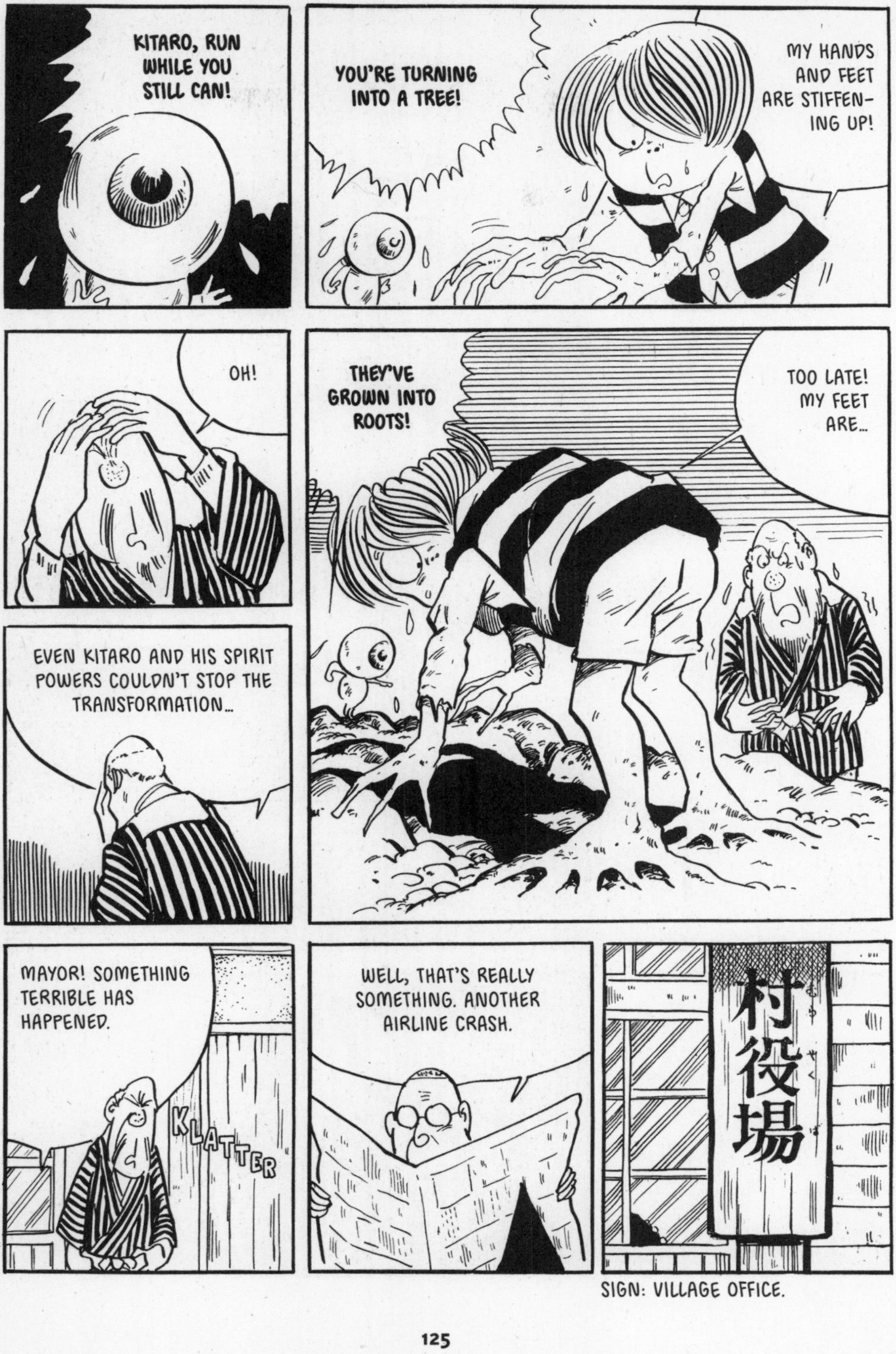
MY HANDS AND FEET ARE STIFFEN-ING UP!
YOU'RE TURNING INTO A TREE!
KITARO, RUN WHILE YOU STILL CAN!
TOO LATE! MY FEET ARE...
THEY'VE GROWN INTO ROOTS!
OH!
EVEN KITARO AND HIS SPIRIT POWERS COULDN'T STOP THE TRANSFORMATION...
村役場
WELL, THAT'S REALLY SOMETHING. ANOTHER AIRLINE CRASH.
MAYOR! SOMETHING TERRIBLE HAS HAPPENED.
KLATTER

SIGN: VILLAGE OFFICE.

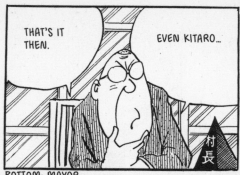

IT REALLY IS TERRIBLE, ISN'T IT?
EVEN KITARO WAS UNABLE TO KEEP FROM TURNING INTO A TREE.
EVEN KITARO...
THAT'S IT THEN.
村長

BOTTOM: MAYOR.

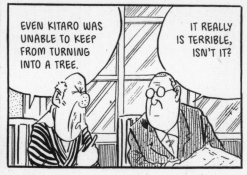

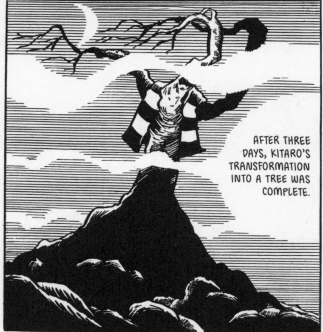

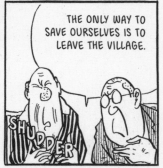

THE ONLY WAY TO SAVE OURSELVES IS TO LEAVE THE VILLAGE.
SHUDDER
AFTER THREE DAYS, KITARO'S TRANSFORMATION INTO A TREE WAS COMPLETE.
KITARO!
BUT NO MATTER HOW MANY TIMES HE CALLED OUT, NO REPLY CAME.
OH, MY SON. THIS REALLY IS A NIGHT-MARE.

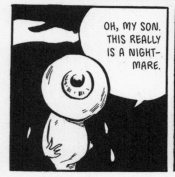

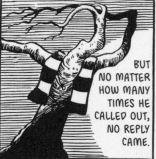

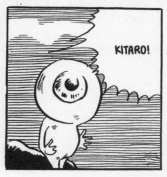

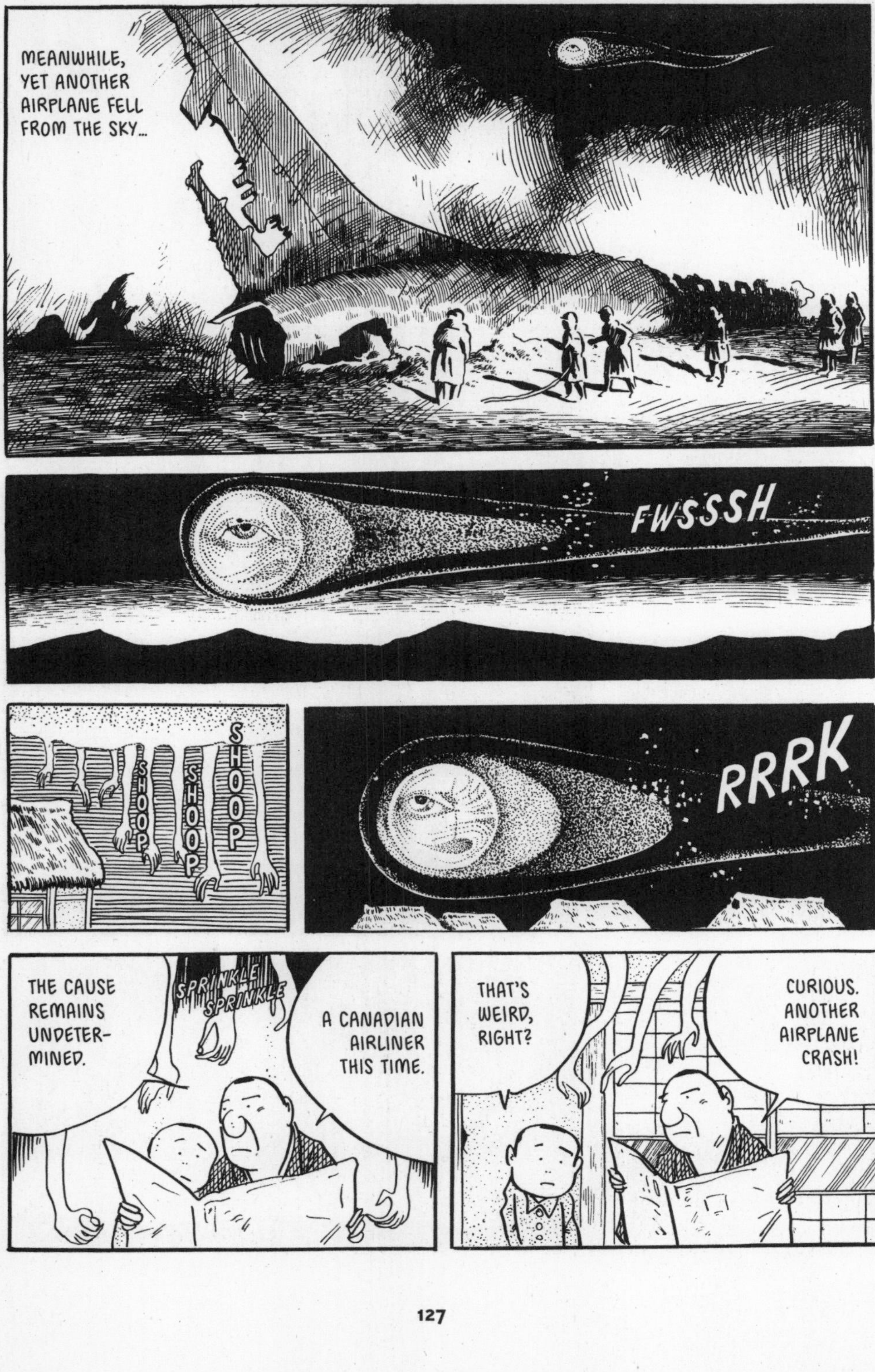
MEANWHILE, YET ANOTHER AIRPLANE FELL FROM THE SKY...
FWSSSH
RRRK
SHOOP
SHOOP
SHOOP
CURIOUS. ANOTHER AIRPLANE CRASH!
THAT'S WEIRD, RIGHT?
A CANADIAN AIRLINER THIS TIME.
SPRINKLE SPRINKLE
THE CAUSE REMAINS UNDETER-MINED.

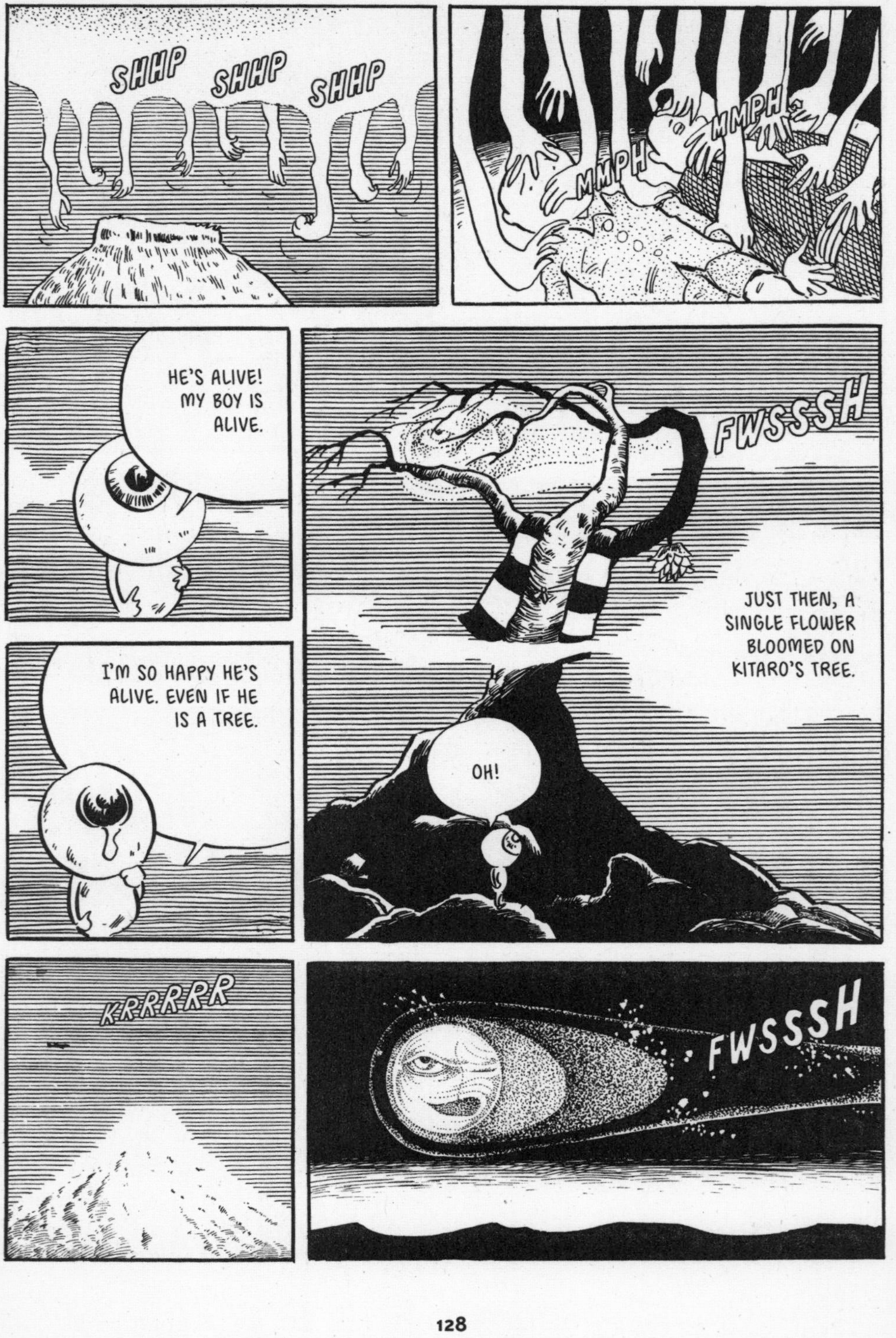
MMPH
MMPH
SHHP
SHHP
SHHP
FWSSSH
JUST THEN, A SINGLE FLOWER BLOOMED ON KITARO'S TREE.
OH!
HE'S ALIVE! MY BOY IS ALIVE.
I'M SO HAPPY HE'S ALIVE. EVEN IF HE IS A TREE.
FWSSSH
KRRRRR

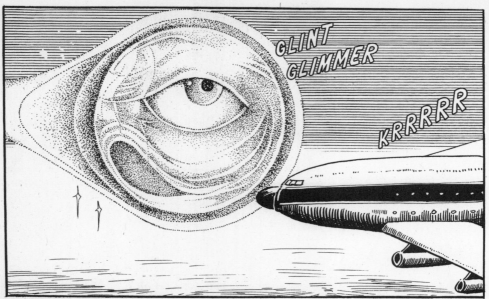

GLINT
GLIMMER
KRRRRR
POP
FWSSSH
ZMMM
村役場
AND YET ANOTHER PLANE CRASH.
A EUROPEAN AIR-LINER HAS CRASHED INTO THE SECOND STATION ON MOUNT FUJI.
THAT'S REALLY STRANGE.

SIGN: VILLAGE OFFICE.

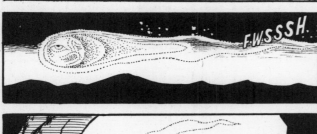

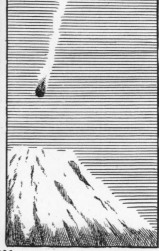

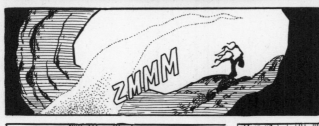

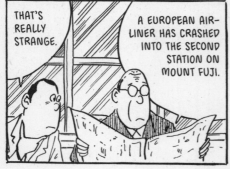

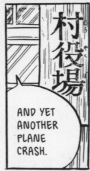

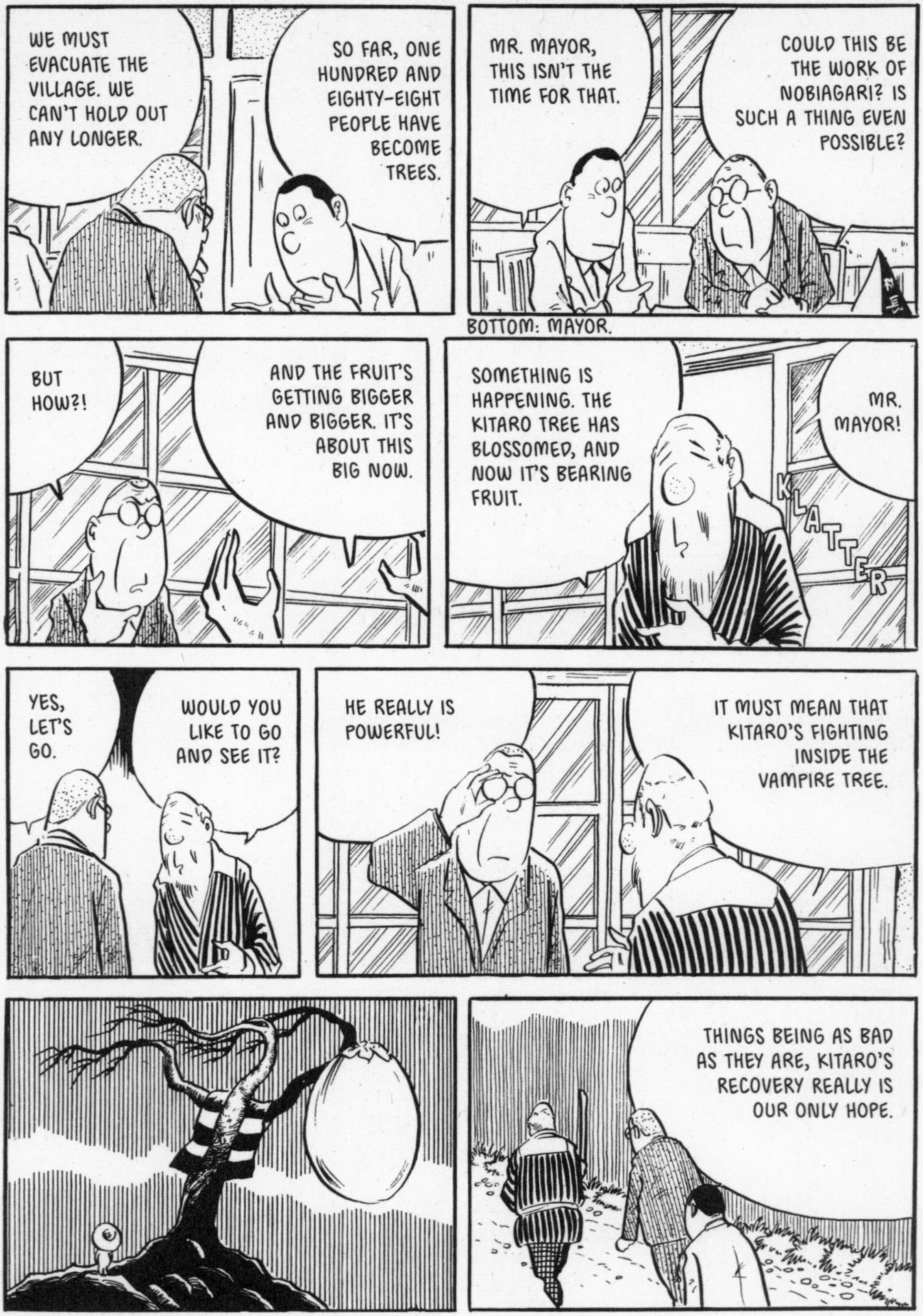
COULD THIS BE THE WORK OF NOBIAGARI? IS SUCH A THING EVEN POSSIBLE?
MR. MAYOR, THIS ISN'T THE TIME FOR THAT.
BOTTOM: MAYOR.
SO FAR, ONE HUNDRED AND EIGHTY-EIGHT PEOPLE HAVE BECOME TREES.
WE MUST EVACUATE THE VILLAGE. WE CAN'T HOLD OUT ANY LONGER.
MR. MAYOR!
KLATTER
SOMETHING IS HAPPENING. THE KITARO TREE HAS BLOSSOMED, AND NOW IT'S BEARING FRUIT.
AND THE FRUIT'S GETTING BIGGER AND BIGGER. IT'S ABOUT THIS BIG NOW.
BUT HOW?!
IT MUST MEAN THAT KITARO'S FIGHTING INSIDE THE VAMPIRE TREE.
HE REALLY IS POWERFUL!
WOULD YOU LIKE TO GO AND SEE IT?
YES, LET'S GO.
THINGS BEING AS BAD AS THEY ARE, KITARO'S RECOVERY REALLY IS OUR ONLY HOPE.

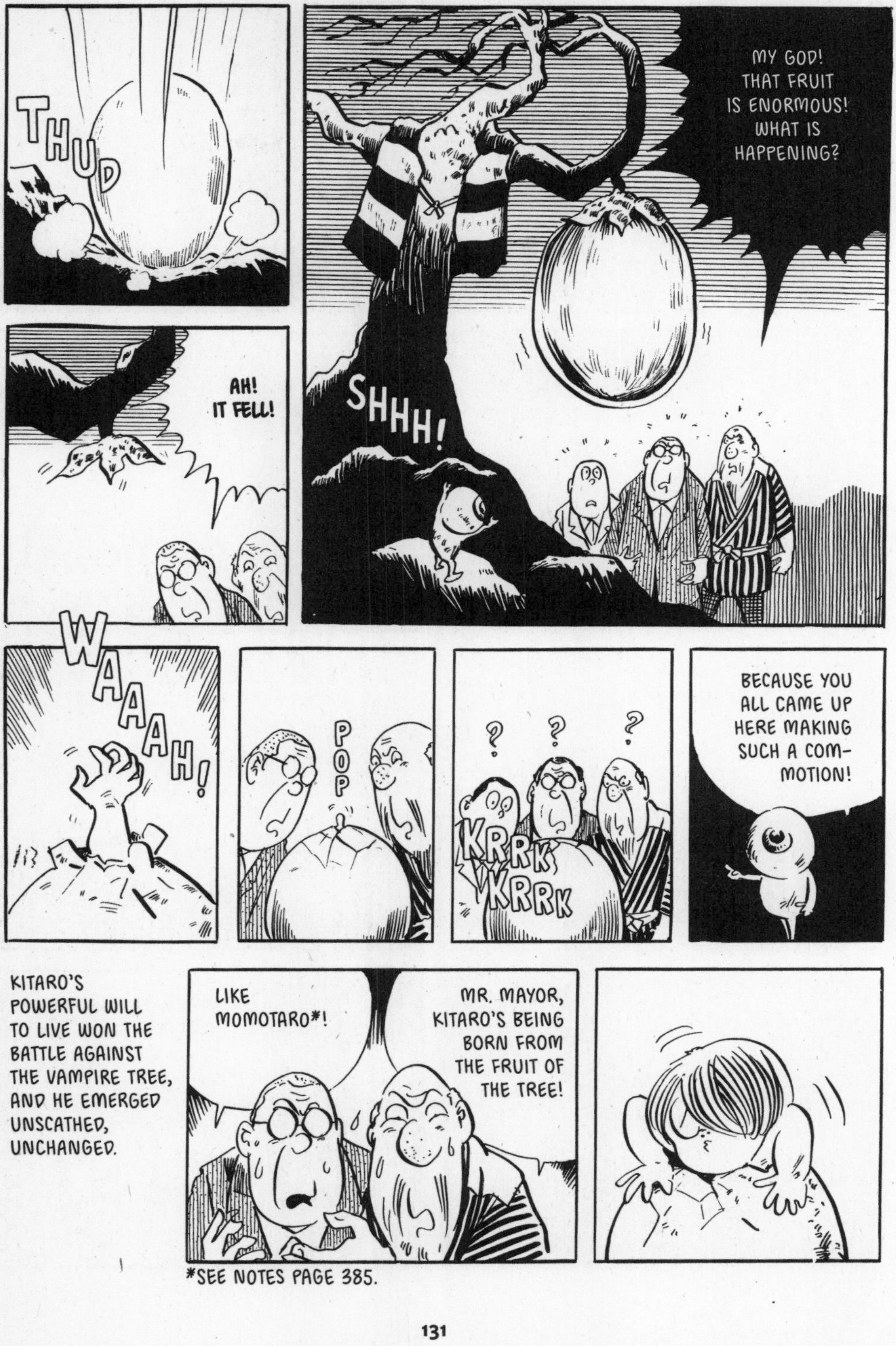
MY GOD! THAT FRUIT IS ENORMOUS! WHAT IS HAPPENING?
SHHHH!
THUD
AH! IT FELL!
BECAUSE YOU ALL CAME UP HERE MAKING SUCH A COM-MOTION!
? ? ?
KRRK KRRK
POP
WAAAAH!
MR. MAYOR, KITARO'S BEING BORN FROM THE FRUIT OF THE TREE!
LIKE MOMOTARO*!
KITARO'S POWERFUL WILL TO LIVE WON THE BATTLE AGAINST THE VAMPIRE TREE, AND HE EMERGED UNSCATHED, UNCHANGED.

*SEE NOTES PAGE 385.

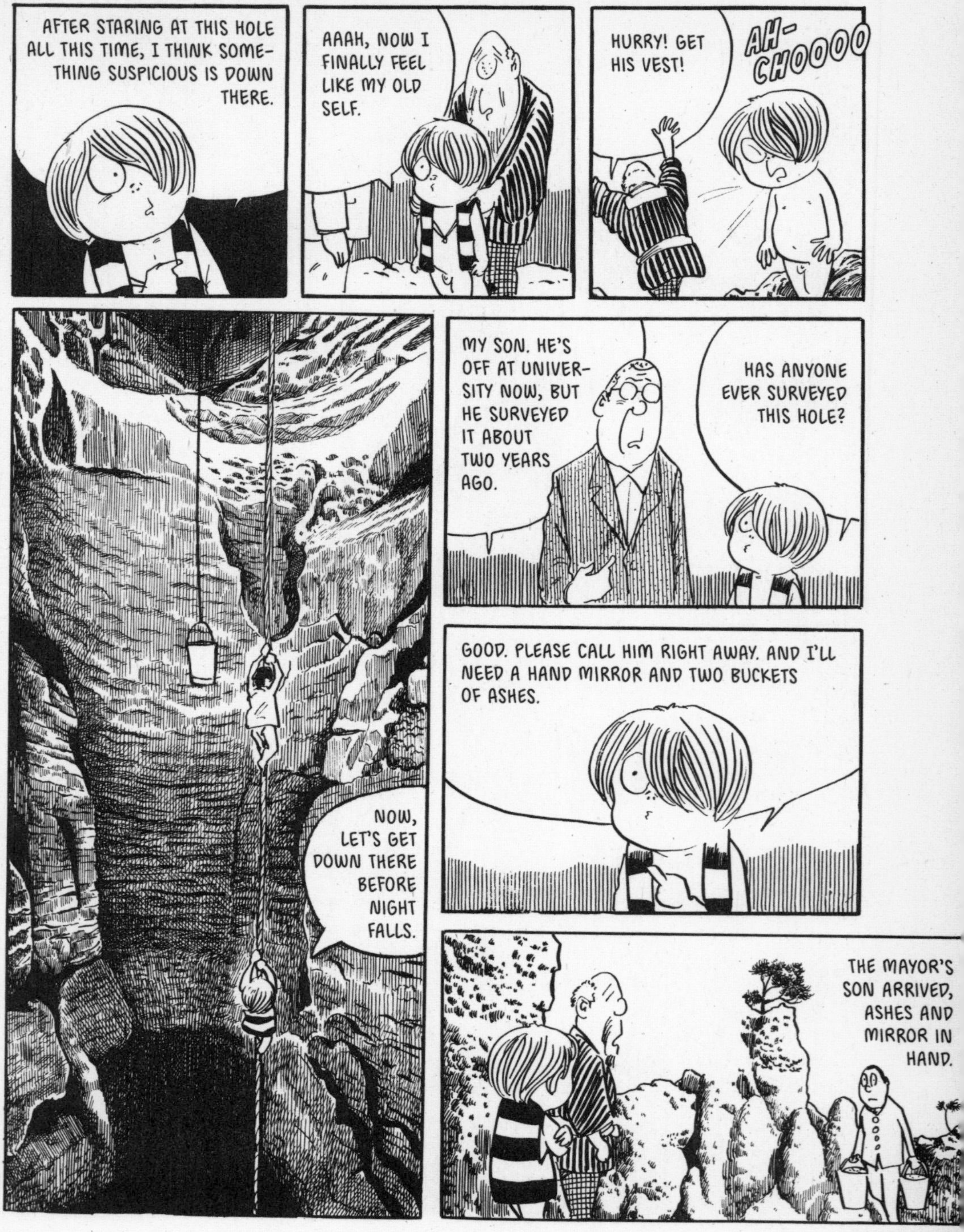
HURRY! GET HIS VEST!
AH-CHOOOO
AAAH, NOW I FINALLY FEEL LIKE MY OLD SELF.
AFTER STARING AT THIS HOLE ALL THIS TIME, I THINK SOMETHING SUSPICIOUS IS DOWN THERE.
HAS ANYONE EVER SURVEYED THIS HOLE?
MY SON. HE'S OFF AT UNIVERSITY NOW, BUT HE SURVEYED IT ABOUT TWO YEARS AGO.
GOOD. PLEASE CALL HIM RIGHT AWAY. AND I'LL NEED A HAND MIRROR AND TWO BUCKETS OF ASHES.
THE MAYOR'S SON ARRIVED, ASHES AND MIRROR IN HAND.
NOW, LET'S GET DOWN THERE BEFORE NIGHT FALLS.

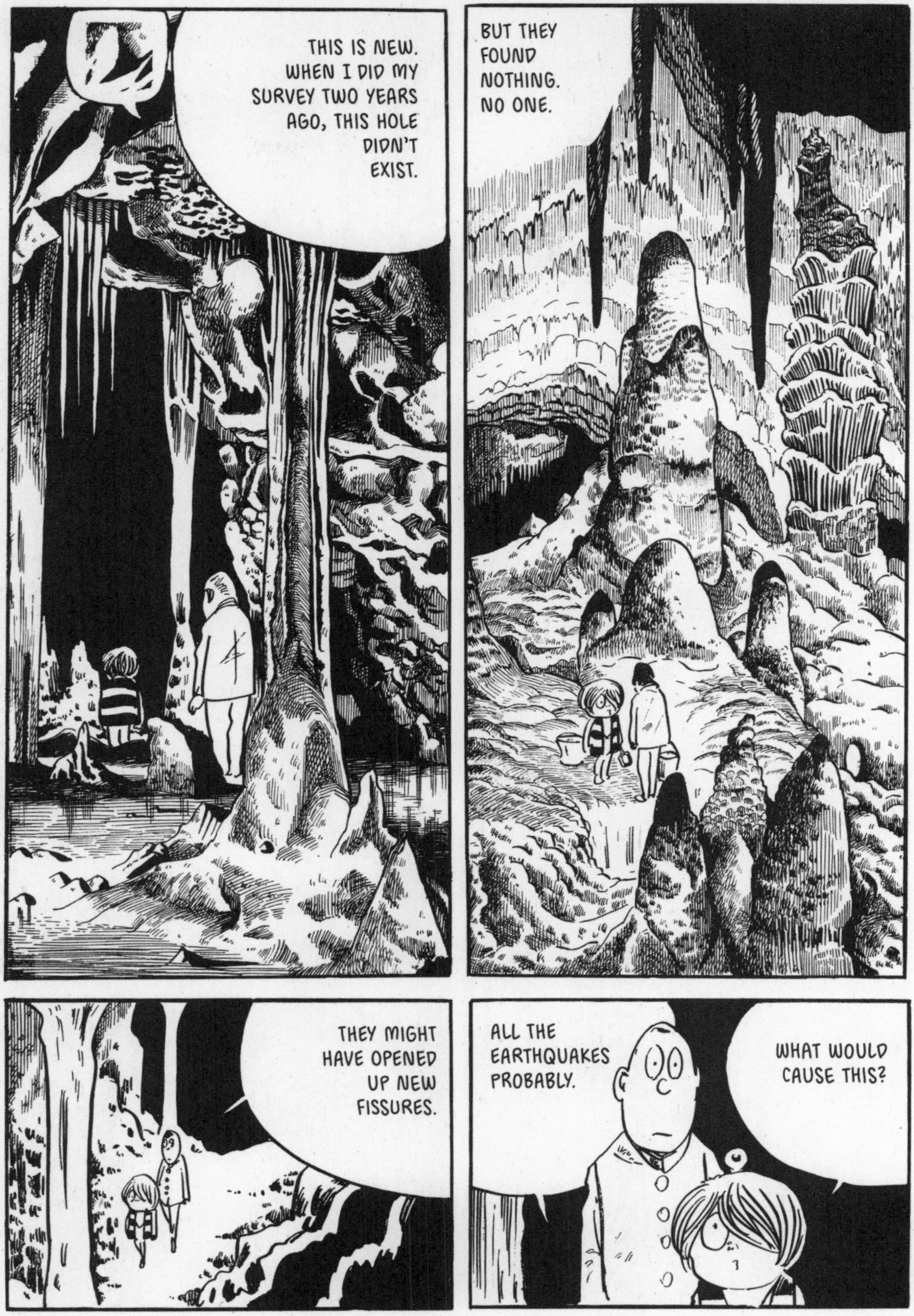
BUT THEY FOUND NOTHING. NO ONE.
THIS IS NEW. WHEN I DID MY SURVEY TWO YEARS AGO, THIS HOLE DIDN'T EXIST.
WHAT WOULD CAUSE THIS?
ALL THE EARTHQUAKES PROBABLY.
THEY MIGHT HAVE OPENED UP NEW FISSURES.

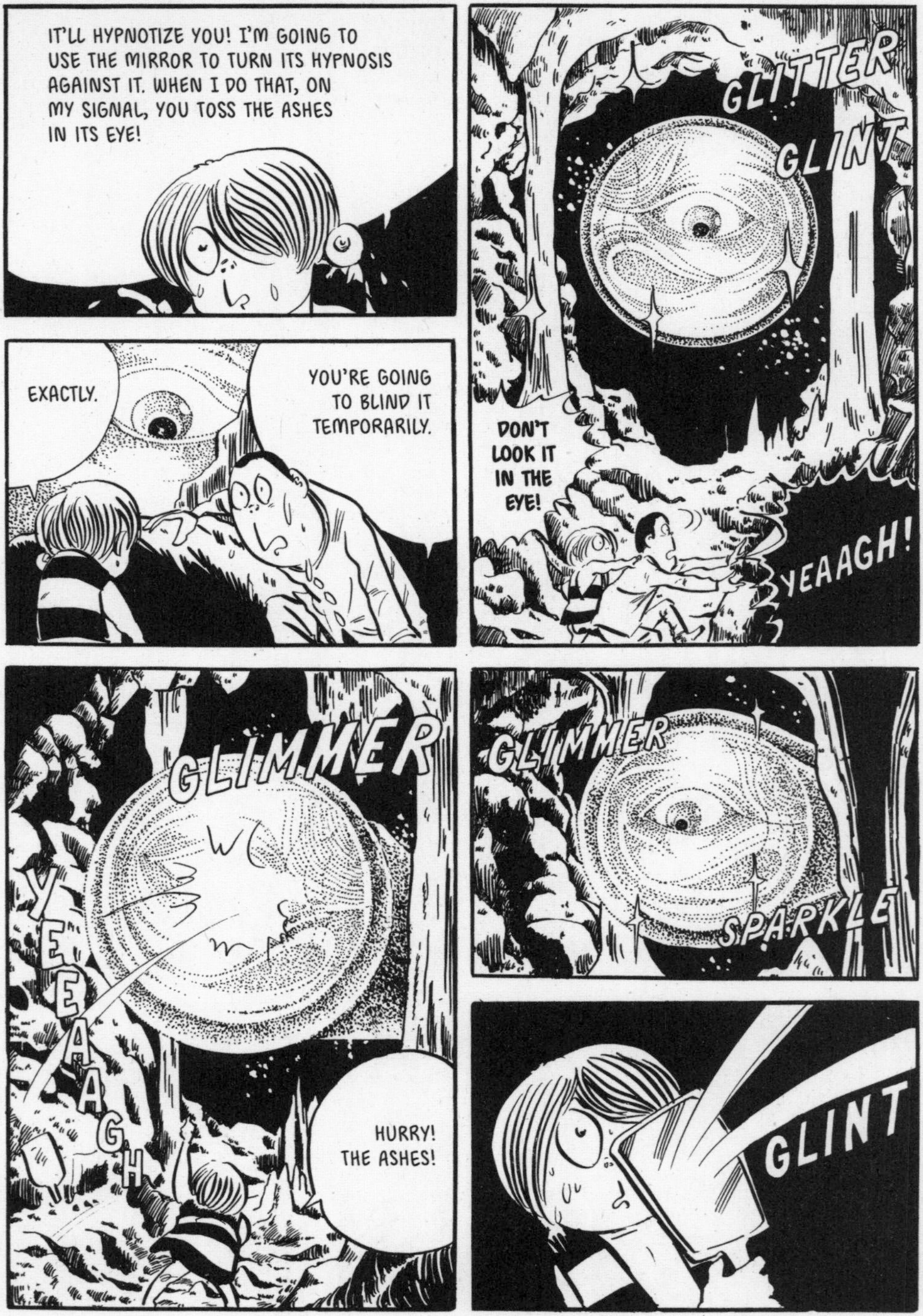
GLITTER
GLINT
DON'T LOOK IT IN THE EYE!
YEAAGH!
IT'LL HYPNOTIZE YOU! I'M GOING TO USE THE MIRROR TO TURN ITS HYPNOSIS AGAINST IT. WHEN I DO THAT, ON MY SIGNAL, YOU TOSS THE ASHES IN ITS EYE!
YOU'RE GOING TO BLIND IT TEMPORARILY.
EXACTLY.
GLIMMER
SPARKLE
GLINT
GLIMMER
HURRY! THE ASHES!
YEEAAGH

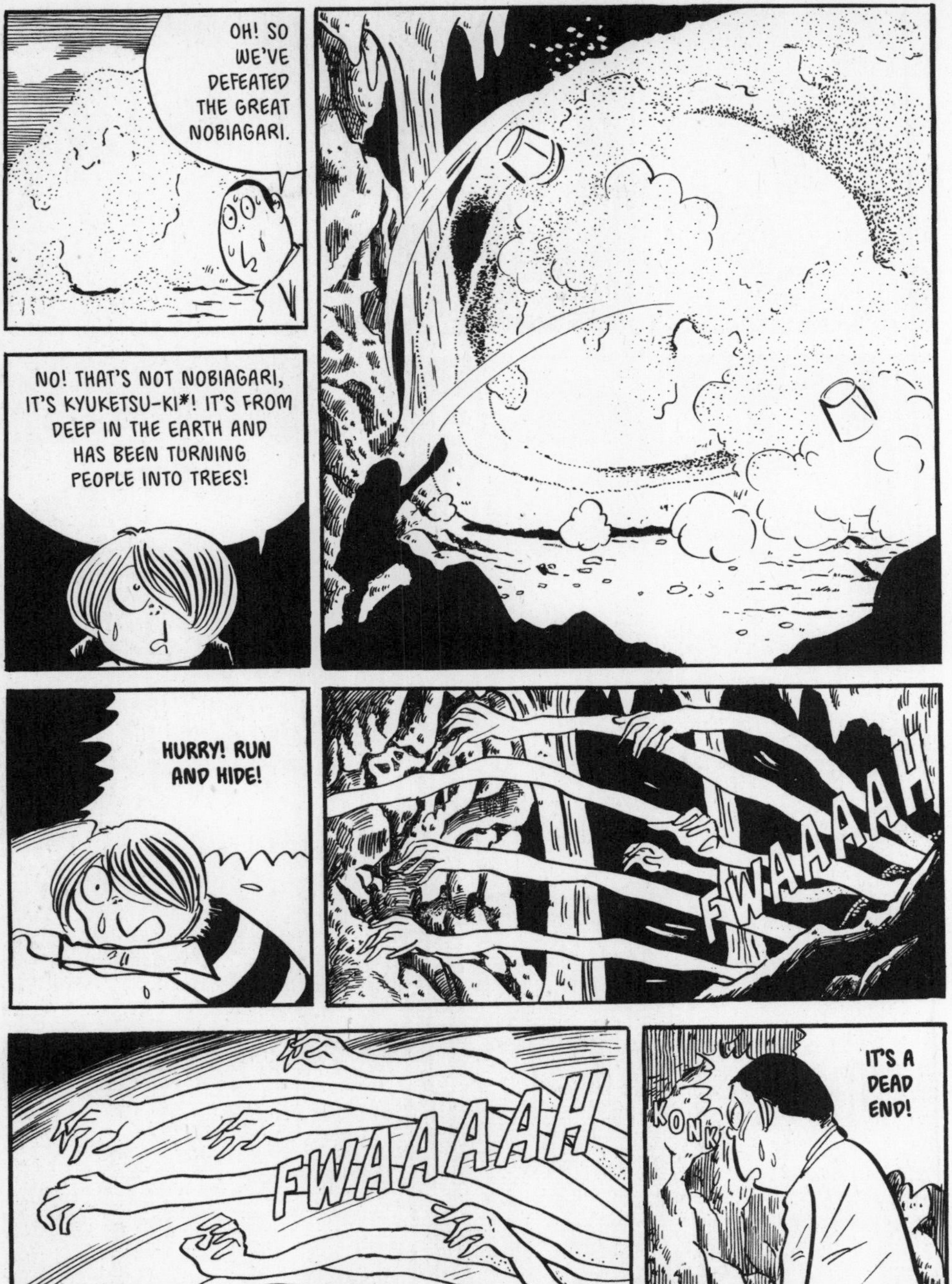
OH! SO WE'VE DEFEATED THE GREAT NOBIAGARI.
NO! THAT'S NOT NOBIAGARI, IT'S KYUKETSU-KI*! IT'S FROM DEEP IN THE EARTH AND HAS BEEN TURNING PEOPLE INTO TREES!
FWAAAAAH
HURRY! RUN AND HIDE!
IT'S A DEAD END!
KONK
FWAAAAAH

*SEE YOKAI GLOSSARY PAGE 390.

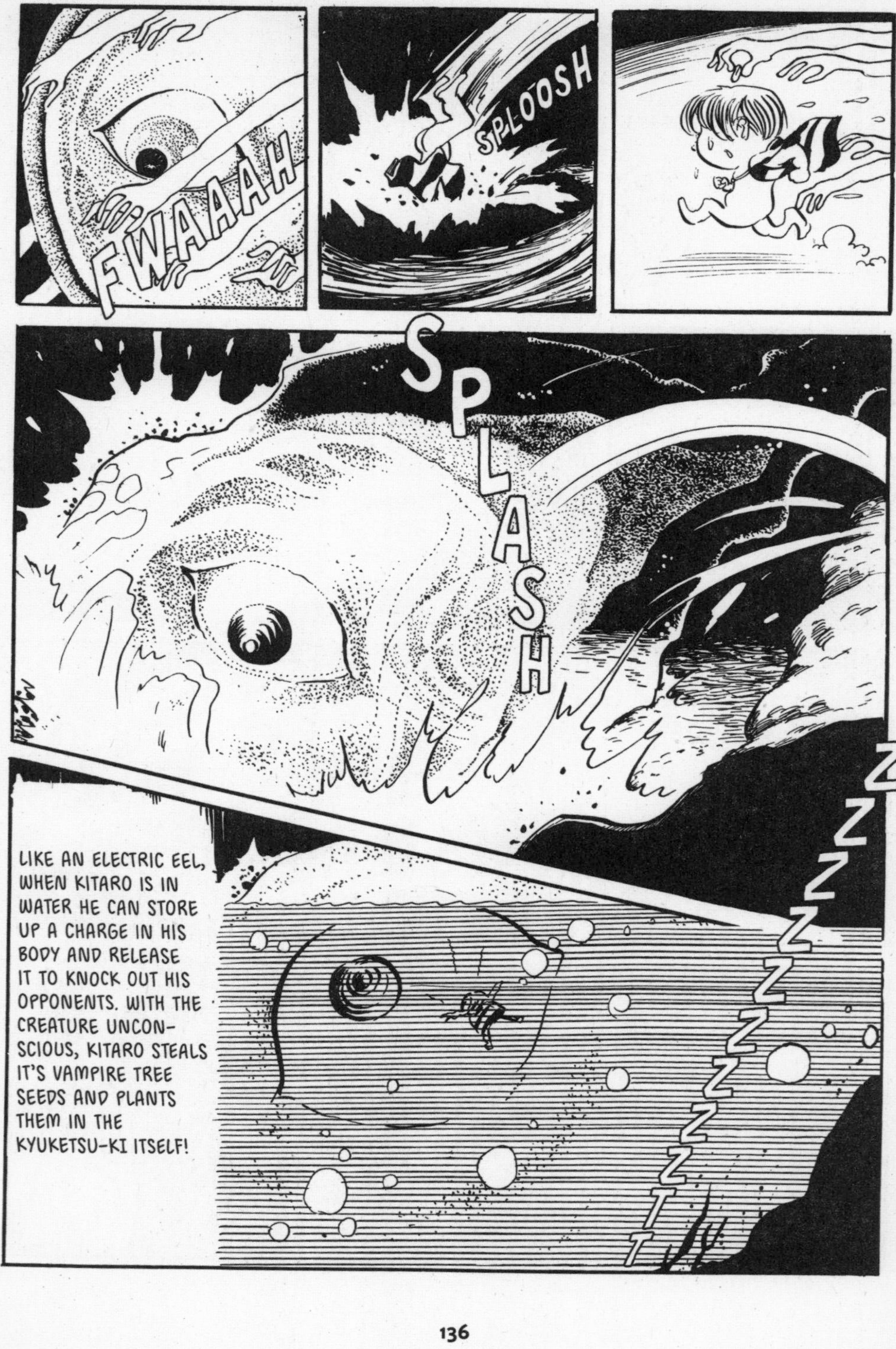
SPLOOSH
FWAAAAH
SPLASH
LIKE AN ELECTRIC EEL, WHEN KITARO IS IN WATER HE CAN STORE UP A CHARGE IN HIS BODY AND RELEASE IT TO KNOCK OUT HIS OPPONENTS. WITH THE CREATURE UNCONSCIOUS, KITARO STEALS IT'S VAMPIRE TREE SEEDS AND PLANTS THEM IN THE KYUKETSU-KI ITSELF!
ZZZZZZZZZTT

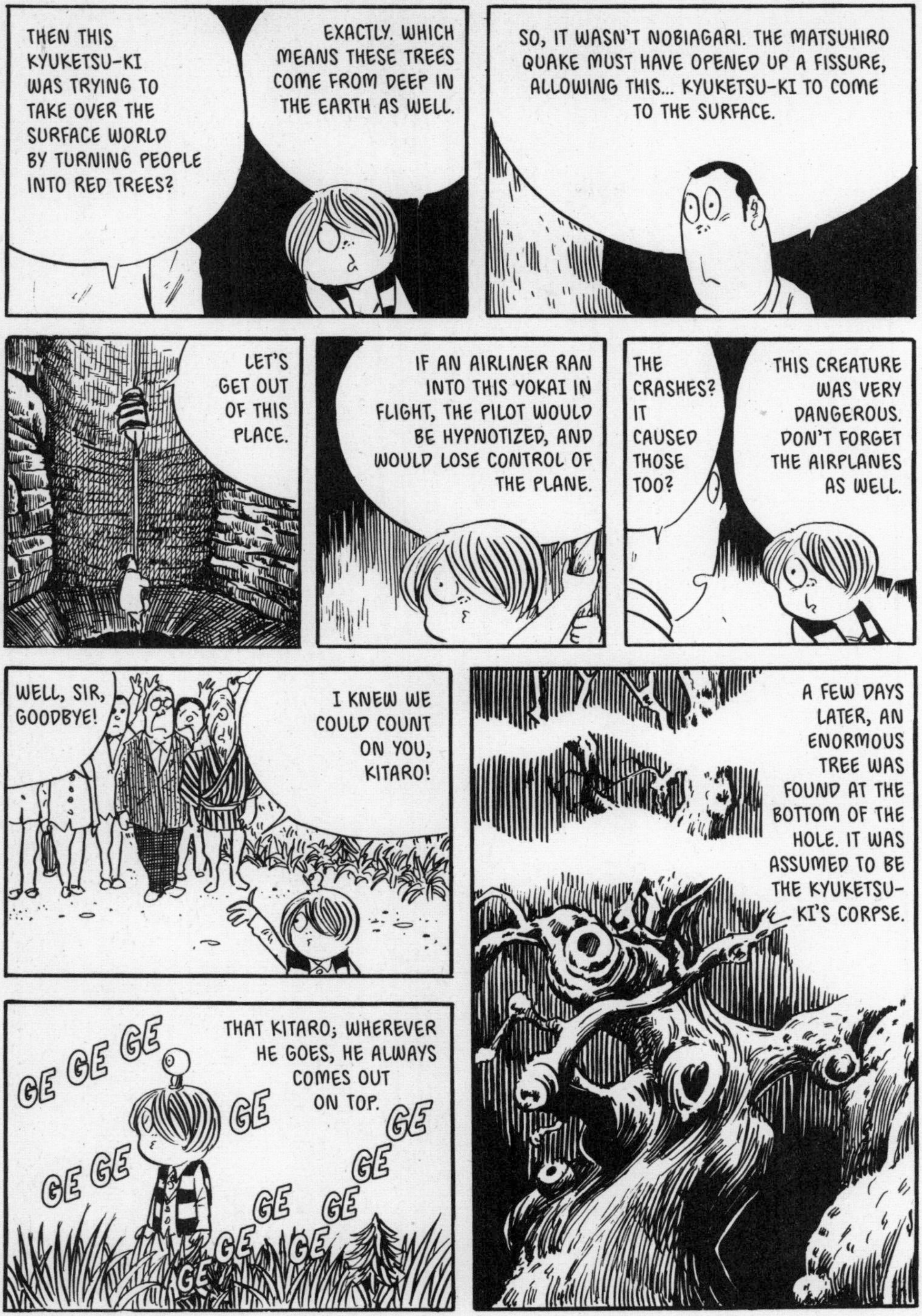

SO, IT WASN'T NOBIAGARI. THE MATSUHIRO QUAKE MUST HAVE OPENED UP A FISSURE, ALLOWING THIS... KYUKETSU-KI TO COME TO THE SURFACE.
EXACTLY. WHICH MEANS THESE TREES COME FROM DEEP IN THE EARTH AS WELL.
THEN THIS KYUKETSU-KI WAS TRYING TO TAKE OVER THE SURFACE WORLD BY TURNING PEOPLE INTO RED TREES?
THIS CREATURE WAS VERY DANGEROUS. DON'T FORGET THE AIRPLANES AS WELL.
THE CRASHES? IT CAUSED THOSE TOO?
IF AN AIRLINER RAN INTO THIS YOKAI IN FLIGHT, THE PILOT WOULD BE HYPNOTIZED, AND WOULD LOSE CONTROL OF THE PLANE.
LET'S GET OUT OF THIS PLACE.
A FEW DAYS LATER, AN ENORMOUS TREE WAS FOUND AT THE BOTTOM OF THE HOLE. IT WAS ASSUMED TO BE THE KYUKETSU-KI'S CORPSE.
I KNEW WE COULD COUNT ON YOU, KITARO!
WELL, SIR, GOODBYE!
THAT KITARO; WHEREVER HE GOES, HE ALWAYS COMES OUT ON TOP.
GE GE GE
GE
GE
GE GE
GE
GE GE
GE GE
GE GE

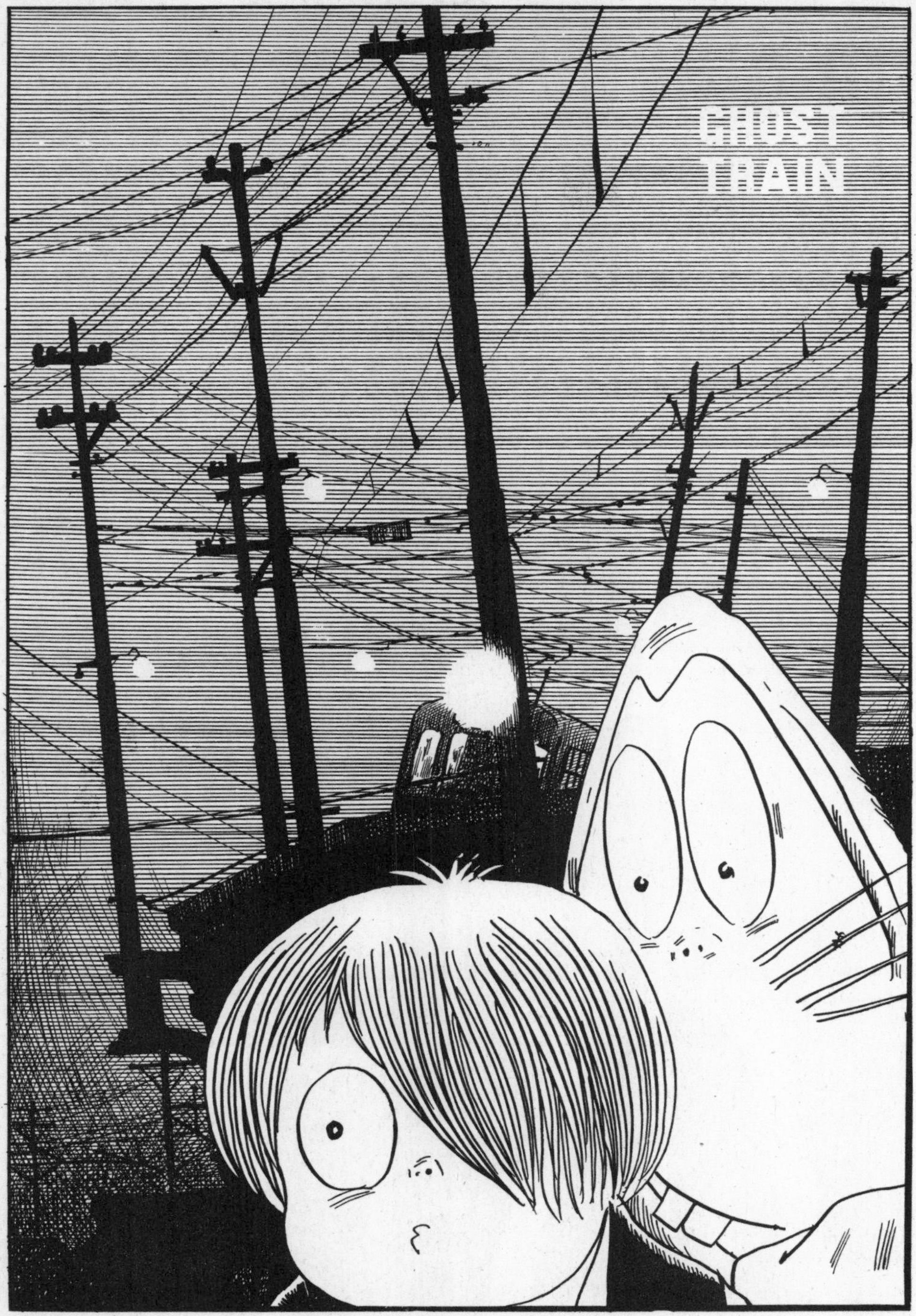
GHOST
TRAIN

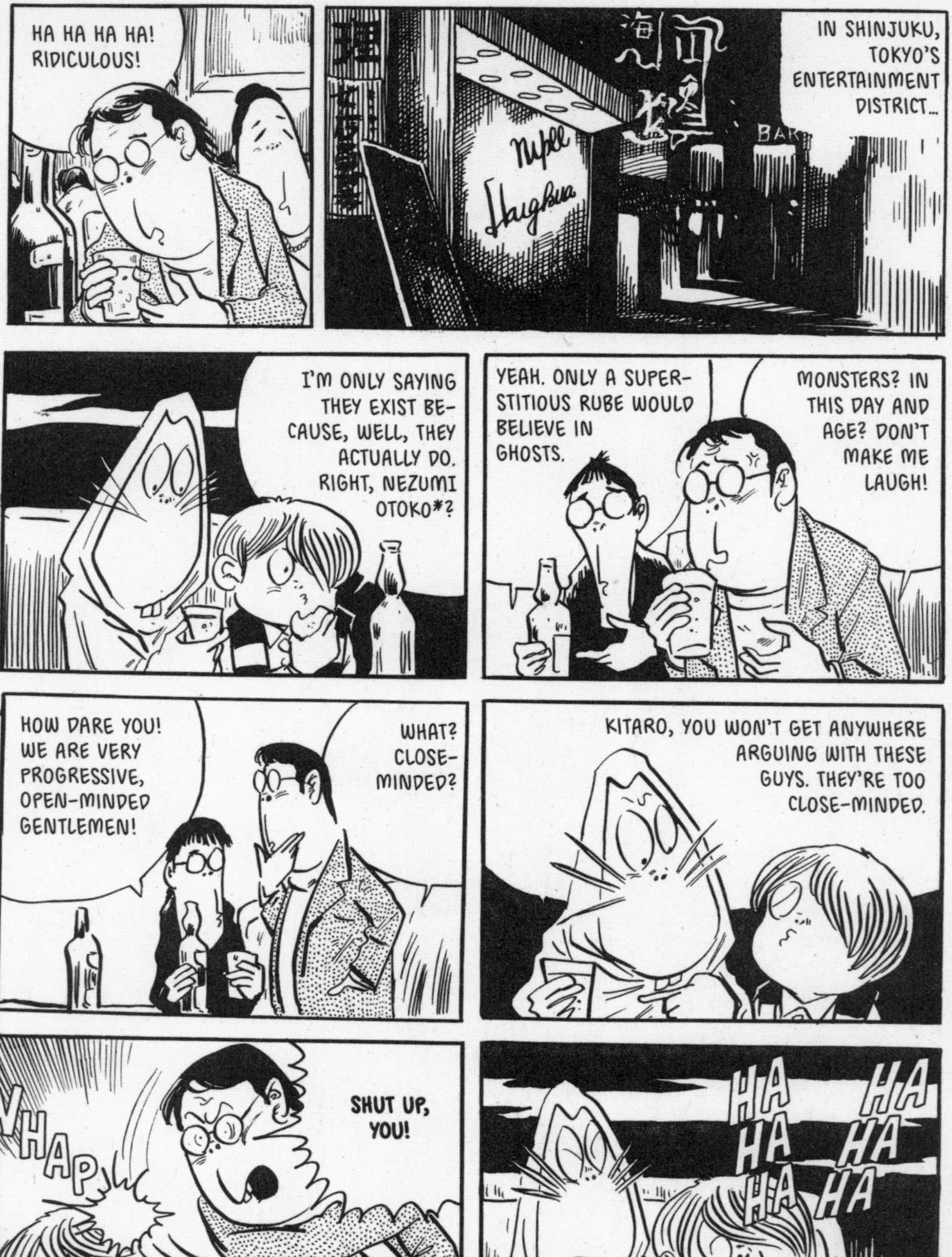
IN SHINJUKU, TOKYO'S ENTERTAINMENT DISTRICT...
HA HA HA HA! RIDICULOUS!
MONSTERS? IN THIS DAY AND AGE? DON'T MAKE ME LAUGH!
YEAH. ONLY A SUPER-STITIOUS RUBE WOULD BELIEVE IN GHOSTS.
I'M ONLY SAYING THEY EXIST BE-CAUSE, WELL, THEY ACTUALLY DO. RIGHT, NEZUMI OTOKO*?
KITARO, YOU WON'T GET ANYWHERE ARGUING WITH THESE GUYS. THEY'RE TOO CLOSE-MINDED.
WHAT? CLOSE-MINDED?
HOW DARE YOU! WE ARE VERY PROGRESSIVE, OPEN-MINDED GENTLEMEN!
HA HA HA HA HA HA HA HA
SHUT UP, YOU!
WHAP

*SEE YOKAI GLOSSARY PAGE 388.

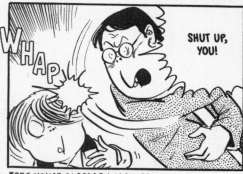

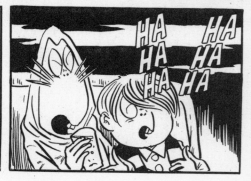

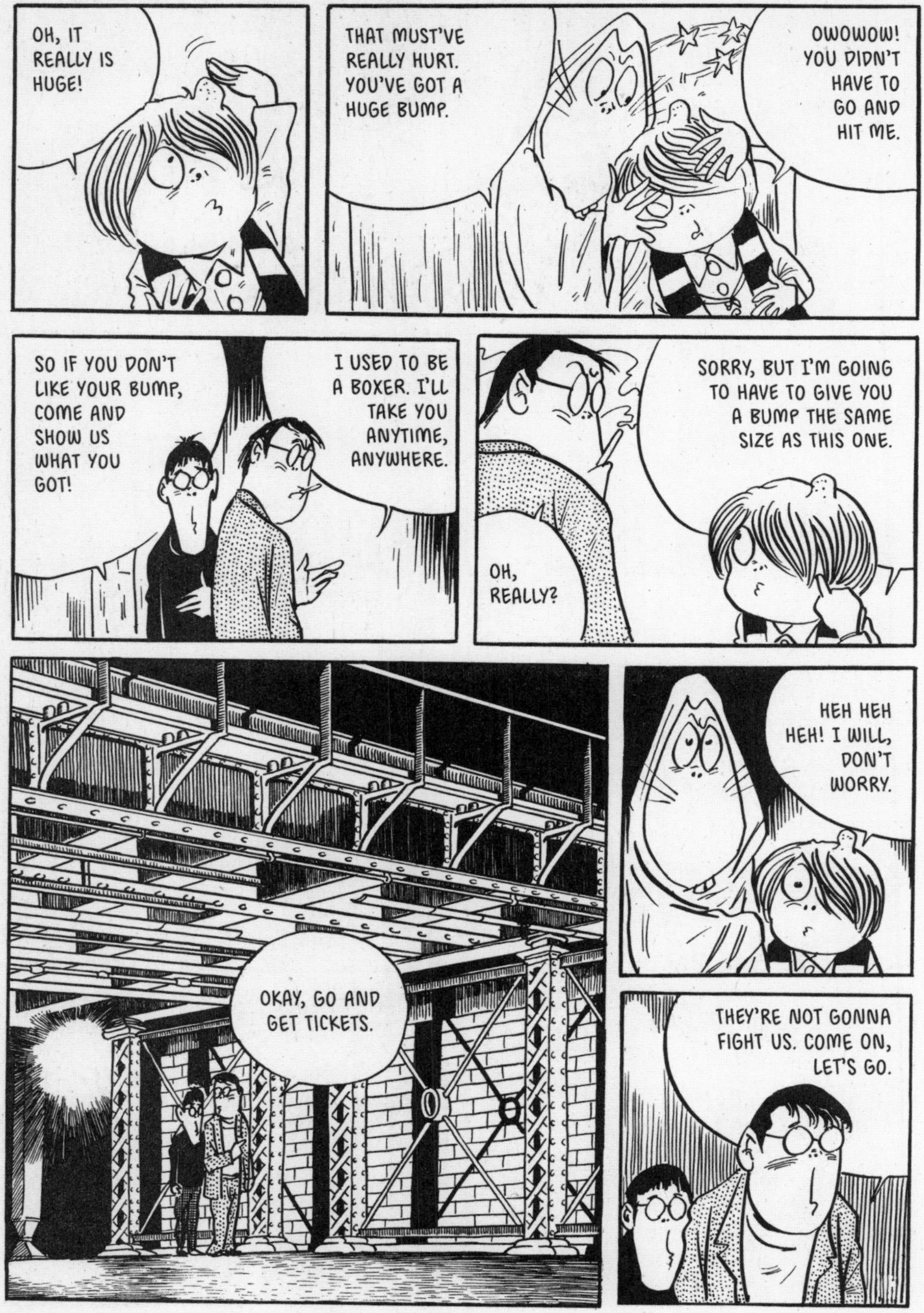
OWOWOW! YOU DIDN'T HAVE TO GO AND HIT ME.
THAT MUST'VE REALLY HURT. YOU'VE GOT A HUGE BUMP.
OH, IT REALLY IS HUGE!
SORRY, BUT I'M GOING TO HAVE TO GIVE YOU A BUMP THE SAME SIZE AS THIS ONE.
OH, REALLY?
I USED TO BE A BOXER. I'LL TAKE YOU ANYTIME, ANYWHERE.
SO IF YOU DON'T LIKE YOUR BUMP, COME AND SHOW US WHAT YOU GOT!
HEH HEH HEH! I WILL, DON'T WORRY.
THEY'RE NOT GONNA FIGHT US. COME ON, LET'S GO.
OKAY, GO AND GET TICKETS.

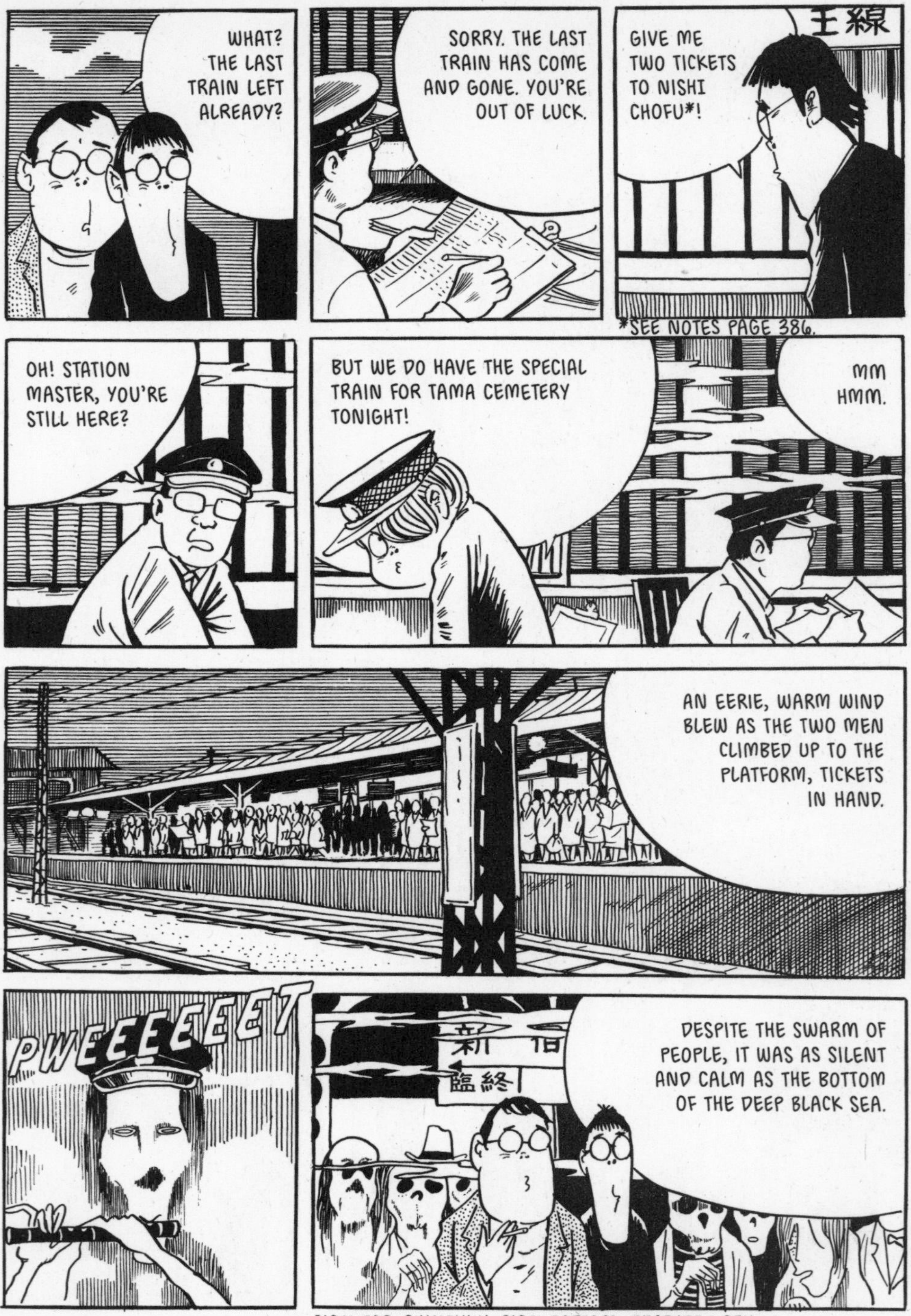
王線
GIVE ME TWO TICKETS TO NISHI CHOFU*!
SORRY. THE LAST TRAIN HAS COME AND GONE. YOU'RE OUT OF LUCK.
WHAT? THE LAST TRAIN LEFT ALREADY?
MM HMM.
BUT WE DO HAVE THE SPECIAL TRAIN FOR TAMA CEMETERY TONIGHT!
OH! STATION MASTER, YOU'RE STILL HERE?
AN EERIE, WARM WIND BLEW AS THE TWO MEN CLIMBED UP TO THE PLATFORM, TICKETS IN HAND.
DESPITE THE SWARM OF PEOPLE, IT WAS AS SILENT AND CALM AS THE BOTTOM OF THE DEEP BLACK SEA.
新 宿
臨終
PWEEEEEEET

*SEE NOTES PAGE 386.

SIGN TOP: SHINJUKU. SIGN BOTTOM: DEATHBED STN.

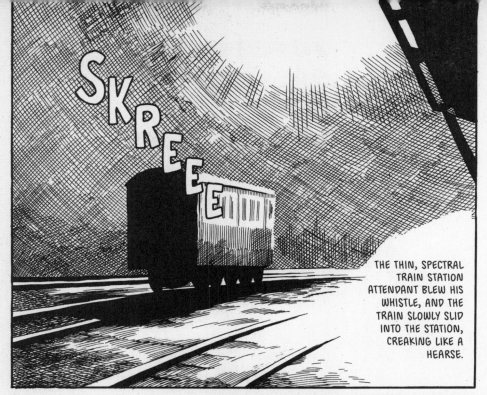

SKREEE
THE THIN, SPECTRAL TRAIN STATION ATTENDANT BLEW HIS WHISTLE, AND THE TRAIN SLOWLY SLID INTO THE STATION, CREAKING LIKE A HEARSE.
THE DOOR CLANKED OPEN LIKE THAT OF A CREMATORIUM.
KUNKA
KUNKA
KUNKA
THE CROWD ENTERED THE TRAIN AS IF THEY WERE BEING SUCKED IN.
IT'S FREEZING IN HERE. THIS TRAIN SEEMS EXTRA CREEPY, DOESN'T IT?
IT'S ALL IN YOUR HEAD.
BEFORE LONG, A HERD OF STATION ATTENDANTS APPEARED OUT OF NOWHERE BEARING STICKS OF INCENSE*.

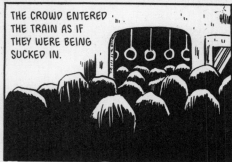

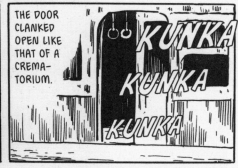

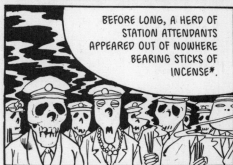

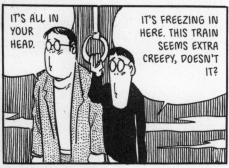

*INCENSE IS A VERY IMPORTANT COMPONENT OF JAPANESE FUNERAL RITES.

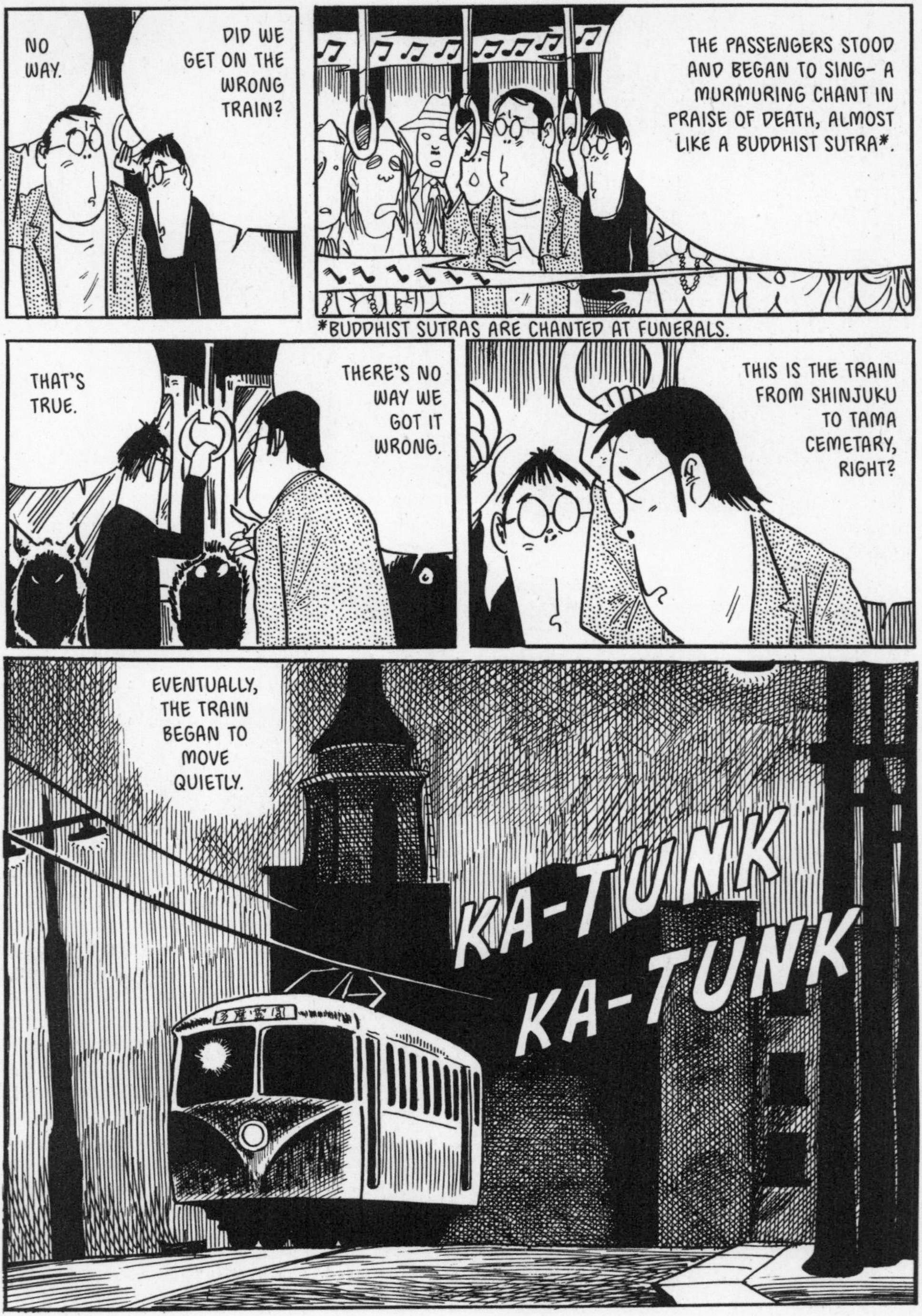
THE PASSENGERS STOOD AND BEGAN TO SING– A MURMURING CHANT IN PRAISE OF DEATH, ALMOST LIKE A BUDDHIST SUTRA*.
DID WE GET ON THE WRONG TRAIN?
NO WAY.
*BUDDHIST SUTRAS ARE CHANTED AT FUNERALS.
THIS IS THE TRAIN FROM SHINJUKU TO TAMA CEMETARY, RIGHT?
THERE'S NO WAY WE GOT IT WRONG.
THAT'S TRUE.
EVENTUALLY, THE TRAIN BEGAN TO MOVE QUIETLY.
KA-TUNK
KA-TUNK

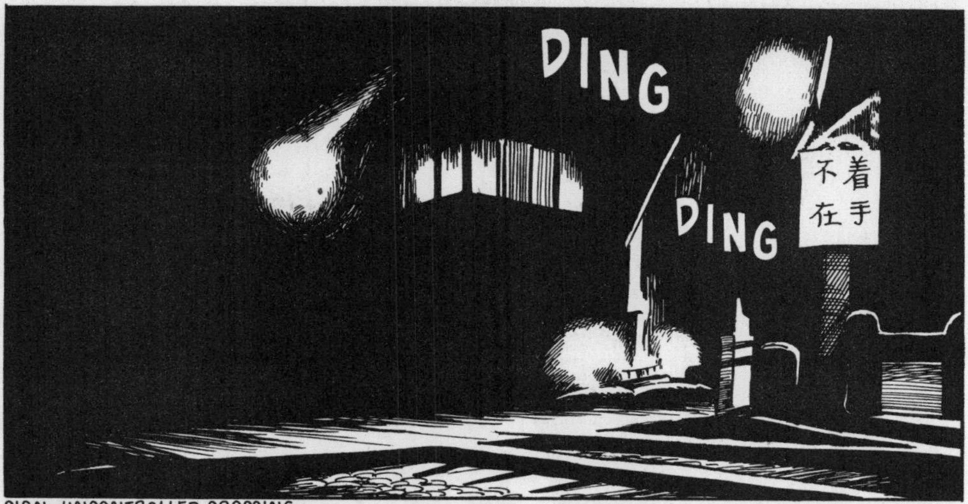
DING
DING
着手不在
SIGN: UNCONTROLLED CROSSING.

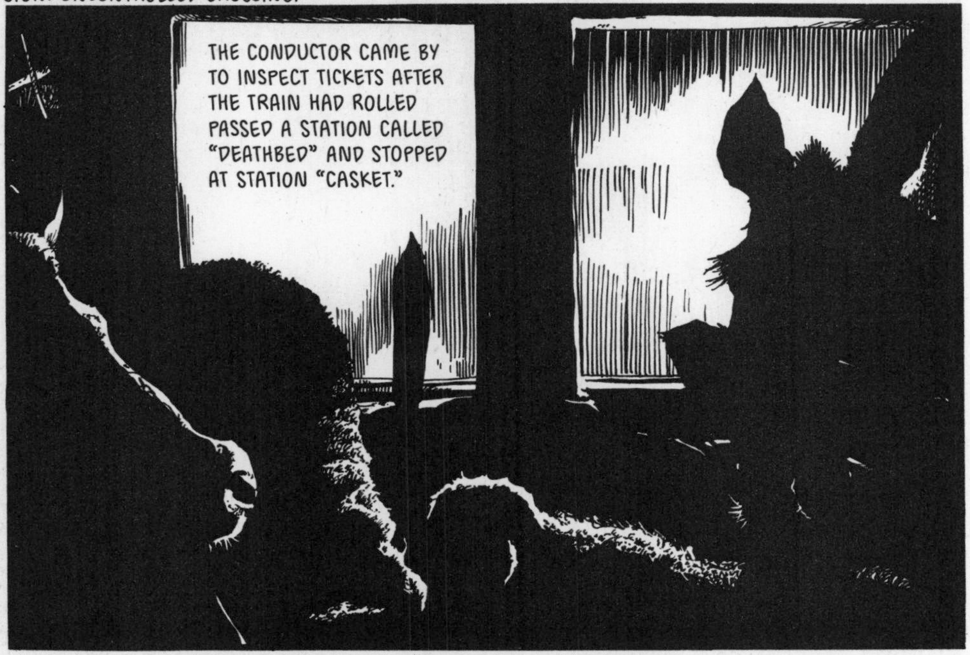
THE CONDUCTOR CAME BY TO INSPECT TICKETS AFTER THE TRAIN HAD ROLLED PASSED A STATION CALLED "DEATHBED" AND STOPPED AT STATION "CASKET."

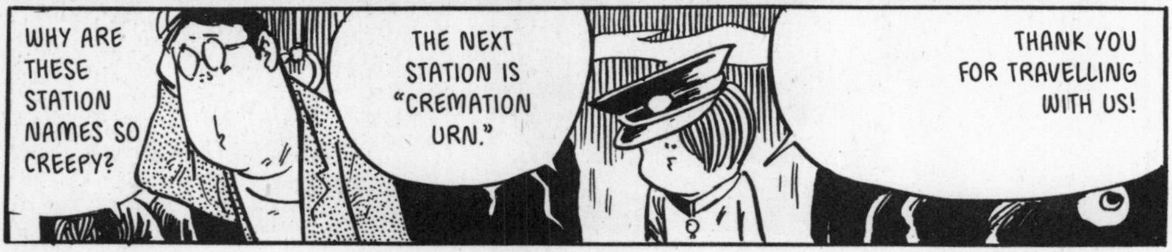
THANK YOU FOR TRAVELLING WITH US!
THE NEXT STATION IS "CREMATION URN."
WHY ARE THESE STATION NAMES SO CREEPY?

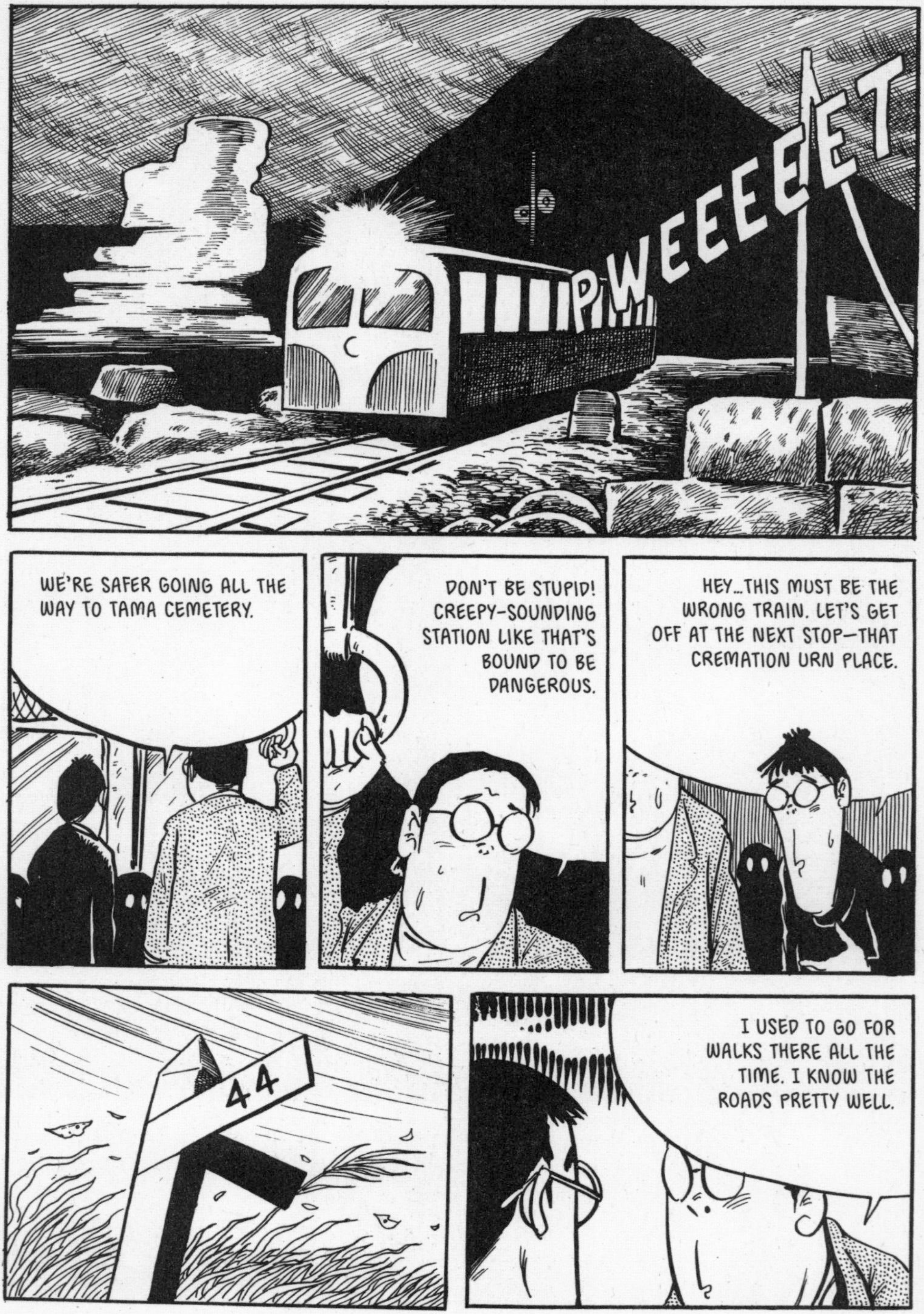
PWEEEEEET
HEY...THIS MUST BE THE WRONG TRAIN. LET'S GET OFF AT THE NEXT STOP—THAT CREMATION URN PLACE.
DON'T BE STUPID! CREEPY-SOUNDING STATION LIKE THAT'S BOUND TO BE DANGEROUS.
WE'RE SAFER GOING ALL THE WAY TO TAMA CEMETERY.
I USED TO GO FOR WALKS THERE ALL THE TIME. I KNOW THE ROADS PRETTY WELL.
44

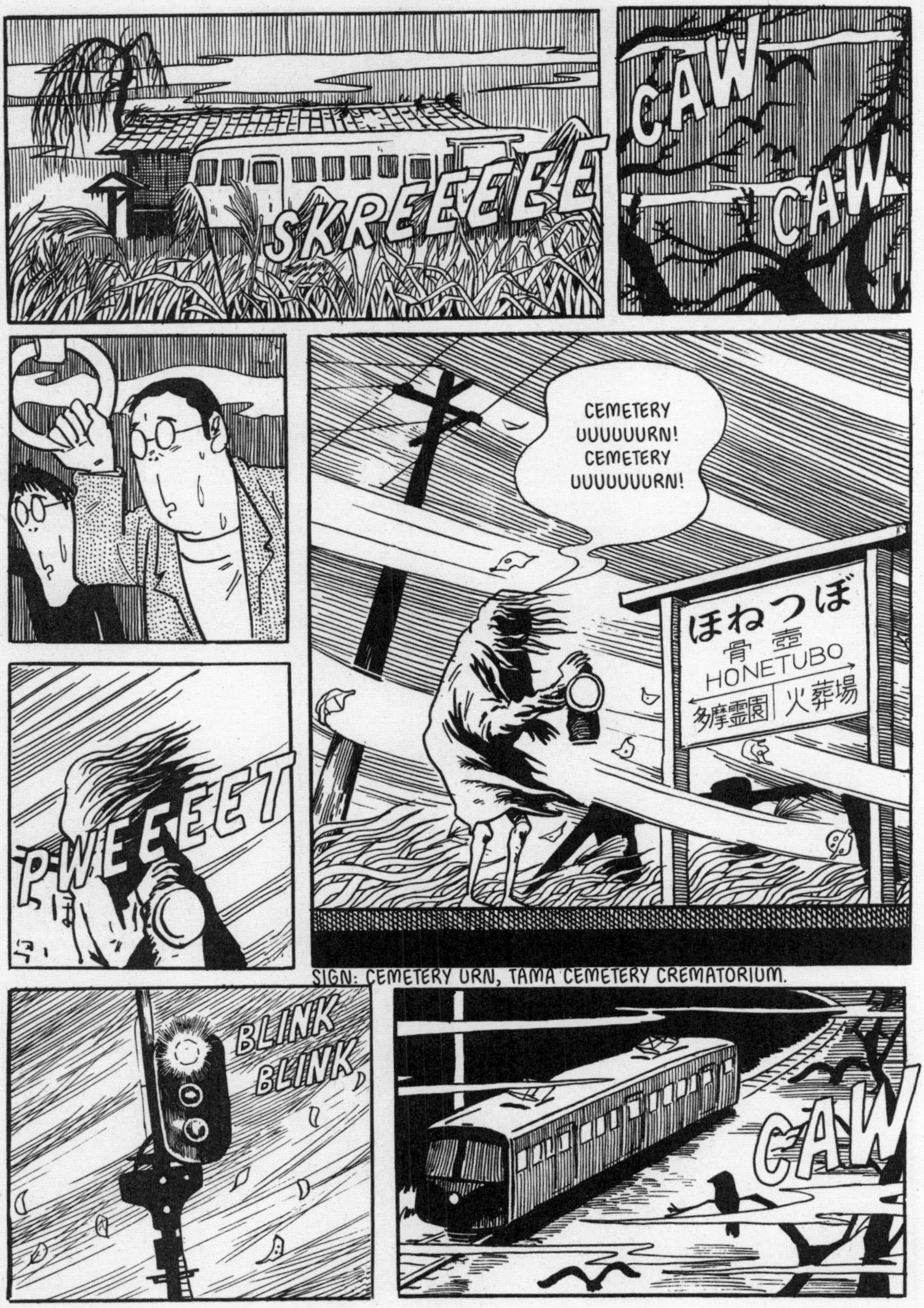
CAW
CAW
SKREEEEEE
CEMETERY UUUUUURN! CEMETERY UUUUUUURN!
ほねつぼ
骨壺
HONETUBO
多摩霊園
火葬場
PWEEEEET
SIGN: CEMETERY URN, TAMA CEMETERY CREMATORIUM.
CAW
BLINK
BLINK

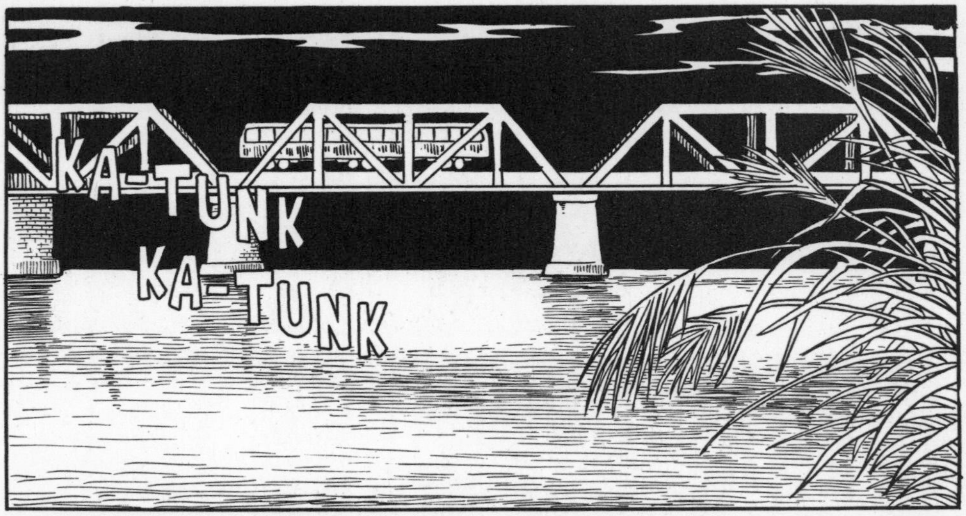
KA-TUNK
KA-TUNK

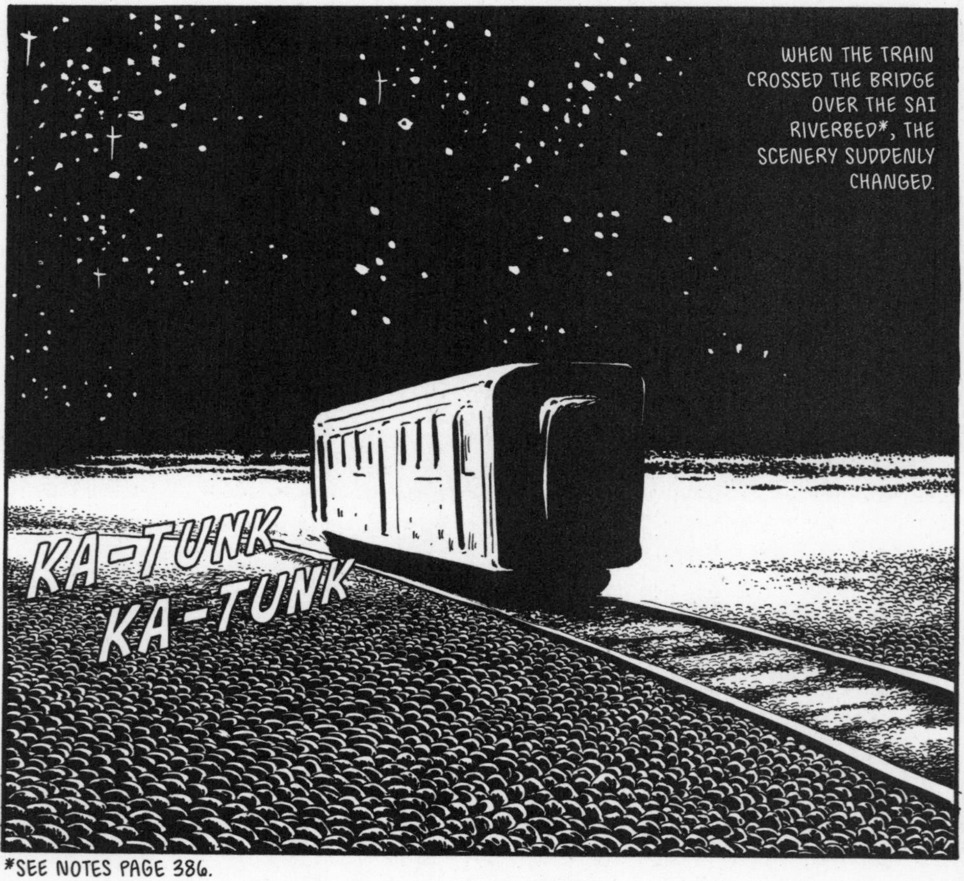
WHEN THE TRAIN CROSSED THE BRIDGE OVER THE SAI RIVERBED*, THE SCENERY SUDDENLY CHANGED.
KA-TUNK
KA-TUNK

*SEE NOTES PAGE 386.

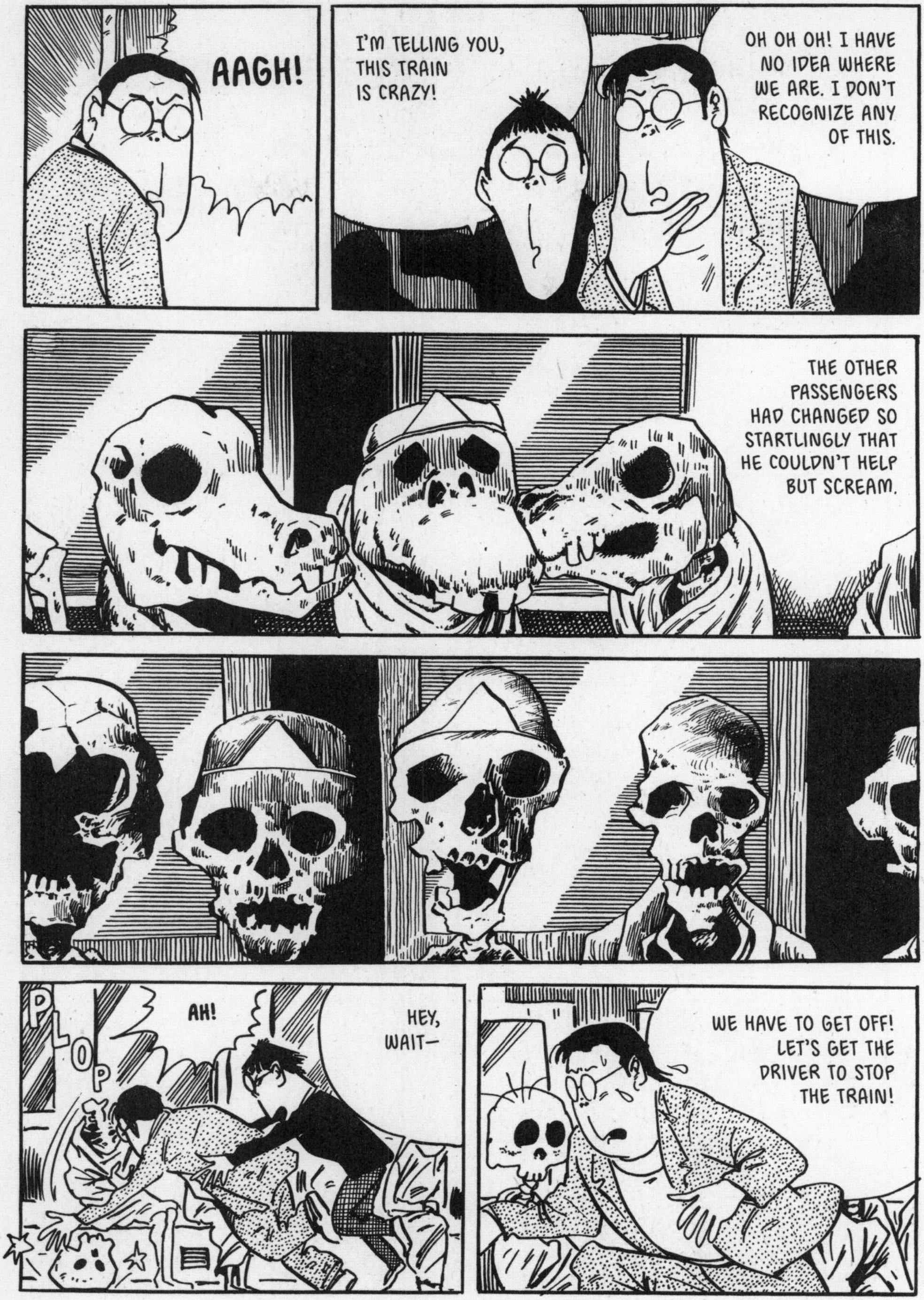
OH OH OH! I HAVE NO IDEA WHERE WE ARE. I DON'T RECOGNIZE ANY OF THIS.
I'M TELLING YOU, THIS TRAIN IS CRAZY!
AAGH!
THE OTHER PASSENGERS HAD CHANGED SO STARTLINGLY THAT HE COULDN'T HELP BUT SCREAM.
WE HAVE TO GET OFF! LET'S GET THE DRIVER TO STOP THE TRAIN!
HEY, WAIT—
AH!
PLOP

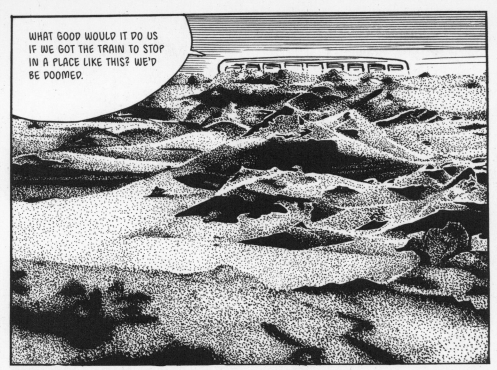

WHAT GOOD WOULD IT DO US IF WE GOT THE TRAIN TO STOP IN A PLACE LIKE THIS? WE'D BE DOOMED.
THINK ABOUT THE LAST STOP FOR A MINUTE! THE CEMETERY...AND WITH THE WAY THINGS HAVE GONE SO FAR...
WE'RE HEADED TO OUR GRAVES!
RAP RAP RAP
乗務員室
WE'VE GOT TO STOP THIS TRAIN!
YOU DON'T HAVE TO POUND ON IT. IT'S ALREADY OPEN.
乗
KRRRK

DOOR: CONDUCTOR'S CABIN.

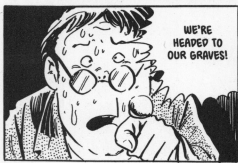

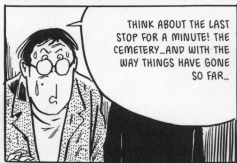

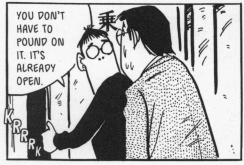

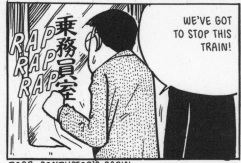

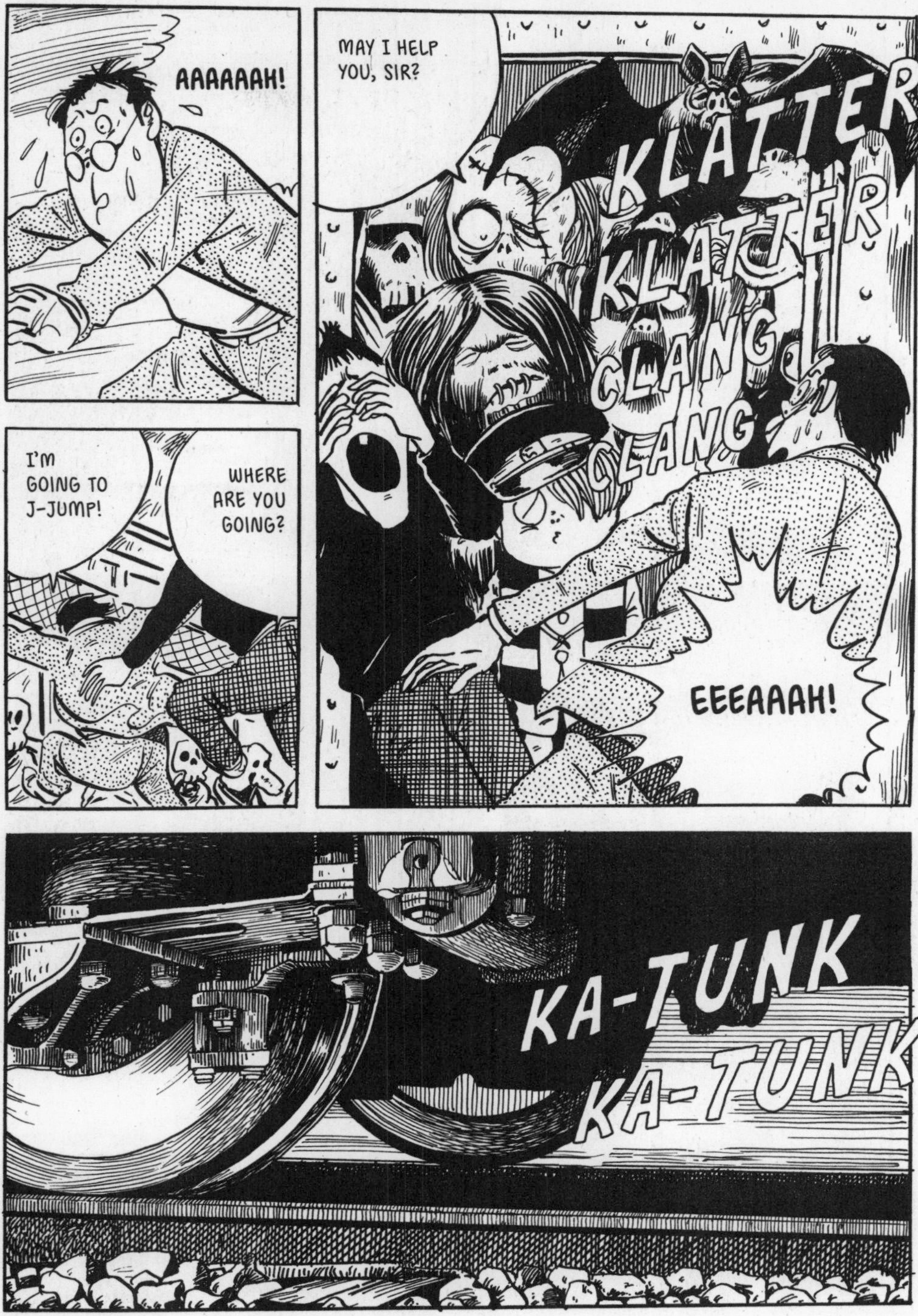
MAY I HELP YOU, SIR?
KLATTER
KLATTER
CLANG
CLANG
EEEAAAH!
AAAAAAH!
WHERE ARE YOU GOING?
I'M GOING TO J-JUMP!
KA-TUNK
KA-TUNK

NO! YOU'LL NEVER SURVIVE A JUMP LIKE THAT!
IDIOT!
I'D RATHER JUMP TO MY DEATH THAN BE EATEN ALIVE OR TORN TO BITS HERE!
YEEEAAAGH!

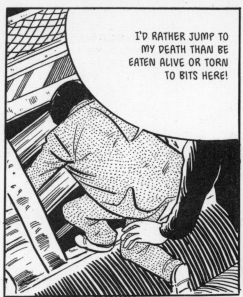

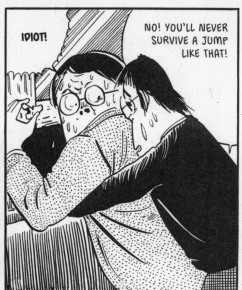

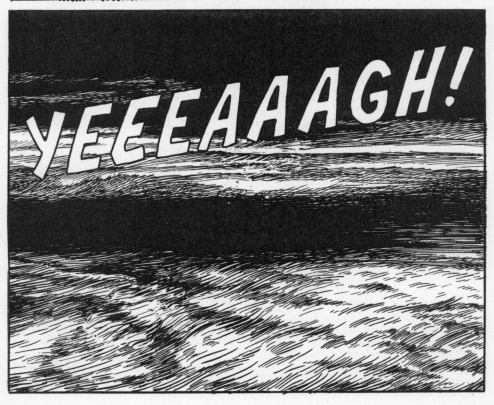

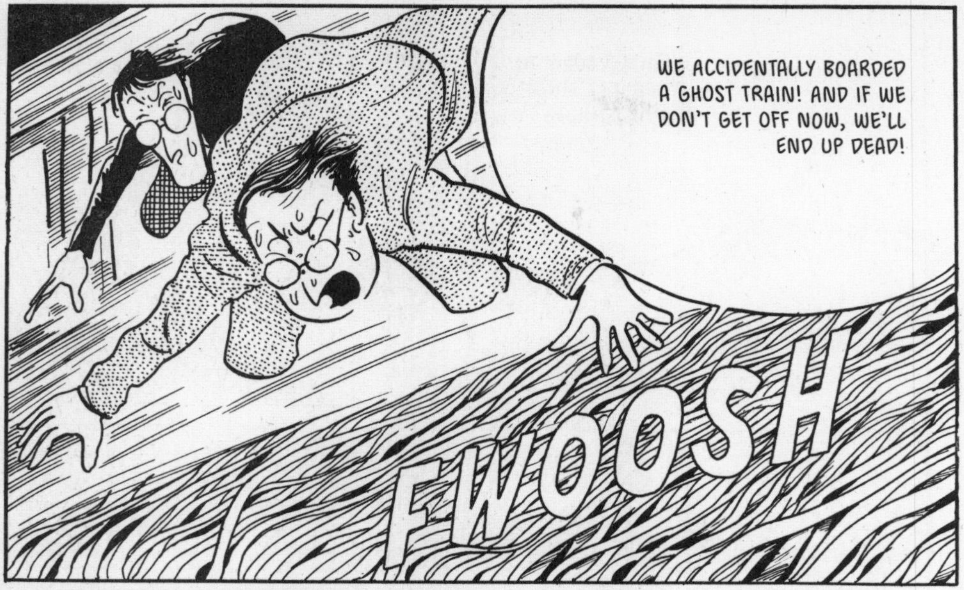
WE ACCIDENTALLY BOARDED A GHOST TRAIN! AND IF WE DON'T GET OFF NOW, WE'LL END UP DEAD!
FWOOSH

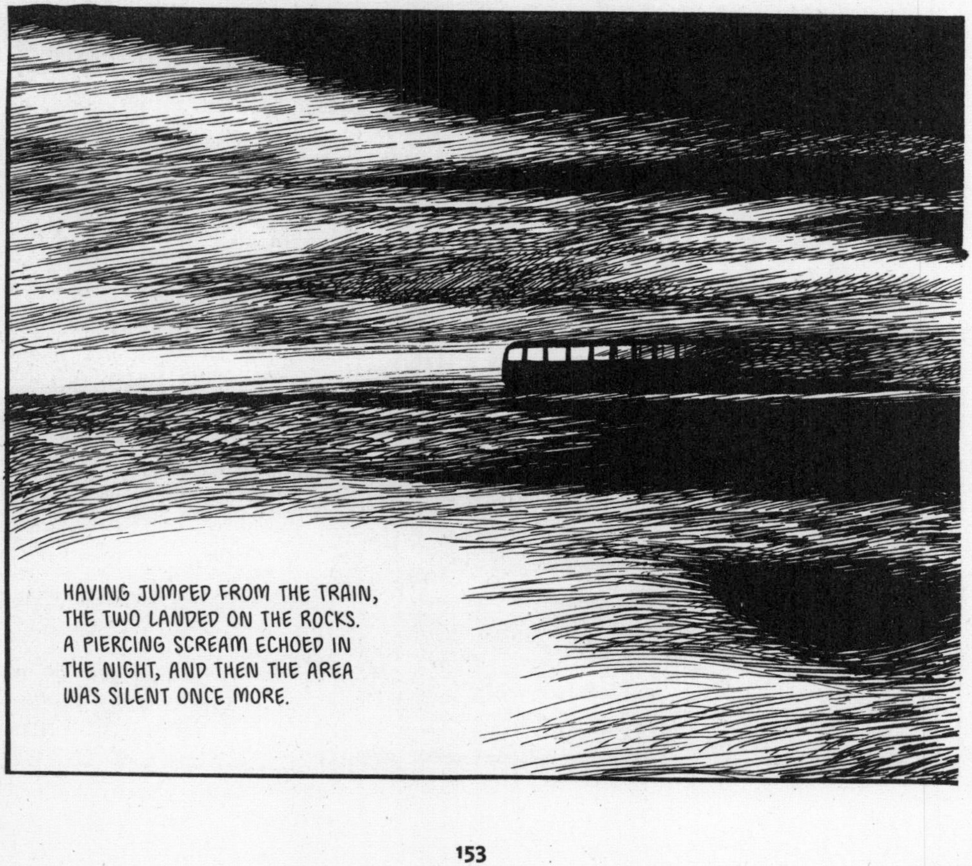
HAVING JUMPED FROM THE TRAIN, THE TWO LANDED ON THE ROCKS. A PIERCING SCREAM ECHOED IN THE NIGHT, AND THEN THE AREA WAS SILENT ONCE MORE.

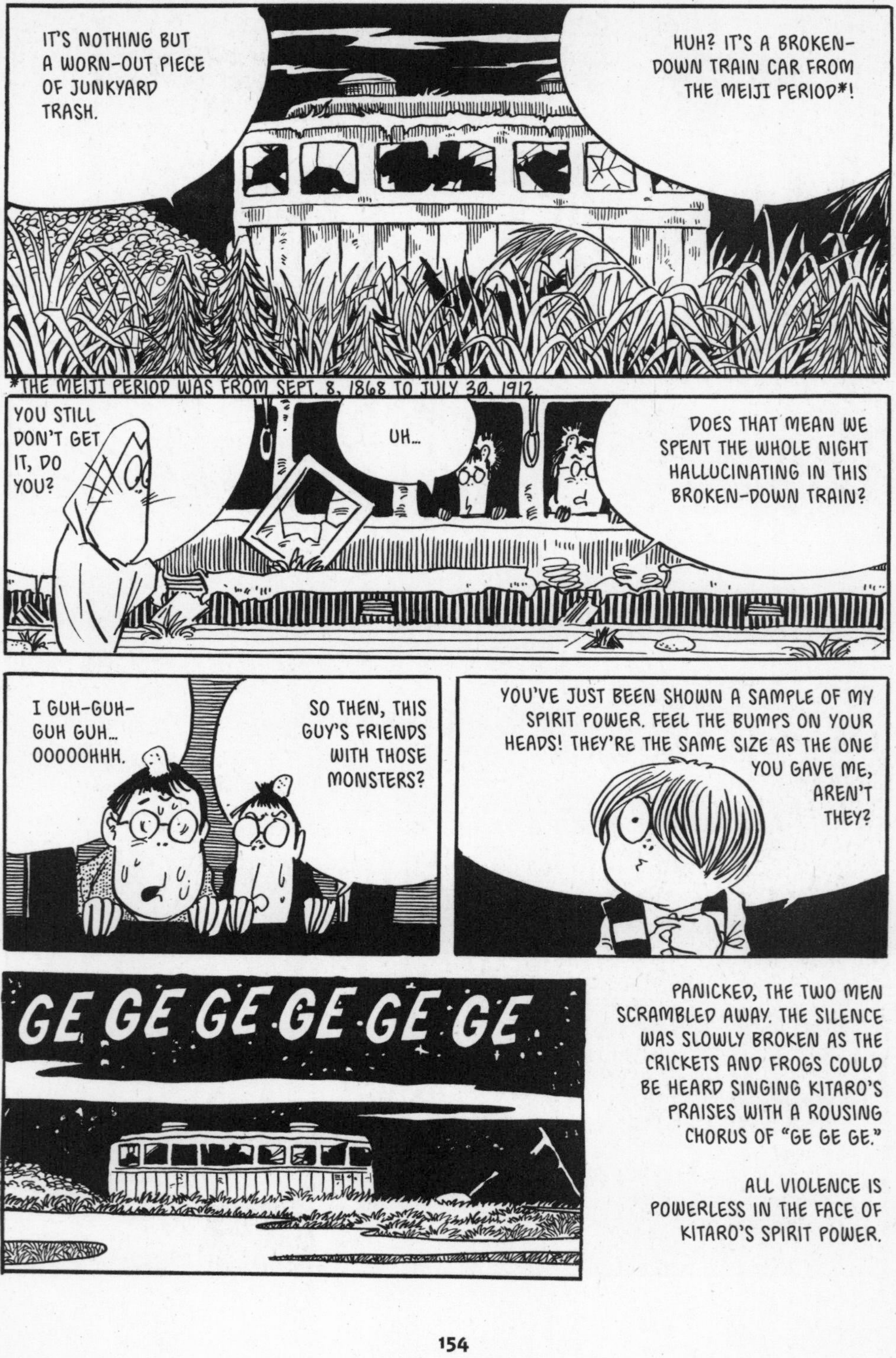
HUH? IT'S A BROKEN-DOWN TRAIN CAR FROM THE MEIJI PERIOD*!
IT'S NOTHING BUT A WORN-OUT PIECE OF JUNKYARD TRASH.
*THE MEIJI PERIOD WAS FROM SEPT. 8, 1868 TO JULY 30, 1912.
DOES THAT MEAN WE SPENT THE WHOLE NIGHT HALLUCINATING IN THIS BROKEN-DOWN TRAIN?
UH...
YOU STILL DON'T GET IT, DO YOU?
YOU'VE JUST BEEN SHOWN A SAMPLE OF MY SPIRIT POWER. FEEL THE BUMPS ON YOUR HEADS! THEY'RE THE SAME SIZE AS THE ONE YOU GAVE ME, AREN'T THEY?
SO THEN, THIS GUY'S FRIENDS WITH THOSE MONSTERS?
I GUH-GUH-GUH GUH... OOOOOHHH.
PANICKED, THE TWO MEN SCRAMBLED AWAY. THE SILENCE WAS SLOWLY BROKEN AS THE CRICKETS AND FROGS COULD BE HEARD SINGING KITARO'S PRAISES WITH A ROUSING CHORUS OF "GE GE GE."
ALL VIOLENCE IS POWERLESS IN THE FACE OF KITARO'S SPIRIT POWER.
GE GE GE GE GE GE

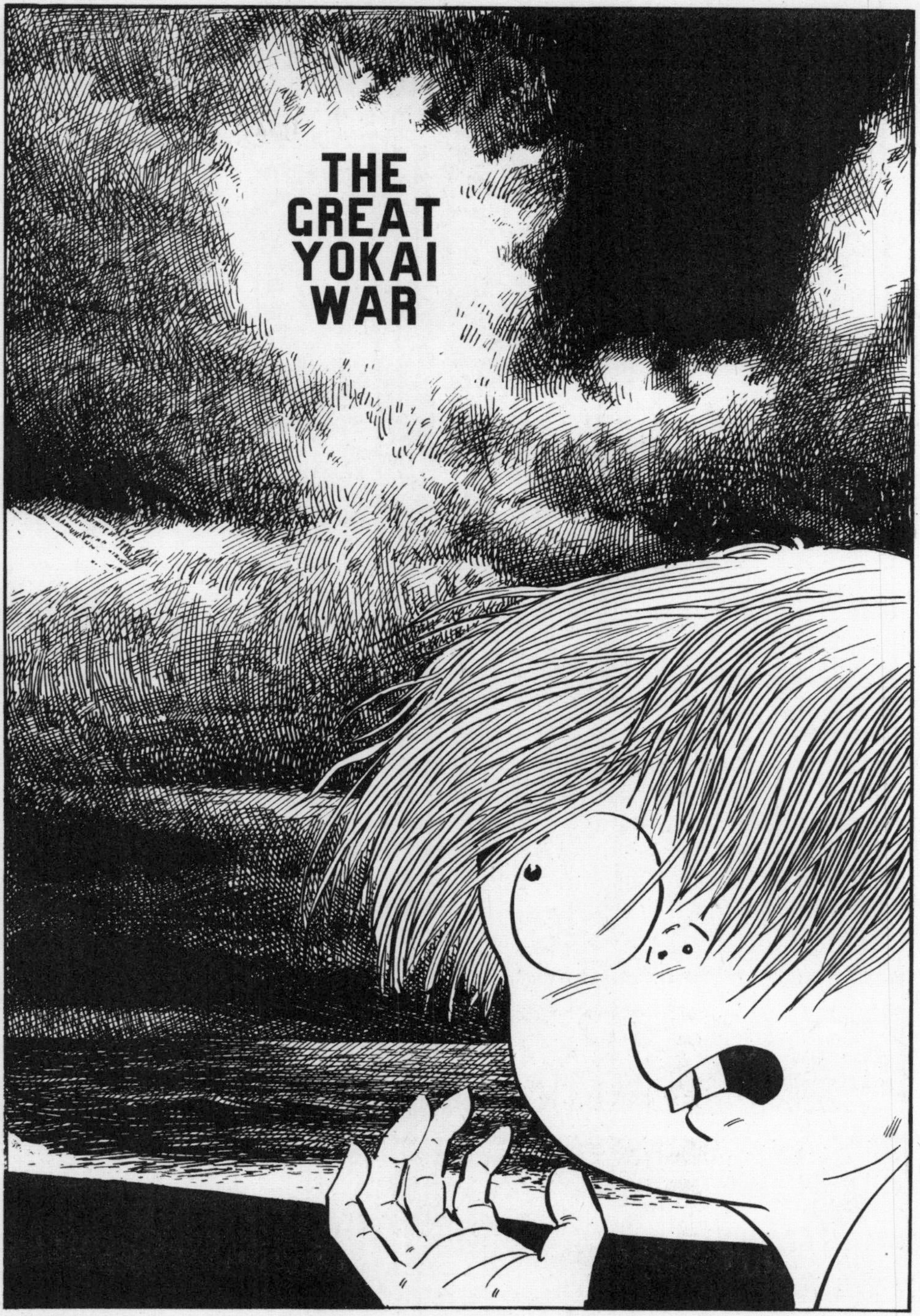
THE GREAT YOKAI WAR

WHAT? WHAT'S GOING ON?
...
KLAK KLEK
PEOPLE OF JAPAN, PLEASE LISTEN! OUR ISLAND HAS BEEN TAKEN OVER BY MONSTERS!
I WENT TO THE GOVERNMENT AND THE POLICE, BUT THEY REFUSE TO DO ANYTHING. THEY THINK I'M CRAZY!
PLEASE, PLEASE, I BEG YOU TO HELP—
MRRR MRRR
HEH, WHAT A KOOK!
MRRR MRRR
IT'S HOPELESS...
A-HUH-HUH! WHY WON'T ANYONE BELIEVE ME...
... ...

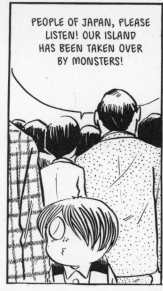

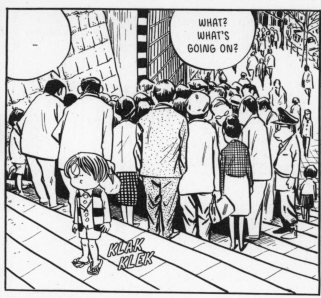

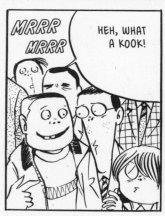

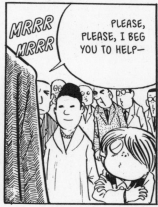

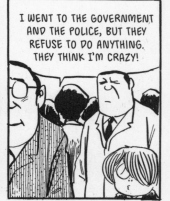

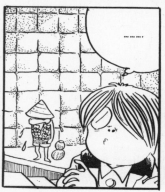

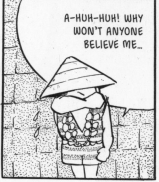

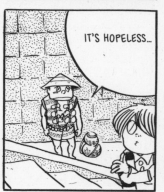

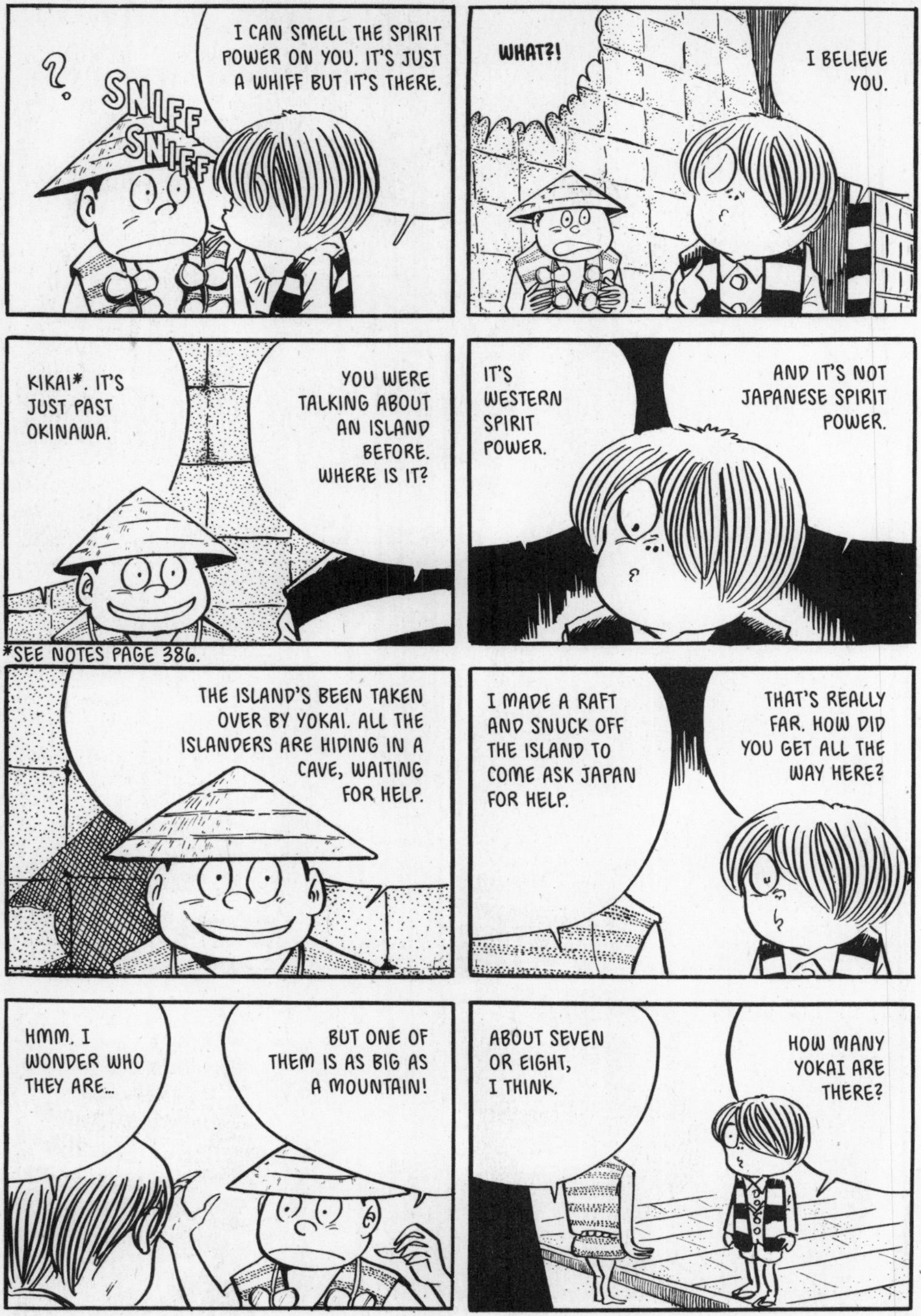
I BELIEVE YOU.
WHAT?!
I CAN SMELL THE SPIRIT POWER ON YOU. IT'S JUST A WHIFF BUT IT'S THERE.
SNIFF SNIFF
?
AND IT'S NOT JAPANESE SPIRIT POWER.
IT'S WESTERN SPIRIT POWER.
YOU WERE TALKING ABOUT AN ISLAND BEFORE. WHERE IS IT?
KIKAI*. IT'S JUST PAST OKINAWA.
THAT'S REALLY FAR. HOW DID YOU GET ALL THE WAY HERE?
I MADE A RAFT AND SNUCK OFF THE ISLAND TO COME ASK JAPAN FOR HELP.
THE ISLAND'S BEEN TAKEN OVER BY YOKAI. ALL THE ISLANDERS ARE HIDING IN A CAVE, WAITING FOR HELP.
HOW MANY YOKAI ARE THERE?
ABOUT SEVEN OR EIGHT, I THINK.
BUT ONE OF THEM IS AS BIG AS A MOUNTAIN!
HMM. I WONDER WHO THEY ARE...

*SEE NOTES PAGE 386.

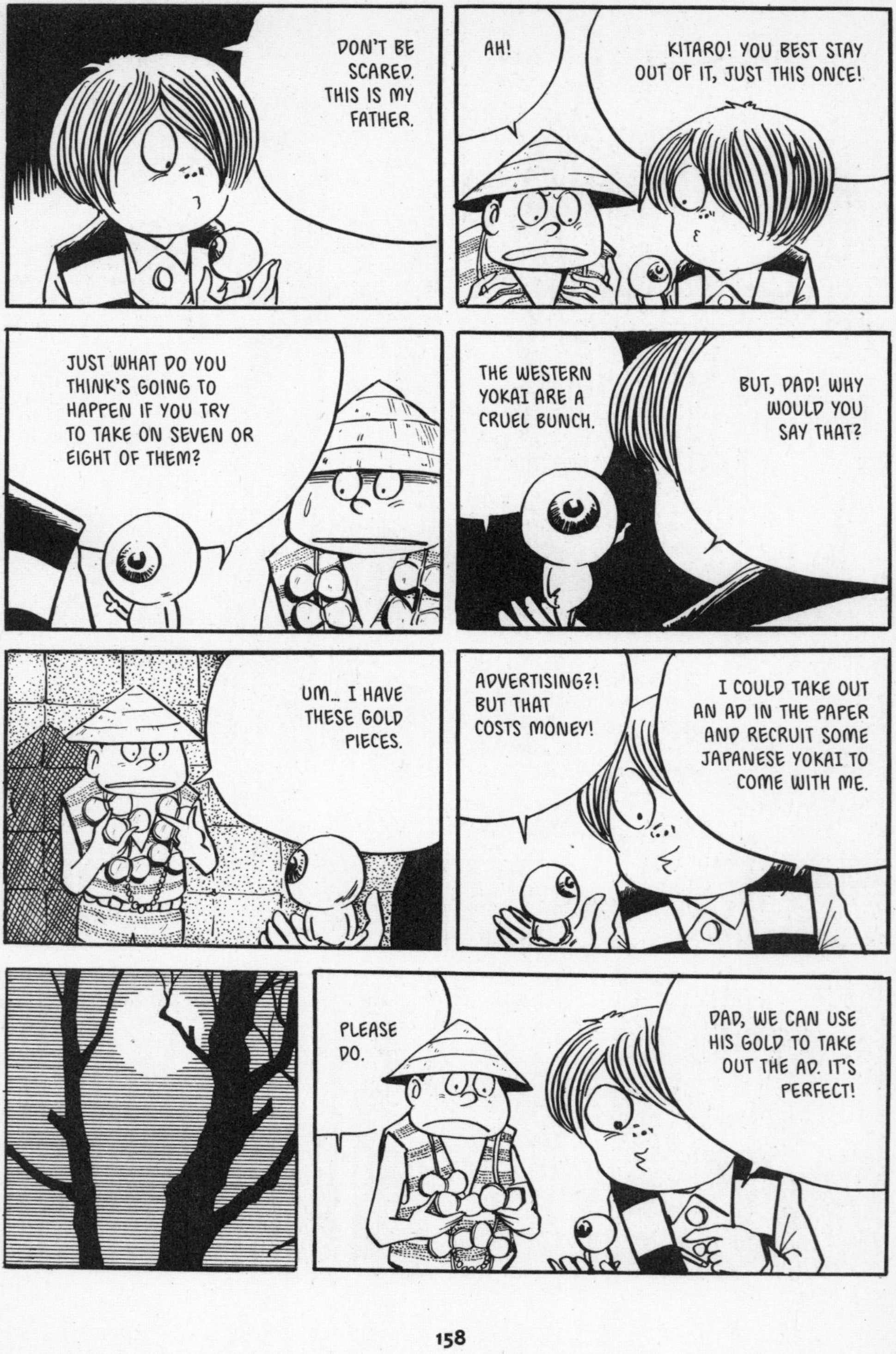
KITARO! YOU BEST STAY OUT OF IT, JUST THIS ONCE!
AH!
DON'T BE SCARED. THIS IS MY FATHER.
BUT, DAD! WHY WOULD YOU SAY THAT?
THE WESTERN YOKAI ARE A CRUEL BUNCH.
JUST WHAT DO YOU THINK'S GOING TO HAPPEN IF YOU TRY TO TAKE ON SEVEN OR EIGHT OF THEM?
I COULD TAKE OUT AN AD IN THE PAPER AND RECRUIT SOME JAPANESE YOKAI TO COME WITH ME.
ADVERTISING?! BUT THAT COSTS MONEY!
UM... I HAVE THESE GOLD PIECES.
DAD, WE CAN USE HIS GOLD TO TAKE OUT THE AD. IT'S PERFECT!
PLEASE DO.

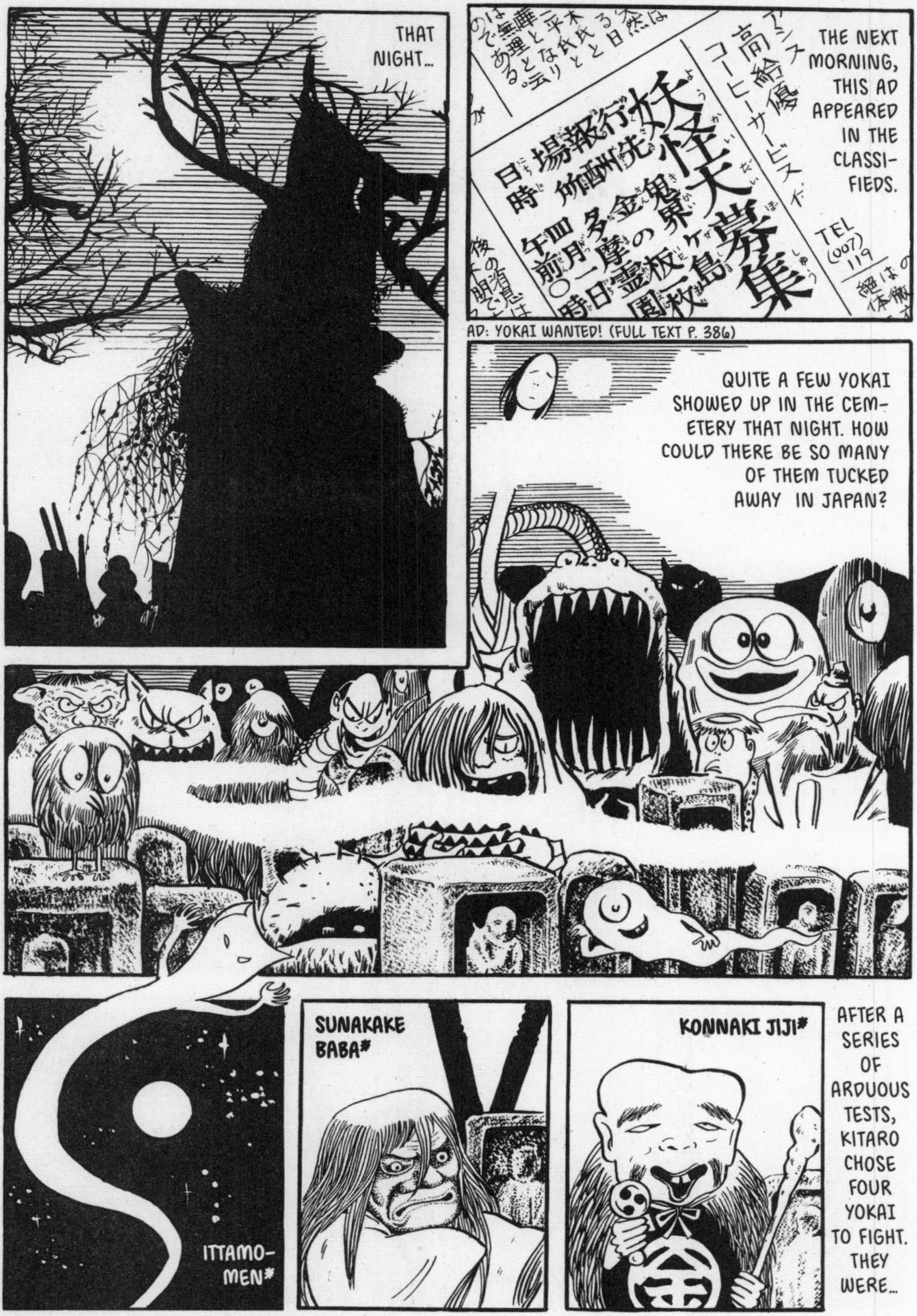
THE NEXT MORNING, THIS AD APPEARED IN THE CLASSIFIEDS.
高給優遇
コーヒーサービス付
妖怪大募集
行先 鬼界ケ島
報酬 金一封
場所 多摩霊園
日時 四月一日 午前〇時
TEL (007) 119
AD: YOKAI WANTED! (FULL TEXT P. 386)
QUITE A FEW YOKAI SHOWED UP IN THE CEMETERY THAT NIGHT. HOW COULD THERE BE SO MANY OF THEM TUCKED AWAY IN JAPAN?
THAT NIGHT...
AFTER A SERIES OF ARDUOUS TESTS, KITARO CHOSE FOUR YOKAI TO FIGHT. THEY WERE...
KONNAKI JIJI*
SUNAKAKE BABA*
ITTAMOMEN*

*SEE YOKAI GLOSSARY PAGE 391.

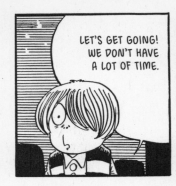

NURIKABE*
LET'S GET GOING! WE DON'T HAVE A LOT OF TIME.
MY RAFT IS THIS WAY.
MARCH
MARCH
HEY! KITARO!
OH! NEZUMI OTOKO!
I'M COMING TOO.

*SEE YOKAI GLOSSARY PAGE 392.

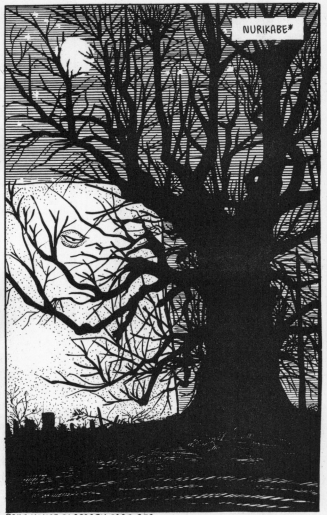

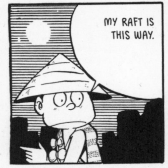

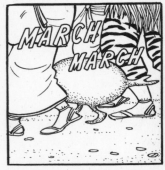

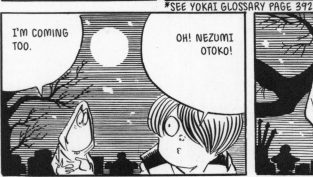

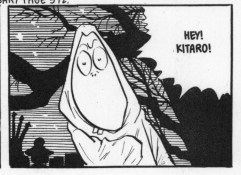

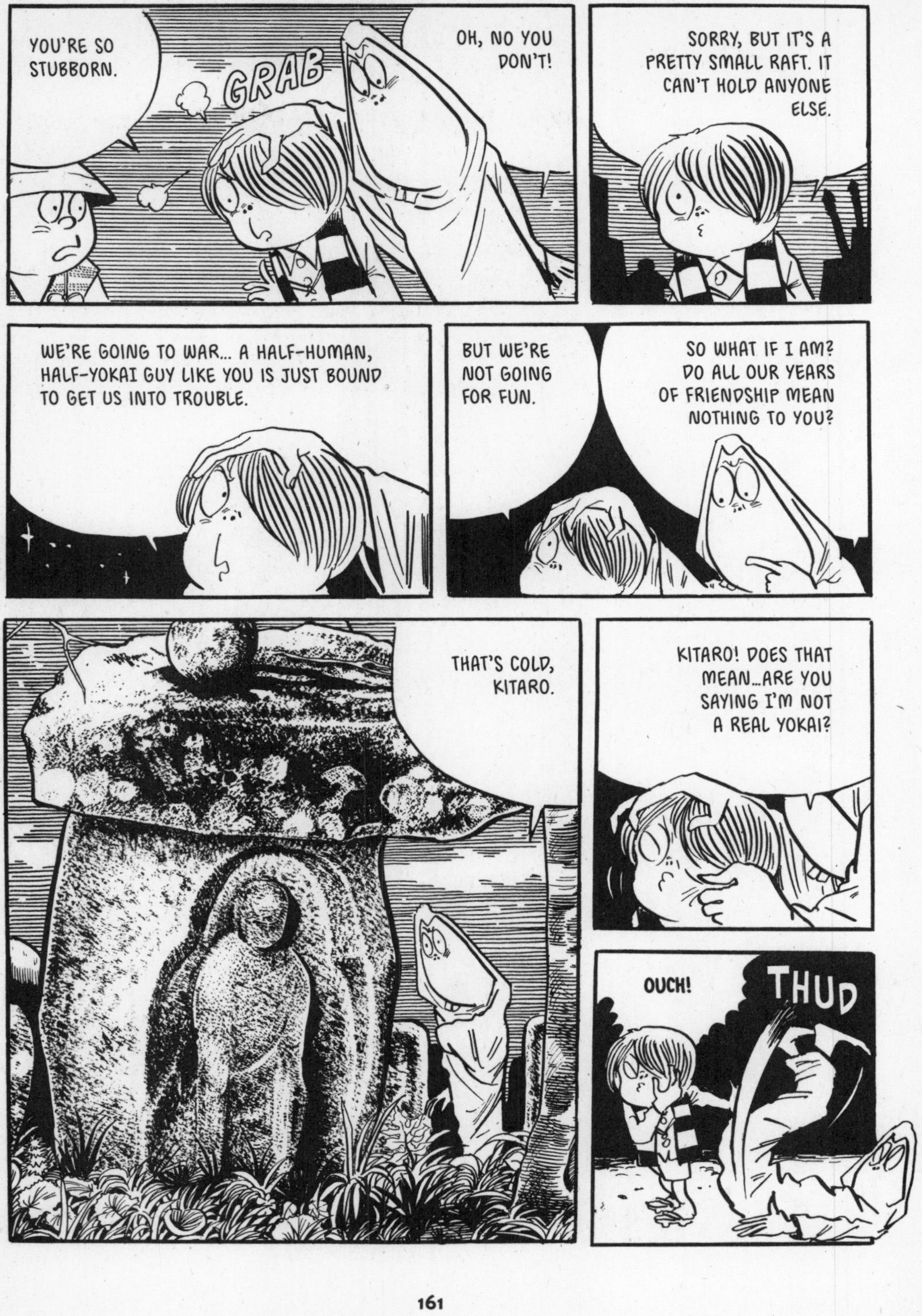
SORRY, BUT IT'S A PRETTY SMALL RAFT. IT CAN'T HOLD ANYONE ELSE.
OH, NO YOU DON'T!
GRAB
YOU'RE SO STUBBORN.
SO WHAT IF I AM? DO ALL OUR YEARS OF FRIENDSHIP MEAN NOTHING TO YOU?
BUT WE'RE NOT GOING FOR FUN.
WE'RE GOING TO WAR... A HALF-HUMAN, HALF-YOKAI GUY LIKE YOU IS JUST BOUND TO GET US INTO TROUBLE.
KITARO! DOES THAT MEAN...ARE YOU SAYING I'M NOT A REAL YOKAI?
THUD
OUCH!
THAT'S COLD, KITARO.

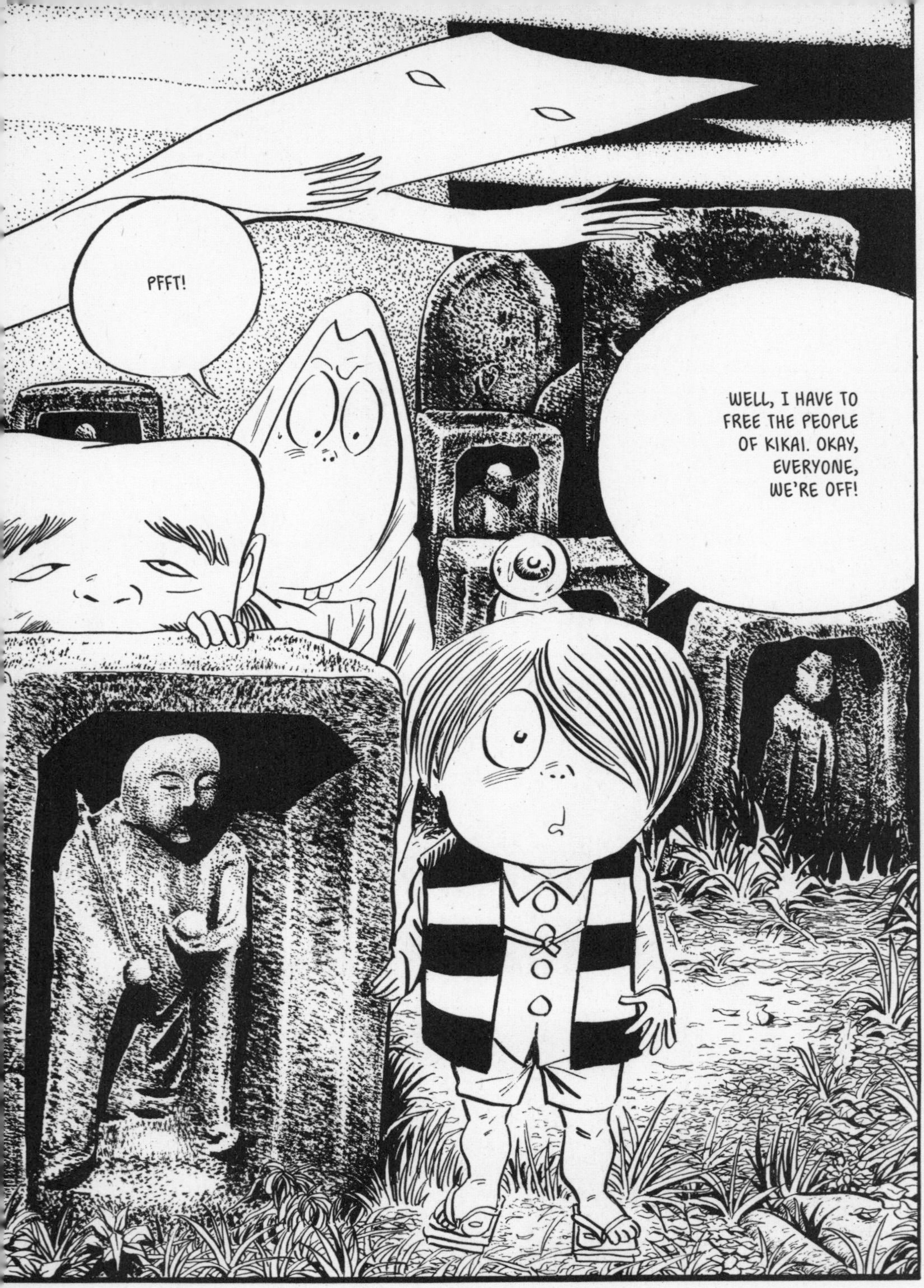
WELL, I HAVE TO FREE THE PEOPLE OF KIKAI. OKAY, EVERYONE, WE'RE OFF!
PFFT!

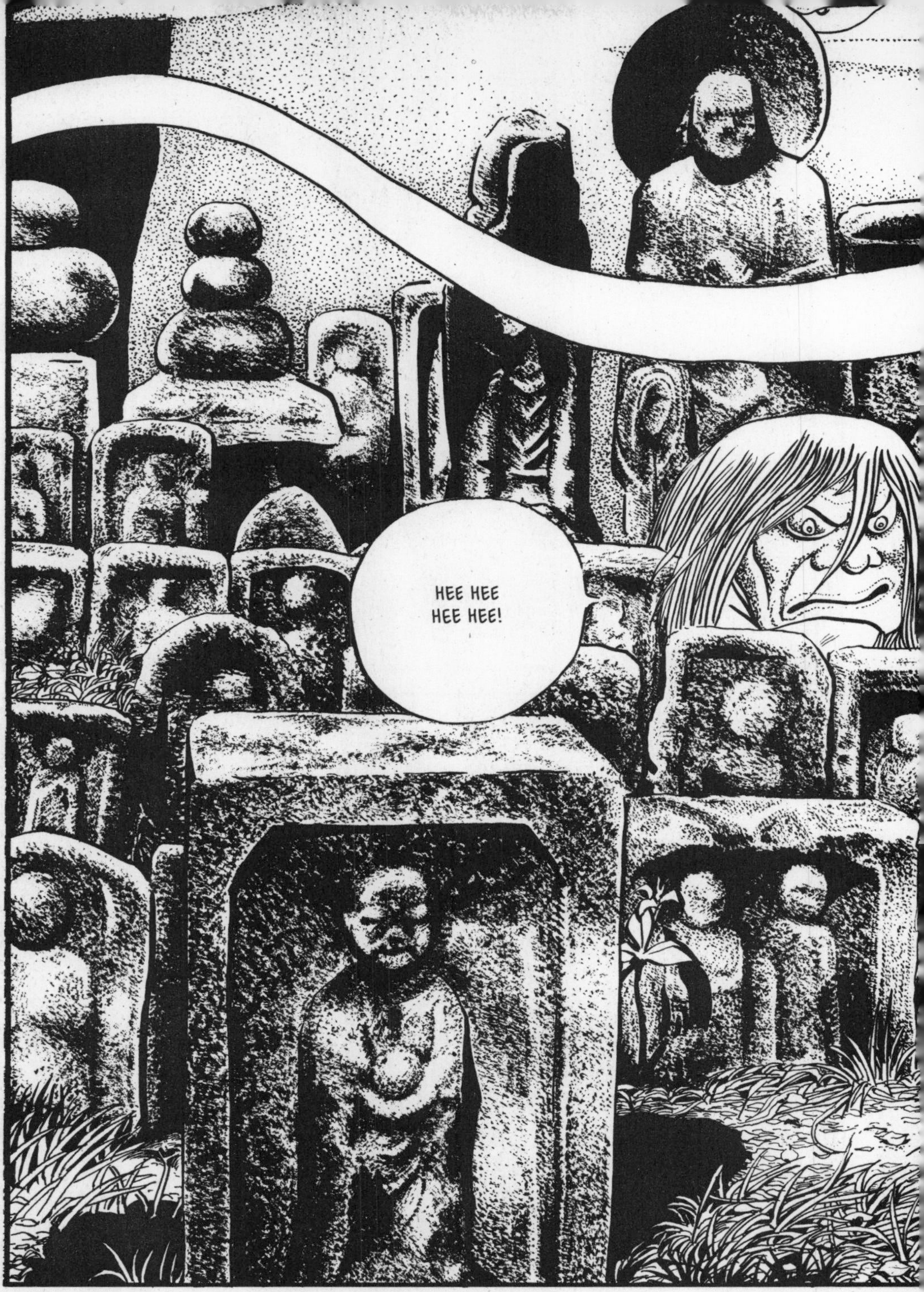
HEE HEE HEE HEE!

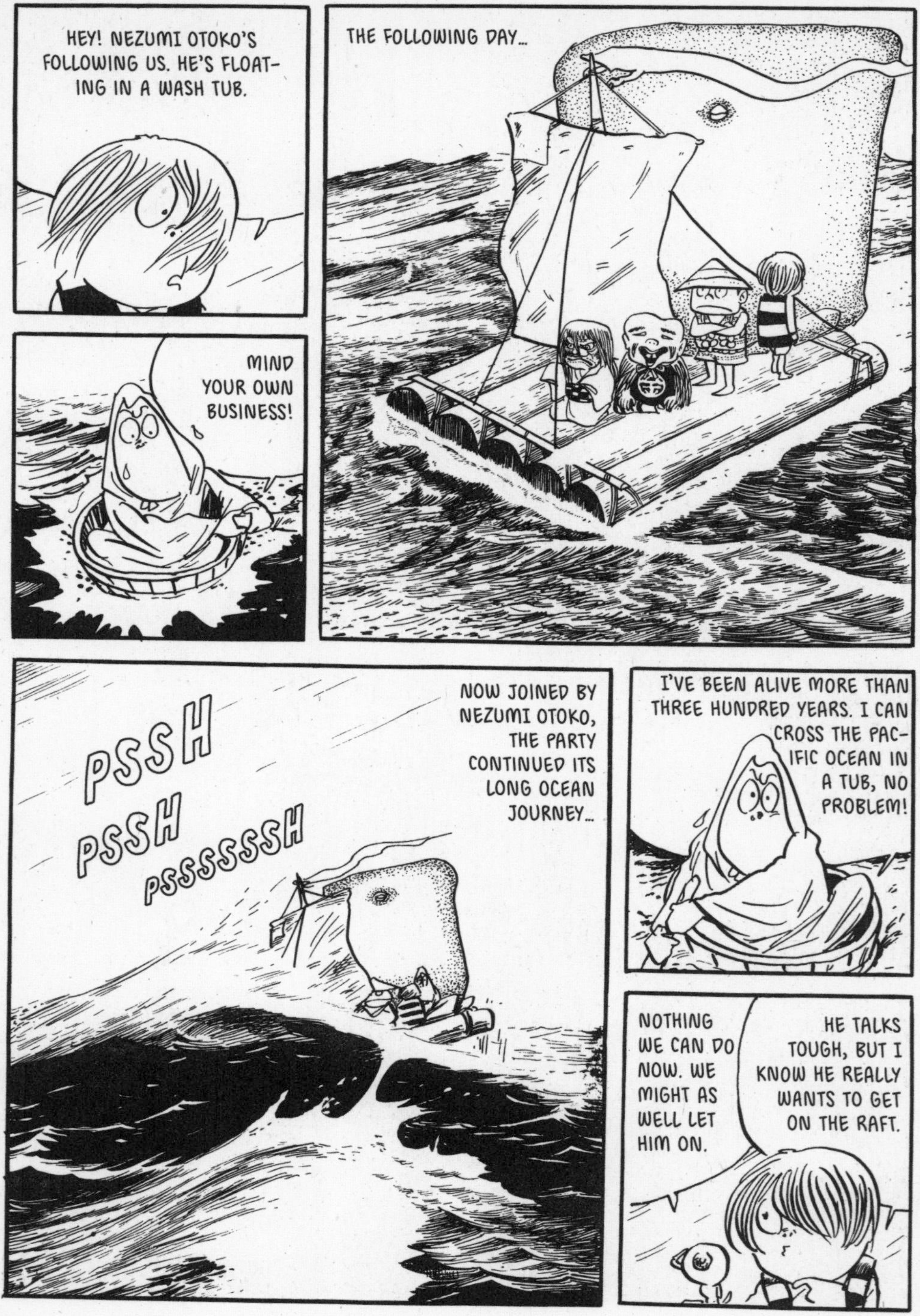
THE FOLLOWING DAY...
HEY! NEZUMI OTOKO'S FOLLOWING US. HE'S FLOAT-ING IN A WASH TUB.
MIND YOUR OWN BUSINESS!
I'VE BEEN ALIVE MORE THAN THREE HUNDRED YEARS. I CAN CROSS THE PAC-IFIC OCEAN IN A TUB, NO PROBLEM!
HE TALKS TOUGH, BUT I KNOW HE REALLY WANTS TO GET ON THE RAFT.
NOTHING WE CAN DO NOW. WE MIGHT AS WELL LET HIM ON.
NOW JOINED BY NEZUMI OTOKO, THE PARTY CONTINUED ITS LONG OCEAN JOURNEY...
PSSH
PSSH
PSSSSSSH

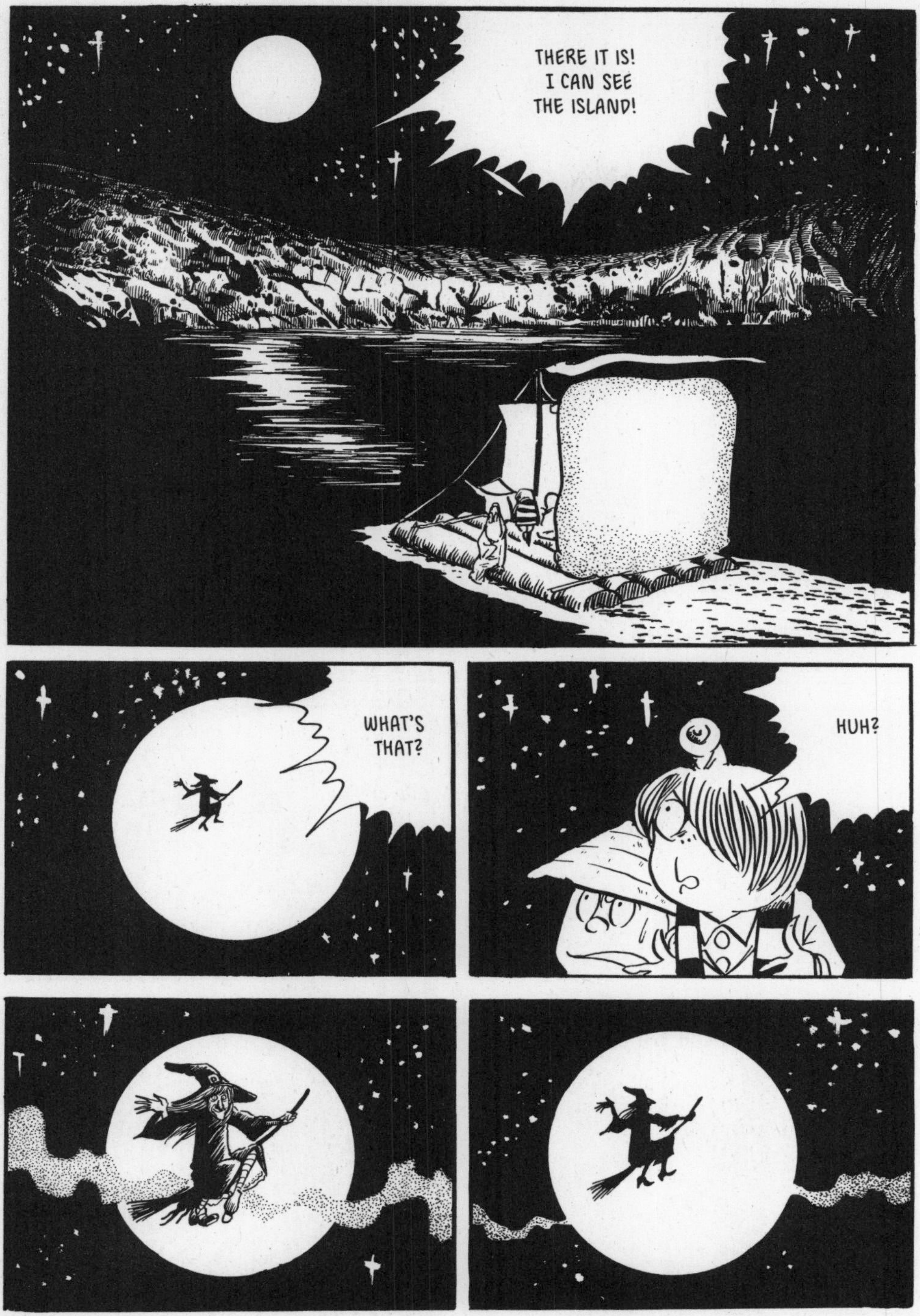
THERE IT IS! I CAN SEE THE ISLAND!
WHAT'S THAT?
HUH?

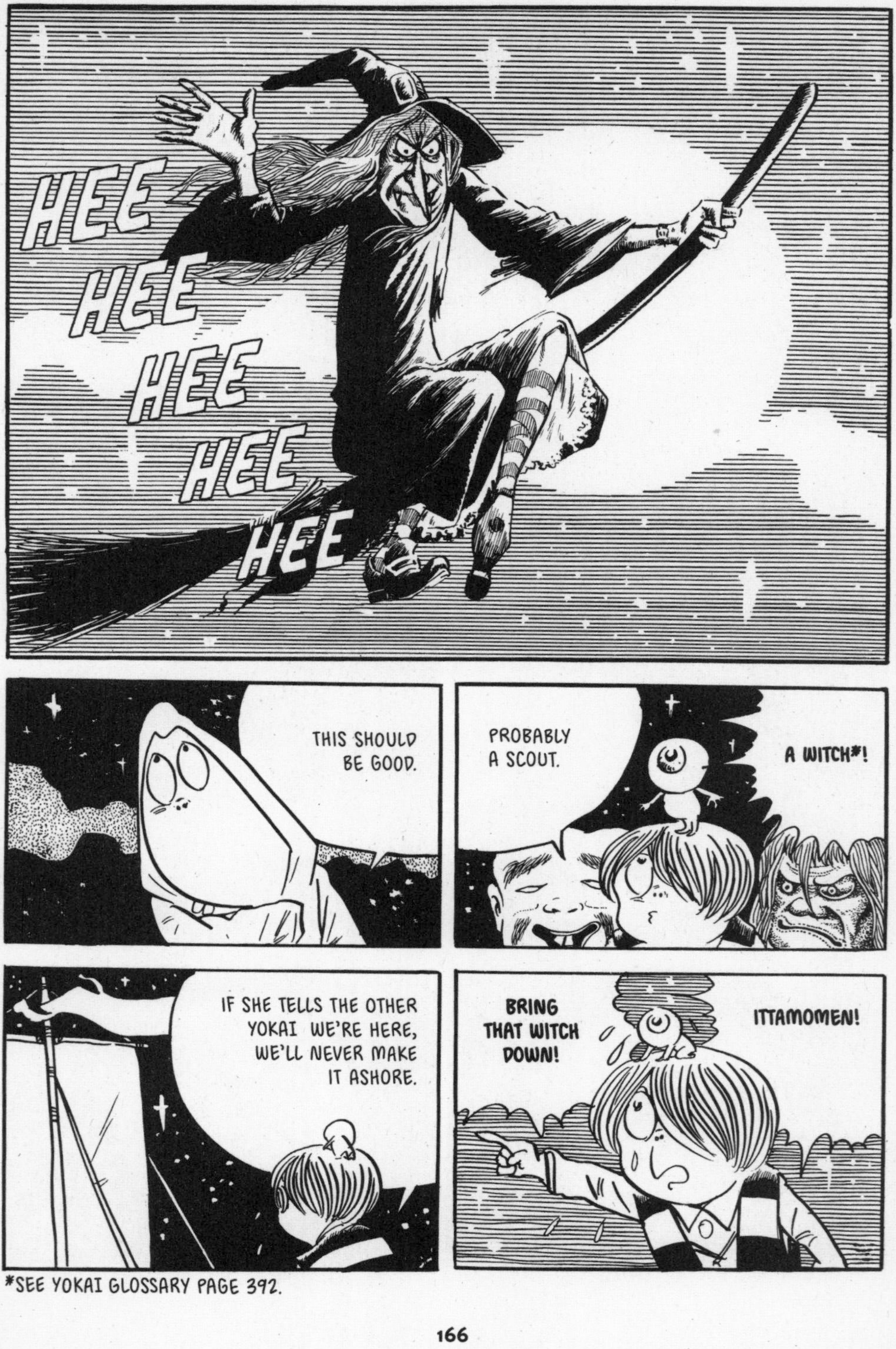
HEE HEE HEE HEE HEE
A WITCH*!
PROBABLY A SCOUT.
THIS SHOULD BE GOOD.
ITTAMOMEN!
BRING THAT WITCH DOWN!
IF SHE TELLS THE OTHER YOKAI WE'RE HERE, WE'LL NEVER MAKE IT ASHORE.

*SEE YOKAI GLOSSARY PAGE 392.

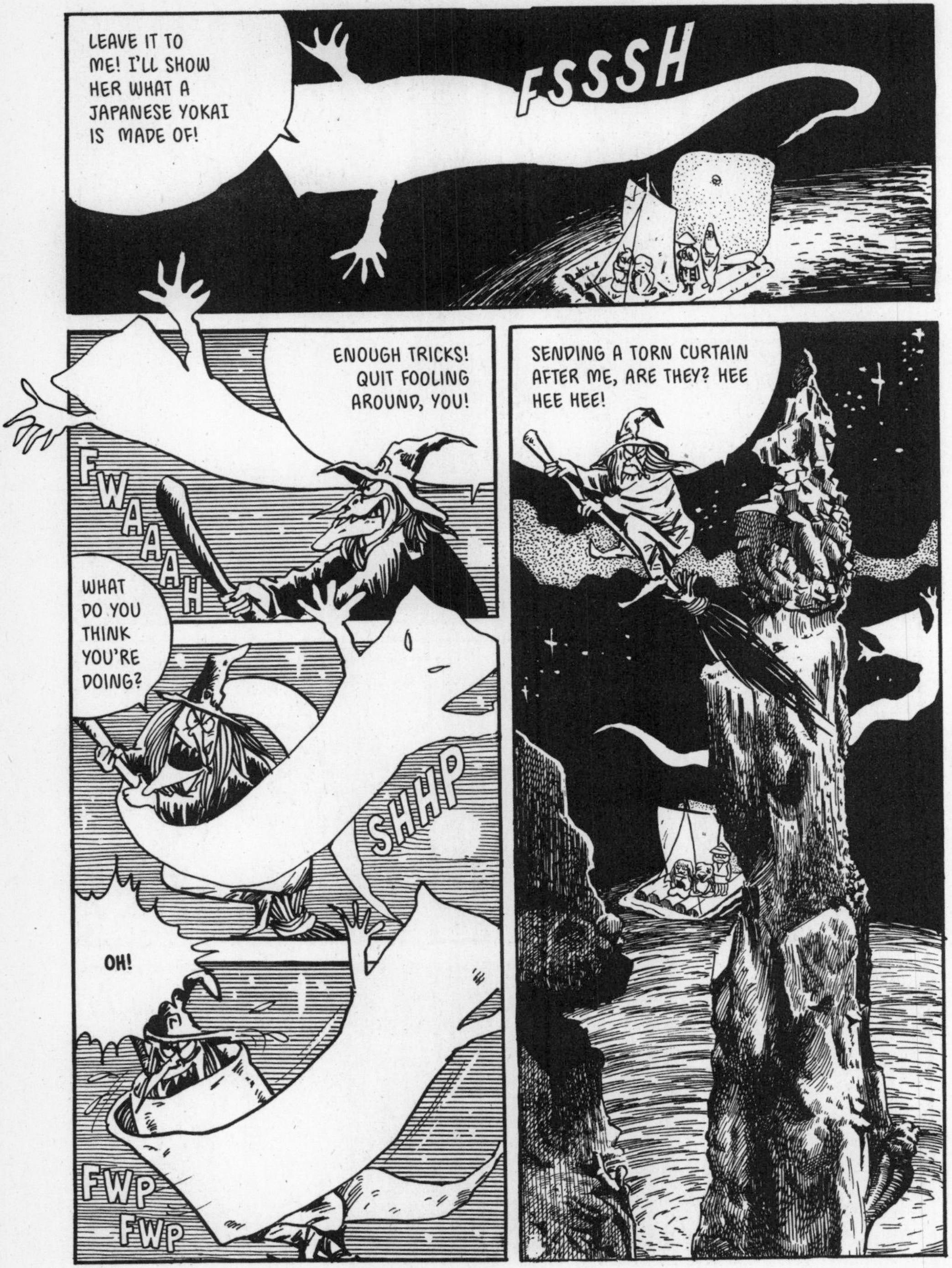
FSSSH
LEAVE IT TO ME! I'LL SHOW HER WHAT A JAPANESE YOKAI IS MADE OF!
SENDING A TORN CURTAIN AFTER ME, ARE THEY? HEE HEE HEE!
ENOUGH TRICKS! QUIT FOOLING AROUND, YOU!
FWAAAAH
WHAT DO YOU THINK YOU'RE DOING?
SHHP
OH!
FWP FWP

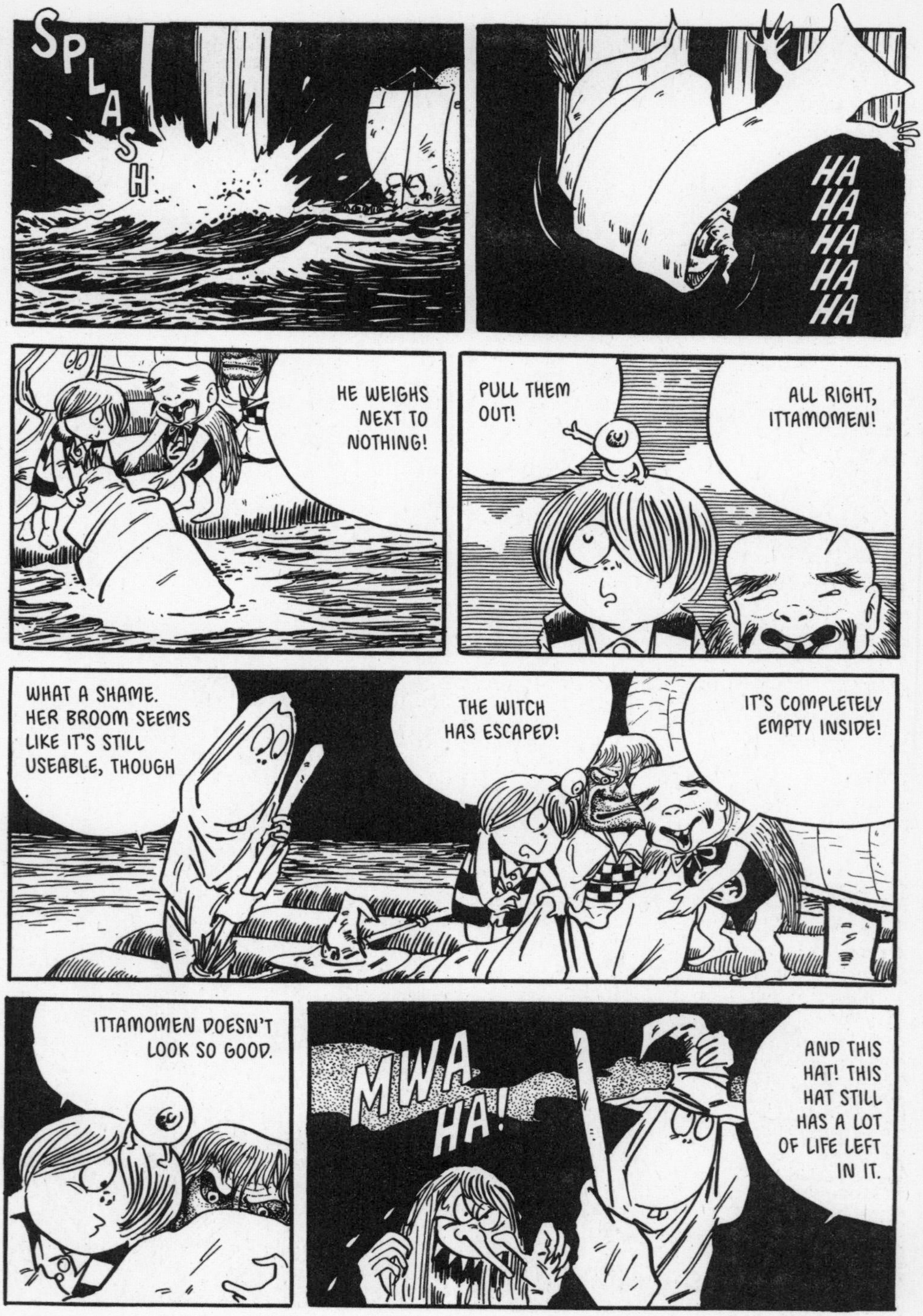

HA HA HA HA HA HA
SPLASH
ALL RIGHT, ITTAMOMEN!
PULL THEM OUT!
HE WEIGHS NEXT TO NOTHING!
IT'S COMPLETELY EMPTY INSIDE!
THE WITCH HAS ESCAPED!
WHAT A SHAME. HER BROOM SEEMS LIKE IT'S STILL USEABLE, THOUGH
AND THIS HAT! THIS HAT STILL HAS A LOT OF LIFE LEFT IN IT.
MWA HA!
ITTAMOMEN DOESN'T LOOK SO GOOD.

HE'S NOT DEAD, IS HE?
THERE'S A NEEDLE THROUGH HIS HEART!
YANK
TAKING A VETERAN LIKE ITTAMOMEN DOWN LIKE THIS...
OUR ENEMY'S THE REAL THING.
AAAAAH!
NEZUMI OTOKO!
EE HEE HEE HEE HEE HEE HEE
HEEEELP!

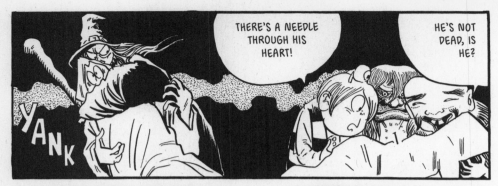

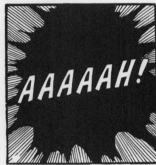

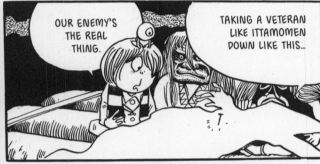

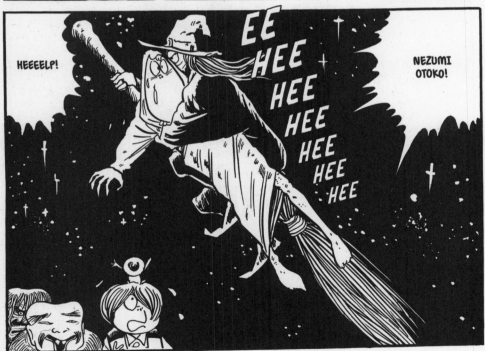

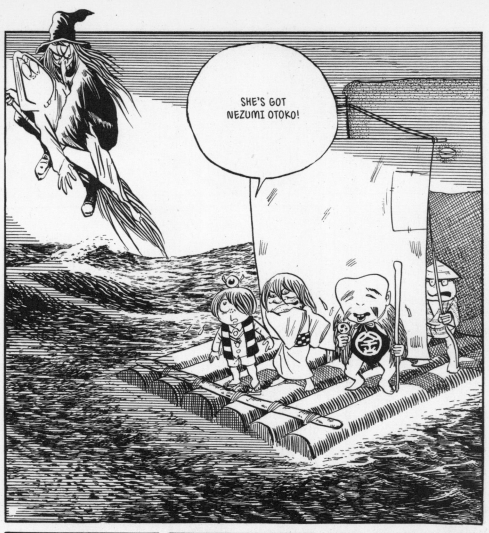

SHE'S GOT NEZUMI OTOKO!
EE HEE HEE HEE HEE HEE HEE HEE
THE FIRST VICTORY IS THEIRS...
KITARO! LOOK! IN FRONT OF US!

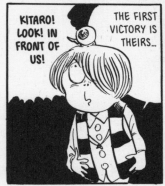

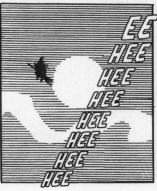

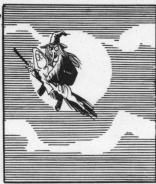

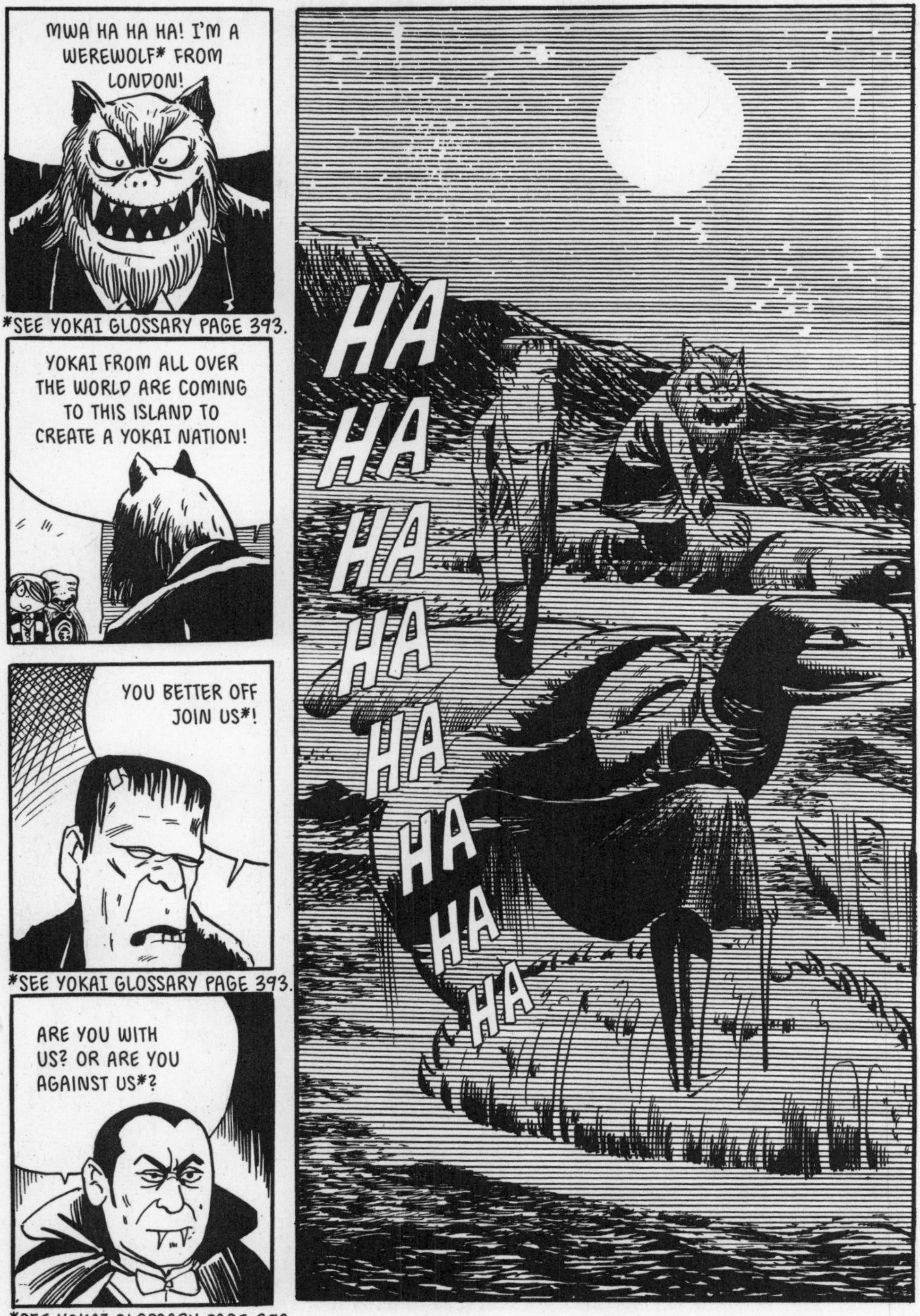
HA HA HA HA HA HA HA HA HA
MWA HA HA HA! I'M A WEREWOLF* FROM LONDON!
*SEE YOKAI GLOSSARY PAGE 393.
YOKAI FROM ALL OVER THE WORLD ARE COMING TO THIS ISLAND TO CREATE A YOKAI NATION!
YOU BETTER OFF JOIN US*!
*SEE YOKAI GLOSSARY PAGE 393.
ARE YOU WITH US? OR ARE YOU AGAINST US*?
*SEE YOKAI GLOSSARY PAGE 392.

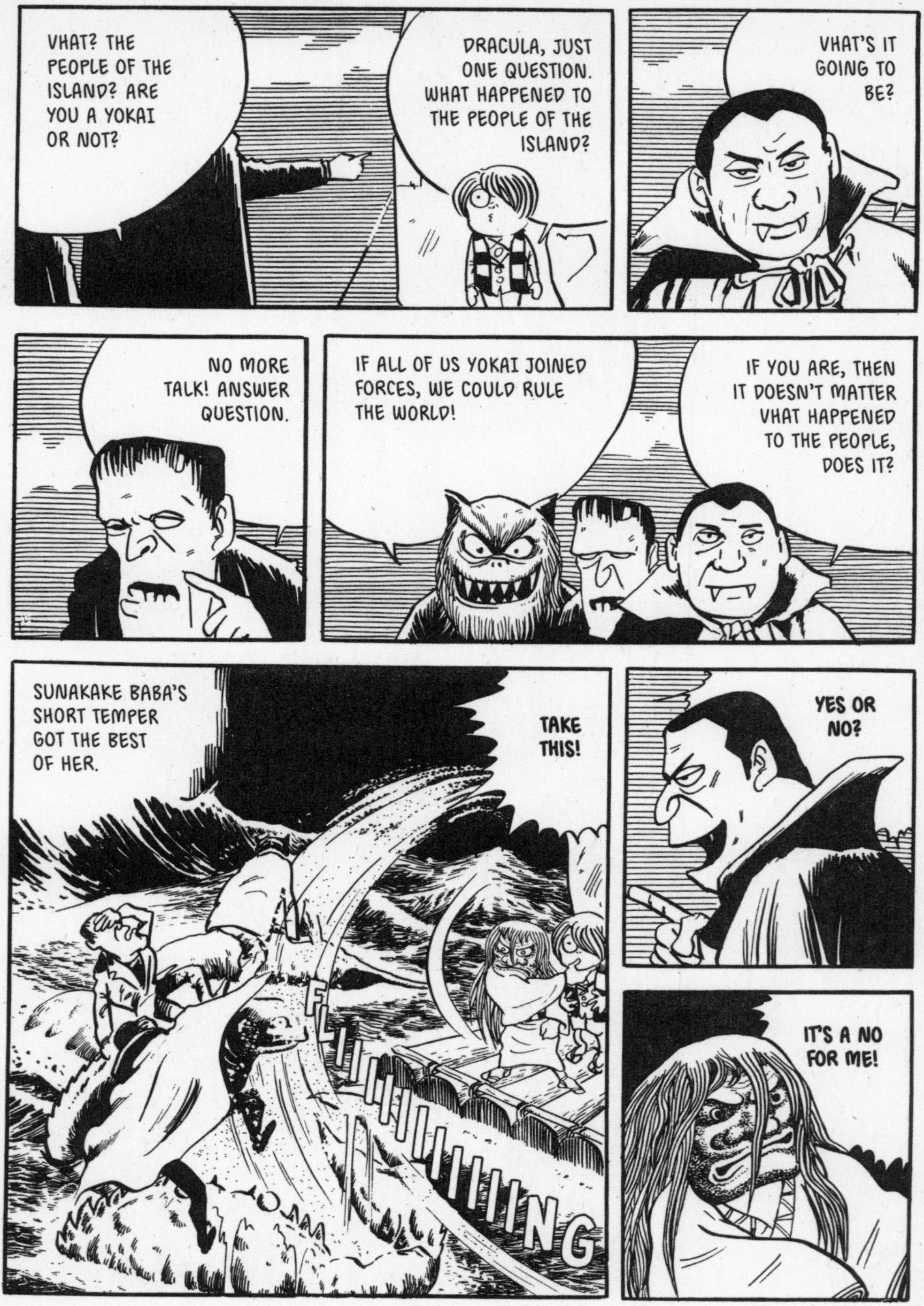
VHAT'S IT GOING TO BE?
DRACULA, JUST ONE QUESTION. WHAT HAPPENED TO THE PEOPLE OF THE ISLAND?
VHAT? THE PEOPLE OF THE ISLAND? ARE YOU A YOKAI OR NOT?
IF YOU ARE, THEN IT DOESN'T MATTER VHAT HAPPENED TO THE PEOPLE, DOES IT?
IF ALL OF US YOKAI JOINED FORCES, WE COULD RULE THE WORLD!
NO MORE TALK! ANSWER QUESTION.
YES OR NO?
IT'S A NO FOR ME!
TAKE THIS!
SUNAKAKE BABA'S SHORT TEMPER GOT THE BEST OF HER.
FLIIIIIIIIIIIIING

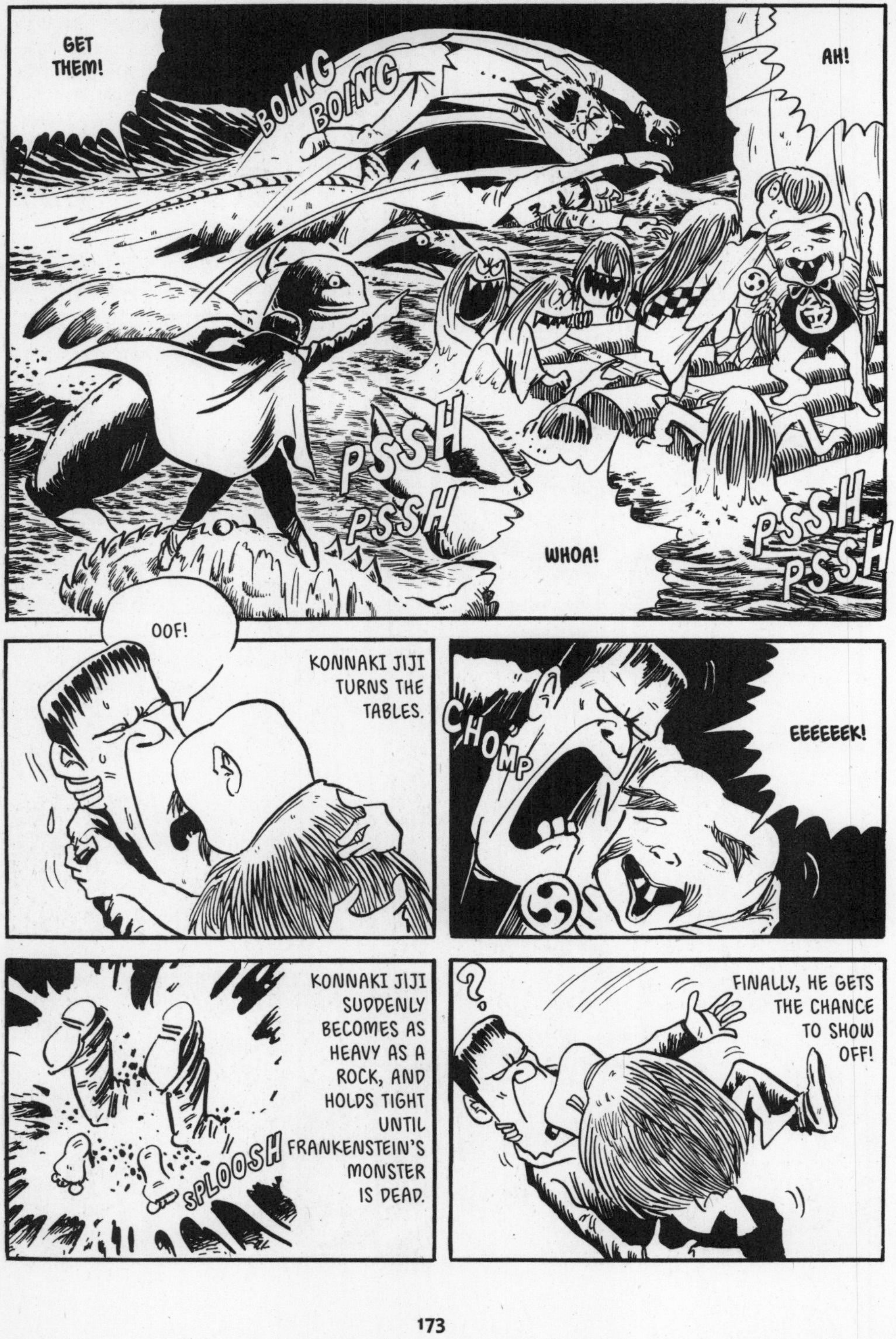
AH!
GET THEM!
BOING
BOING
PSSH
PSSH
WHOA!
PSSH
PSSH
EEEEEEK!
CHOMP
KONNAKI JIJI TURNS THE TABLES.
OOF!
FINALLY, HE GETS THE CHANCE TO SHOW OFF!
?
KONNAKI JIJI SUDDENLY BECOMES AS HEAVY AS A ROCK, AND HOLDS TIGHT UNTIL FRANKENSTEIN'S MONSTER IS DEAD.
SPLOOSH

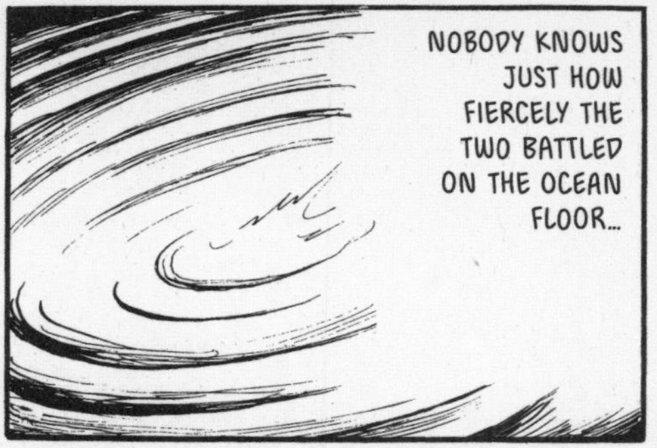
NOBODY KNOWS JUST HOW FIERCELY THE TWO BATTLED ON THE OCEAN FLOOR...

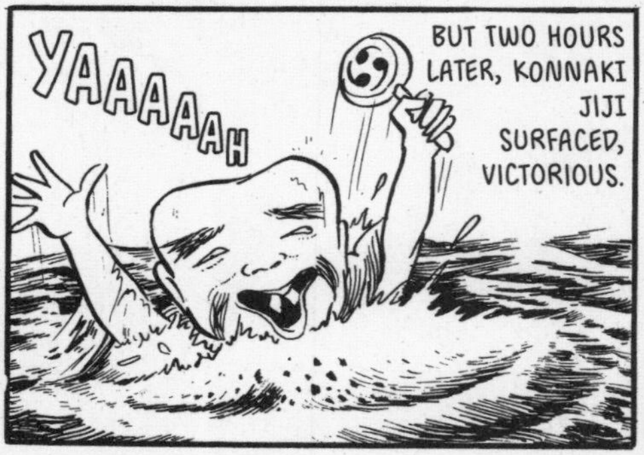
BUT TWO HOURS LATER, KONNAKI JIJI SURFACED, VICTORIOUS.
YAAAAAAH

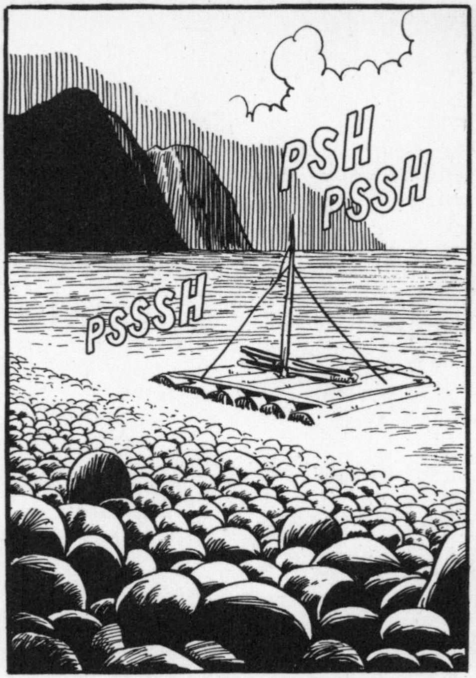
PSH
PSSH
PSSSH

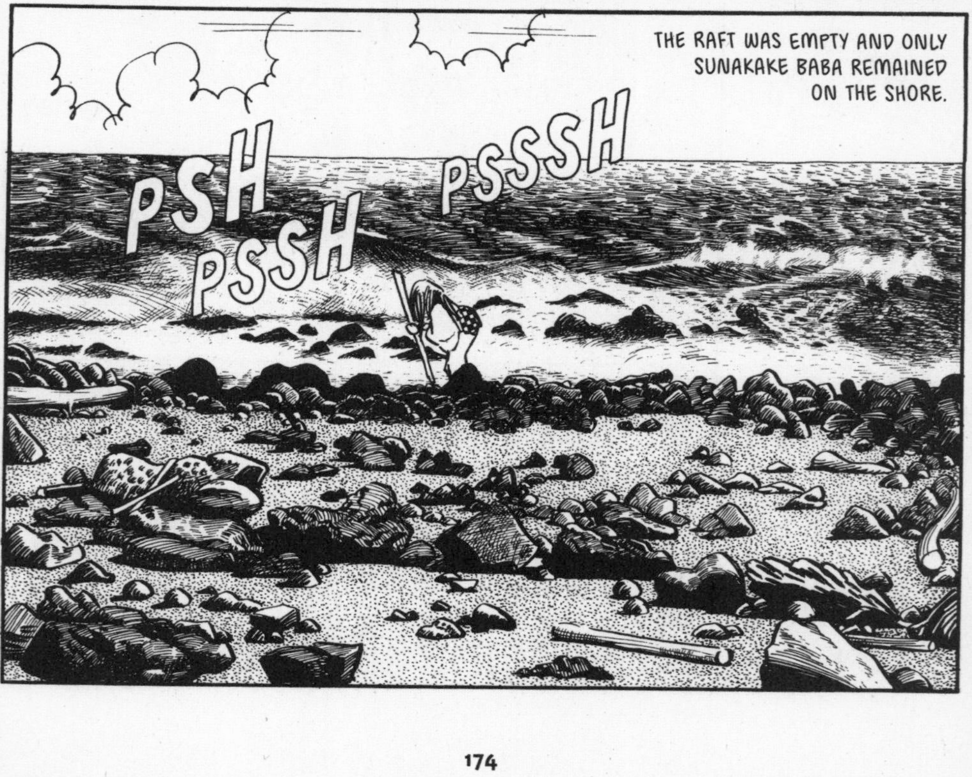
THE RAFT WAS EMPTY AND ONLY SUNAKAKE BABA REMAINED ON THE SHORE.
PSSSH
PSH
PSSH

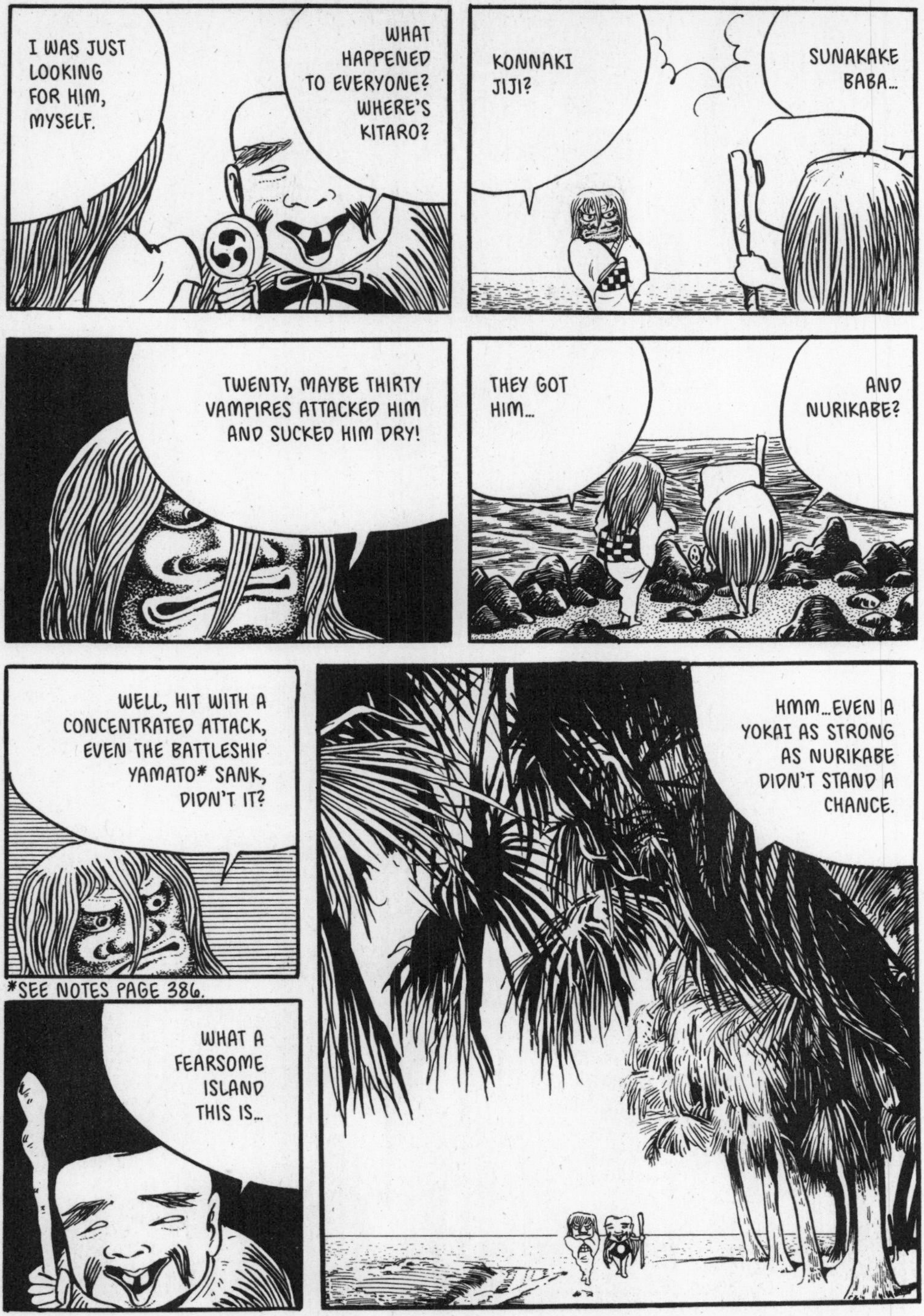
SUNAKAKE BABA...
KONNAKI JIJI?
WHAT HAPPENED TO EVERYONE? WHERE'S KITARO?
I WAS JUST LOOKING FOR HIM, MYSELF.
AND NURIKABE?
THEY GOT HIM...
TWENTY, MAYBE THIRTY VAMPIRES ATTACKED HIM AND SUCKED HIM DRY!
HMM...EVEN A YOKAI AS STRONG AS NURIKABE DIDN'T STAND A CHANCE.
WELL, HIT WITH A CONCENTRATED ATTACK, EVEN THE BATTLESHIP YAMATO* SANK, DIDN'T IT?
WHAT A FEARSOME ISLAND THIS IS...

*SEE NOTES PAGE 386.

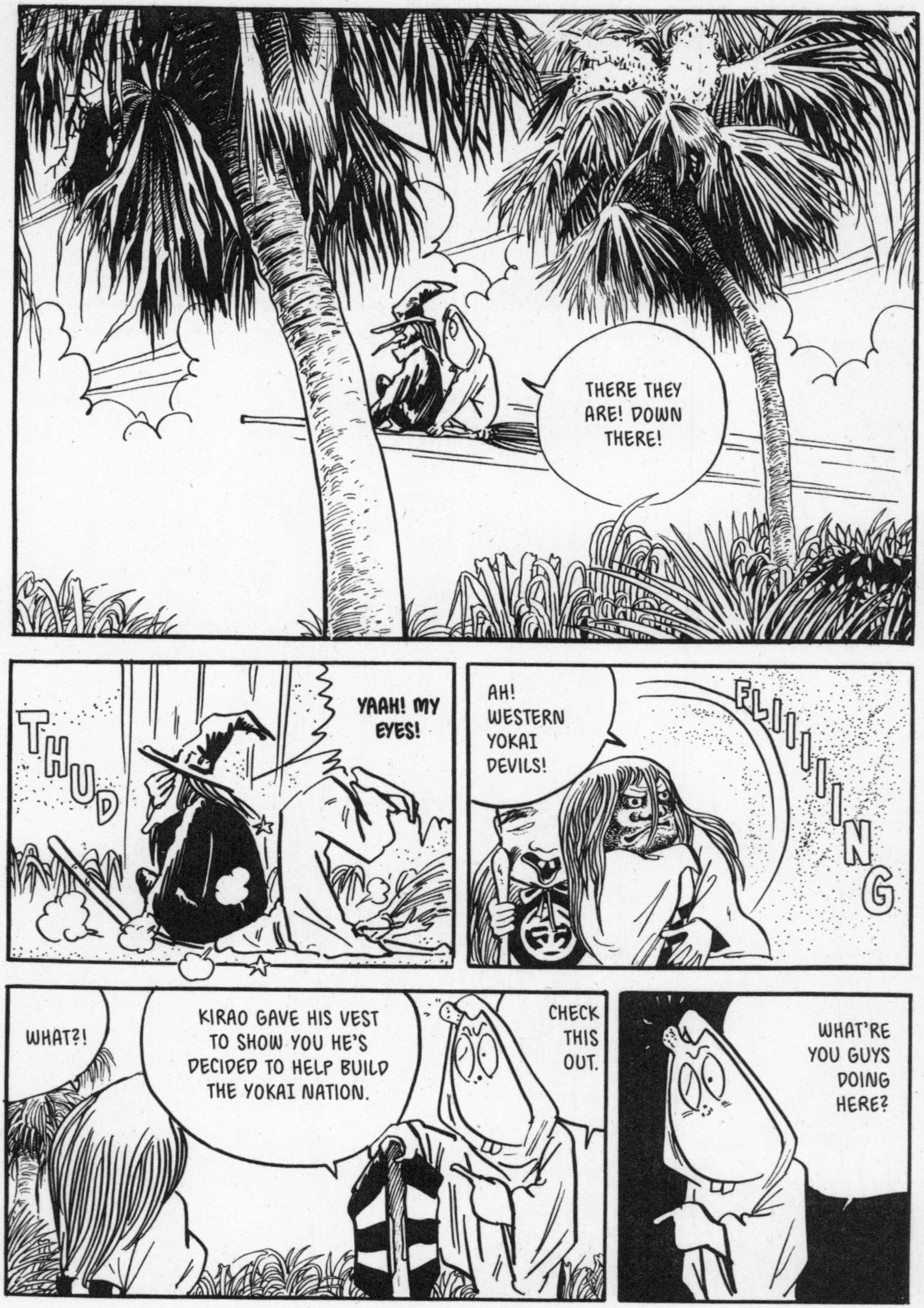
THERE THEY ARE! DOWN THERE!
AH! WESTERN YOKAI DEVILS!
FLIIIIING
YAAH! MY EYES!
THUD
WHAT'RE YOU GUYS DOING HERE?
CHECK THIS OUT.
KIRAO GAVE HIS VEST TO SHOW YOU HE'S DECIDED TO HELP BUILD THE YOKAI NATION.
WHAT?!

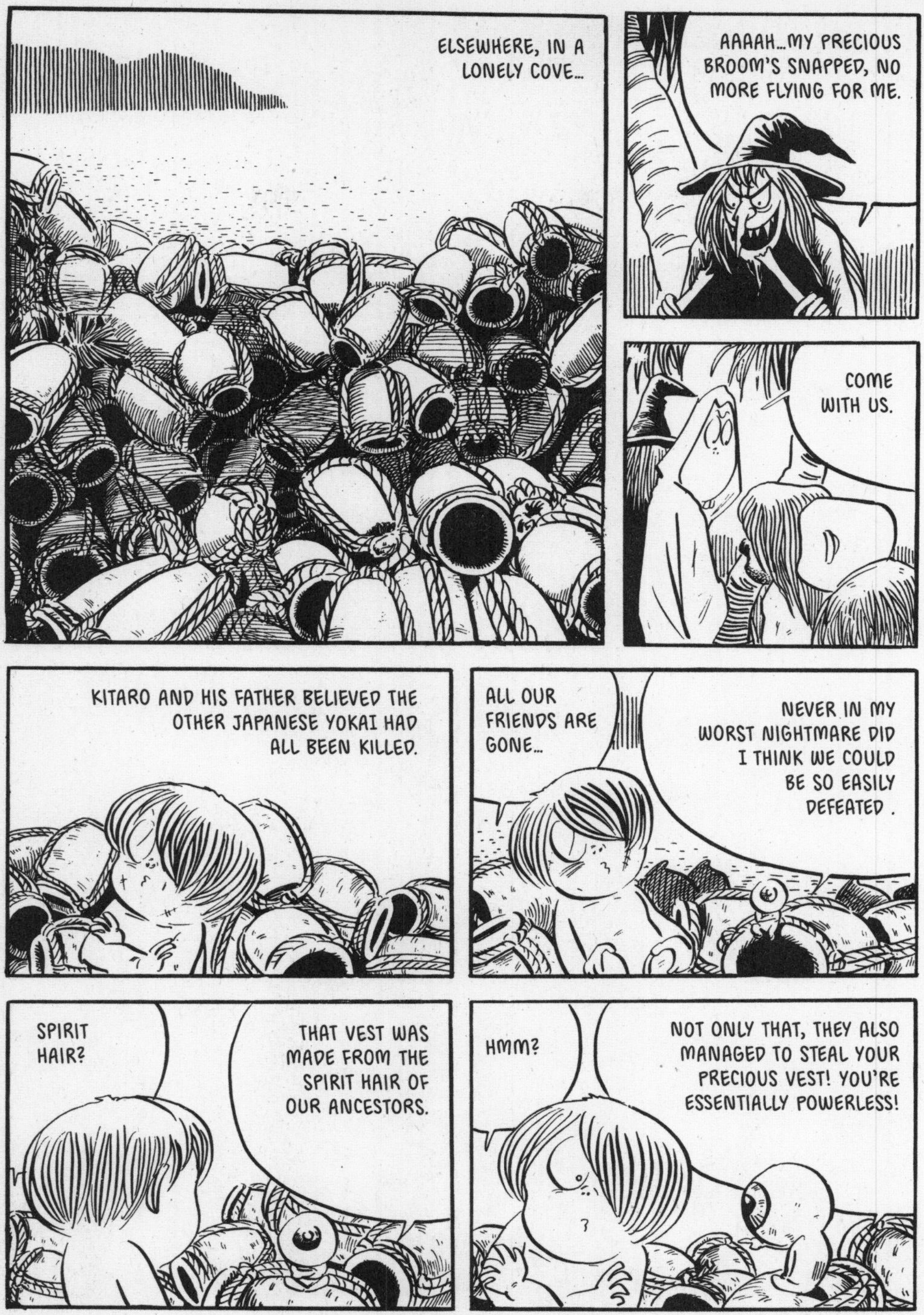
AAAAH...MY PRECIOUS BROOM'S SNAPPED, NO MORE FLYING FOR ME.
COME WITH US.
ELSEWHERE, IN A LONELY COVE...
NEVER IN MY WORST NIGHTMARE DID I THINK WE COULD BE SO EASILY DEFEATED .
ALL OUR FRIENDS ARE GONE...
KITARO AND HIS FATHER BELIEVED THE OTHER JAPANESE YOKAI HAD ALL BEEN KILLED.
NOT ONLY THAT, THEY ALSO MANAGED TO STEAL YOUR PRECIOUS VEST! YOU'RE ESSENTIALLY POWERLESS!
HMM?
THAT VEST WAS MADE FROM THE SPIRIT HAIR OF OUR ANCESTORS.
SPIRIT HAIR?

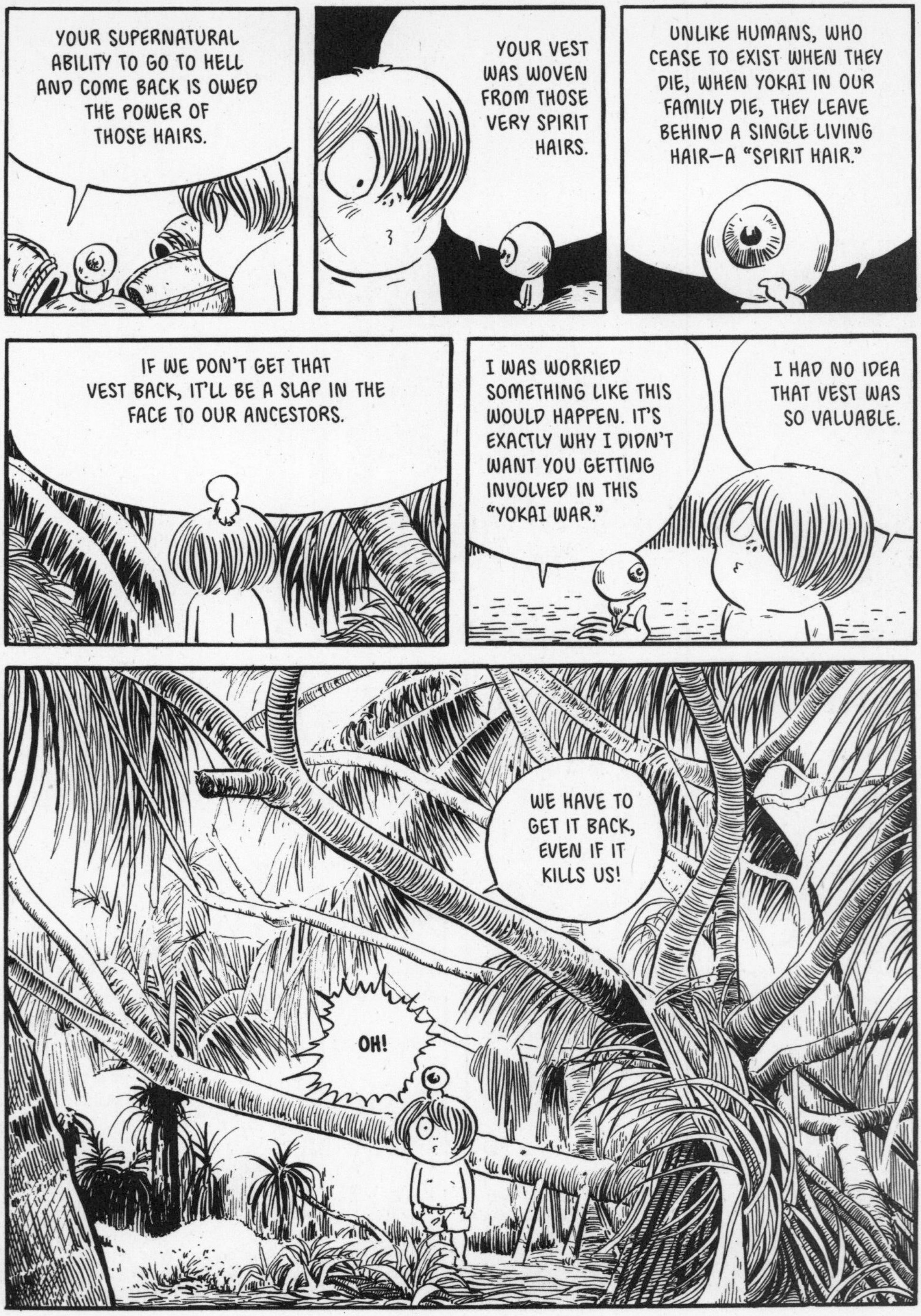
UNLIKE HUMANS, WHO CEASE TO EXIST WHEN THEY DIE, WHEN YOKAI IN OUR FAMILY DIE, THEY LEAVE BEHIND A SINGLE LIVING HAIR—A "SPIRIT HAIR."
YOUR VEST WAS WOVEN FROM THOSE VERY SPIRIT HAIRS.
YOUR SUPERNATURAL ABILITY TO GO TO HELL AND COME BACK IS OWED THE POWER OF THOSE HAIRS.
I HAD NO IDEA THAT VEST WAS SO VALUABLE.
I WAS WORRIED SOMETHING LIKE THIS WOULD HAPPEN. IT'S EXACTLY WHY I DIDN'T WANT YOU GETTING INVOLVED IN THIS "YOKAI WAR."
IF WE DON'T GET THAT VEST BACK, IT'LL BE A SLAP IN THE FACE TO OUR ANCESTORS.
WE HAVE TO GET IT BACK, EVEN IF IT KILLS US!
OH!

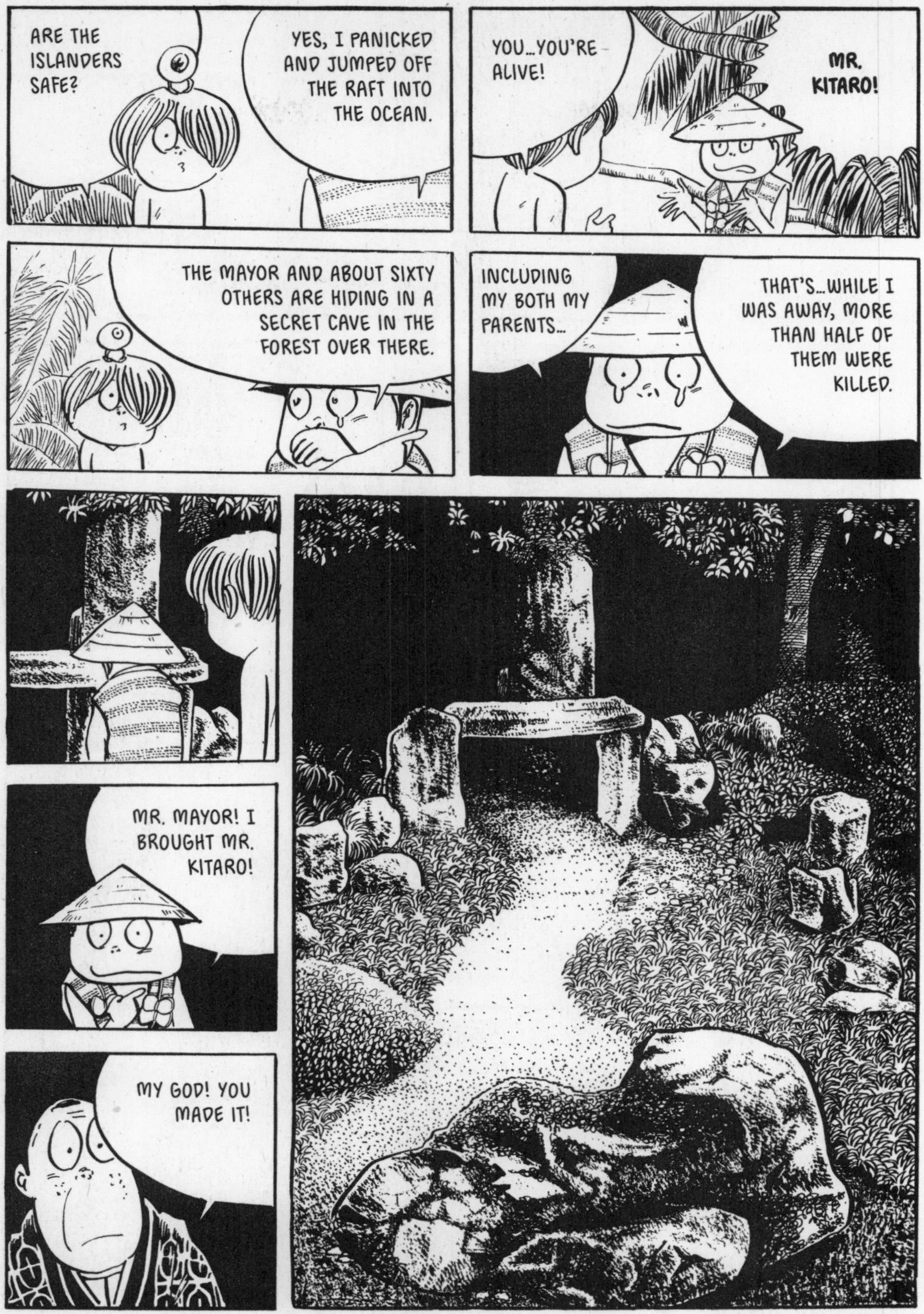
MR. KITARO!
YOU...YOU'RE ALIVE!
YES, I PANICKED AND JUMPED OFF THE RAFT INTO THE OCEAN.
ARE THE ISLANDERS SAFE?
THAT'S...WHILE I WAS AWAY, MORE THAN HALF OF THEM WERE KILLED.
INCLUDING MY BOTH MY PARENTS...
THE MAYOR AND ABOUT SIXTY OTHERS ARE HIDING IN A SECRET CAVE IN THE FOREST OVER THERE.
MR. MAYOR! I BROUGHT MR. KITARO!
MY GOD! YOU MADE IT!

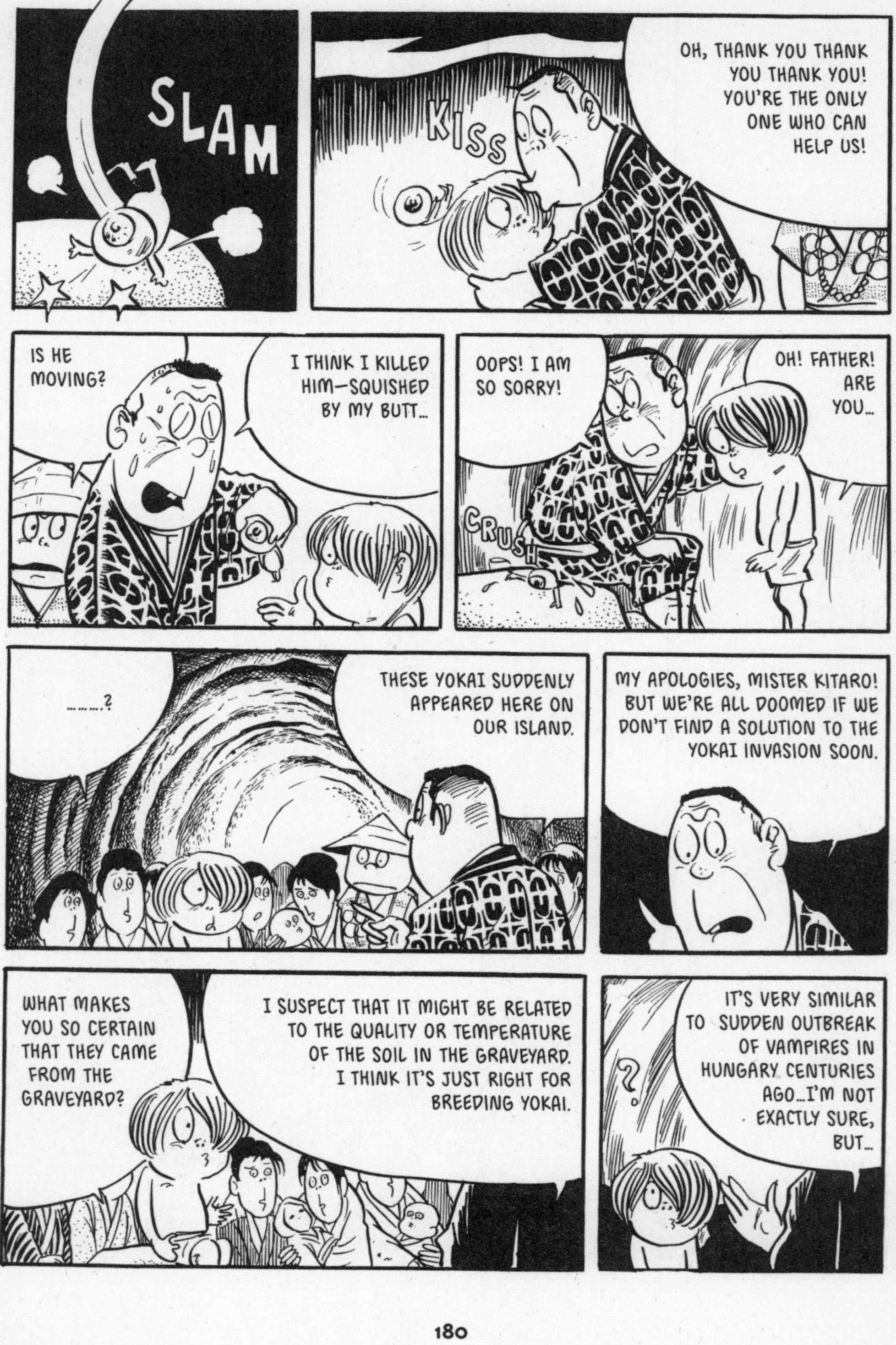
OH, THANK YOU THANK YOU THANK YOU! YOU'RE THE ONLY ONE WHO CAN HELP US!
KISS
SLAM
OH! FATHER! ARE YOU...
OOPS! I AM SO SORRY!
CRUSH
I THINK I KILLED HIM—SQUISHED BY MY BUTT...
IS HE MOVING?
MY APOLOGIES, MISTER KITARO! BUT WE'RE ALL DOOMED IF WE DON'T FIND A SOLUTION TO THE YOKAI INVASION SOON.
THESE YOKAI SUDDENLY APPEARED HERE ON OUR ISLAND.
………?
IT'S VERY SIMILAR TO SUDDEN OUTBREAK OF VAMPIRES IN HUNGARY CENTURIES AGO...I'M NOT EXACTLY SURE, BUT...
?
I SUSPECT THAT IT MIGHT BE RELATED TO THE QUALITY OR TEMPERATURE OF THE SOIL IN THE GRAVEYARD. I THINK IT'S JUST RIGHT FOR BREEDING YOKAI.
WHAT MAKES YOU SO CERTAIN THAT THEY CAME FROM THE GRAVEYARD?

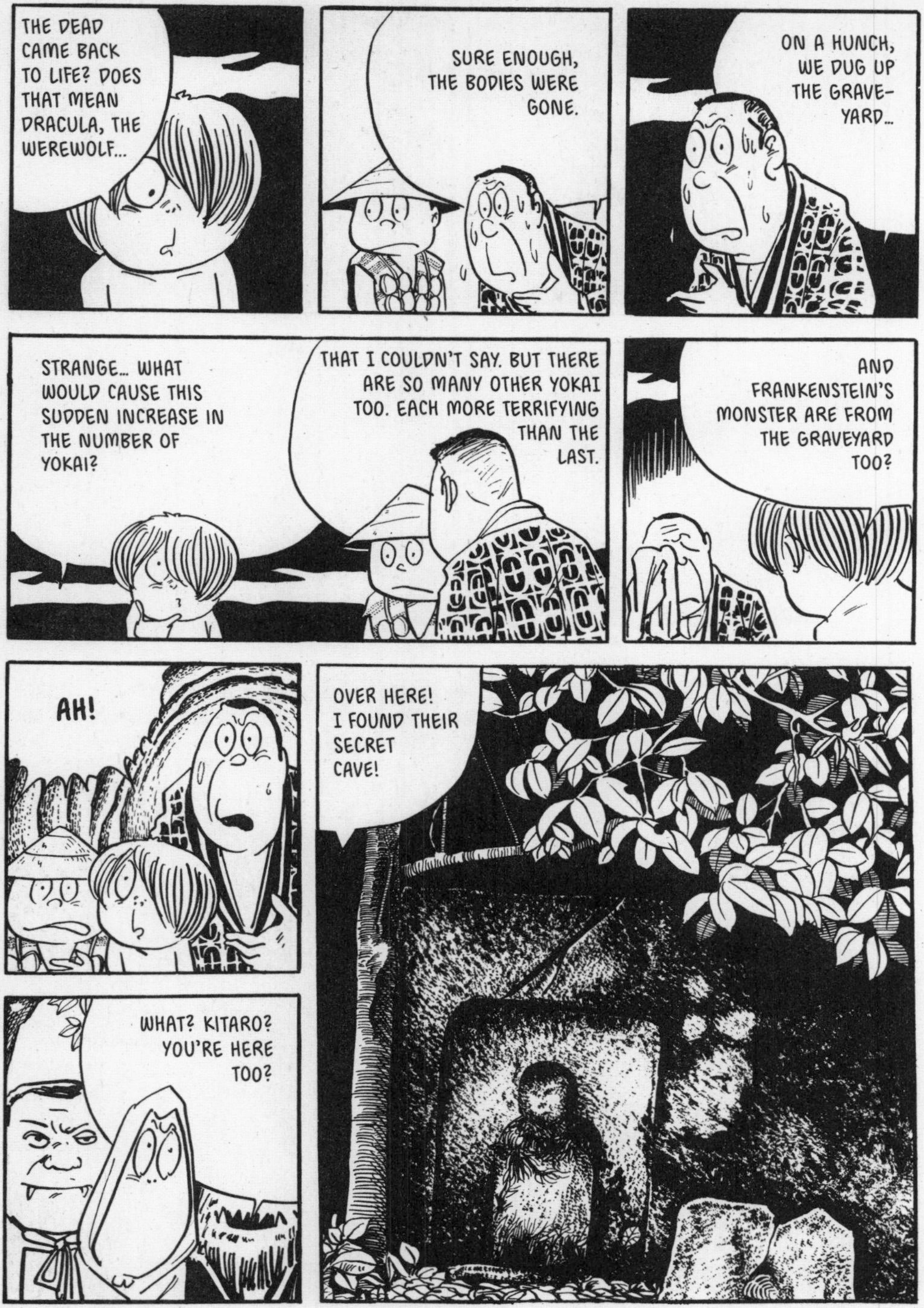
ON A HUNCH, WE DUG UP THE GRAVE-YARD...
SURE ENOUGH, THE BODIES WERE GONE.
THE DEAD CAME BACK TO LIFE? DOES THAT MEAN DRACULA, THE WEREWOLF...
AND FRANKENSTEIN'S MONSTER ARE FROM THE GRAVEYARD TOO?
THAT I COULDN'T SAY. BUT THERE ARE SO MANY OTHER YOKAI TOO. EACH MORE TERRIFYING THAN THE LAST.
STRANGE... WHAT WOULD CAUSE THIS SUDDEN INCREASE IN THE NUMBER OF YOKAI?
OVER HERE! I FOUND THEIR SECRET CAVE!
AH!
WHAT? KITARO? YOU'RE HERE TOO?

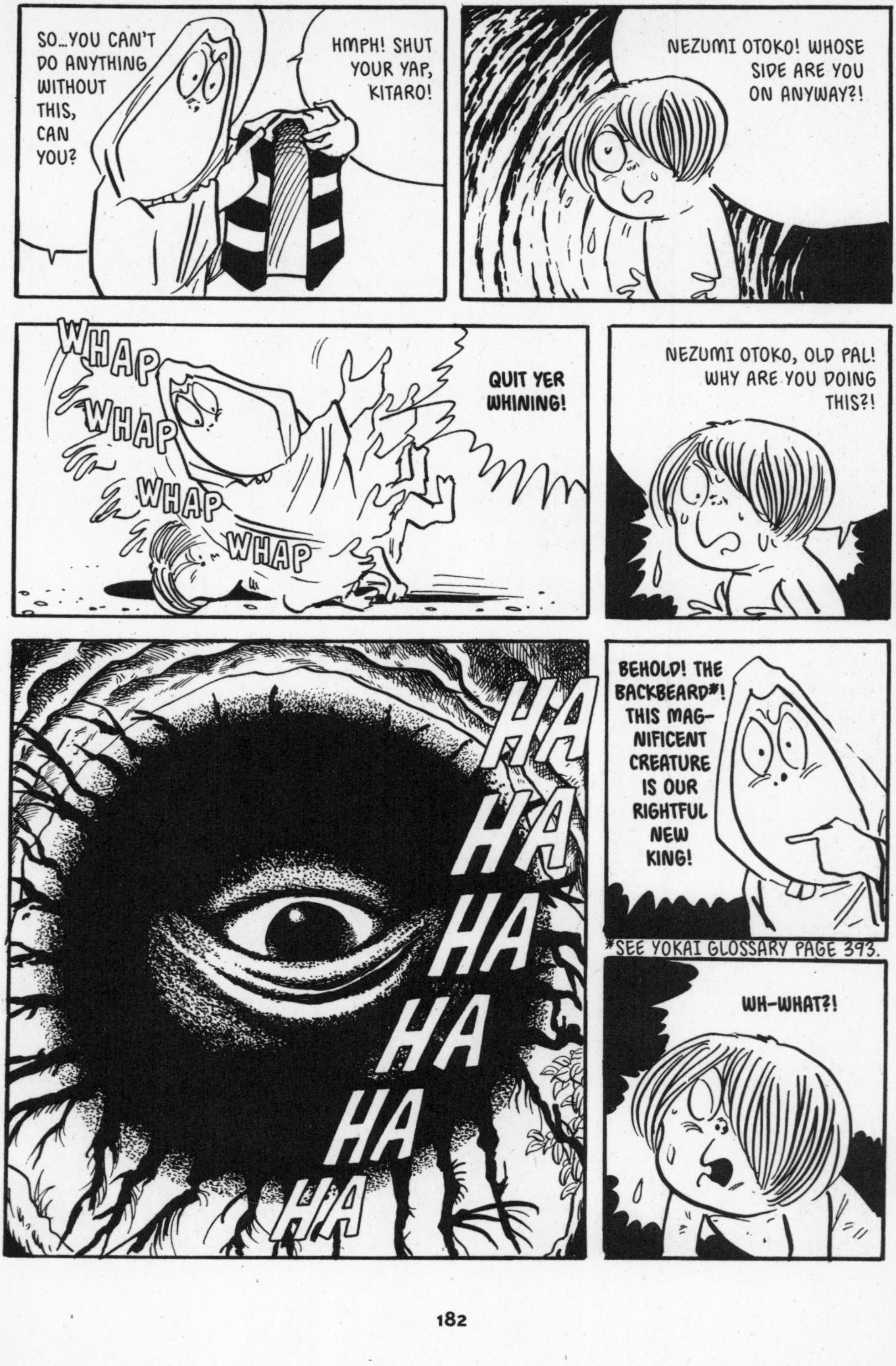
NEZUMI OTOKO! WHOSE SIDE ARE YOU ON ANYWAY?!
HMPH! SHUT YOUR YAP, KITARO!
SO...YOU CAN'T DO ANYTHING WITHOUT THIS, CAN YOU?
NEZUMI OTOKO, OLD PAL! WHY ARE YOU DOING THIS?!
QUIT YER WHINING!
WHAP
WHAP
WHAP
WHAP
BEHOLD! THE BACKBEARD*! THIS MAGNIFICENT CREATURE IS OUR RIGHTFUL NEW KING!
*SEE YOKAI GLOSSARY PAGE 393.
WH-WHAT?!
HA HA HA HA HA HA HA

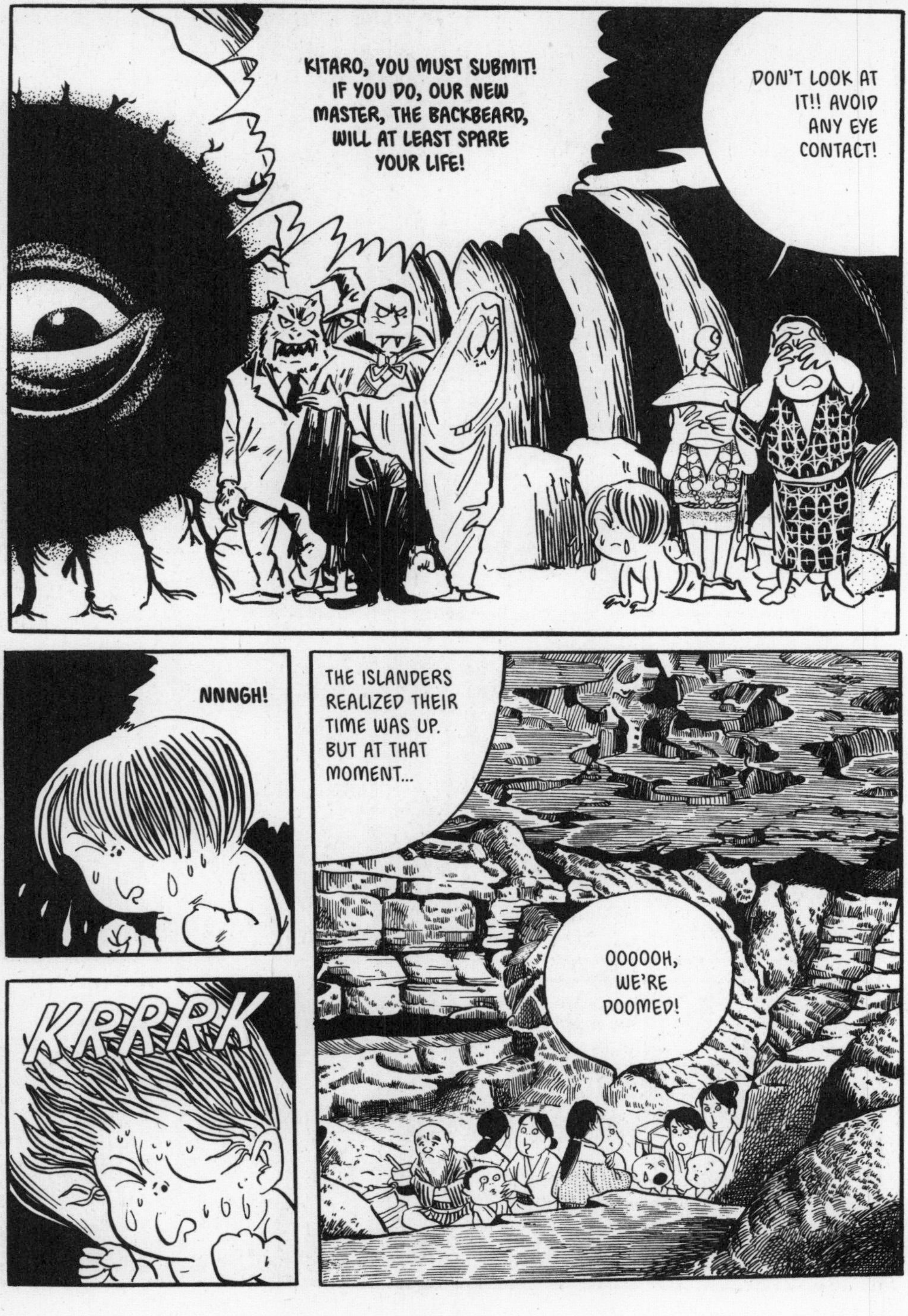
KITARO, YOU MUST SUBMIT! IF YOU DO, OUR NEW MASTER, THE BACKBEARD, WILL AT LEAST SPARE YOUR LIFE!
DON'T LOOK AT IT!! AVOID ANY EYE CONTACT!
NNNGH!
KRRRK
THE ISLANDERS REALIZED THEIR TIME WAS UP. BUT AT THAT MOMENT...
OOOOOH, WE'RE DOOMED!

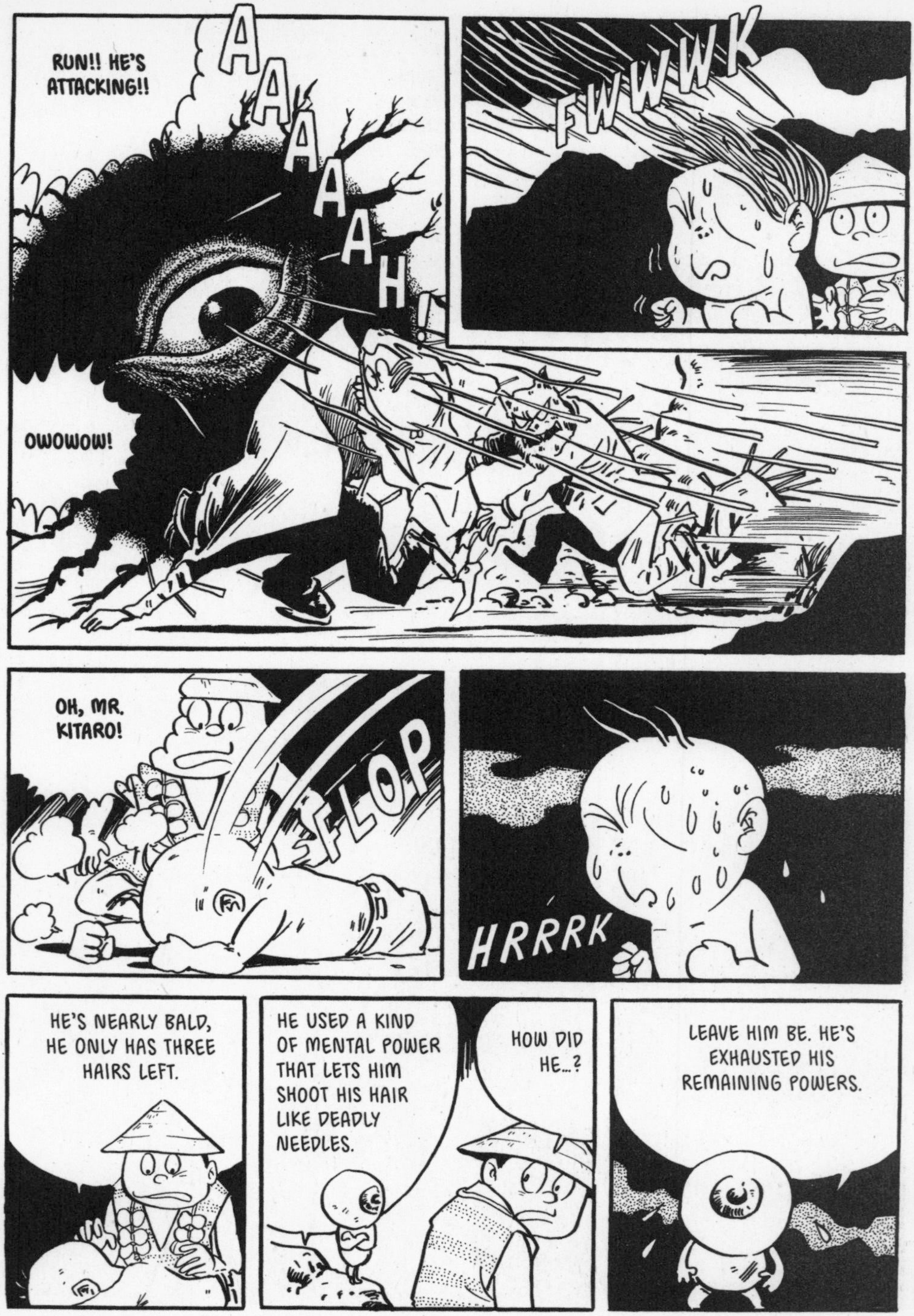
FWWWK
RUN!! HE'S ATTACKING!!
AAAAAAH!
OWOWOW!
HRRRK
OH, MR. KITARO!
FLOP
LEAVE HIM BE. HE'S EXHAUSTED HIS REMAINING POWERS.
HOW DID HE...?
HE USED A KIND OF MENTAL POWER THAT LETS HIM SHOOT HIS HAIR LIKE DEADLY NEEDLES.
HE'S NEARLY BALD, HE ONLY HAS THREE HAIRS LEFT.

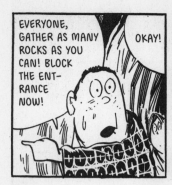

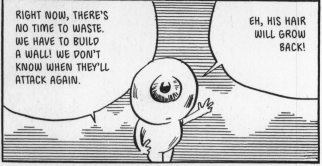

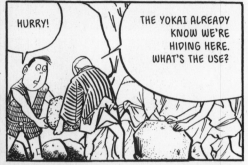

EH, HIS HAIR WILL GROW BACK!
RIGHT NOW, THERE'S NO TIME TO WASTE. WE HAVE TO BUILD A WALL! WE DON'T KNOW WHEN THEY'LL ATTACK AGAIN.
OKAY!
EVERYONE, GATHER AS MANY ROCKS AS YOU CAN! BLOCK THE ENT-RANCE NOW!
THE YOKAI ALREADY KNOW WE'RE HIDING HERE. WHAT'S THE USE?
HURRY!
LET KITARO REST FOR NOW. WE NEED TO KNOW WHERE THE ENEMY'S GONE OFF TO IF WE'RE GOING TO GET ANY SLEEP TONIGHT.
WELL?
WE'LL GO TOGETHER. I'LL RIDE ON YOUR SHOULDER.
BOING

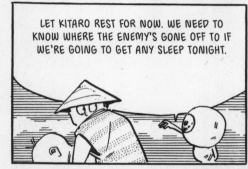

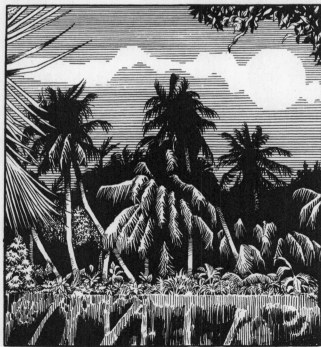

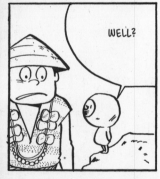

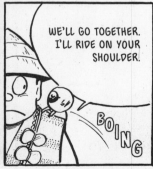

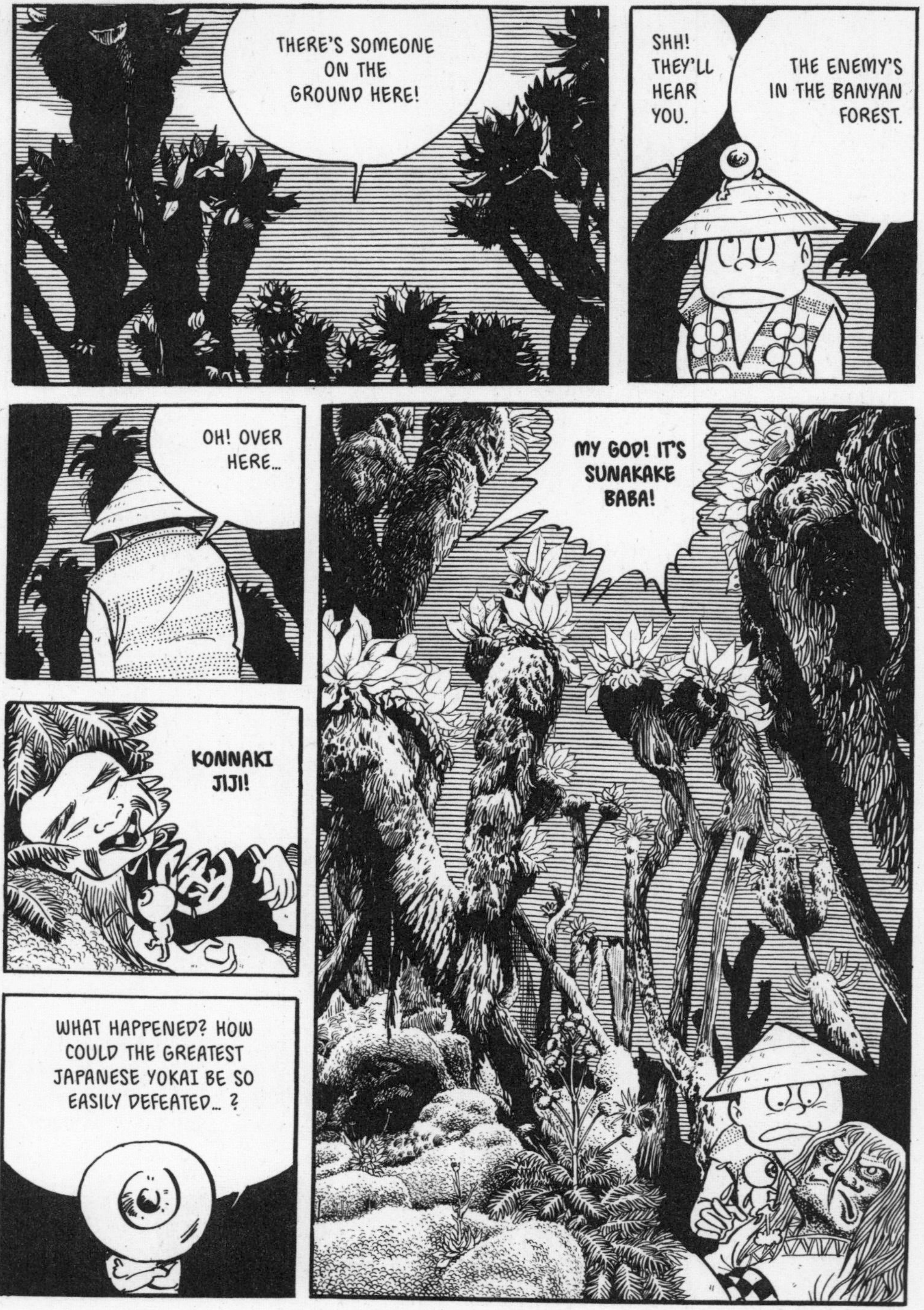
THE ENEMY'S IN THE BANYAN FOREST.
SHH! THEY'LL HEAR YOU.
THERE'S SOMEONE ON THE GROUND HERE!
MY GOD! IT'S SUNAKAKE BABA!
OH! OVER HERE...
KONNAKI JIJI!
WHAT HAPPENED? HOW COULD THE GREATEST JAPANESE YOKAI BE SO EASILY DEFEATED... ?

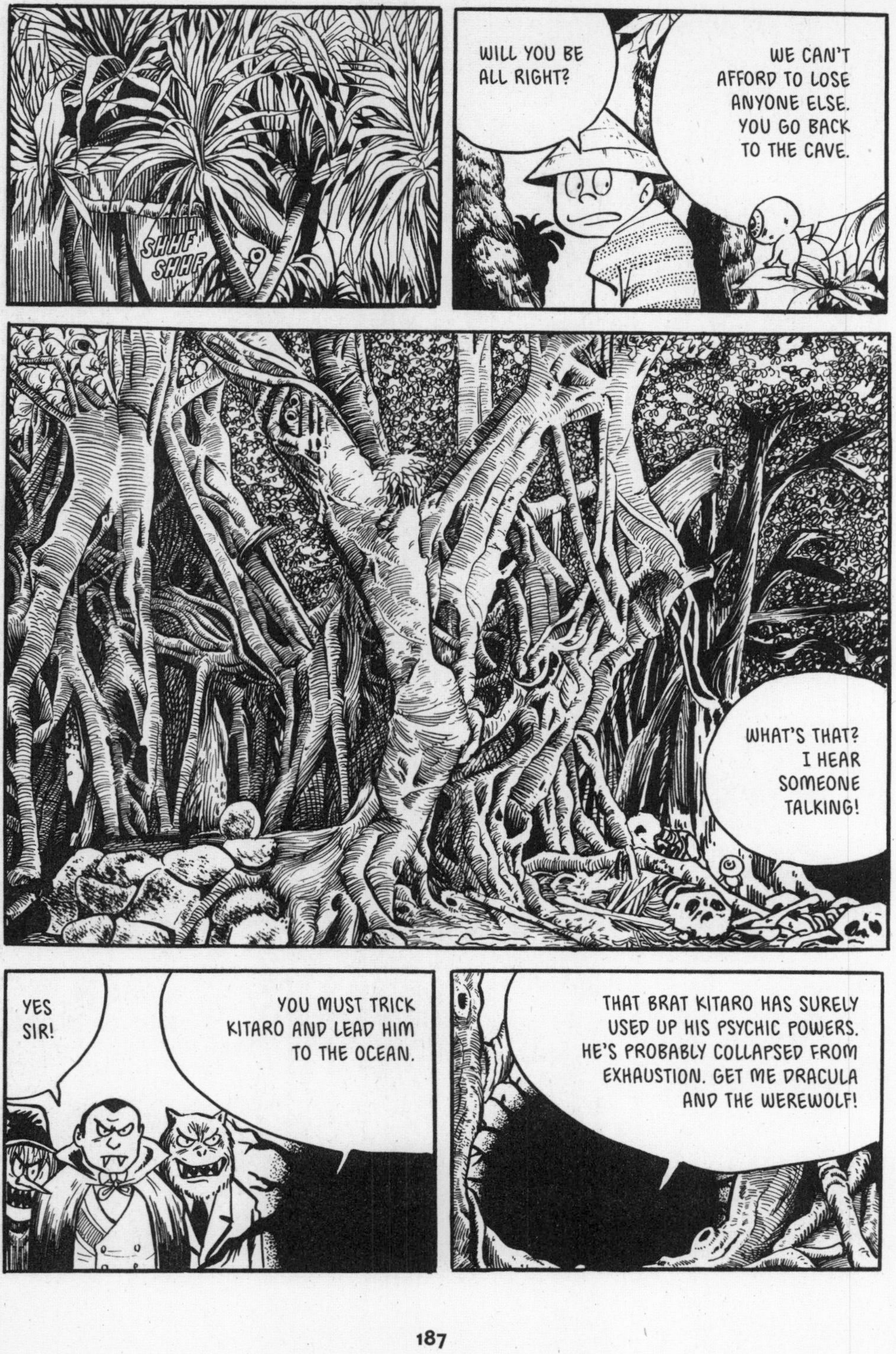
WE CAN'T AFFORD TO LOSE ANYONE ELSE. YOU GO BACK TO THE CAVE.
WILL YOU BE ALL RIGHT?
SHHF SHHF
WHAT'S THAT? I HEAR SOMEONE TALKING!
THAT BRAT KITARO HAS SURELY USED UP HIS PSYCHIC POWERS. HE'S PROBABLY COLLAPSED FROM EXHAUSTION. GET ME DRACULA AND THE WEREWOLF!
YOU MUST TRICK KITARO AND LEAD HIM TO THE OCEAN.
YES SIR!

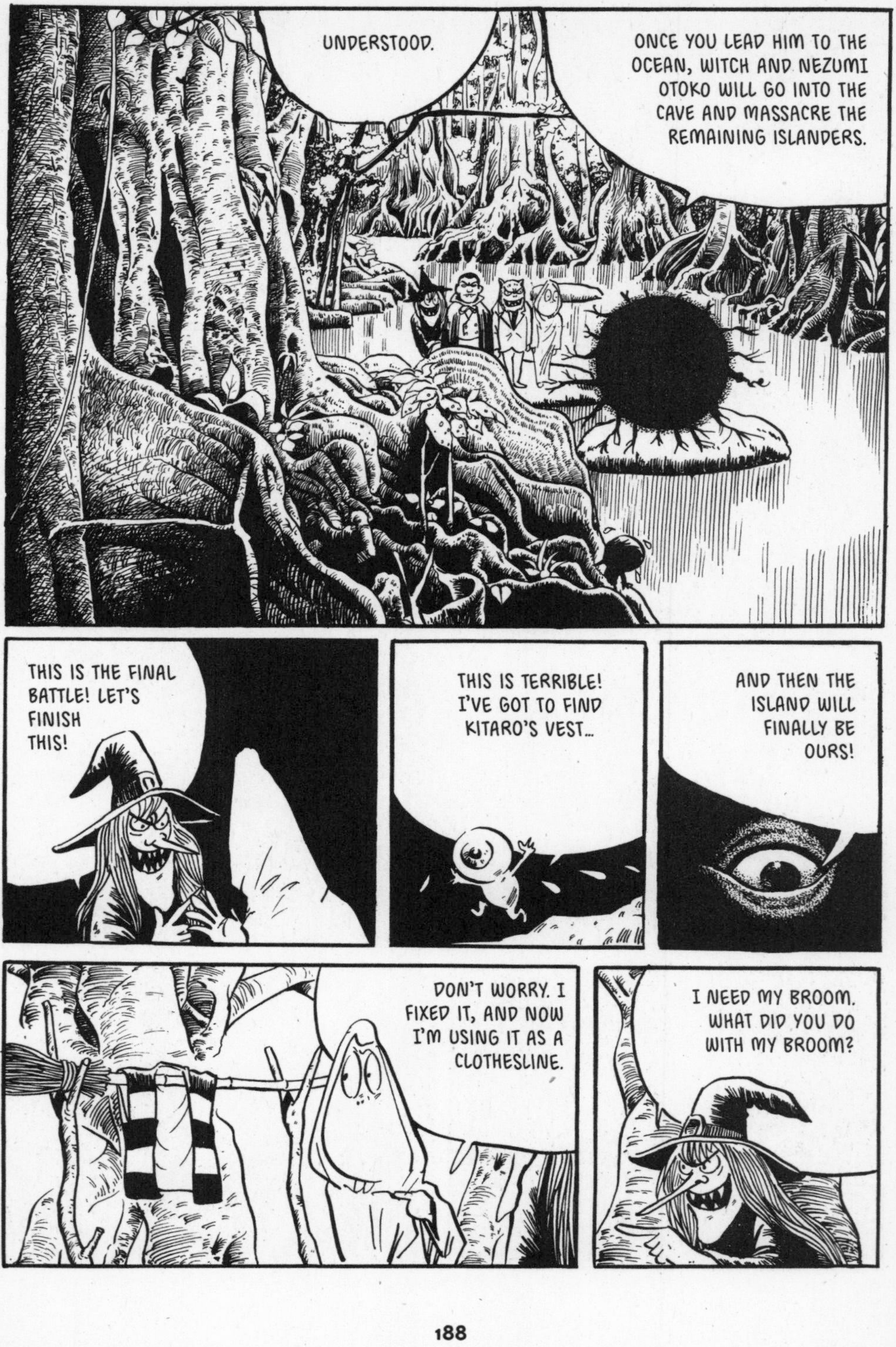
ONCE YOU LEAD HIM TO THE OCEAN, WITCH AND NEZUMI OTOKO WILL GO INTO THE CAVE AND MASSACRE THE REMAINING ISLANDERS.
UNDERSTOOD.
AND THEN THE ISLAND WILL FINALLY BE OURS!
THIS IS TERRIBLE! I'VE GOT TO FIND KITARO'S VEST...
THIS IS THE FINAL BATTLE! LET'S FINISH THIS!
I NEED MY BROOM. WHAT DID YOU DO WITH MY BROOM?
DON'T WORRY. I FIXED IT, AND NOW I'M USING IT AS A CLOTHESLINE.

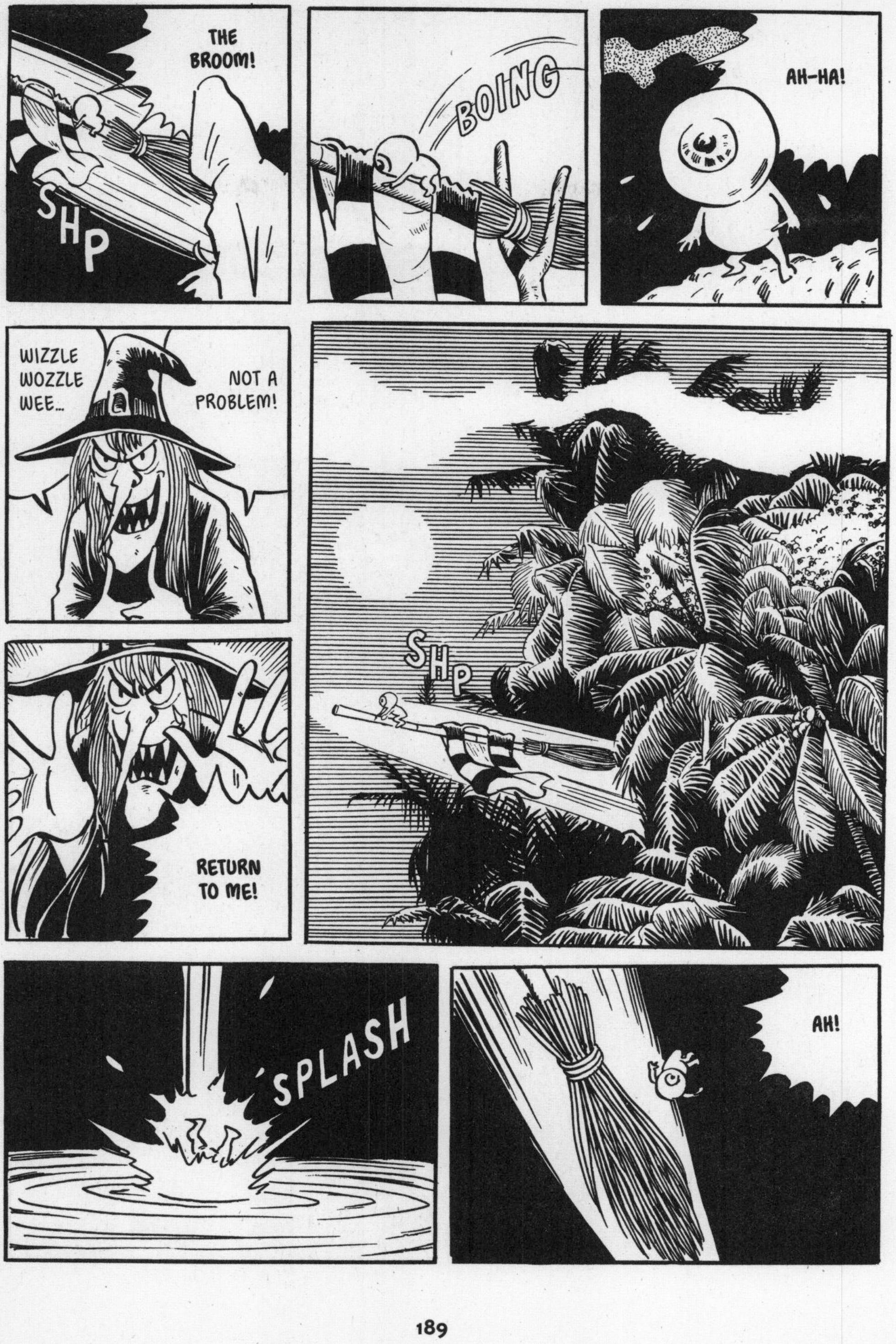
AH-HA!
BOING
THE BROOM!
SHP
SHP
WIZZLE WOZZLE WEE...
NOT A PROBLEM!
RETURN TO ME!
AH!
SPLASH

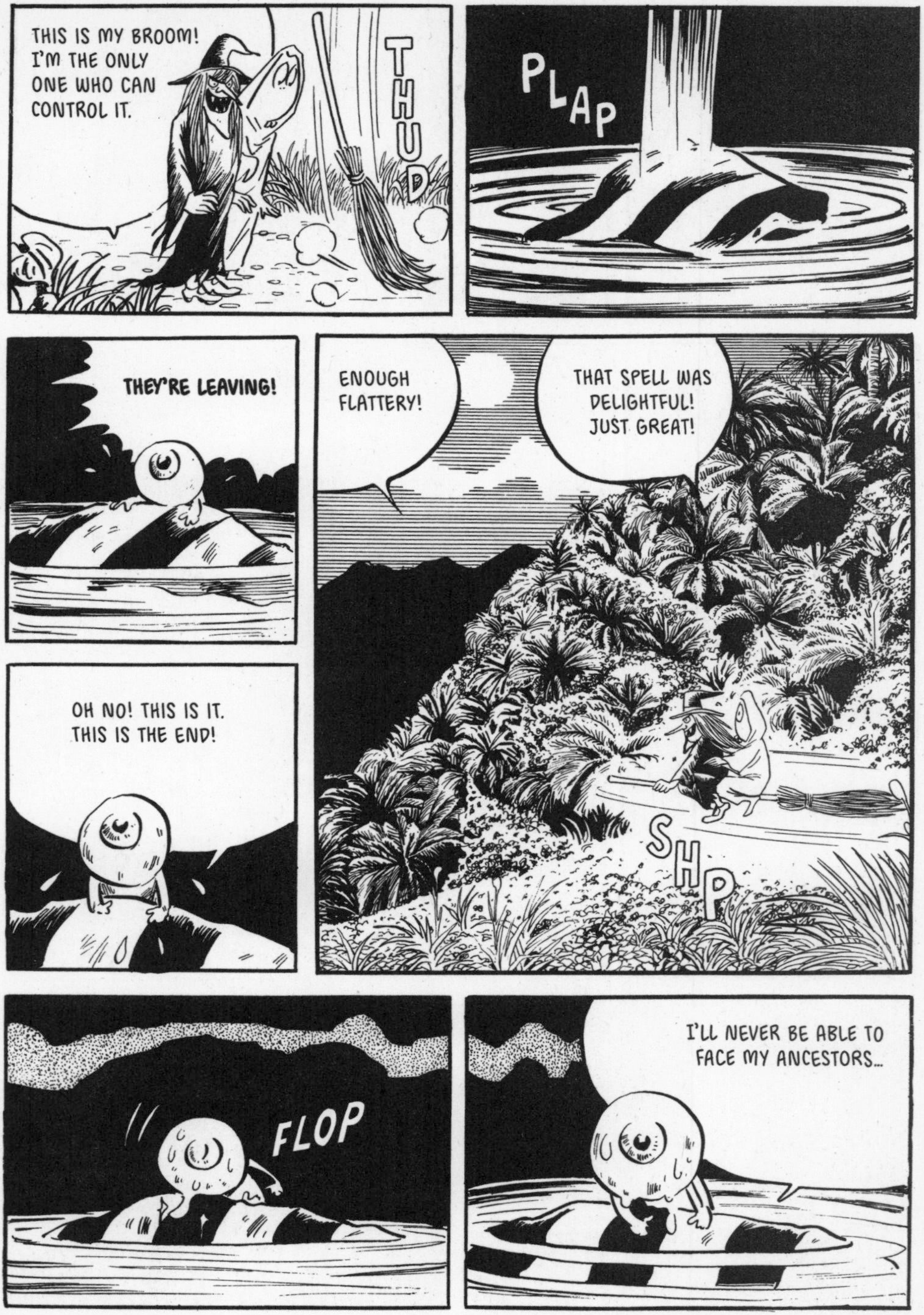
PLAP
THUD
THIS IS MY BROOM! I'M THE ONLY ONE WHO CAN CONTROL IT.
THAT SPELL WAS DELIGHTFUL! JUST GREAT!
ENOUGH FLATTERY!
SHP
THEY'RE LEAVING!
OH NO! THIS IS IT. THIS IS THE END!
I'LL NEVER BE ABLE TO FACE MY ANCESTORS...
FLOP

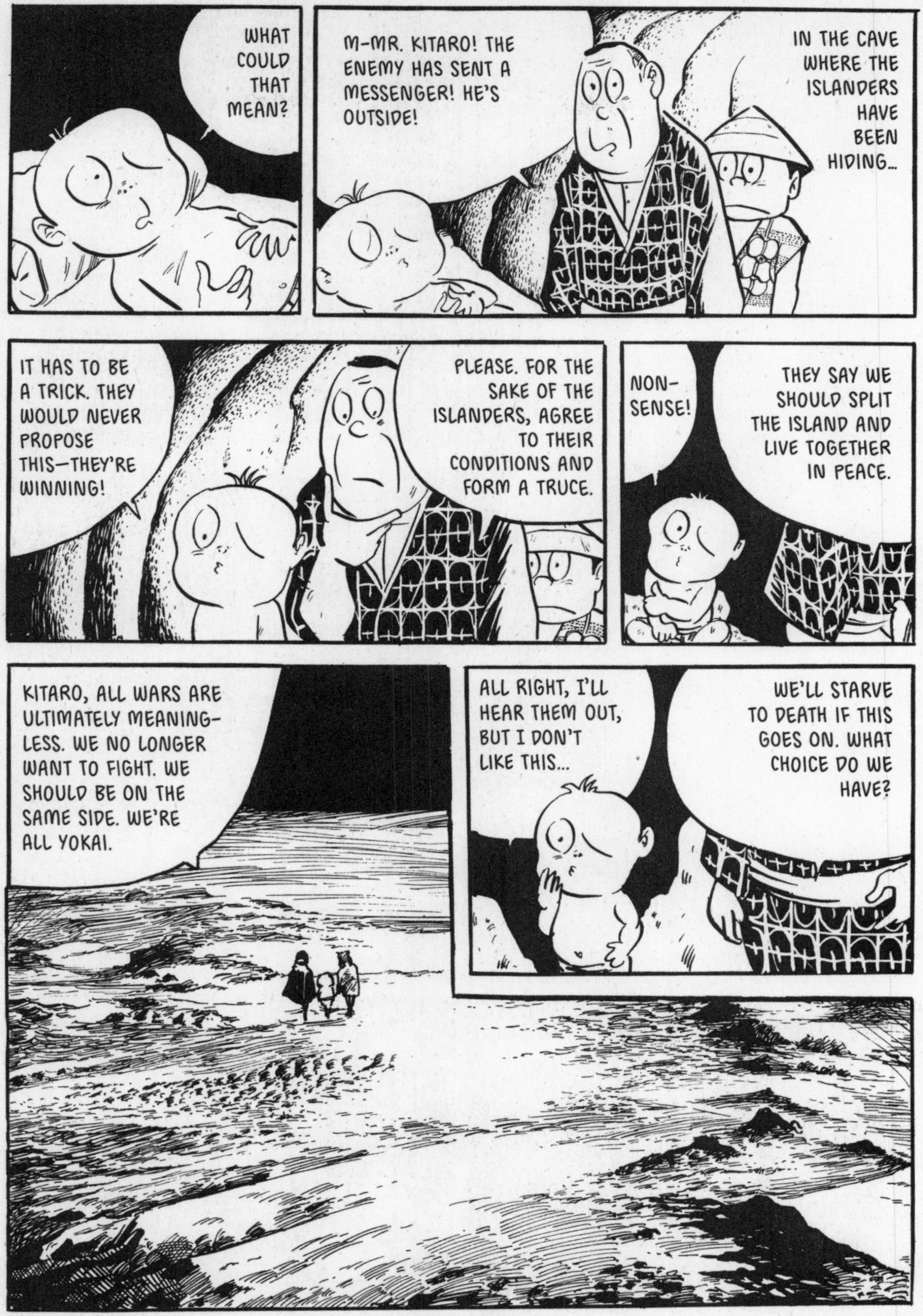
IN THE CAVE WHERE THE ISLANDERS HAVE BEEN HIDING...
M-MR. KITARO! THE ENEMY HAS SENT A MESSENGER! HE'S OUTSIDE!
WHAT COULD THAT MEAN?
THEY SAY WE SHOULD SPLIT THE ISLAND AND LIVE TOGETHER IN PEACE.
NON-SENSE!
PLEASE. FOR THE SAKE OF THE ISLANDERS, AGREE TO THEIR CONDITIONS AND FORM A TRUCE.
IT HAS TO BE A TRICK. THEY WOULD NEVER PROPOSE THIS—THEY'RE WINNING!
WE'LL STARVE TO DEATH IF THIS GOES ON. WHAT CHOICE DO WE HAVE?
ALL RIGHT, I'LL HEAR THEM OUT, BUT I DON'T LIKE THIS...
KITARO, ALL WARS ARE ULTIMATELY MEANING-LESS. WE NO LONGER WANT TO FIGHT. WE SHOULD BE ON THE SAME SIDE. WE'RE ALL YOKAI.

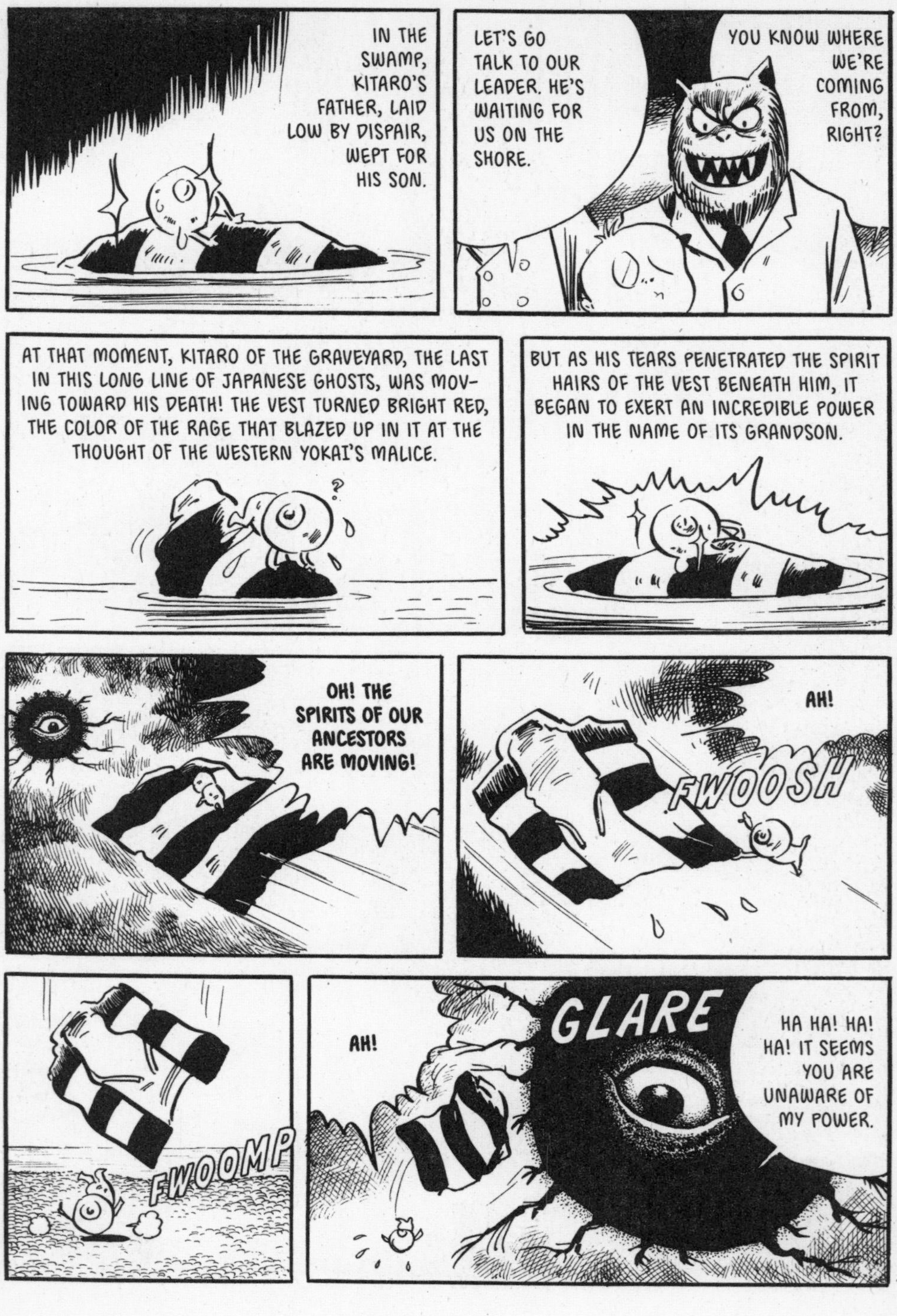
YOU KNOW WHERE WE'RE COMING FROM, RIGHT?
LET'S GO TALK TO OUR LEADER. HE'S WAITING FOR US ON THE SHORE.
IN THE SWAMP, KITARO'S FATHER, LAID LOW BY DISPAIR, WEPT FOR HIS SON.
BUT AS HIS TEARS PENETRATED THE SPIRIT HAIRS OF THE VEST BENEATH HIM, IT BEGAN TO EXERT AN INCREDIBLE POWER IN THE NAME OF ITS GRANDSON.
AT THAT MOMENT, KITARO OF THE GRAVEYARD, THE LAST IN THIS LONG LINE OF JAPANESE GHOSTS, WAS MOVING TOWARD HIS DEATH! THE VEST TURNED BRIGHT RED, THE COLOR OF THE RAGE THAT BLAZED UP IN IT AT THE THOUGHT OF THE WESTERN YOKAI'S MALICE.
?
AH!
FWOOSH
OH! THE SPIRITS OF OUR ANCESTORS ARE MOVING!
HA HA! HA! HA! IT SEEMS YOU ARE UNAWARE OF MY POWER.
GLARE
AH!
FWOOMP

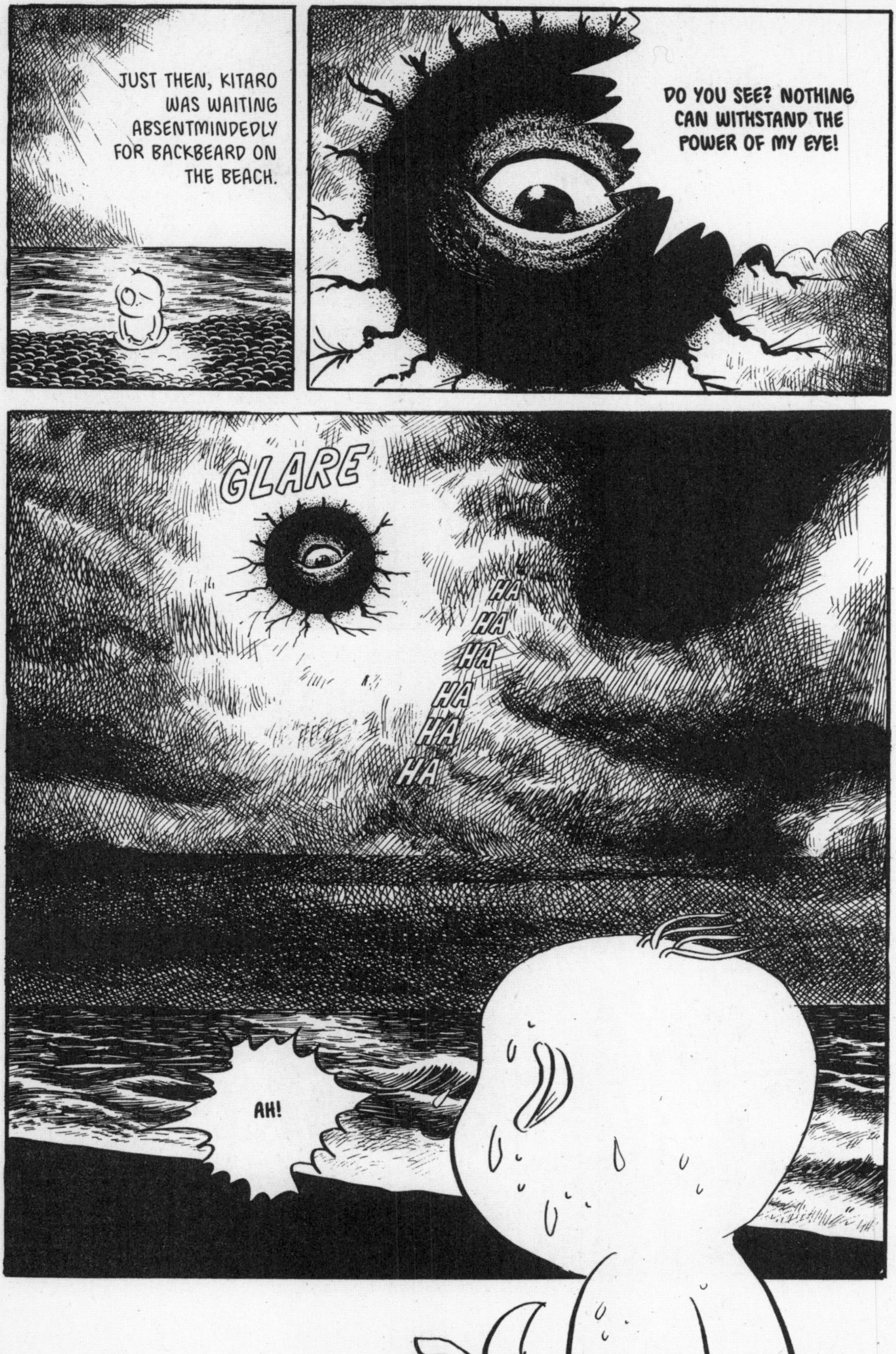

DO YOU SEE? NOTHING CAN WITHSTAND THE POWER OF MY EYE!
JUST THEN, KITARO WAS WAITING ABSENTMINDEDLY FOR BACKBEARD ON THE BEACH.
GLARE
HA HA HA HA HA HA
AH!

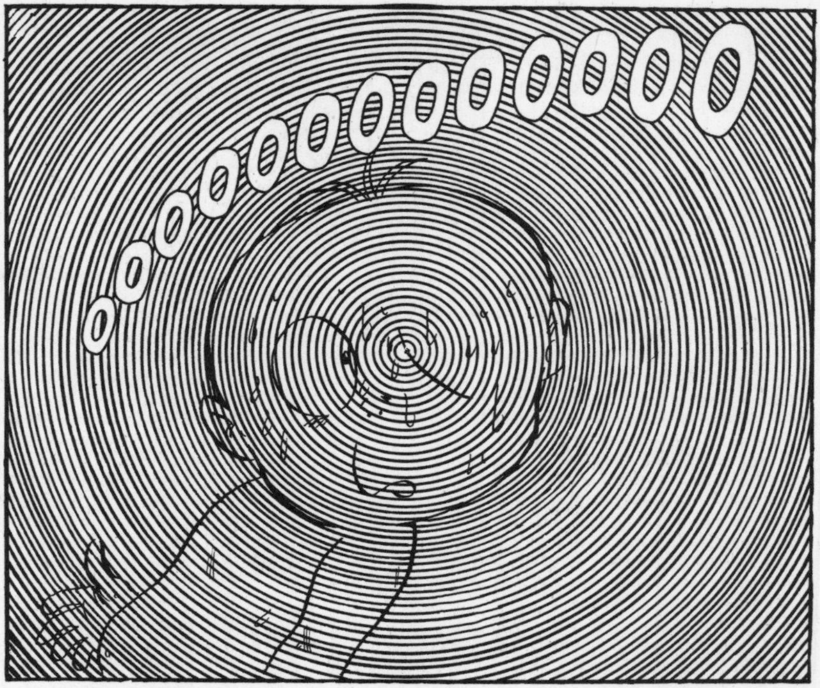
OOOOOOOOOOOOO

TURNING AROUND WITH A GASP AT THE SOUND OF UNEXPECTED LAUGHTER IN THE SKY, KITARO ACCIDENTALLY LOOKED INTO BACKBEARD'S EYE, FALLING NEATLY INTO HIS ENEMY'S TRAP!

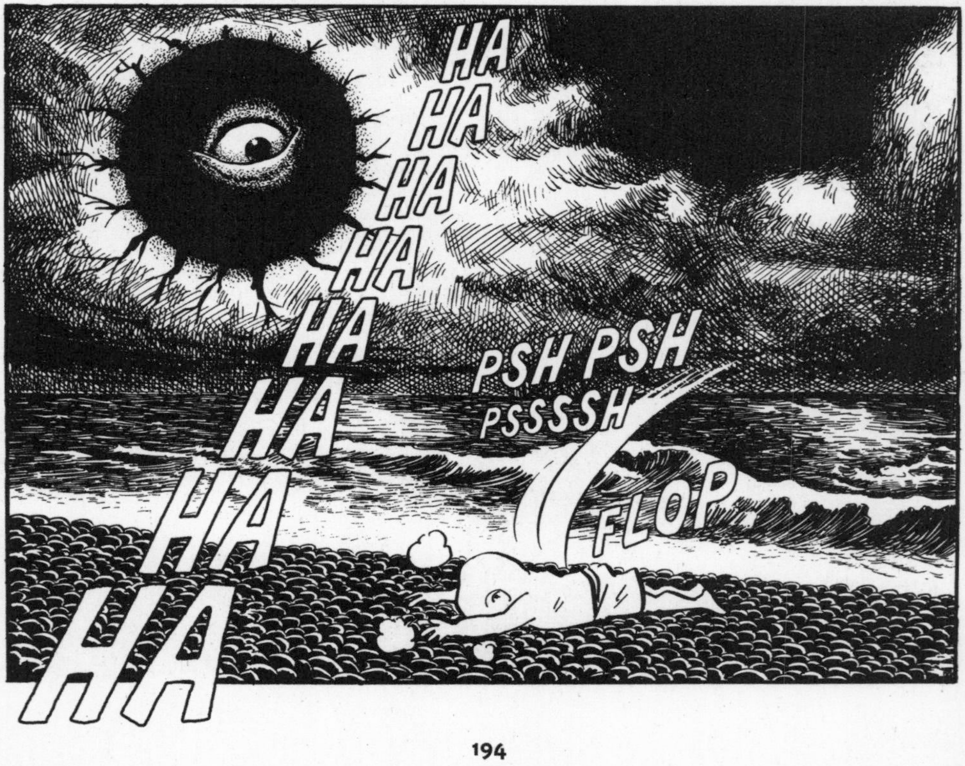
HA
HA
HA
HA
HA
HA
HA
HA
PSH PSH
PSSSSH
FLOP

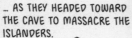

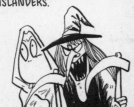

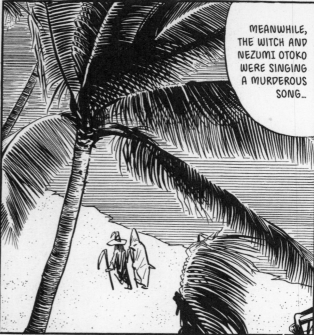

MEANWHILE, THE WITCH AND NEZUMI OTOKO WERE SINGING A MURDEROUS SONG...
... AS THEY HEADED TOWARD THE CAVE TO MASSACRE THE ISLANDERS.
LITTLE DID THEY REALIZE THE ERROR OF STEPPING ON KITARO'S VEST...
WHICH SUDDENLY SNAPPED BACK TO LIFE!
FLUTTER
FORTUNATELY, WITHOUT EYES, THE VEST ESCAPED ANY FATAL WOUNDS. AND ONCE KITARO'S FATHER HAD CLIMBED ABOARD, THEY CHASED AFTER THE PAIR OF WOULD-BE MURDERERS.

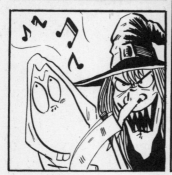

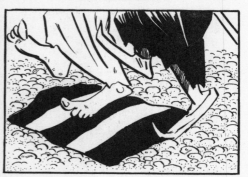

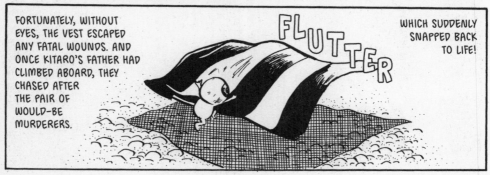

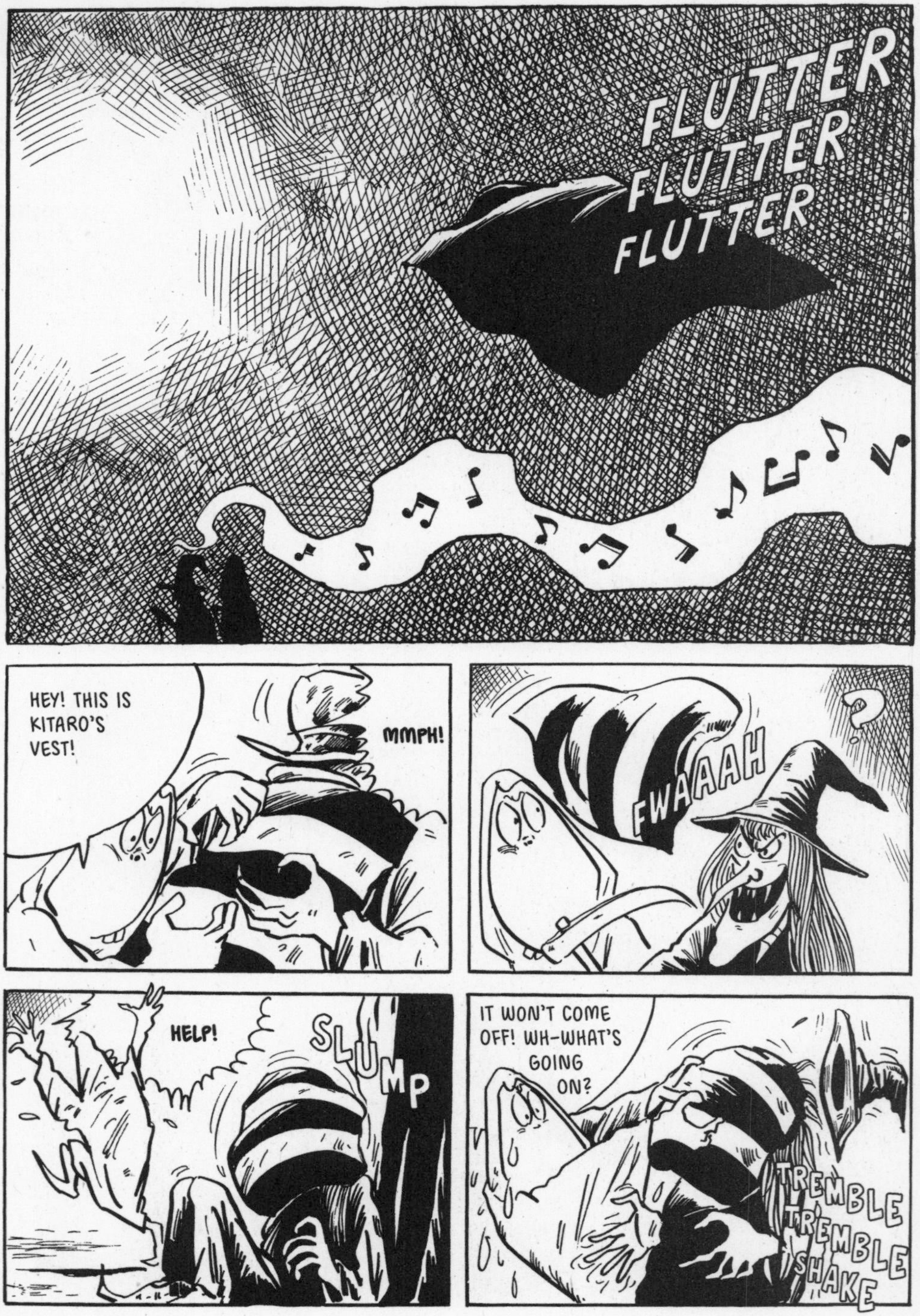
FLUTTER FLUTTER FLUTTER
?
FWAAAH
HEY! THIS IS KITARO'S VEST!
MMPH!
IT WON'T COME OFF! WH-WHAT'S GOING ON?
TREMBLE TREMBLE SHAKE
HELP!
SLUMP

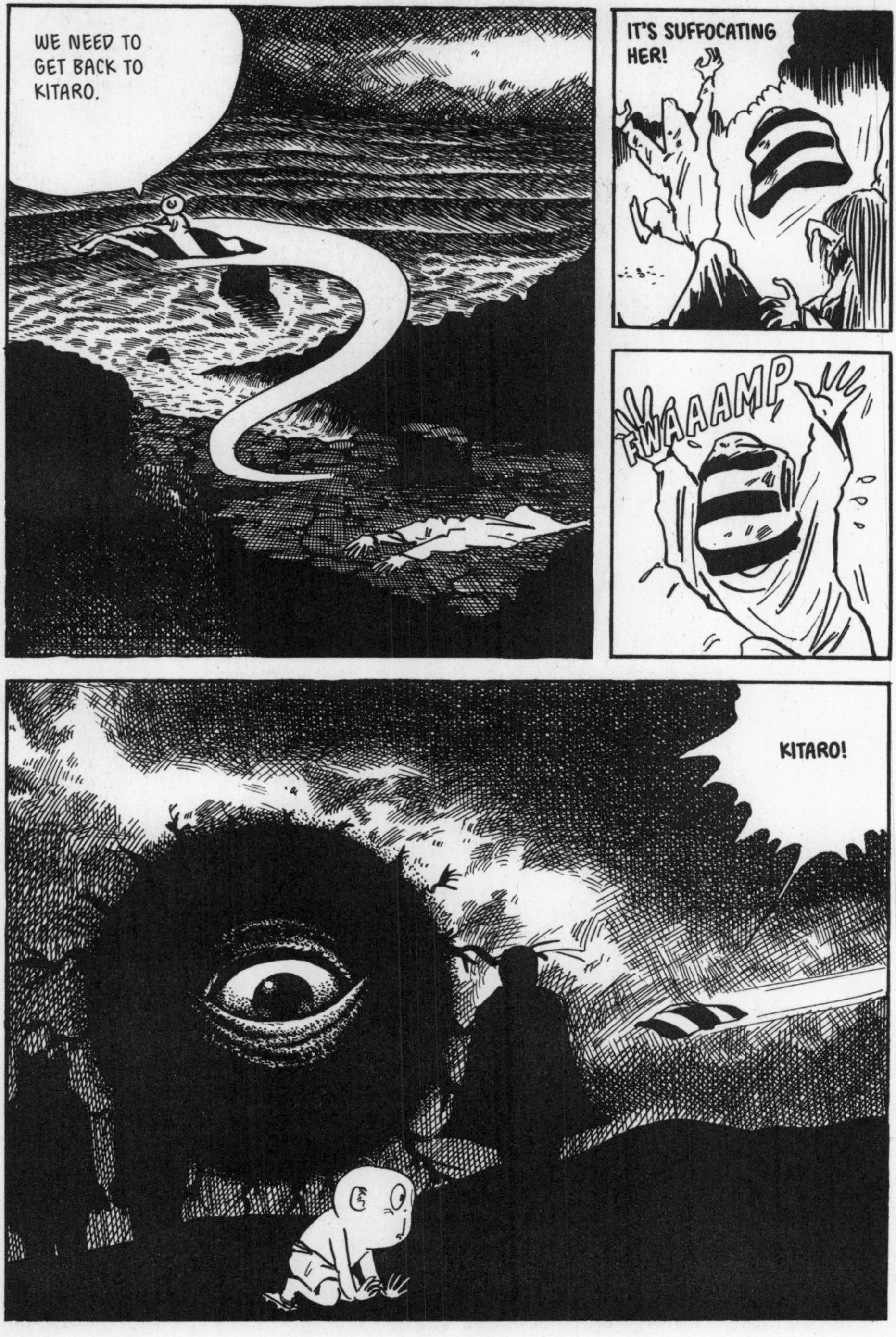
IT'S SUFFOCATING HER!
FWAAAMP
WE NEED TO GET BACK TO KITARO.
KITARO!

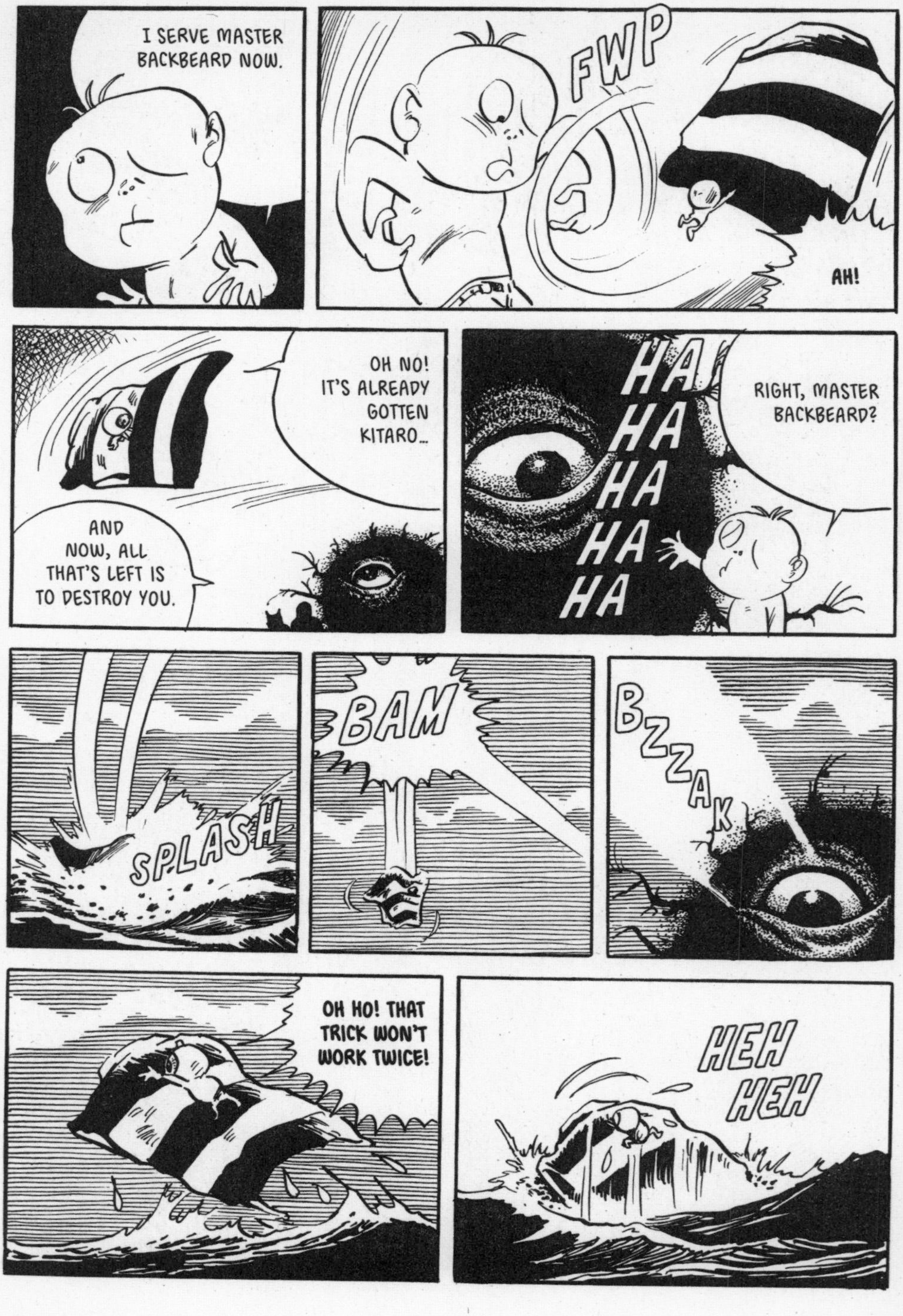
FWP
AH!
I SERVE MASTER BACKBEARD NOW.
RIGHT, MASTER BACKBEARD?
HA HA HA HA HA HA
OH NO! IT'S ALREADY GOTTEN KITARO...
AND NOW, ALL THAT'S LEFT IS TO DESTROY YOU.
BZZAK
BAM
SPLASH
HEH HEH
OH HO! THAT TRICK WON'T WORK TWICE!

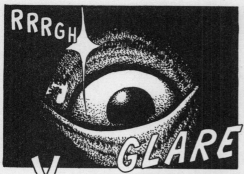

RRRGH
GLARE
FLUTTER
BOING
STAB
YEEAAAAAAGH
KITARO'S FATHER LANDED A SHARP BLOW TO BACK-BEARD'S WEAK SPOT.
GET THAT LITTLE EYEBALL!
FLOP
I GOTCHA!
AS BACKBEARD BREATHED ITS LAST, KITARO WAS OVERCOME WITH A STRANGE FEELING.

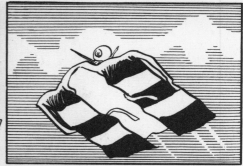

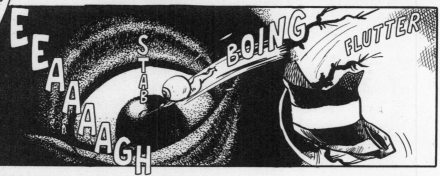

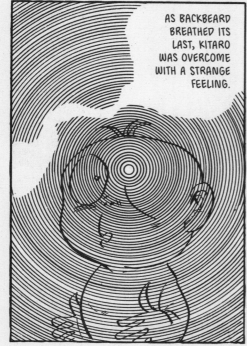

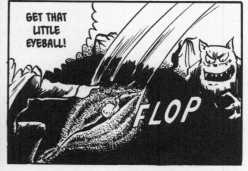

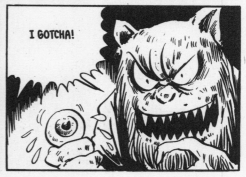

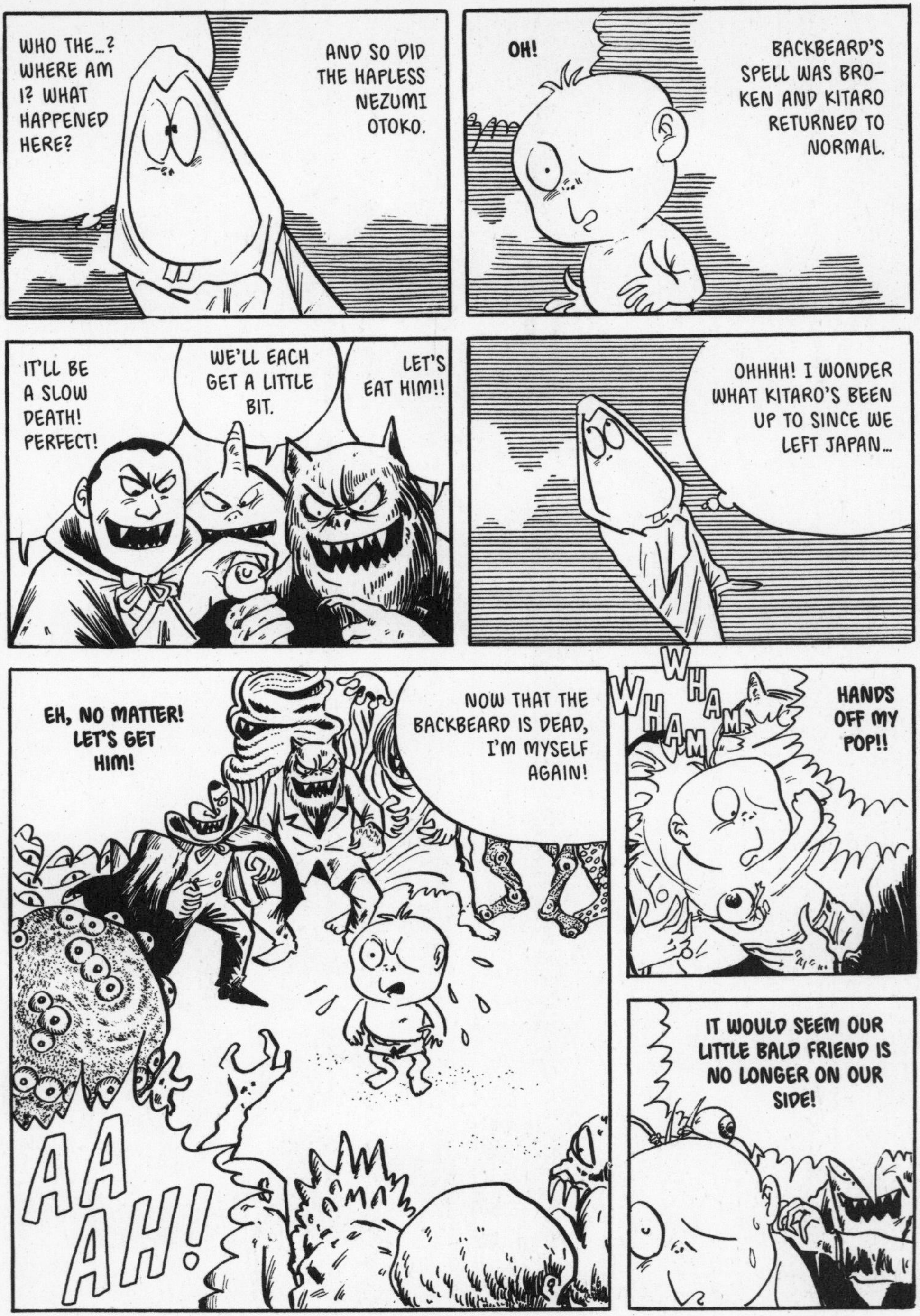
BACKBEARD'S SPELL WAS BRO- KEN AND KITARO RETURNED TO NORMAL.
OH!
AND SO DID THE HAPLESS NEZUMI OTOKO.
WHO THE...? WHERE AM I? WHAT HAPPENED HERE?
OHHHH! I WONDER WHAT KITARO'S BEEN UP TO SINCE WE LEFT JAPAN...
LET'S EAT HIM!!
WE'LL EACH GET A LITTLE BIT.
IT'LL BE A SLOW DEATH! PERFECT!
HANDS OFF MY POP!!
WHAM WHAM WHAM
IT WOULD SEEM OUR LITTLE BALD FRIEND IS NO LONGER ON OUR SIDE!
NOW THAT THE BACKBEARD IS DEAD, I'M MYSELF AGAIN!
EH, NO MATTER! LET'S GET HIM!
AAAAH!

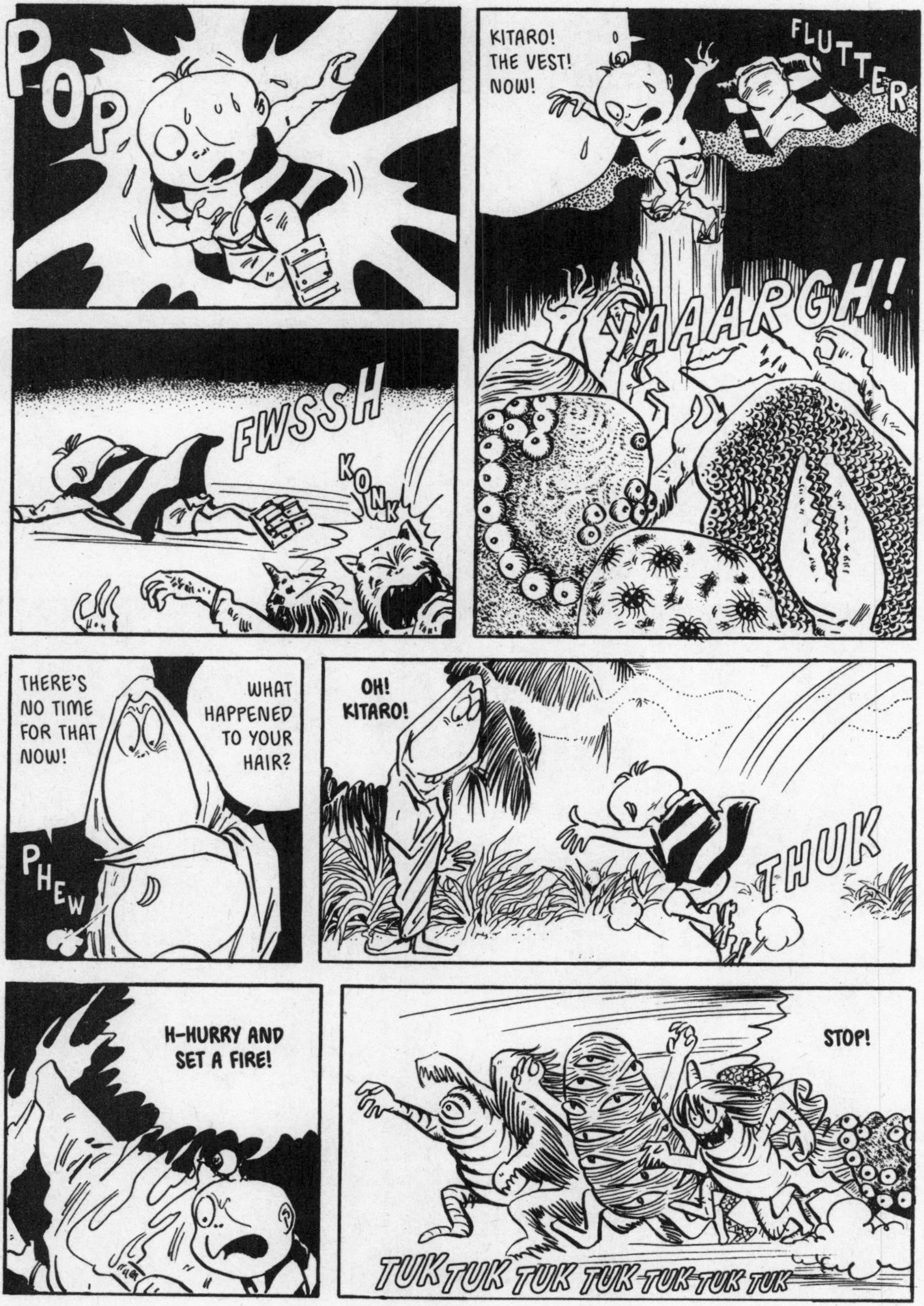
KITARO! THE VEST! NOW!
FLUTTER
YAAARGH!
POP
FWSSH
KONK
OH! KITARO!
THUK
WHAT HAPPENED TO YOUR HAIR?
THERE'S NO TIME FOR THAT NOW!
PHEW
STOP!
TUK TUK TUK TUK TUK TUK TUK
H-HURRY AND SET A FIRE!

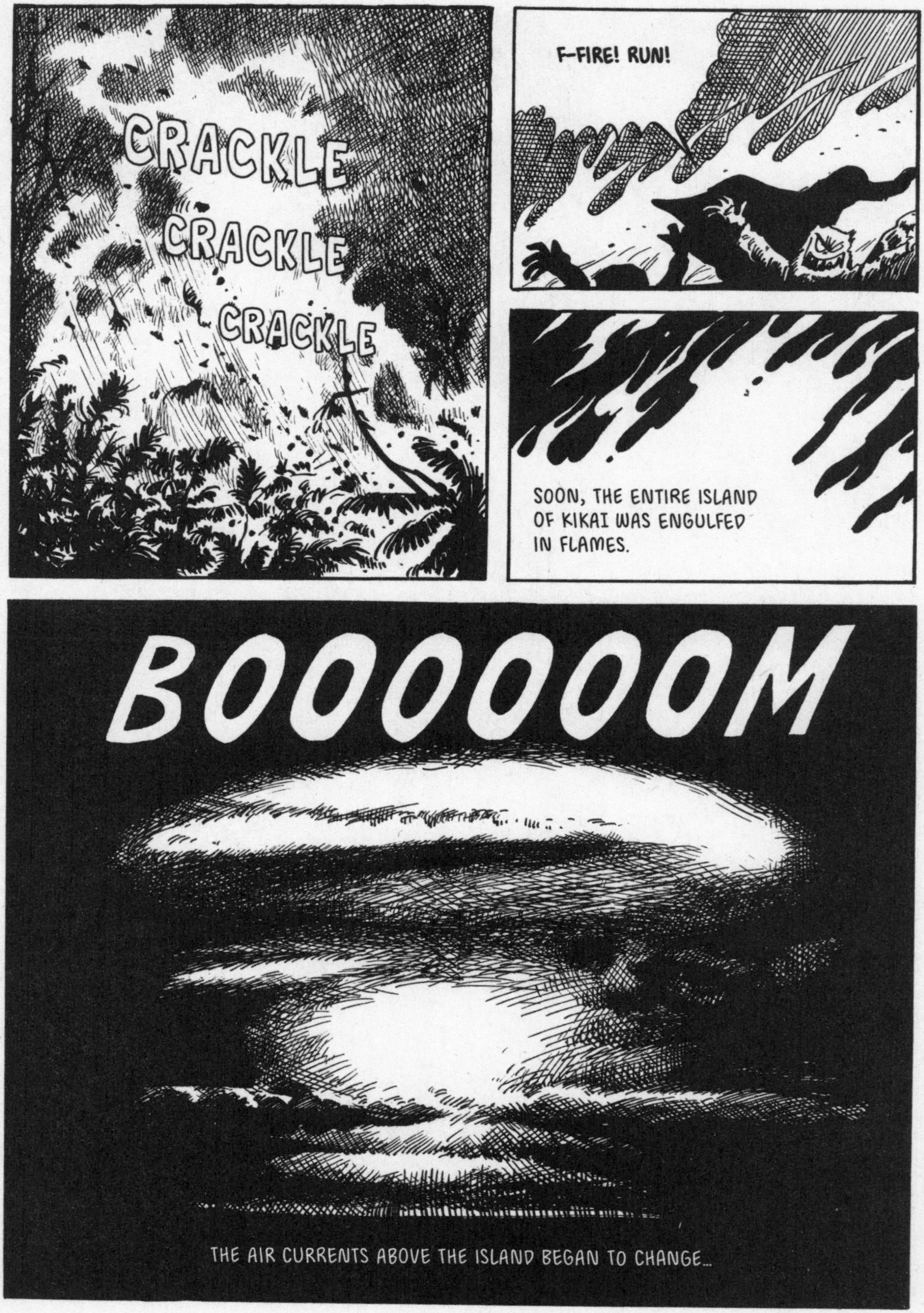
F-FIRE! RUN!
SOON, THE ENTIRE ISLAND OF KIKAI WAS ENGULFED IN FLAMES.
CRACKLE
CRACKLE
CRACKLE
BOOOOOOM
THE AIR CURRENTS ABOVE THE ISLAND BEGAN TO CHANGE...

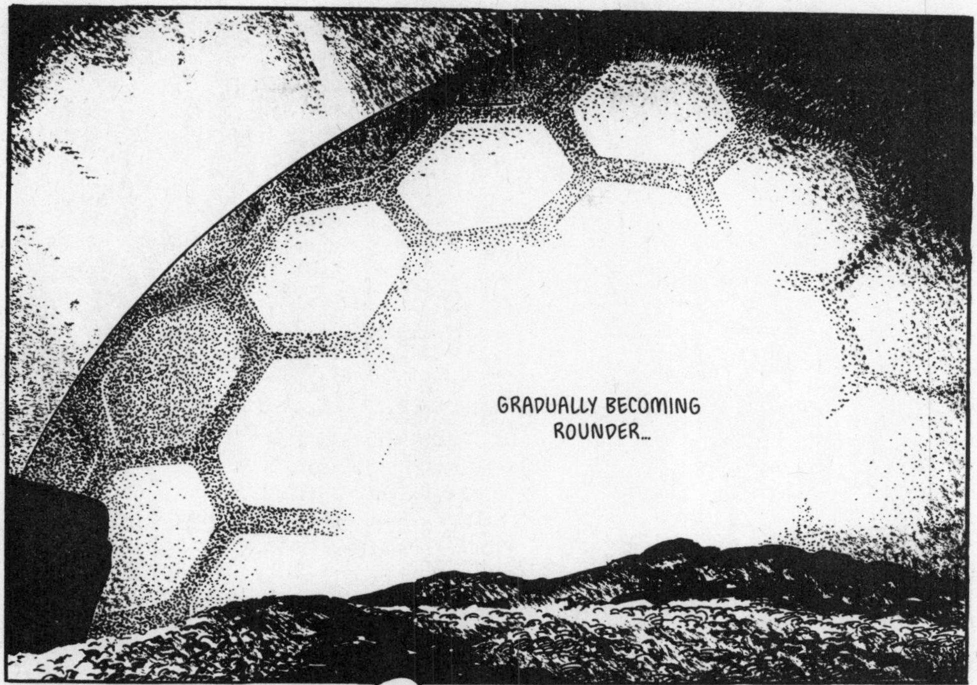
GRADUALLY BECOMING ROUNDER...

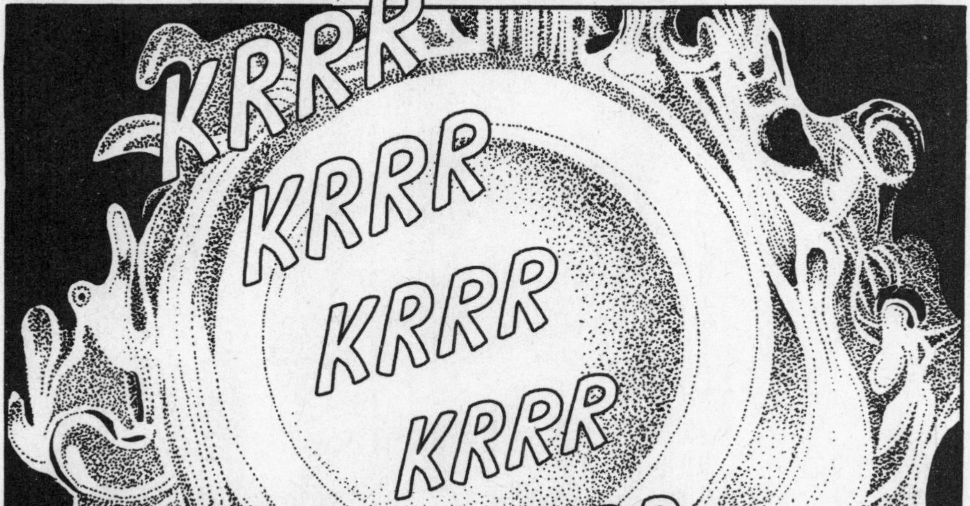
KRRR
KRRR
KRRR
KRRR
KRRR
KRRR

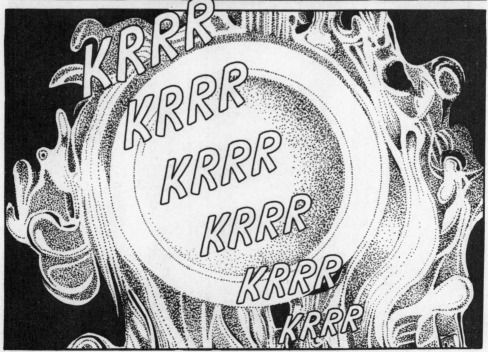

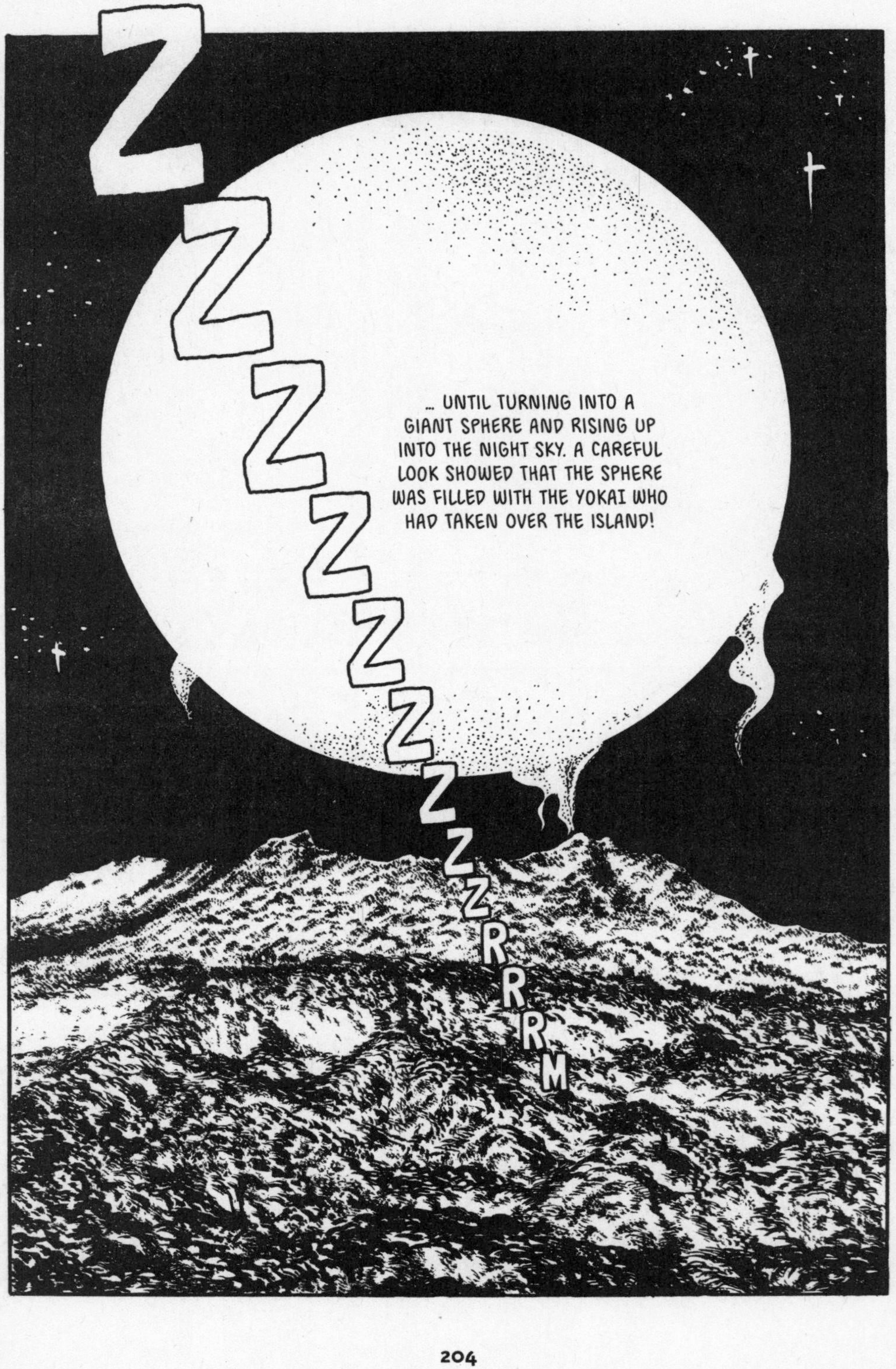
ZZZZZZZZZZZZRRRM
... UNTIL TURNING INTO A GIANT SPHERE AND RISING UP INTO THE NIGHT SKY. A CAREFUL LOOK SHOWED THAT THE SPHERE WAS FILLED WITH THE YOKAI WHO HAD TAKEN OVER THE ISLAND!

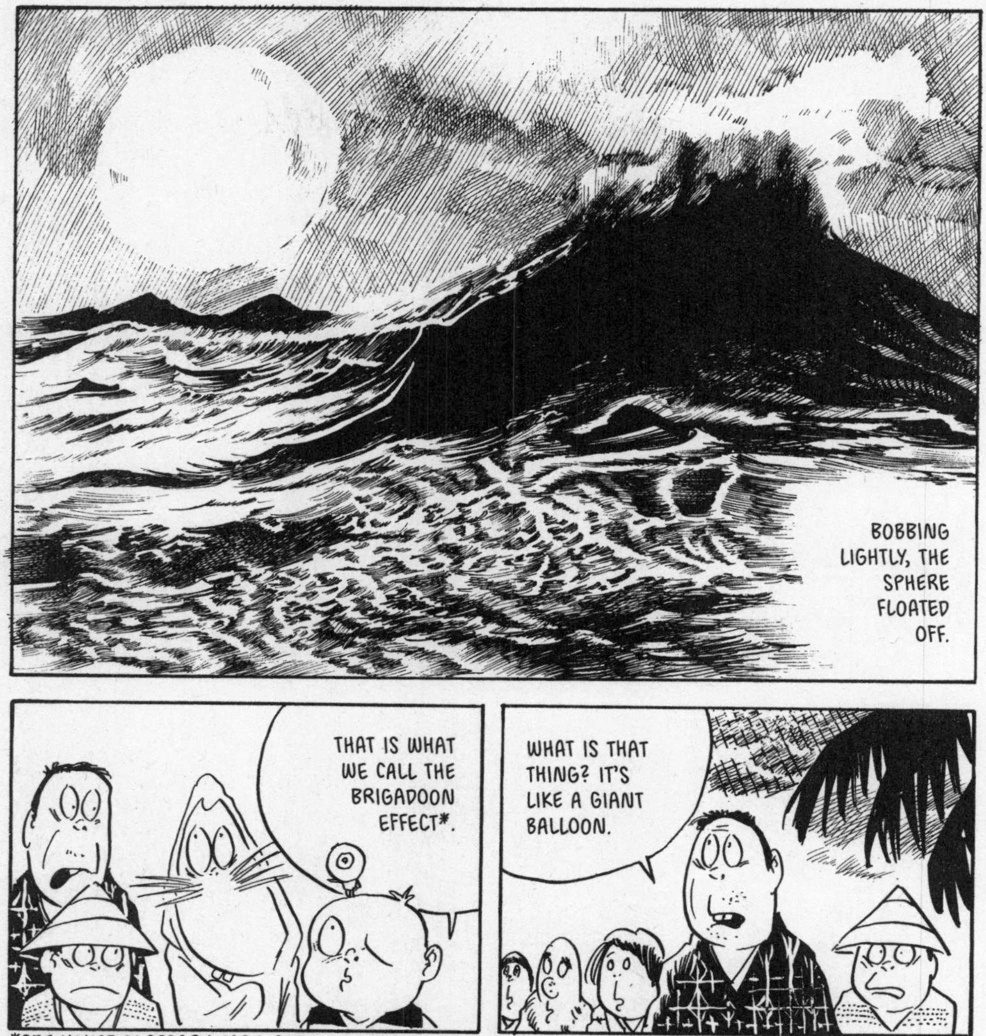
BOBBING LIGHTLY, THE SPHERE FLOATED OFF.
WHAT IS THAT THING? IT'S LIKE A GIANT BALLOON.
THAT IS WHAT WE CALL THE BRIGADOON EFFECT*.

*SEE YOKAI GLOSSARY PAGE 395.

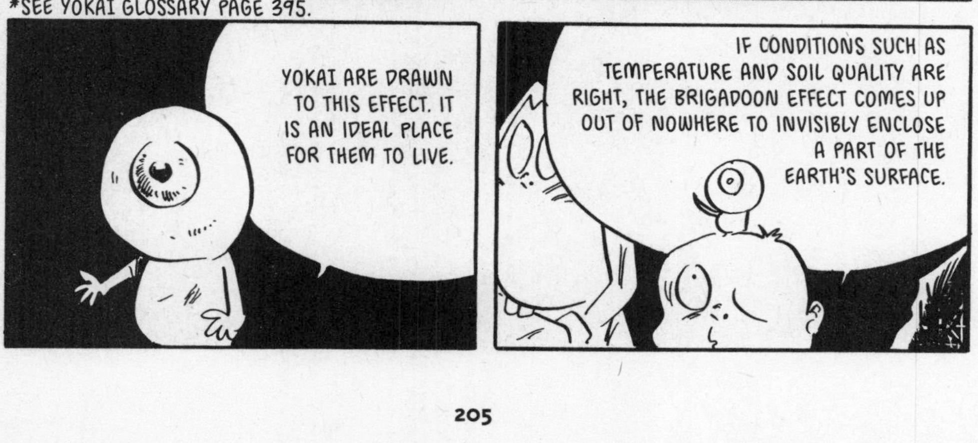
IF CONDITIONS SUCH AS TEMPERATURE AND SOIL QUALITY ARE RIGHT, THE BRIGADOON EFFECT COMES UP OUT OF NOWHERE TO INVISIBLY ENCLOSE A PART OF THE EARTH'S SURFACE.
YOKAI ARE DRAWN TO THIS EFFECT. IT IS AN IDEAL PLACE FOR THEM TO LIVE.

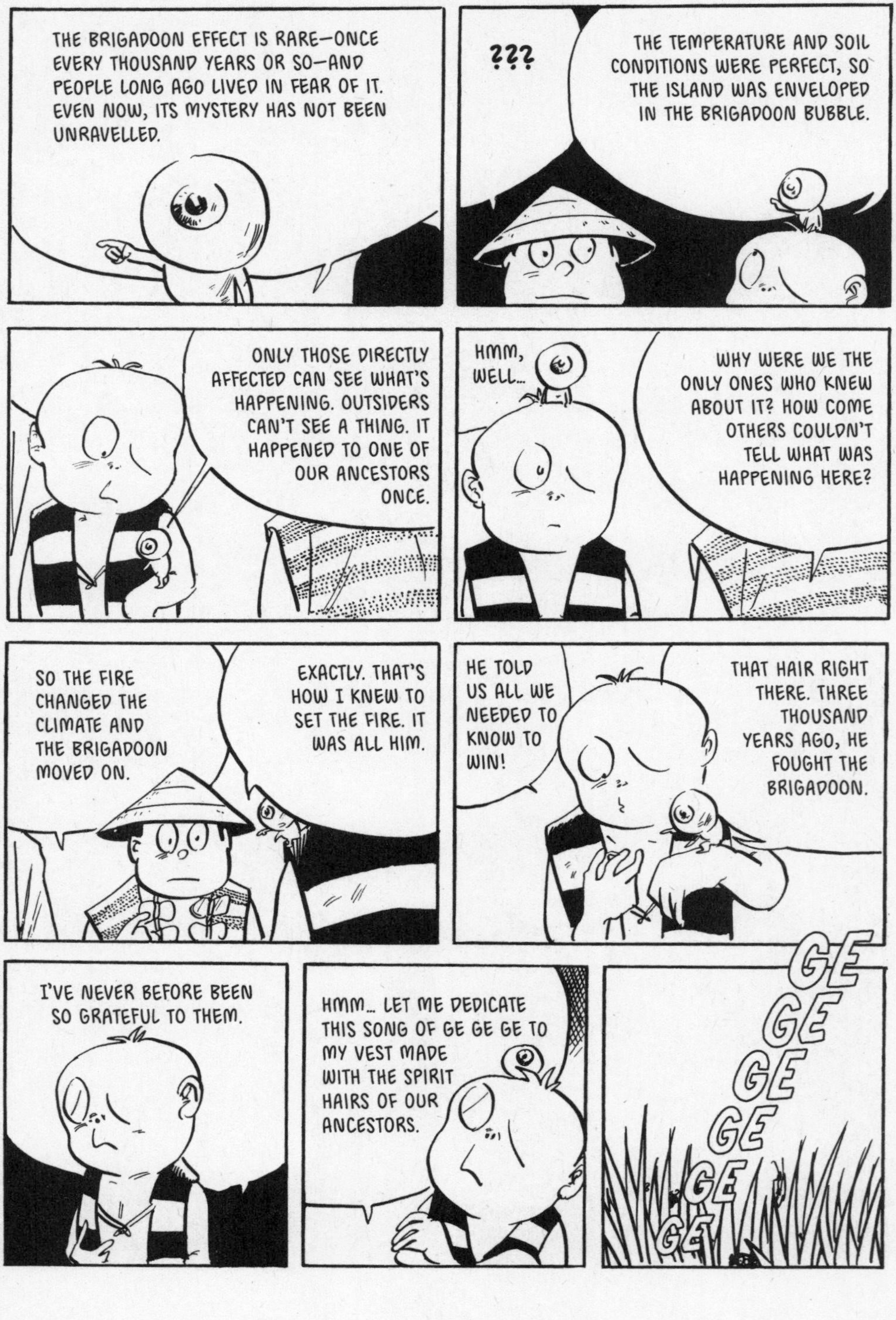
THE TEMPERATURE AND SOIL CONDITIONS WERE PERFECT, SO THE ISLAND WAS ENVELOPED IN THE BRIGADOON BUBBLE.
???
THE BRIGADOON EFFECT IS RARE—ONCE EVERY THOUSAND YEARS OR SO—AND PEOPLE LONG AGO LIVED IN FEAR OF IT. EVEN NOW, ITS MYSTERY HAS NOT BEEN UNRAVELLED.
WHY WERE WE THE ONLY ONES WHO KNEW ABOUT IT? HOW COME OTHERS COULDN'T TELL WHAT WAS HAPPENING HERE?
HMM, WELL...
ONLY THOSE DIRECTLY AFFECTED CAN SEE WHAT'S HAPPENING. OUTSIDERS CAN'T SEE A THING. IT HAPPENED TO ONE OF OUR ANCESTORS ONCE.
THAT HAIR RIGHT THERE. THREE THOUSAND YEARS AGO, HE FOUGHT THE BRIGADOON.
HE TOLD US ALL WE NEEDED TO KNOW TO WIN!
EXACTLY. THAT'S HOW I KNEW TO SET THE FIRE. IT WAS ALL HIM.
SO THE FIRE CHANGED THE CLIMATE AND THE BRIGADOON MOVED ON.
GE GE GE GE GE GE
HMM... LET ME DEDICATE THIS SONG OF GE GE GE TO MY VEST MADE WITH THE SPIRIT HAIRS OF OUR ANCESTORS.
I'VE NEVER BEFORE BEEN SO GRATEFUL TO THEM.

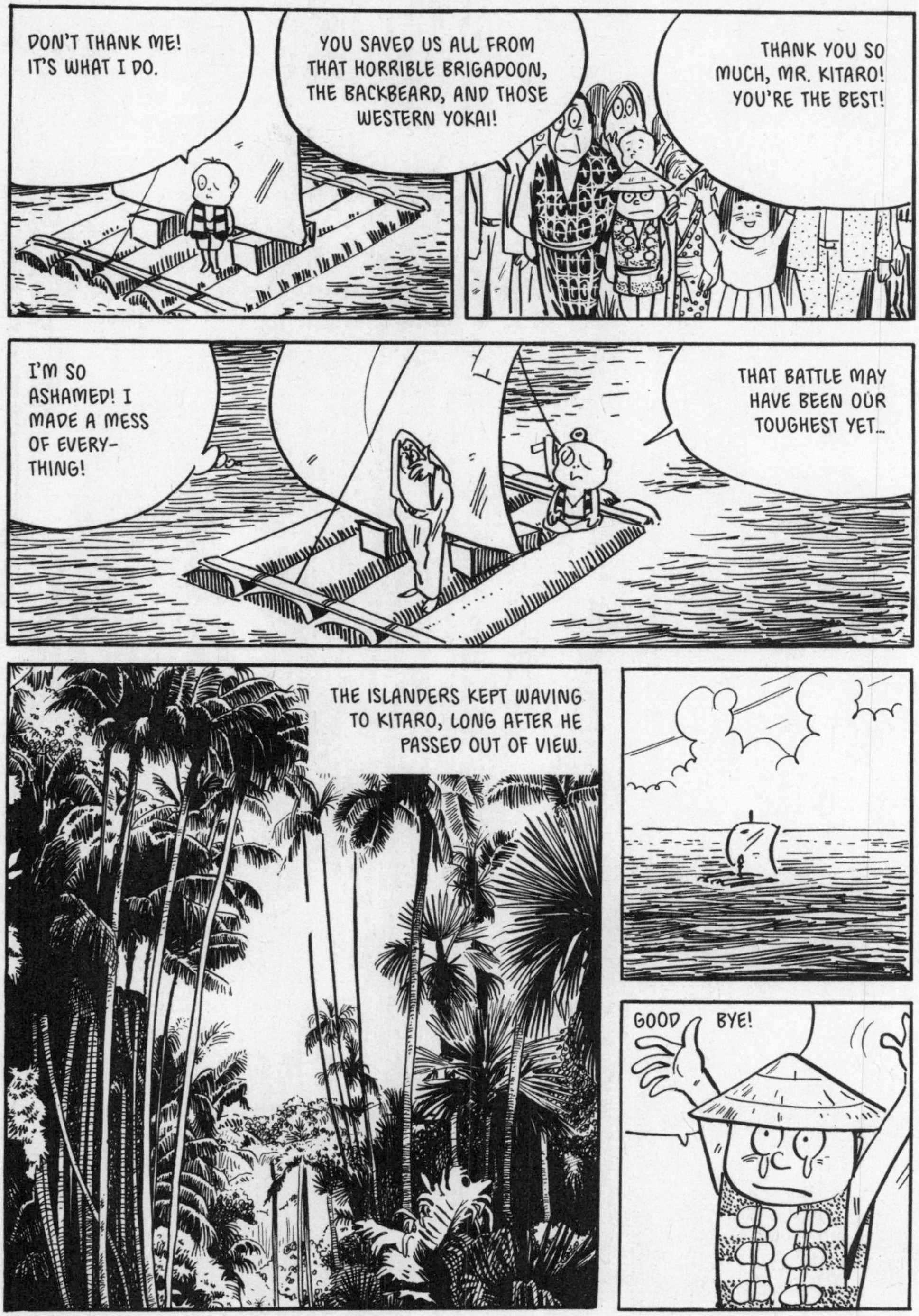
THANK YOU SO MUCH, MR. KITARO! YOU'RE THE BEST!
YOU SAVED US ALL FROM THAT HORRIBLE BRIGADOON, THE BACKBEARD, AND THOSE WESTERN YOKAI!
DON'T THANK ME! IT'S WHAT I DO.
THAT BATTLE MAY HAVE BEEN OUR TOUGHEST YET...
I'M SO ASHAMED! I MADE A MESS OF EVERY-THING!
GOOD BYE!
THE ISLANDERS KEPT WAVING TO KITARO, LONG AFTER HE PASSED OUT OF VIEW.

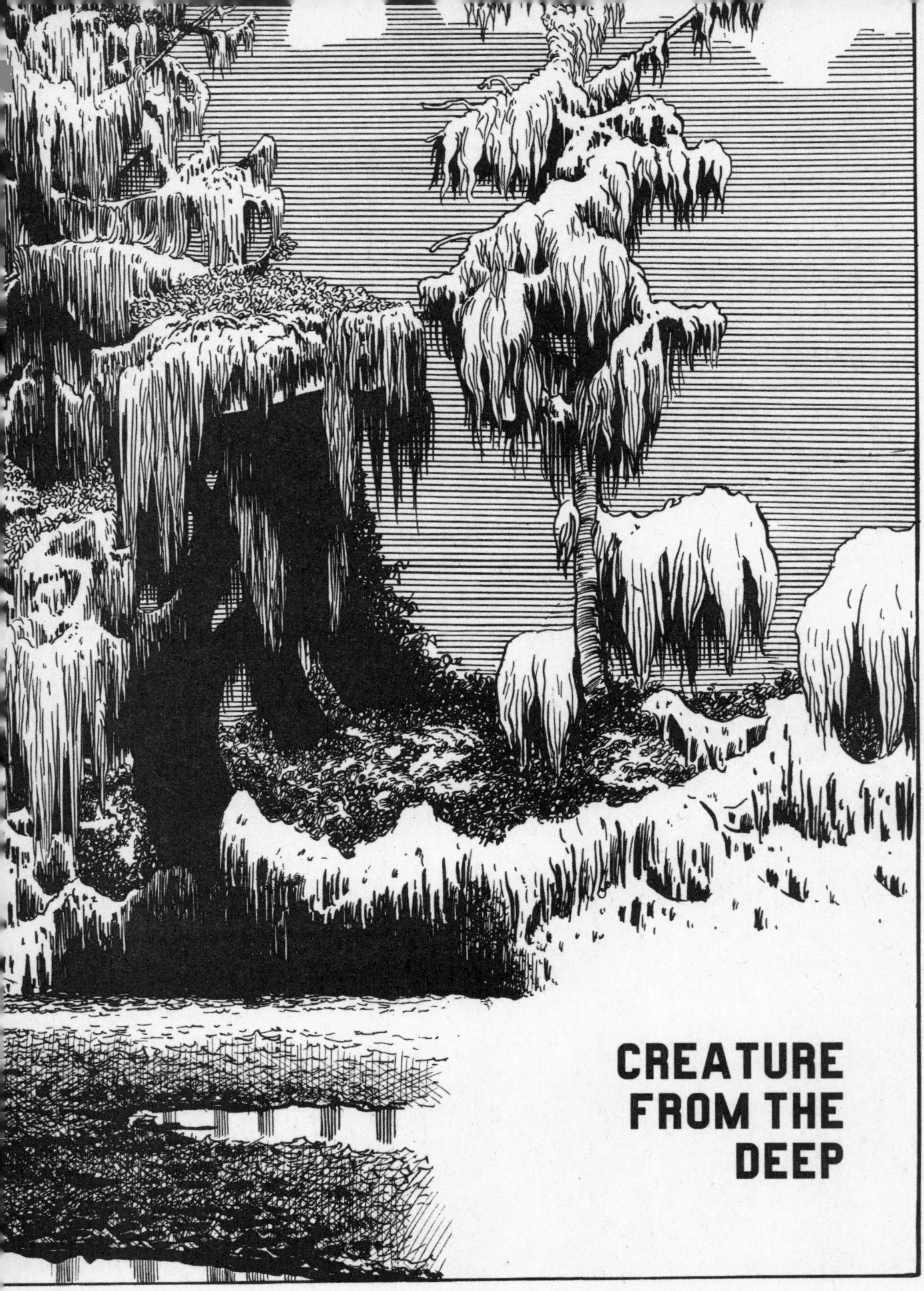
CREATURE
FROM THE
DEEP

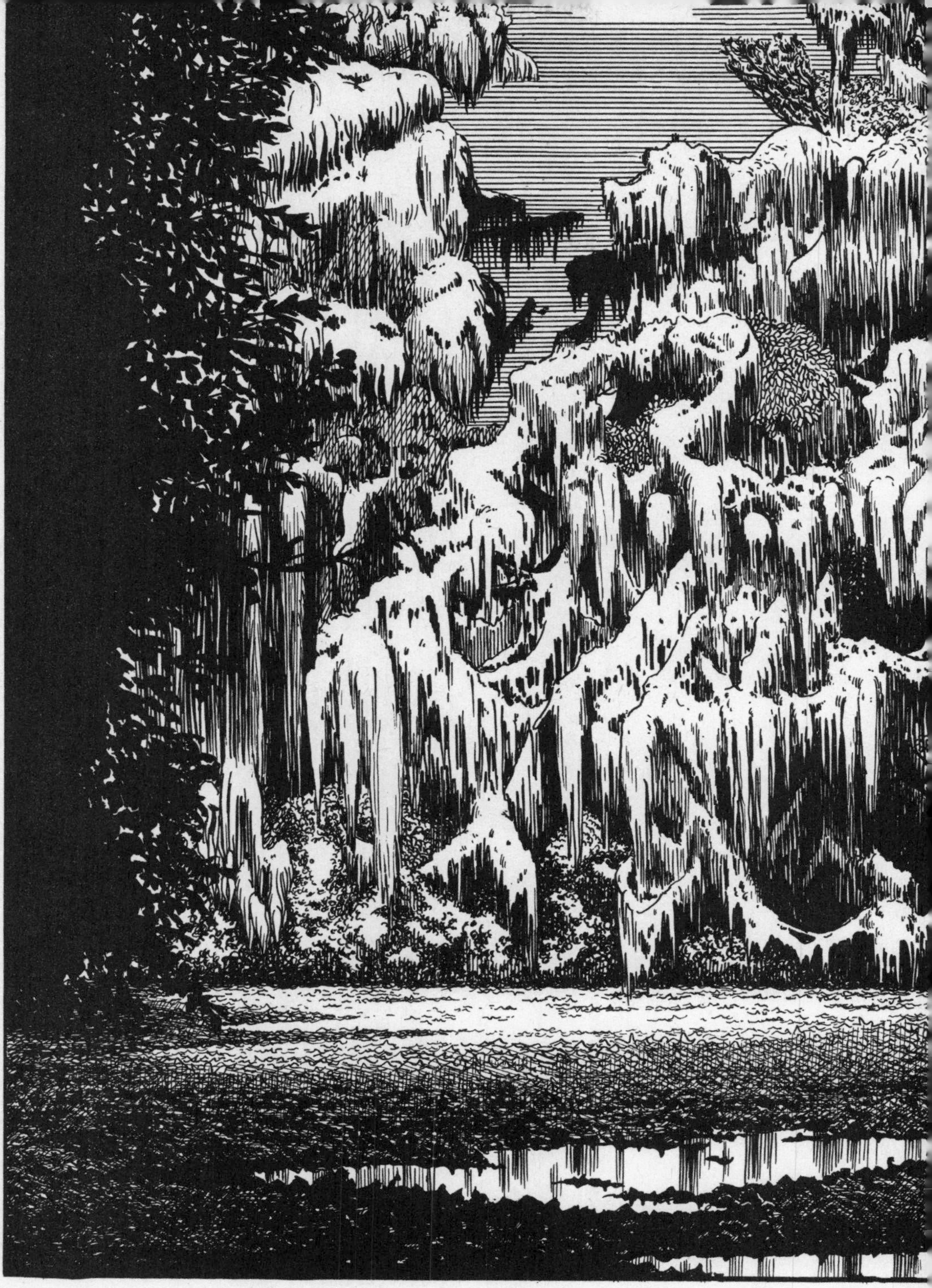

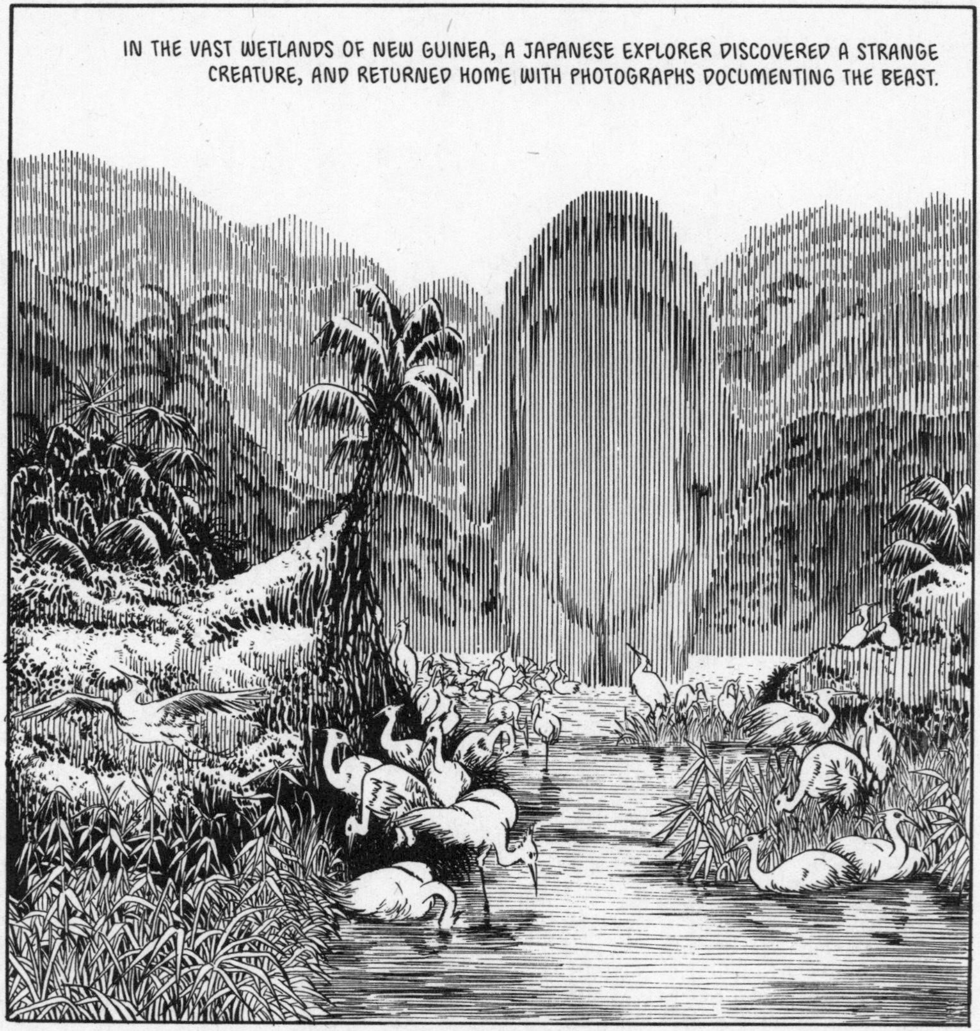
IN THE VAST WETLANDS OF NEW GUINEA, A JAPANESE EXPLORER DISCOVERED A STRANGE CREATURE, AND RETURNED HOME WITH PHOTOGRAPHS DOCUMENTING THE BEAST.

MANY SCIENTISTS STUDIED THE PHOTO AND DETERMINED THAT THE CREATURE WAS IN FACT A ZEUGLODON*, AN ANCESTOR TO THE MODERN WHALE THAT HAD LIVED MORE THAN THREE HUNDRED MILLION YEARS AGO. BUT HOW COULD IT STILL BE ALIVE WITHOUT HAVING EVOLVED AT ALL?

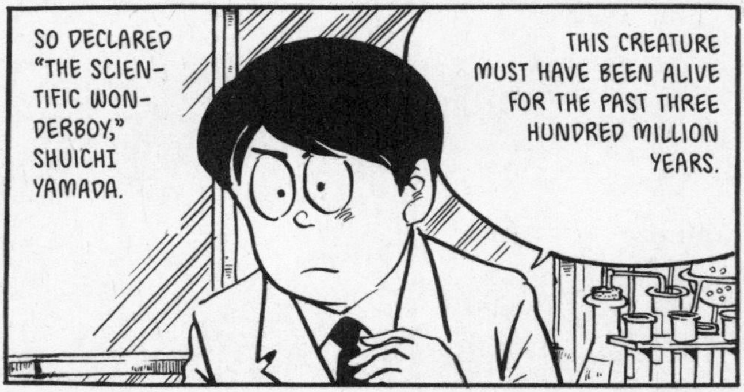
THIS CREATURE MUST HAVE BEEN ALIVE FOR THE PAST THREE HUNDRED MILLION YEARS.
SO DECLARED "THE SCIENTIFIC WONDERBOY," SHUICHI YAMADA.

*SEE YOKAI GLOSSARY PAGE 394.

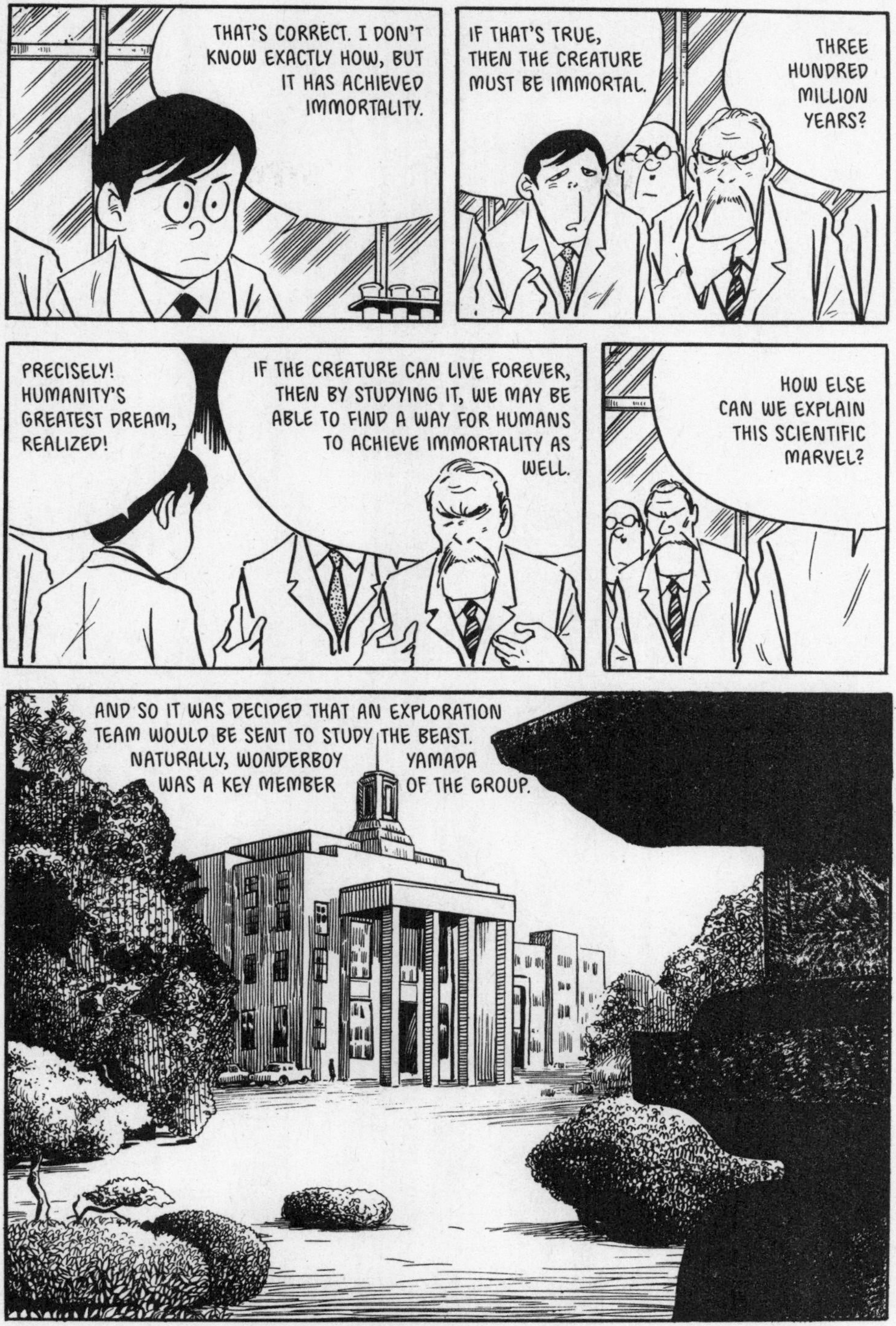
THREE HUNDRED MILLION YEARS?
IF THAT'S TRUE, THEN THE CREATURE MUST BE IMMORTAL.
THAT'S CORRECT. I DON'T KNOW EXACTLY HOW, BUT IT HAS ACHIEVED IMMORTALITY.
HOW ELSE CAN WE EXPLAIN THIS SCIENTIFIC MARVEL?
IF THE CREATURE CAN LIVE FOREVER, THEN BY STUDYING IT, WE MAY BE ABLE TO FIND A WAY FOR HUMANS TO ACHIEVE IMMORTALITY AS WELL.
PRECISELY! HUMANITY'S GREATEST DREAM, REALIZED!
AND SO IT WAS DECIDED THAT AN EXPLORATION TEAM WOULD BE SENT TO STUDY THE BEAST. NATURALLY, WONDERBOY YAMADA WAS A KEY MEMBER OF THE GROUP.

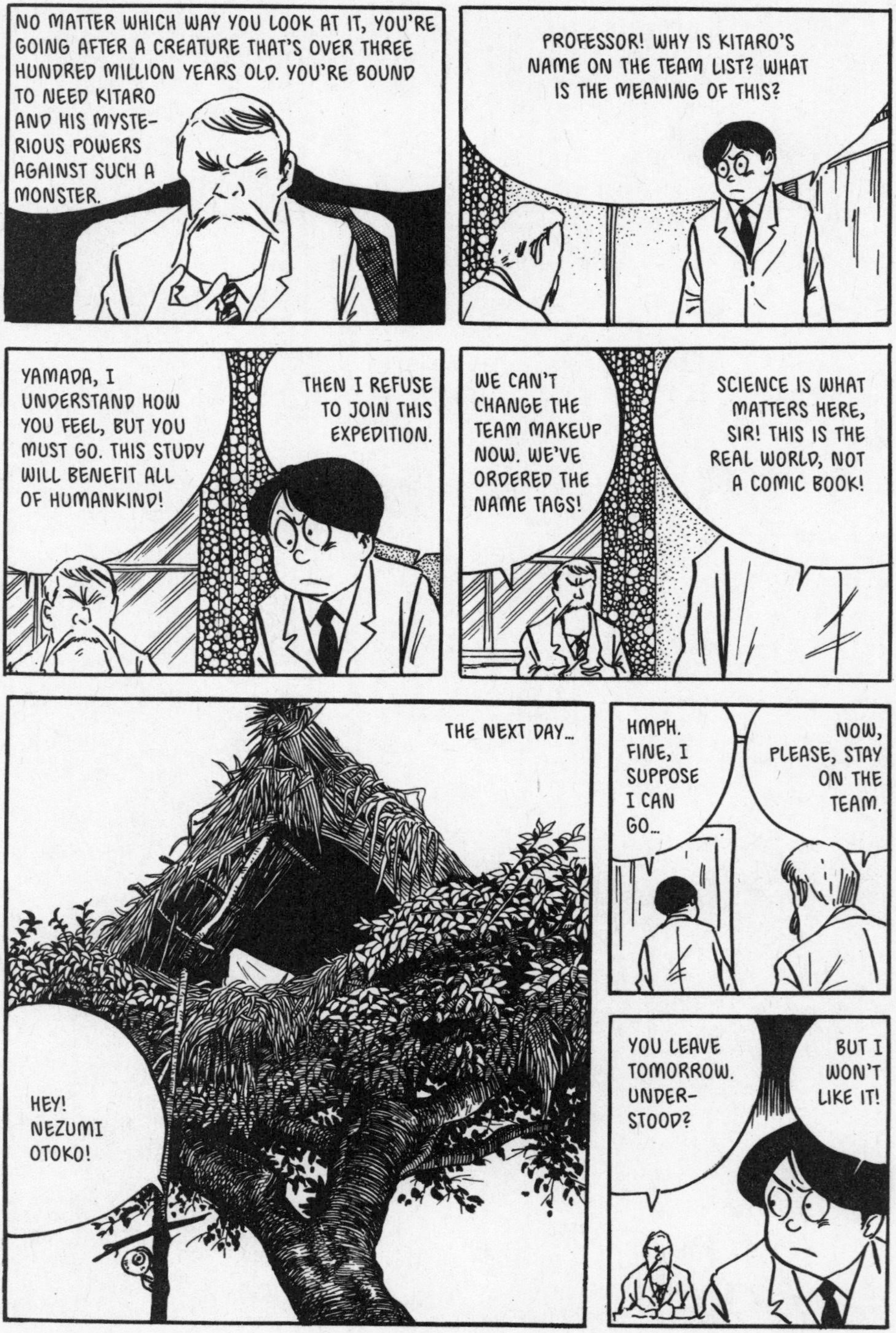
PROFESSOR! WHY IS KITARO'S NAME ON THE TEAM LIST? WHAT IS THE MEANING OF THIS?
NO MATTER WHICH WAY YOU LOOK AT IT, YOU'RE GOING AFTER A CREATURE THAT'S OVER THREE HUNDRED MILLION YEARS OLD. YOU'RE BOUND TO NEED KITARO AND HIS MYSTERIOUS POWERS AGAINST SUCH A MONSTER.
SCIENCE IS WHAT MATTERS HERE, SIR! THIS IS THE REAL WORLD, NOT A COMIC BOOK!
WE CAN'T CHANGE THE TEAM MAKEUP NOW. WE'VE ORDERED THE NAME TAGS!
THEN I REFUSE TO JOIN THIS EXPEDITION.
YAMADA, I UNDERSTAND HOW YOU FEEL, BUT YOU MUST GO. THIS STUDY WILL BENEFIT ALL OF HUMANKIND!
NOW, PLEASE, STAY ON THE TEAM.
HMPH. FINE, I SUPPOSE I CAN GO...
BUT I WON'T LIKE IT!
YOU LEAVE TOMORROW. UNDERSTOOD?
THE NEXT DAY...
HEY! NEZUMI OTOKO!

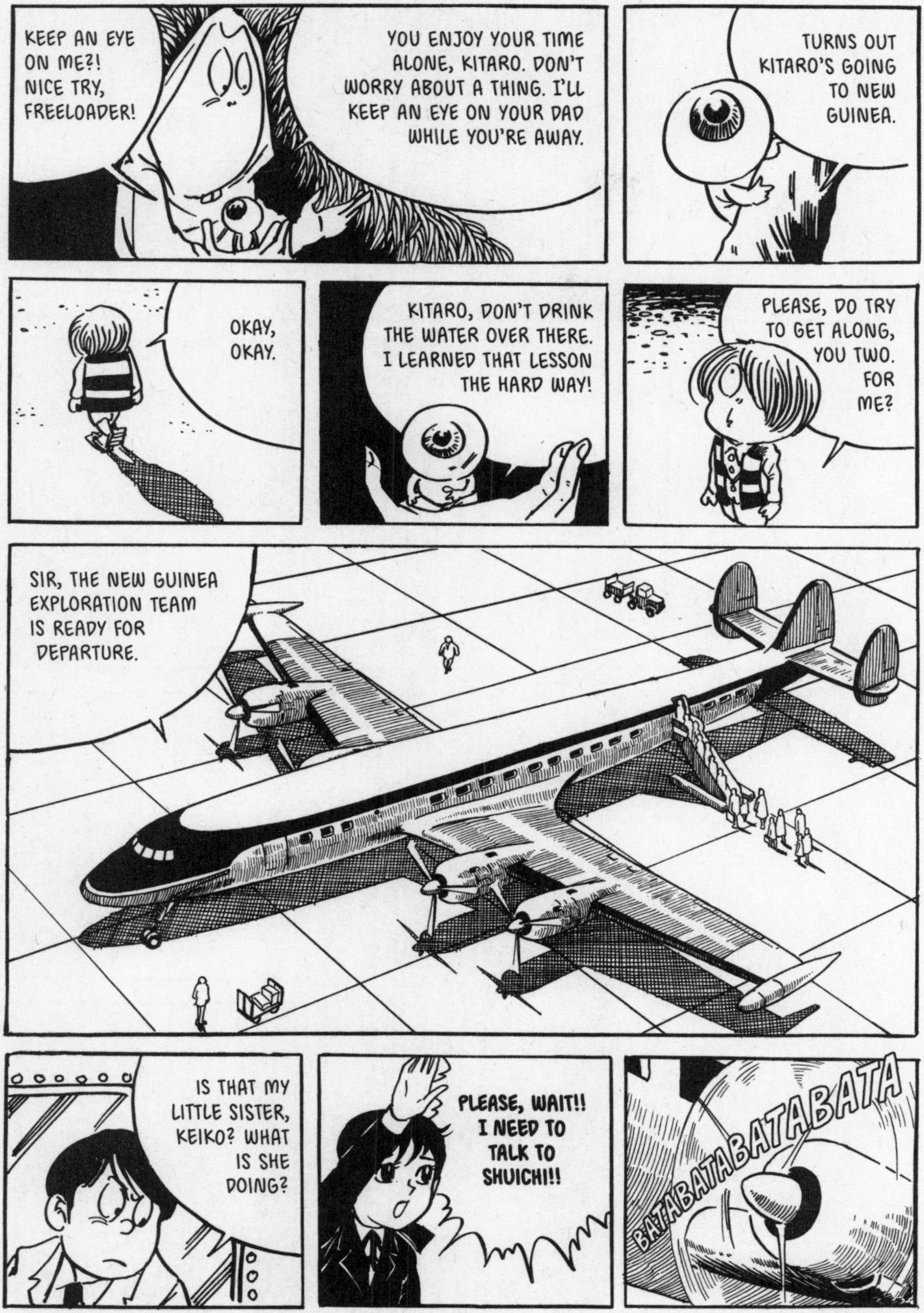
TURNS OUT KITARO'S GOING TO NEW GUINEA.
YOU ENJOY YOUR TIME ALONE, KITARO. DON'T WORRY ABOUT A THING. I'LL KEEP AN EYE ON YOUR DAD WHILE YOU'RE AWAY.
KEEP AN EYE ON ME?! NICE TRY, FREELOADER!
PLEASE, DO TRY TO GET ALONG, YOU TWO. FOR ME?
KITARO, DON'T DRINK THE WATER OVER THERE. I LEARNED THAT LESSON THE HARD WAY!
OKAY, OKAY.
SIR, THE NEW GUINEA EXPLORATION TEAM IS READY FOR DEPARTURE.
BATABATABATABATA
PLEASE, WAIT!! I NEED TO TALK TO SHUICHI!!!
IS THAT MY LITTLE SISTER, KEIKO? WHAT IS SHE DOING?

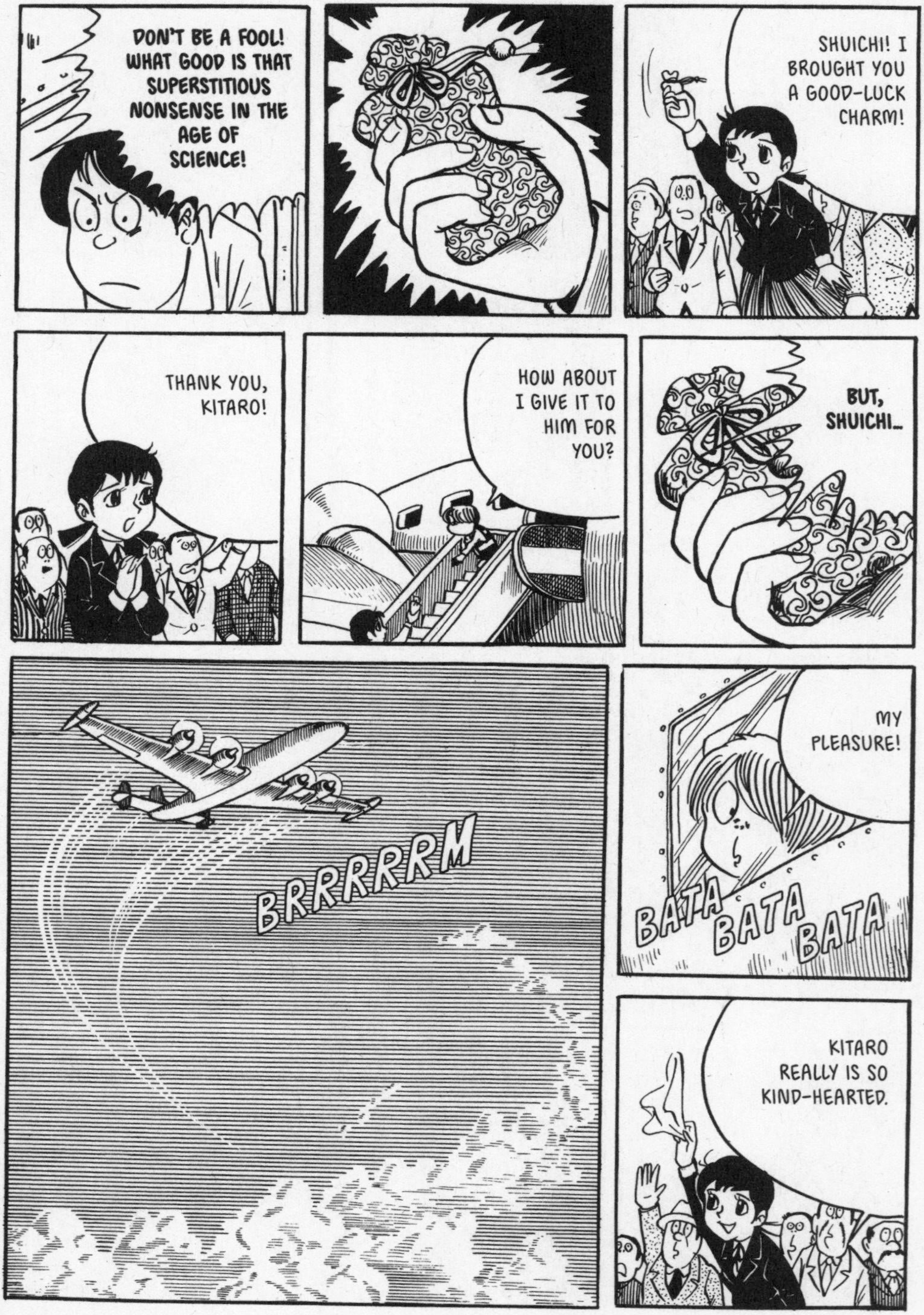
SHUICHI! I BROUGHT YOU A GOOD-LUCK CHARM!
DON'T BE A FOOL! WHAT GOOD IS THAT SUPERSTITIOUS NONSENSE IN THE AGE OF SCIENCE!
BUT, SHUICHI...
HOW ABOUT I GIVE IT TO HIM FOR YOU?
THANK YOU, KITARO!
MY PLEASURE!
BATA BATA BATA
KITARO REALLY IS SO KIND-HEARTED.
BRRRRRM

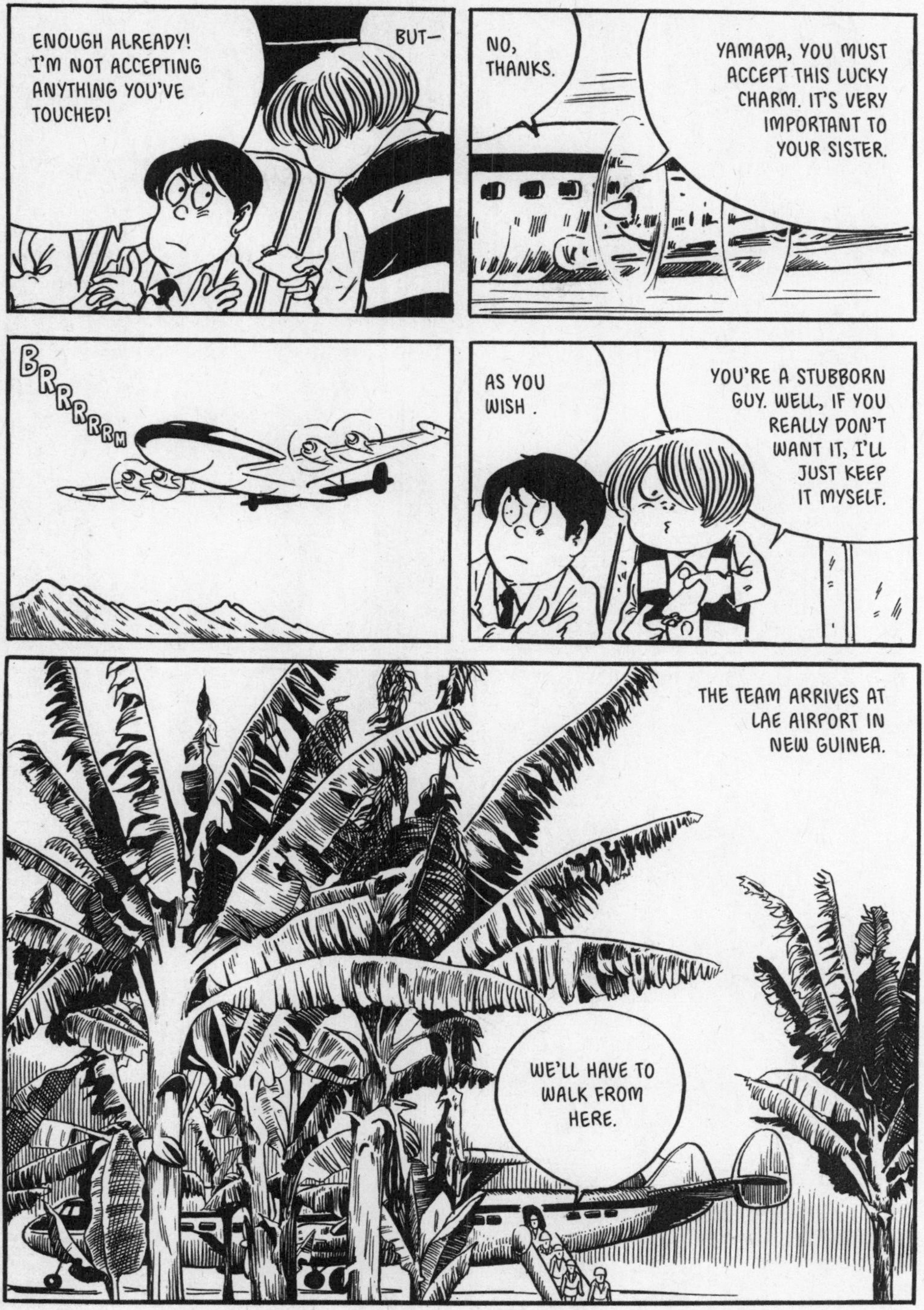
YAMADA, YOU MUST ACCEPT THIS LUCKY CHARM. IT'S VERY IMPORTANT TO YOUR SISTER.
NO, THANKS.
BUT—
ENOUGH ALREADY! I'M NOT ACCEPTING ANYTHING YOU'VE TOUCHED!
YOU'RE A STUBBORN GUY. WELL, IF YOU REALLY DON'T WANT IT, I'LL JUST KEEP IT MYSELF.
AS YOU WISH .
BRRRRRM
THE TEAM ARRIVES AT LAE AIRPORT IN NEW GUINEA.
WE'LL HAVE TO WALK FROM HERE.

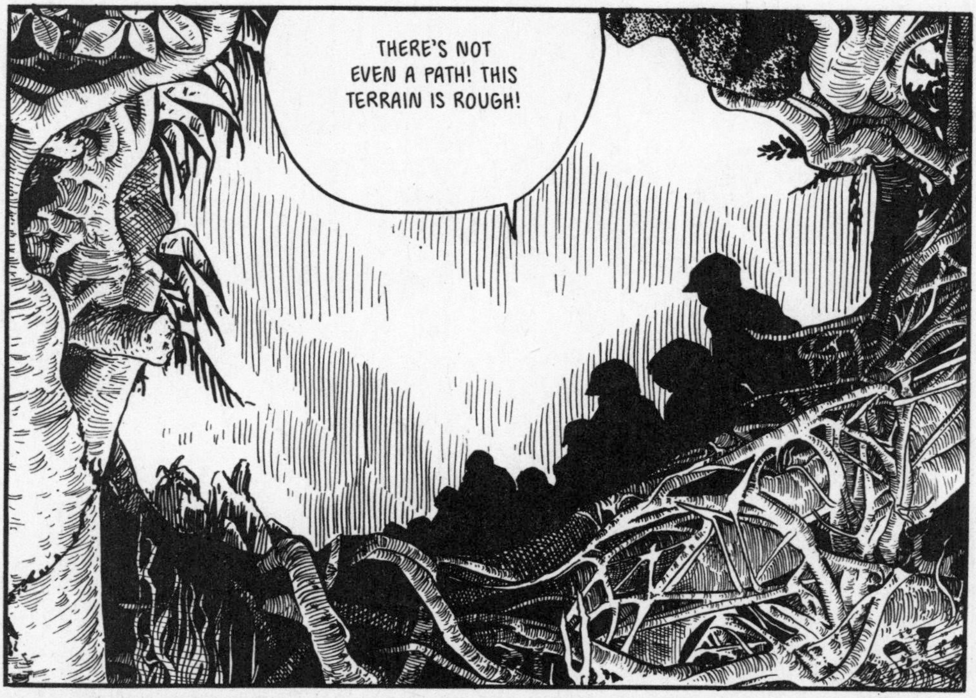
THERE'S NOT EVEN A PATH! THIS TERRAIN IS ROUGH!

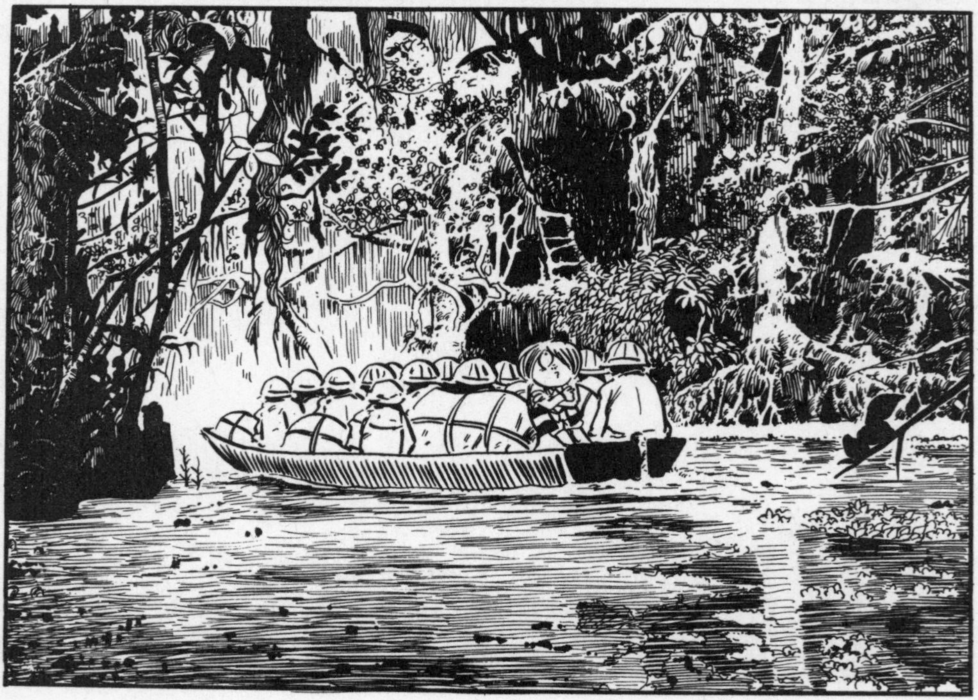

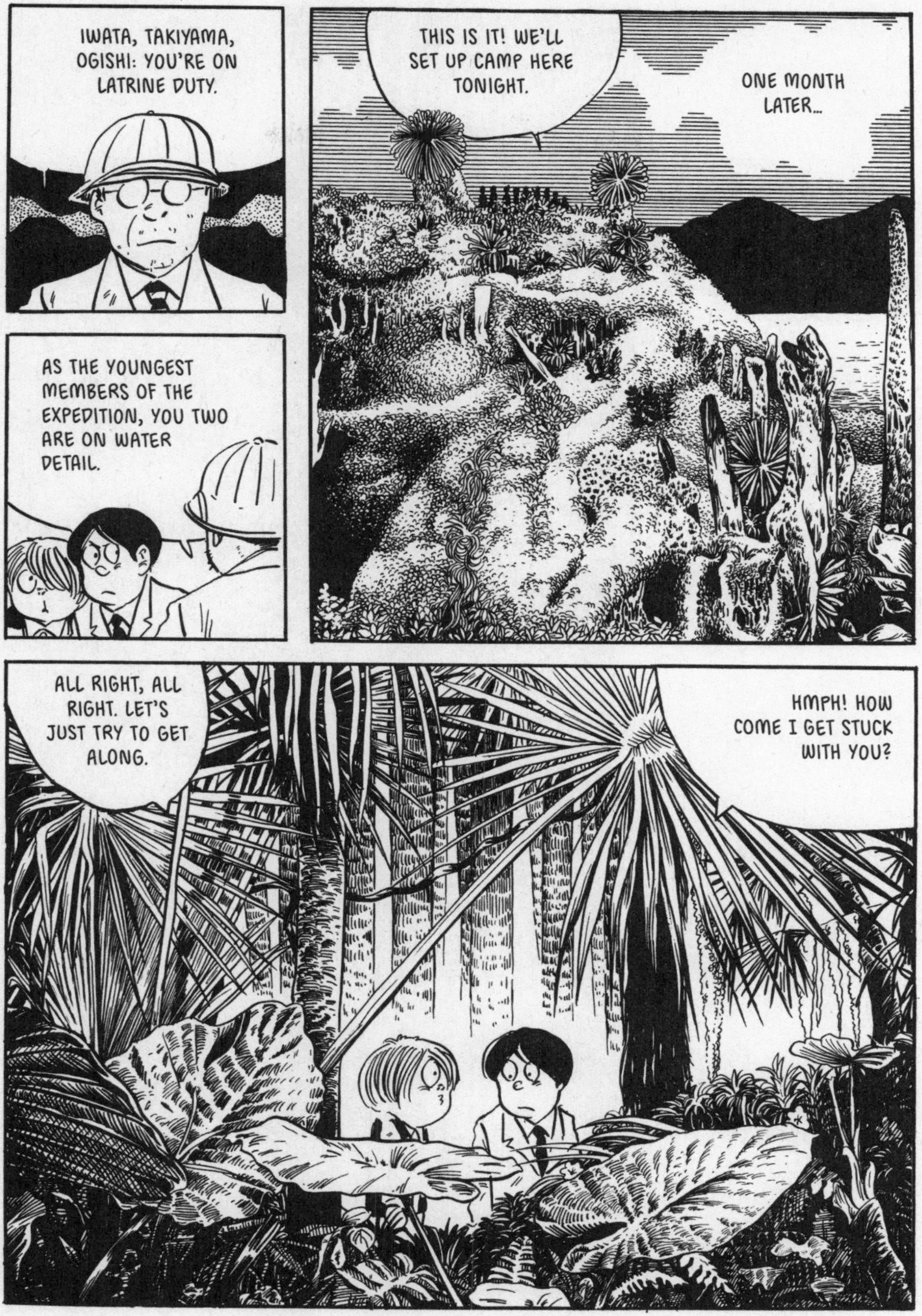
ONE MONTH LATER...
THIS IS IT! WE'LL SET UP CAMP HERE TONIGHT.
IWATA, TAKIYAMA, OGISHI: YOU'RE ON LATRINE DUTY.
AS THE YOUNGEST MEMBERS OF THE EXPEDITION, YOU TWO ARE ON WATER DETAIL.
HMPH! HOW COME I GET STUCK WITH YOU?
ALL RIGHT, ALL RIGHT. LET'S JUST TRY TO GET ALONG.

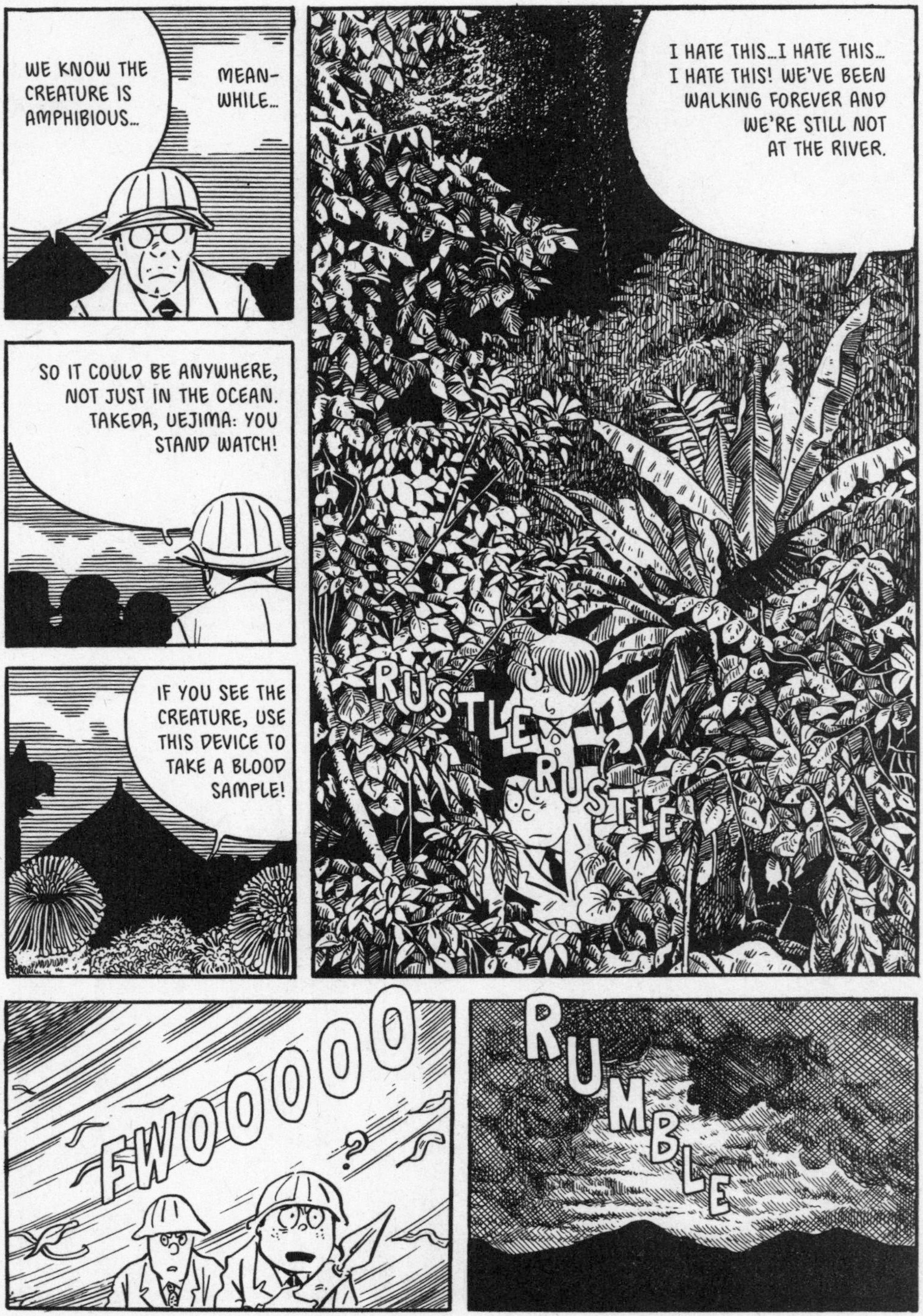
I HATE THIS...I HATE THIS... I HATE THIS! WE'VE BEEN WALKING FOREVER AND WE'RE STILL NOT AT THE RIVER.
RUSTLE
RUSTLE
MEAN-WHILE...
WE KNOW THE CREATURE IS AMPHIBIOUS...
SO IT COULD BE ANYWHERE, NOT JUST IN THE OCEAN. TAKEDA, UEJIMA: YOU STAND WATCH!
IF YOU SEE THE CREATURE, USE THIS DEVICE TO TAKE A BLOOD SAMPLE!
RUMBLE
FWOOOOOO
?

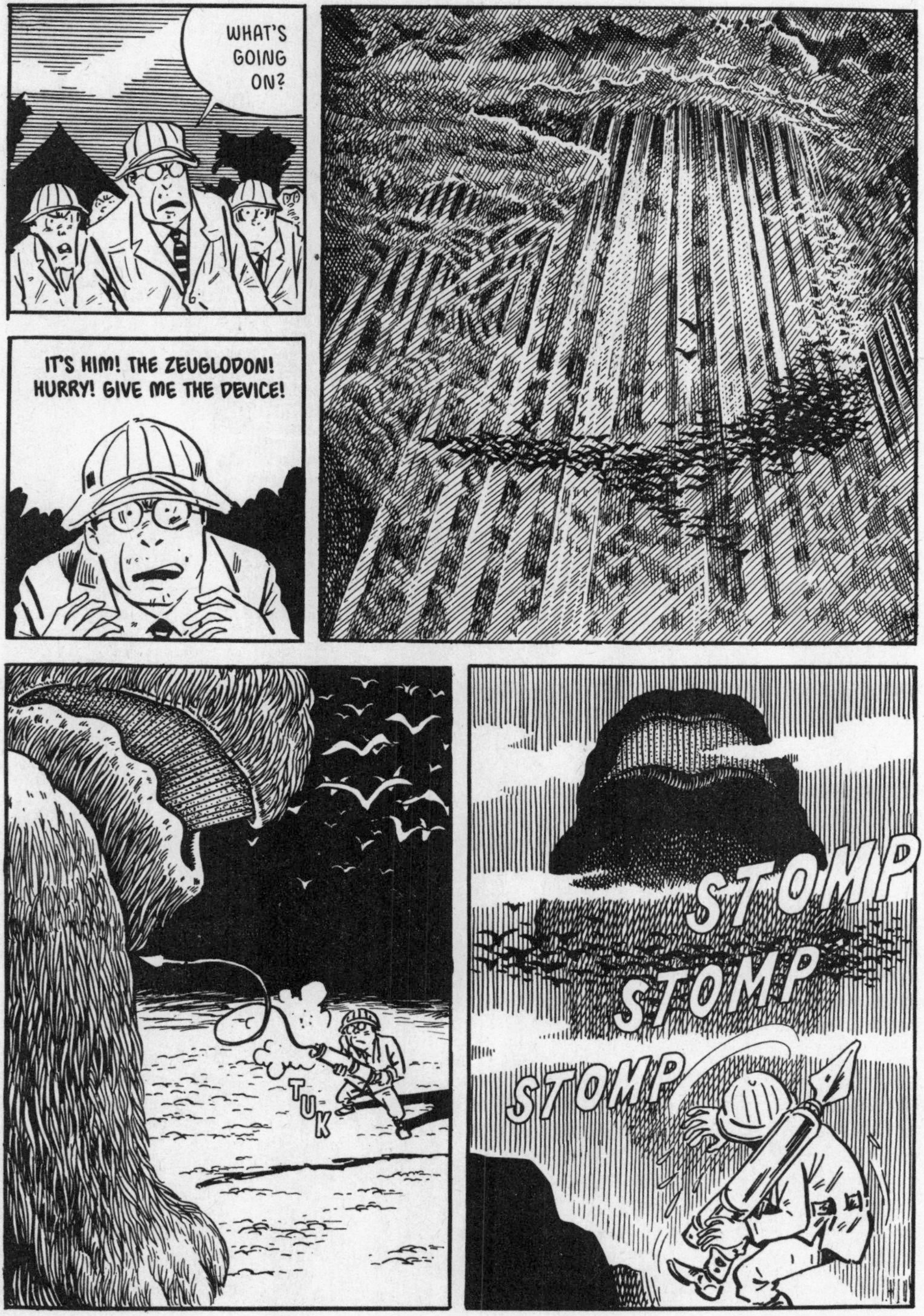
WHAT'S GOING ON?
IT'S HIM! THE ZEUGLODON! HURRY! GIVE ME THE DEVICE!
STOMP
STOMP
STOMP
TUK

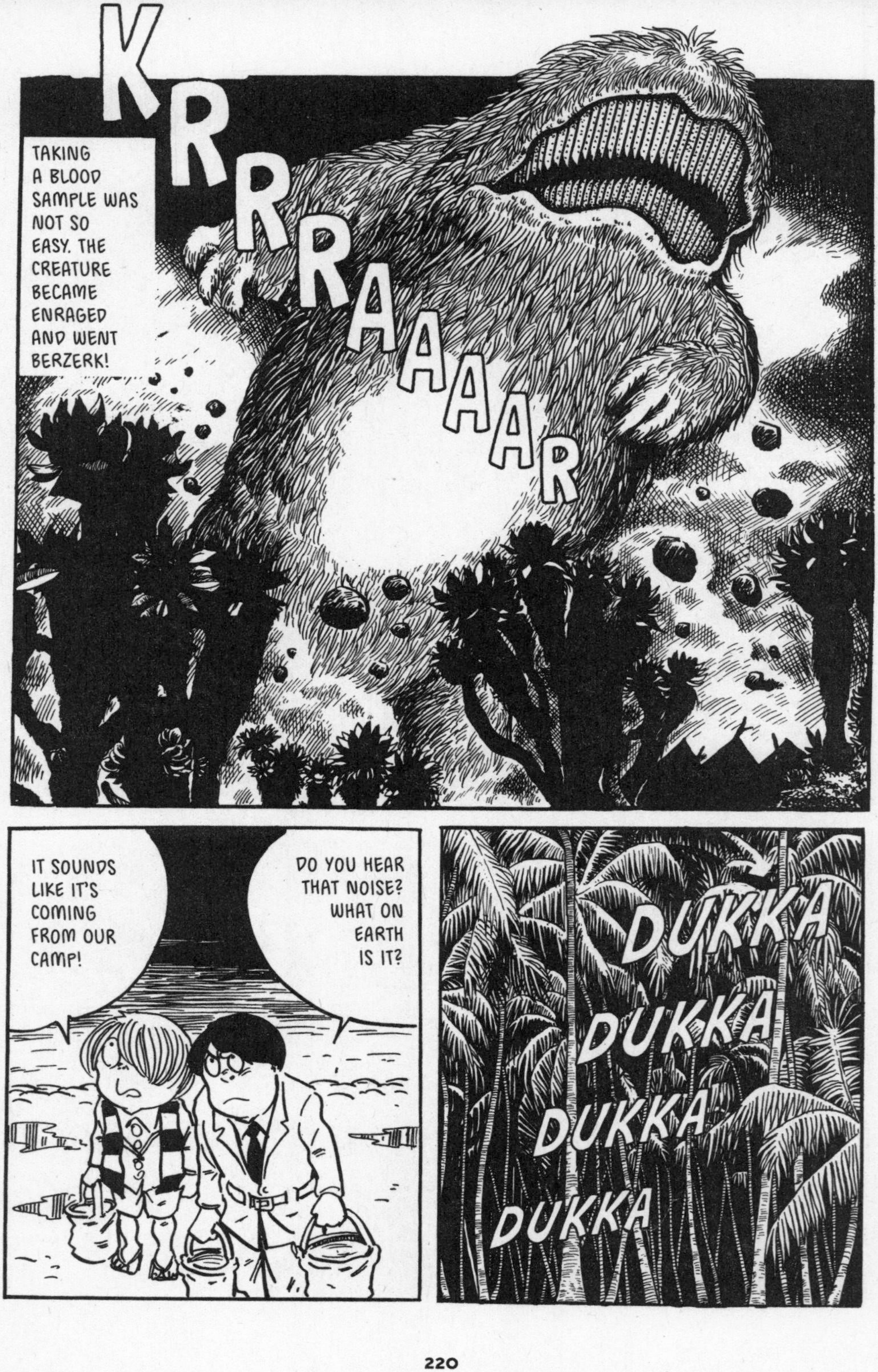
KRRRAAAAR
TAKING A BLOOD SAMPLE WAS NOT SO EASY. THE CREATURE BECAME ENRAGED AND WENT BERZERK!
DUKKA
DUKKA
DUKKA
DUKKA
DO YOU HEAR THAT NOISE? WHAT ON EARTH IS IT?
IT SOUNDS LIKE IT'S COMING FROM OUR CAMP!

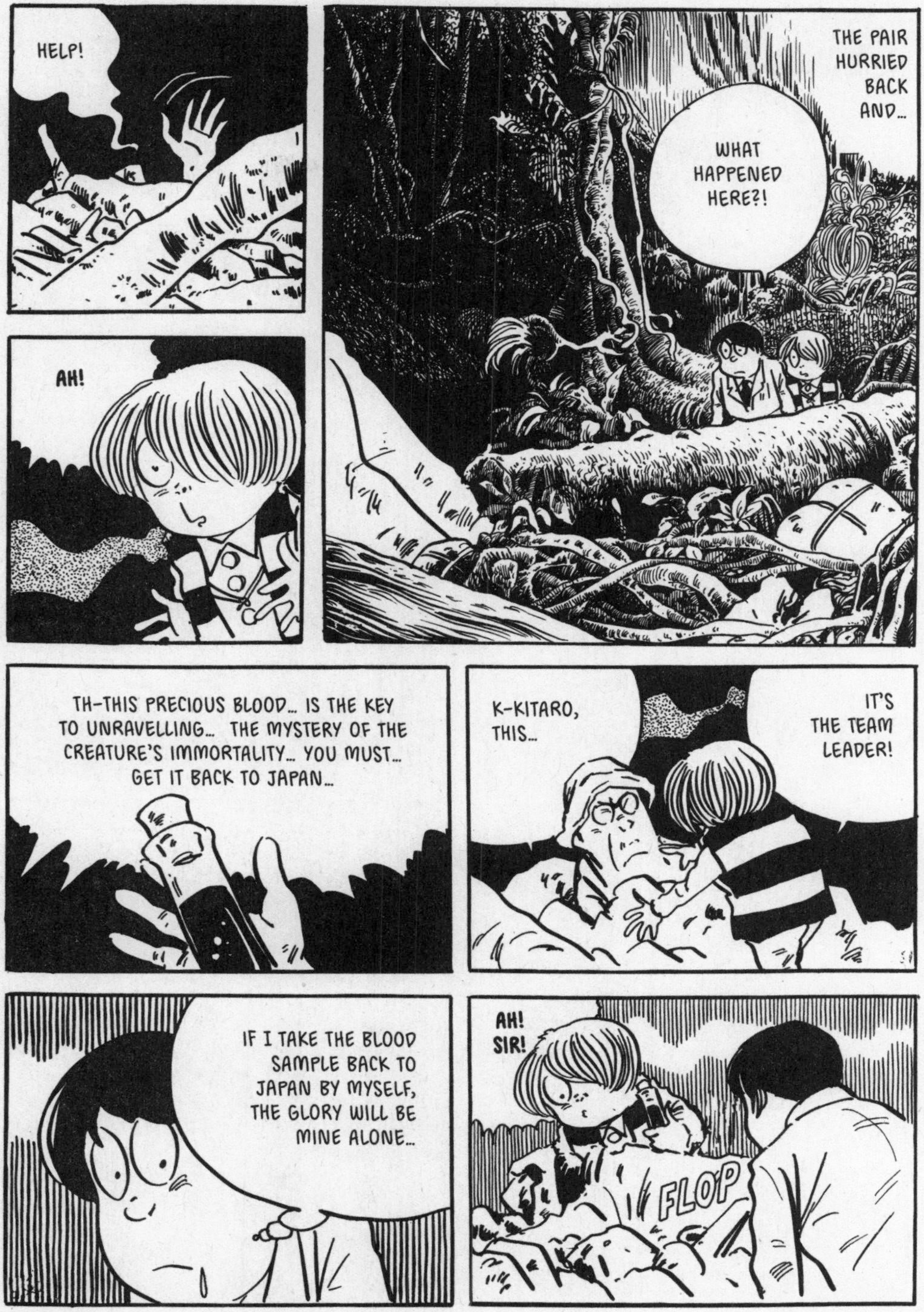
THE PAIR HURRIED BACK AND...
WHAT HAPPENED HERE?!
HELP!
AH!
IT'S THE TEAM LEADER!
K-KITARO, THIS...
TH-THIS PRECIOUS BLOOD... IS THE KEY TO UNRAVELLING... THE MYSTERY OF THE CREATURE'S IMMORTALITY... YOU MUST... GET IT BACK TO JAPAN...
AH! SIR!
FLOP
IF I TAKE THE BLOOD SAMPLE BACK TO JAPAN BY MYSELF, THE GLORY WILL BE MINE ALONE...

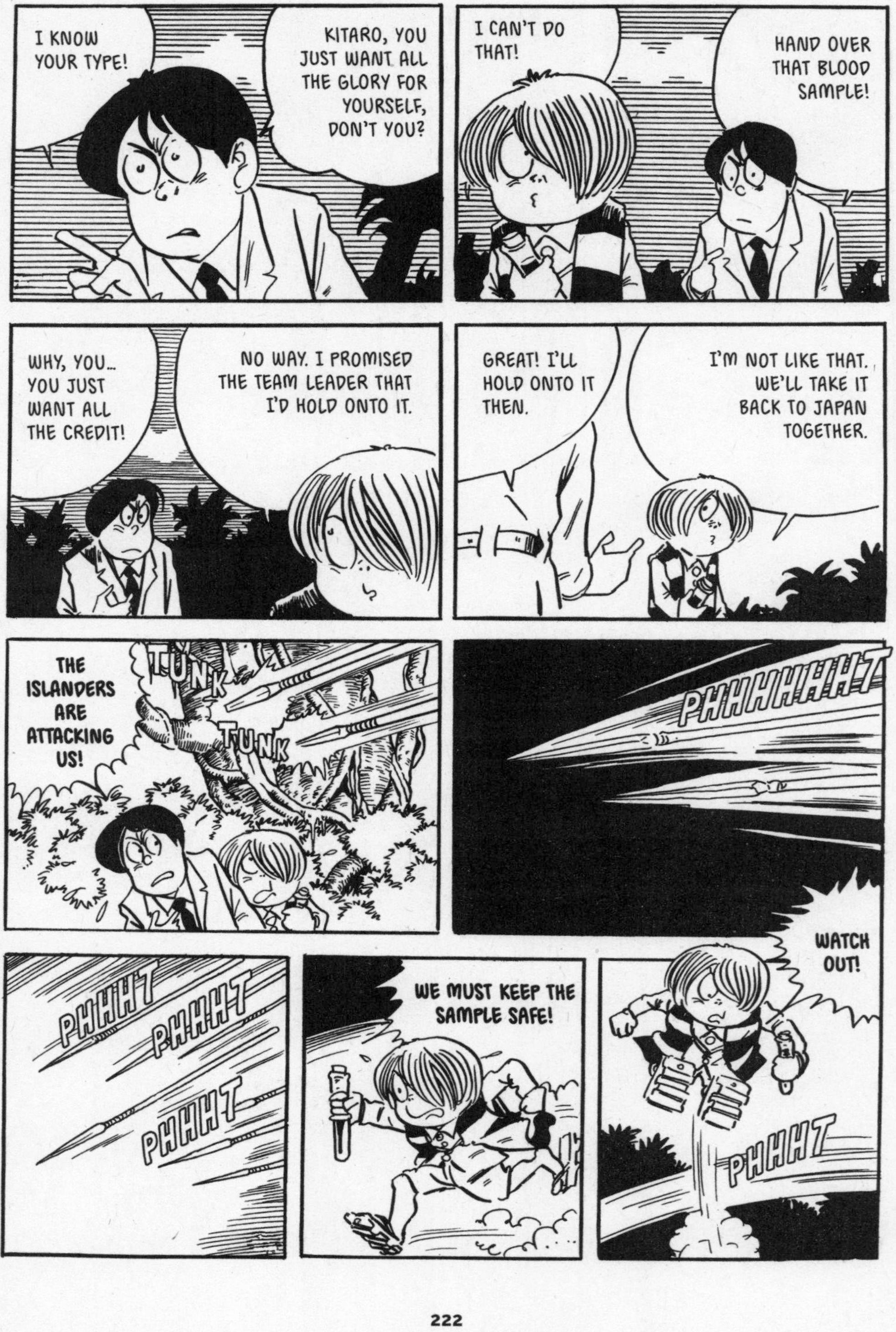
HAND OVER THAT BLOOD SAMPLE!
I CAN'T DO THAT!
KITARO, YOU JUST WANT ALL THE GLORY FOR YOURSELF, DON'T YOU?
I KNOW YOUR TYPE!
I'M NOT LIKE THAT. WE'LL TAKE IT BACK TO JAPAN TOGETHER.
GREAT! I'LL HOLD ONTO IT THEN.
NO WAY. I PROMISED THE TEAM LEADER THAT I'D HOLD ONTO IT.
WHY, YOU... YOU JUST WANT ALL THE CREDIT!
PHHHHHHHT
TUNK
TUNK
THE ISLANDERS ARE ATTACKING US!
WATCH OUT!
PHHHT
WE MUST KEEP THE SAMPLE SAFE!
PHHHT
PHHHT
PHHHT

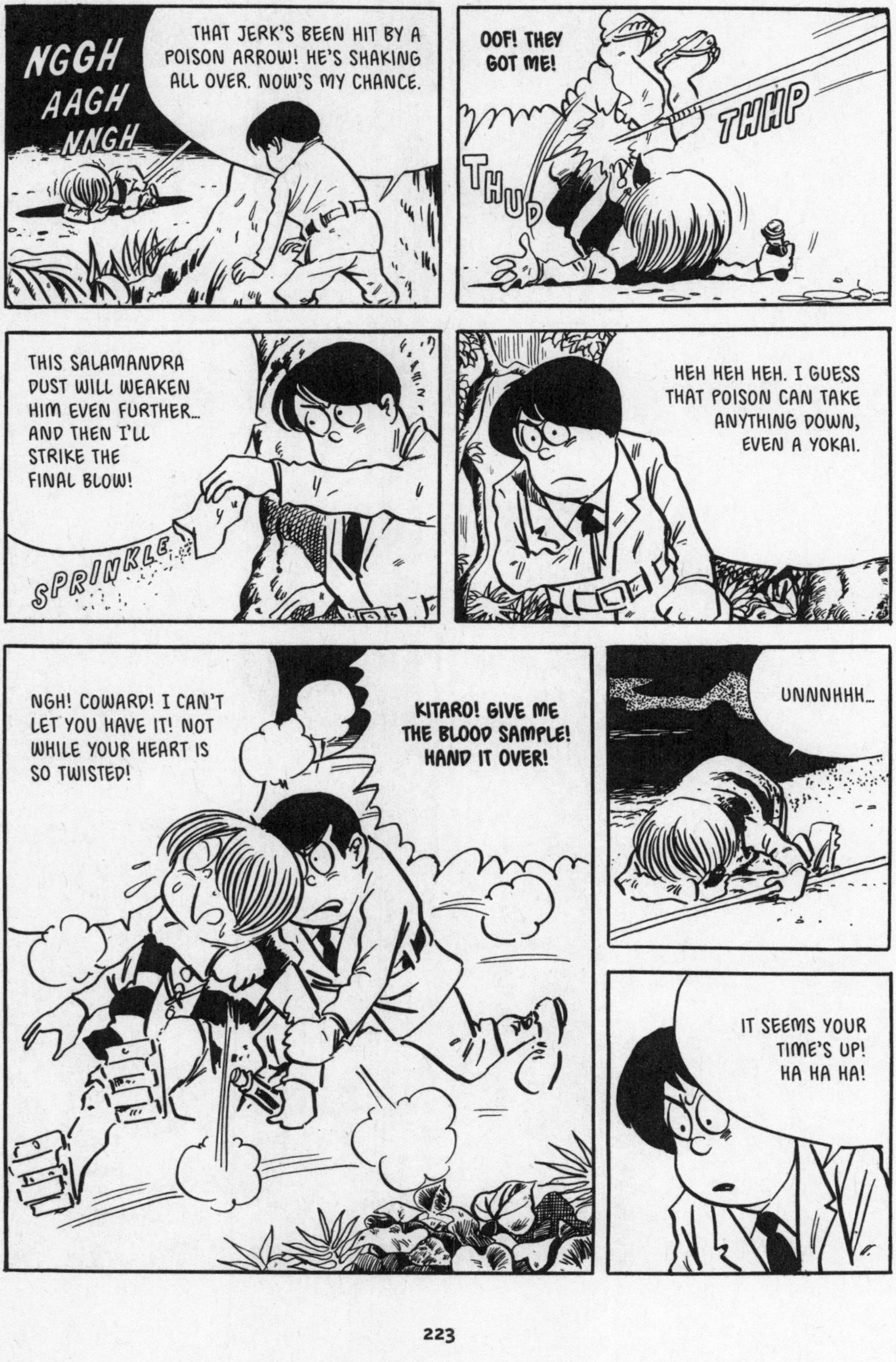
OOF! THEY GOT ME!
THHP
THUD
THAT JERK'S BEEN HIT BY A POISON ARROW! HE'S SHAKING ALL OVER. NOW'S MY CHANCE.
NGGH AAGH NNGH
HEH HEH HEH. I GUESS THAT POISON CAN TAKE ANYTHING DOWN, EVEN A YOKAI.
THIS SALAMANDRA DUST WILL WEAKEN HIM EVEN FURTHER... AND THEN I'LL STRIKE THE FINAL BLOW!
SPRINKLE
UNNNHHH...
IT SEEMS YOUR TIME'S UP! HA HA HA!
KITARO! GIVE ME THE BLOOD SAMPLE! HAND IT OVER!
NGH! COWARD! I CAN'T LET YOU HAVE IT! NOT WHILE YOUR HEART IS SO TWISTED!

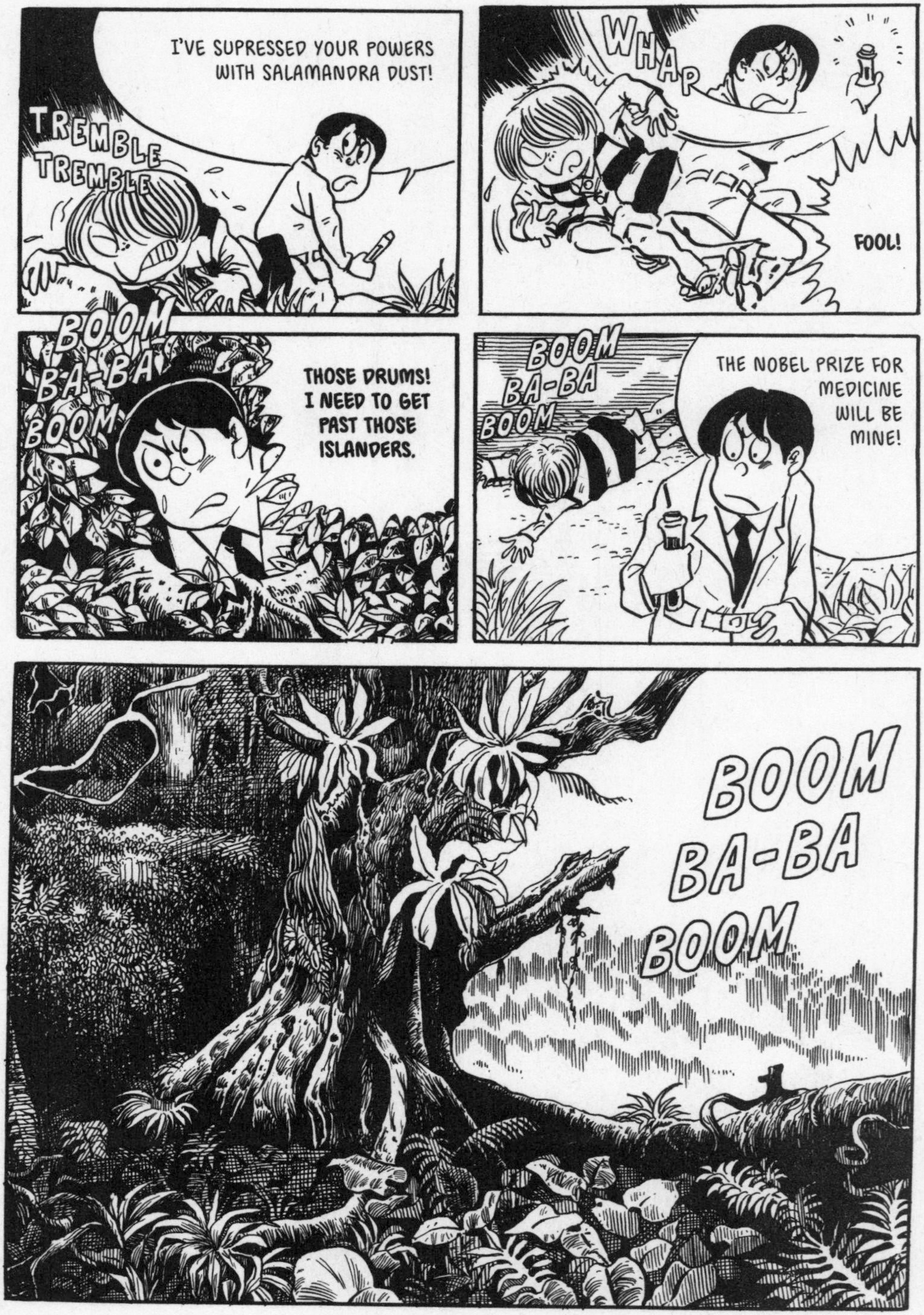
WHAP
FOOL!
I'VE SUPRESSED YOUR POWERS WITH SALAMANDRA DUST!
TREMBLE TREMBLE
THE NOBEL PRIZE FOR MEDICINE WILL BE MINE!
BOOM BA-BA BOOM
THOSE DRUMS! I NEED TO GET PAST THOSE ISLANDERS.
BOOM BA-BA BOOM
BOOM BA-BA BOOM

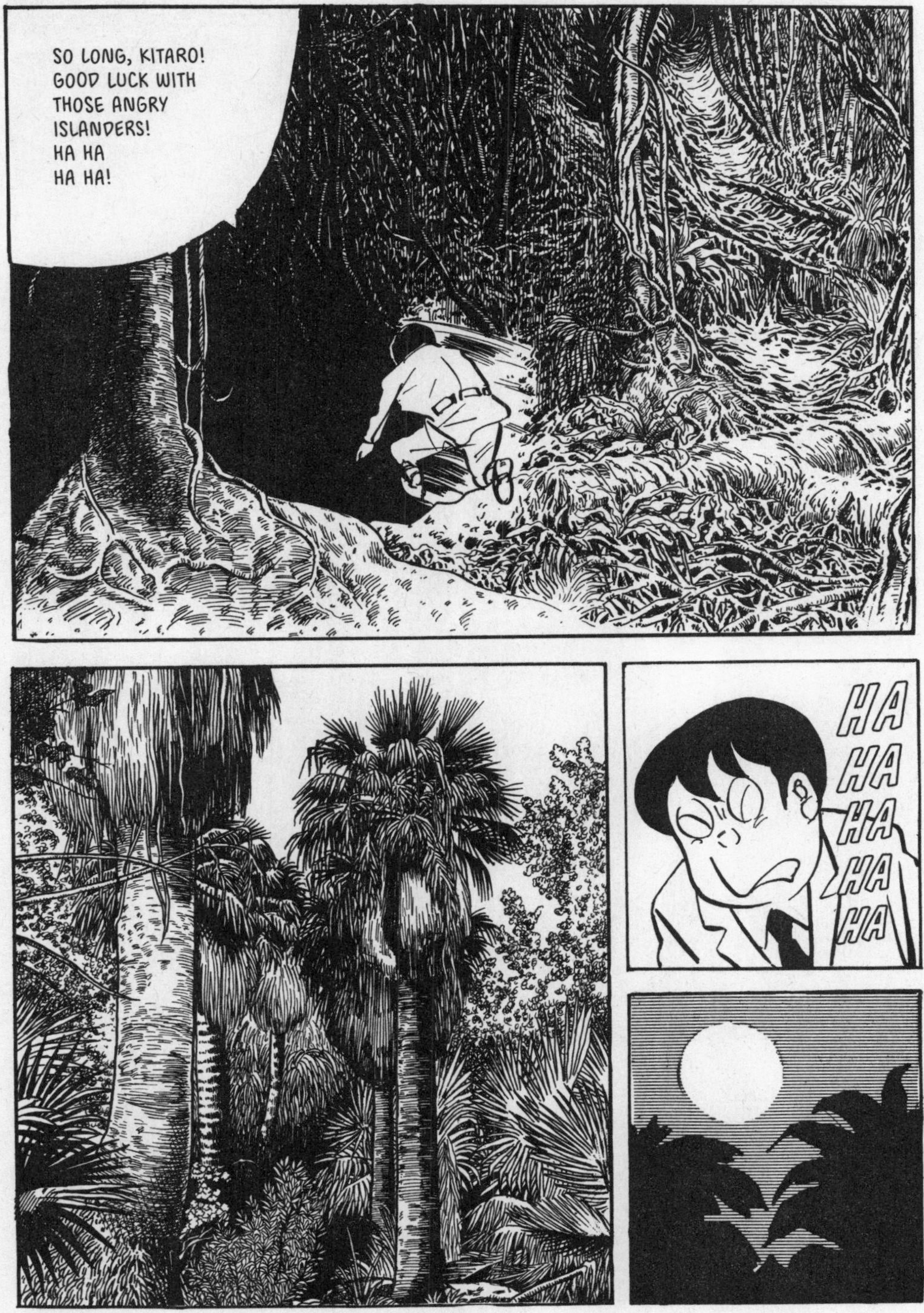
SO LONG, KITARO! GOOD LUCK WITH THOSE ANGRY ISLANDERS! HA HA HA HA!
HA HA HA HA HA

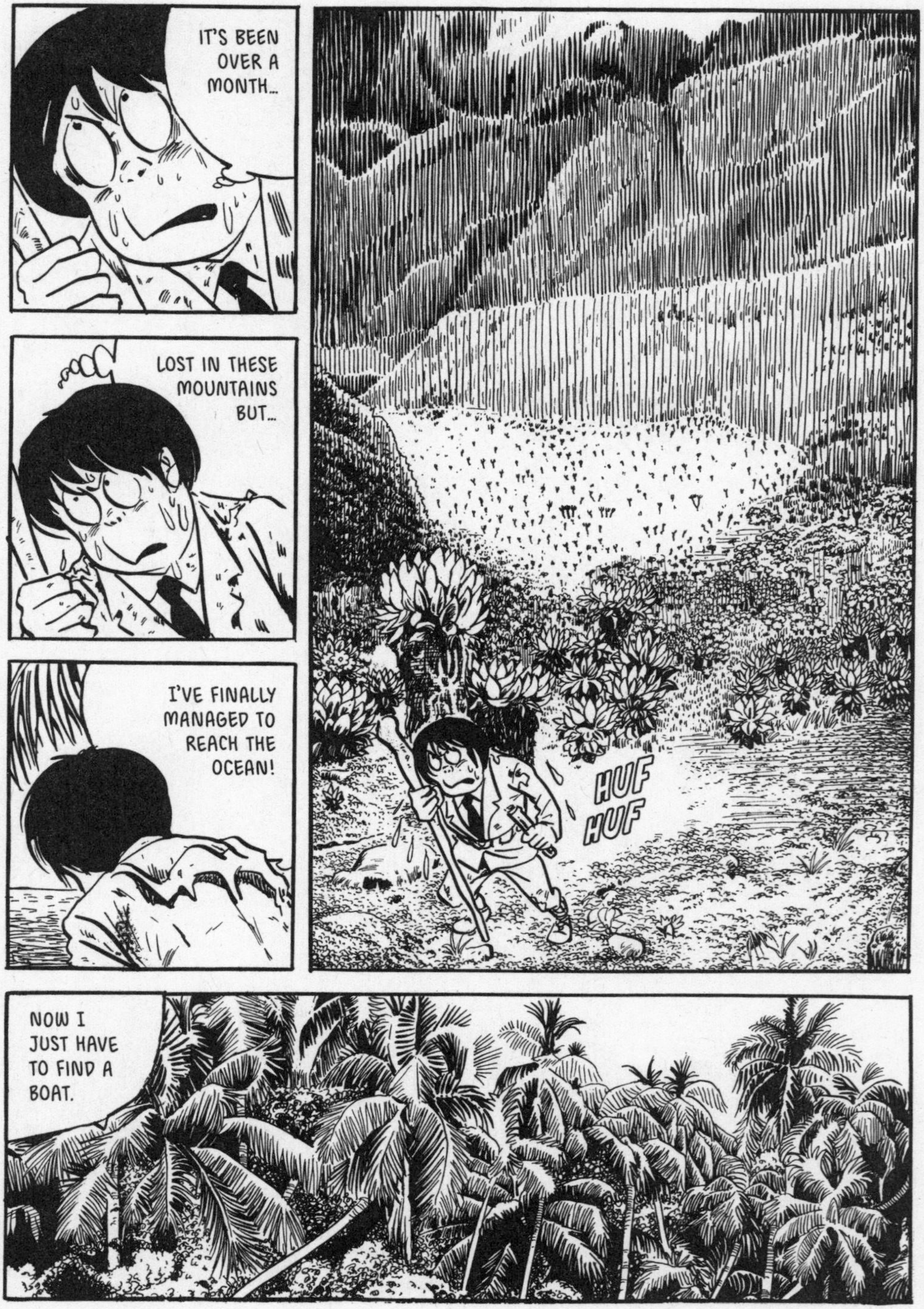
HUF
HUF
IT'S BEEN OVER A MONTH...
LOST IN THESE MOUNTAINS BUT...
I'VE FINALLY MANAGED TO REACH THE OCEAN!
NOW I JUST HAVE TO FIND A BOAT.

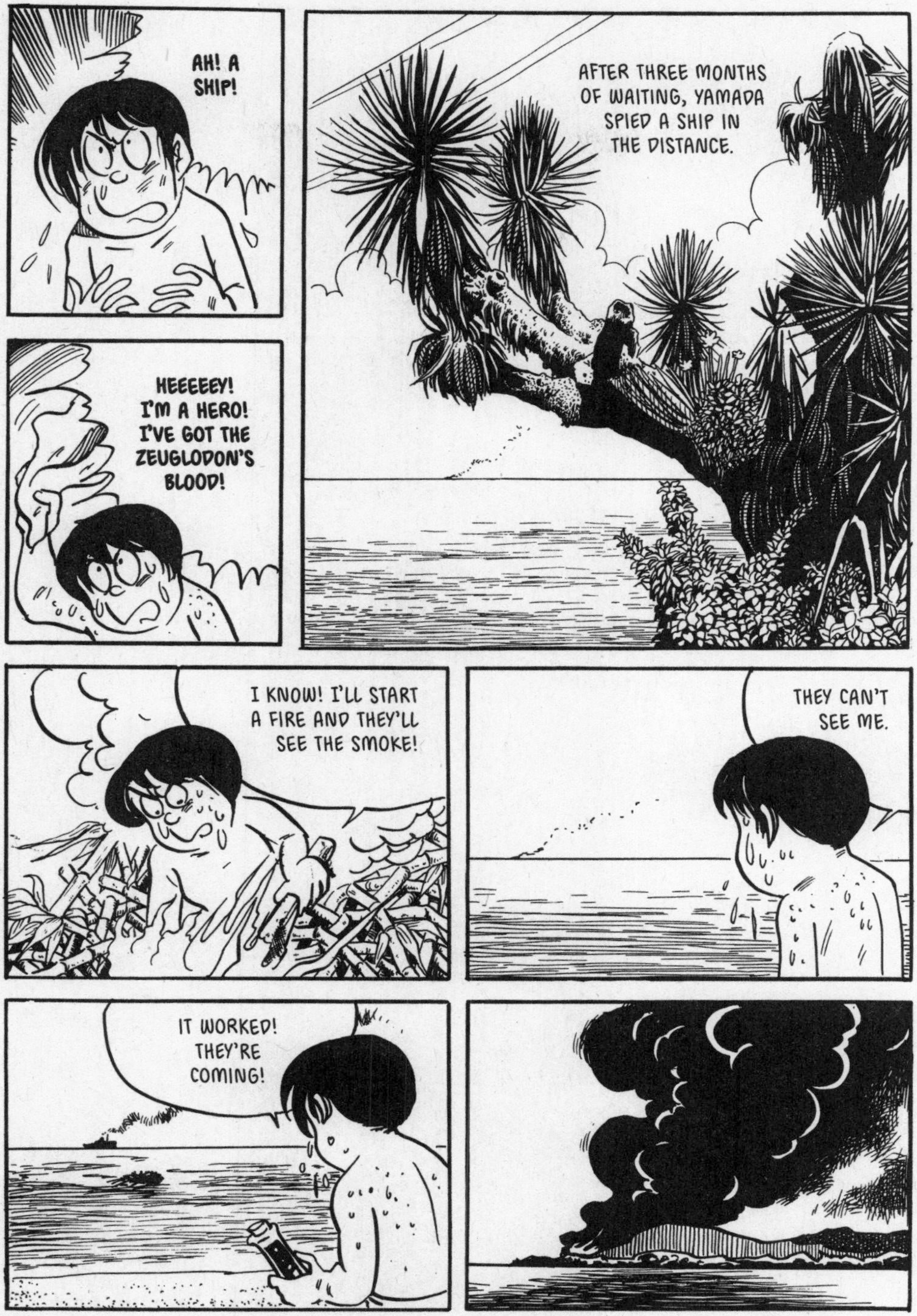
AFTER THREE MONTHS OF WAITING, YAMADA SPIED A SHIP IN THE DISTANCE.
AH! A SHIP!
HEEEEEY! I'M A HERO! I'VE GOT THE ZEUGLODON'S BLOOD!
THEY CAN'T SEE ME.
I KNOW! I'LL START A FIRE AND THEY'LL SEE THE SMOKE!
IT WORKED! THEY'RE COMING!

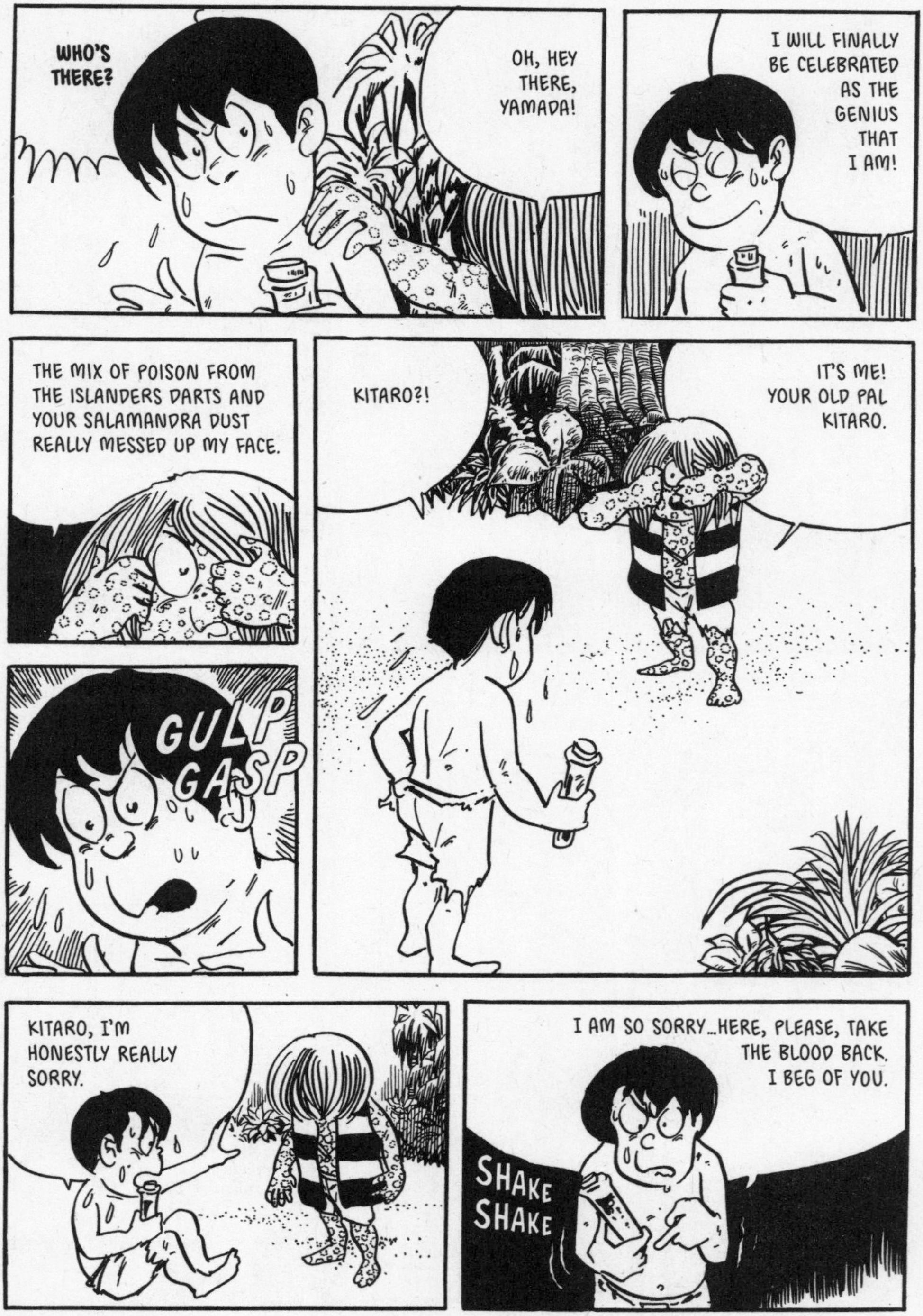
I WILL FINALLY BE CELEBRATED AS THE GENIUS THAT I AM!
OH, HEY THERE, YAMADA!
WHO'S THERE?
IT'S ME! YOUR OLD PAL KITARO.
KITARO?!
THE MIX OF POISON FROM THE ISLANDERS DARTS AND YOUR SALAMANDRA DUST REALLY MESSED UP MY FACE.
GULP
GASP
I AM SO SORRY...HERE, PLEASE, TAKE THE BLOOD BACK. I BEG OF YOU.
SHAKE
SHAKE
KITARO, I'M HONESTLY REALLY SORRY.

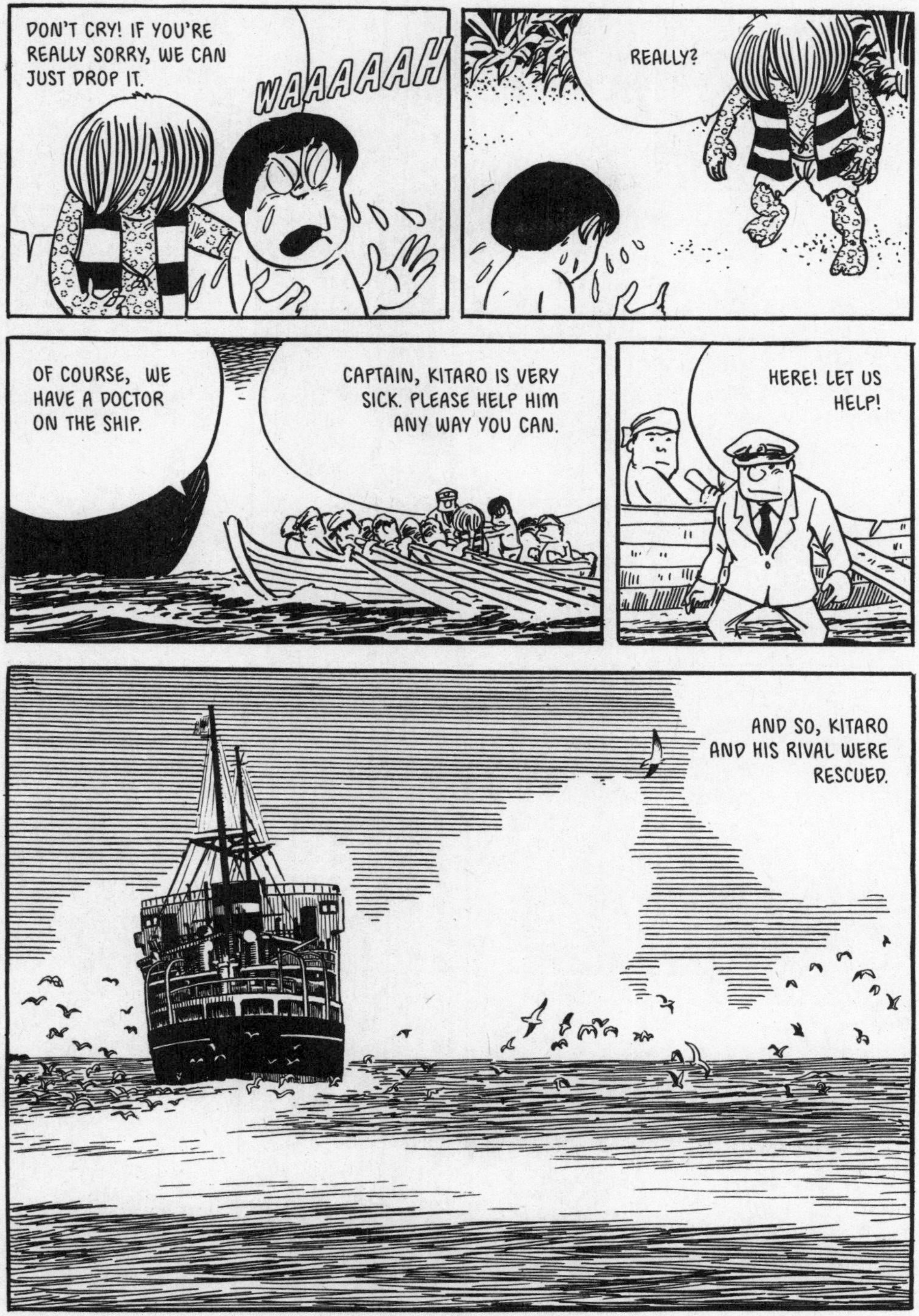
REALLY?
WAAAAAH
DON'T CRY! IF YOU'RE REALLY SORRY, WE CAN JUST DROP IT.
HERE! LET US HELP!
CAPTAIN, KITARO IS VERY SICK. PLEASE HELP HIM ANY WAY YOU CAN.
OF COURSE, WE HAVE A DOCTOR ON THE SHIP.
AND SO, KITARO AND HIS RIVAL WERE RESCUED.

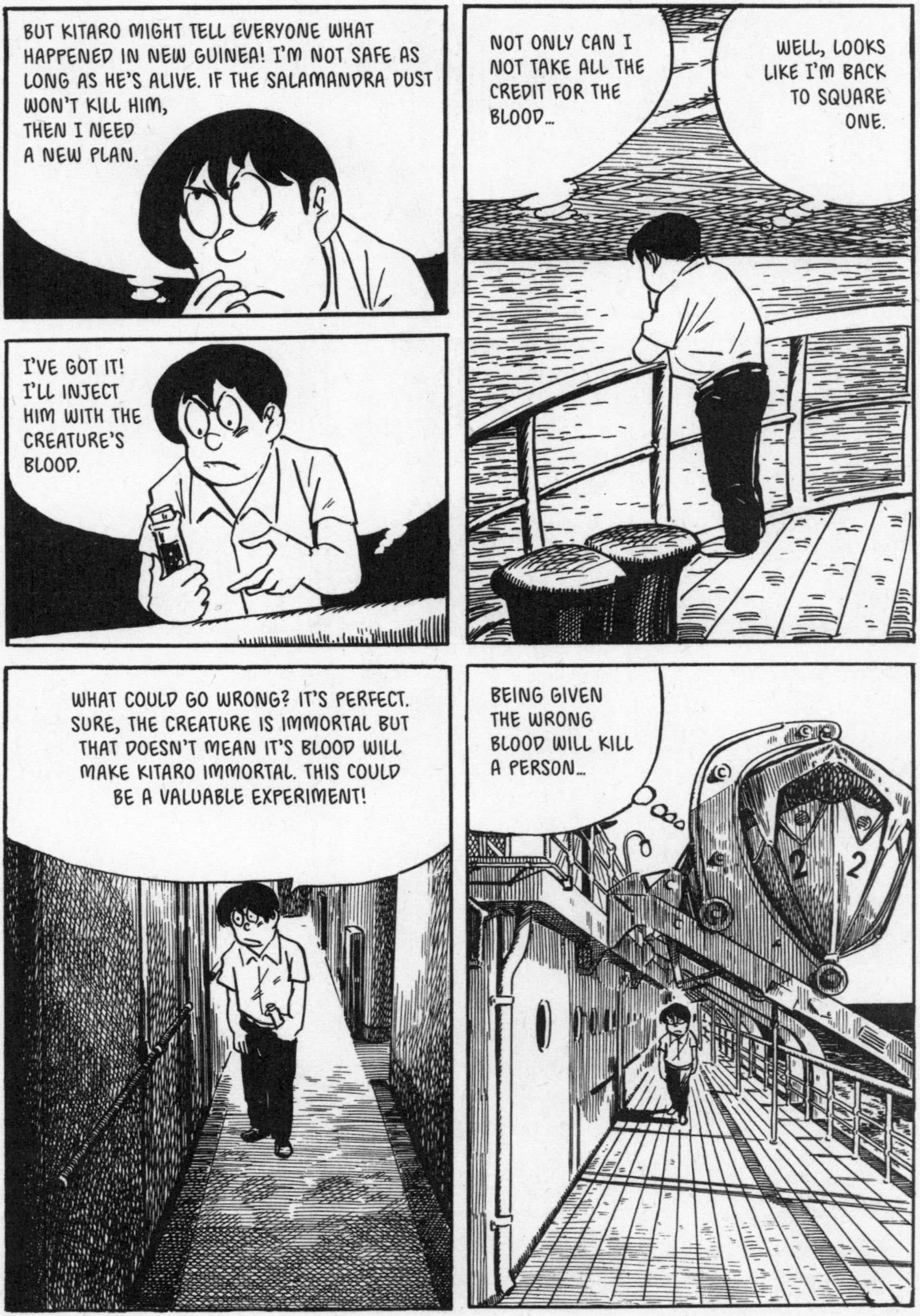
WELL, LOOKS LIKE I'M BACK TO SQUARE ONE.
NOT ONLY CAN I NOT TAKE ALL THE CREDIT FOR THE BLOOD...
BUT KITARO MIGHT TELL EVERYONE WHAT HAPPENED IN NEW GUINEA! I'M NOT SAFE AS LONG AS HE'S ALIVE. IF THE SALAMANDRA DUST WON'T KILL HIM, THEN I NEED A NEW PLAN.
I'VE GOT IT! I'LL INJECT HIM WITH THE CREATURE'S BLOOD.
BEING GIVEN THE WRONG BLOOD WILL KILL A PERSON...
WHAT COULD GO WRONG? IT'S PERFECT. SURE, THE CREATURE IS IMMORTAL BUT THAT DOESN'T MEAN IT'S BLOOD WILL MAKE KITARO IMMORTAL. THIS COULD BE A VALUABLE EXPERIMENT!

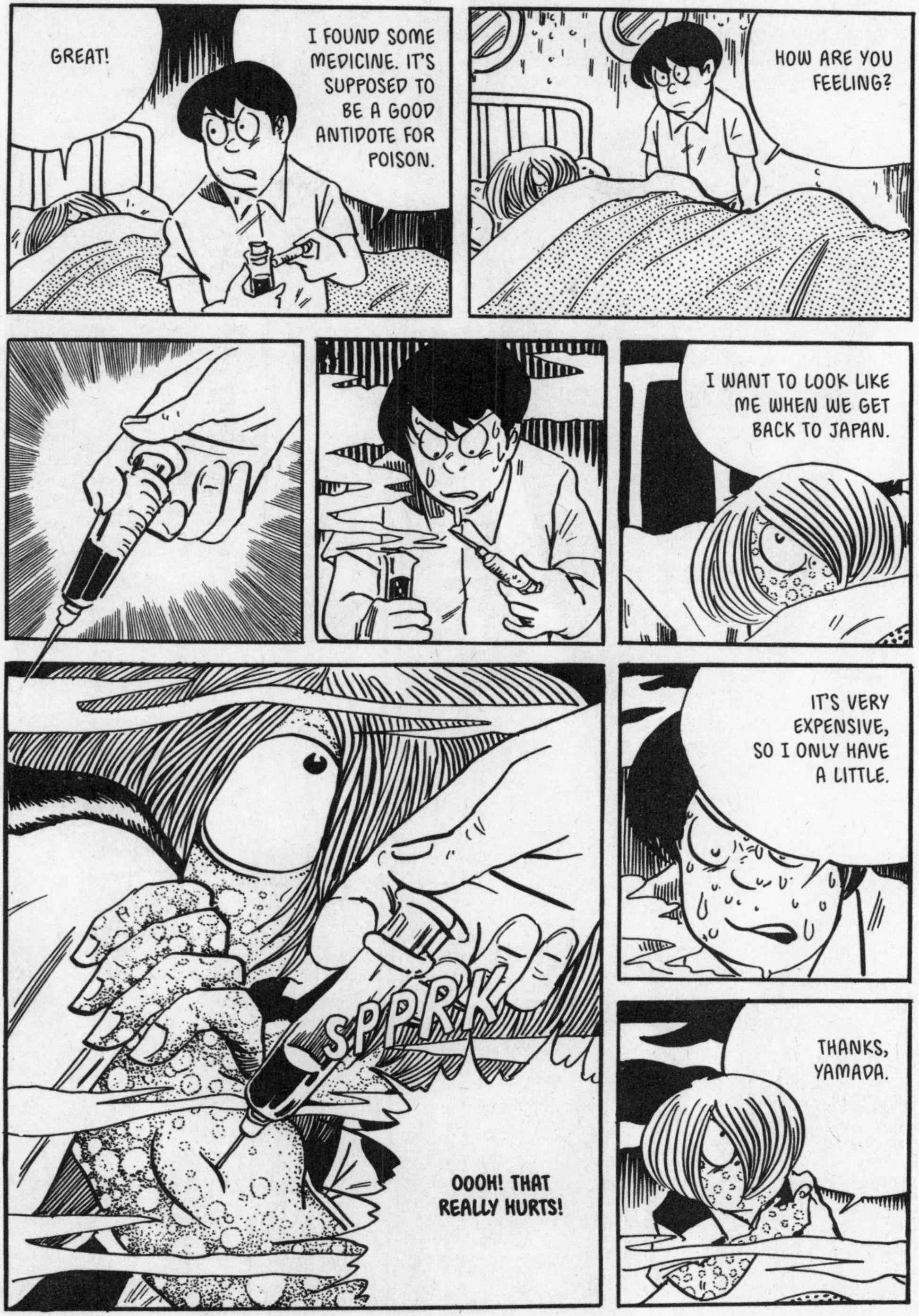
HOW ARE YOU FEELING?
I FOUND SOME MEDICINE. IT'S SUPPOSED TO BE A GOOD ANTIDOTE FOR POISON.
GREAT!
I WANT TO LOOK LIKE ME WHEN WE GET BACK TO JAPAN.
IT'S VERY EXPENSIVE, SO I ONLY HAVE A LITTLE.
THANKS, YAMADA.
SPPRK
OOOH! THAT REALLY HURTS!

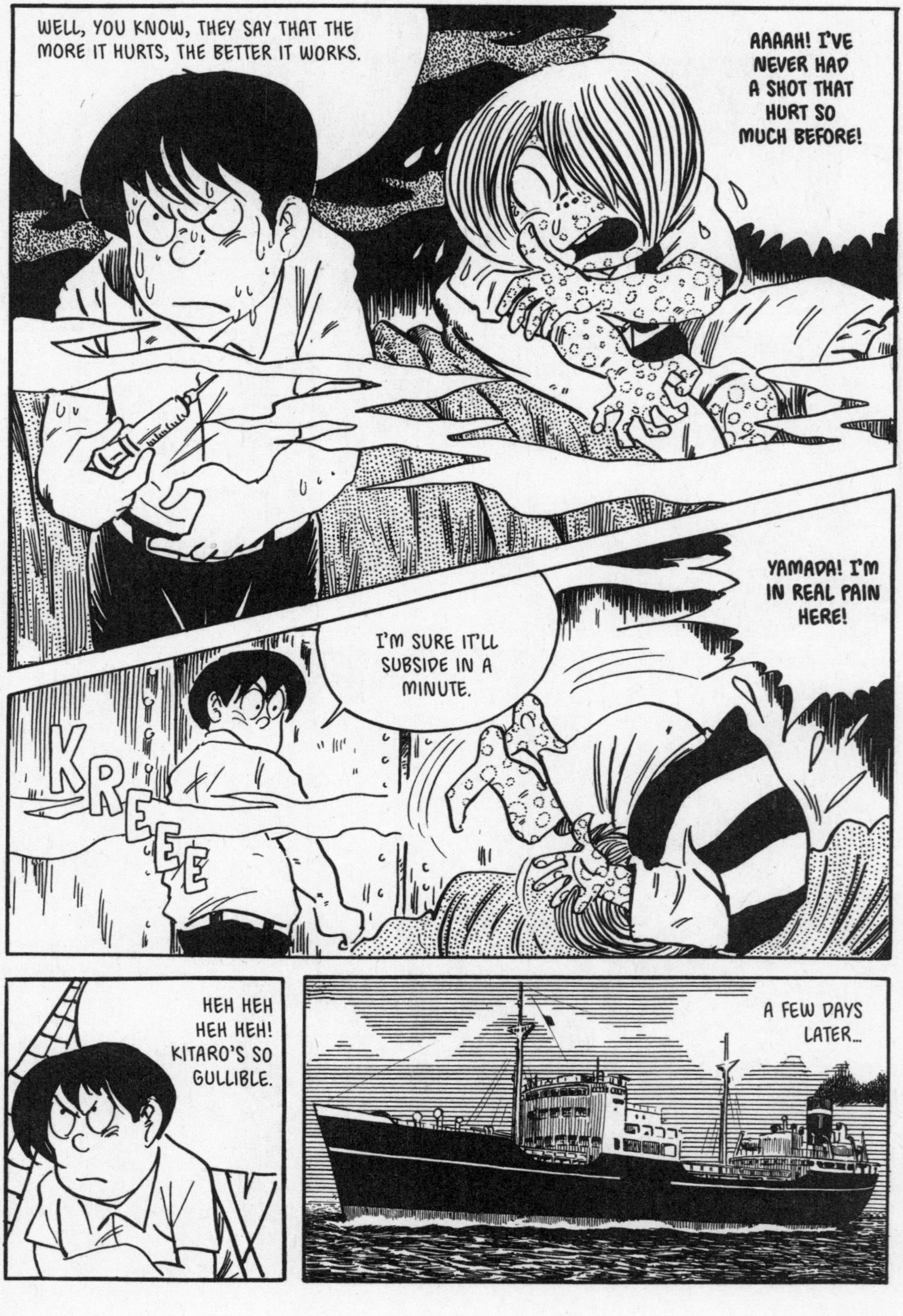
AAAAH! I'VE NEVER HAD A SHOT THAT HURT SO MUCH BEFORE!
WELL, YOU KNOW, THEY SAY THAT THE MORE IT HURTS, THE BETTER IT WORKS.
YAMADA! I'M IN REAL PAIN HERE!
I'M SURE IT'LL SUBSIDE IN A MINUTE.
KREEEE
A FEW DAYS LATER...
HEH HEH HEH HEH! KITARO'S SO GULLIBLE.

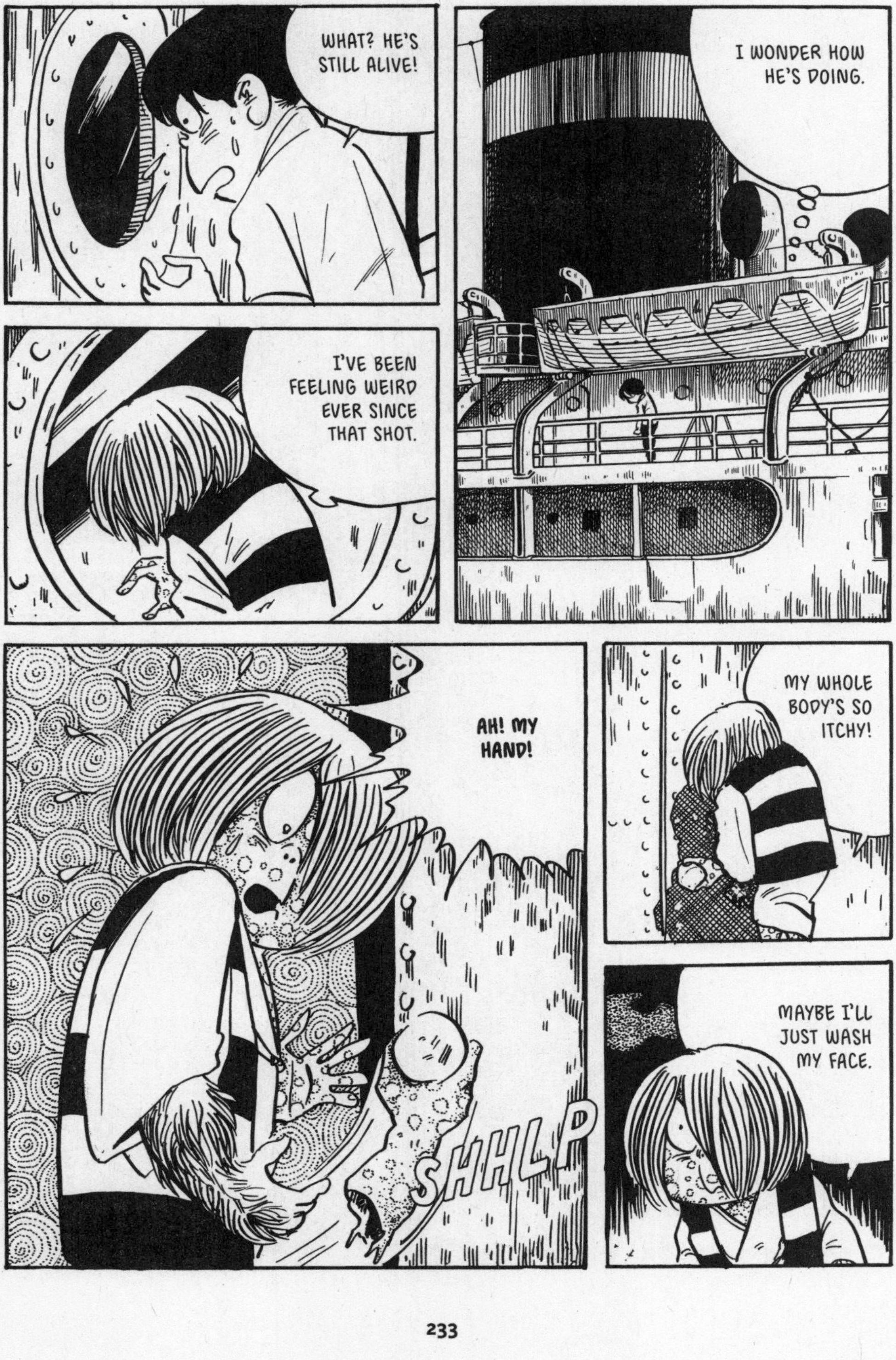
I WONDER HOW HE'S DOING.
WHAT? HE'S STILL ALIVE!
I'VE BEEN FEELING WEIRD EVER SINCE THAT SHOT.
MY WHOLE BODY'S SO ITCHY!
MAYBE I'LL JUST WASH MY FACE.
AH! MY HAND!
SHHLP

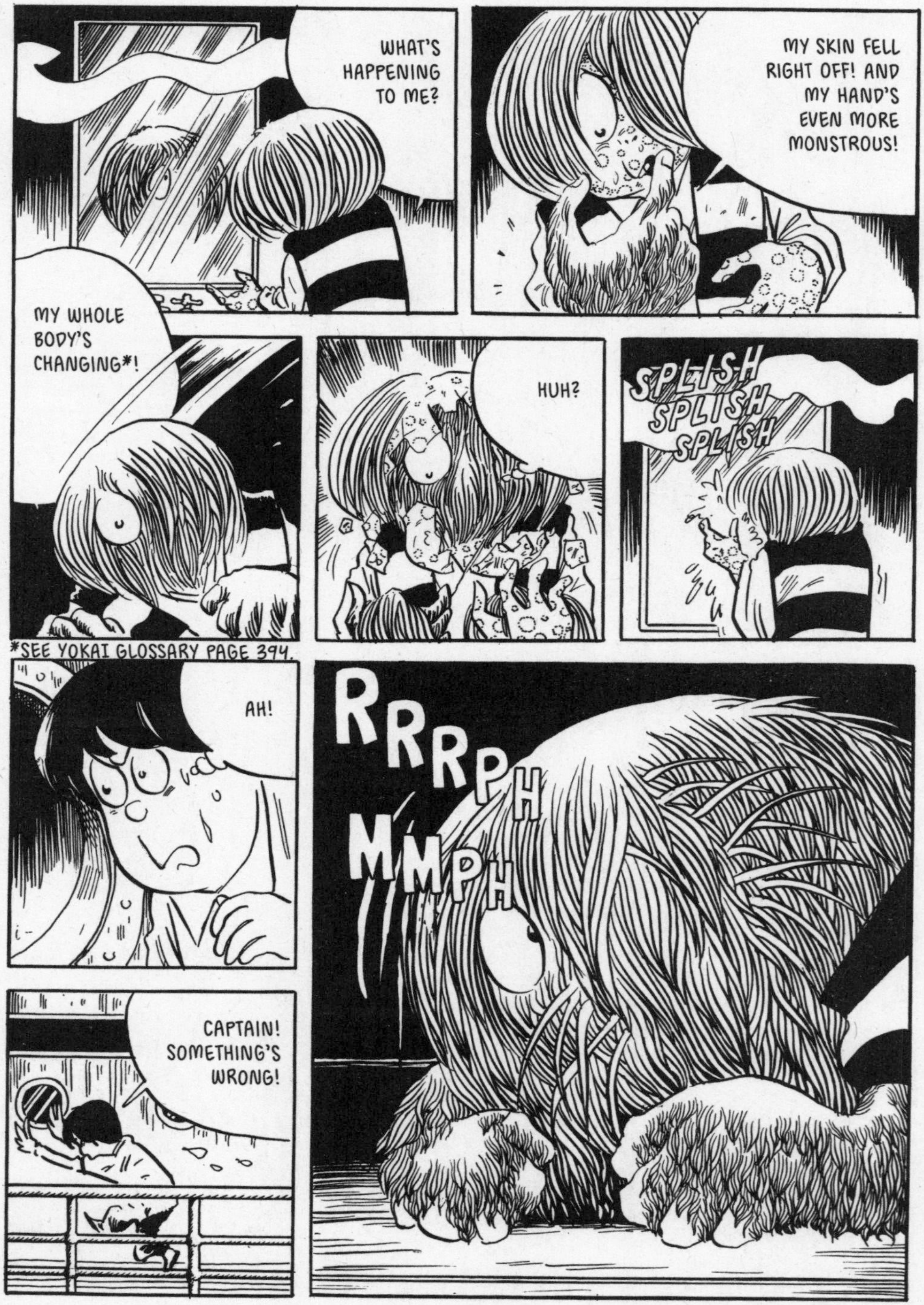
MY SKIN FELL RIGHT OFF! AND MY HAND'S EVEN MORE MONSTROUS!
WHAT'S HAPPENING TO ME?
SPLISH SPLISH SPLISH
HUH?
MY WHOLE BODY'S CHANGING*!
RRRPH MMMPH
AH!
CAPTAIN! SOMETHING'S WRONG!

*SEE YOKAI GLOSSARY PAGE 394.

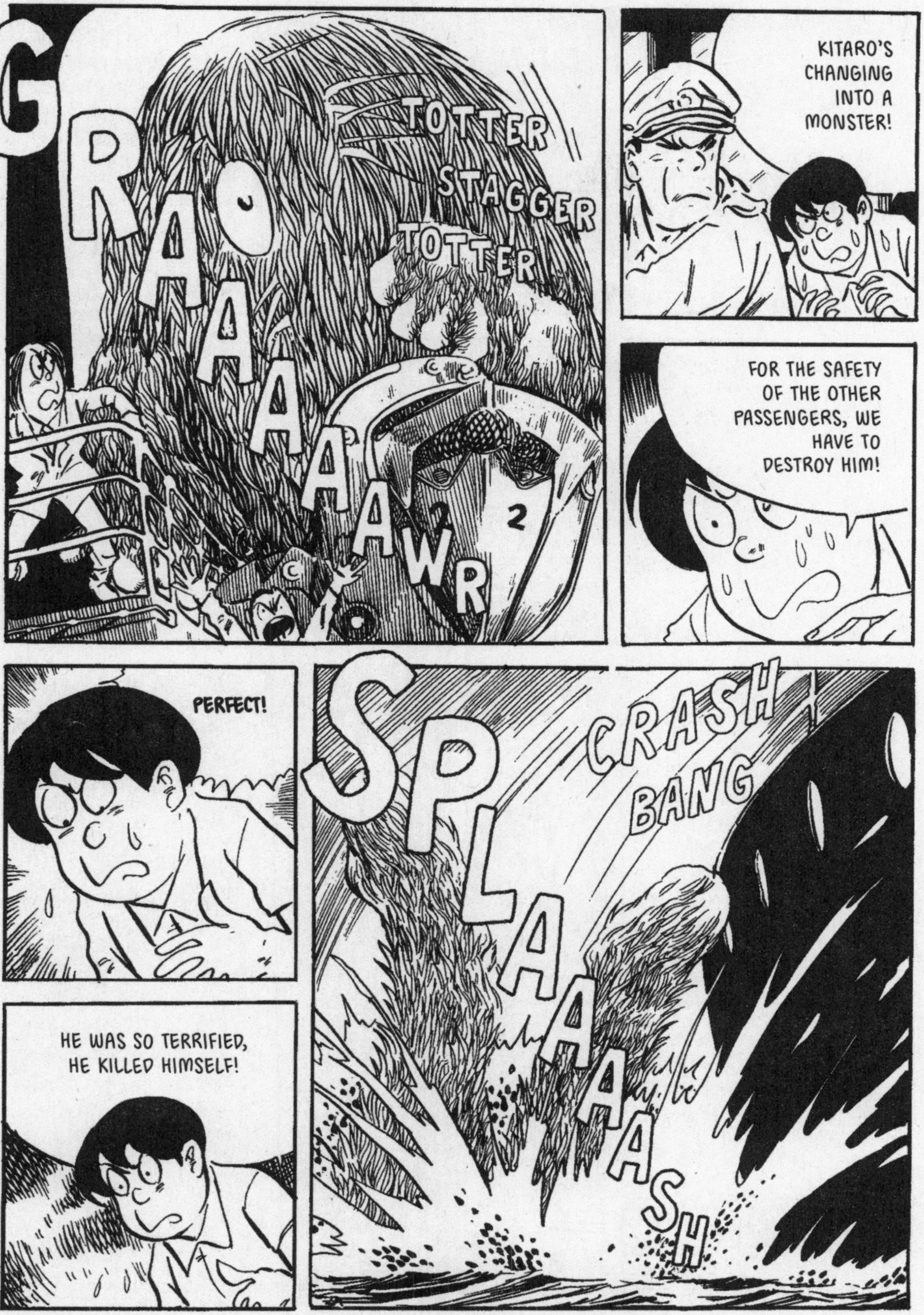
KITARO'S CHANGING INTO A MONSTER!
FOR THE SAFETY OF THE OTHER PASSENGERS, WE HAVE TO DESTROY HIM!
GRAAAAAAAWR
TOTTER
STAGGER
TOTTER
SPLAAAAASH
CRASH
BANG
PERFECT!
HE WAS SO TERRIFIED, HE KILLED HIMSELF!

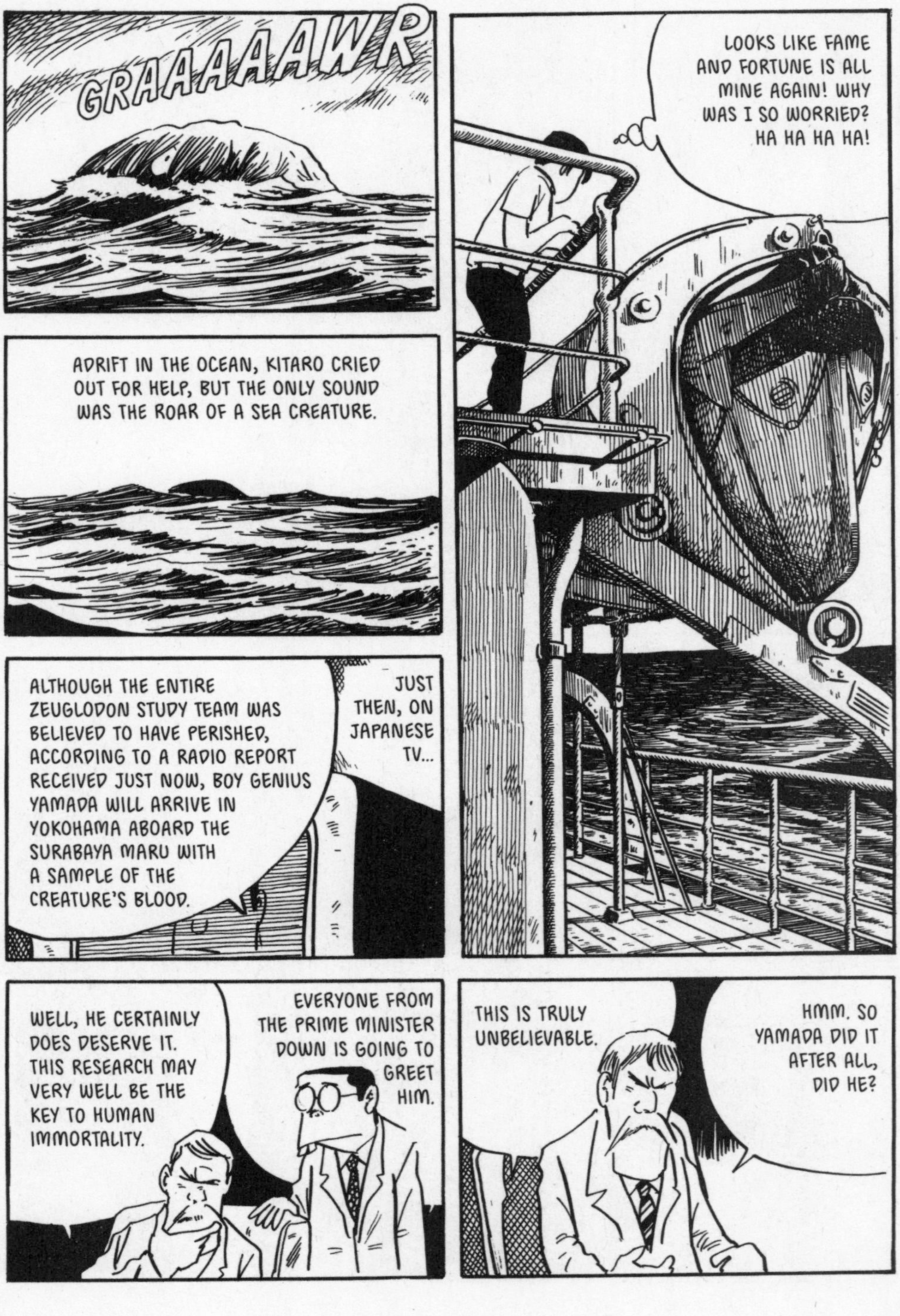

LOOKS LIKE FAME AND FORTUNE IS ALL MINE AGAIN! WHY WAS I SO WORRIED? HA HA HA HA!
GRAAAAAAWR
ADRIFT IN THE OCEAN, KITARO CRIED OUT FOR HELP, BUT THE ONLY SOUND WAS THE ROAR OF A SEA CREATURE.
JUST THEN, ON JAPANESE TV...
ALTHOUGH THE ENTIRE ZEUGLODON STUDY TEAM WAS BELIEVED TO HAVE PERISHED, ACCORDING TO A RADIO REPORT RECEIVED JUST NOW, BOY GENIUS YAMADA WILL ARRIVE IN YOKOHAMA ABOARD THE SURABAYA MARU WITH A SAMPLE OF THE CREATURE'S BLOOD.
HMM. SO YAMADA DID IT AFTER ALL, DID HE?
THIS IS TRULY UNBELIEVABLE.
EVERYONE FROM THE PRIME MINISTER DOWN IS GOING TO GREET HIM.
WELL, HE CERTAINLY DOES DESERVE IT. THIS RESEARCH MAY VERY WELL BE THE KEY TO HUMAN IMMORTALITY.

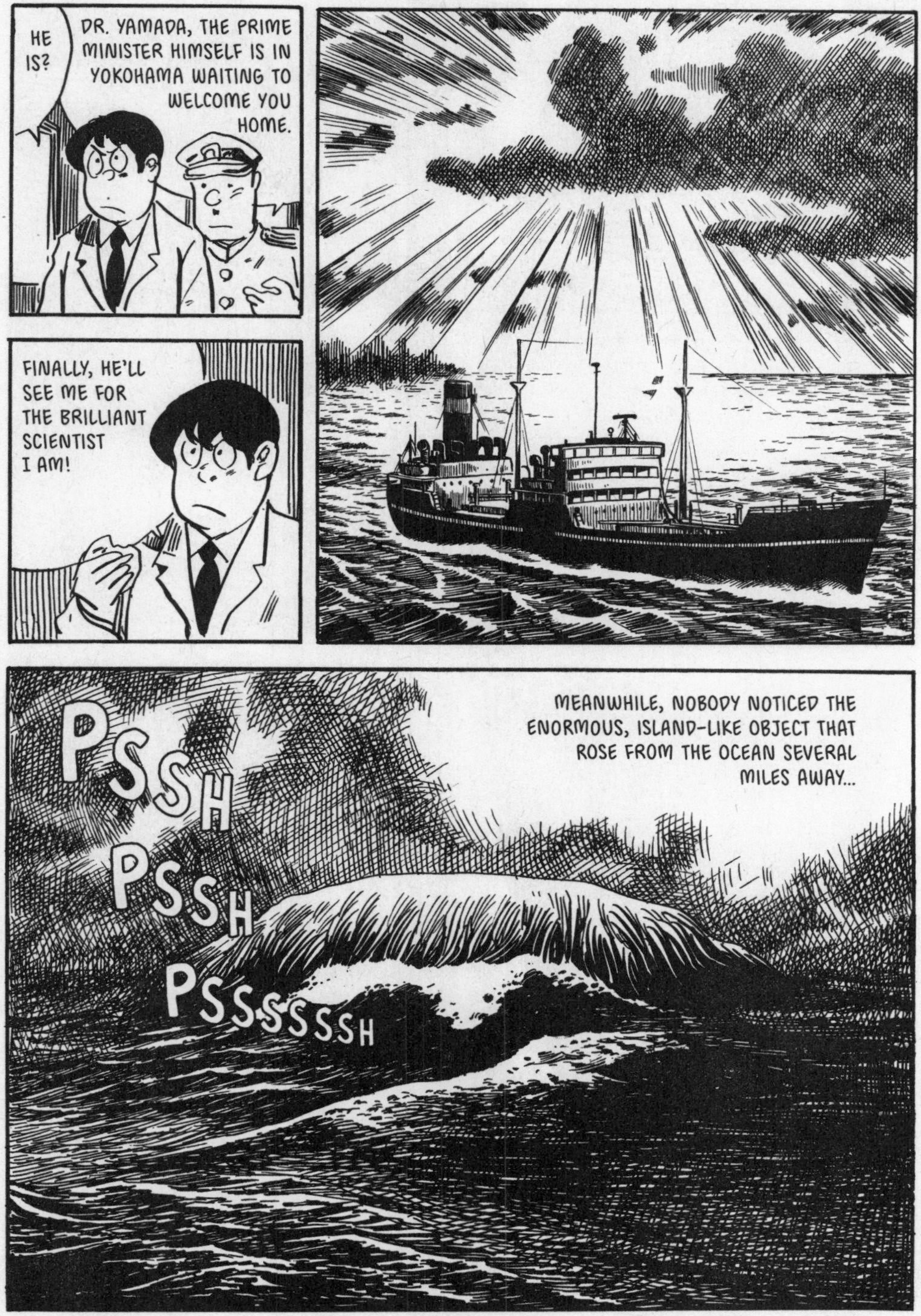
DR. YAMADA, THE PRIME MINISTER HIMSELF IS IN YOKOHAMA WAITING TO WELCOME YOU HOME.
HE IS?
FINALLY, HE'LL SEE ME FOR THE BRILLIANT SCIENTIST I AM!
MEANWHILE, NOBODY NOTICED THE ENORMOUS, ISLAND-LIKE OBJECT THAT ROSE FROM THE OCEAN SEVERAL MILES AWAY...
PSSH
PSSH
PSSSSSSSH

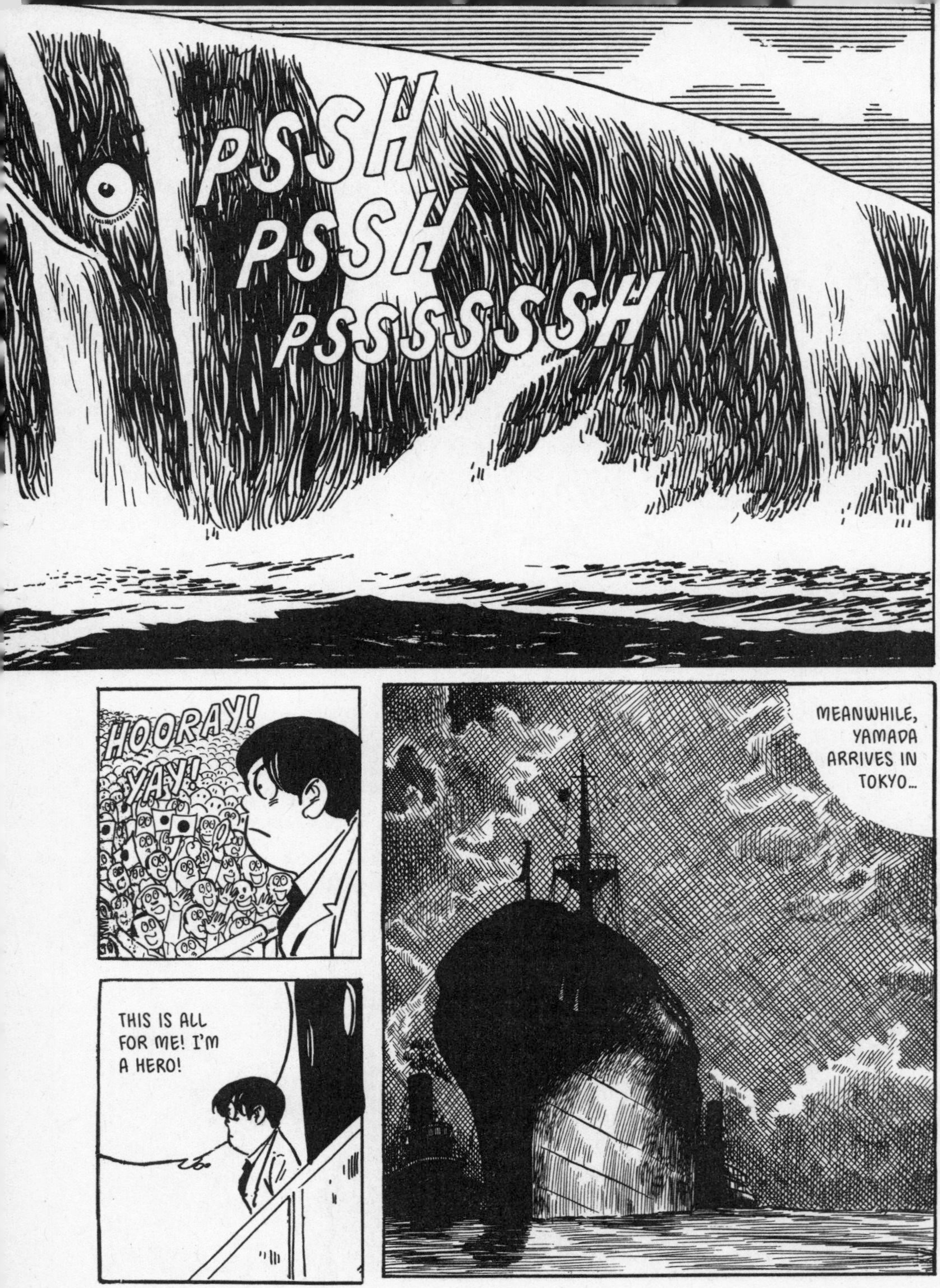
PSSH
PSSH
PSSSSSSH
MEANWHILE, YAMADA ARRIVES IN TOKYO...
HOORAY!
YAY!
THIS IS ALL FOR ME! I'M A HERO!

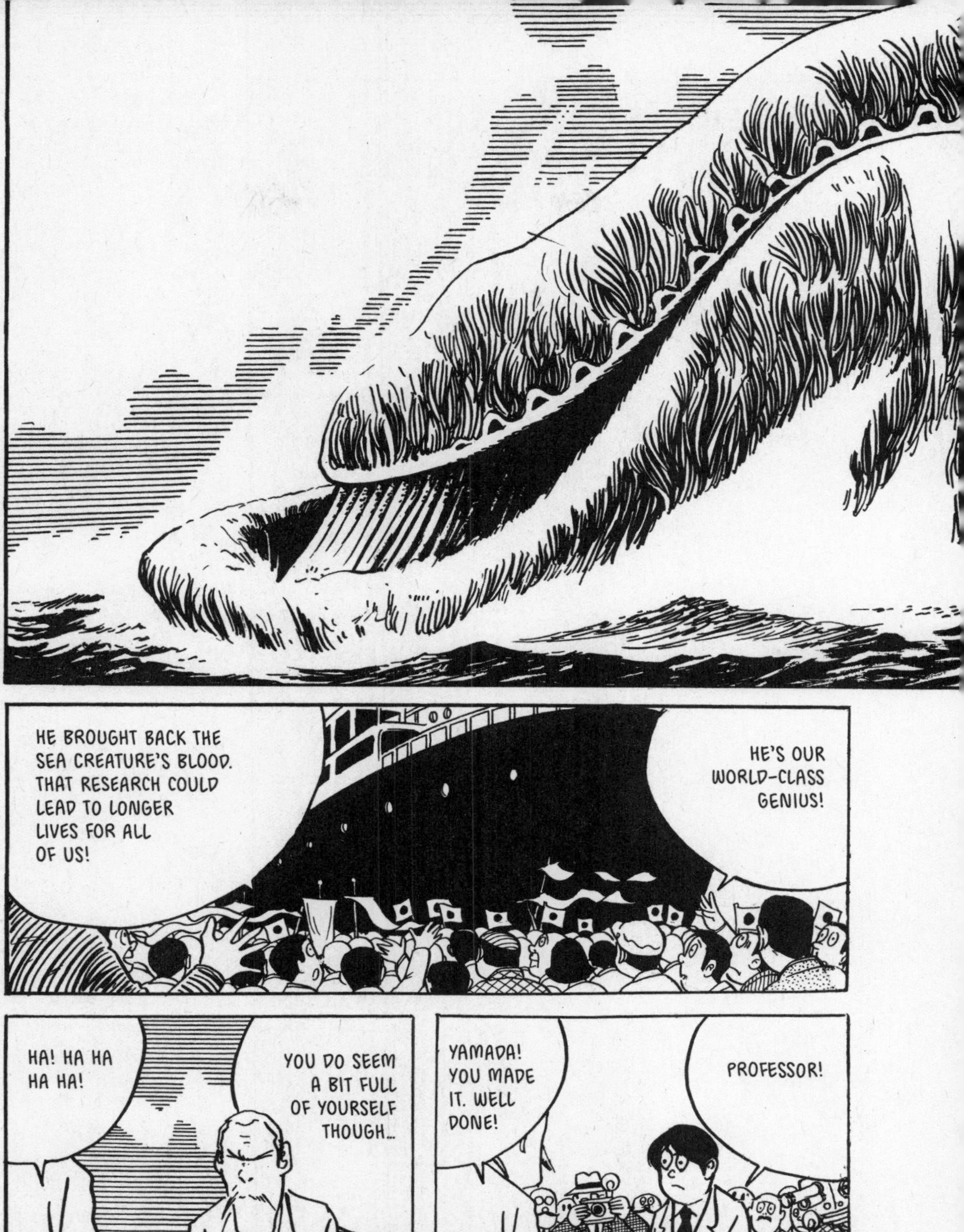
HE'S OUR WORLD-CLASS GENIUS!
HE BROUGHT BACK THE SEA CREATURE'S BLOOD. THAT RESEARCH COULD LEAD TO LONGER LIVES FOR ALL OF US!
PROFESSOR!
YAMADA! YOU MADE IT. WELL DONE!
YOU DO SEEM A BIT FULL OF YOURSELF THOUGH...
HA! HA HA HA HA!

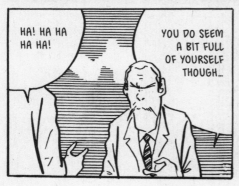

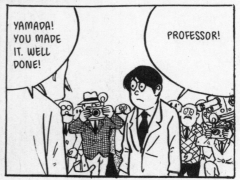

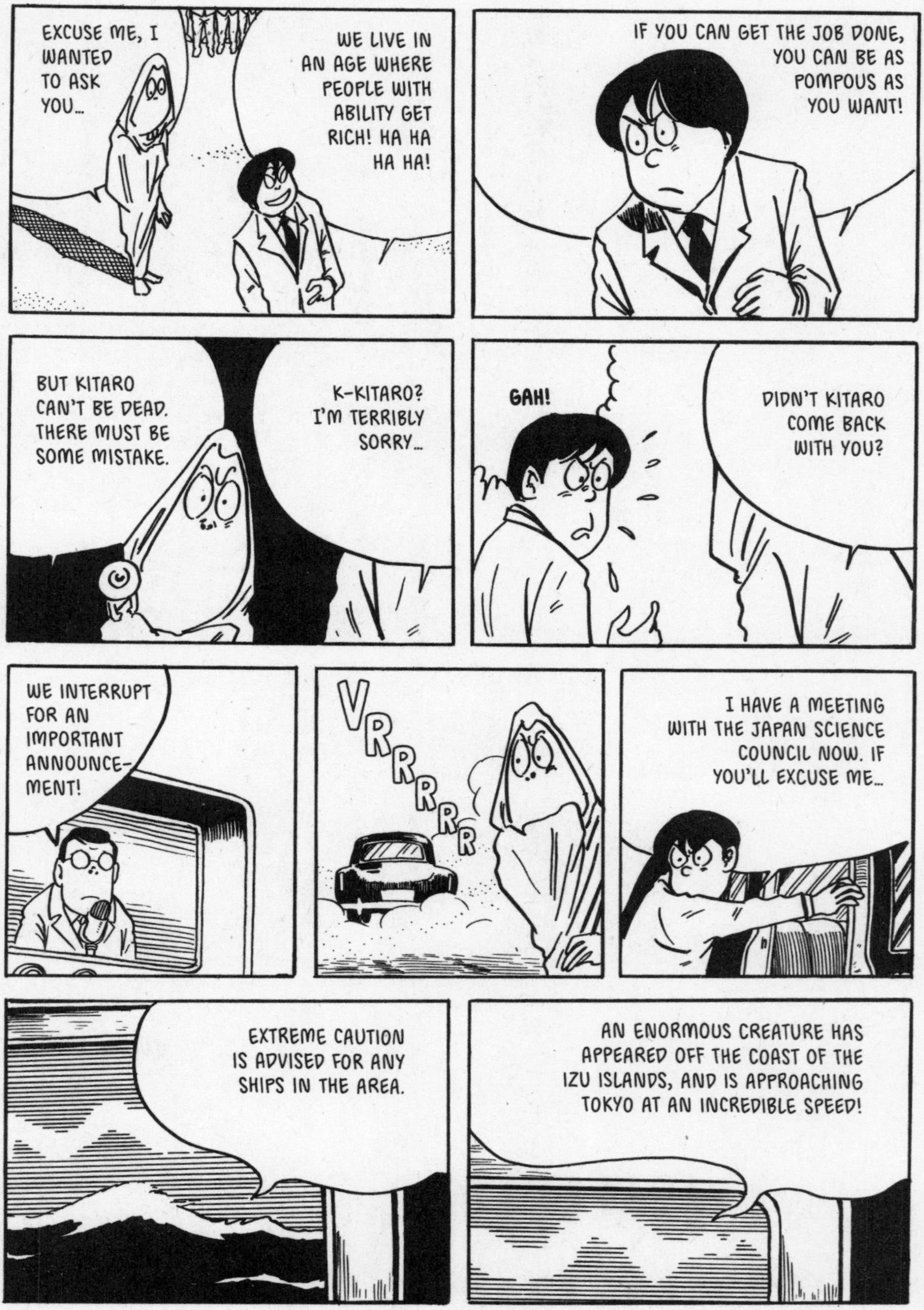
IF YOU CAN GET THE JOB DONE, YOU CAN BE AS POMPOUS AS YOU WANT!
WE LIVE IN AN AGE WHERE PEOPLE WITH ABILITY GET RICH! HA HA HA HA!
EXCUSE ME, I WANTED TO ASK YOU...
DIDN'T KITARO COME BACK WITH YOU?
GAH!
K-KITARO? I'M TERRIBLY SORRY...
BUT KITARO CAN'T BE DEAD. THERE MUST BE SOME MISTAKE.
I HAVE A MEETING WITH THE JAPAN SCIENCE COUNCIL NOW. IF YOU'LL EXCUSE ME...
VRRRRR
WE INTERRUPT FOR AN IMPORTANT ANNOUNCE-MENT!
AN ENORMOUS CREATURE HAS APPEARED OFF THE COAST OF THE IZU ISLANDS, AND IS APPROACHING TOKYO AT AN INCREDIBLE SPEED!
EXTREME CAUTION IS ADVISED FOR ANY SHIPS IN THE AREA.

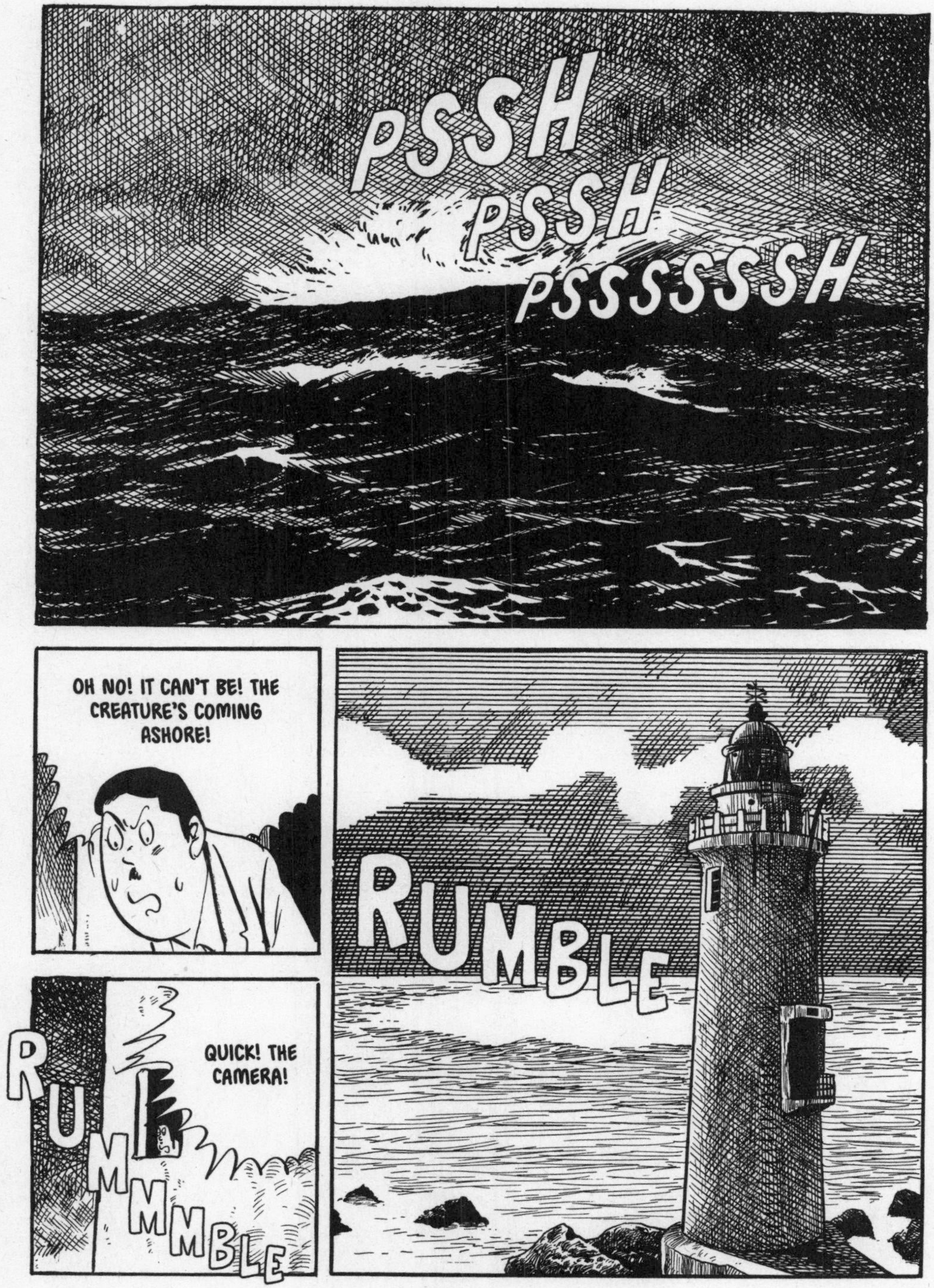
PSSH
PSSH
PSSSSSSH
RUMBLE
OH NO! IT CAN'T BE! THE CREATURE'S COMING ASHORE!
QUICK! THE CAMERA!
RUMMMBLE

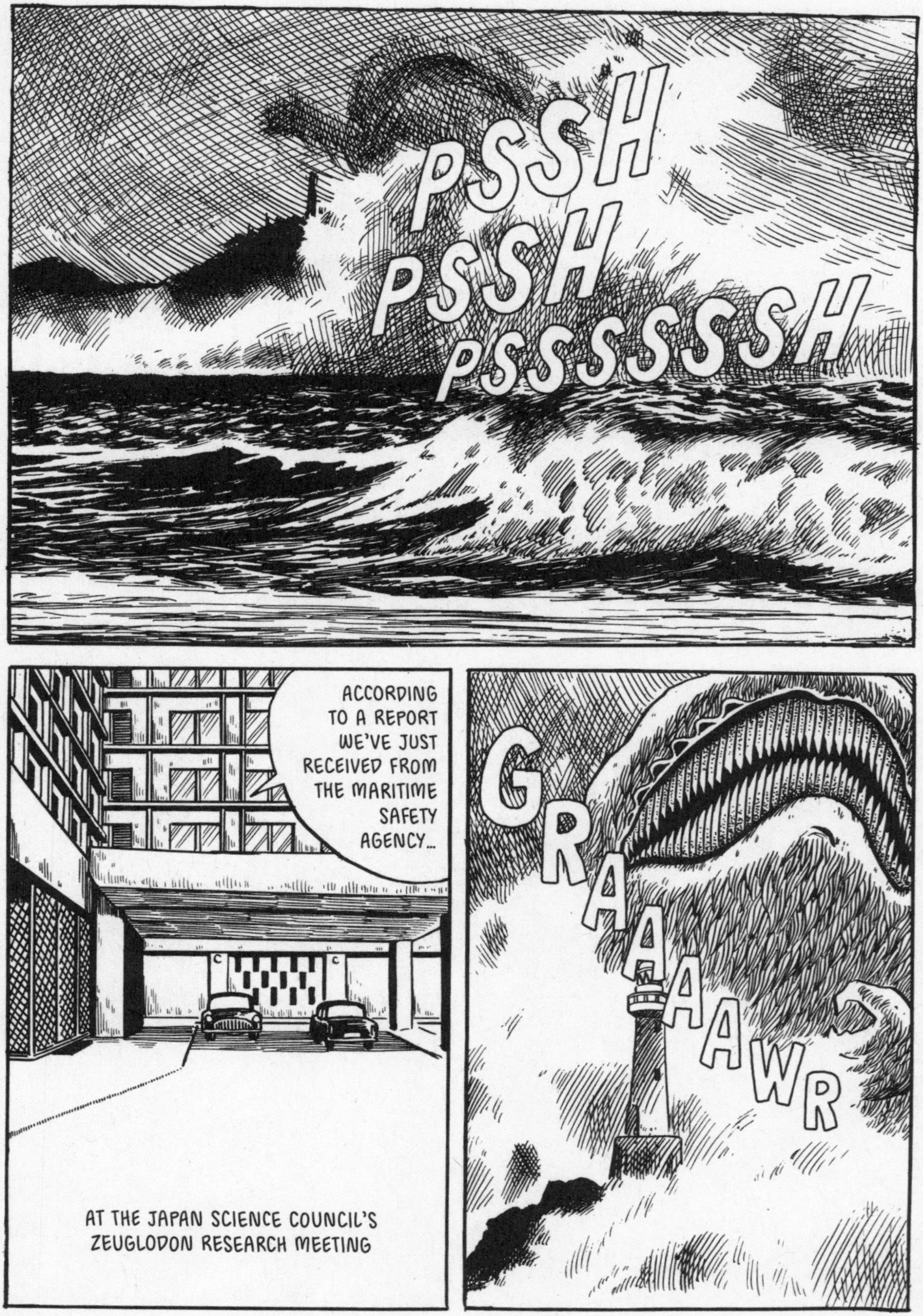
PSSH
PSSH
PSSSSSSH
GRAAAAAAWR
ACCORDING TO A REPORT WE'VE JUST RECEIVED FROM THE MARITIME SAFETY AGENCY...
AT THE JAPAN SCIENCE COUNCIL'S ZEUGLODON RESEARCH MEETING

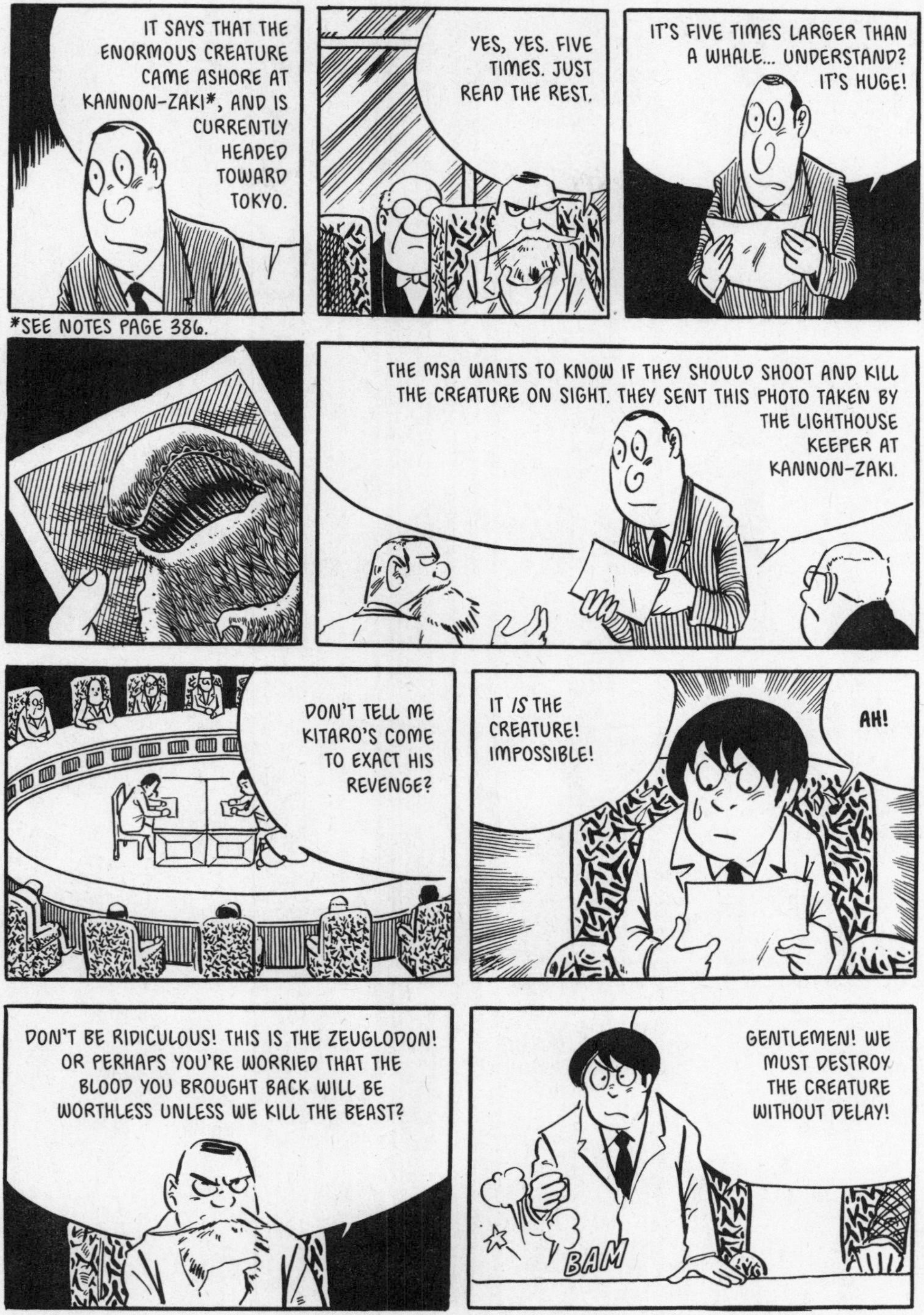
IT'S FIVE TIMES LARGER THAN A WHALE... UNDERSTAND? IT'S HUGE!
YES, YES. FIVE TIMES. JUST READ THE REST.
IT SAYS THAT THE ENORMOUS CREATURE CAME ASHORE AT KANNON-ZAKI*, AND IS CURRENTLY HEADED TOWARD TOKYO.
THE MSA WANTS TO KNOW IF THEY SHOULD SHOOT AND KILL THE CREATURE ON SIGHT. THEY SENT THIS PHOTO TAKEN BY THE LIGHTHOUSE KEEPER AT KANNON-ZAKI.
AH!
IT *IS* THE CREATURE! IMPOSSIBLE!
DON'T TELL ME KITARO'S COME TO EXACT HIS REVENGE?
GENTLEMEN! WE MUST DESTROY THE CREATURE WITHOUT DELAY!
BAM
DON'T BE RIDICULOUS! THIS IS THE ZEUGLODON! OR PERHAPS YOU'RE WORRIED THAT THE BLOOD YOU BROUGHT BACK WILL BE WORTHLESS UNLESS WE KILL THE BEAST?

*SEE NOTES PAGE 386.

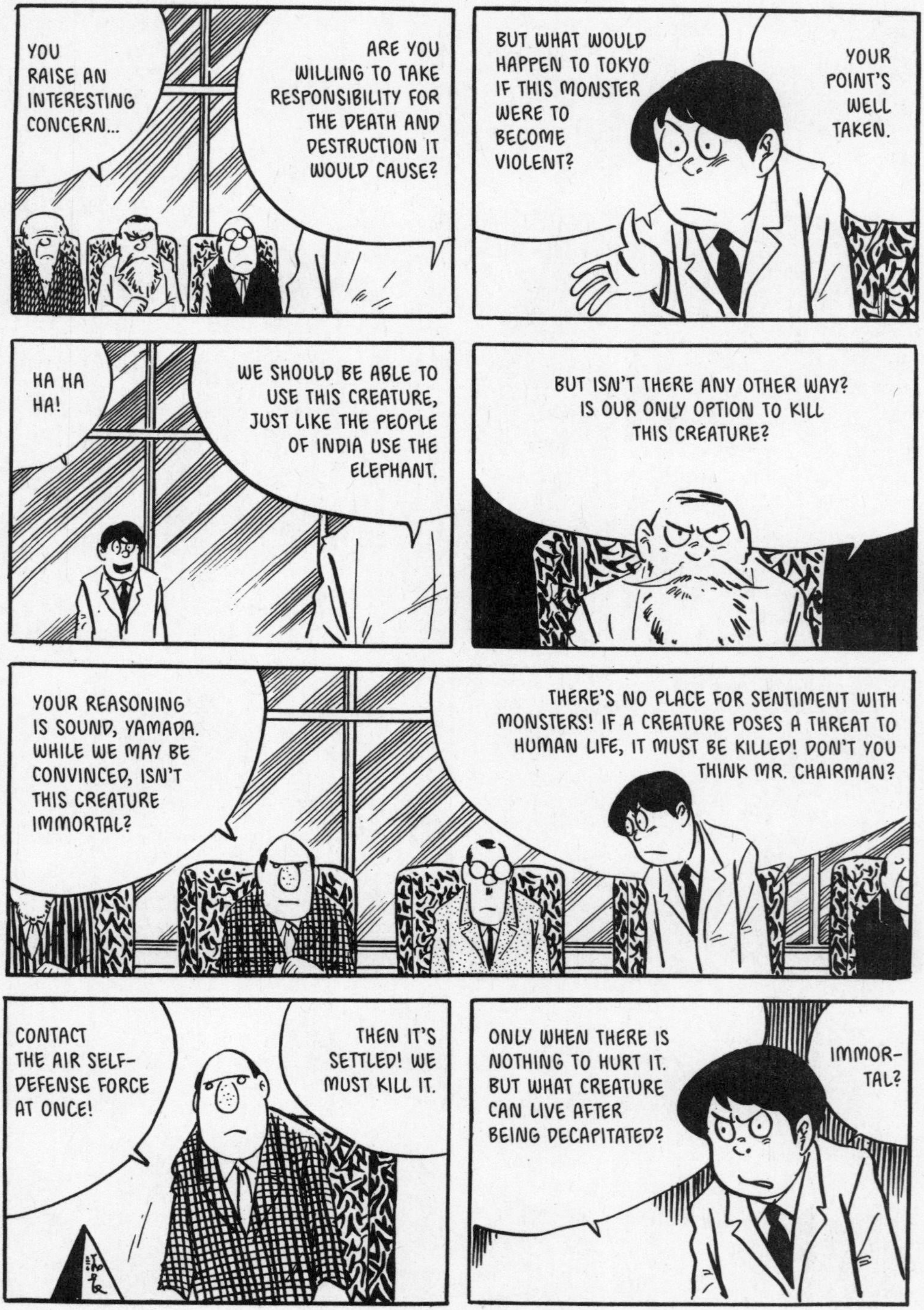
YOUR POINT'S WELL TAKEN.
BUT WHAT WOULD HAPPEN TO TOKYO IF THIS MONSTER WERE TO BECOME VIOLENT?
ARE YOU WILLING TO TAKE RESPONSIBILITY FOR THE DEATH AND DESTRUCTION IT WOULD CAUSE?
YOU RAISE AN INTERESTING CONCERN...
BUT ISN'T THERE ANY OTHER WAY? IS OUR ONLY OPTION TO KILL THIS CREATURE?
WE SHOULD BE ABLE TO USE THIS CREATURE, JUST LIKE THE PEOPLE OF INDIA USE THE ELEPHANT.
HA HA HA!
THERE'S NO PLACE FOR SENTIMENT WITH MONSTERS! IF A CREATURE POSES A THREAT TO HUMAN LIFE, IT MUST BE KILLED! DON'T YOU THINK MR. CHAIRMAN?
YOUR REASONING IS SOUND, YAMADA. WHILE WE MAY BE CONVINCED, ISN'T THIS CREATURE IMMORTAL?
IMMOR-TAL?
ONLY WHEN THERE IS NOTHING TO HURT IT. BUT WHAT CREATURE CAN LIVE AFTER BEING DECAPITATED?
THEN IT'S SETTLED! WE MUST KILL IT.
CONTACT THE AIR SELF-DEFENSE FORCE AT ONCE!

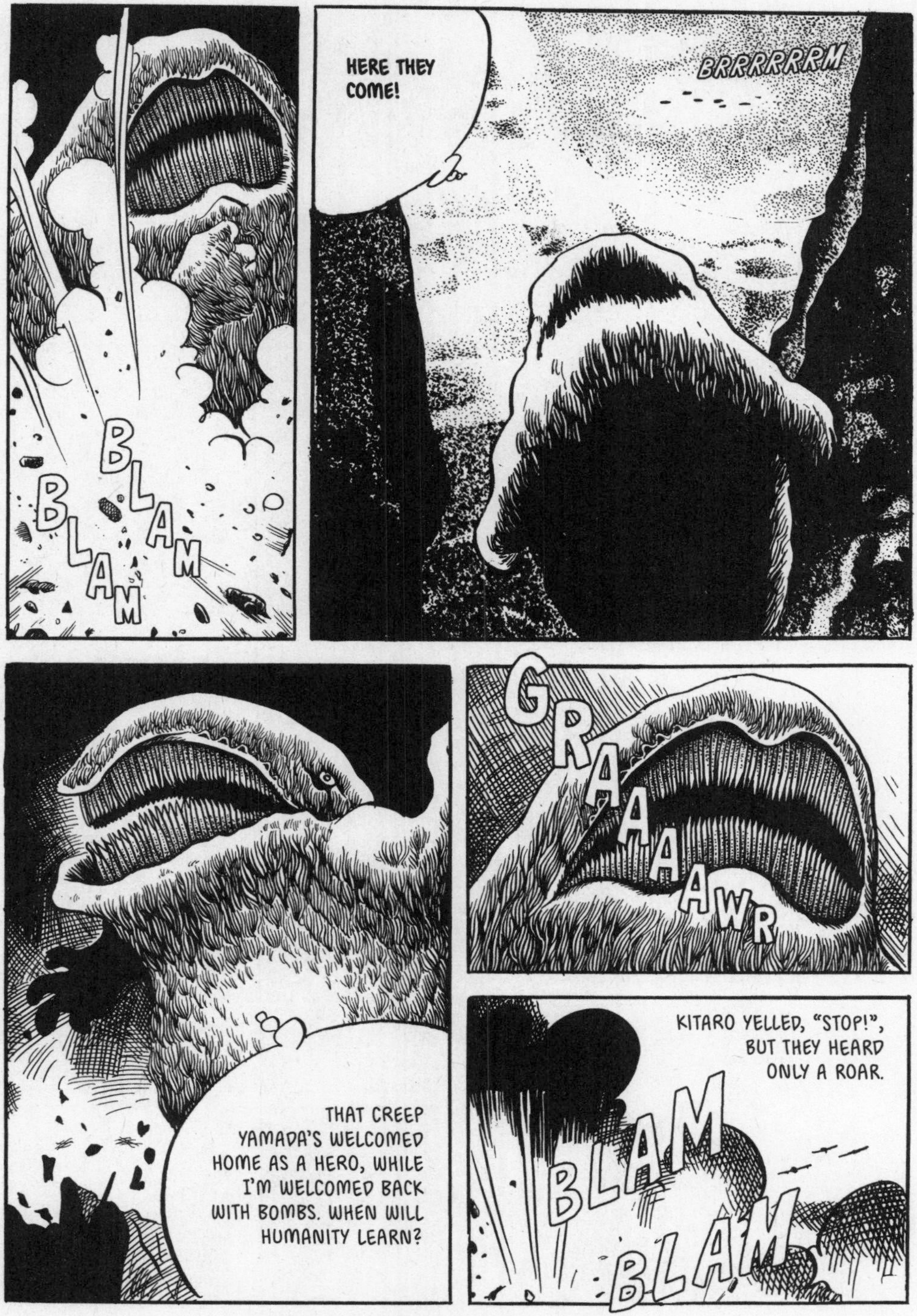
HERE THEY COME!
BRRRRRRM
BLAM BLAM
GRAAAAAWR
KITARO YELLED, "STOP!", BUT THEY HEARD ONLY A ROAR.
BLAM BLAM
THAT CREEP YAMADA'S WELCOMED HOME AS A HERO, WHILE I'M WELCOMED BACK WITH BOMBS. WHEN WILL HUMANITY LEARN?

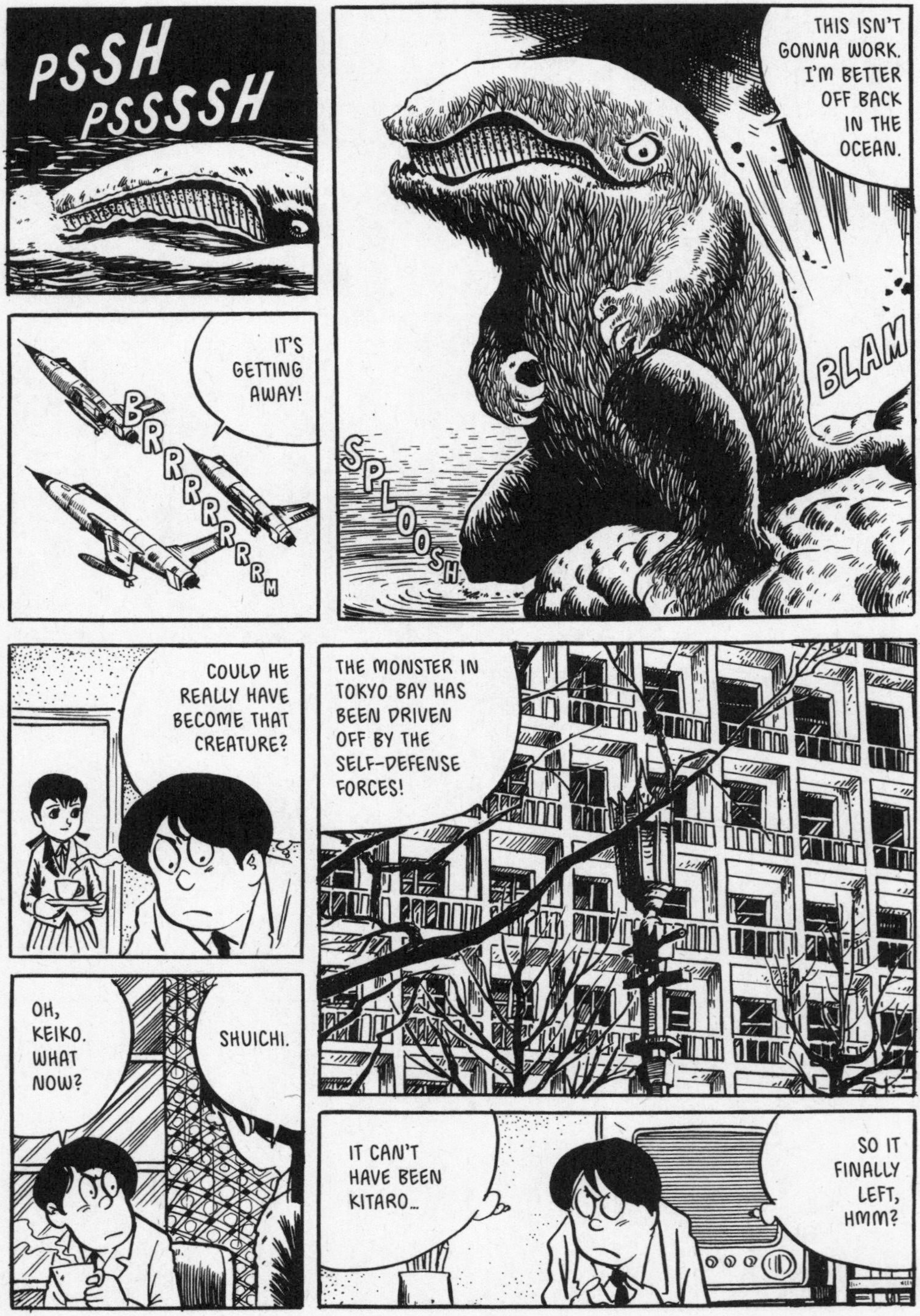
THIS ISN'T GONNA WORK. I'M BETTER OFF BACK IN THE OCEAN.
BLAM
SPLOOSH
PSSH PSSSSH
IT'S GETTING AWAY!
BRRRRRRRRM
THE MONSTER IN TOKYO BAY HAS BEEN DRIVEN OFF BY THE SELF-DEFENSE FORCES!
COULD HE REALLY HAVE BECOME THAT CREATURE?
SHUICHI.
OH, KEIKO. WHAT NOW?
SO IT FINALLY LEFT, HMM?
IT CAN'T HAVE BEEN KITARO...

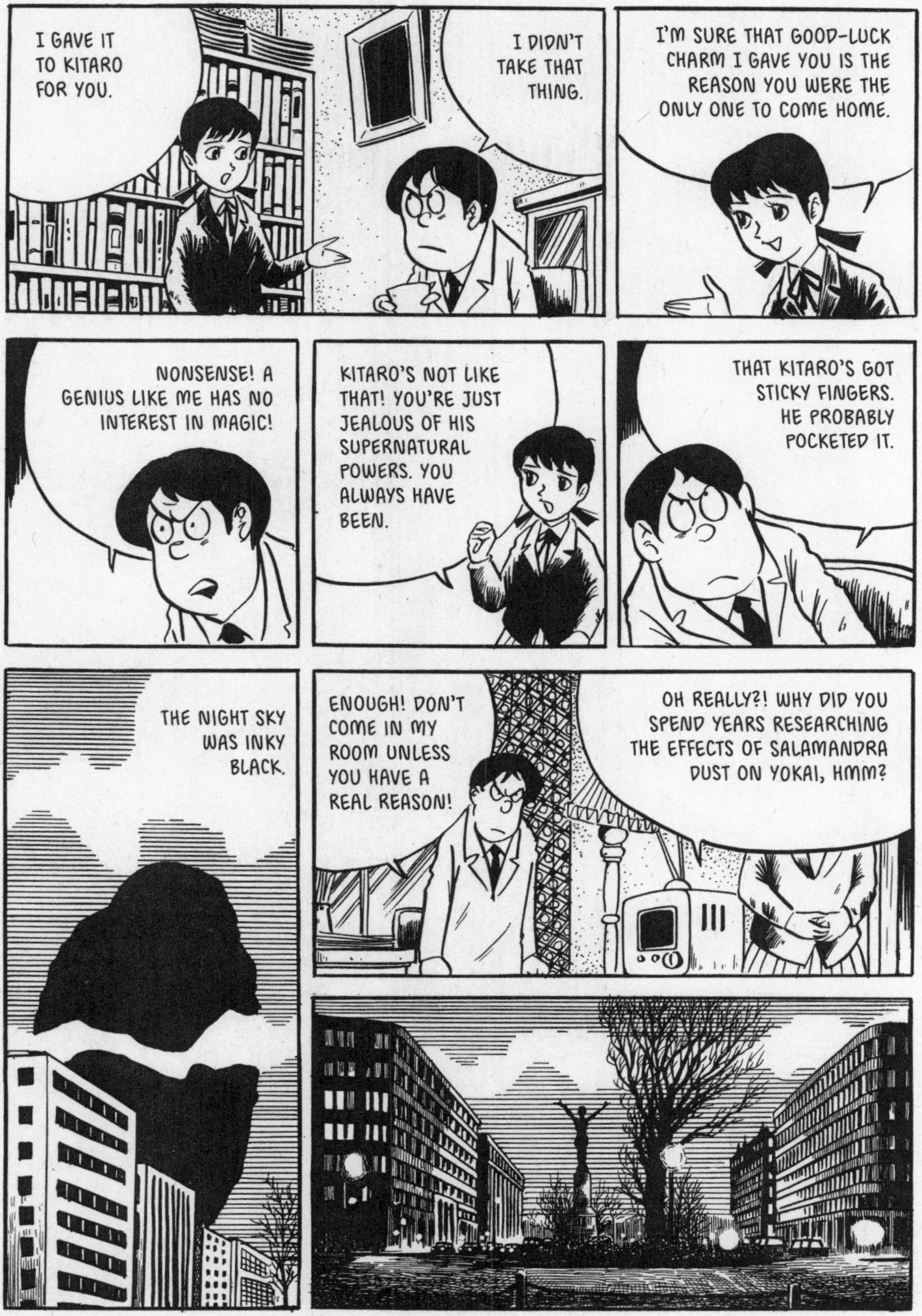
I'M SURE THAT GOOD-LUCK CHARM I GAVE YOU IS THE REASON YOU WERE THE ONLY ONE TO COME HOME.
I DIDN'T TAKE THAT THING.
I GAVE IT TO KITARO FOR YOU.
THAT KITARO'S GOT STICKY FINGERS. HE PROBABLY POCKETED IT.
KITARO'S NOT LIKE THAT! YOU'RE JUST JEALOUS OF HIS SUPERNATURAL POWERS. YOU ALWAYS HAVE BEEN.
NONSENSE! A GENIUS LIKE ME HAS NO INTEREST IN MAGIC!
OH REALLY?! WHY DID YOU SPEND YEARS RESEARCHING THE EFFECTS OF SALAMANDRA DUST ON YOKAI, HMM?
ENOUGH! DON'T COME IN MY ROOM UNLESS YOU HAVE A REAL REASON!
THE NIGHT SKY WAS INKY BLACK.

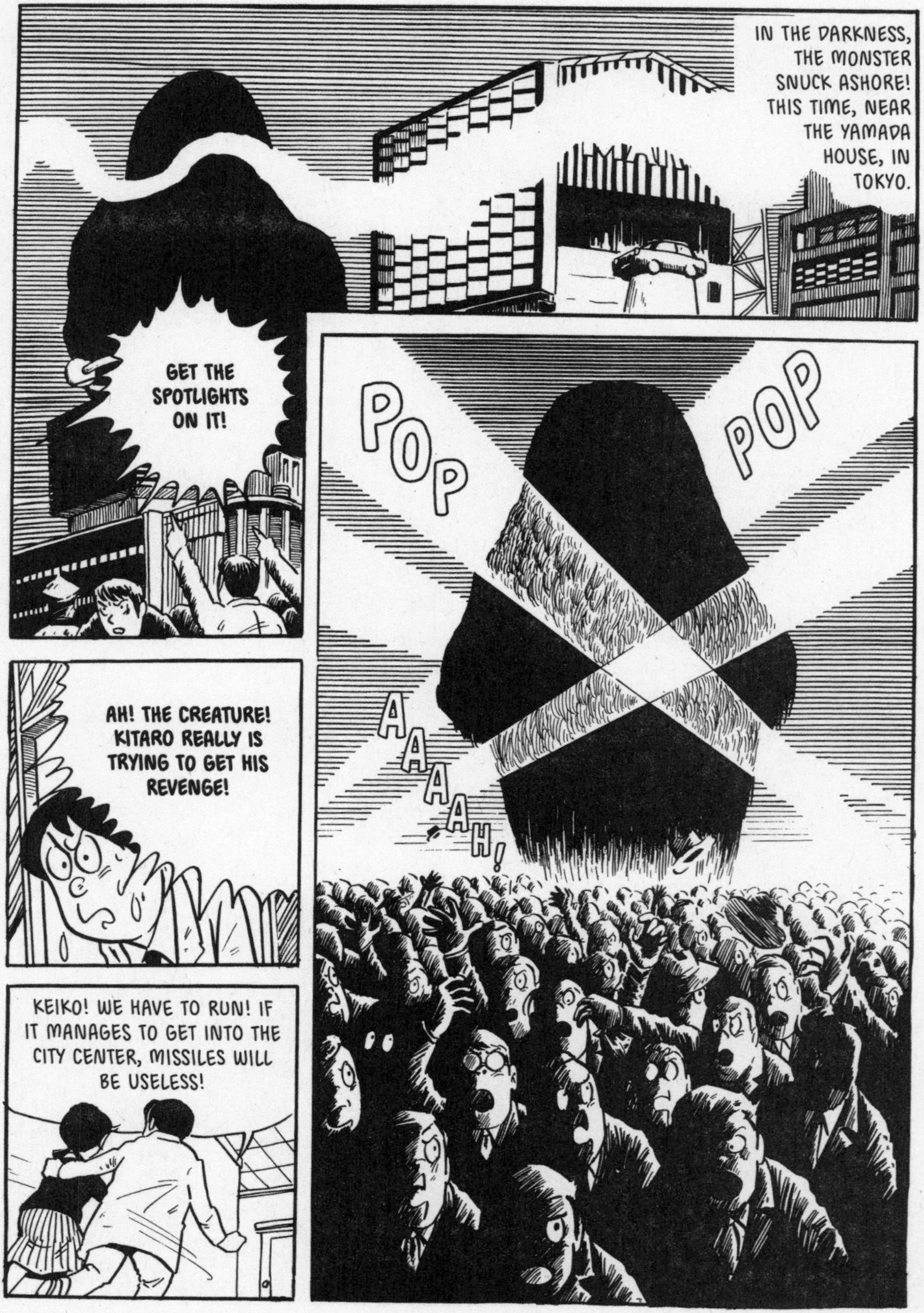
IN THE DARKNESS, THE MONSTER SNUCK ASHORE! THIS TIME, NEAR THE YAMADA HOUSE, IN TOKYO.
POP
POP
AAAAAH!
GET THE SPOTLIGHTS ON IT!
AH! THE CREATURE! KITARO REALLY IS TRYING TO GET HIS REVENGE!
KEIKO! WE HAVE TO RUN! IF IT MANAGES TO GET INTO THE CITY CENTER, MISSILES WILL BE USELESS!

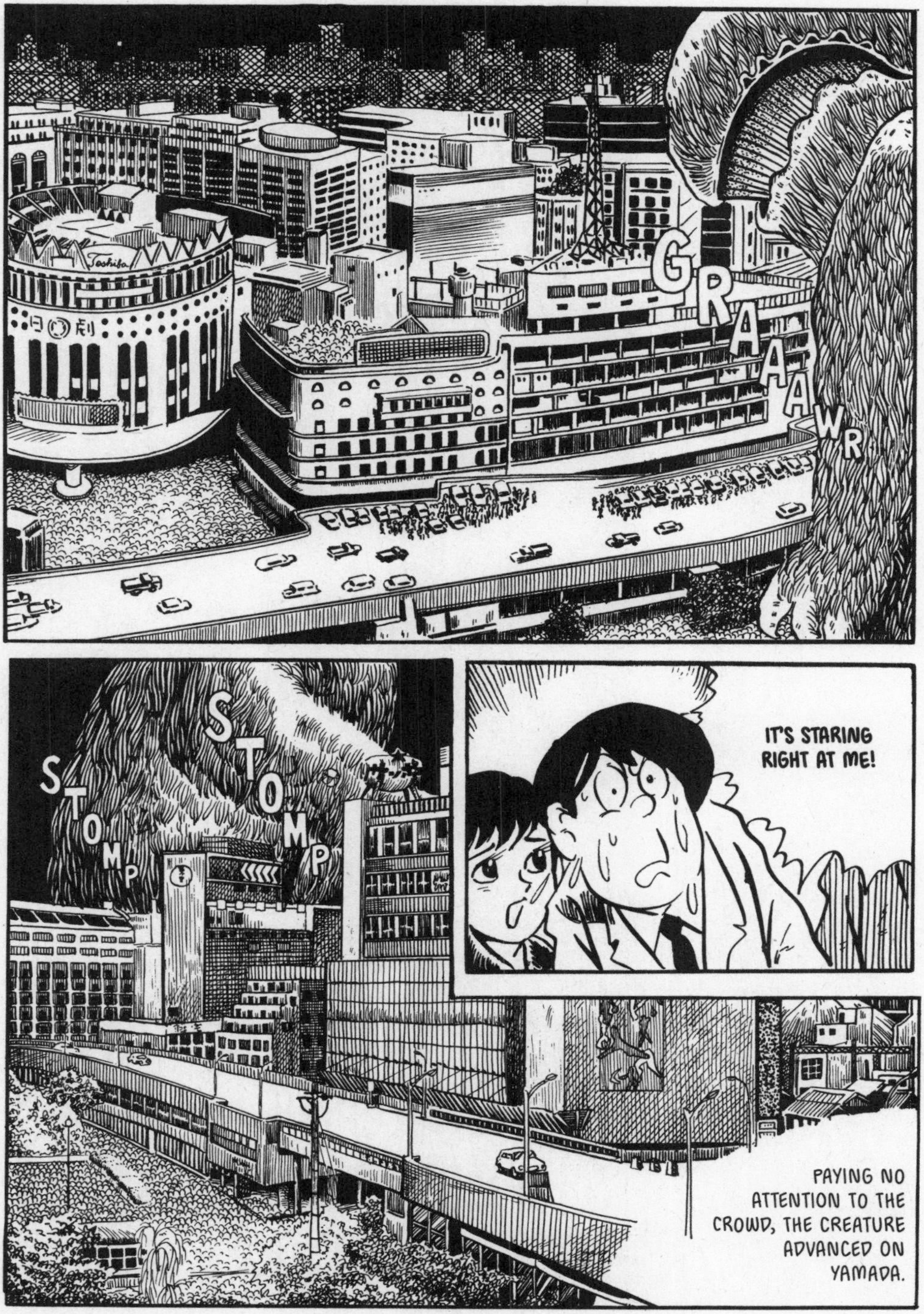
GRAAAAWR
IT'S STARING RIGHT AT ME!
STOMP
STOMP
PAYING NO ATTENTION TO THE CROWD, THE CREATURE ADVANCED ON YAMADA.

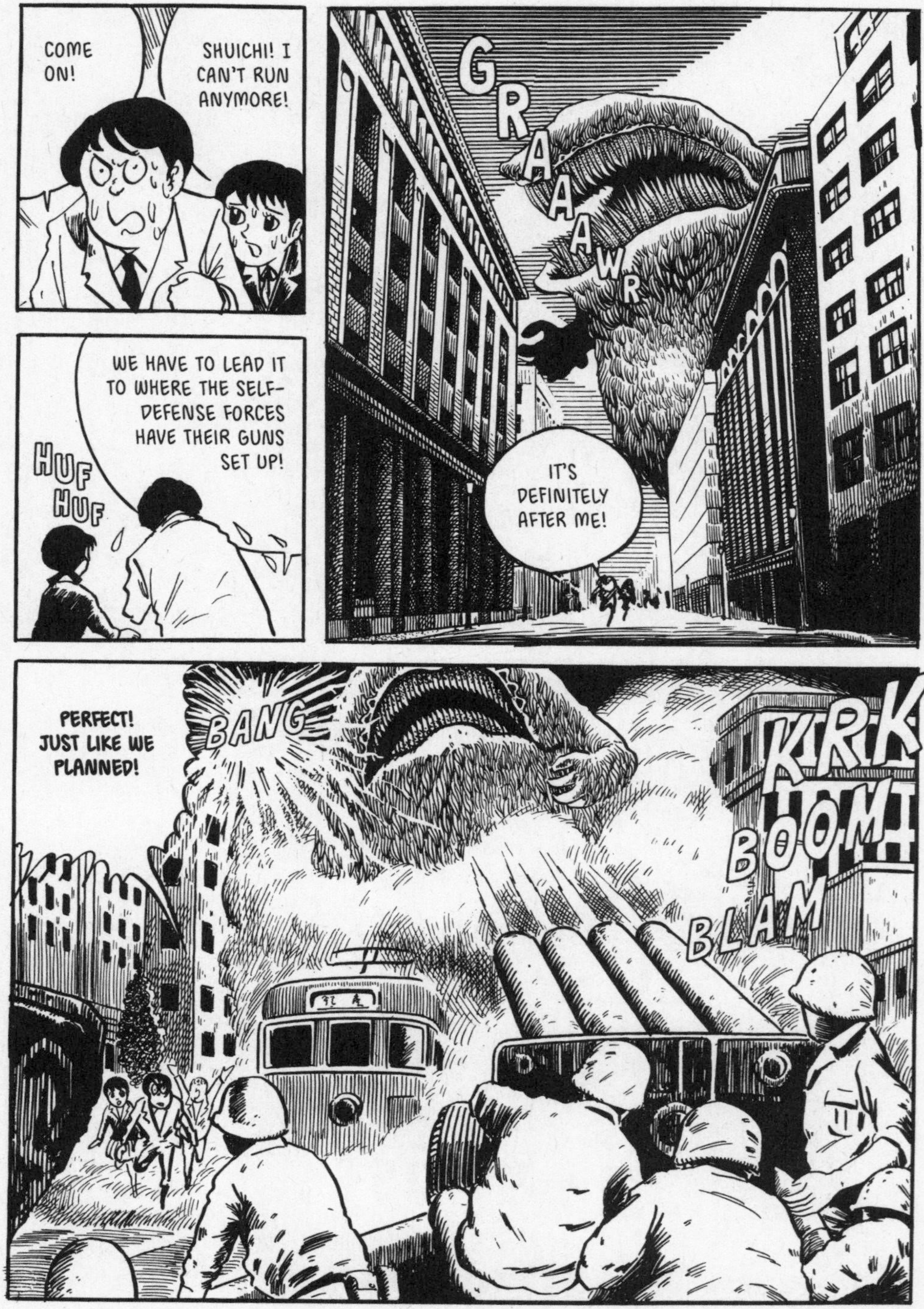
GRAAAWR
IT'S DEFINITELY AFTER ME!
SHUICHI! I CAN'T RUN ANYMORE!
COME ON!
WE HAVE TO LEAD IT TO WHERE THE SELF-DEFENSE FORCES HAVE THEIR GUNS SET UP!
HUF HUF
KRK
BANG
PERFECT! JUST LIKE WE PLANNED!
BOOM
BLAM

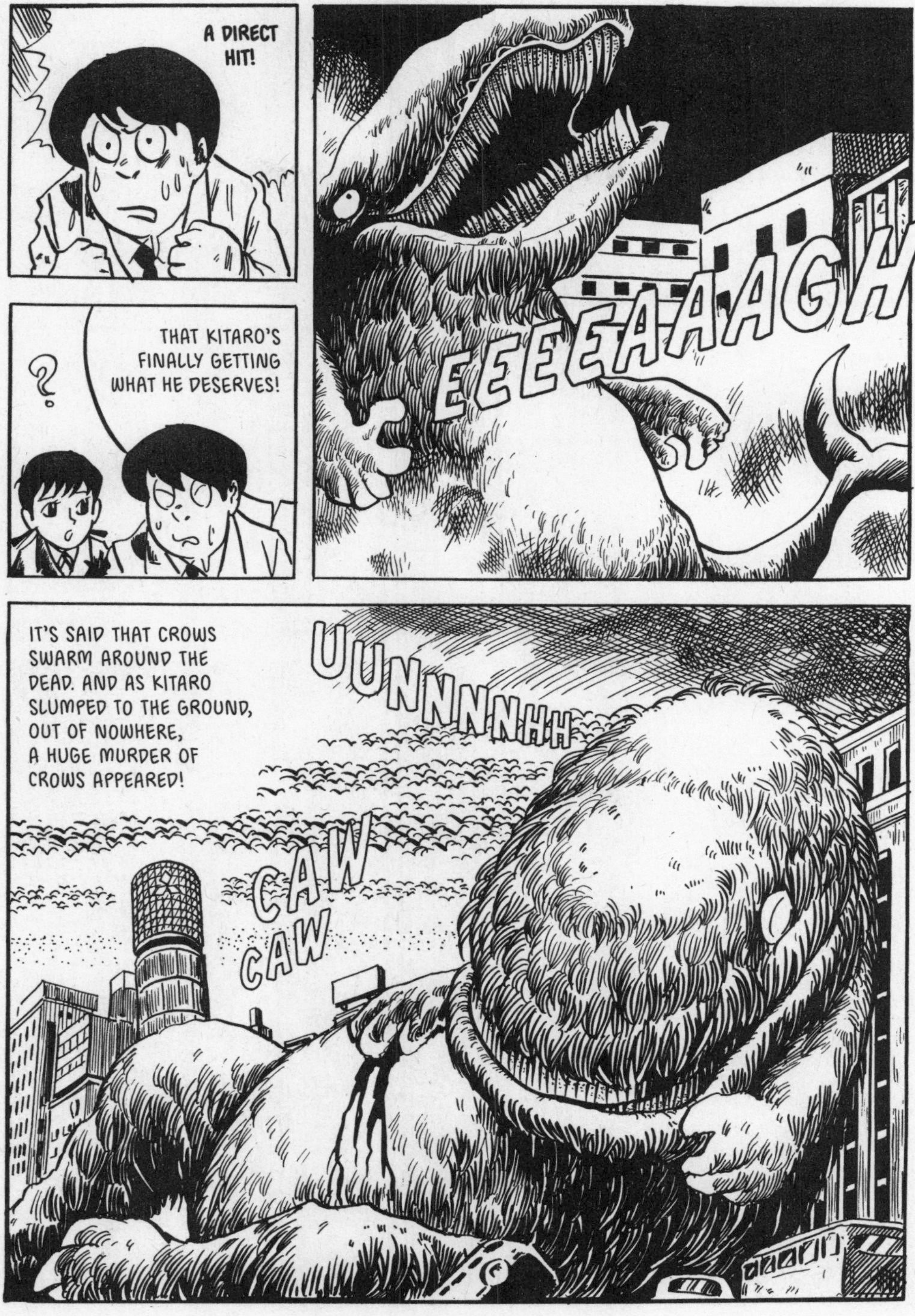
EEEEAAAAGH
A DIRECT HIT!
?
THAT KITARO'S FINALLY GETTING WHAT HE DESERVES!
UUNNNNNHH
IT'S SAID THAT CROWS SWARM AROUND THE DEAD. AND AS KITARO SLUMPED TO THE GROUND, OUT OF NOWHERE, A HUGE MURDER OF CROWS APPEARED!
CAW
CAW

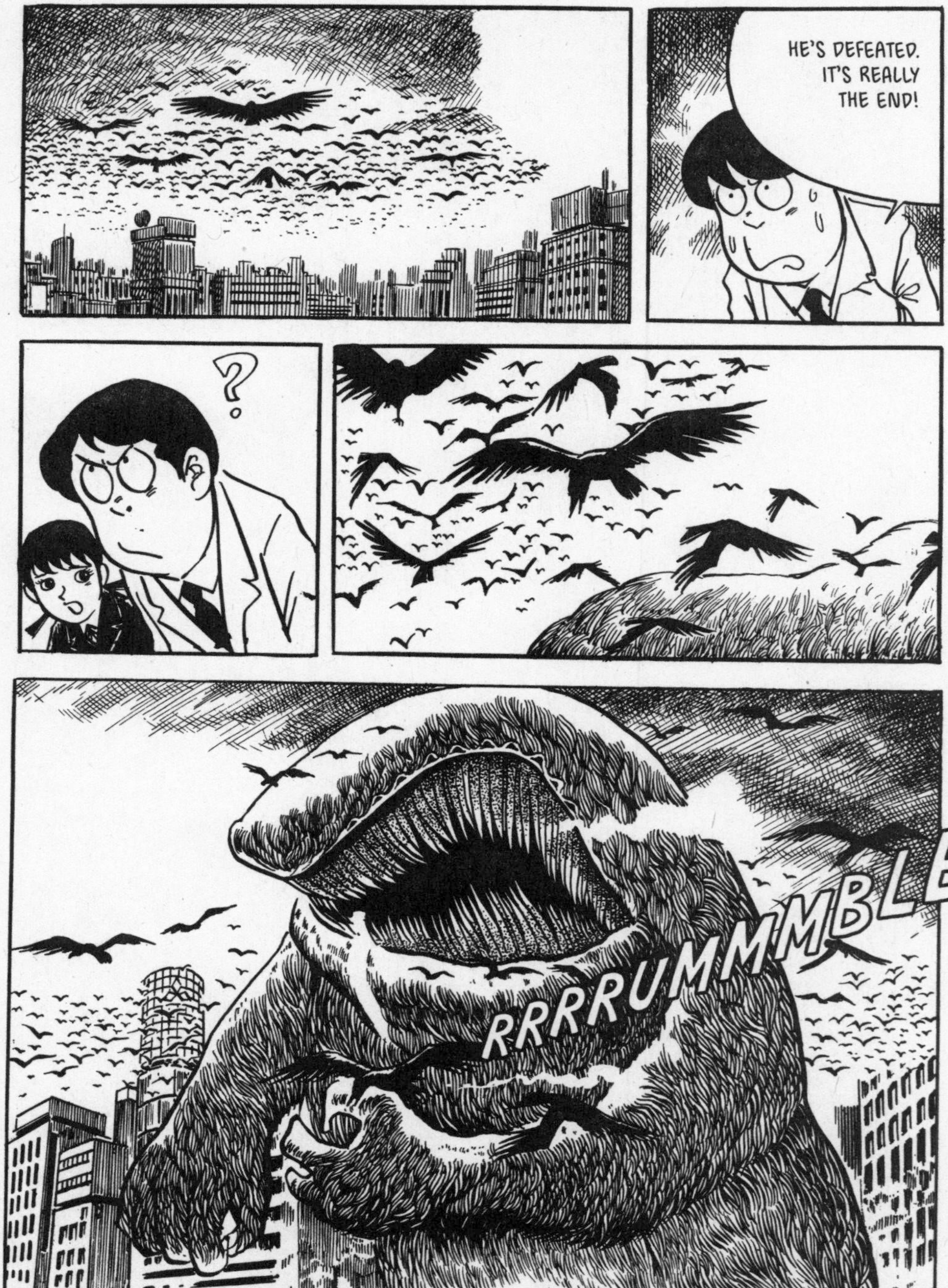
HE'S DEFEATED. IT'S REALLY THE END!
?
RRRRUMMMMBLE

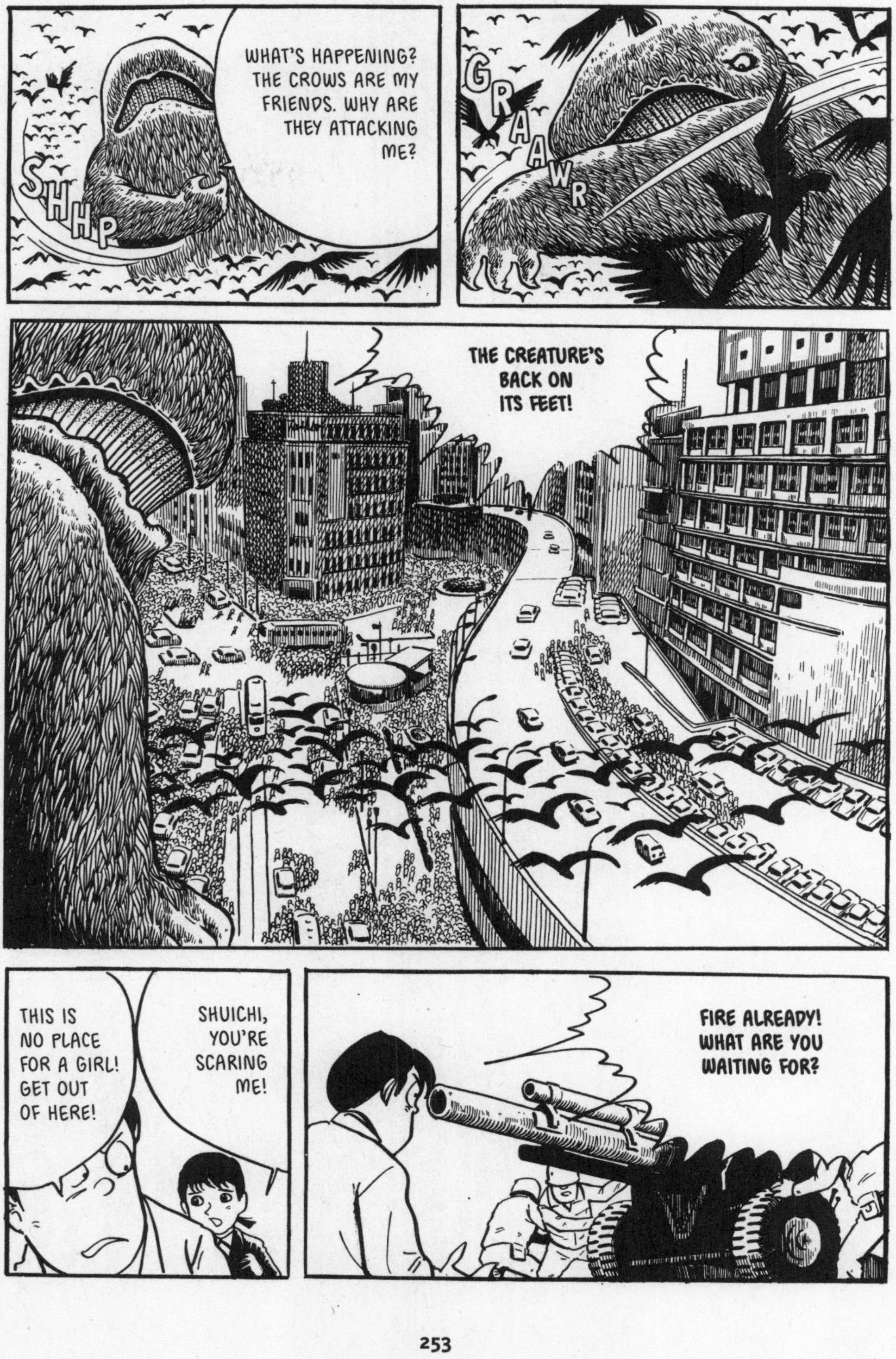
GRAAWR
WHAT'S HAPPENING? THE CROWS ARE MY FRIENDS. WHY ARE THEY ATTACKING ME?
SHHP
THE CREATURE'S BACK ON ITS FEET!
FIRE ALREADY! WHAT ARE YOU WAITING FOR?
SHUICHI, YOU'RE SCARING ME!
THIS IS NO PLACE FOR A GIRL! GET OUT OF HERE!

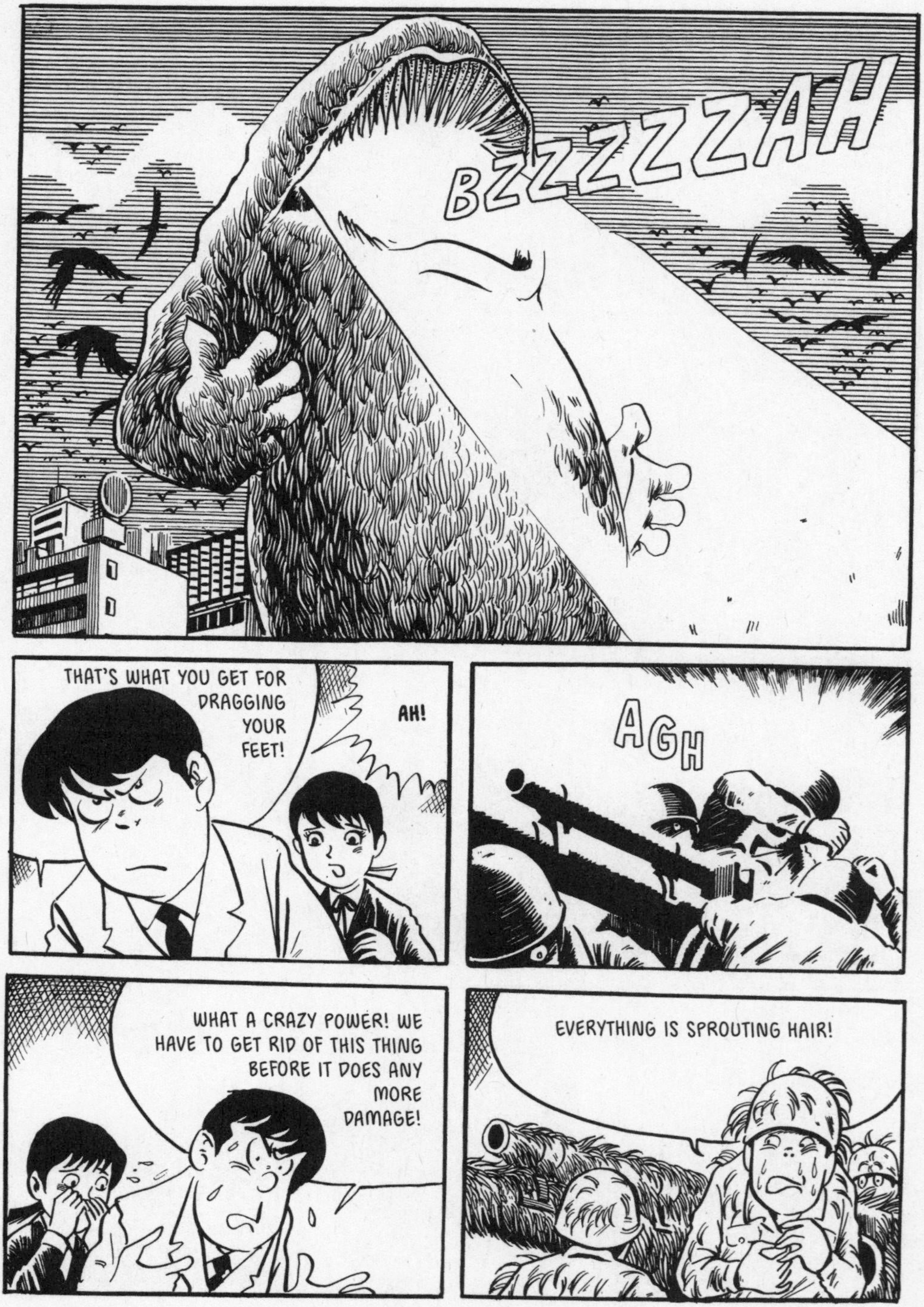
BZZZZZZAH
AGH
AH!
THAT'S WHAT YOU GET FOR DRAGGING YOUR FEET!
EVERYTHING IS SPROUTING HAIR!
WHAT A CRAZY POWER! WE HAVE TO GET RID OF THIS THING BEFORE IT DOES ANY MORE DAMAGE!

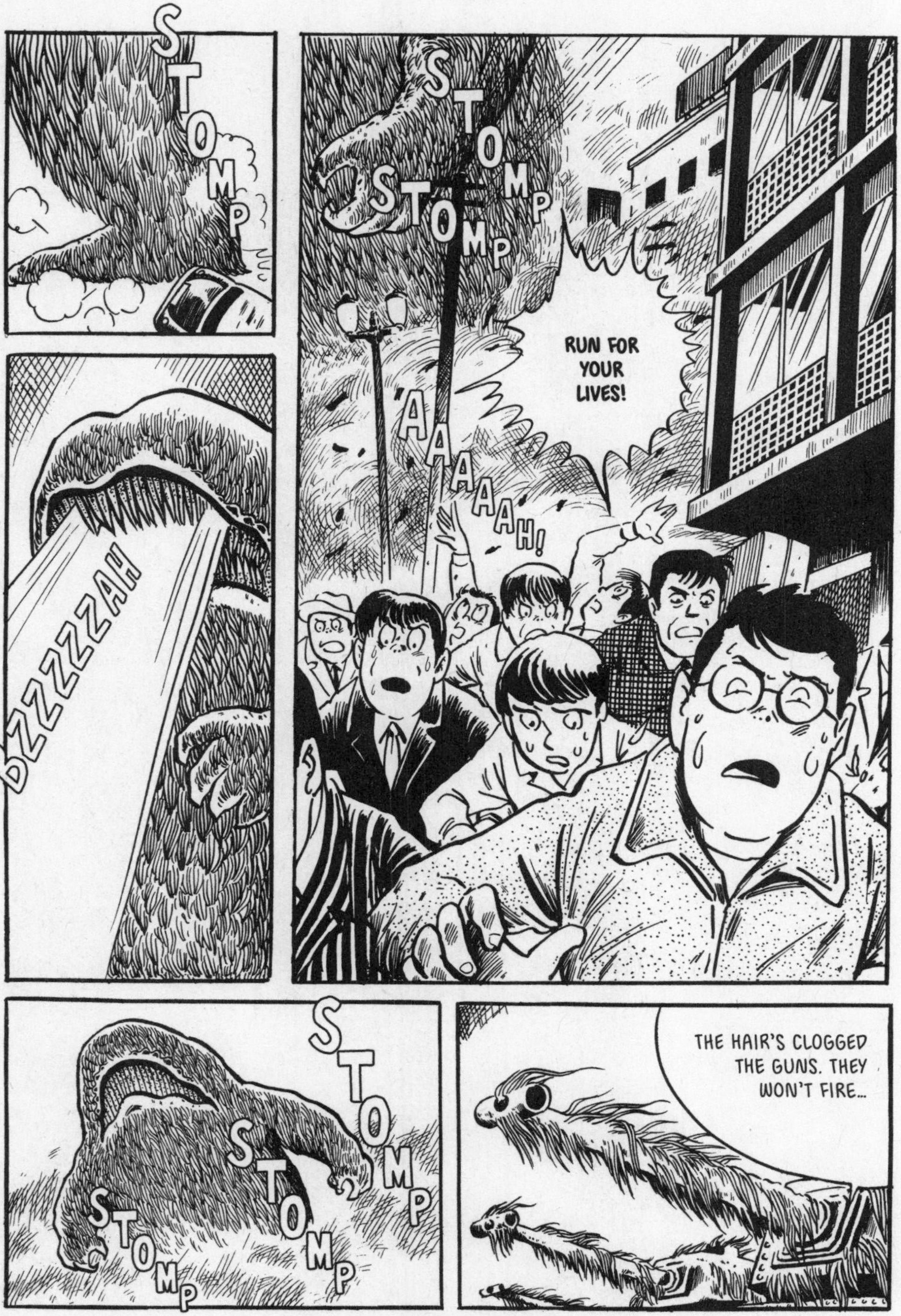
STOMP
STOMP
STOMP
RUN FOR YOUR LIVES!
AAAAAAH!
STOMP
BZZZZZZAH
THE HAIR'S CLOGGED THE GUNS. THEY WON'T FIRE...
STOMP
STOMP
STOMP

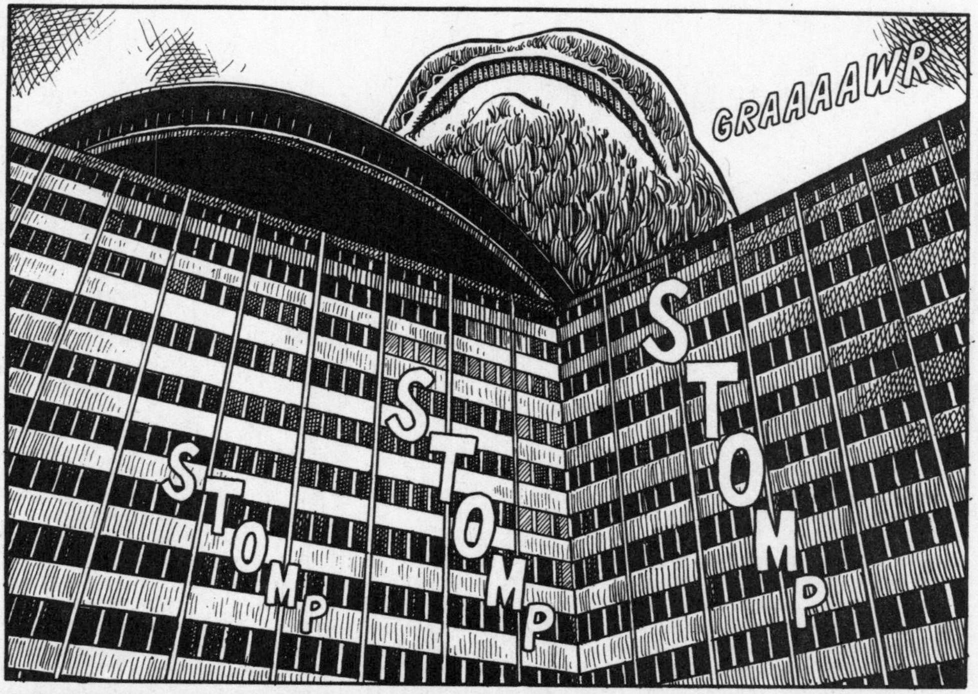
GRAAAAWR
STOMP
STOMP
STOMP
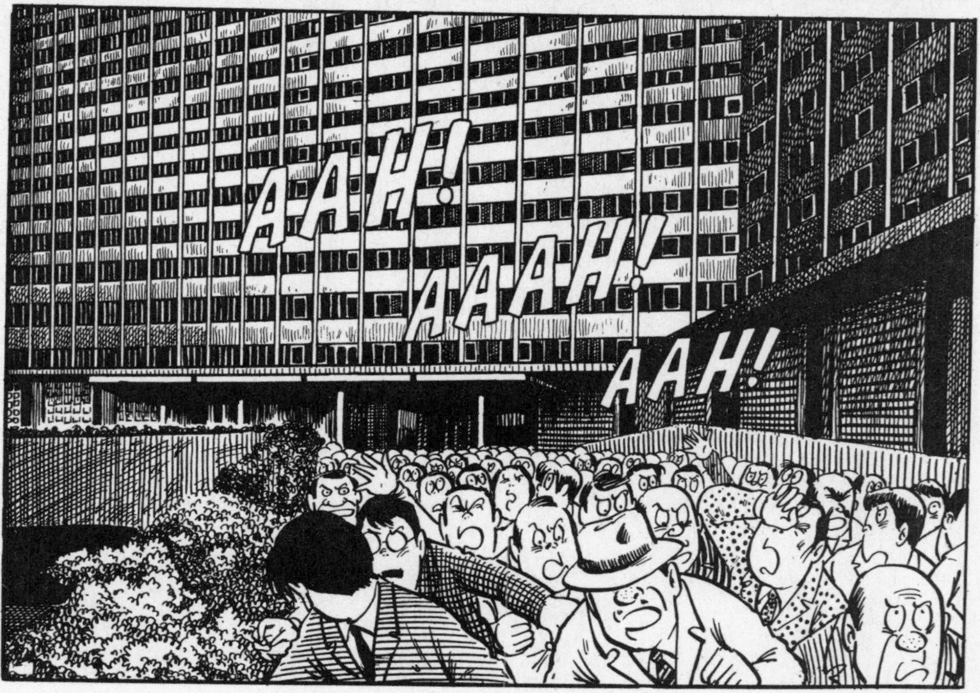
AAH!
AAAAH!
AAH!

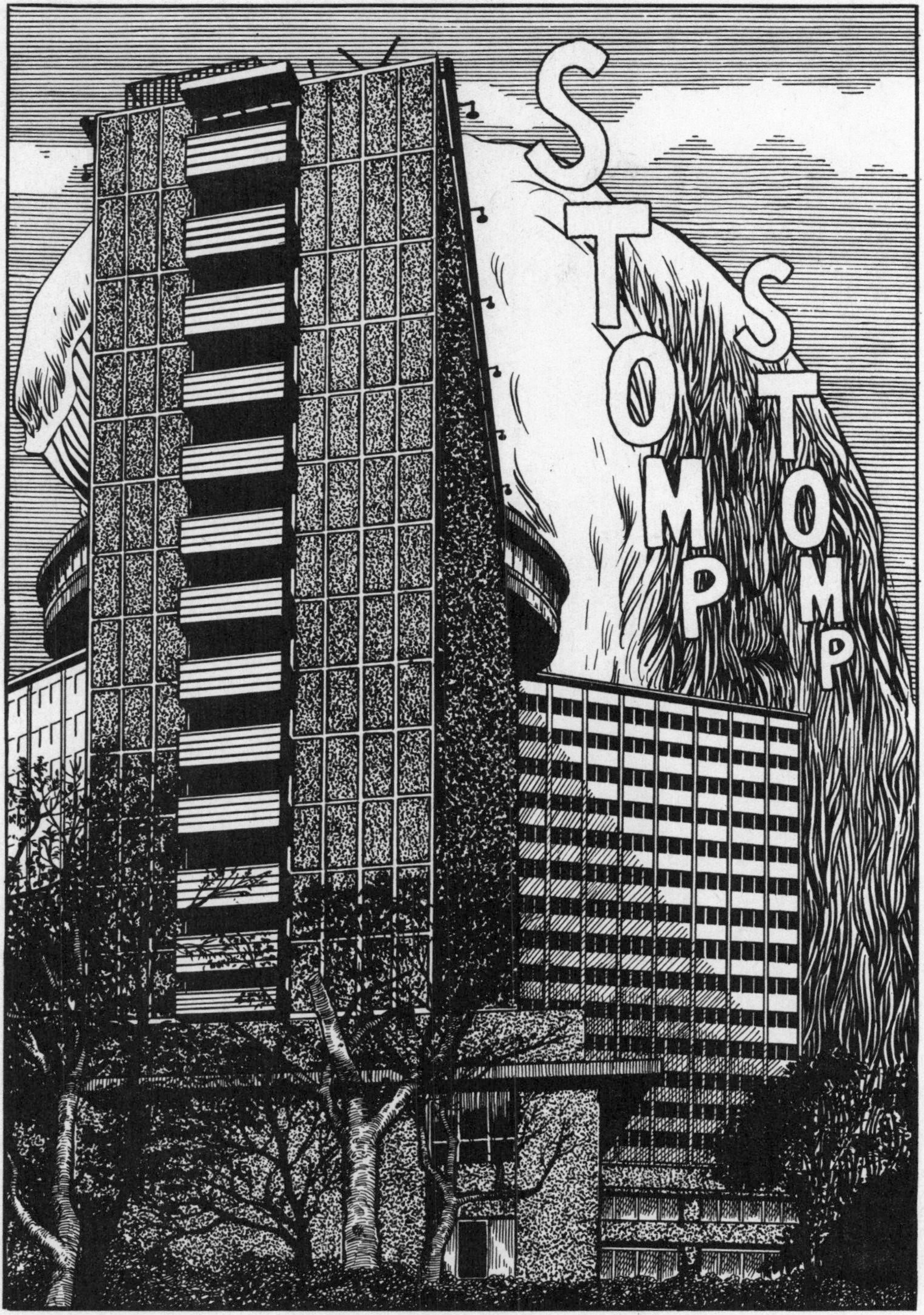
STOMP
STOMP

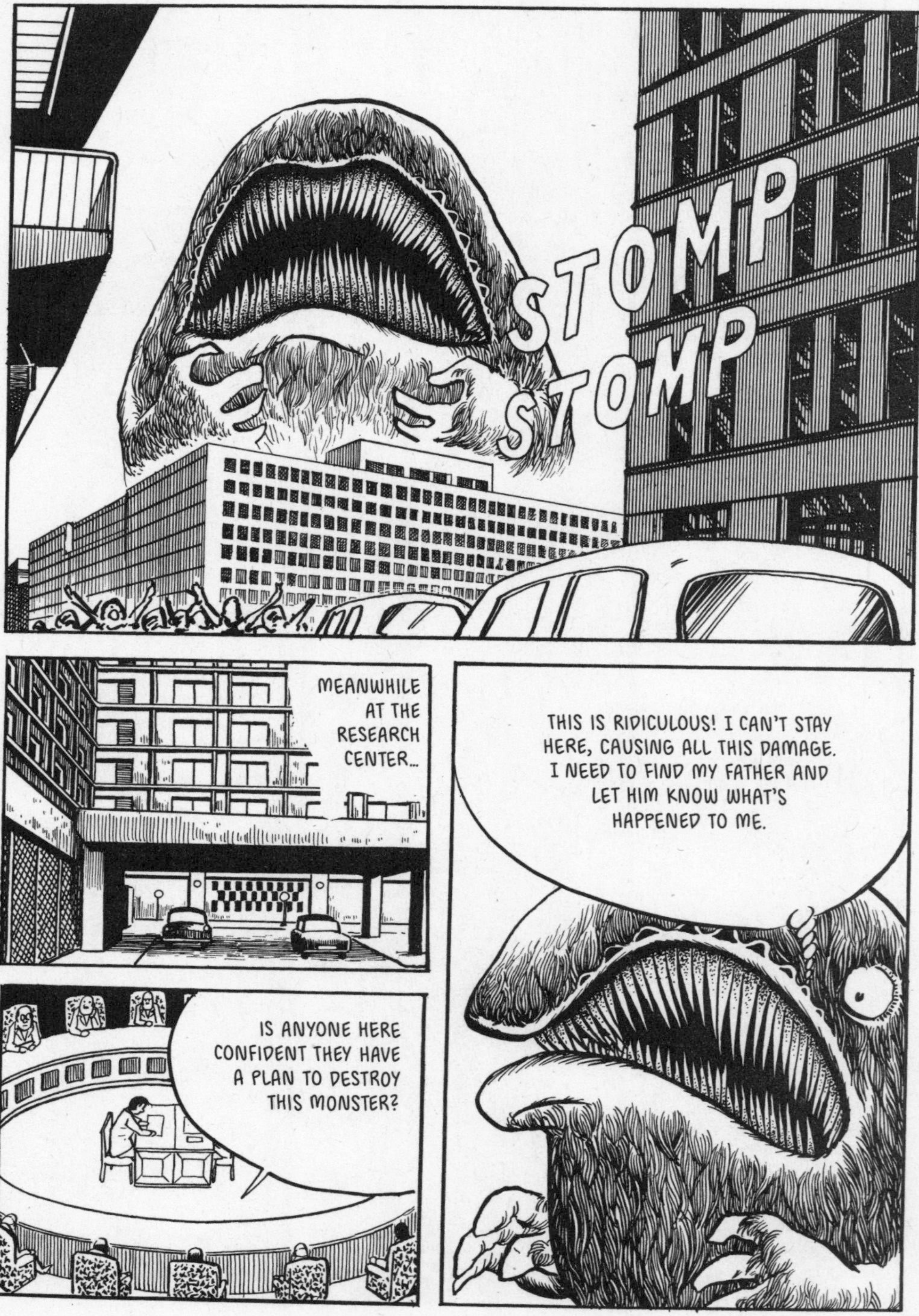
STOMP
STOMP
THIS IS RIDICULOUS! I CAN'T STAY HERE, CAUSING ALL THIS DAMAGE. I NEED TO FIND MY FATHER AND LET HIM KNOW WHAT'S HAPPENED TO ME.
MEANWHILE AT THE RESEARCH CENTER...
IS ANYONE HERE CONFIDENT THEY HAVE A PLAN TO DESTROY THIS MONSTER?

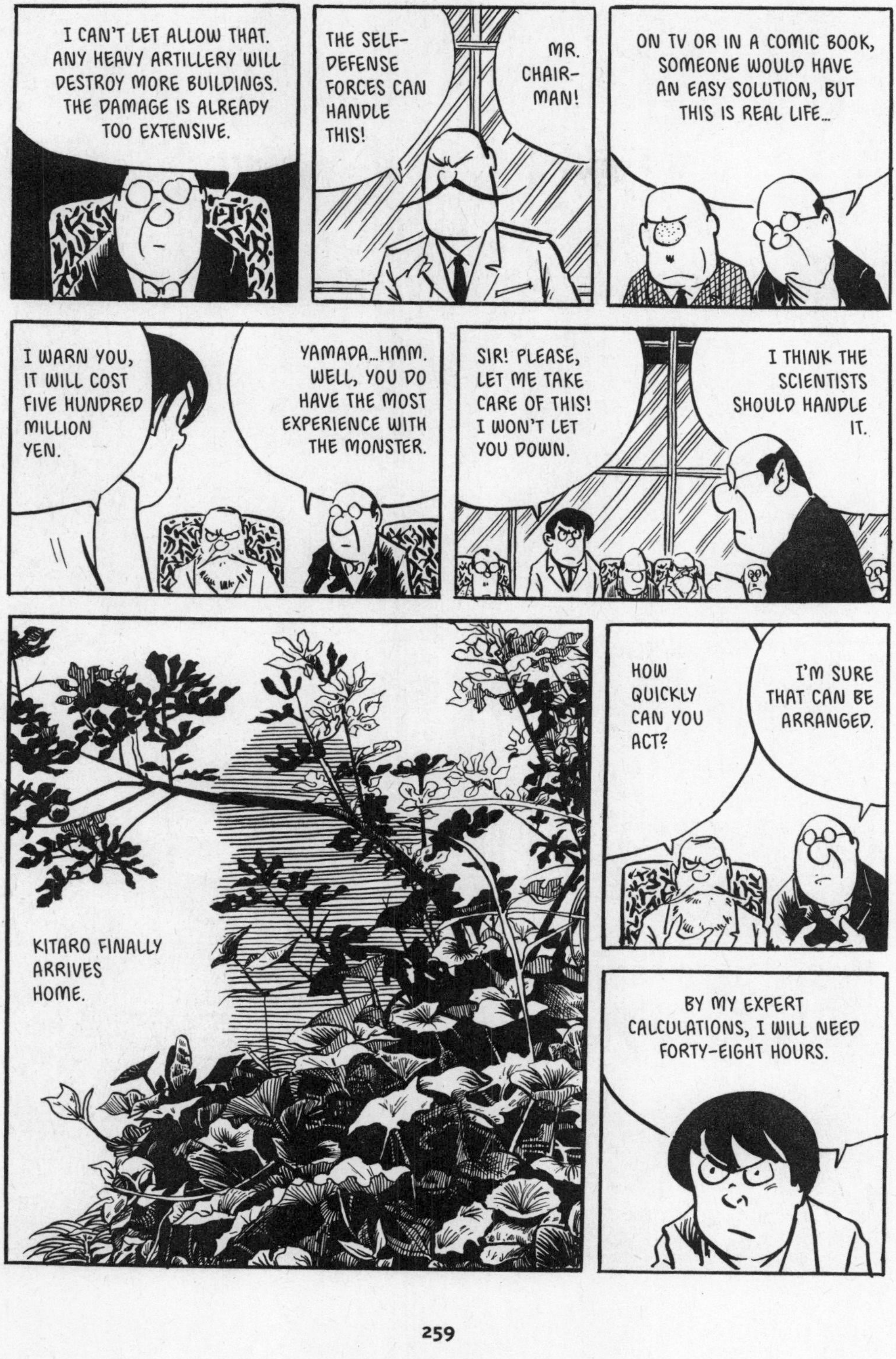
ON TV OR IN A COMIC BOOK, SOMEONE WOULD HAVE AN EASY SOLUTION, BUT THIS IS REAL LIFE...
MR. CHAIRMAN!
THE SELF-DEFENSE FORCES CAN HANDLE THIS!
I CAN'T LET ALLOW THAT. ANY HEAVY ARTILLERY WILL DESTROY MORE BUILDINGS. THE DAMAGE IS ALREADY TOO EXTENSIVE.
I THINK THE SCIENTISTS SHOULD HANDLE IT.
SIR! PLEASE, LET ME TAKE CARE OF THIS! I WON'T LET YOU DOWN.
YAMADA...HMM. WELL, YOU DO HAVE THE MOST EXPERIENCE WITH THE MONSTER.
I WARN YOU, IT WILL COST FIVE HUNDRED MILLION YEN.
I'M SURE THAT CAN BE ARRANGED.
HOW QUICKLY CAN YOU ACT?
BY MY EXPERT CALCULATIONS, I WILL NEED FORTY-EIGHT HOURS.
KITARO FINALLY ARRIVES HOME.

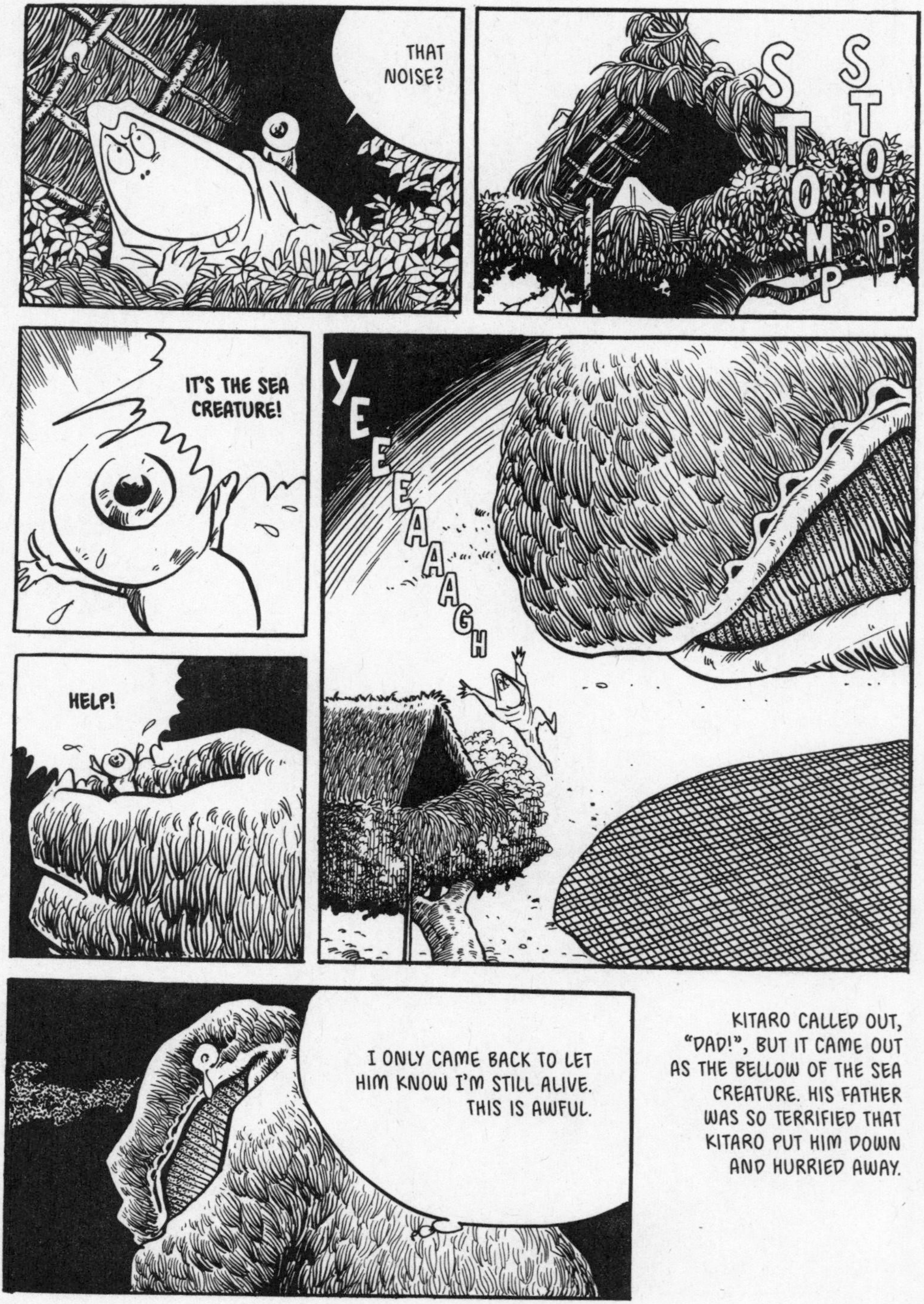
STOMP
STOMP
THAT NOISE?
YEEEAAAAGH
IT'S THE SEA CREATURE!
HELP!
KITARO CALLED OUT, "DAD!", BUT IT CAME OUT AS THE BELLOW OF THE SEA CREATURE. HIS FATHER WAS SO TERRIFIED THAT KITARO PUT HIM DOWN AND HURRIED AWAY.
I ONLY CAME BACK TO LET HIM KNOW I'M STILL ALIVE. THIS IS AWFUL.

THE GRAVITY OF THE SITUATION FINALLY HIT KITARO. HERE HE WAS, A POWERFUL YOKAI, LAID LOW BY THIS MONSTROUS TRANSFORMATION. HE NEVER THOUGHT THIS SORT OF THING WOULD BOTHER HIM, BUT IT DID. NOBODY—NOT HIS FATHER, NOT HIS FRIENDS, NOT EVEN THE CROWS—RECOGNIZED HIM. THE OLD KITARO WAS GONE.

SUDDENLY, KITARO REMEMBERED THE GOOD-LUCK CHARM WEDGED BETWEEN HIS FINGERS.

OF COURSE! YAMADA'S YOUNGER SISTER KEIKO WAS SURE TO RECOGNIZE HIM. SHE WAS HIS LAST CHANCE, HIS ONLY HOPE.

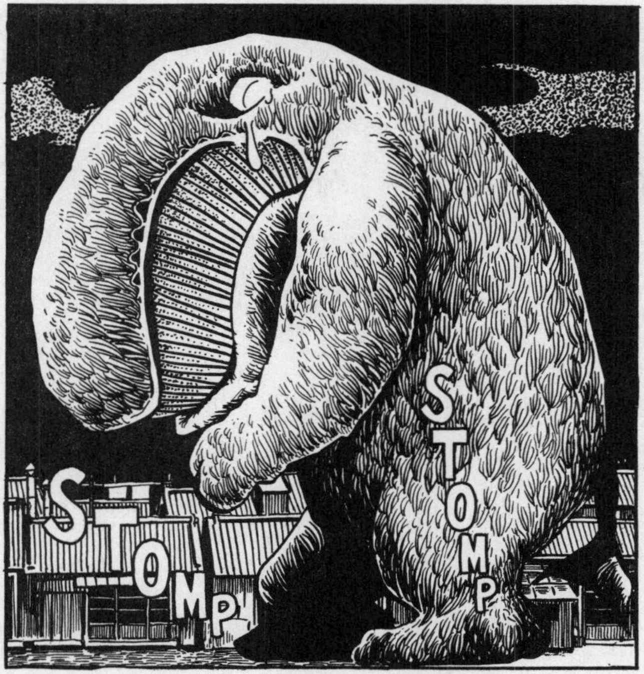
STOMP
STOMP

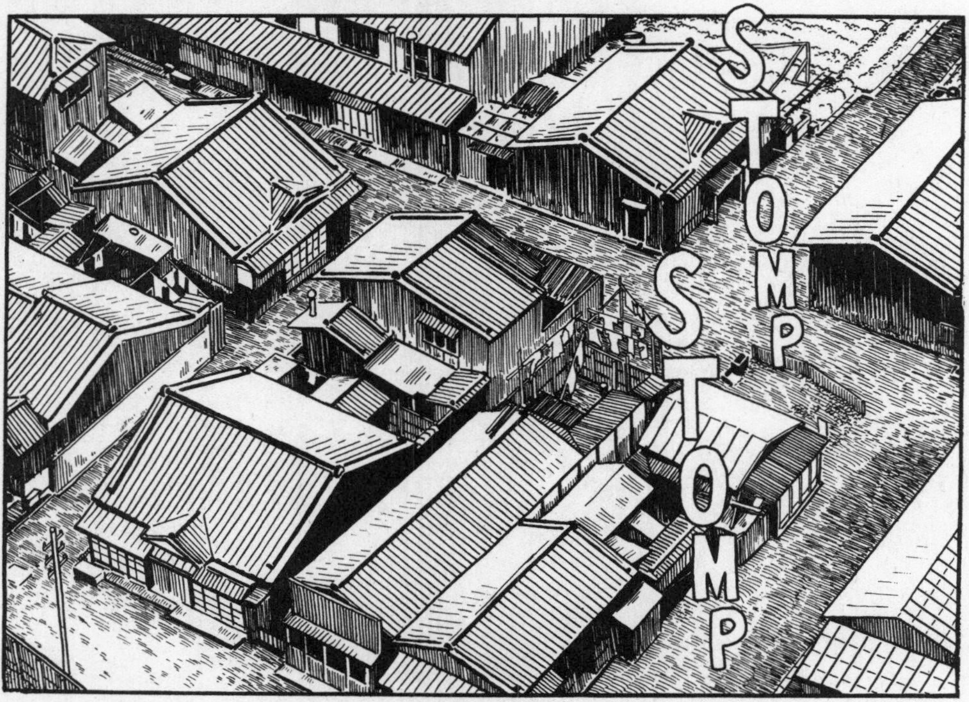
STOMP
STOMP

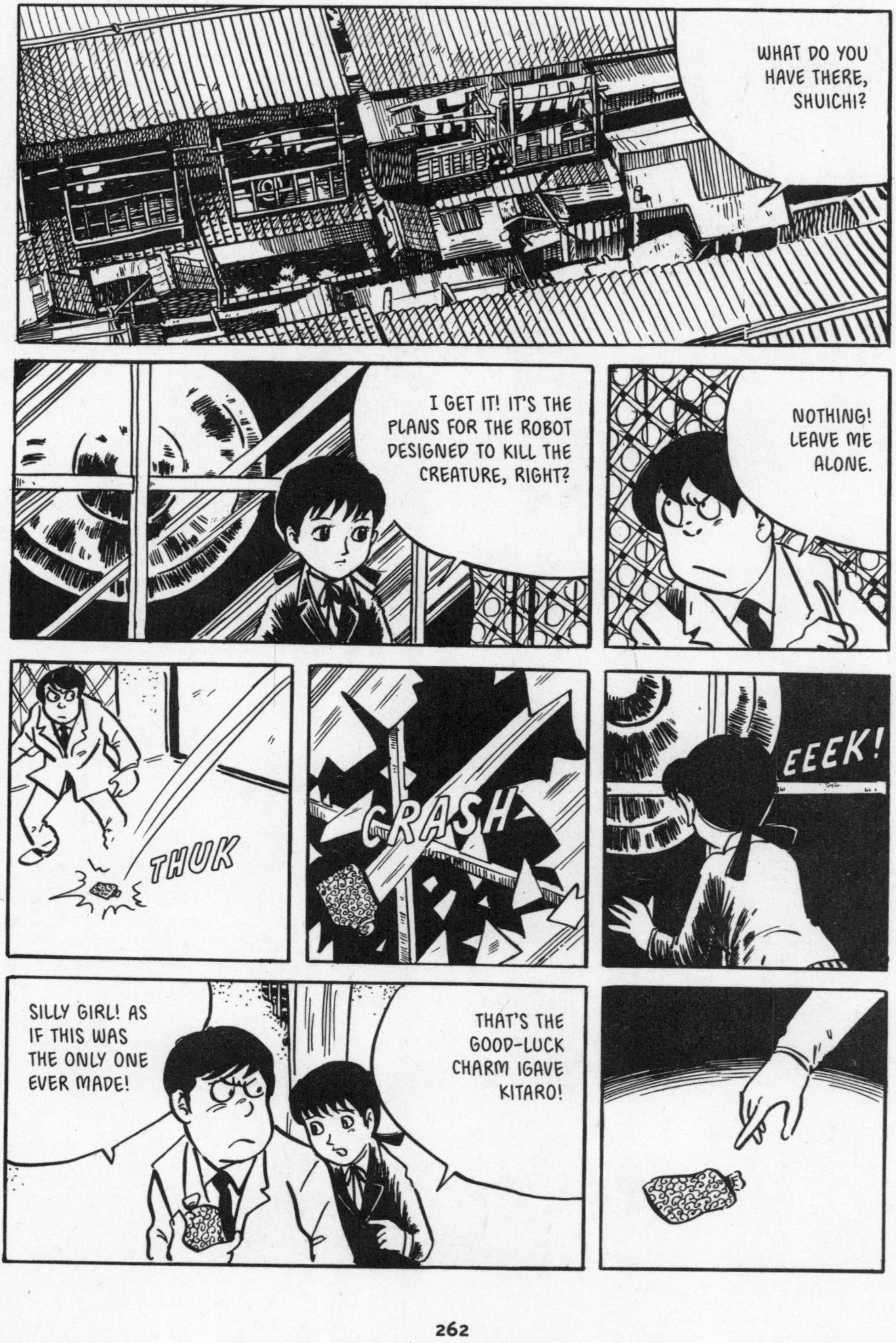
WHAT DO YOU HAVE THERE, SHUICHI?
NOTHING! LEAVE ME ALONE.
I GET IT! IT'S THE PLANS FOR THE ROBOT DESIGNED TO KILL THE CREATURE, RIGHT?
EEEK!
CRASH
THUK
THAT'S THE GOOD-LUCK CHARM I GAVE KITARO!
SILLY GIRL! AS IF THIS WAS THE ONLY ONE EVER MADE!

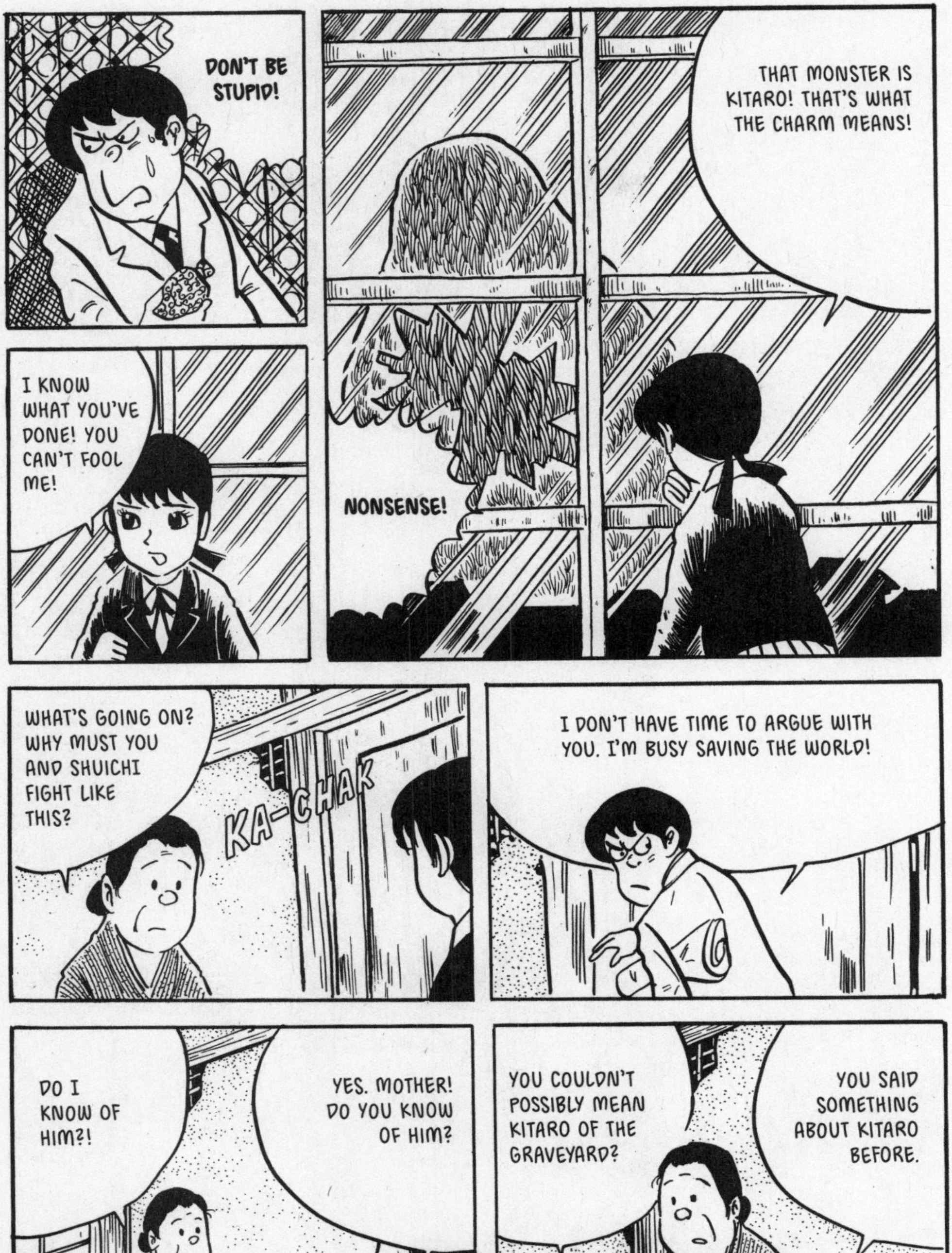
THAT MONSTER IS KITARO! THAT'S WHAT THE CHARM MEANS!
NONSENSE!
DON'T BE STUPID!
I KNOW WHAT YOU'VE DONE! YOU CAN'T FOOL ME!
I DON'T HAVE TIME TO ARGUE WITH YOU. I'M BUSY SAVING THE WORLD!
WHAT'S GOING ON? WHY MUST YOU AND SHUICHI FIGHT LIKE THIS?
KA-CHAK
YOU SAID SOMETHING ABOUT KITARO BEFORE.
YOU COULDN'T POSSIBLY MEAN KITARO OF THE GRAVEYARD?
YES. MOTHER! DO YOU KNOW OF HIM?
DO I KNOW OF HIM?!

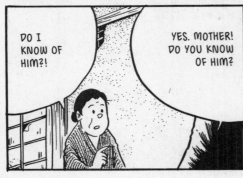

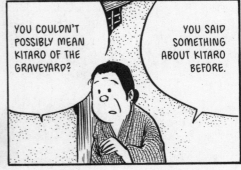

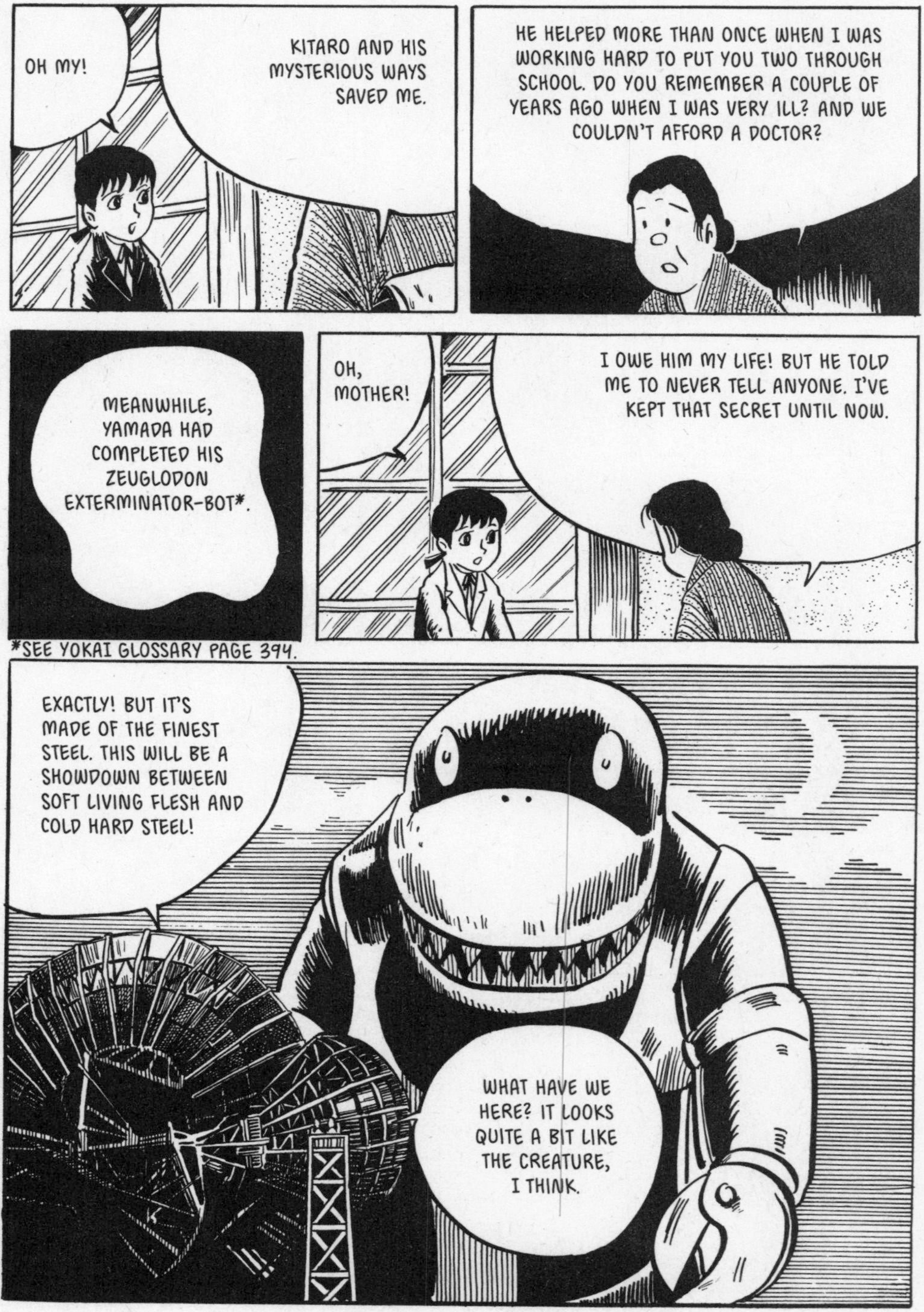
HE HELPED MORE THAN ONCE WHEN I WAS WORKING HARD TO PUT YOU TWO THROUGH SCHOOL. DO YOU REMEMBER A COUPLE OF YEARS AGO WHEN I WAS VERY ILL? AND WE COULDN'T AFFORD A DOCTOR?
KITARO AND HIS MYSTERIOUS WAYS SAVED ME.
OH MY!
I OWE HIM MY LIFE! BUT HE TOLD ME TO NEVER TELL ANYONE. I'VE KEPT THAT SECRET UNTIL NOW.
OH, MOTHER!
MEANWHILE, YAMADA HAD COMPLETED HIS ZEUGLODON EXTERMINATOR-BOT*.
WHAT HAVE WE HERE? IT LOOKS QUITE A BIT LIKE THE CREATURE, I THINK.
EXACTLY! BUT IT'S MADE OF THE FINEST STEEL. THIS WILL BE A SHOWDOWN BETWEEN SOFT LIVING FLESH AND COLD HARD STEEL!

*SEE YOKAI GLOSSARY PAGE 394.

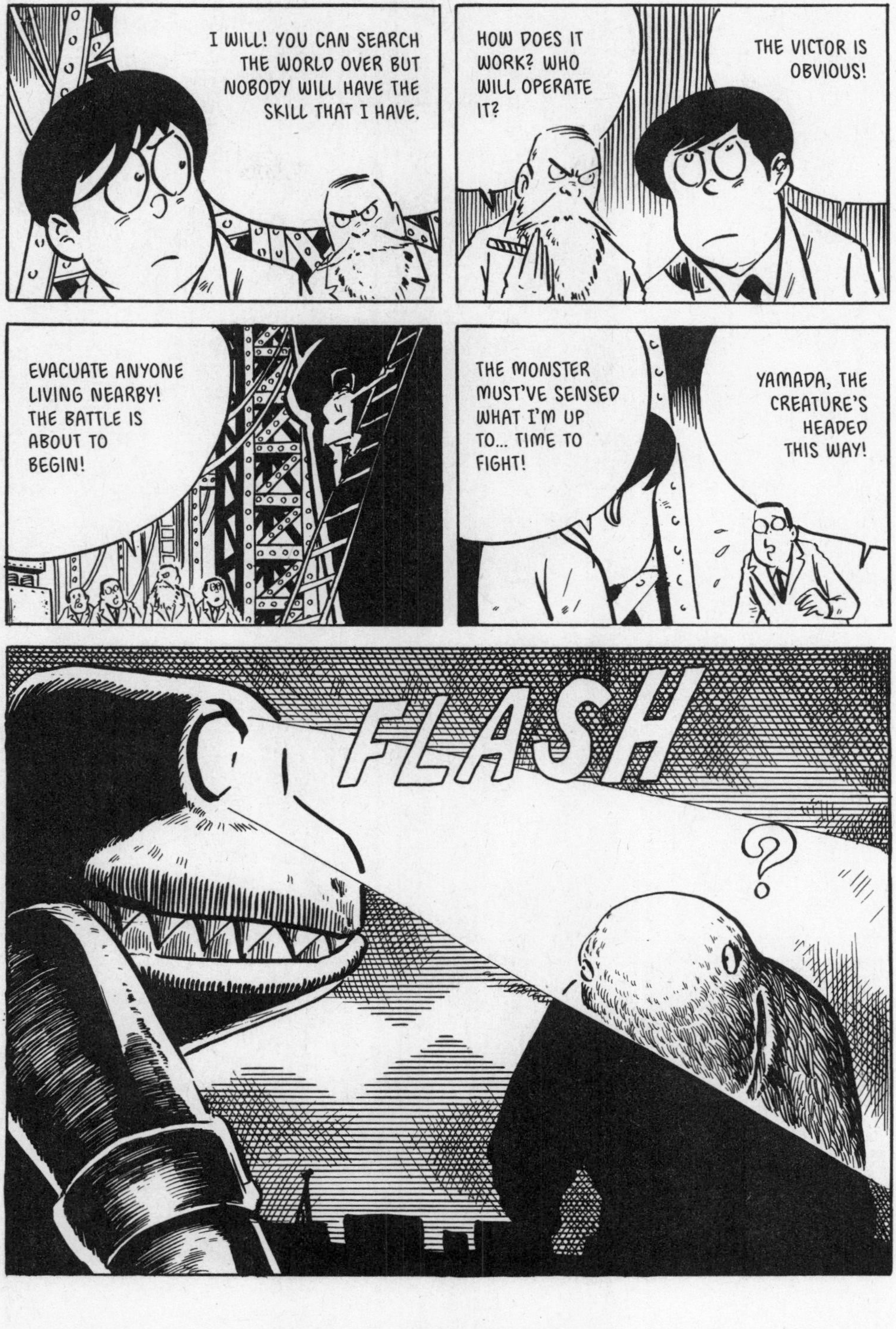
THE VICTOR IS OBVIOUS!
HOW DOES IT WORK? WHO WILL OPERATE IT?
I WILL! YOU CAN SEARCH THE WORLD OVER BUT NOBODY WILL HAVE THE SKILL THAT I HAVE.
YAMADA, THE CREATURE'S HEADED THIS WAY!
THE MONSTER MUST'VE SENSED WHAT I'M UP TO... TIME TO FIGHT!
EVACUATE ANYONE LIVING NEARBY! THE BATTLE IS ABOUT TO BEGIN!
FLASH
?

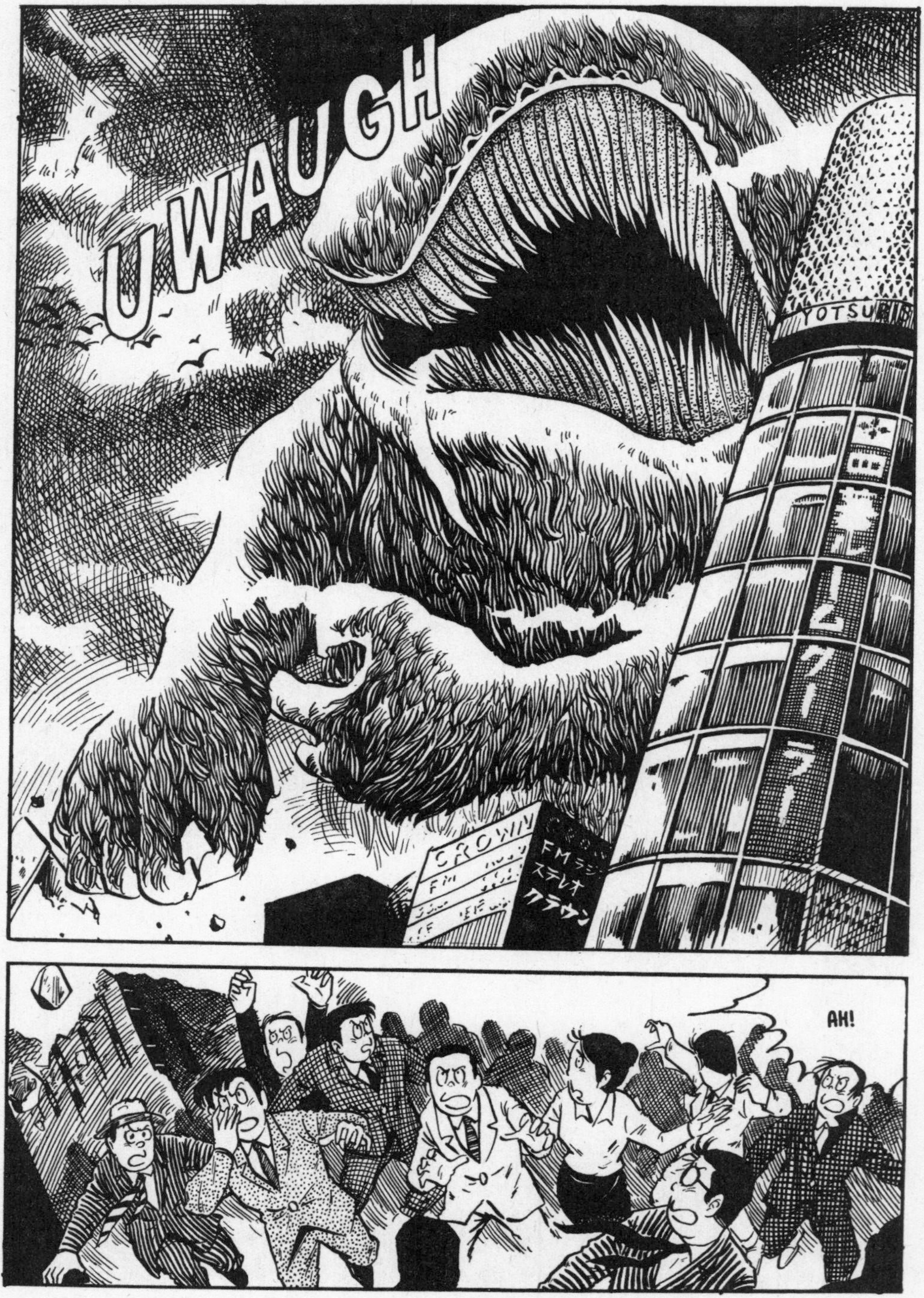
UWAUGH
CROWN
ステレオ
クラウン
AH!

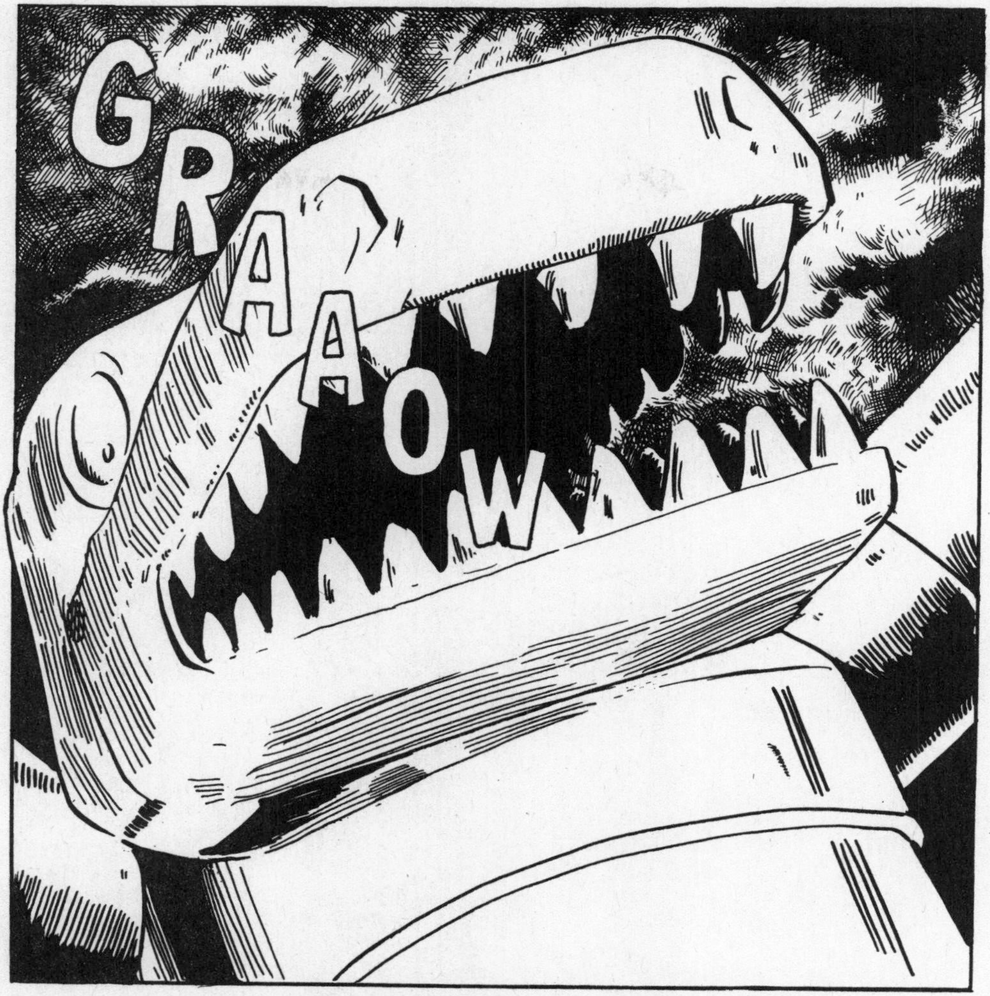
GRAAAOW

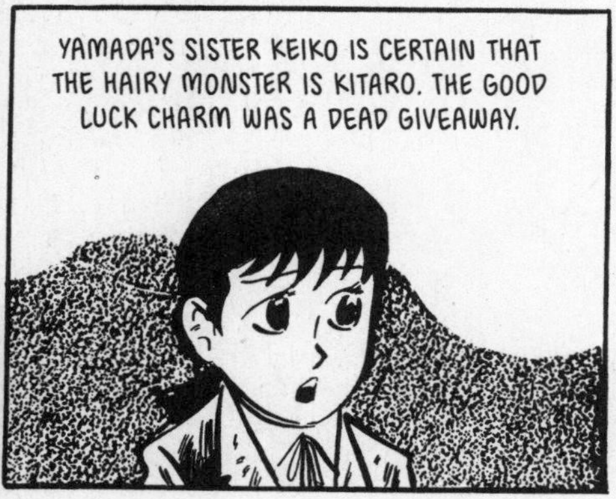
YAMADA'S SISTER KEIKO IS CERTAIN THAT THE HAIRY MONSTER IS KITARO. THE GOOD LUCK CHARM WAS A DEAD GIVEAWAY.

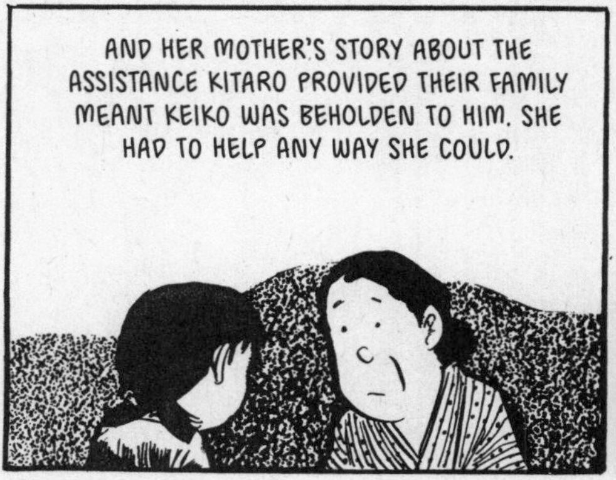
AND HER MOTHER'S STORY ABOUT THE ASSISTANCE KITARO PROVIDED THEIR FAMILY MEANT KEIKO WAS BEHOLDEN TO HIM. SHE HAD TO HELP ANY WAY SHE COULD.

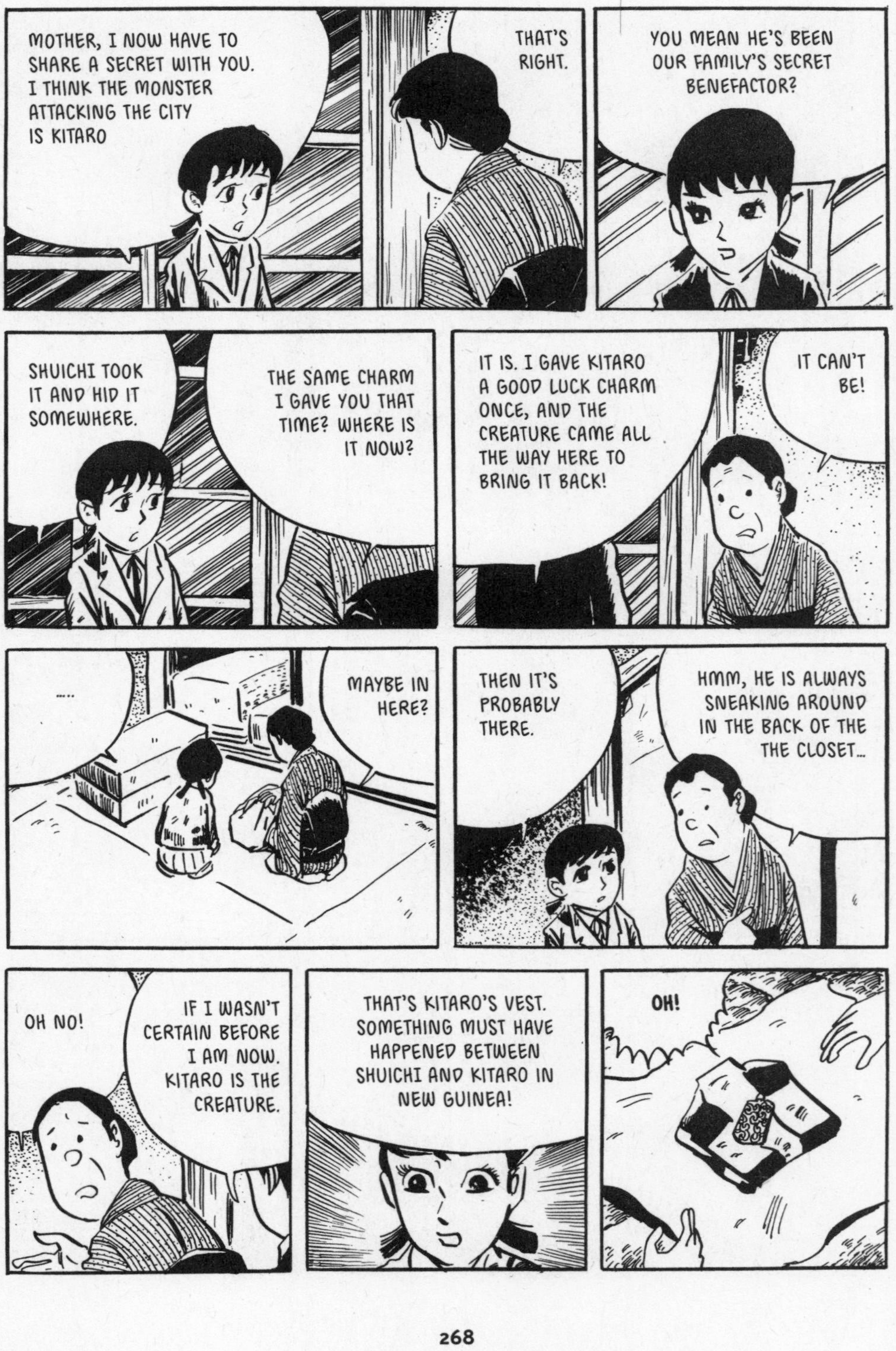
YOU MEAN HE'S BEEN OUR FAMILY'S SECRET BENEFACTOR?
THAT'S RIGHT.
MOTHER, I NOW HAVE TO SHARE A SECRET WITH YOU. I THINK THE MONSTER ATTACKING THE CITY IS KITARO
IT CAN'T BE!
IT IS. I GAVE KITARO A GOOD LUCK CHARM ONCE, AND THE CREATURE CAME ALL THE WAY HERE TO BRING IT BACK!
THE SAME CHARM I GAVE YOU THAT TIME? WHERE IS IT NOW?
SHUICHI TOOK IT AND HID IT SOMEWHERE.
HMM, HE IS ALWAYS SNEAKING AROUND IN THE BACK OF THE THE CLOSET...
THEN IT'S PROBABLY THERE.
MAYBE IN HERE?
.....
OH!
THAT'S KITARO'S VEST. SOMETHING MUST HAVE HAPPENED BETWEEN SHUICHI AND KITARO IN NEW GUINEA!
IF I WASN'T CERTAIN BEFORE I AM NOW. KITARO IS THE CREATURE.
OH NO!

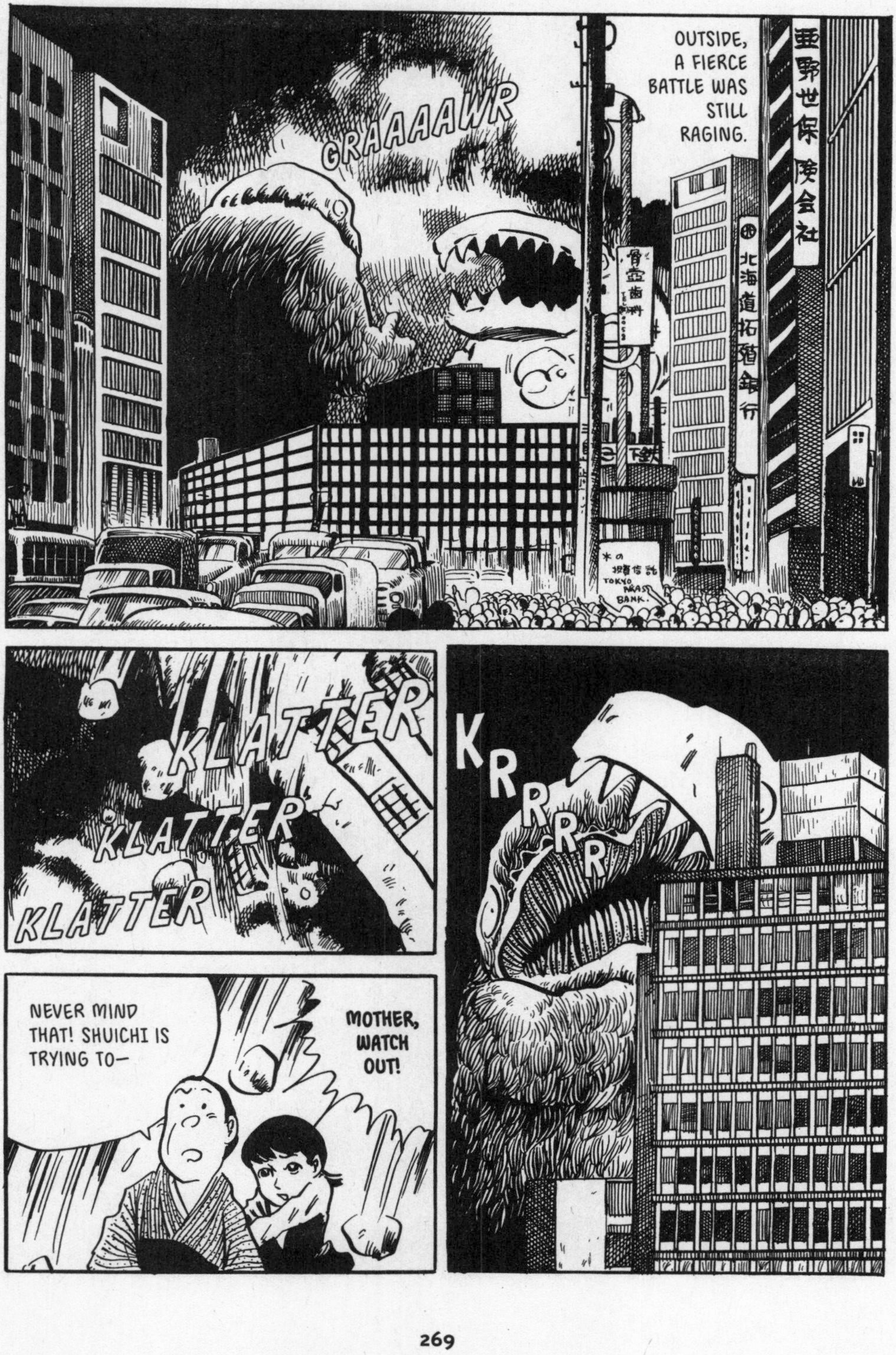
OUTSIDE, A FIERCE BATTLE WAS STILL RAGING.
GRAAAAWR
北海道拓殖銀行
KRRRRR
KLATTER
KLATTER
KLATTER
MOTHER, WATCH OUT!
NEVER MIND THAT! SHUICHI IS TRYING TO—

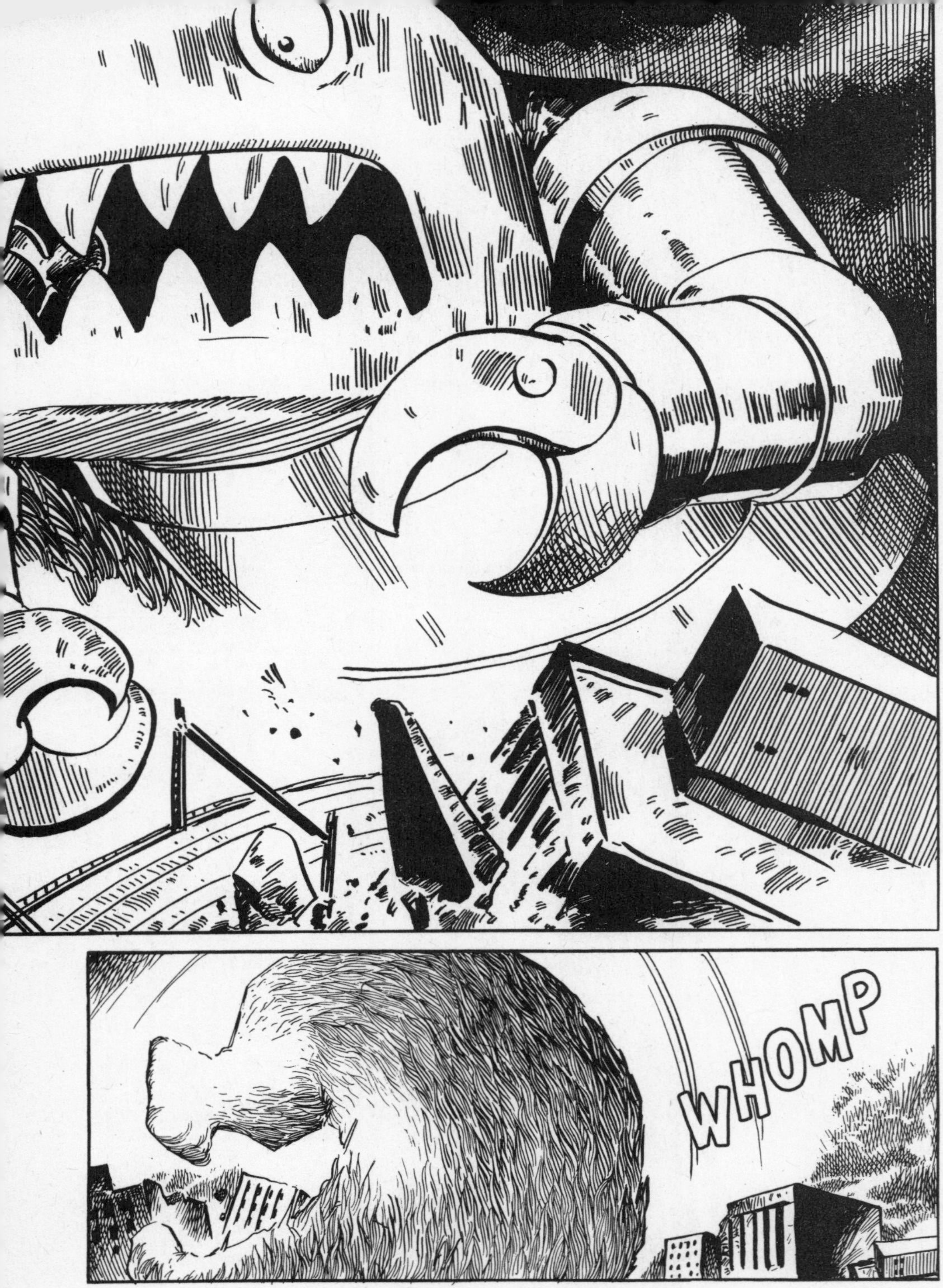
WHOMP

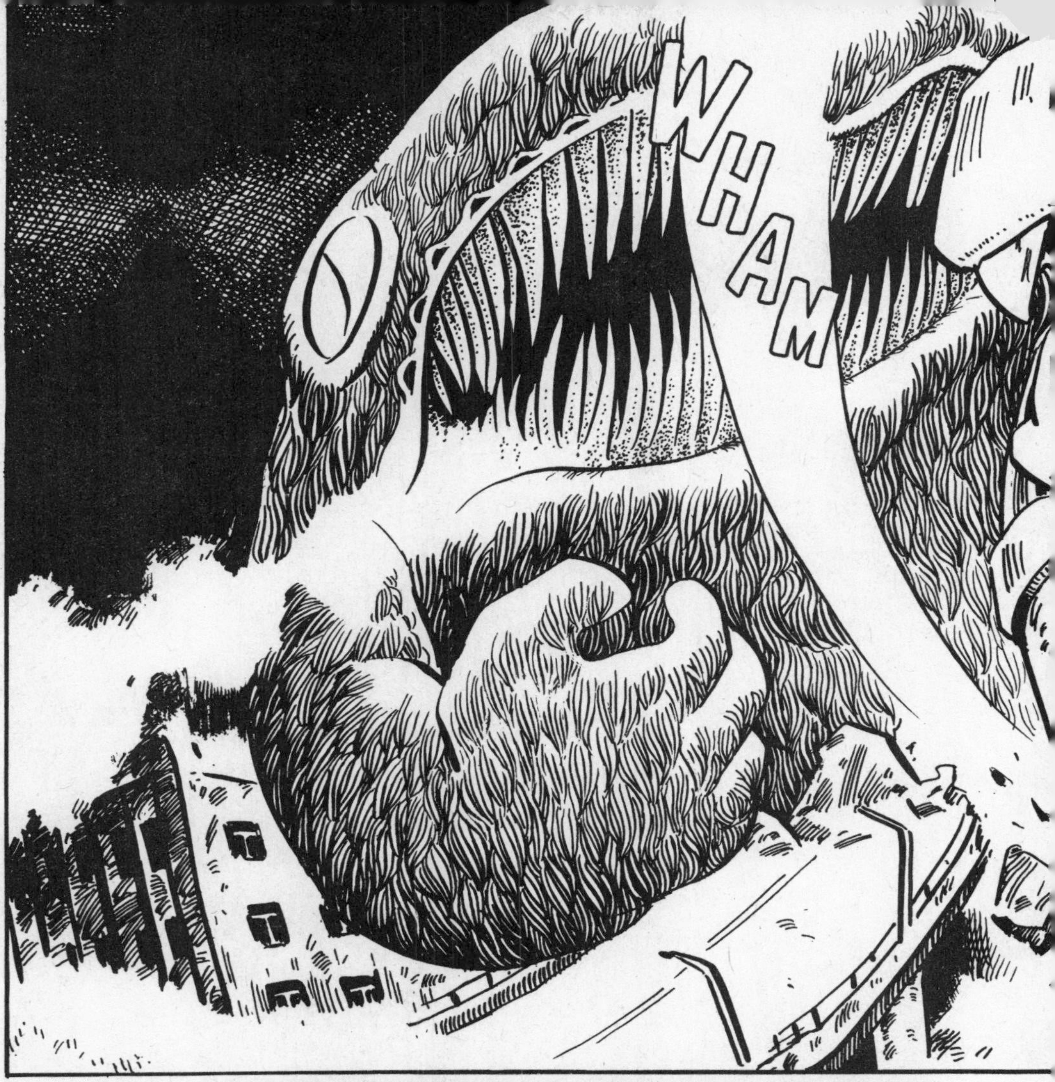
WHAM
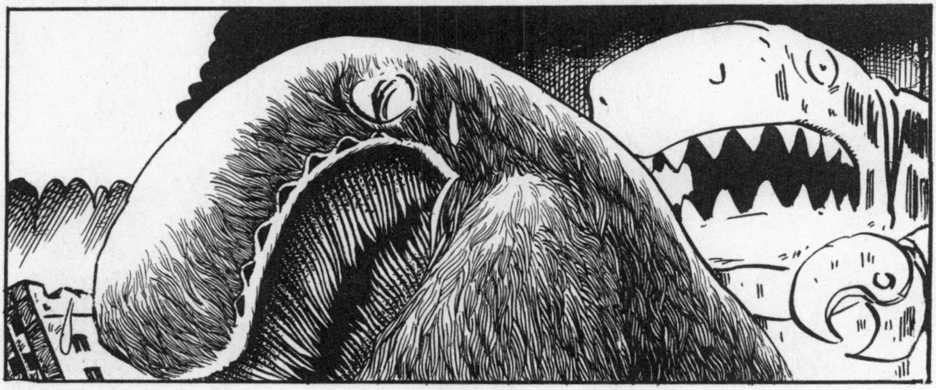

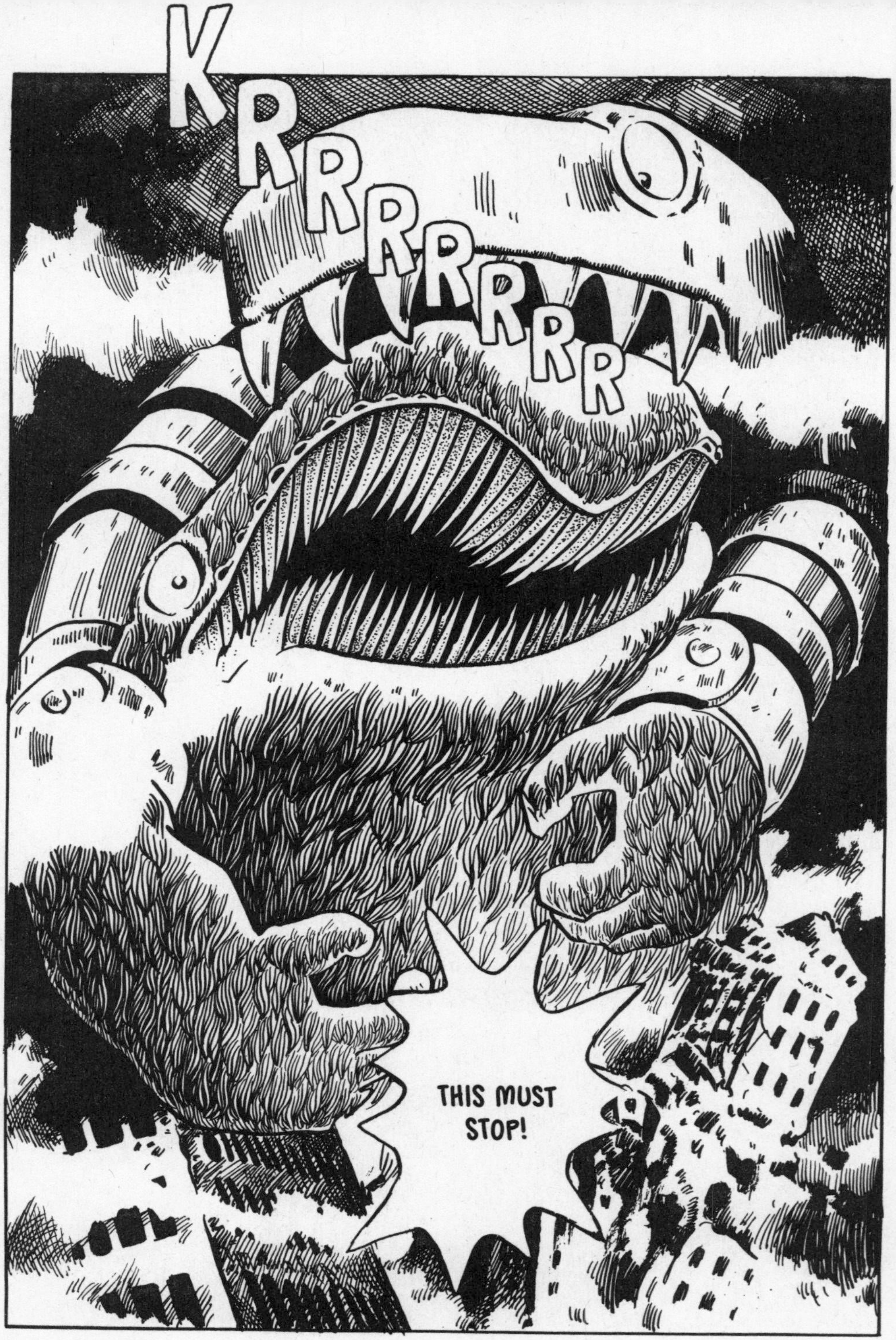
KRRRRRRRRR
THIS MUST STOP!

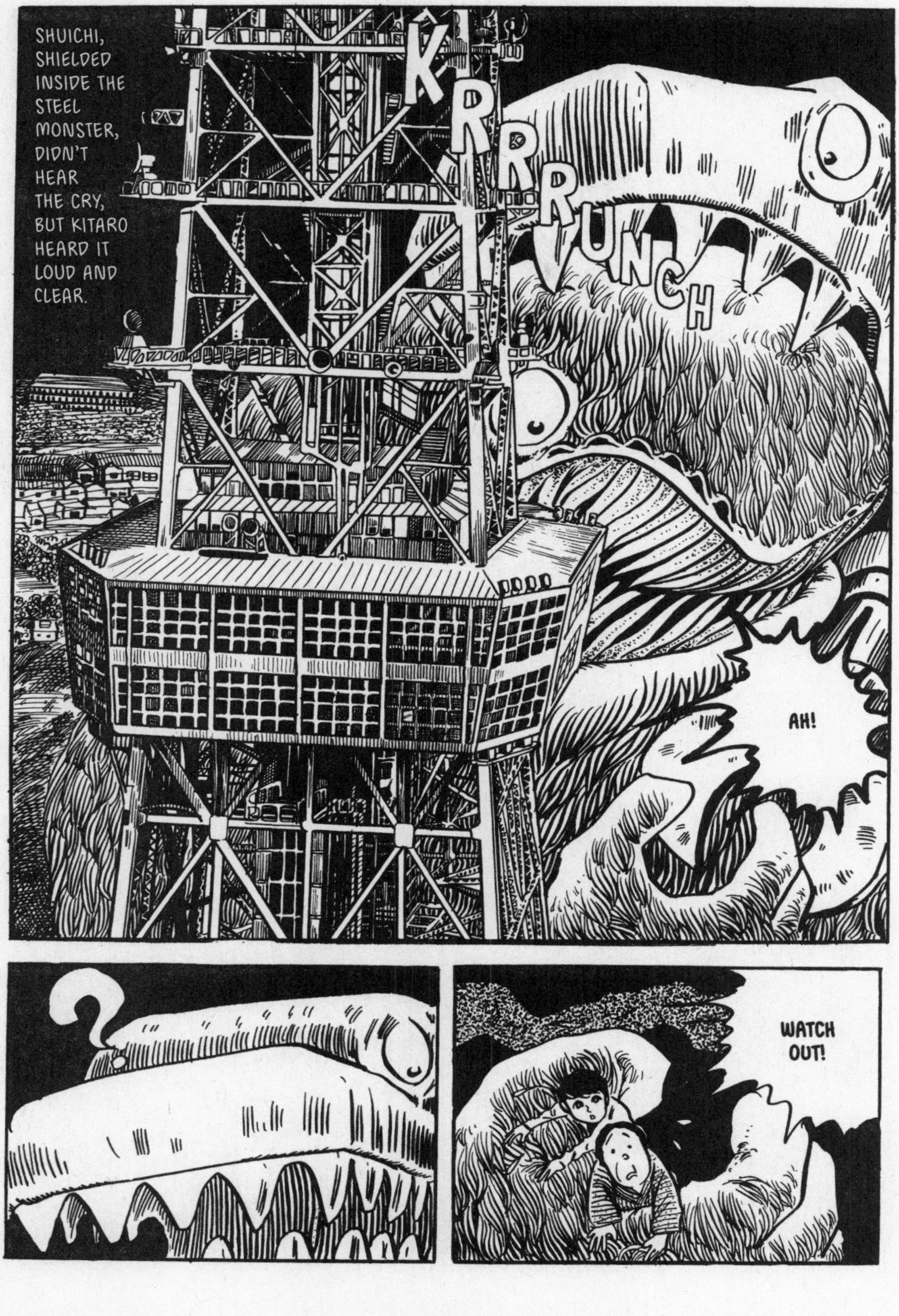
KRRRUNCH
SHUICHI, SHIELDED INSIDE THE STEEL MONSTER, DIDN'T HEAR THE CRY, BUT KITARO HEARD IT LOUD AND CLEAR.
AH!
WATCH OUT!
?

KITARO'S GOT KEIKO AND MY MOTHER!
BZZZZZAH
GIVE THEM BACK!
THE SCISSORS I BUILT IN WILL TAKE CARE OF YOUR HAIR POWER.
SNIP
SNIP
SNIP
FOOL!

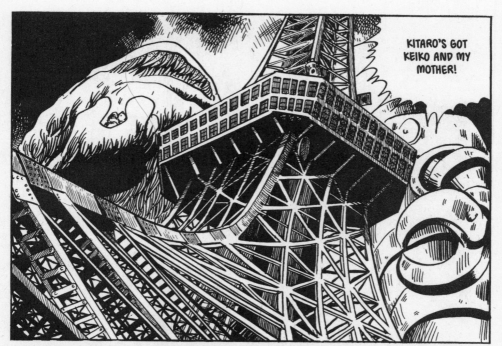

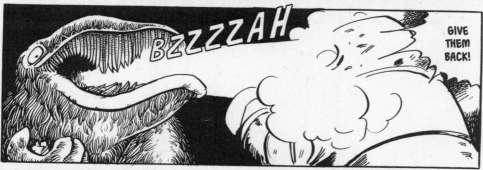

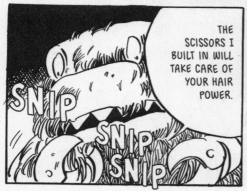

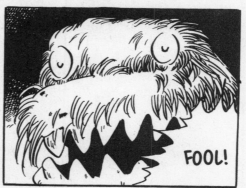

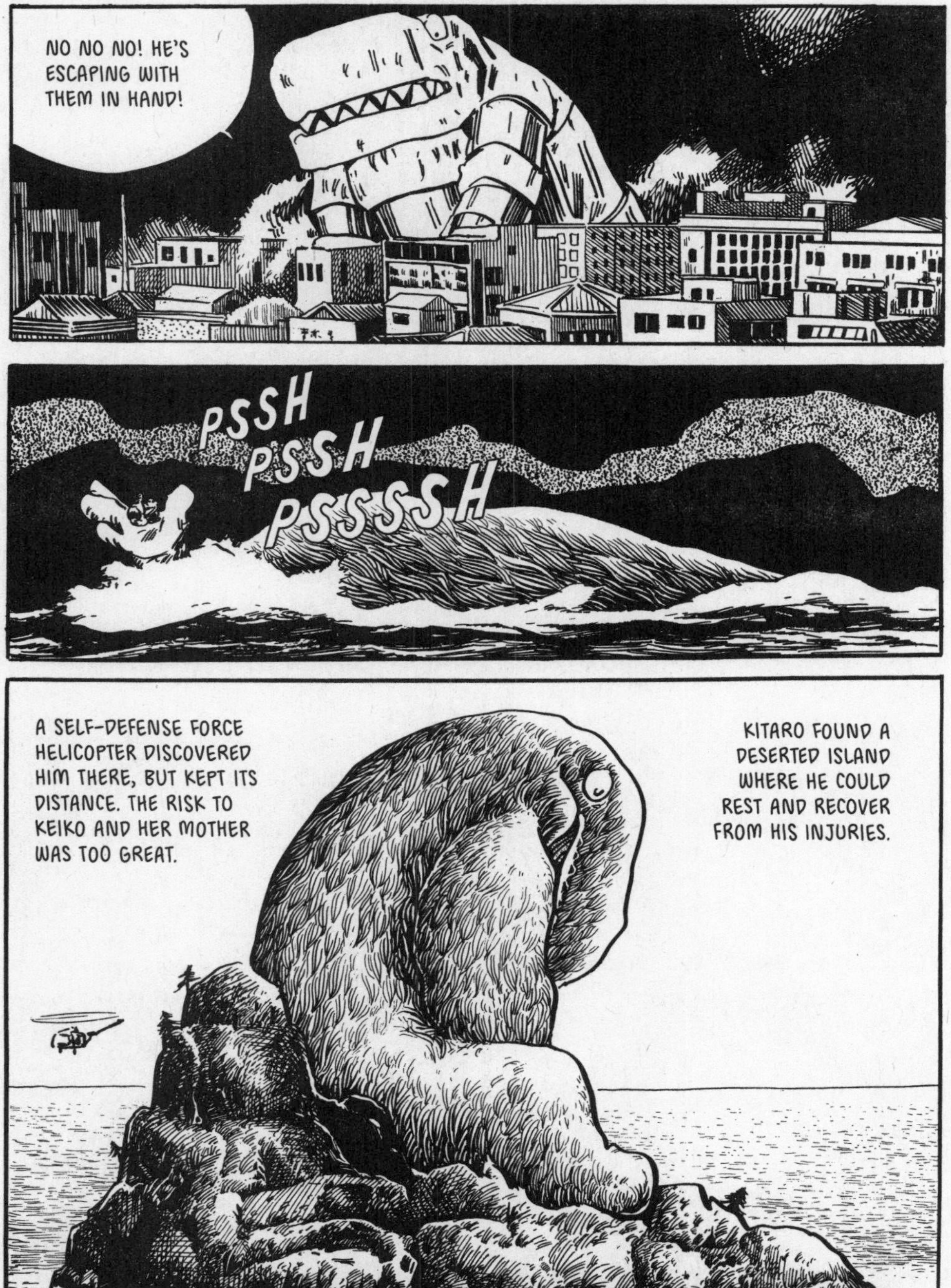
NO NO NO! HE'S ESCAPING WITH THEM IN HAND!
PSSH PSSH PSSSSSH
KITARO FOUND A DESERTED ISLAND WHERE HE COULD REST AND RECOVER FROM HIS INJURIES.
A SELF-DEFENSE FORCE HELICOPTER DISCOVERED HIM THERE, BUT KEPT ITS DISTANCE. THE RISK TO KEIKO AND HER MOTHER WAS TOO GREAT.

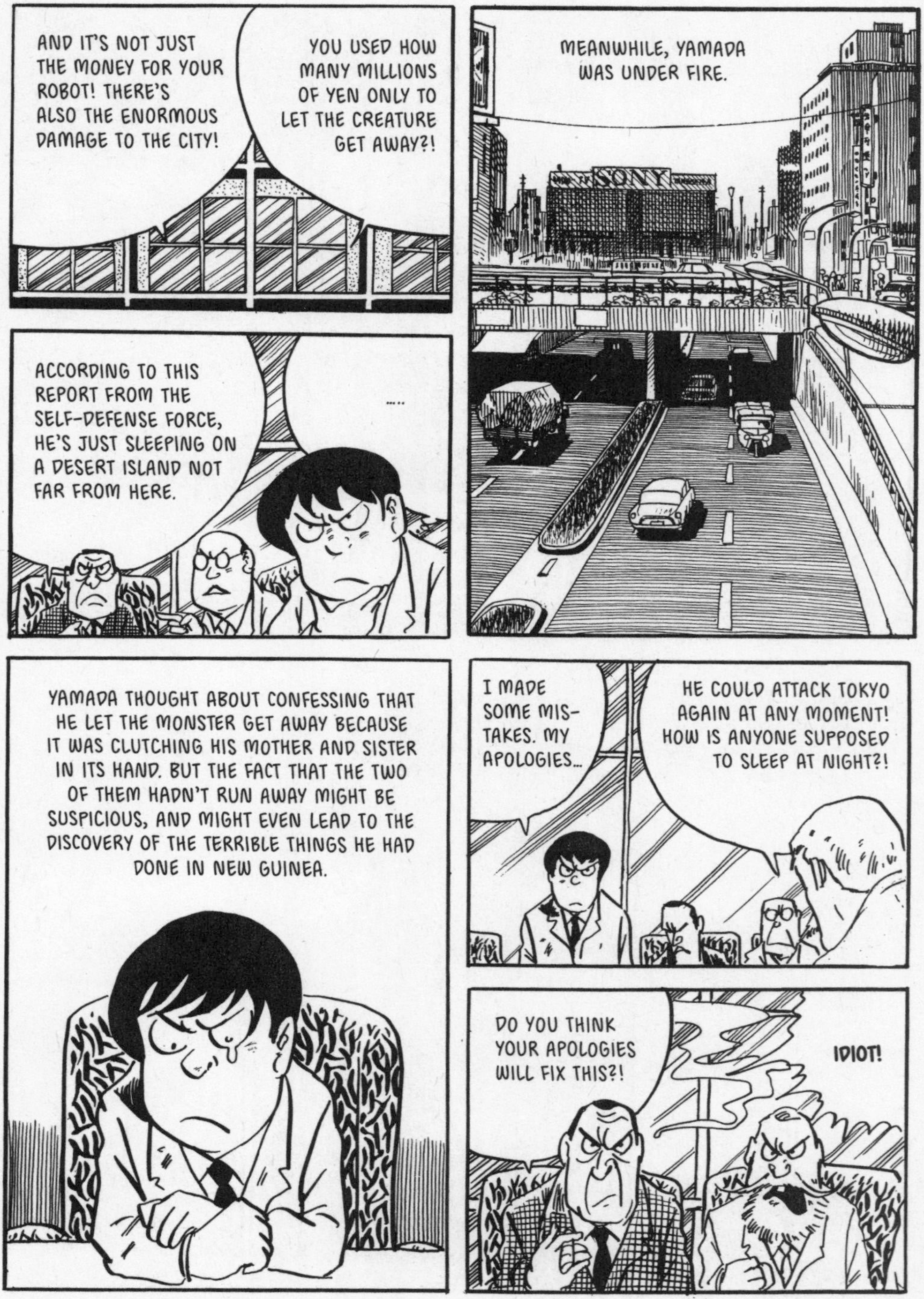
MEANWHILE, YAMADA WAS UNDER FIRE.
SONY
YOU USED HOW MANY MILLIONS OF YEN ONLY TO LET THE CREATURE GET AWAY?!
AND IT'S NOT JUST THE MONEY FOR YOUR ROBOT! THERE'S ALSO THE ENORMOUS DAMAGE TO THE CITY!
....
ACCORDING TO THIS REPORT FROM THE SELF-DEFENSE FORCE, HE'S JUST SLEEPING ON A DESERT ISLAND NOT FAR FROM HERE.
HE COULD ATTACK TOKYO AGAIN AT ANY MOMENT! HOW IS ANYONE SUPPOSED TO SLEEP AT NIGHT?!
I MADE SOME MIS-TAKES. MY APOLOGIES...
IDIOT!
DO YOU THINK YOUR APOLOGIES WILL FIX THIS?!
YAMADA THOUGHT ABOUT CONFESSING THAT HE LET THE MONSTER GET AWAY BECAUSE IT WAS CLUTCHING HIS MOTHER AND SISTER IN ITS HAND. BUT THE FACT THAT THE TWO OF THEM HADN'T RUN AWAY MIGHT BE SUSPICIOUS, AND MIGHT EVEN LEAD TO THE DISCOVERY OF THE TERRIBLE THINGS HE HAD DONE IN NEW GUINEA.

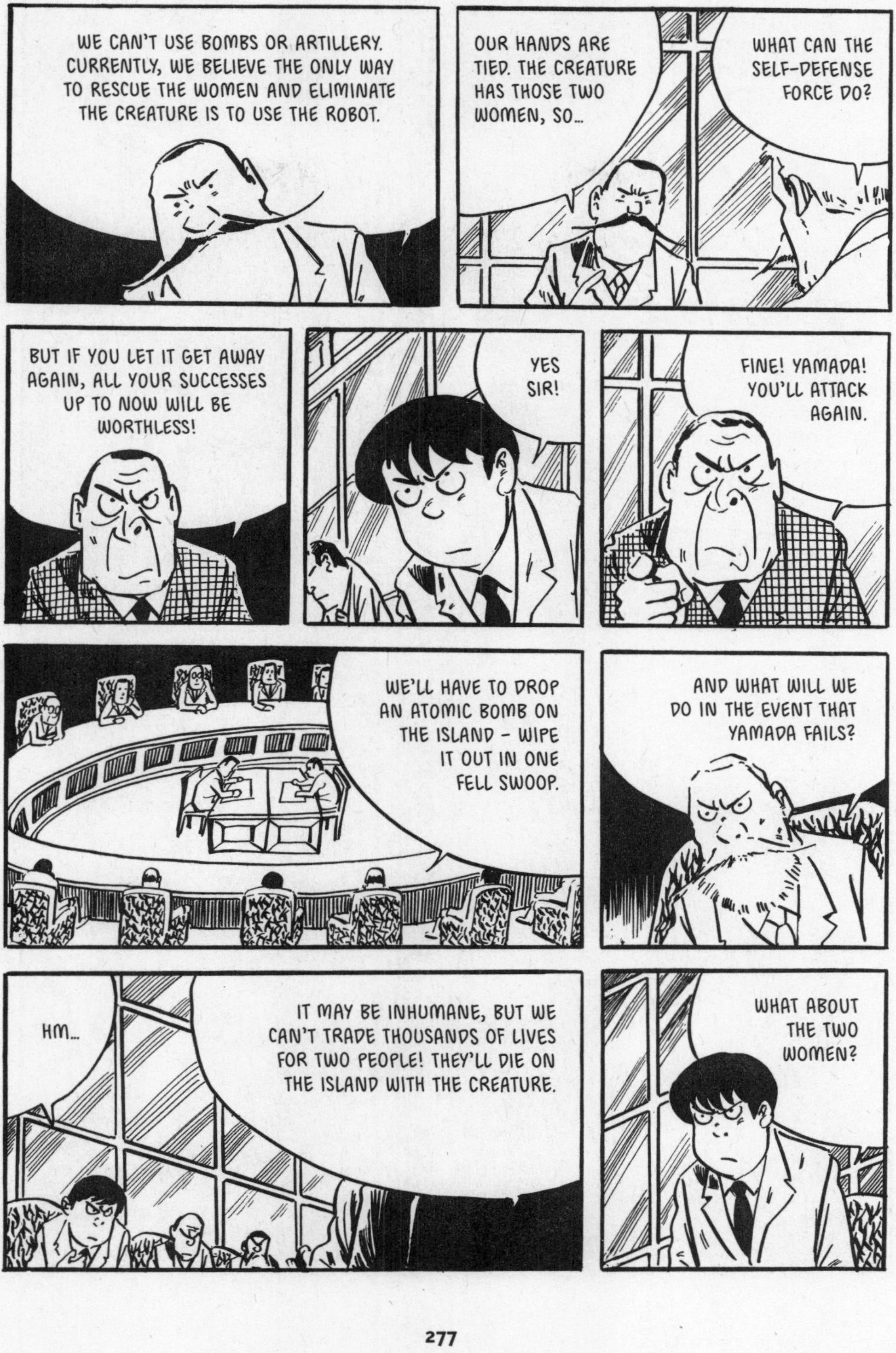
WHAT CAN THE SELF-DEFENSE FORCE DO?
OUR HANDS ARE TIED. THE CREATURE HAS THOSE TWO WOMEN, SO...
WE CAN'T USE BOMBS OR ARTILLERY. CURRENTLY, WE BELIEVE THE ONLY WAY TO RESCUE THE WOMEN AND ELIMINATE THE CREATURE IS TO USE THE ROBOT.
FINE! YAMADA! YOU'LL ATTACK AGAIN.
YES SIR!
BUT IF YOU LET IT GET AWAY AGAIN, ALL YOUR SUCCESSES UP TO NOW WILL BE WORTHLESS!
AND WHAT WILL WE DO IN THE EVENT THAT YAMADA FAILS?
WE'LL HAVE TO DROP AN ATOMIC BOMB ON THE ISLAND - WIPE IT OUT IN ONE FELL SWOOP.
WHAT ABOUT THE TWO WOMEN?
IT MAY BE INHUMANE, BUT WE CAN'T TRADE THOUSANDS OF LIVES FOR TWO PEOPLE! THEY'LL DIE ON THE ISLAND WITH THE CREATURE.
HM...

PSSH
PSSH
PSSSSH

I MUST KILL KITARO AND SAVE MY FAMILY.

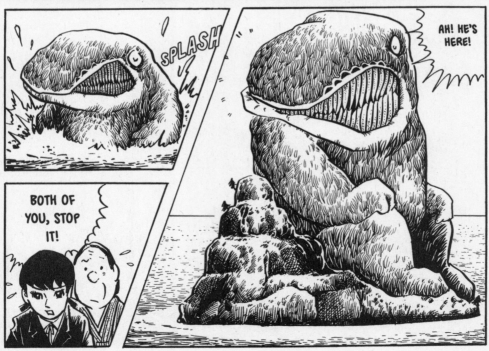

SPLASH

AH! HE'S HERE!

BOTH OF YOU, STOP IT!

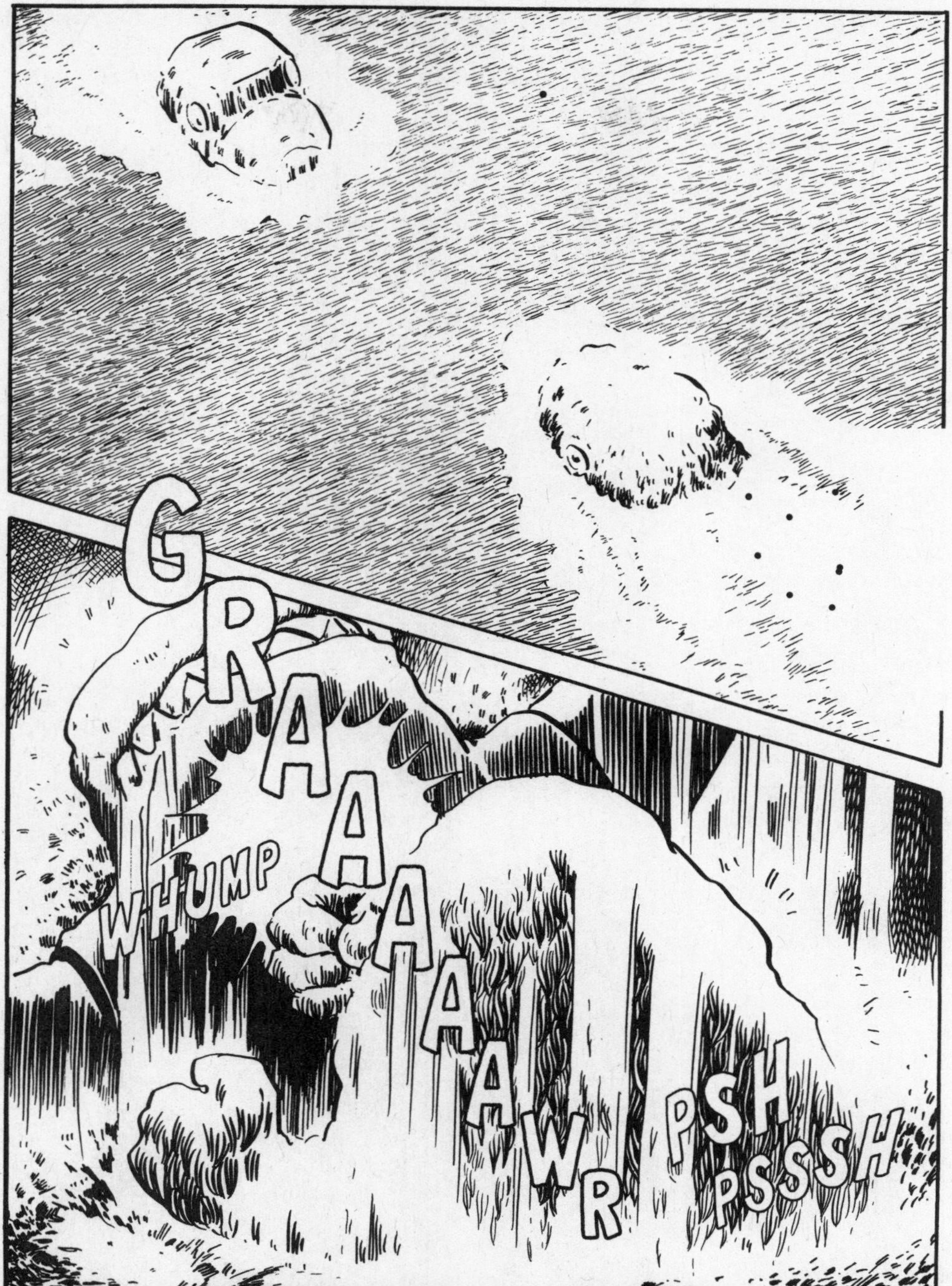
GRAAAAAWR
WHUMP
PSH
PSSSH

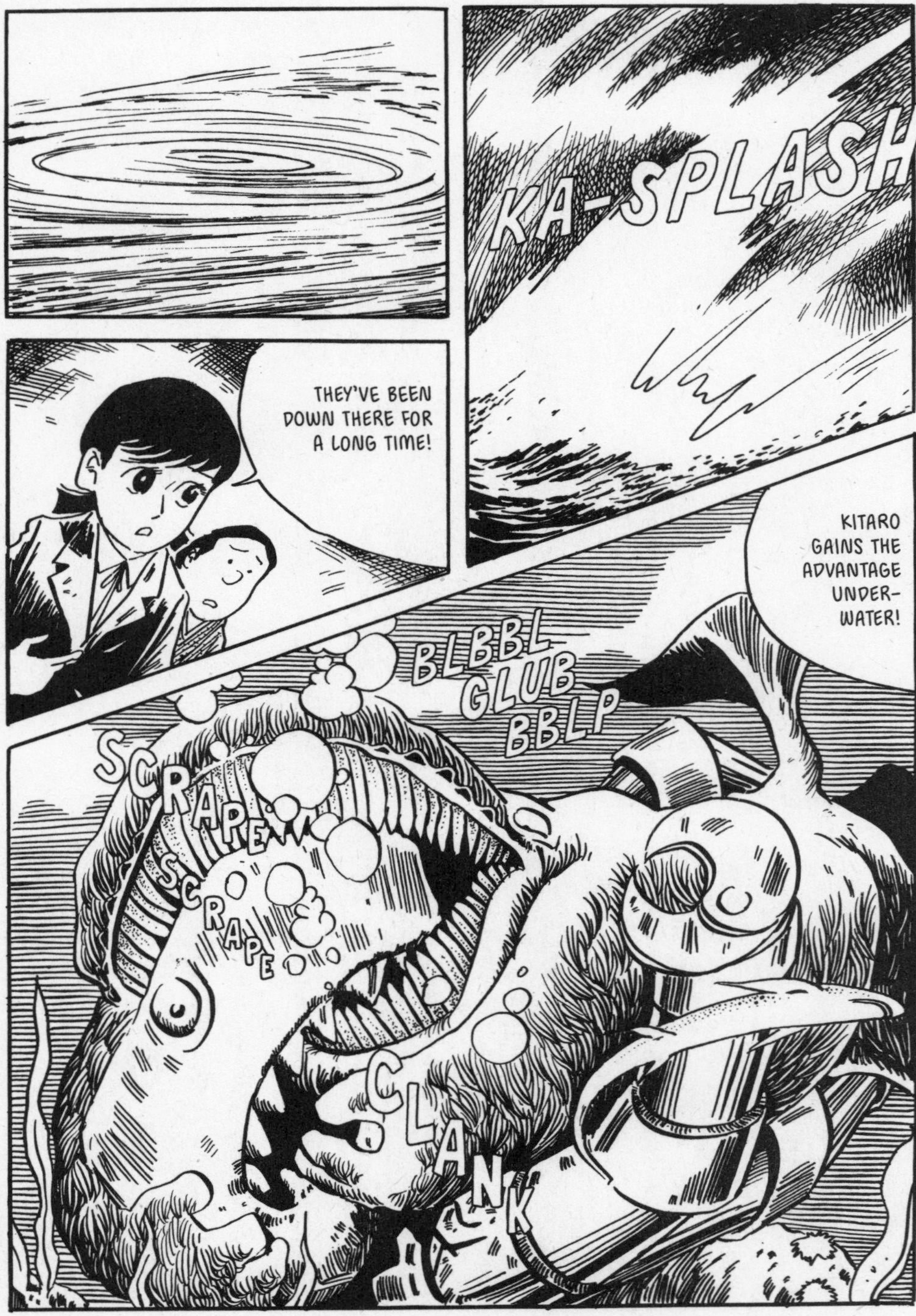
KA-SPLASH
THEY'VE BEEN DOWN THERE FOR A LONG TIME!
KITARO GAINS THE ADVANTAGE UNDER-WATER!
BLBBL GLUB BBLP
SCRAPE SCRAPE
CLANK

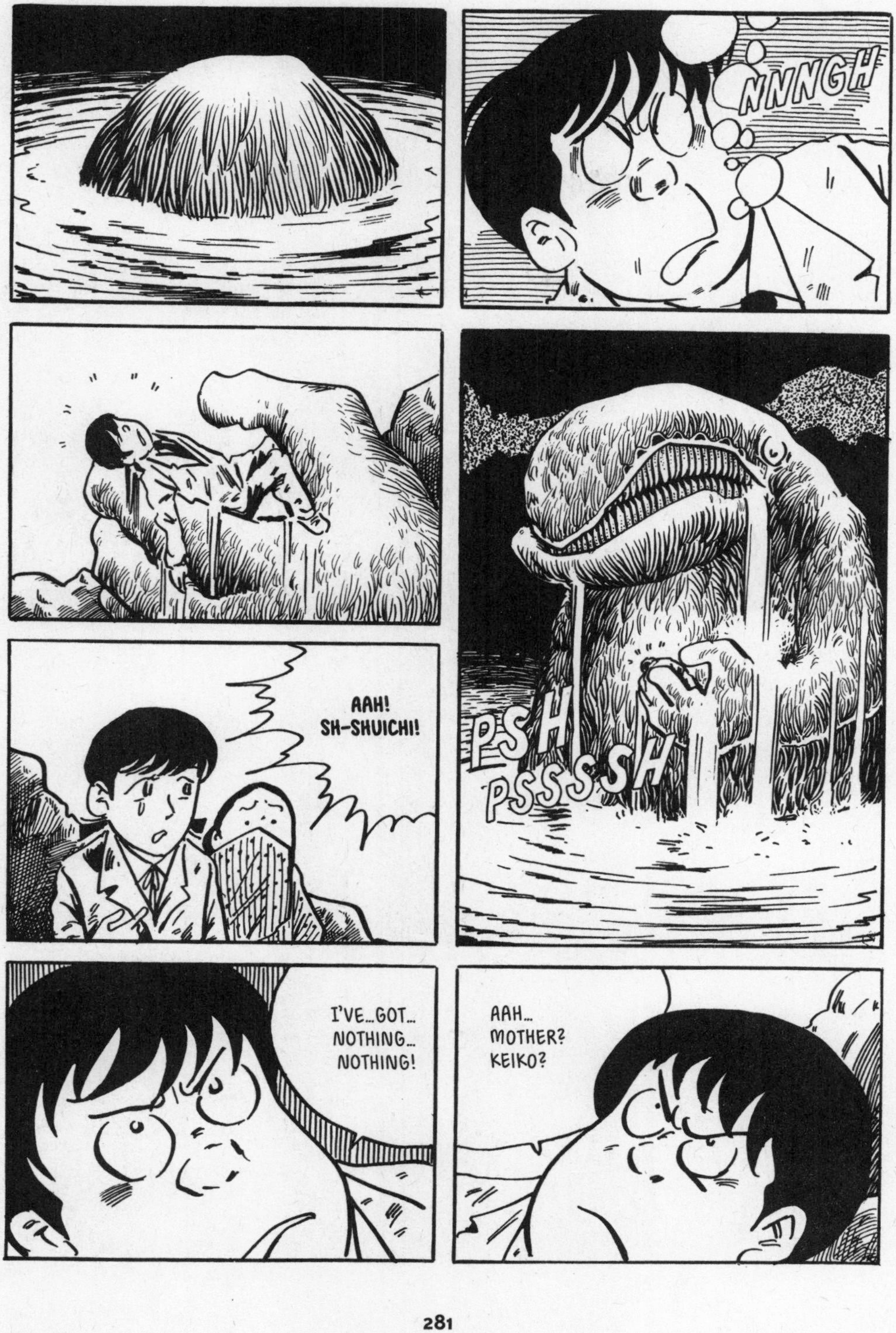
NNNGH
PSH
PSSSSH
AAH! SH-SHUICHI!
AAH... MOTHER? KEIKO?
I'VE...GOT... NOTHING... NOTHING!

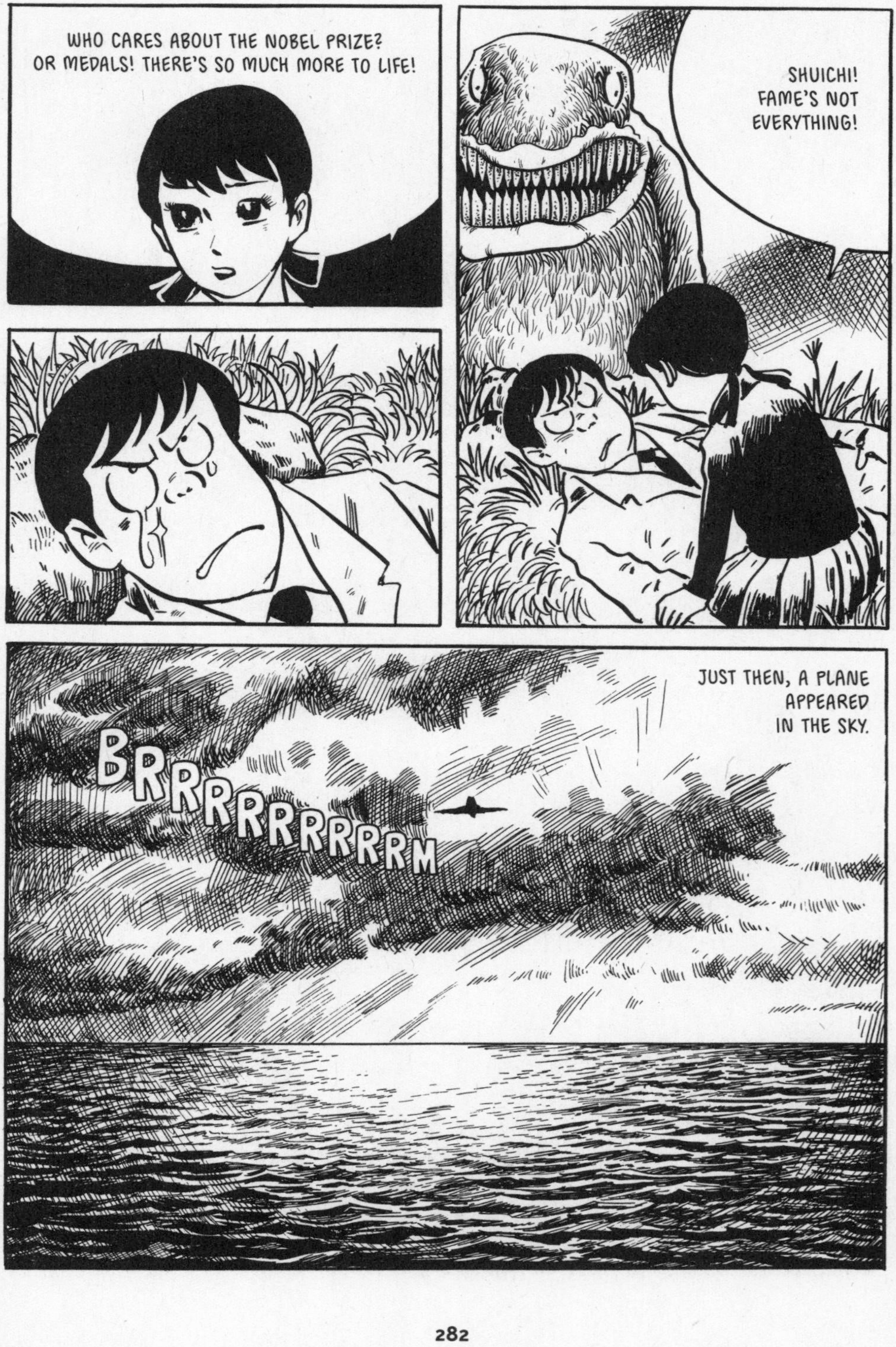
SHUICHI! FAME'S NOT EVERYTHING!
WHO CARES ABOUT THE NOBEL PRIZE? OR MEDALS! THERE'S SO MUCH MORE TO LIFE!
JUST THEN, A PLANE APPEARED IN THE SKY.
BRRRRRRRRRRM

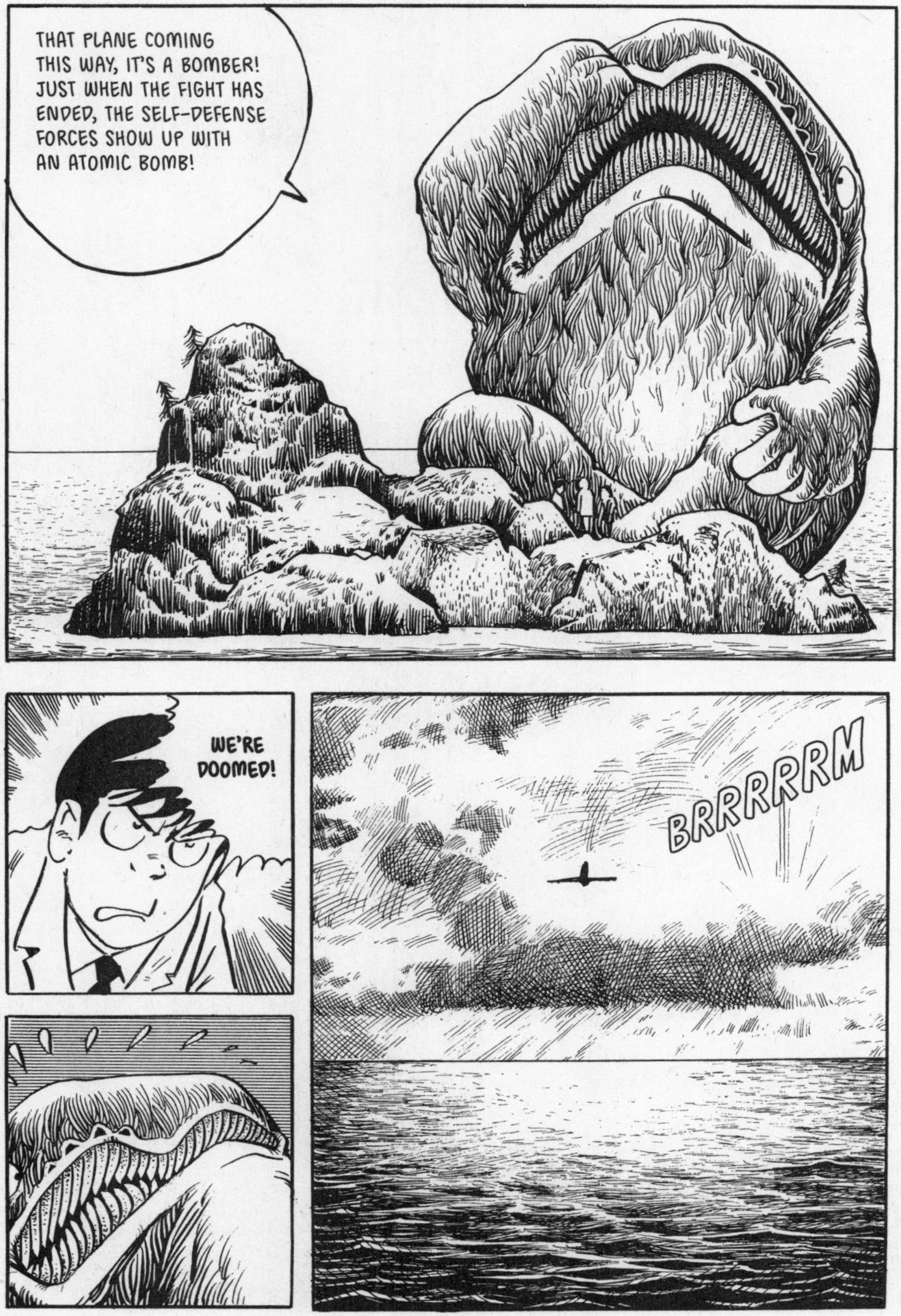
THAT PLANE COMING THIS WAY, IT'S A BOMBER! JUST WHEN THE FIGHT HAS ENDED, THE SELF-DEFENSE FORCES SHOW UP WITH AN ATOMIC BOMB!
BRRRRRM
WE'RE DOOMED!

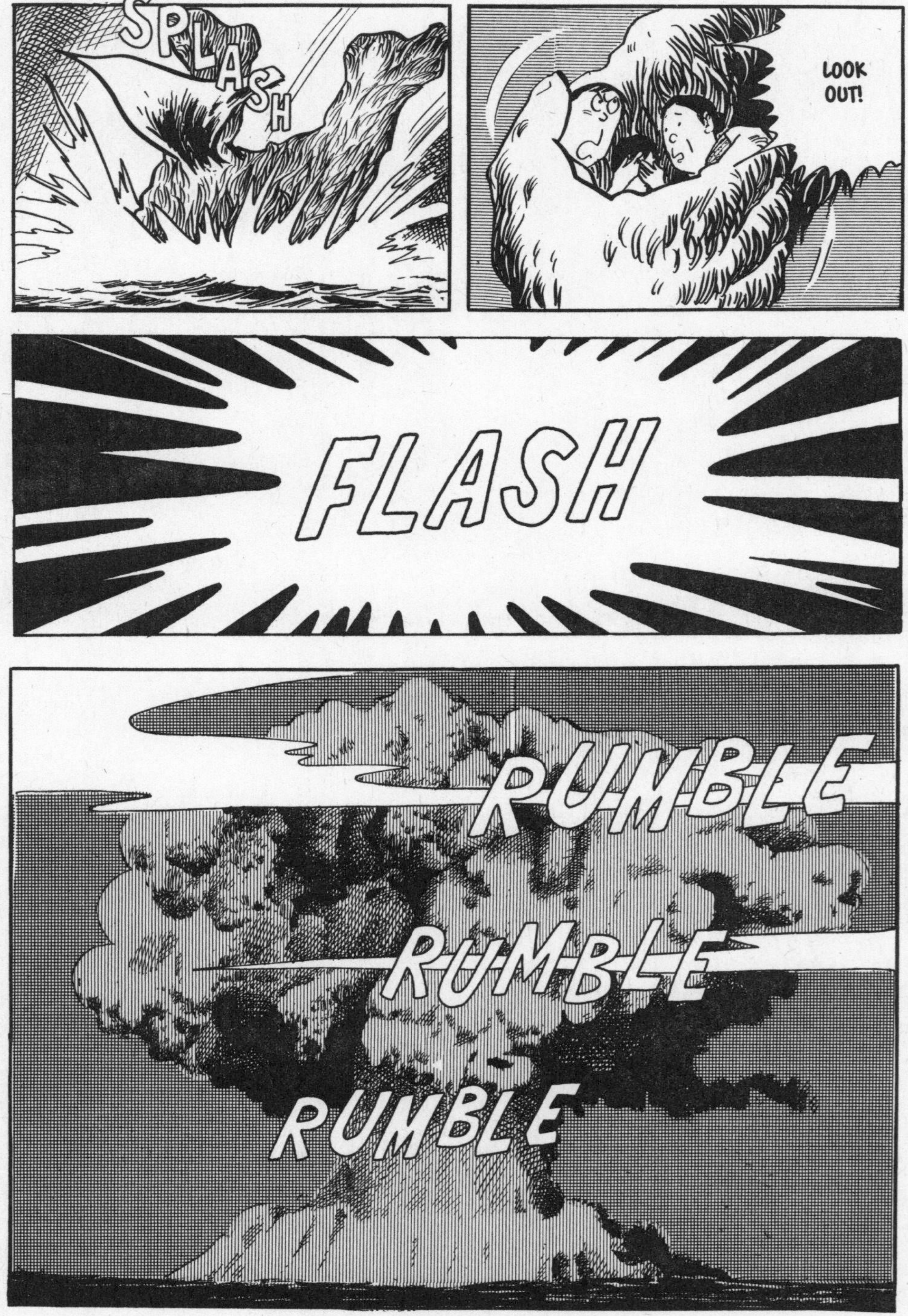
LOOK OUT!
SPLASH
FLASH
RUMBLE
RUMBLE
RUMBLE

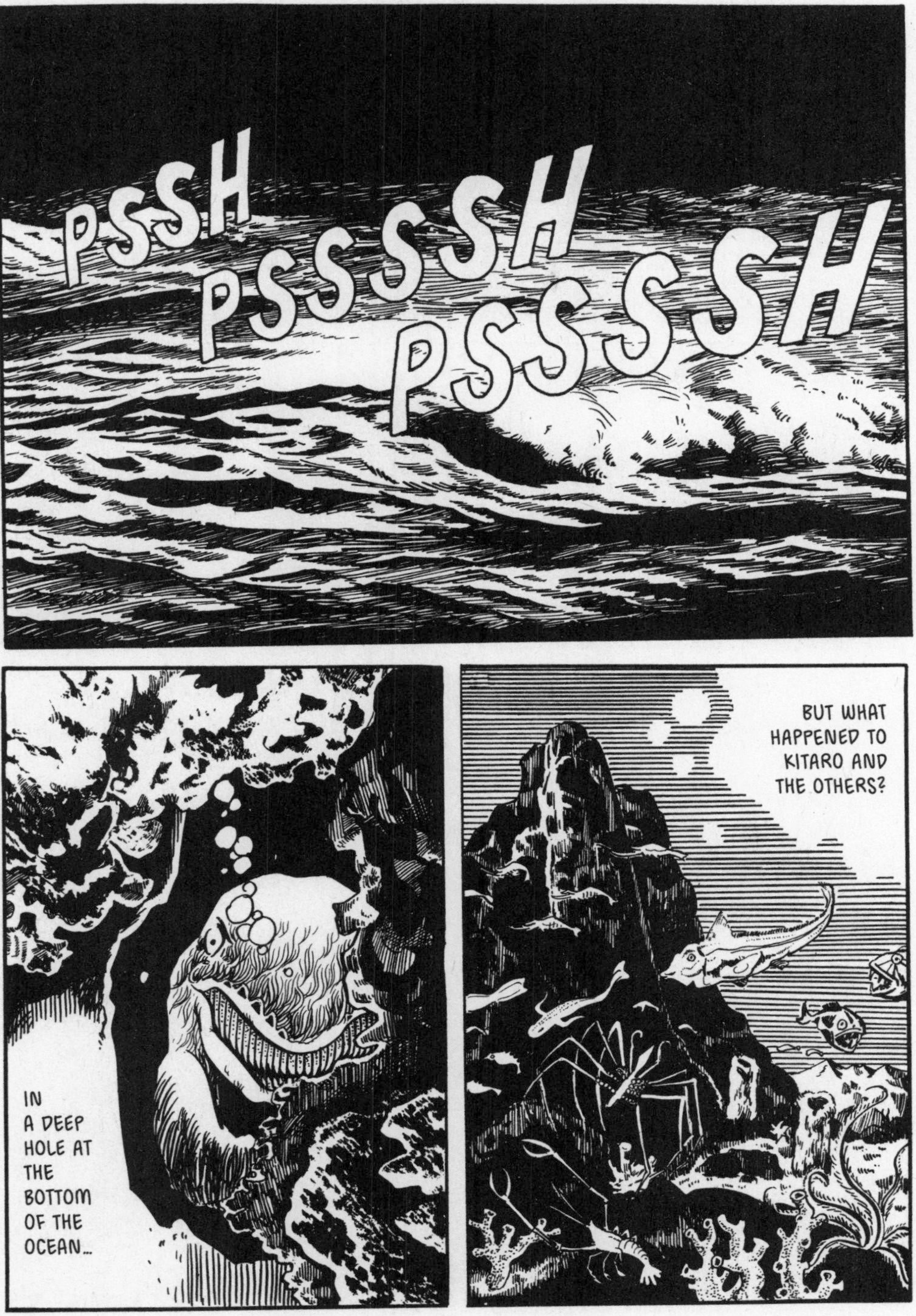
PSSH
PSSSSH
PSSSSSH
BUT WHAT HAPPENED TO KITARO AND THE OTHERS?
IN A DEEP HOLE AT THE BOTTOM OF THE OCEAN...

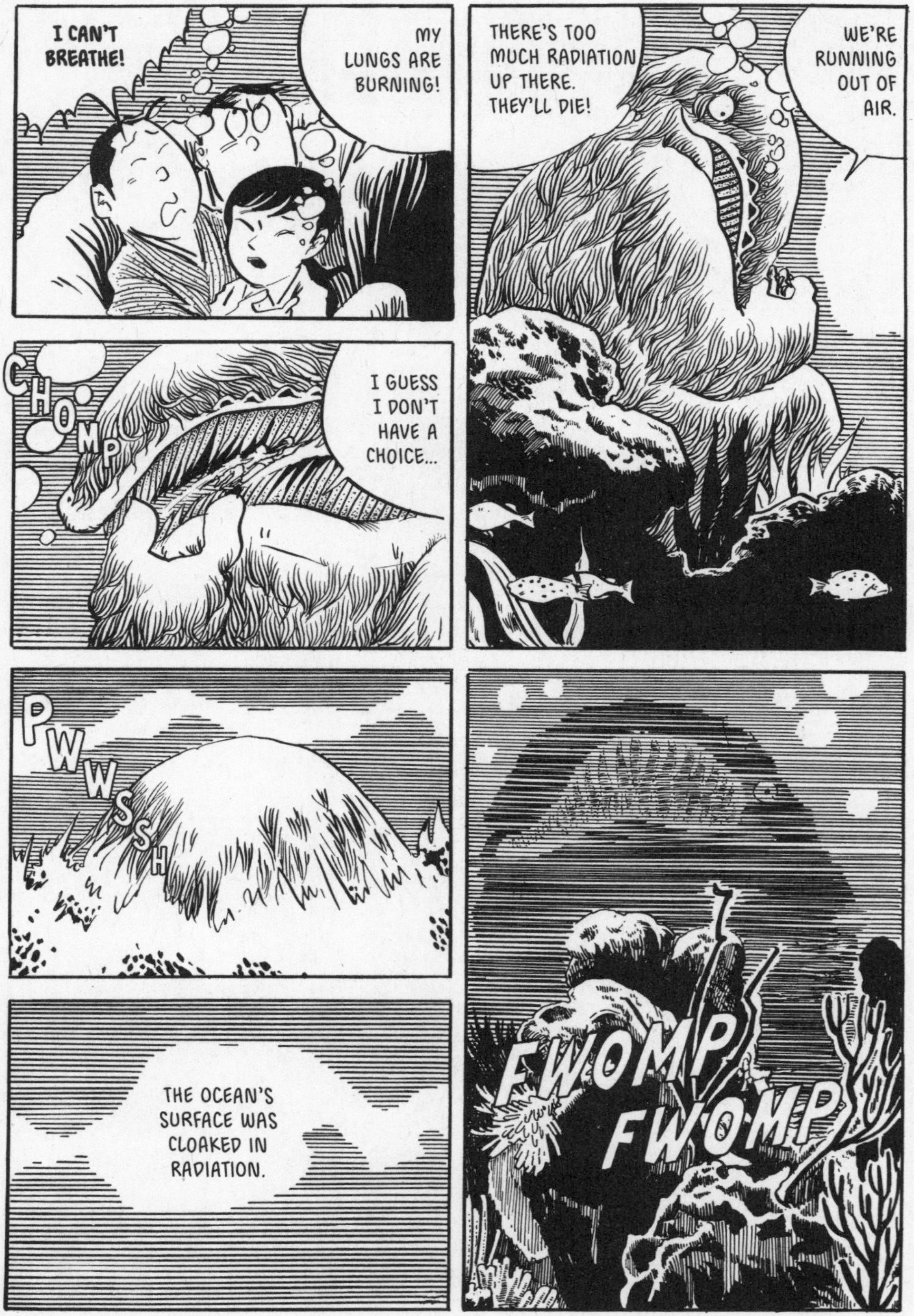
WE'RE RUNNING OUT OF AIR.
THERE'S TOO MUCH RADIATION UP THERE. THEY'LL DIE!
MY LUNGS ARE BURNING!
I CAN'T BREATHE!
I GUESS I DON'T HAVE A CHOICE...
CHOMP
FWOMP FWOMP
PWWSSH
THE OCEAN'S SURFACE WAS CLOAKED IN RADIATION.

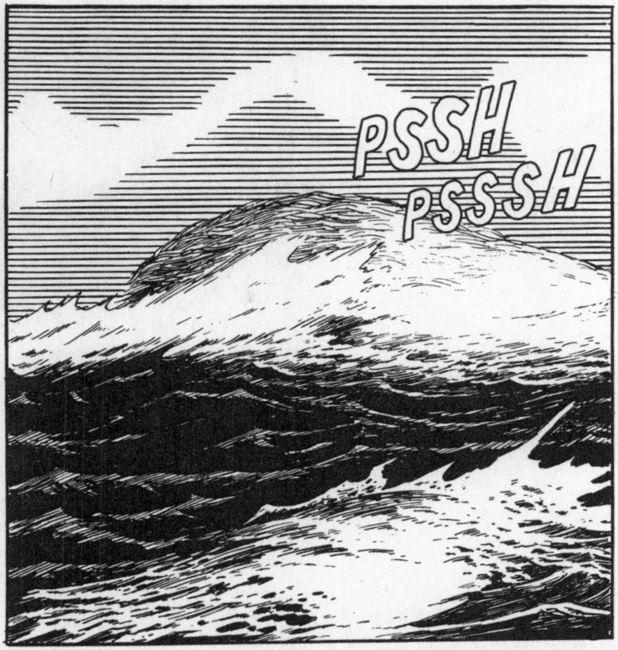
PSSH
PSSSH

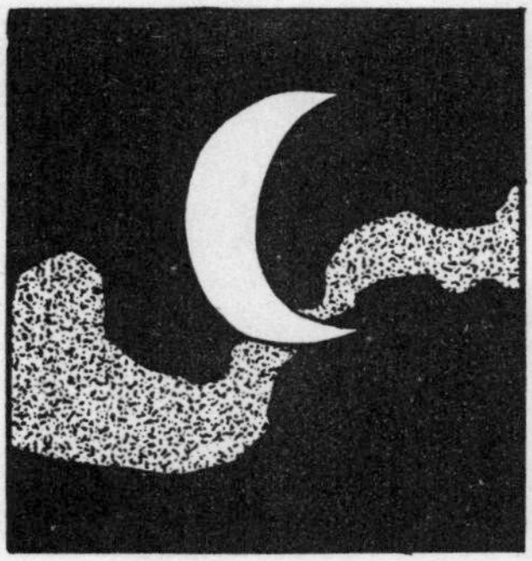

AT THE SURFACE, KITARO WAS EXPOSED TO DANGEROUS AMOUNTS OF RADIATION, BUT THE THREE PEOPLE INSIDE HIS MOUTH WERE SAFE. HE CARRIED THE YAMADA FAMILY TO A BEACH WITH SAFE RADIATION LEVELS AND RELEASED THEM.

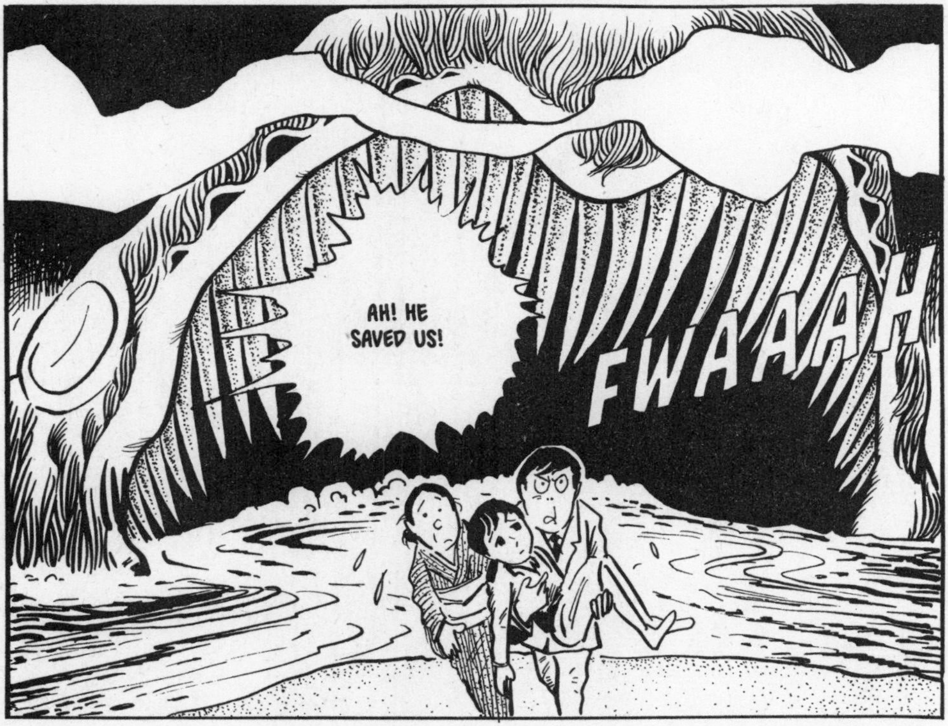
FWAAAAH
AH! HE SAVED US!

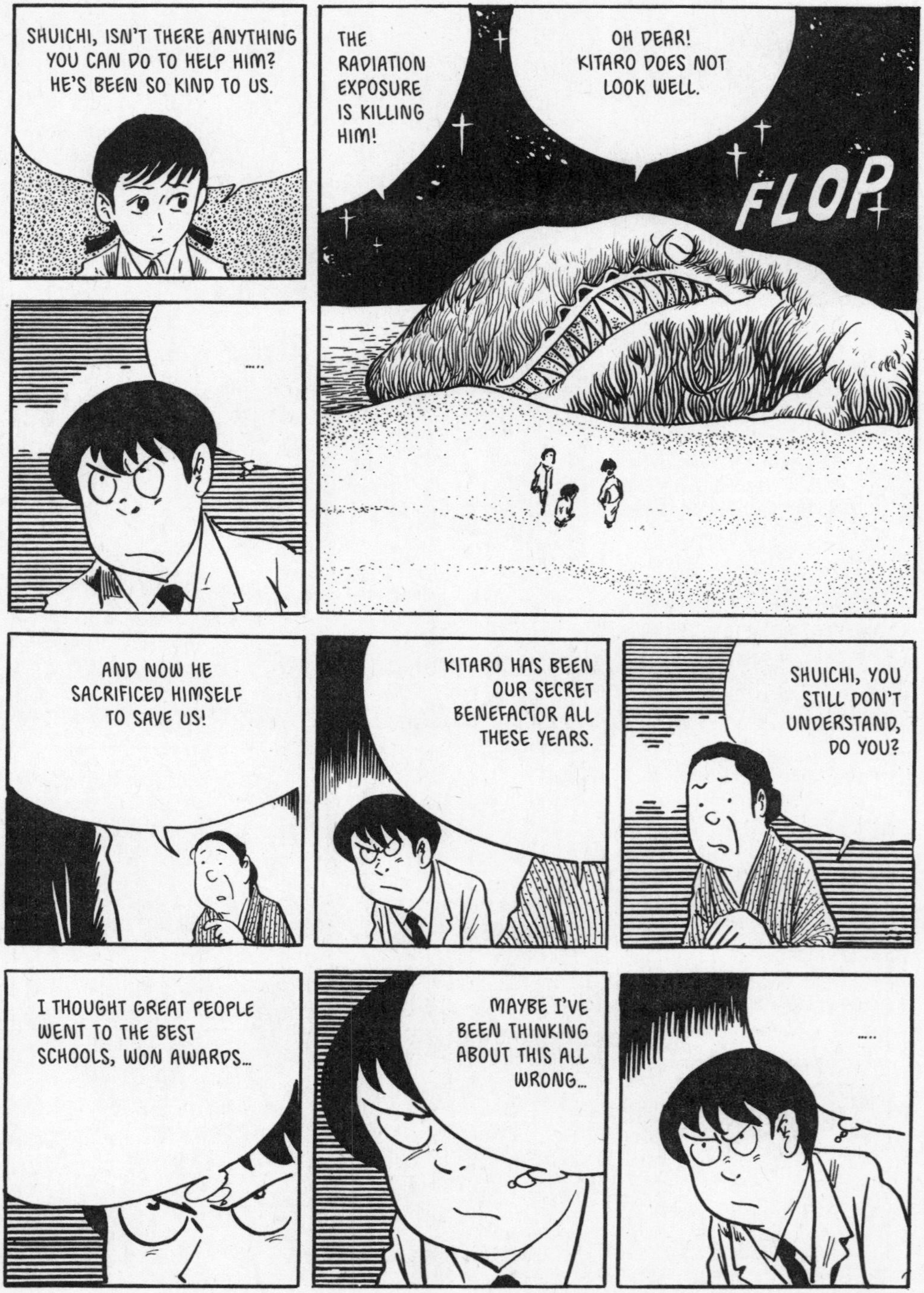

OH DEAR! KITARO DOES NOT LOOK WELL.
THE RADIATION EXPOSURE IS KILLING HIM!
FLOP
SHUICHI, ISN'T THERE ANYTHING YOU CAN DO TO HELP HIM? HE'S BEEN SO KIND TO US.
.....
SHUICHI, YOU STILL DON'T UNDERSTAND, DO YOU?
KITARO HAS BEEN OUR SECRET BENEFACTOR ALL THESE YEARS.
AND NOW HE SACRIFICED HIMSELF TO SAVE US!
....
MAYBE I'VE BEEN THINKING ABOUT THIS ALL WRONG...
I THOUGHT GREAT PEOPLE WENT TO THE BEST SCHOOLS, WON AWARDS...

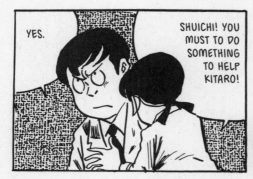

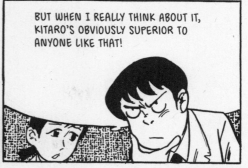

BUT WHEN I REALLY THINK ABOUT IT, KITARO'S OBVIOUSLY SUPERIOR TO ANYONE LIKE THAT!
SHUICHI! YOU MUST TO DO SOMETHING TO HELP KITARO!
YES.
SHUICHI HURRIED BACK TO HIS TOKYO LABORATORY, AND BEGAN STUDYING SALAMANDRA DUST AND THE SEA CREATURE'S BLOOD.
YAMADA, YOU'VE DEVISED SO MANY PLANS TO RID JAPAN OF THE THREAT OF THIS MONSTER...
OH! PROFESSOR!
AND NOW YOU'RE LOOKING FOR A WAY TO HELP THE CREATURE? WHAT A WASTE OF TIME!
THE CREATURE'S RADIOACTIVE! IT'S STILL COLLAPSED ON THE IZU COAST. THE SELF-DEFENSE FORCES ARE GOING TO DISPOSE OF IT IN THE PACIFIC OCEAN.
THIS IS NEWS TO ME. BUT...

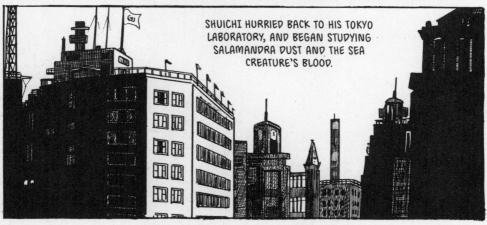

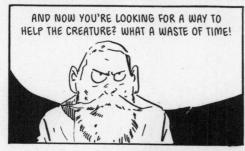

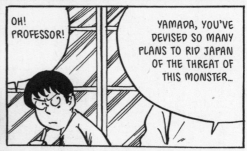

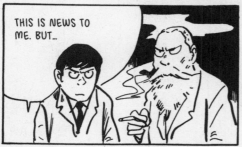

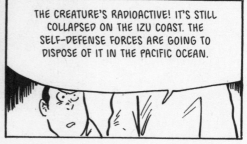

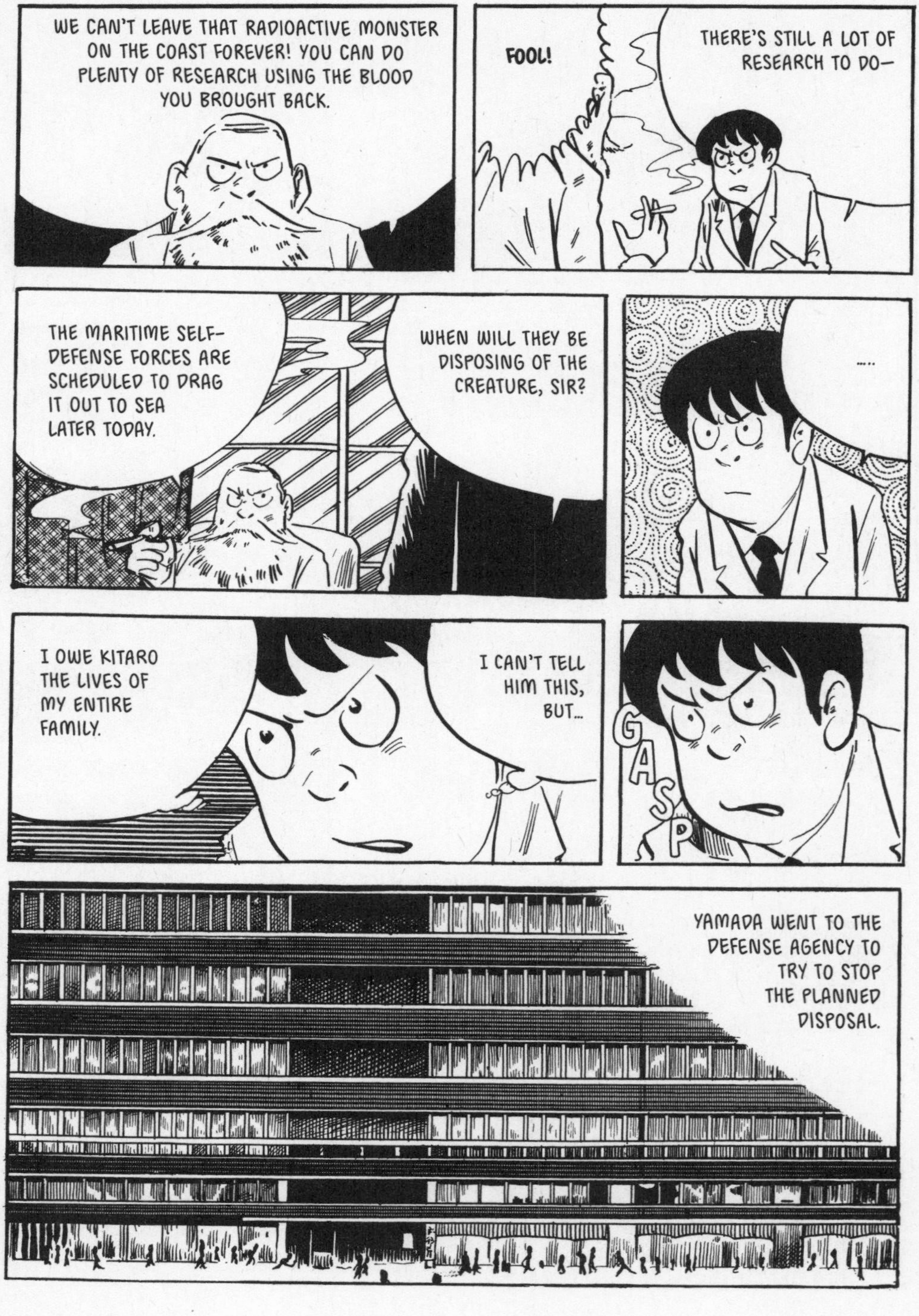
THERE'S STILL A LOT OF RESEARCH TO DO—
FOOL!
WE CAN'T LEAVE THAT RADIOACTIVE MONSTER ON THE COAST FOREVER! YOU CAN DO PLENTY OF RESEARCH USING THE BLOOD YOU BROUGHT BACK.
....
WHEN WILL THEY BE DISPOSING OF THE CREATURE, SIR?
THE MARITIME SELF-DEFENSE FORCES ARE SCHEDULED TO DRAG IT OUT TO SEA LATER TODAY.
GASP
I CAN'T TELL HIM THIS, BUT...
I OWE KITARO THE LIVES OF MY ENTIRE FAMILY.
YAMADA WENT TO THE DEFENSE AGENCY TO TRY TO STOP THE PLANNED DISPOSAL.

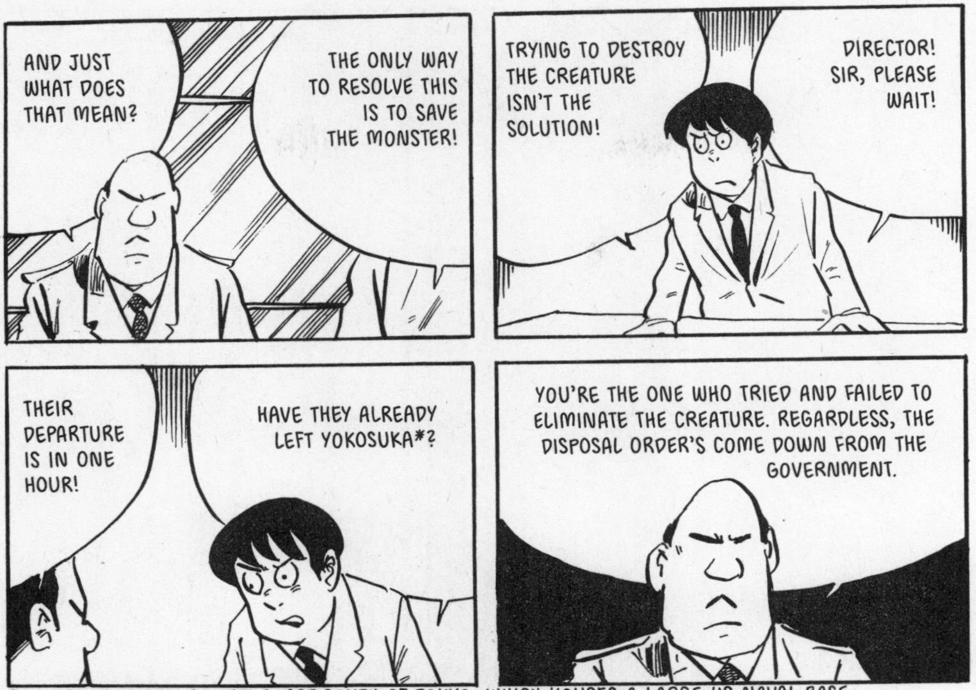
DIRECTOR! SIR, PLEASE WAIT!
TRYING TO DESTROY THE CREATURE ISN'T THE SOLUTION!
THE ONLY WAY TO RESOLVE THIS IS TO SAVE THE MONSTER!
AND JUST WHAT DOES THAT MEAN?
YOU'RE THE ONE WHO TRIED AND FAILED TO ELIMINATE THE CREATURE. REGARDLESS, THE DISPOSAL ORDER'S COME DOWN FROM THE GOVERNMENT.
HAVE THEY ALREADY LEFT YOKOSUKA*?
THEIR DEPARTURE IS IN ONE HOUR!

*YOKOSUKA IS CITY ON THE COAST SOUTH OF TOKYO, WHICH HOUSES A LARGE US NAVAL BASE.

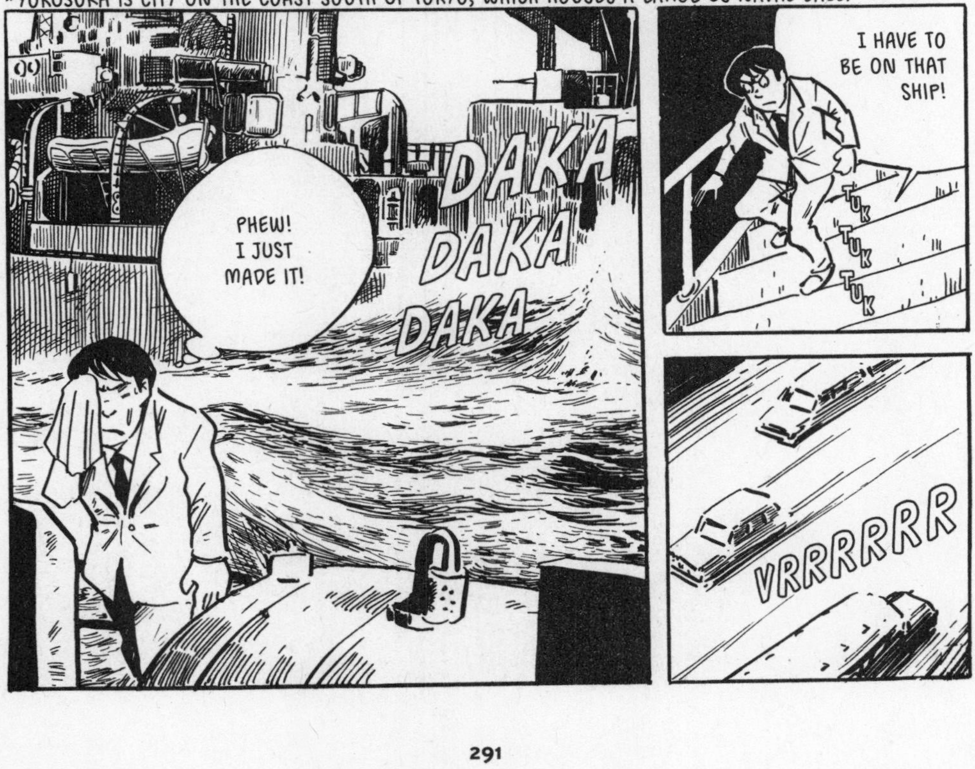
I HAVE TO BE ON THAT SHIP!
TUK
TUK
TUK
VRRRRRR
DAKA
DAKA
DAKA
PHEW! I JUST MADE IT!

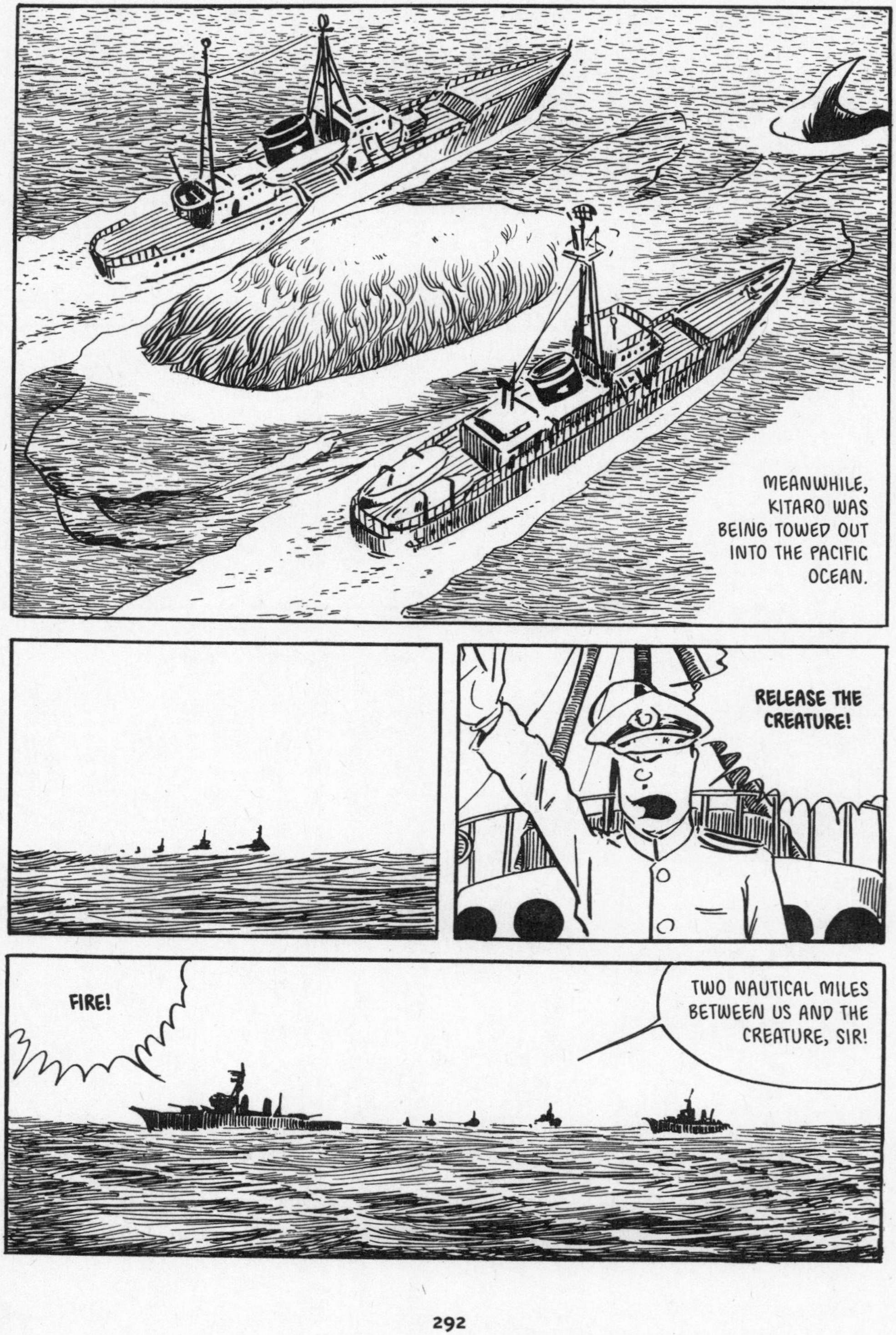
MEANWHILE, KITARO WAS BEING TOWED OUT INTO THE PACIFIC OCEAN.
RELEASE THE CREATURE!
TWO NAUTICAL MILES BETWEEN US AND THE CREATURE, SIR!
FIRE!

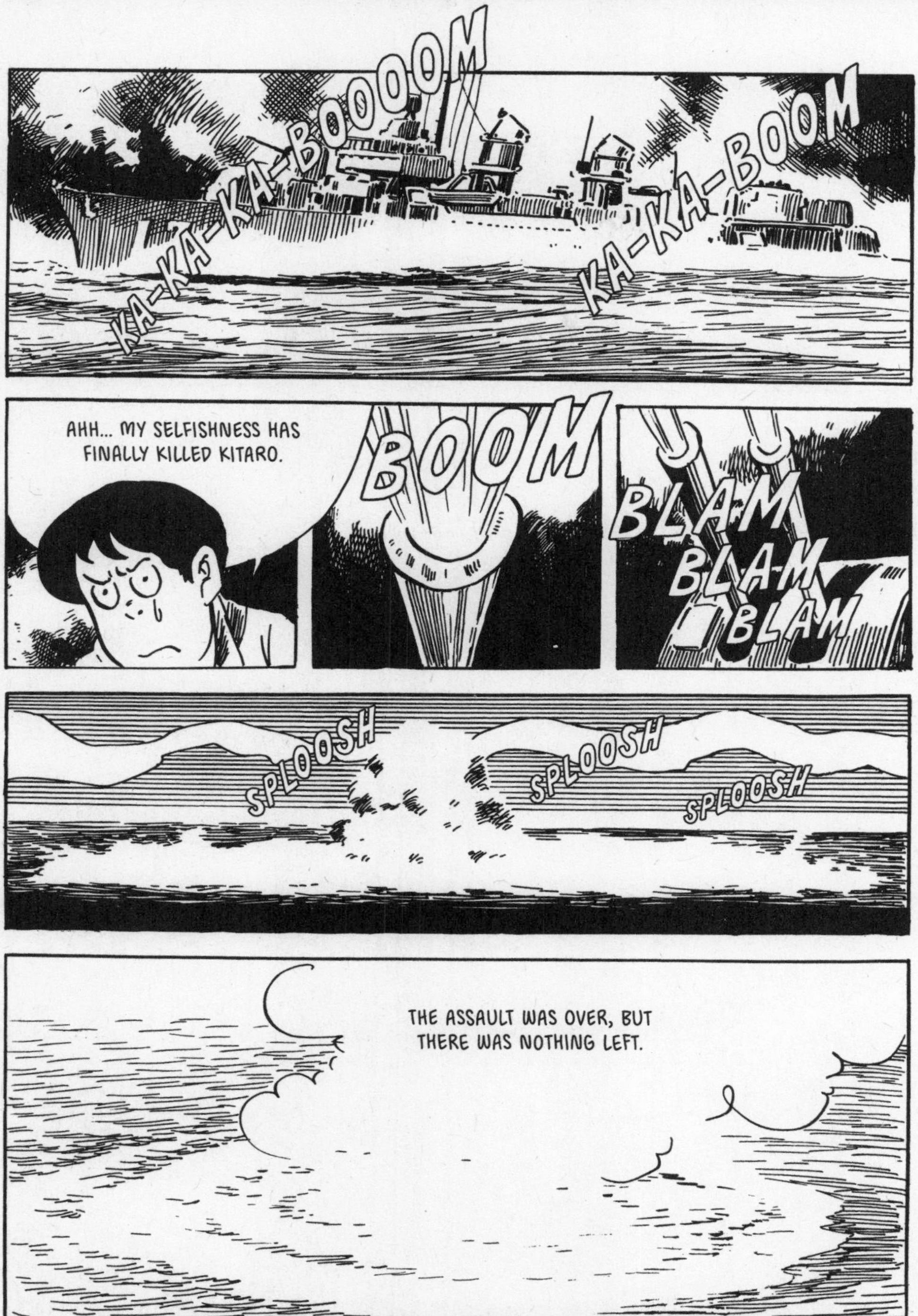
KA-KA-BOOM
KA-KA-KA-BOOOOM
BLAM
BLAM
BLAM
BOOM
AHH... MY SELFISHNESS HAS FINALLY KILLED KITARO.
SPLOOSH
SPLOOSH
SPLOOSH
THE ASSAULT WAS OVER, BUT THERE WAS NOTHING LEFT.

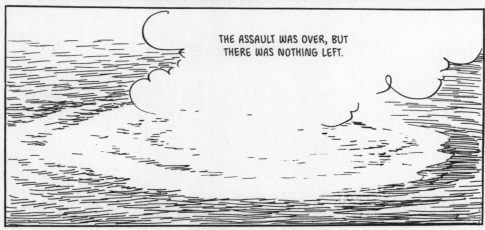

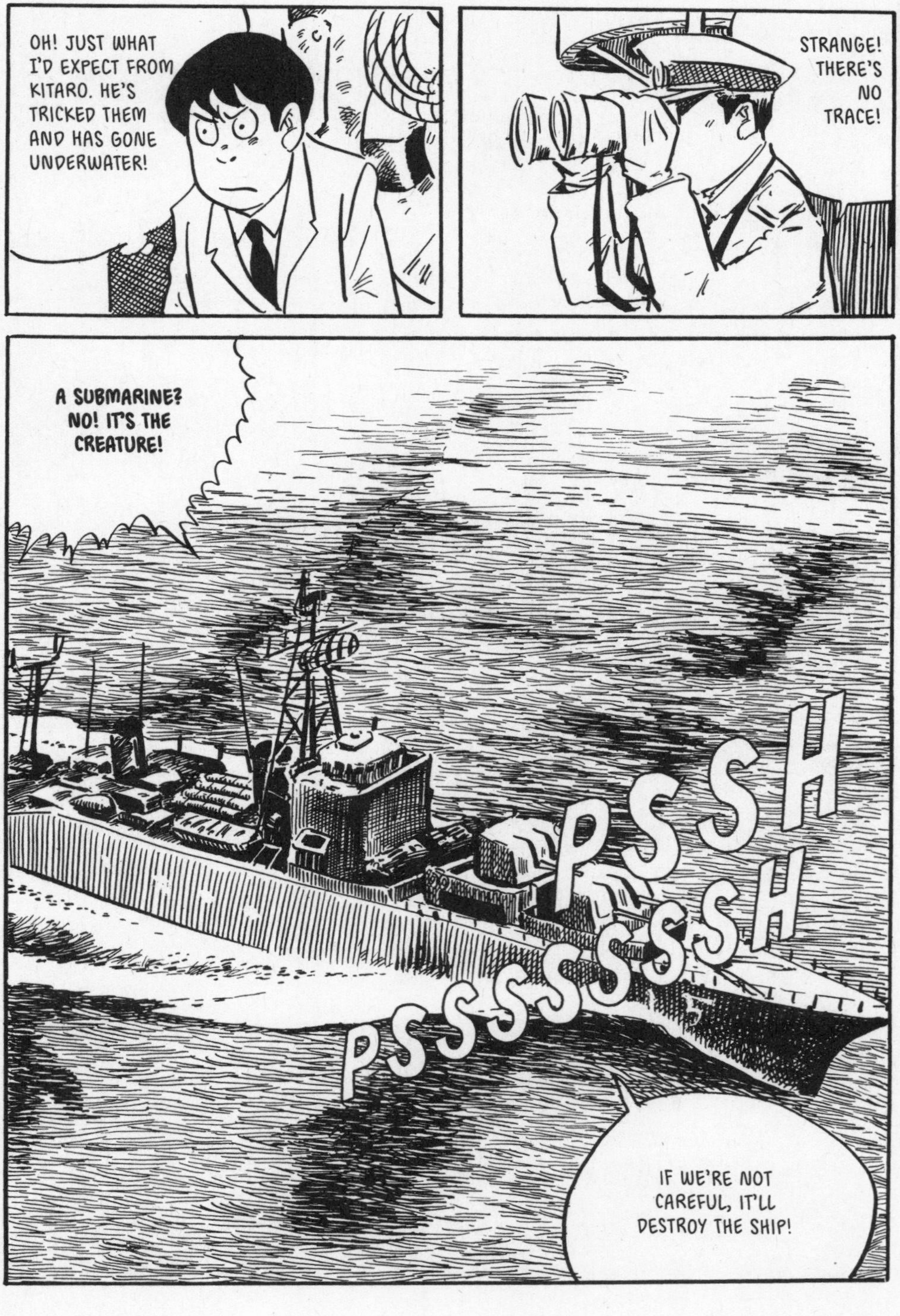
STRANGE! THERE'S NO TRACE!
OH! JUST WHAT I'D EXPECT FROM KITARO. HE'S TRICKED THEM AND HAS GONE UNDERWATER!
A SUBMARINE? NO! IT'S THE CREATURE!
PSSH
PSSSSSSSSH
IF WE'RE NOT CAREFUL, IT'LL DESTROY THE SHIP!

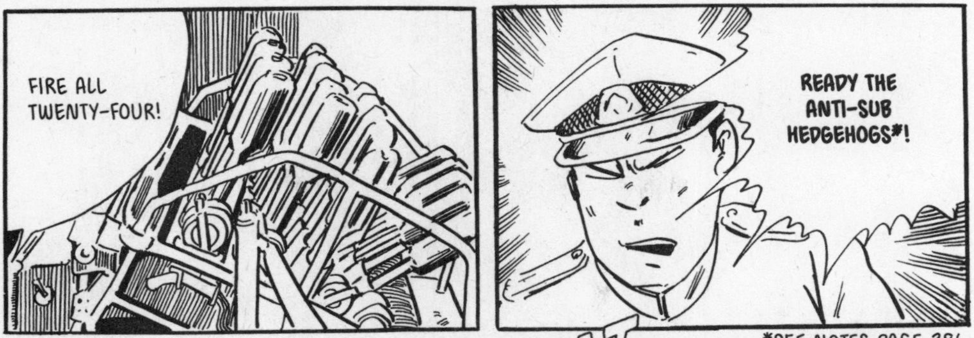
READY THE ANTI-SUB HEDGEHOGS*!
FIRE ALL TWENTY-FOUR!

*SEE NOTES PAGE 386.

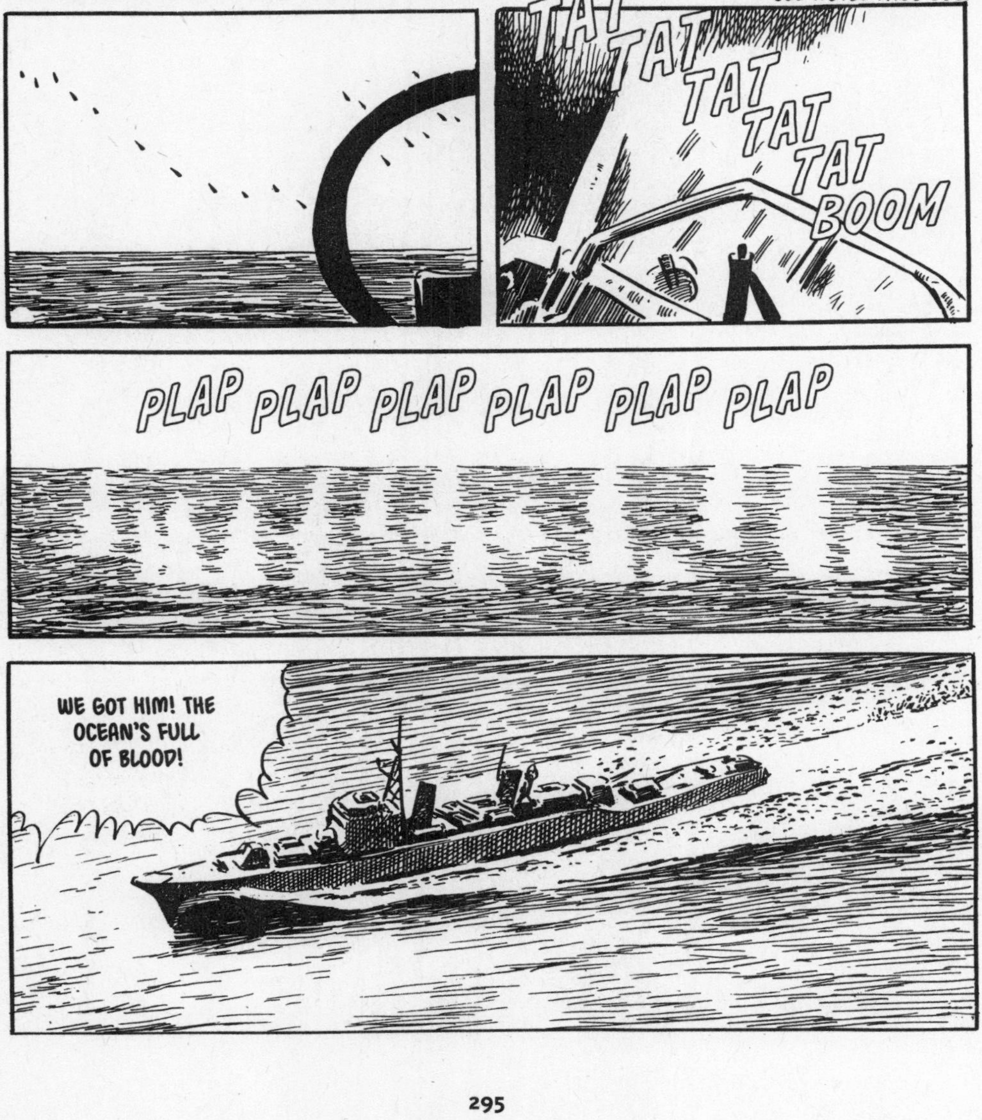
TAT TAT TAT TAT TAT BOOM
PLAP PLAP PLAP PLAP PLAP PLAP
WE GOT HIM! THE OCEAN'S FULL OF BLOOD!

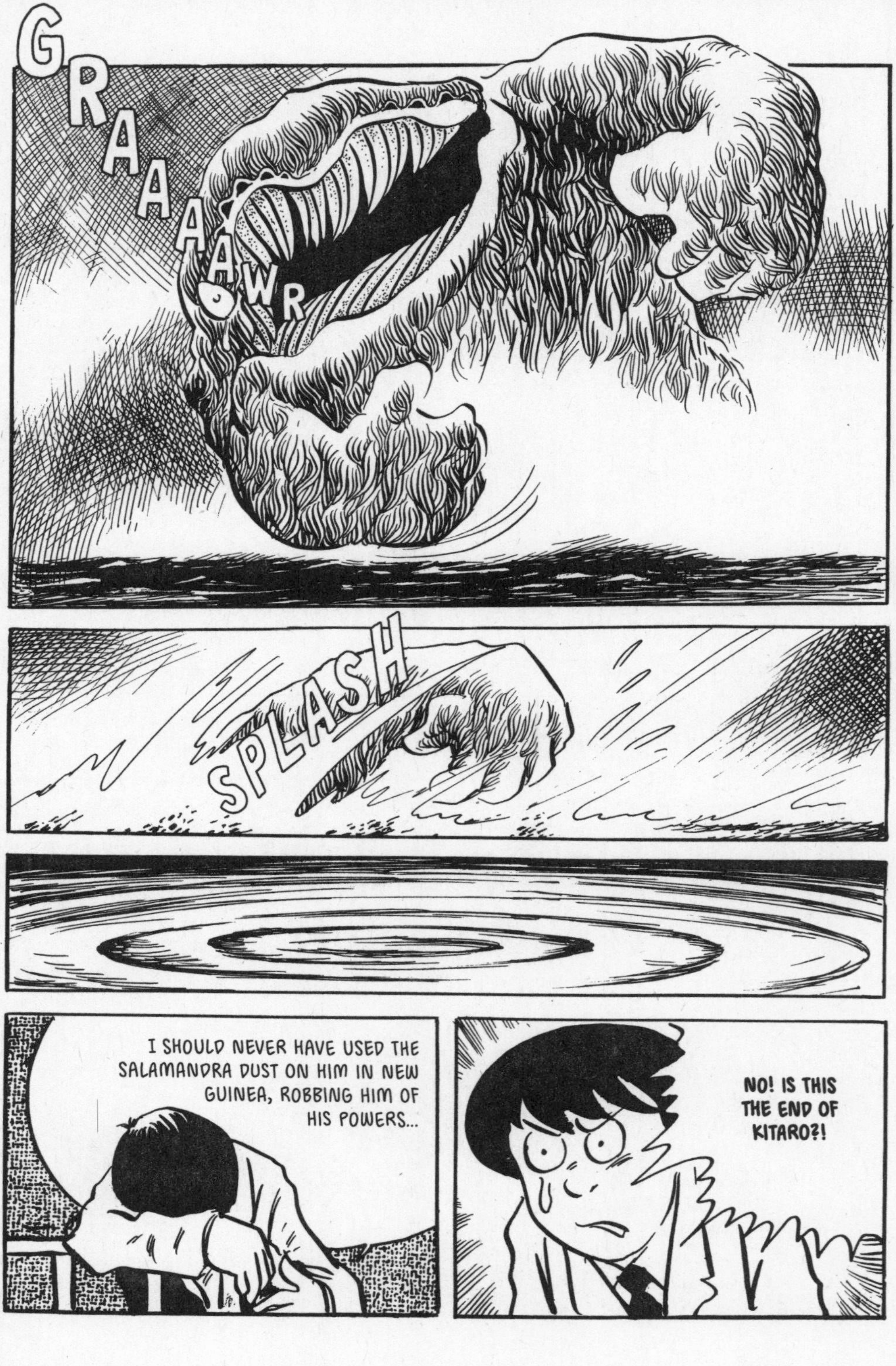
GRAAAAAWR
SPLASH
NO! IS THIS THE END OF KITARO?!
I SHOULD NEVER HAVE USED THE SALAMANDRA DUST ON HIM IN NEW GUINEA, ROBBING HIM OF HIS POWERS...

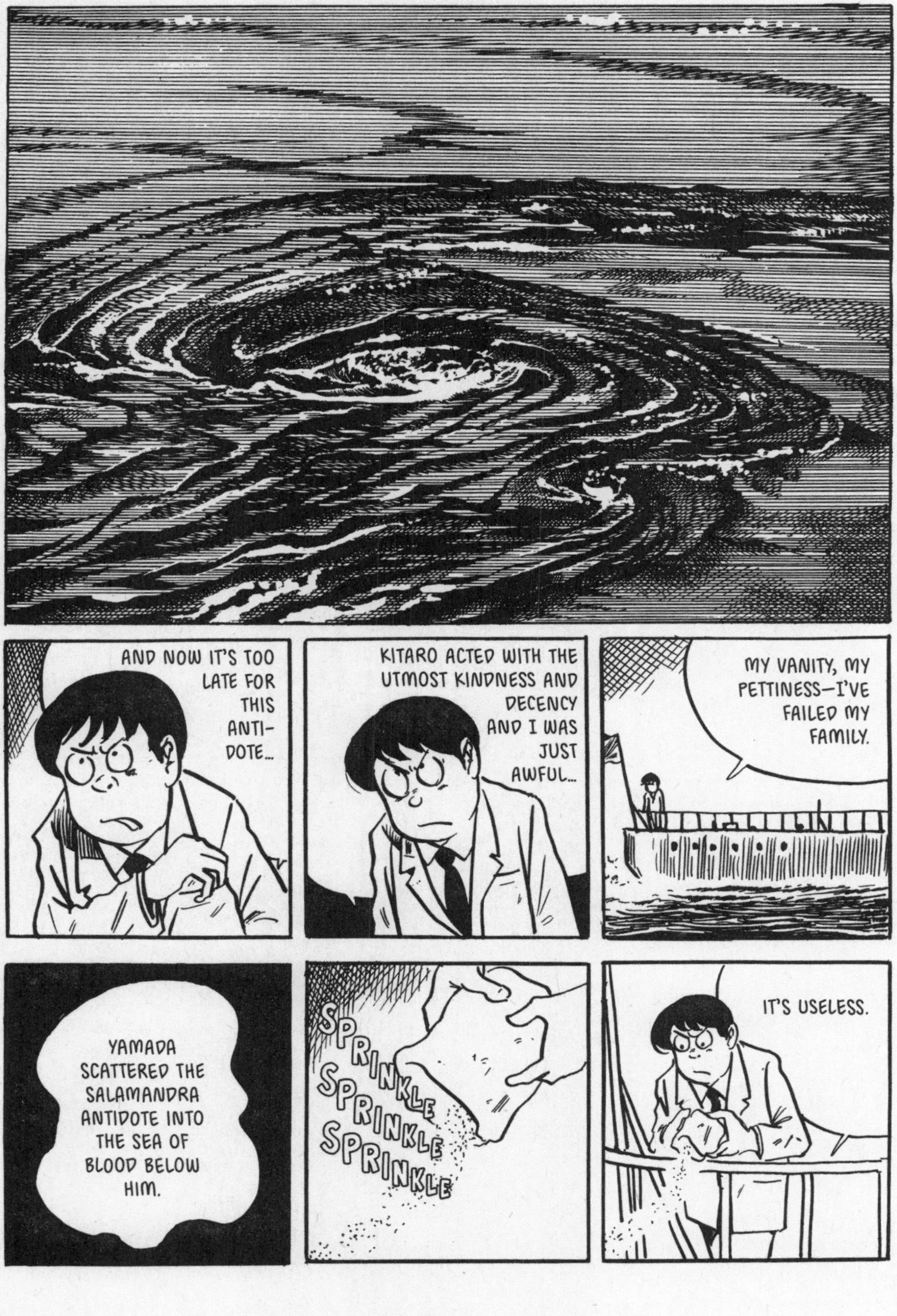
MY VANITY, MY PETTINESS—I'VE FAILED MY FAMILY.
KITARO ACTED WITH THE UTMOST KINDNESS AND DECENCY AND I WAS JUST AWFUL...
AND NOW IT'S TOO LATE FOR THIS ANTI-DOTE...
IT'S USELESS.
SPRINKLE SPRINKLE SPRINKLE
YAMADA SCATTERED THE SALAMANDRA ANTIDOTE INTO THE SEA OF BLOOD BELOW HIM.

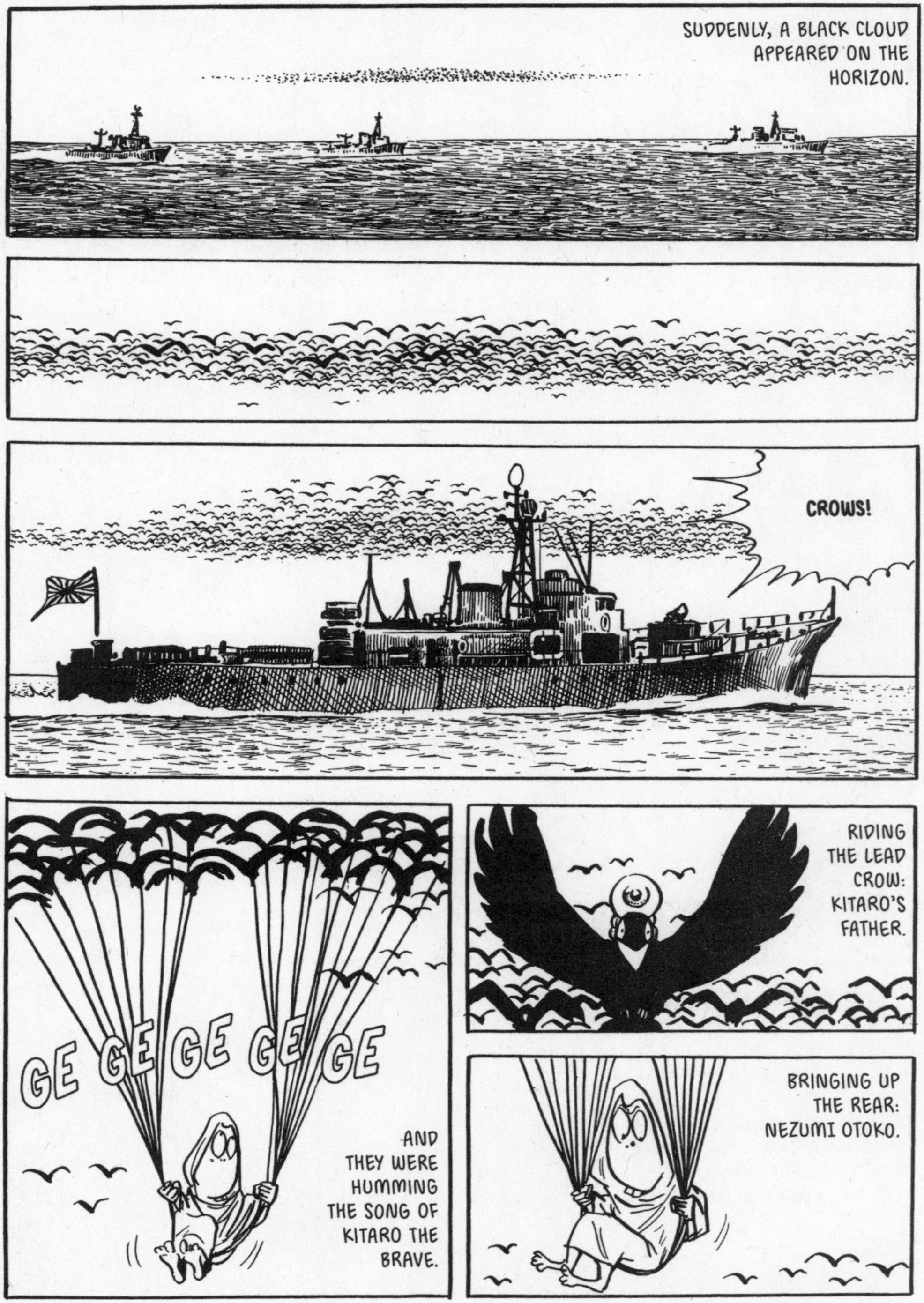
SUDDENLY, A BLACK CLOUD APPEARED ON THE HORIZON.
CROWS!
RIDING THE LEAD CROW: KITARO'S FATHER.
BRINGING UP THE REAR: NEZUMI OTOKO.
GE GE GE GE GE GE
AND THEY WERE HUMMING THE SONG OF KITARO THE BRAVE.

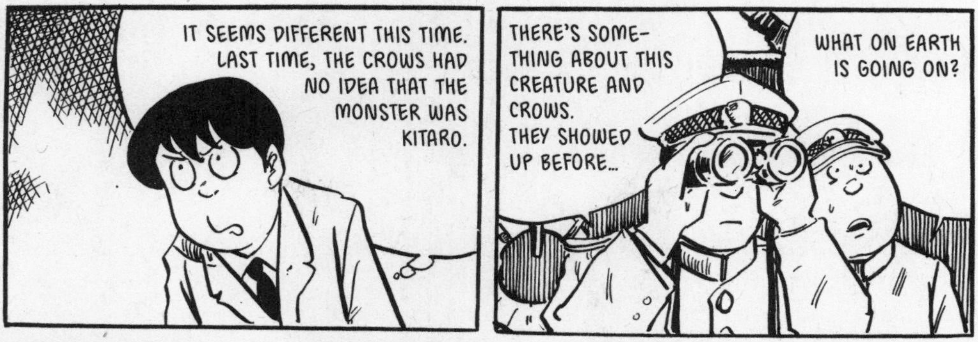
WHAT ON EARTH IS GOING ON?
THERE'S SOMETHING ABOUT THIS CREATURE AND CROWS. THEY SHOWED UP BEFORE...
IT SEEMS DIFFERENT THIS TIME. LAST TIME, THE CROWS HAD NO IDEA THAT THE MONSTER WAS KITARO.

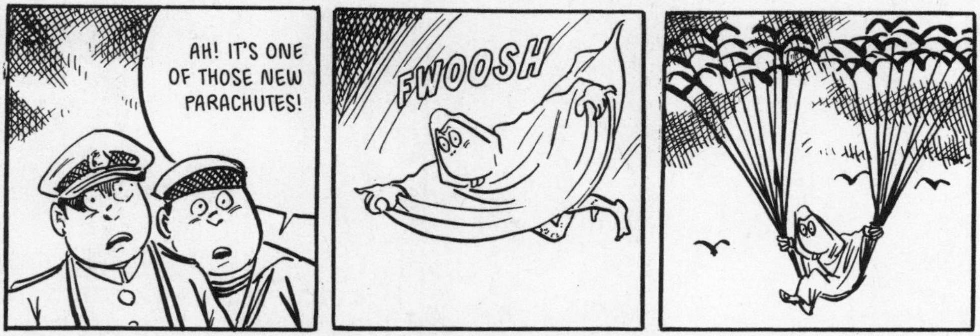
FWOOSH
AH! IT'S ONE OF THOSE NEW PARACHUTES!

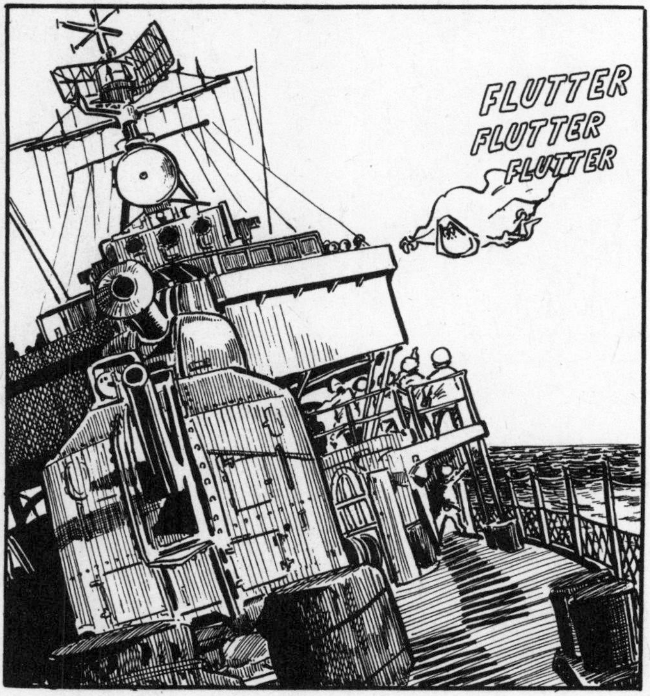
FLUTTER FLUTTER FLUTTER

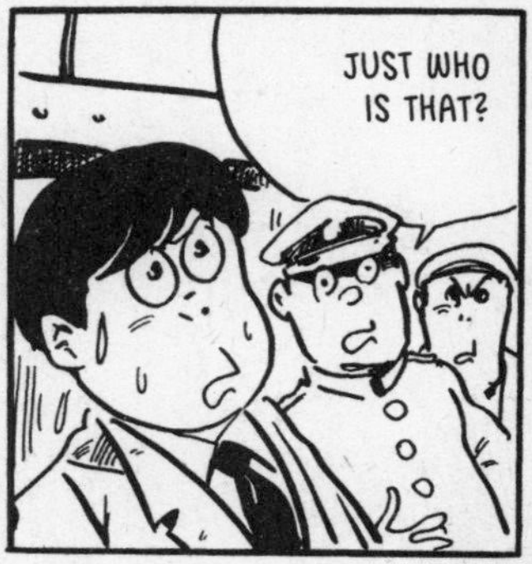
JUST WHO IS THAT?

YAMADA HAD UNDERESTIMATED THE EFFICACY OF THE ANTIDOTE. IT BEGAN HEALING KITARO ALMOST IMMEDIATELY.

AS HIS POWERS RETURNED, KITARO'S DAD AND NEZUMI OTOKO WERE ABLE TO SENSE THAT KITARO NEEDED THEM.

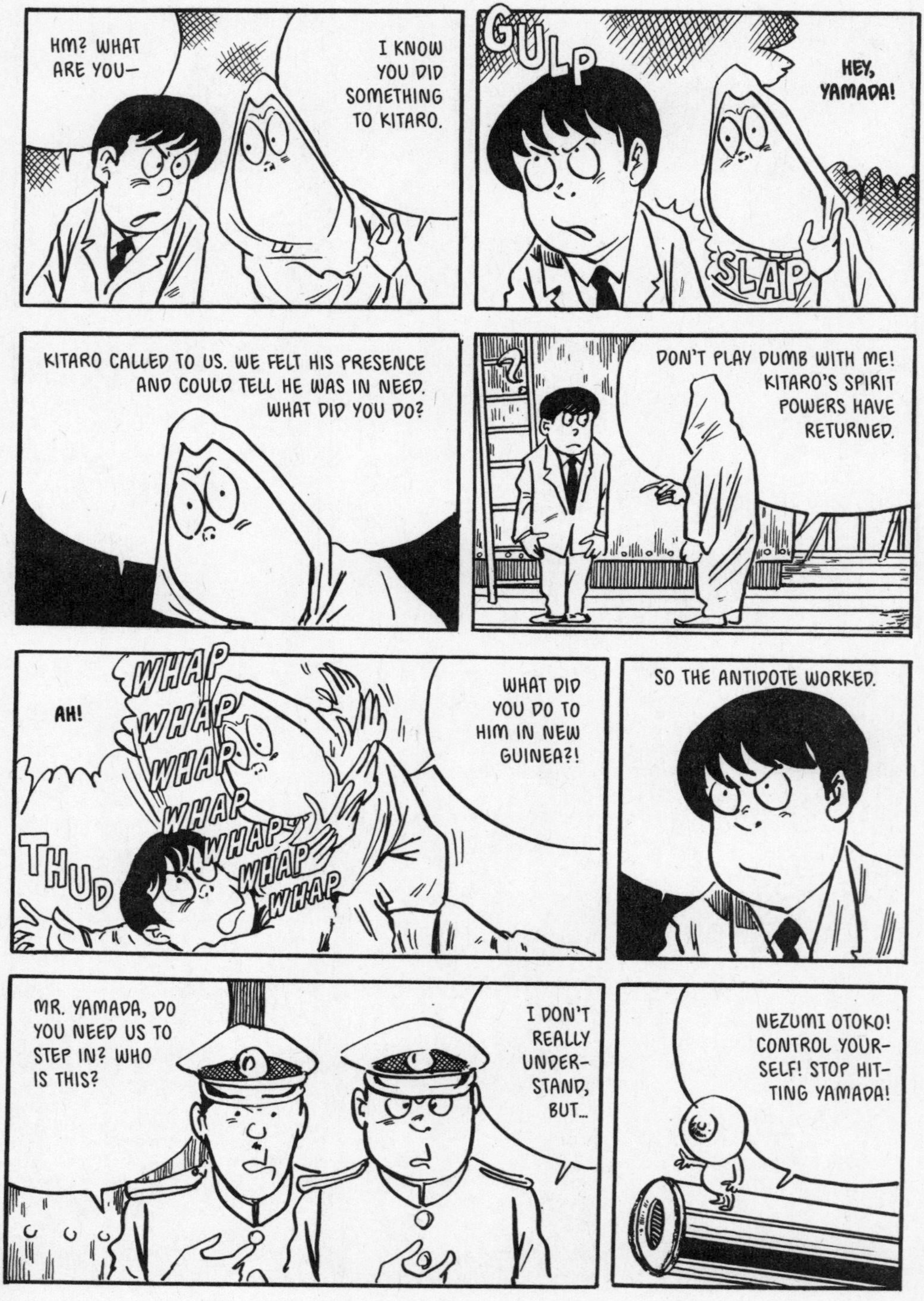
GULP
HEY, YAMADA!
SLAP
I KNOW YOU DID SOMETHING TO KITARO.
HM? WHAT ARE YOU—
DON'T PLAY DUMB WITH ME! KITARO'S SPIRIT POWERS HAVE RETURNED.
?
KITARO CALLED TO US. WE FELT HIS PRESENCE AND COULD TELL HE WAS IN NEED. WHAT DID YOU DO?
SO THE ANTIDOTE WORKED.
WHAT DID YOU DO TO HIM IN NEW GUINEA?!
WHAP WHAP WHAP WHAP WHAP WHAP WHAP
AH!
THUD
NEZUMI OTOKO! CONTROL YOURSELF! STOP HITTING YAMADA!
I DON'T REALLY UNDERSTAND, BUT...
MR. YAMADA, DO YOU NEED US TO STEP IN? WHO IS THIS?

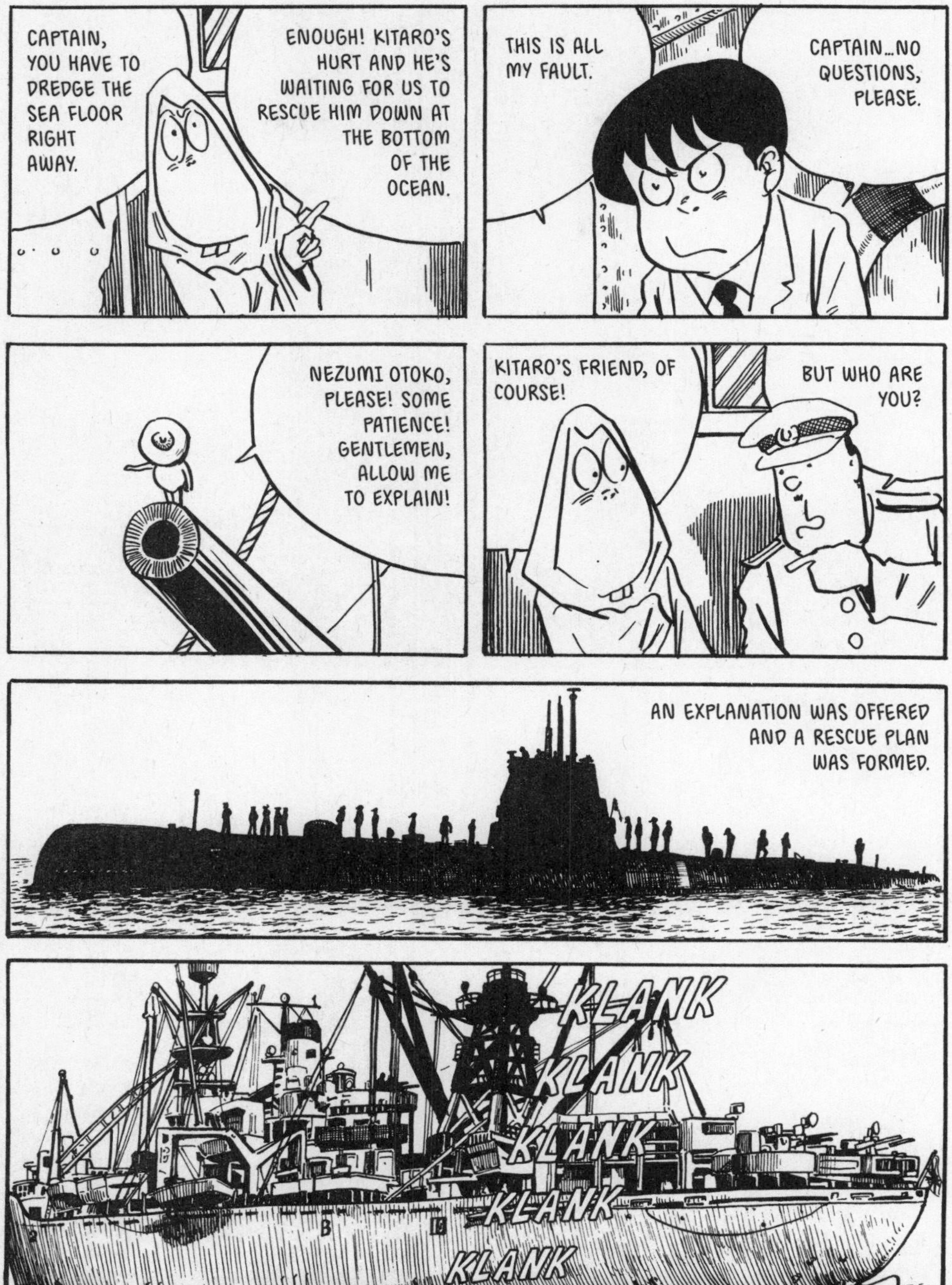
CAPTAIN…NO QUESTIONS, PLEASE.
THIS IS ALL MY FAULT.
ENOUGH! KITARO'S HURT AND HE'S WAITING FOR US TO RESCUE HIM DOWN AT THE BOTTOM OF THE OCEAN.
CAPTAIN, YOU HAVE TO DREDGE THE SEA FLOOR RIGHT AWAY.
BUT WHO ARE YOU?
KITARO'S FRIEND, OF COURSE!
NEZUMI OTOKO, PLEASE! SOME PATIENCE! GENTLEMEN, ALLOW ME TO EXPLAIN!
AN EXPLANATION WAS OFFERED AND A RESCUE PLAN WAS FORMED.
KLANK
KLANK
KLANK
KLANK
KLANK

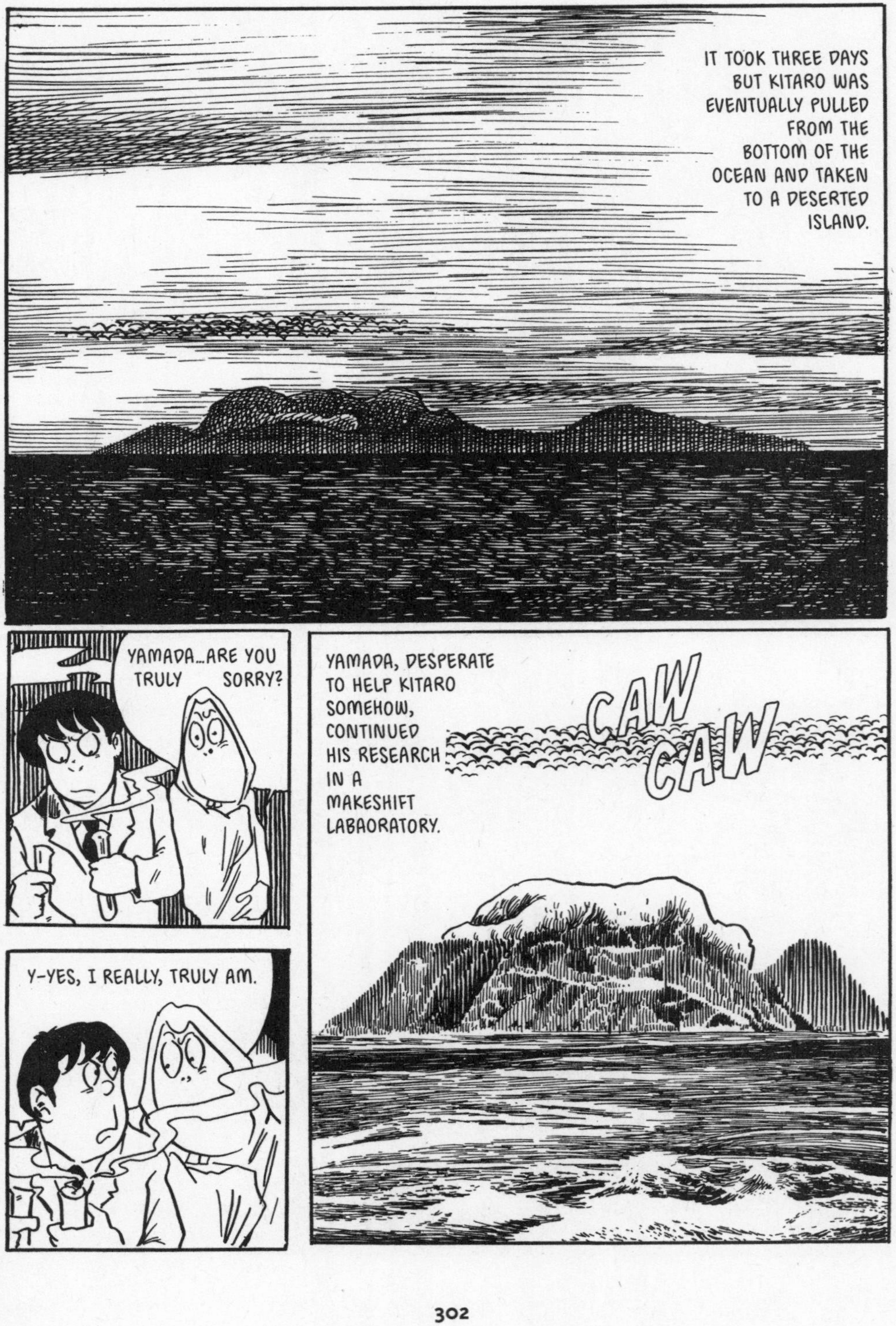
IT TOOK THREE DAYS BUT KITARO WAS EVENTUALLY PULLED FROM THE BOTTOM OF THE OCEAN AND TAKEN TO A DESERTED ISLAND.
YAMADA, DESPERATE TO HELP KITARO SOMEHOW, CONTINUED HIS RESEARCH IN A MAKESHIFT LABAORATORY.
CAW CAW
YAMADA...ARE YOU TRULY SORRY?
Y-YES, I REALLY, TRULY AM.

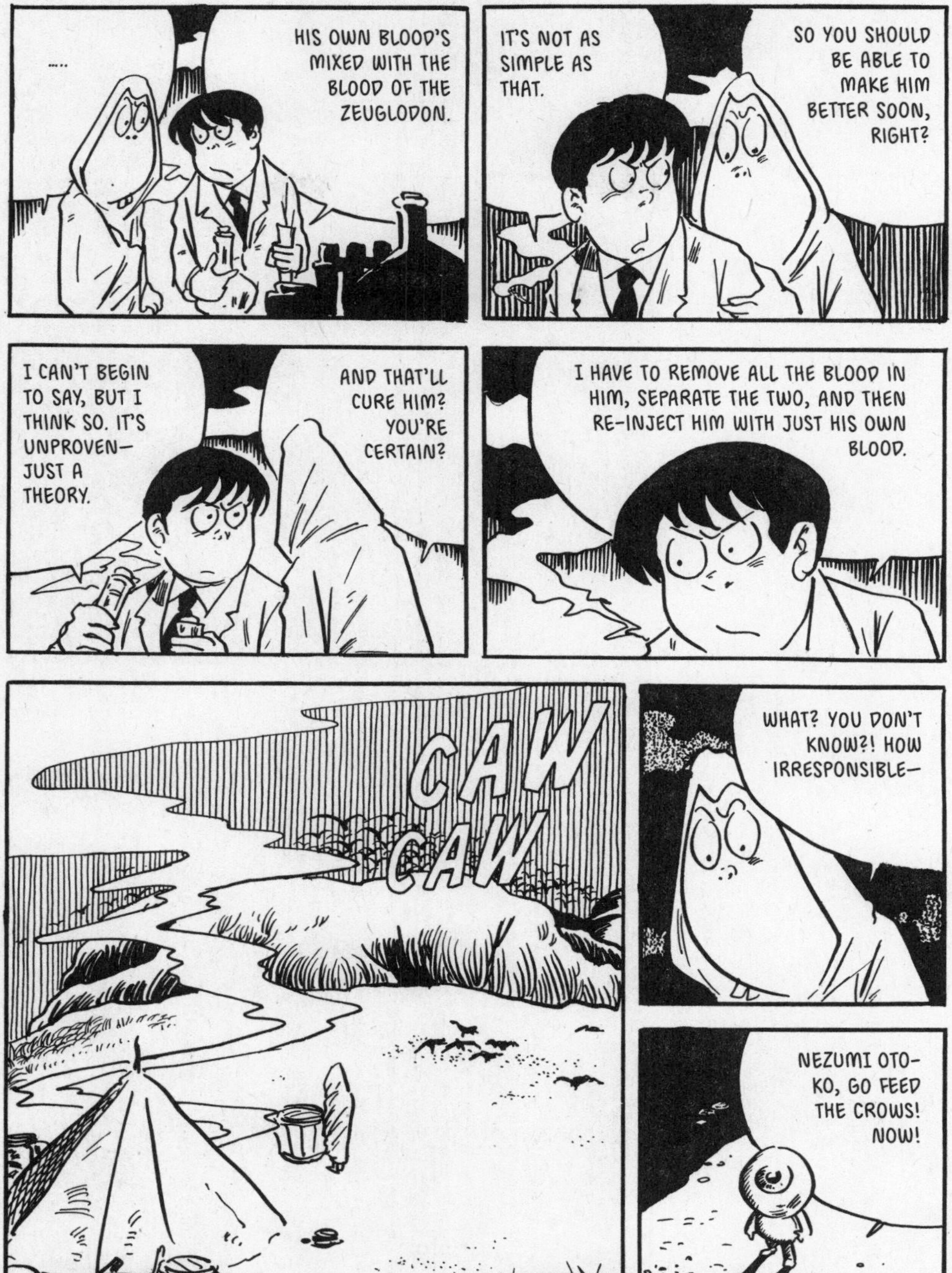
SO YOU SHOULD BE ABLE TO MAKE HIM BETTER SOON, RIGHT?
IT'S NOT AS SIMPLE AS THAT.
HIS OWN BLOOD'S MIXED WITH THE BLOOD OF THE ZEUGLODON.
.....
I HAVE TO REMOVE ALL THE BLOOD IN HIM, SEPARATE THE TWO, AND THEN RE-INJECT HIM WITH JUST HIS OWN BLOOD.
AND THAT'LL CURE HIM? YOU'RE CERTAIN?
I CAN'T BEGIN TO SAY, BUT I THINK SO. IT'S UNPROVEN— JUST A THEORY.
WHAT? YOU DON'T KNOW?! HOW IRRESPONSIBLE—
NEZUMI OTO-KO, GO FEED THE CROWS! NOW!
CAW
CAW

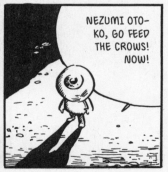

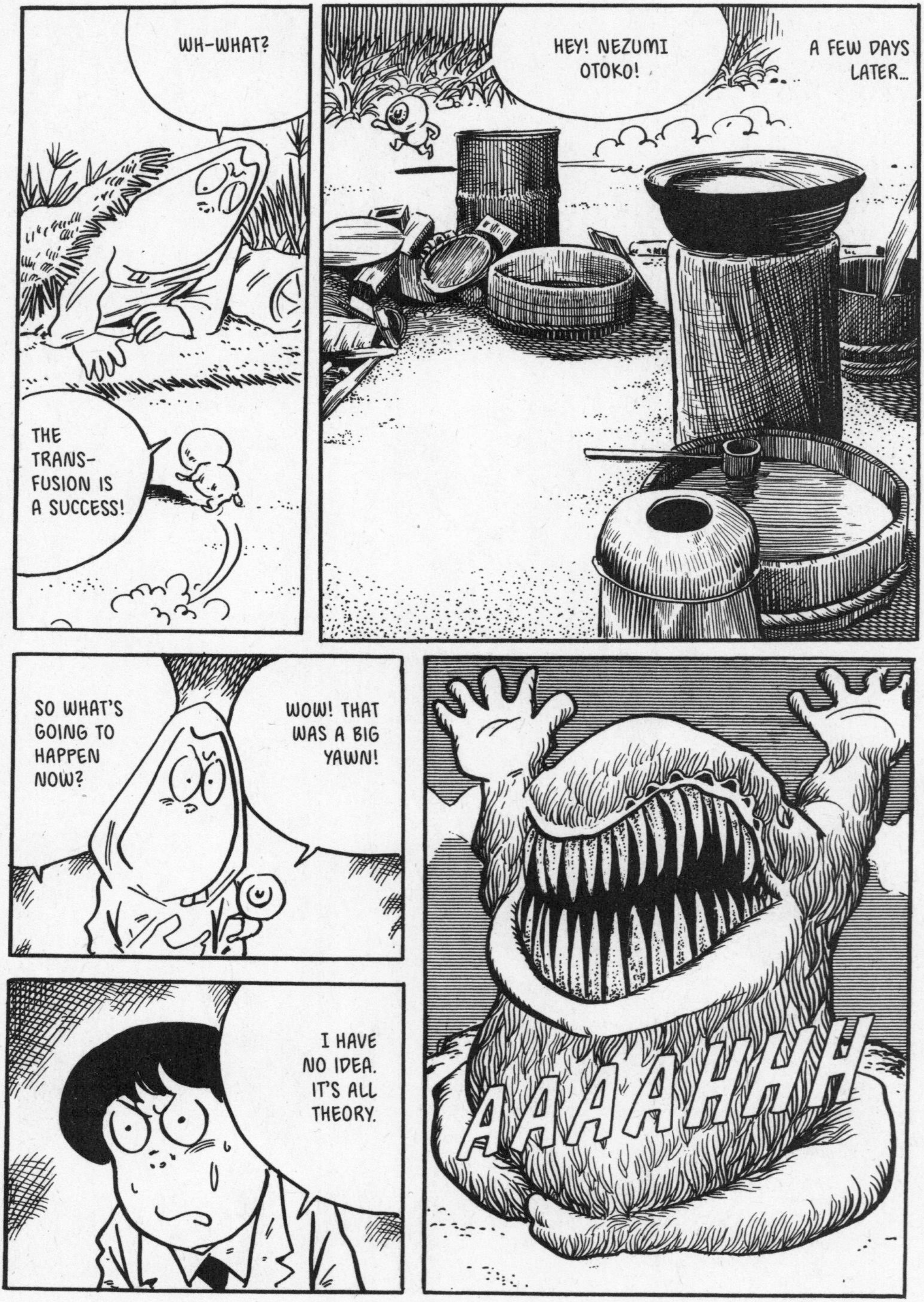
A FEW DAYS LATER...
HEY! NEZUMI OTOKO!
WH-WHAT?
THE TRANS-FUSION IS A SUCCESS!
AAAAHHH
WOW! THAT WAS A BIG YAWN!
SO WHAT'S GOING TO HAPPEN NOW?
I HAVE NO IDEA. IT'S ALL THEORY.

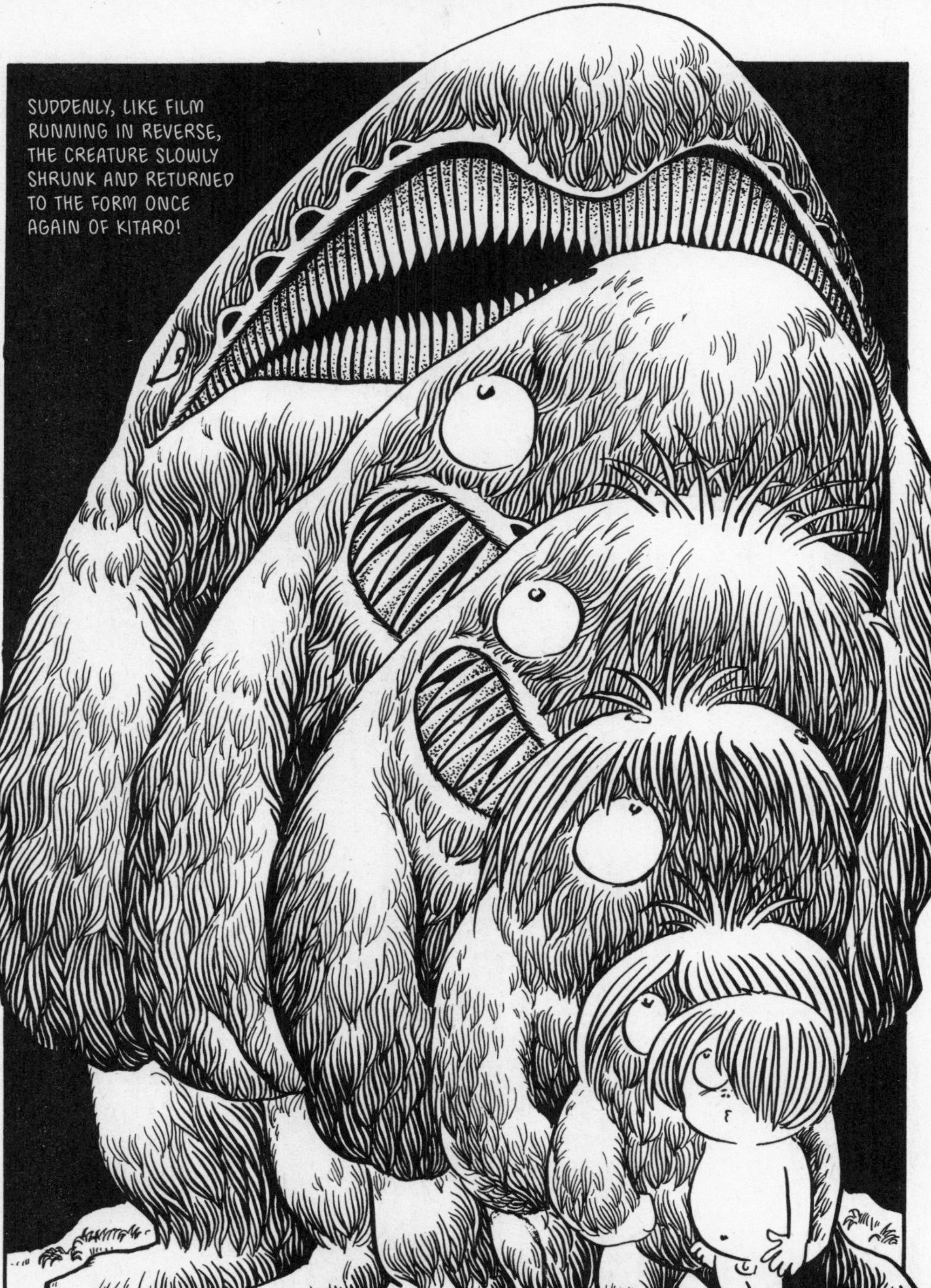
SUDDENLY, LIKE FILM RUNNING IN REVERSE, THE CREATURE SLOWLY SHRUNK AND RETURNED TO THE FORM ONCE AGAIN OF KITARO!

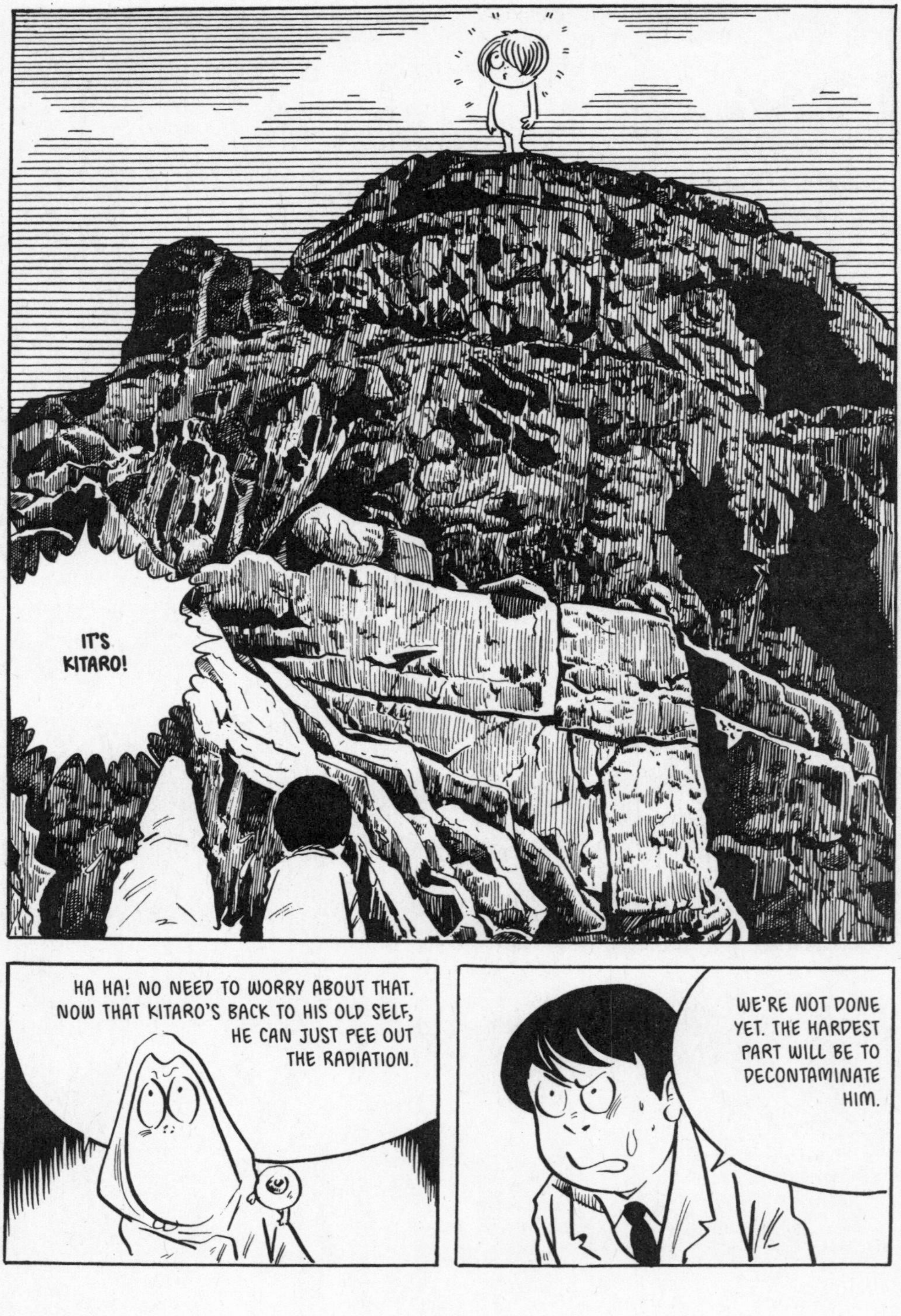
IT'S KITARO!
WE'RE NOT DONE YET. THE HARDEST PART WILL BE TO DECONTAMINATE HIM.
HA HA! NO NEED TO WORRY ABOUT THAT. NOW THAT KITARO'S BACK TO HIS OLD SELF, HE CAN JUST PEE OUT THE RADIATION.

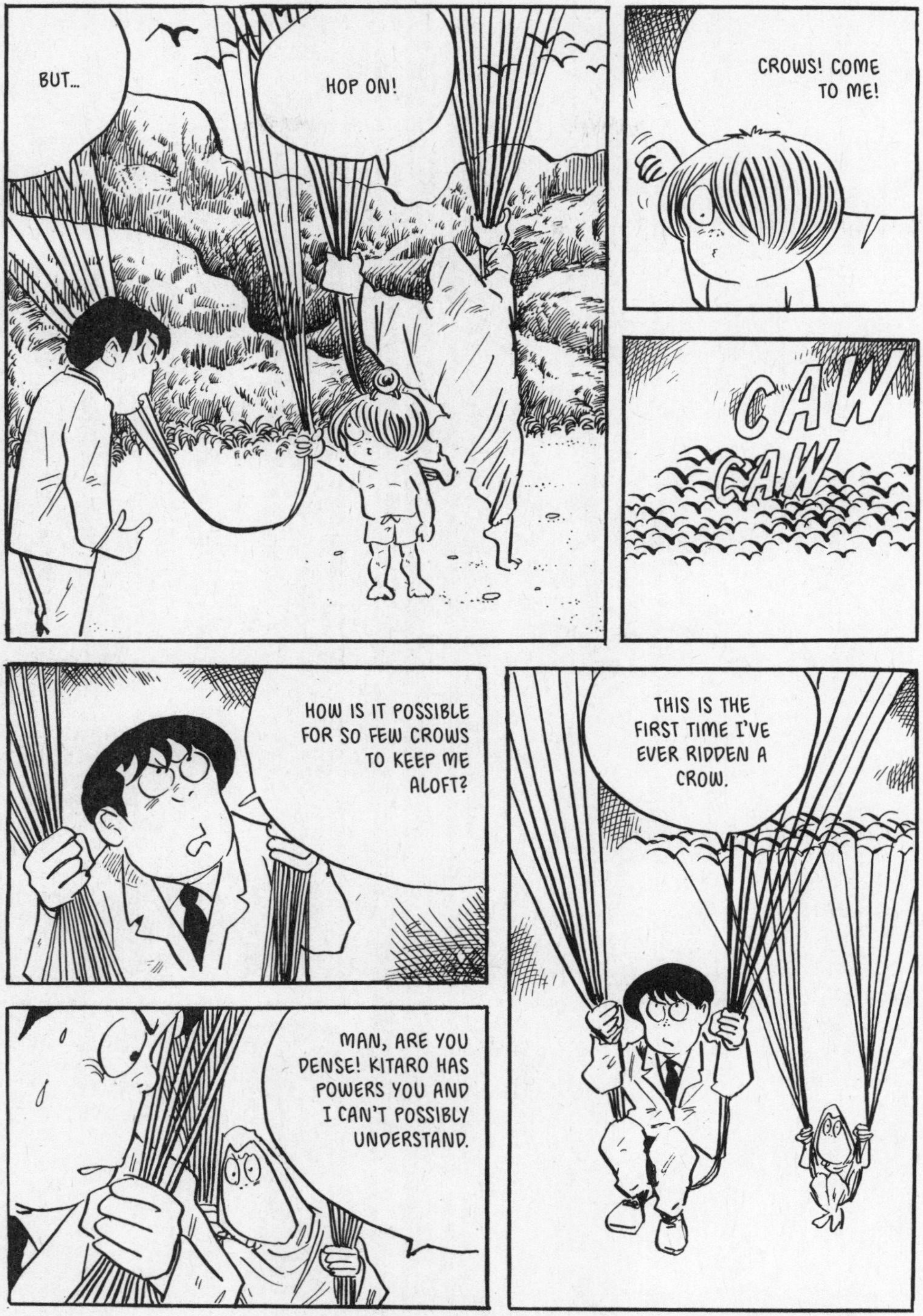
CROWS! COME TO ME!
CAW CAW
HOP ON!
BUT...
THIS IS THE FIRST TIME I'VE EVER RIDDEN A CROW.
HOW IS IT POSSIBLE FOR SO FEW CROWS TO KEEP ME ALOFT?
MAN, ARE YOU DENSE! KITARO HAS POWERS YOU AND I CAN'T POSSIBLY UNDERSTAND.

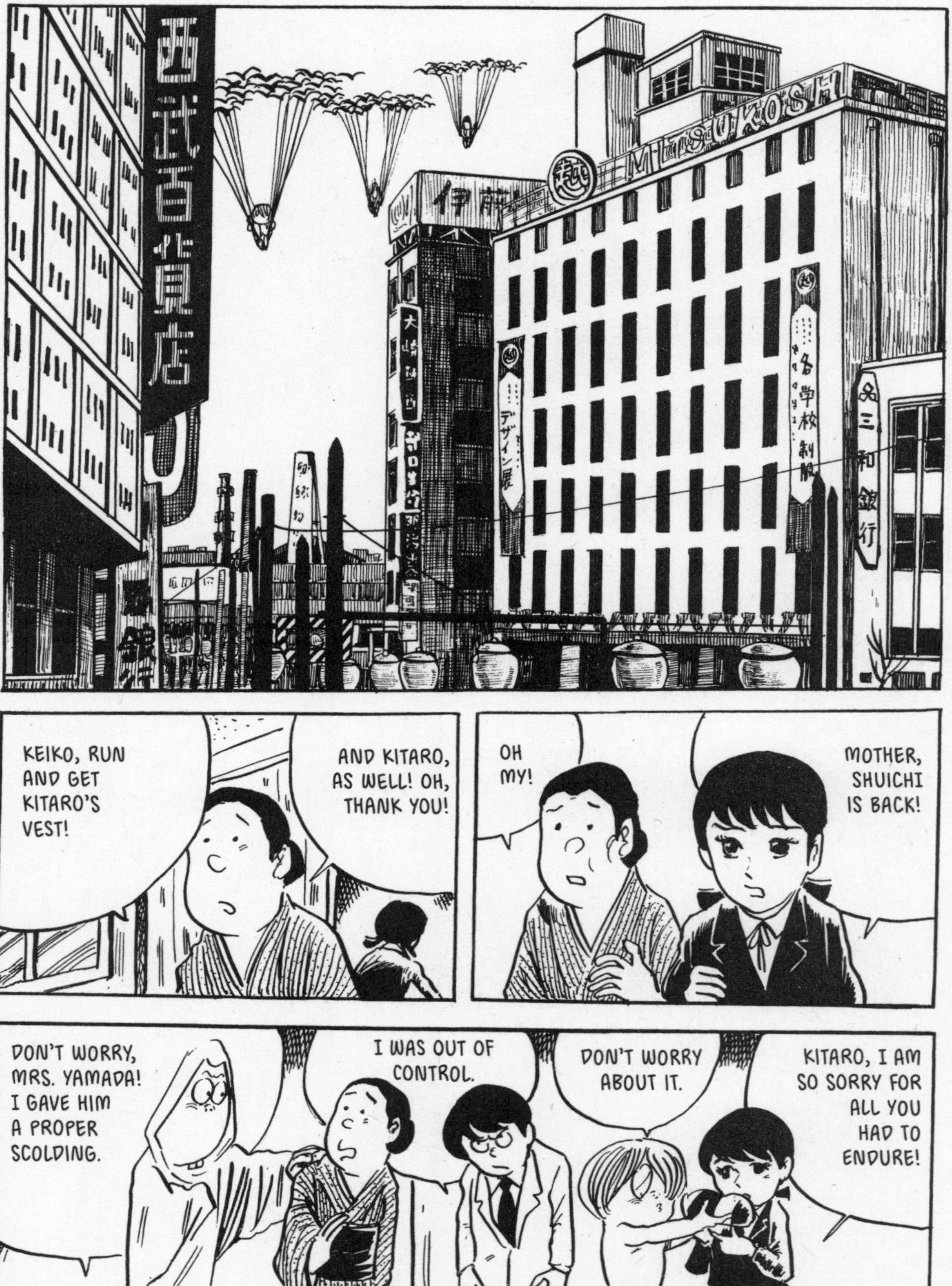
西武百貨店
MITSUKOSHI
各学校制服
デザイン展
三和銀行
MOTHER, SHUICHI IS BACK!
OH MY!
AND KITARO, AS WELL! OH, THANK YOU!
KEIKO, RUN AND GET KITARO'S VEST!
KITARO, I AM SO SORRY FOR ALL YOU HAD TO ENDURE!
DON'T WORRY ABOUT IT.
I WAS OUT OF CONTROL.
DON'T WORRY, MRS. YAMADA! I GAVE HIM A PROPER SCOLDING.

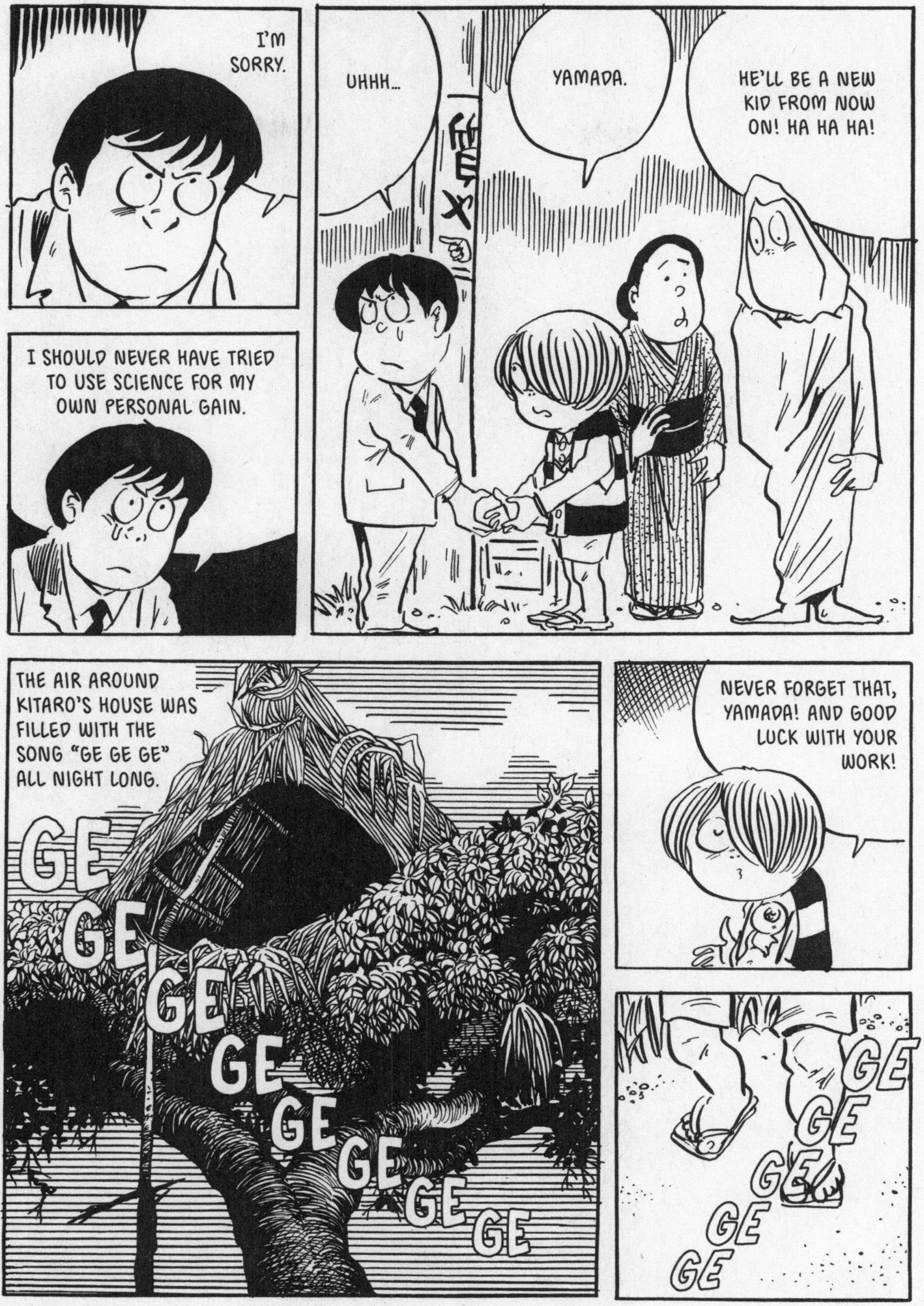
HE'LL BE A NEW KID FROM NOW ON! HA HA HA!
YAMADA.
UHHH...
I'M SORRY.
I SHOULD NEVER HAVE TRIED TO USE SCIENCE FOR MY OWN PERSONAL GAIN.
NEVER FORGET THAT, YAMADA! AND GOOD LUCK WITH YOUR WORK!
GE GE GE GE GE GE
THE AIR AROUND KITARO'S HOUSE WAS FILLED WITH THE SONG "GE GE GE" ALL NIGHT LONG.
GE GE GE GE GE GE GE GE

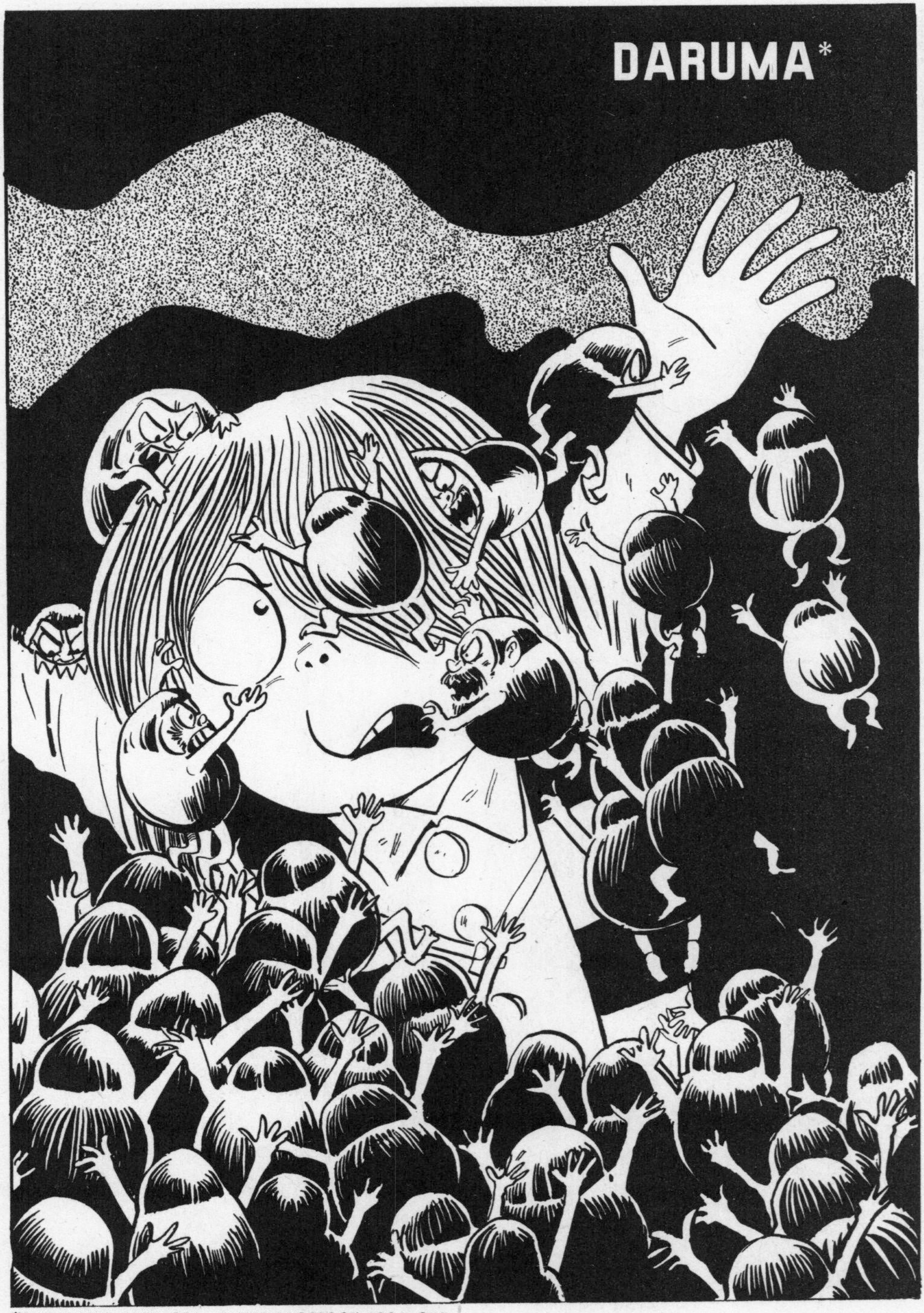
DARUMA*
*SEE NOTES PAGE 386, YOKAI GLOSSARY PAGE 395.

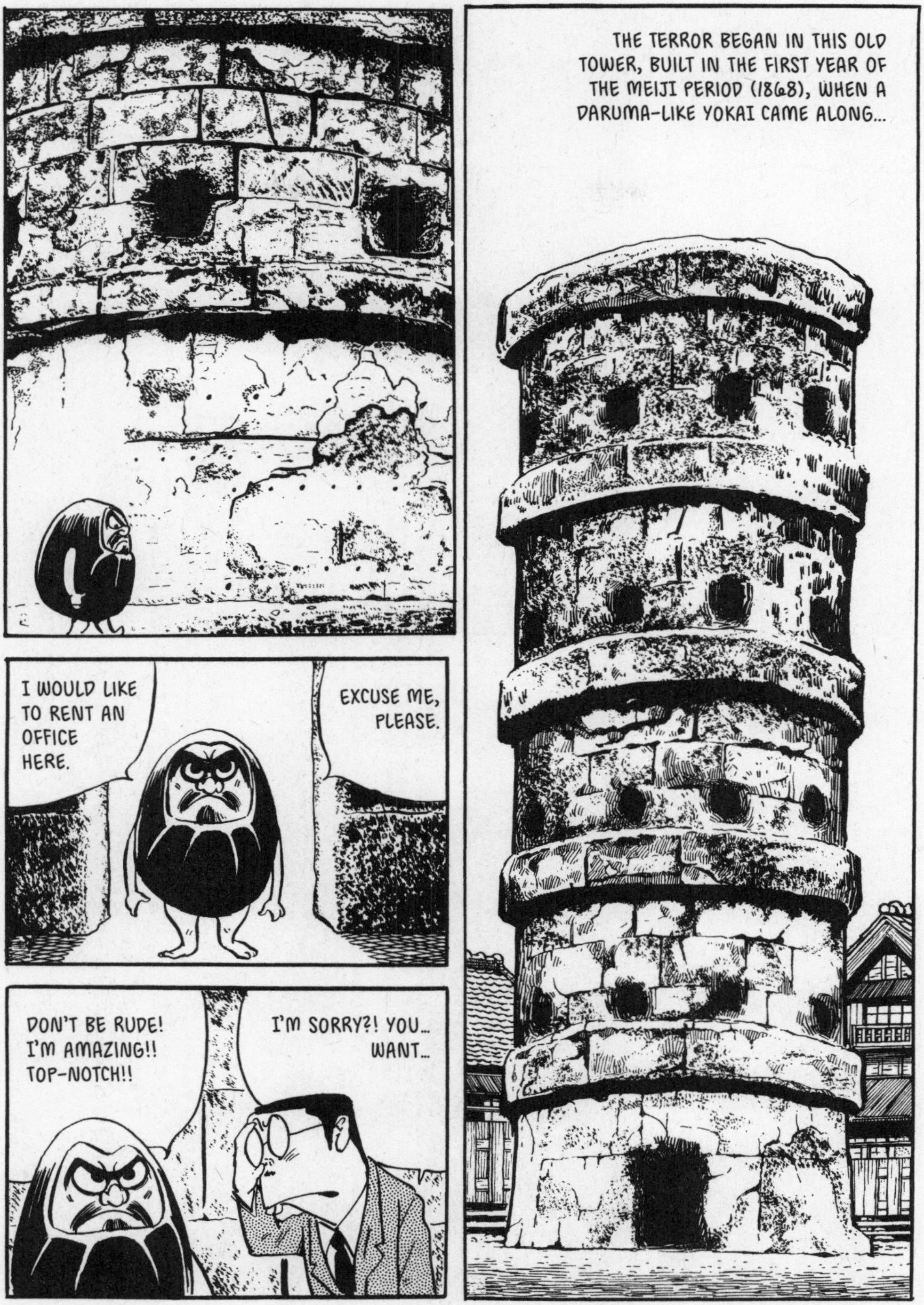
THE TERROR BEGAN IN THIS OLD TOWER, BUILT IN THE FIRST YEAR OF THE MEIJI PERIOD (1868), WHEN A DARUMA-LIKE YOKAI CAME ALONG...
EXCUSE ME, PLEASE.
I WOULD LIKE TO RENT AN OFFICE HERE.
I'M SORRY?! YOU... WANT...
DON'T BE RUDE! I'M AMAZING!! TOP-NOTCH!!

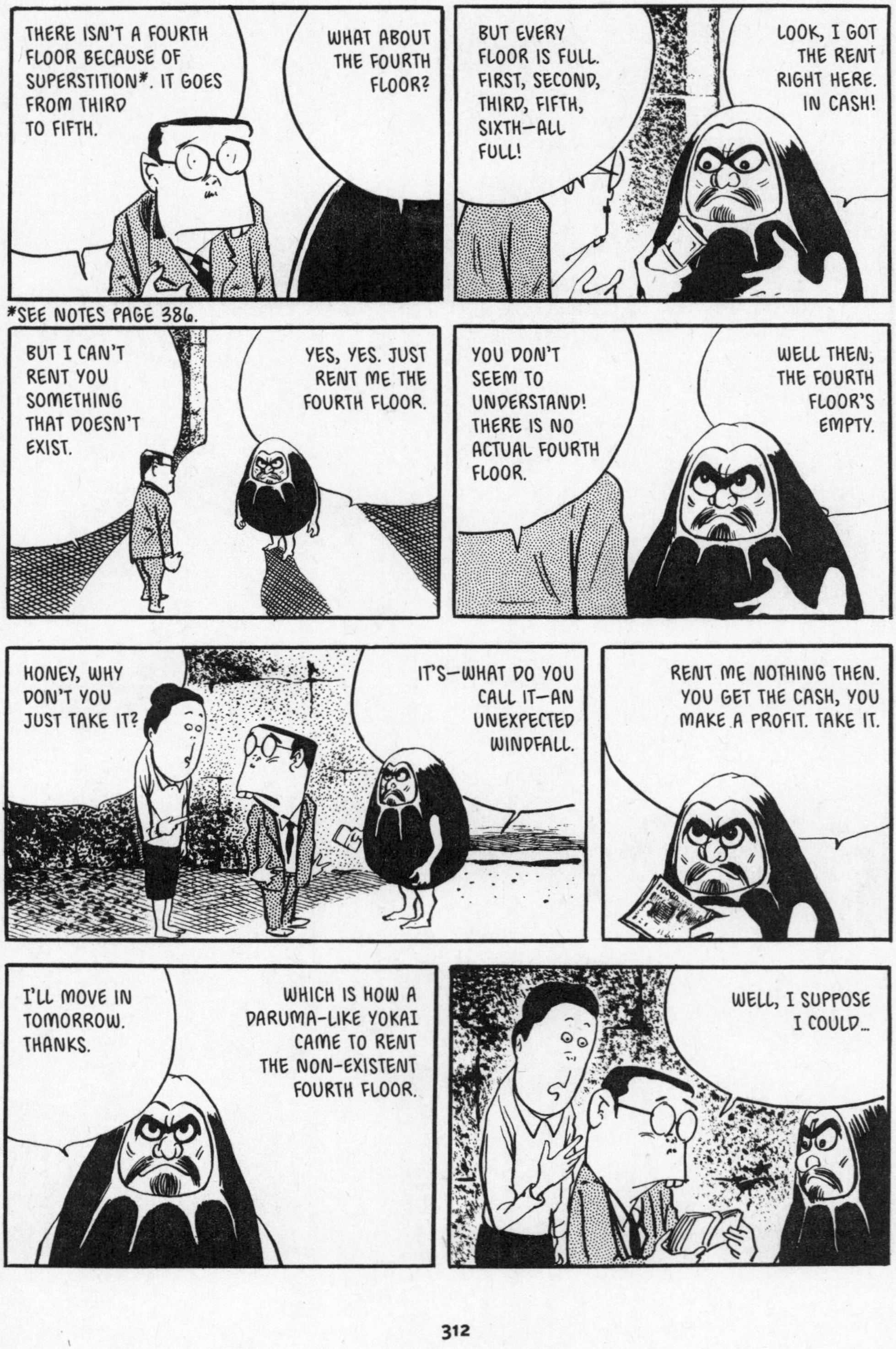
LOOK, I GOT THE RENT RIGHT HERE. IN CASH!
BUT EVERY FLOOR IS FULL. FIRST, SECOND, THIRD, FIFTH, SIXTH—ALL FULL!
WHAT ABOUT THE FOURTH FLOOR?
THERE ISN'T A FOURTH FLOOR BECAUSE OF SUPERSTITION*. IT GOES FROM THIRD TO FIFTH.
WELL THEN, THE FOURTH FLOOR'S EMPTY.
YOU DON'T SEEM TO UNDERSTAND! THERE IS NO ACTUAL FOURTH FLOOR.
YES, YES. JUST RENT ME THE FOURTH FLOOR.
BUT I CAN'T RENT YOU SOMETHING THAT DOESN'T EXIST.
RENT ME NOTHING THEN. YOU GET THE CASH, YOU MAKE A PROFIT. TAKE IT.
IT'S—WHAT DO YOU CALL IT—AN UNEXPECTED WINDFALL.
HONEY, WHY DON'T YOU JUST TAKE IT?
WELL, I SUPPOSE I COULD...
I'LL MOVE IN TOMORROW. THANKS.
WHICH IS HOW A DARUMA-LIKE YOKAI CAME TO RENT THE NON-EXISTENT FOURTH FLOOR.

*SEE NOTES PAGE 386.

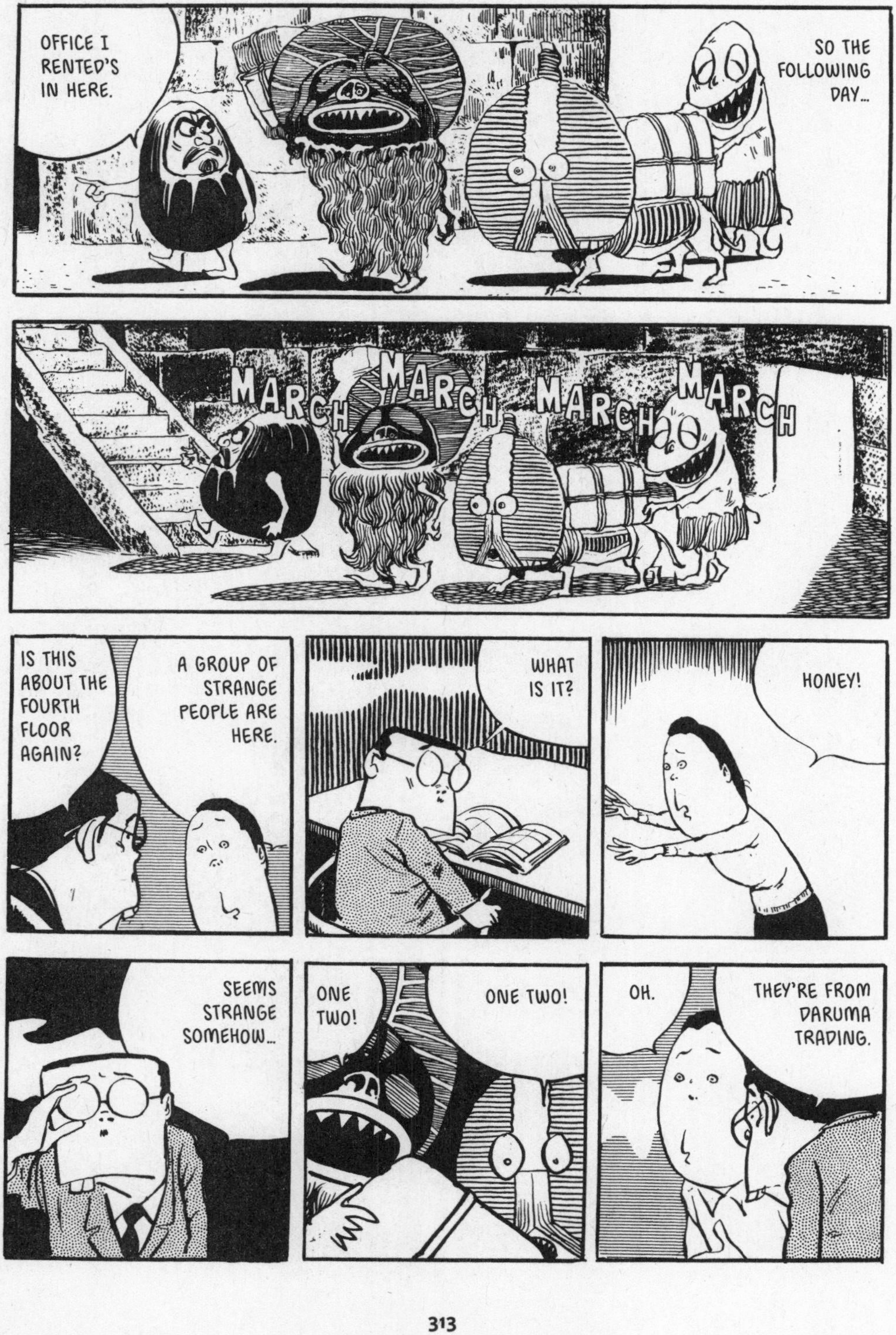
SO THE FOLLOWING DAY...
OFFICE I RENTED'S IN HERE.
MARCH
MARCH
MARCH
MARCH
HONEY!
WHAT IS IT?
A GROUP OF STRANGE PEOPLE ARE HERE.
IS THIS ABOUT THE FOURTH FLOOR AGAIN?
THEY'RE FROM DARUMA TRADING.
OH.
ONE TWO!
ONE TWO!
SEEMS STRANGE SOMEHOW...

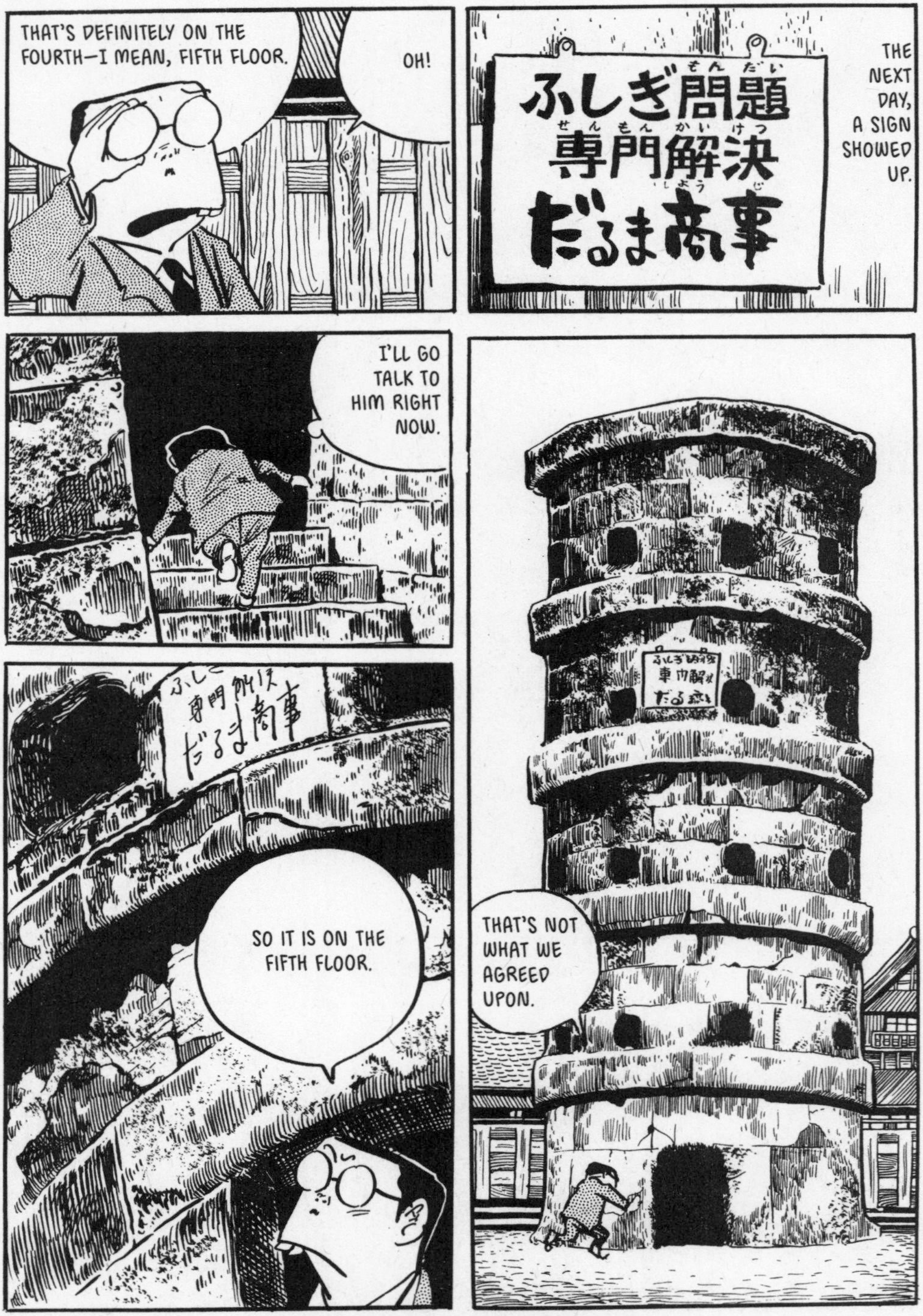
ふしぎ問題
専門解決
だるま商事
THE NEXT DAY, A SIGN SHOWED UP.
OH!
THAT'S DEFINITELY ON THE FOURTH—I MEAN, FIFTH FLOOR.
THAT'S NOT WHAT WE AGREED UPON.
I'LL GO TALK TO HIM RIGHT NOW.
SO IT IS ON THE FIFTH FLOOR.
SIGN: DARUMA TRADING, EXPERT SOLUTIONS TO MYSTERIOUS PROBLEMS.

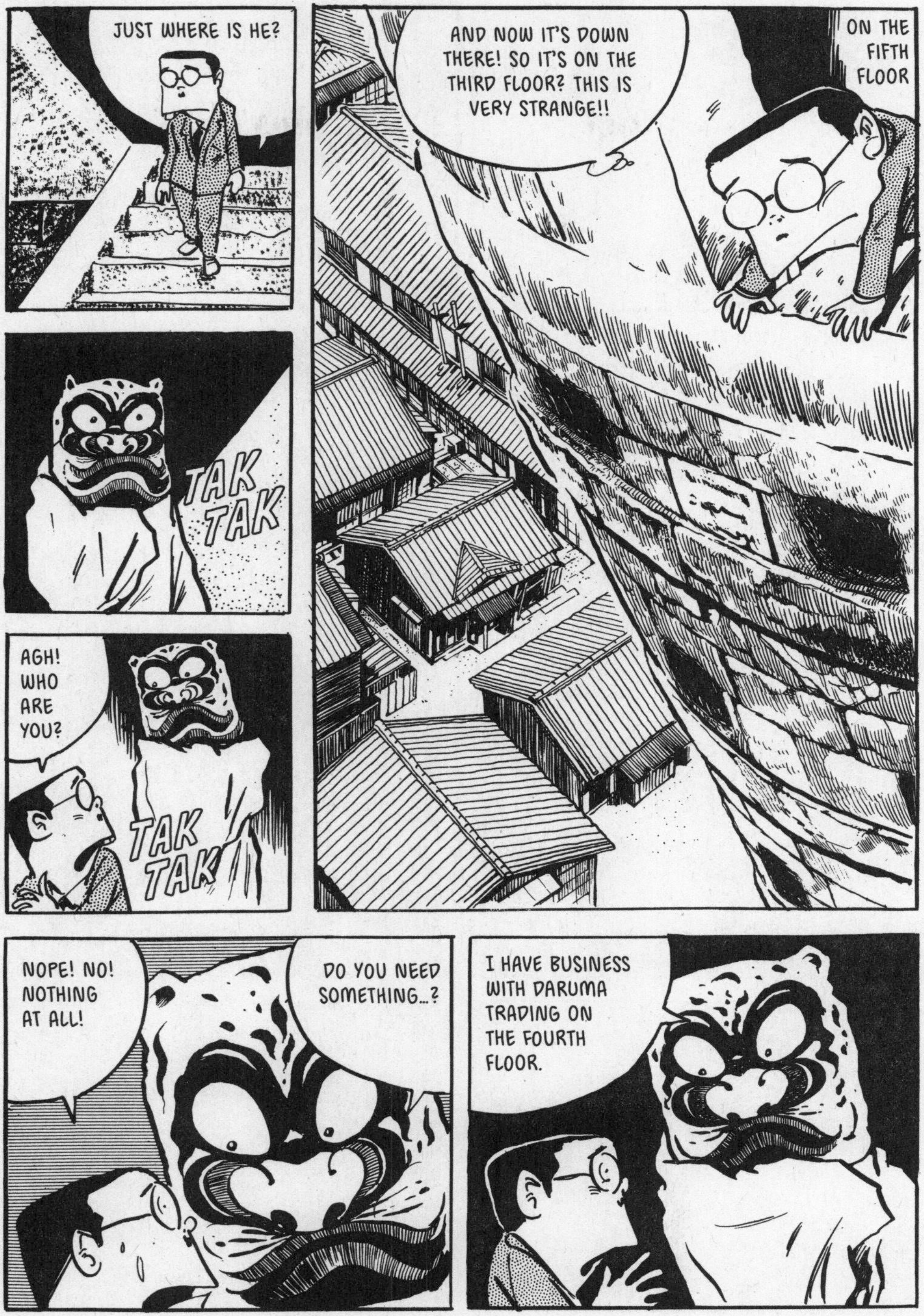
ON THE FIFTH FLOOR
AND NOW IT'S DOWN THERE! SO IT'S ON THE THIRD FLOOR? THIS IS VERY STRANGE!!
JUST WHERE IS HE?
TAK TAK
AGH! WHO ARE YOU?
TAK TAK
I HAVE BUSINESS WITH DARUMA TRADING ON THE FOURTH FLOOR.
DO YOU NEED SOMETHING...?
NOPE! NO! NOTHING AT ALL!

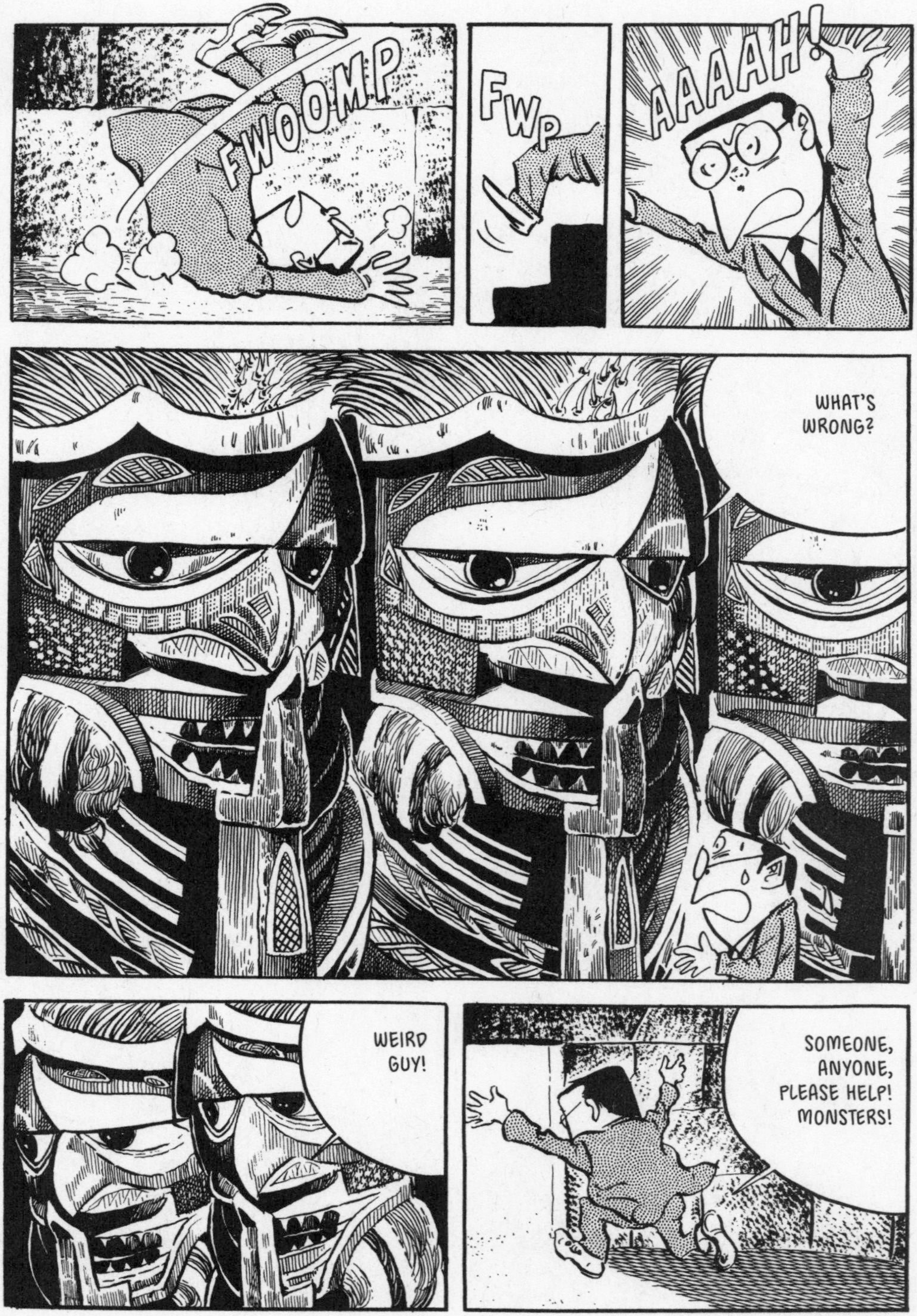
AAAAH!
FWP
FWOOMP
WHAT'S WRONG?
SOMEONE, ANYONE, PLEASE HELP! MONSTERS!
WEIRD GUY!

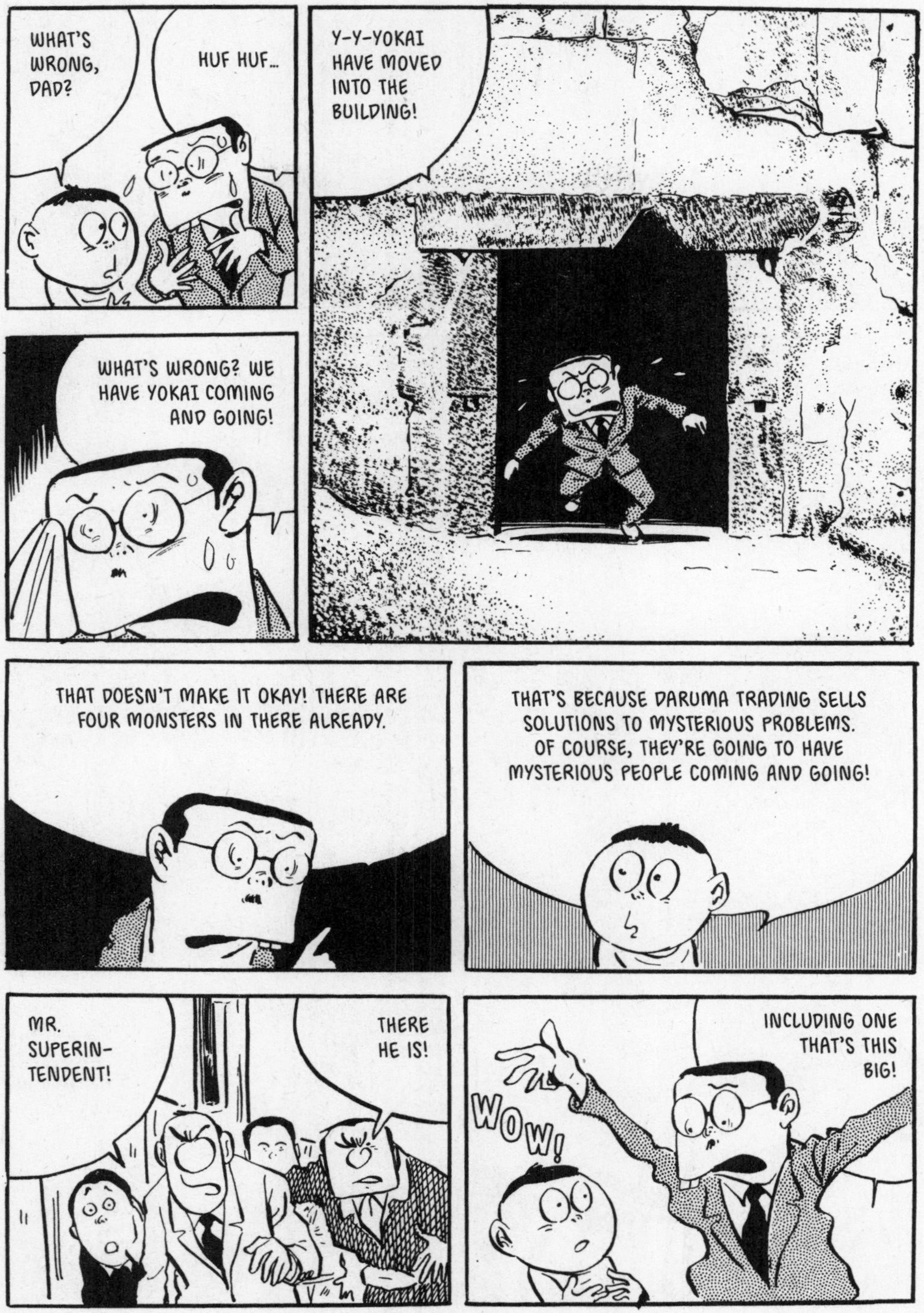
Y-Y-YOKAI HAVE MOVED INTO THE BUILDING!
HUF HUF...
WHAT'S WRONG, DAD?
WHAT'S WRONG? WE HAVE YOKAI COMING AND GOING!
THAT'S BECAUSE DARUMA TRADING SELLS SOLUTIONS TO MYSTERIOUS PROBLEMS. OF COURSE, THEY'RE GOING TO HAVE MYSTERIOUS PEOPLE COMING AND GOING!
THAT DOESN'T MAKE IT OKAY! THERE ARE FOUR MONSTERS IN THERE ALREADY.
INCLUDING ONE THAT'S THIS BIG!
WOW!
THERE HE IS!
MR. SUPERIN-TENDENT!

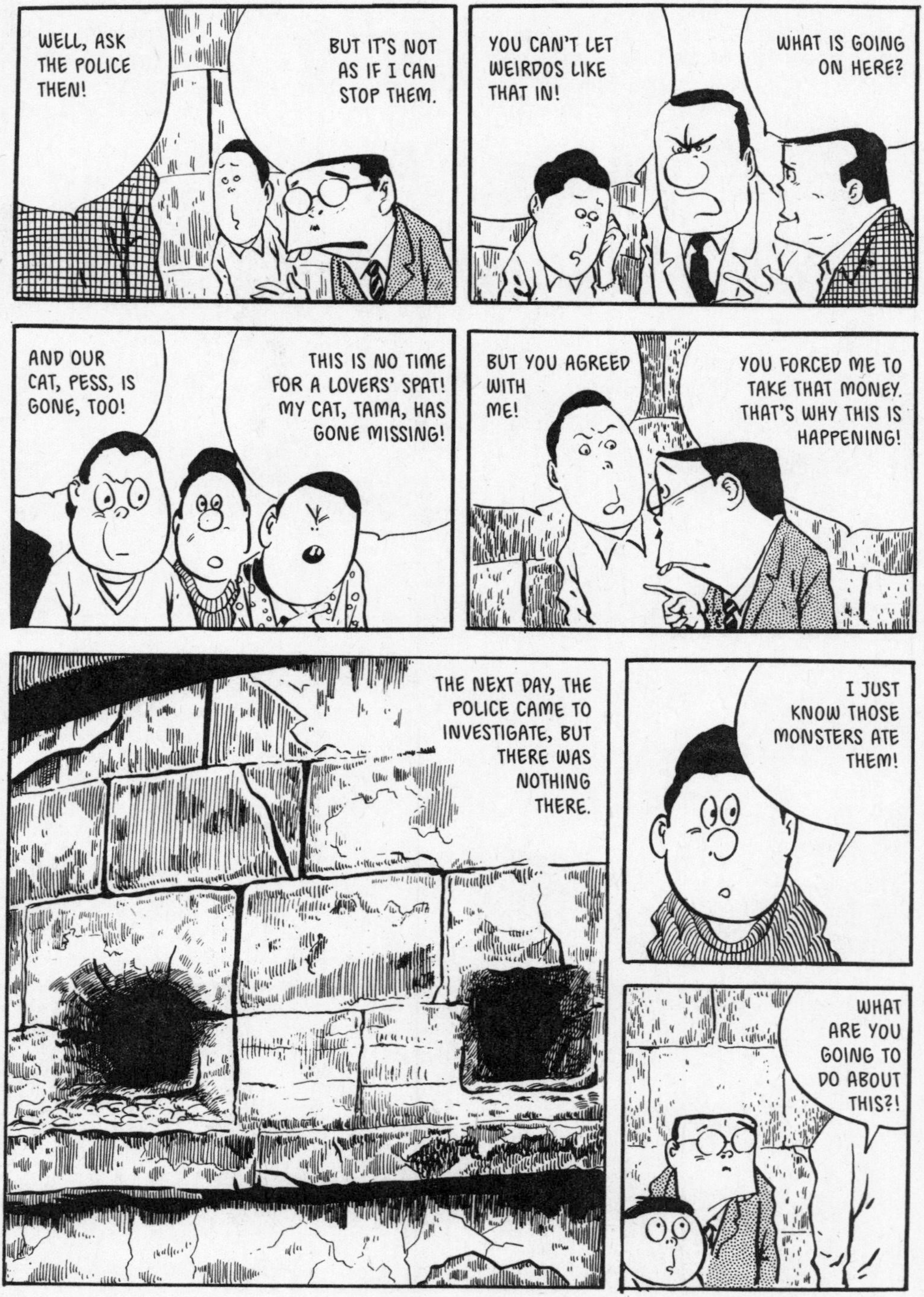
WHAT IS GOING ON HERE?
YOU CAN'T LET WEIRDOS LIKE THAT IN!
BUT IT'S NOT AS IF I CAN STOP THEM.
WELL, ASK THE POLICE THEN!
YOU FORCED ME TO TAKE THAT MONEY. THAT'S WHY THIS IS HAPPENING!
BUT YOU AGREED WITH ME!
THIS IS NO TIME FOR A LOVERS' SPAT! MY CAT, TAMA, HAS GONE MISSING!
AND OUR CAT, PESS, IS GONE, TOO!
I JUST KNOW THOSE MONSTERS ATE THEM!
WHAT ARE YOU GOING TO DO ABOUT THIS?!
THE NEXT DAY, THE POLICE CAME TO INVESTIGATE, BUT THERE WAS NOTHING THERE.

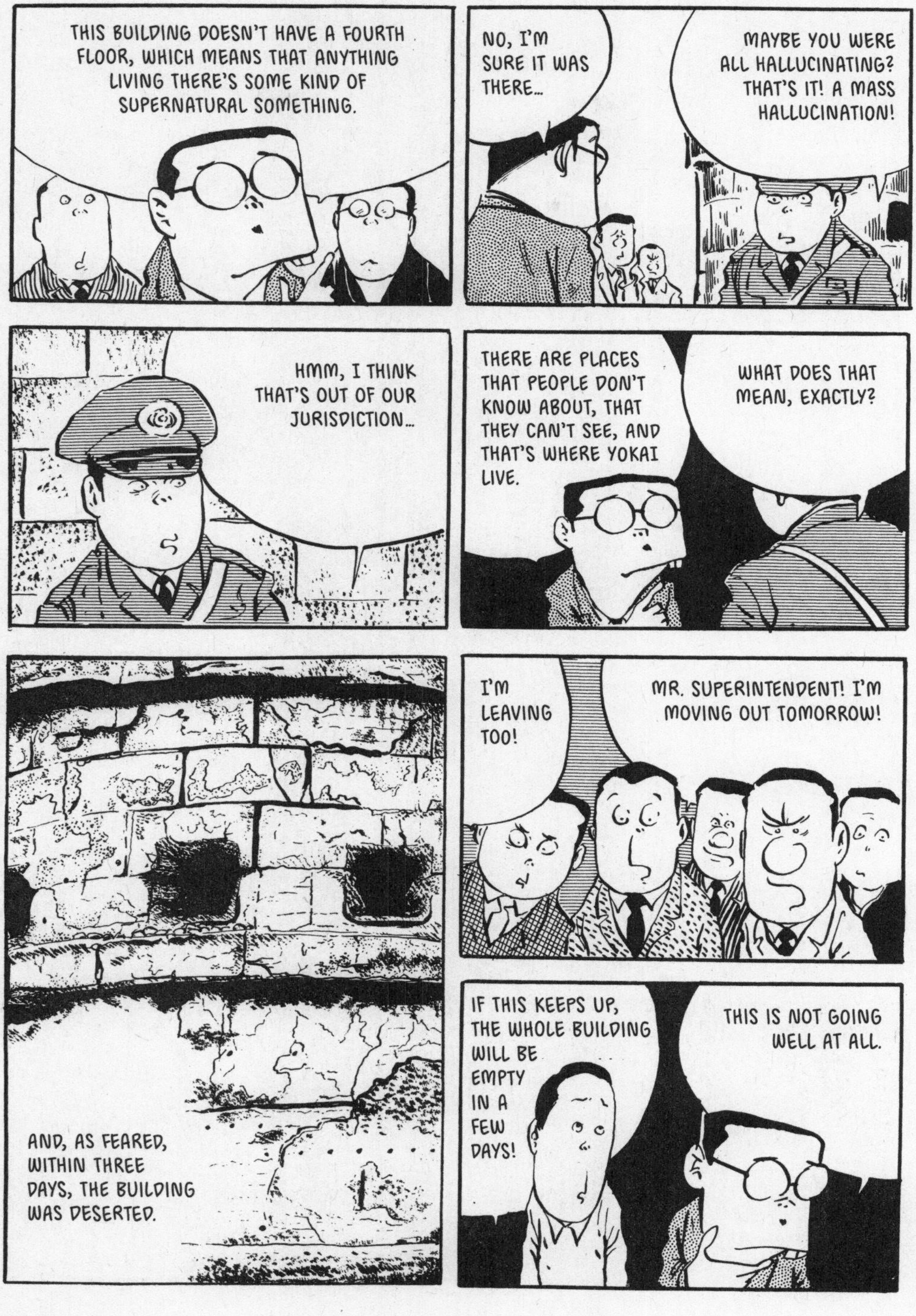
MAYBE YOU WERE ALL HALLUCINATING? THAT'S IT! A MASS HALLUCINATION!
NO, I'M SURE IT WAS THERE...
THIS BUILDING DOESN'T HAVE A FOURTH FLOOR, WHICH MEANS THAT ANYTHING LIVING THERE'S SOME KIND OF SUPERNATURAL SOMETHING.
WHAT DOES THAT MEAN, EXACTLY?
THERE ARE PLACES THAT PEOPLE DON'T KNOW ABOUT, THAT THEY CAN'T SEE, AND THAT'S WHERE YOKAI LIVE.
HMM, I THINK THAT'S OUT OF OUR JURISDICTION...
MR. SUPERINTENDENT! I'M MOVING OUT TOMORROW!
I'M LEAVING TOO!
THIS IS NOT GOING WELL AT ALL.
IF THIS KEEPS UP, THE WHOLE BUILDING WILL BE EMPTY IN A FEW DAYS!
AND, AS FEARED, WITHIN THREE DAYS, THE BUILDING WAS DESERTED.

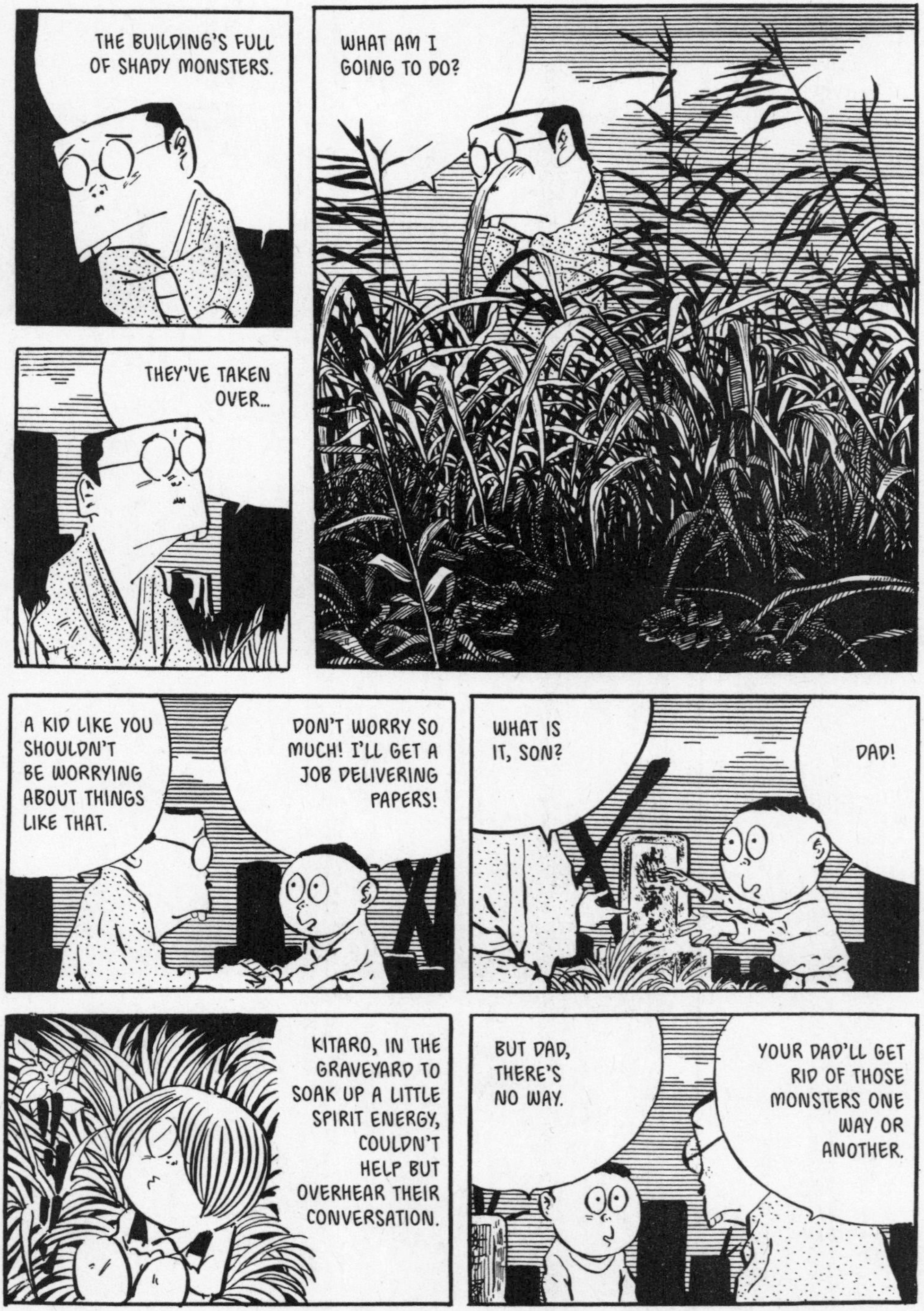
WHAT AM I GOING TO DO?
THE BUILDING'S FULL OF SHADY MONSTERS.
THEY'VE TAKEN OVER...
DAD!
WHAT IS IT, SON?
DON'T WORRY SO MUCH! I'LL GET A JOB DELIVERING PAPERS!
A KID LIKE YOU SHOULDN'T BE WORRYING ABOUT THINGS LIKE THAT.
YOUR DAD'LL GET RID OF THOSE MONSTERS ONE WAY OR ANOTHER.
BUT DAD, THERE'S NO WAY.
KITARO, IN THE GRAVEYARD TO SOAK UP A LITTLE SPIRIT ENERGY, COULDN'T HELP BUT OVERHEAR THEIR CONVERSATION.

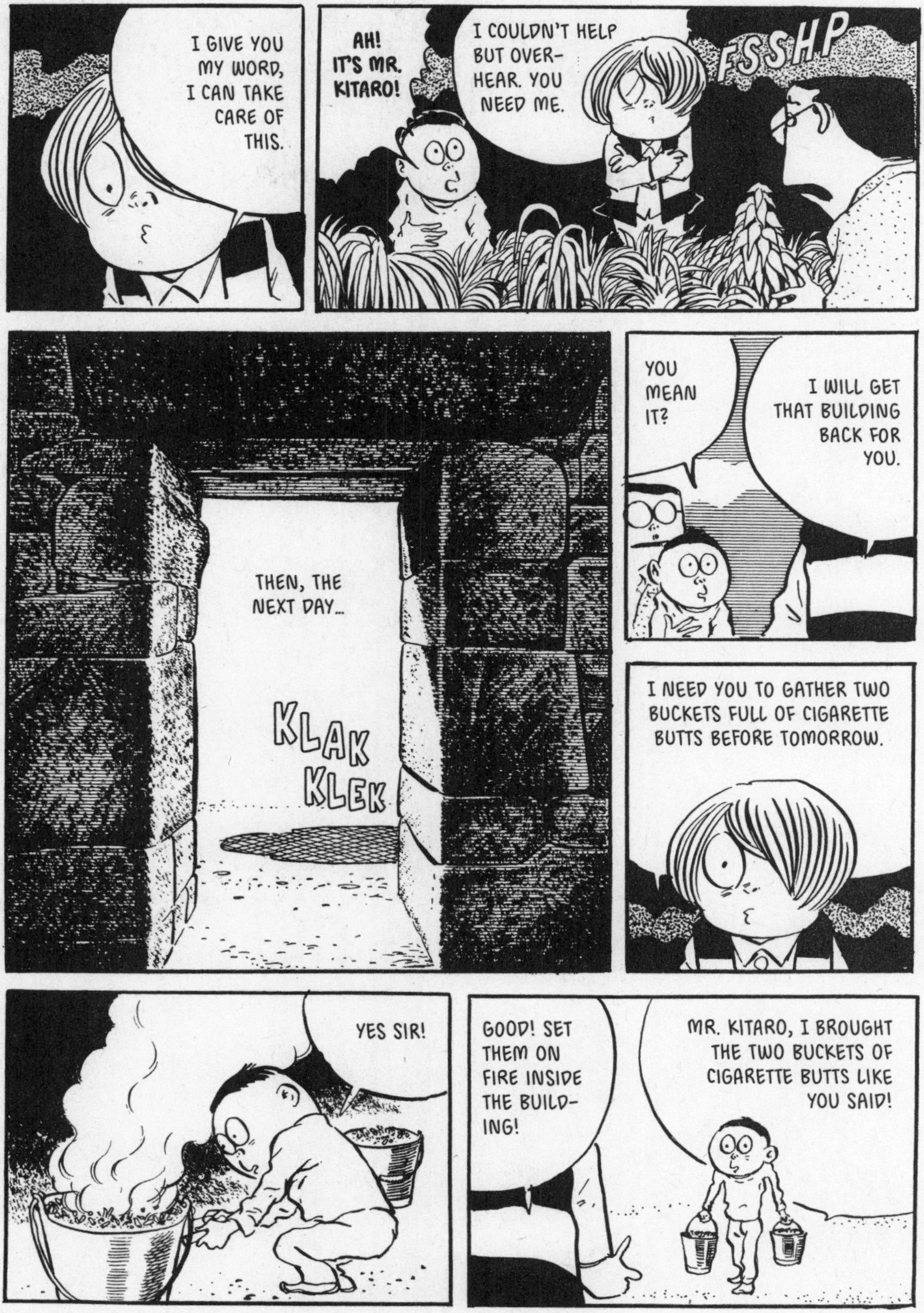
FSSHP
I COULDN'T HELP BUT OVER-HEAR. YOU NEED ME.
AH! IT'S MR. KITARO!
I GIVE YOU MY WORD, I CAN TAKE CARE OF THIS.
I WILL GET THAT BUILDING BACK FOR YOU.
YOU MEAN IT?
I NEED YOU TO GATHER TWO BUCKETS FULL OF CIGARETTE BUTTS BEFORE TOMORROW.
THEN, THE NEXT DAY...
KLAK
KLEK
MR. KITARO, I BROUGHT THE TWO BUCKETS OF CIGARETTE BUTTS LIKE YOU SAID!
GOOD! SET THEM ON FIRE INSIDE THE BUILD-ING!
YES SIR!

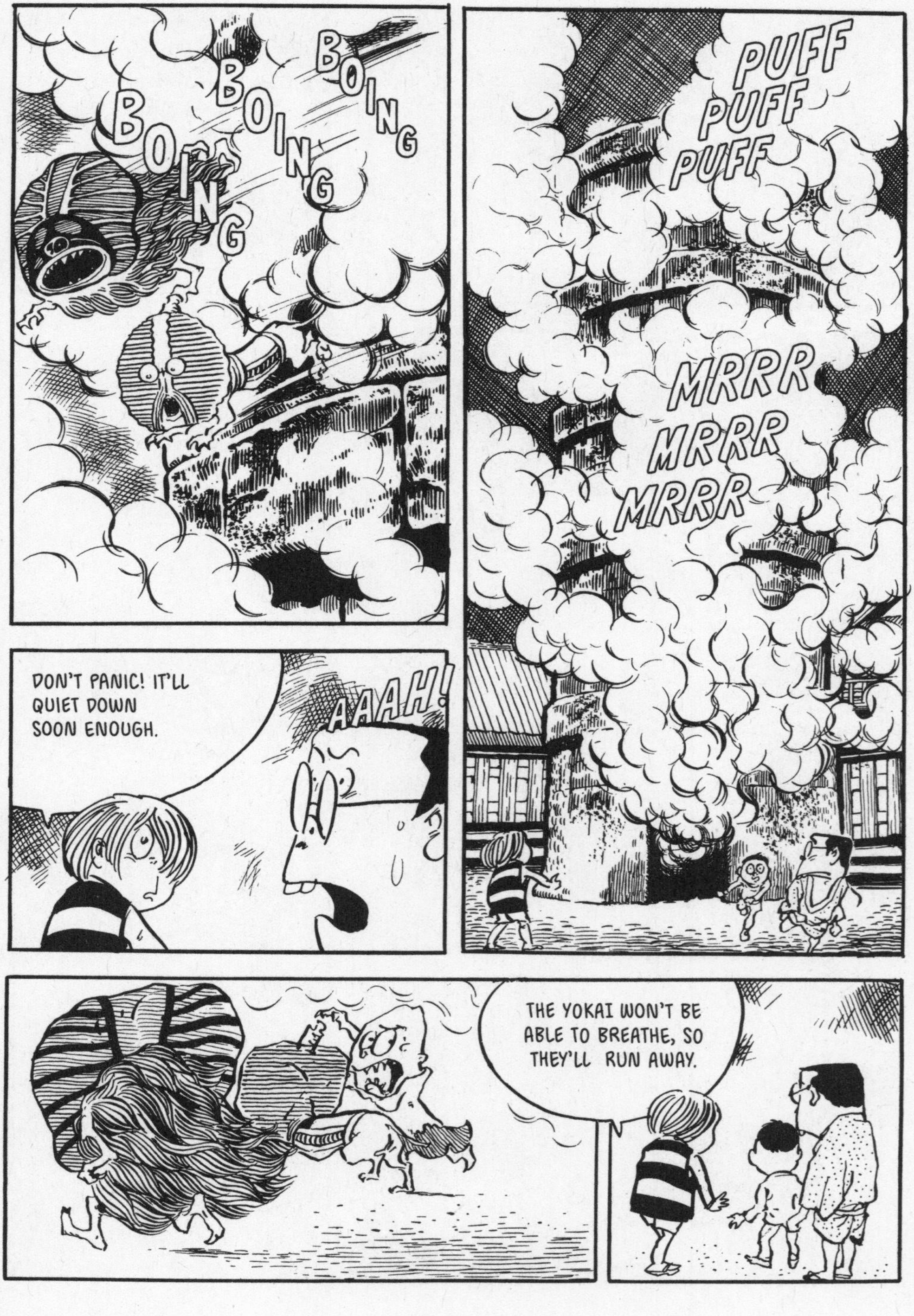
PUFF PUFF PUFF
MRRR MRRR MRRR
BOING BOING BOING
DON'T PANIC! IT'LL QUIET DOWN SOON ENOUGH.
AAAH!
THE YOKAI WON'T BE ABLE TO BREATHE, SO THEY'LL RUN AWAY.

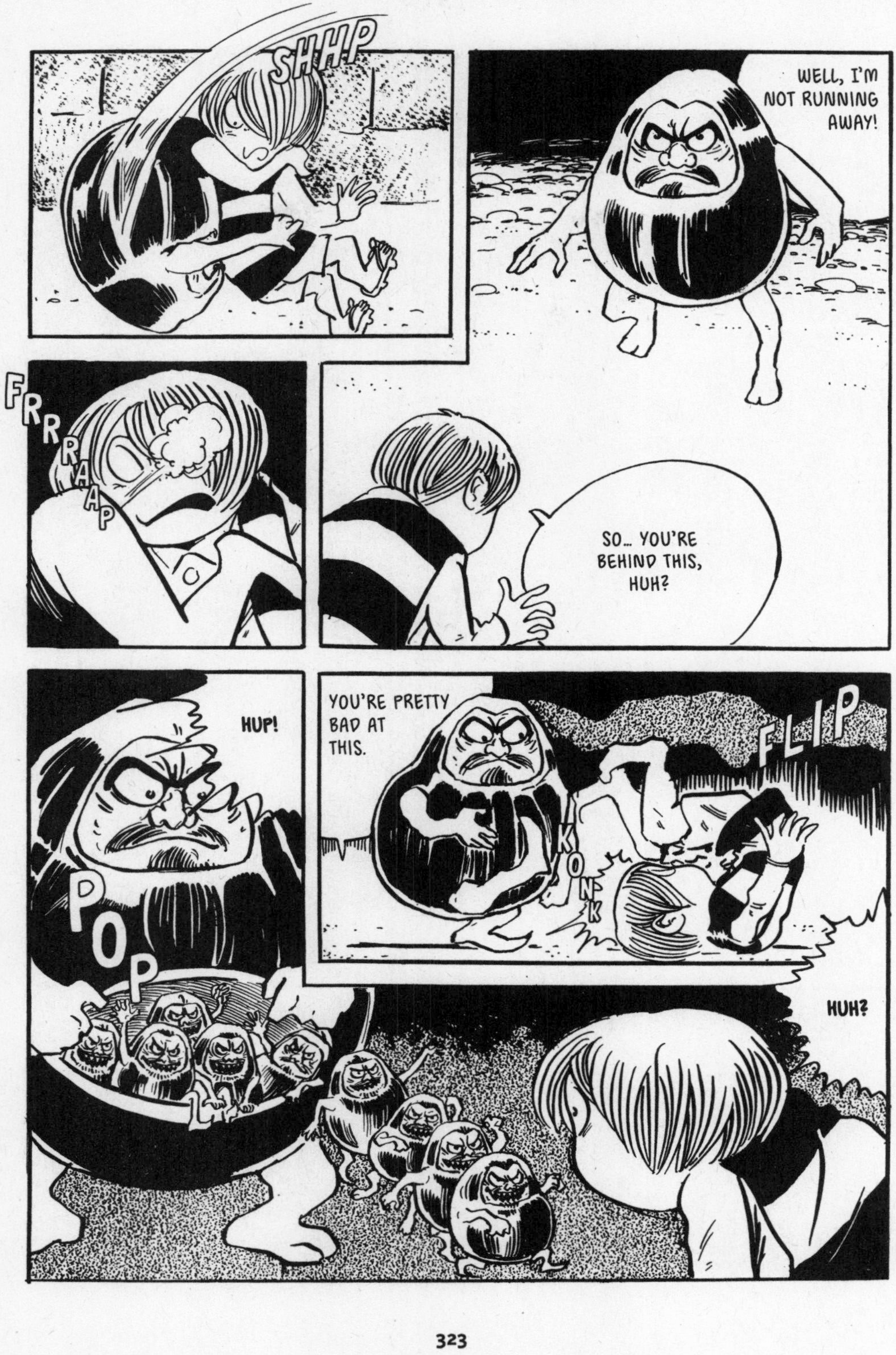
WELL, I'M NOT RUNNING AWAY!
SHHP
SO... YOU'RE BEHIND THIS, HUH?
FRRRRAAP
FLIP
YOU'RE PRETTY BAD AT THIS.
KONK
HUP!
POP
HUH?

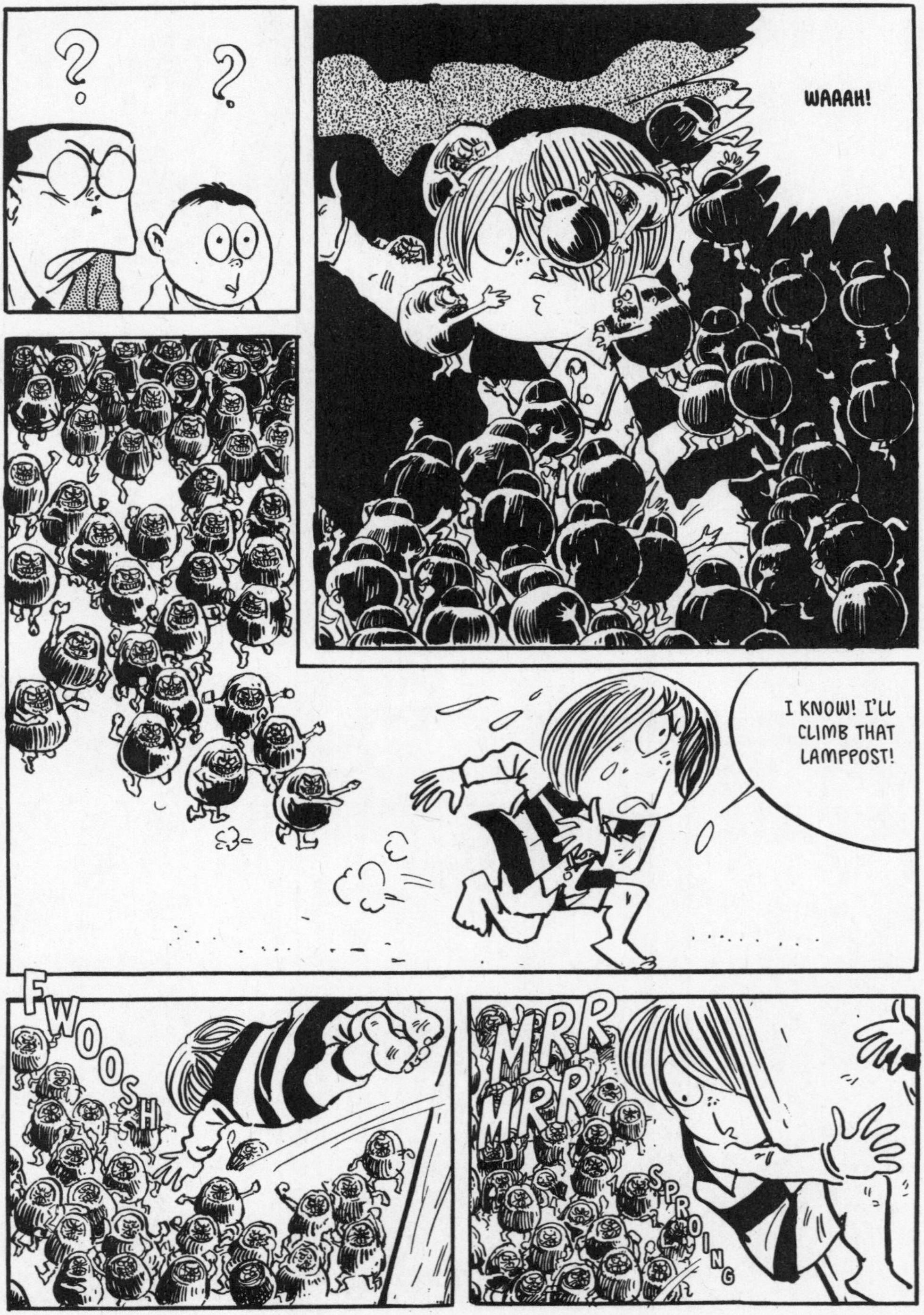
WAAAH!
?
?
I KNOW! I'LL CLIMB THAT LAMPPOST!
MRR
MRR
SPROING
FWOOSH

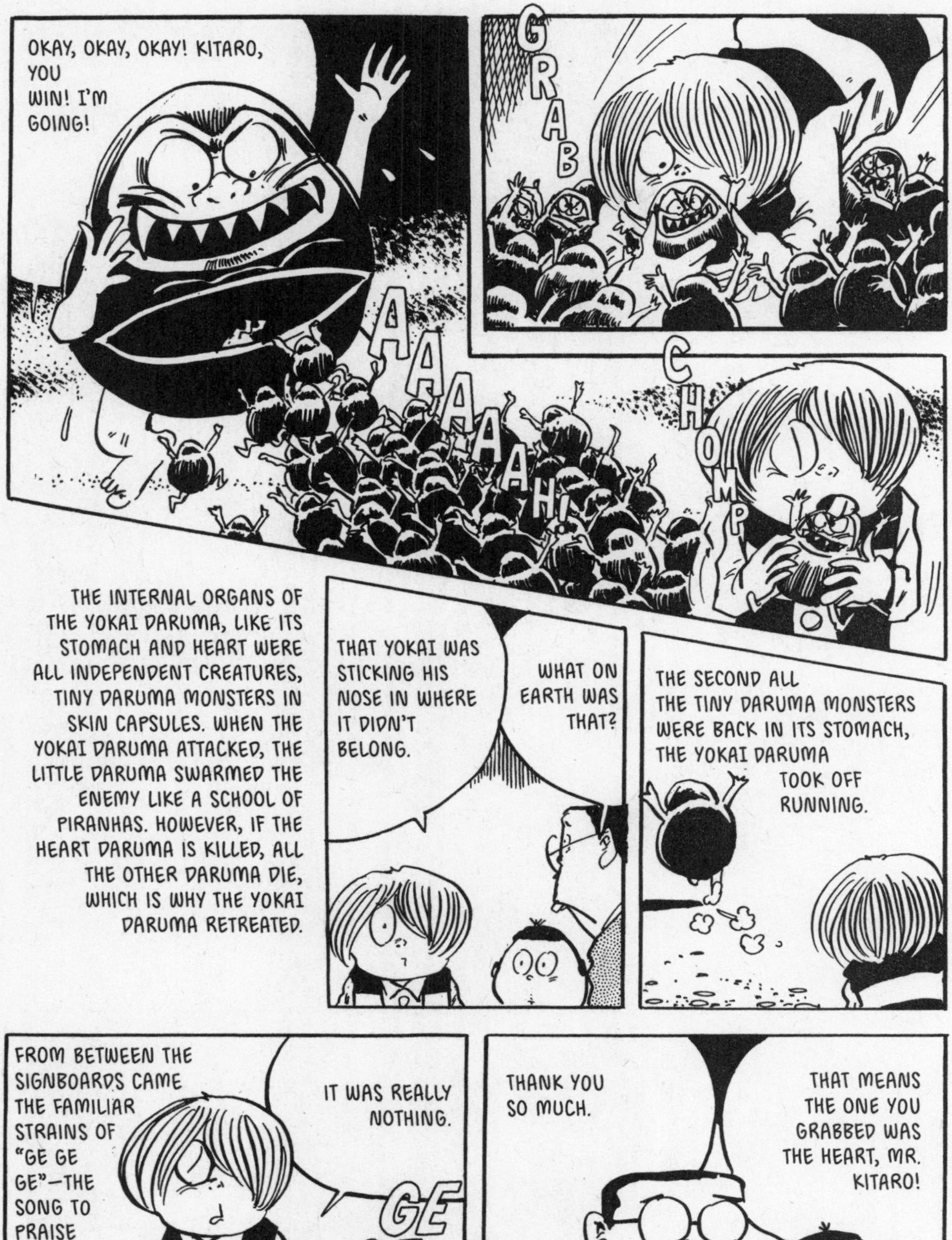
GRAB
OKAY, OKAY, OKAY! KITARO, YOU WIN! I'M GOING!
AAAAAAAH!
CHOMP
THE SECOND ALL THE TINY DARUMA MONSTERS WERE BACK IN ITS STOMACH, THE YOKAI DARUMA TOOK OFF RUNNING.
WHAT ON EARTH WAS THAT?
THAT YOKAI WAS STICKING HIS NOSE IN WHERE IT DIDN'T BELONG.
THE INTERNAL ORGANS OF THE YOKAI DARUMA, LIKE ITS STOMACH AND HEART WERE ALL INDEPENDENT CREATURES, TINY DARUMA MONSTERS IN SKIN CAPSULES. WHEN THE YOKAI DARUMA ATTACKED, THE LITTLE DARUMA SWARMED THE ENEMY LIKE A SCHOOL OF PIRANHAS. HOWEVER, IF THE HEART DARUMA IS KILLED, ALL THE OTHER DARUMA DIE, WHICH IS WHY THE YOKAI DARUMA RETREATED.
THAT MEANS THE ONE YOU GRABBED WAS THE HEART, MR. KITARO!
THANK YOU SO MUCH.
IT WAS REALLY NOTHING.
FROM BETWEEN THE SIGNBOARDS CAME THE FAMILIAR STRAINS OF "GE GE GE"—THE SONG TO PRAISE KITARO.
GE GE GE GE GE

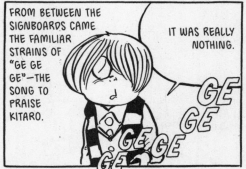

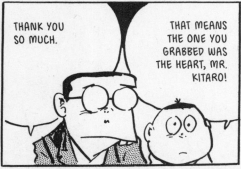

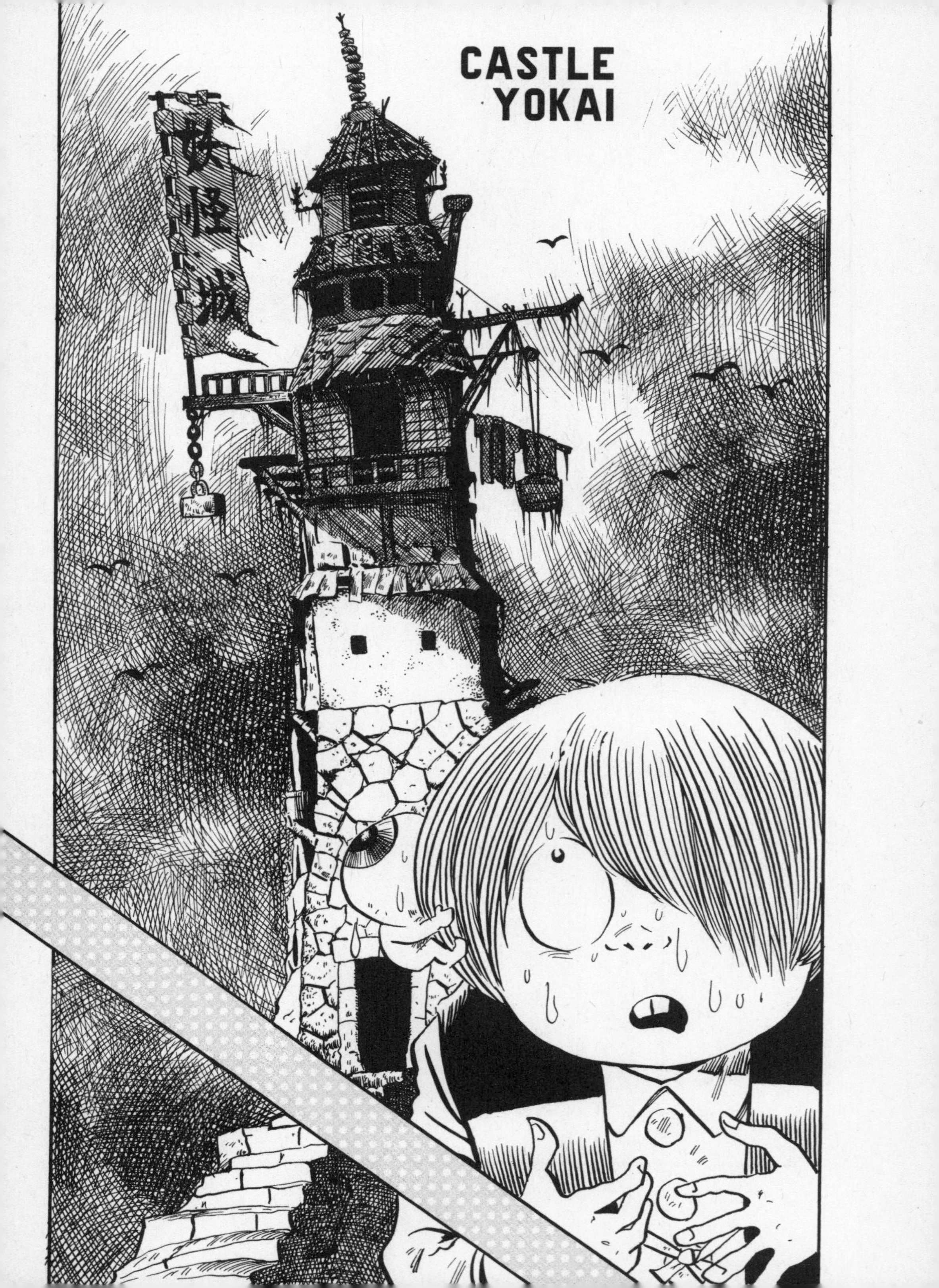
CASTLE YOKAI
妖怪城

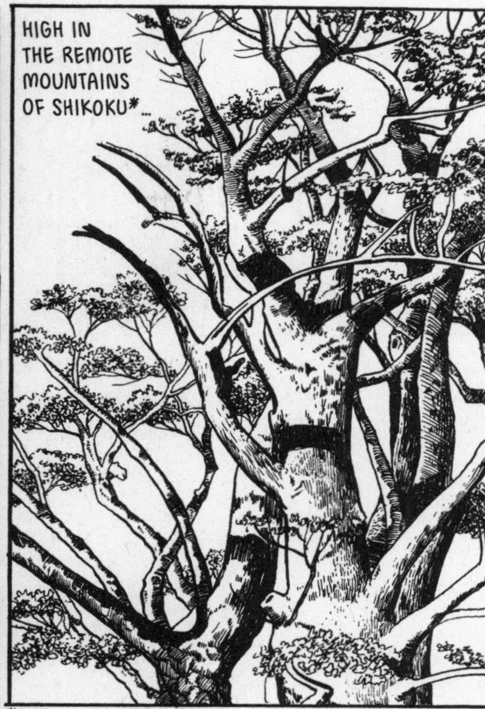
HIGH IN THE REMOTE MOUNTAINS OF SHIKOKU*...

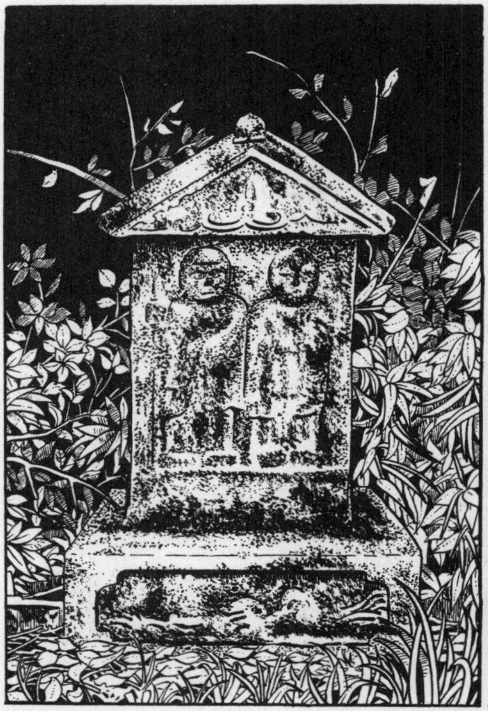

*SEE NOTES PAGE 386.

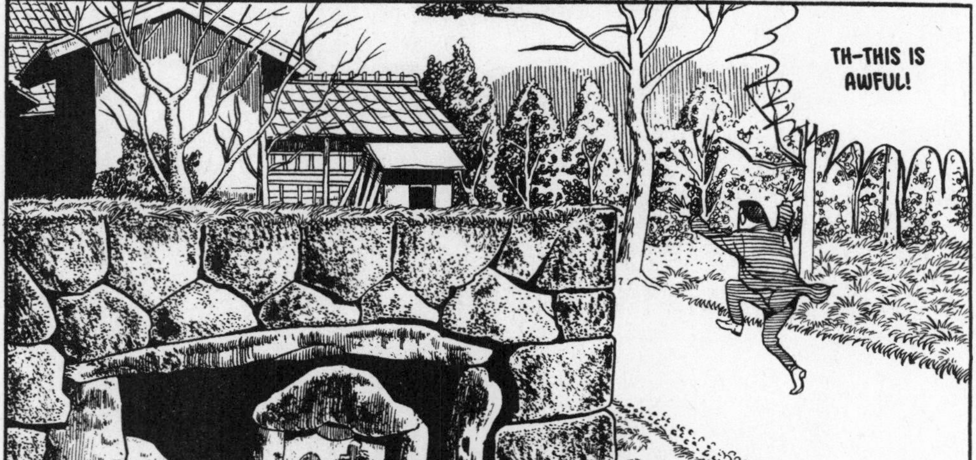
TH-THIS IS AWFUL!

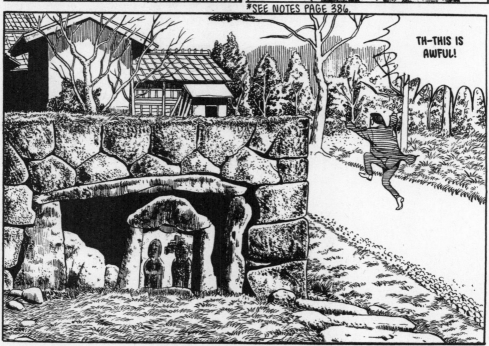

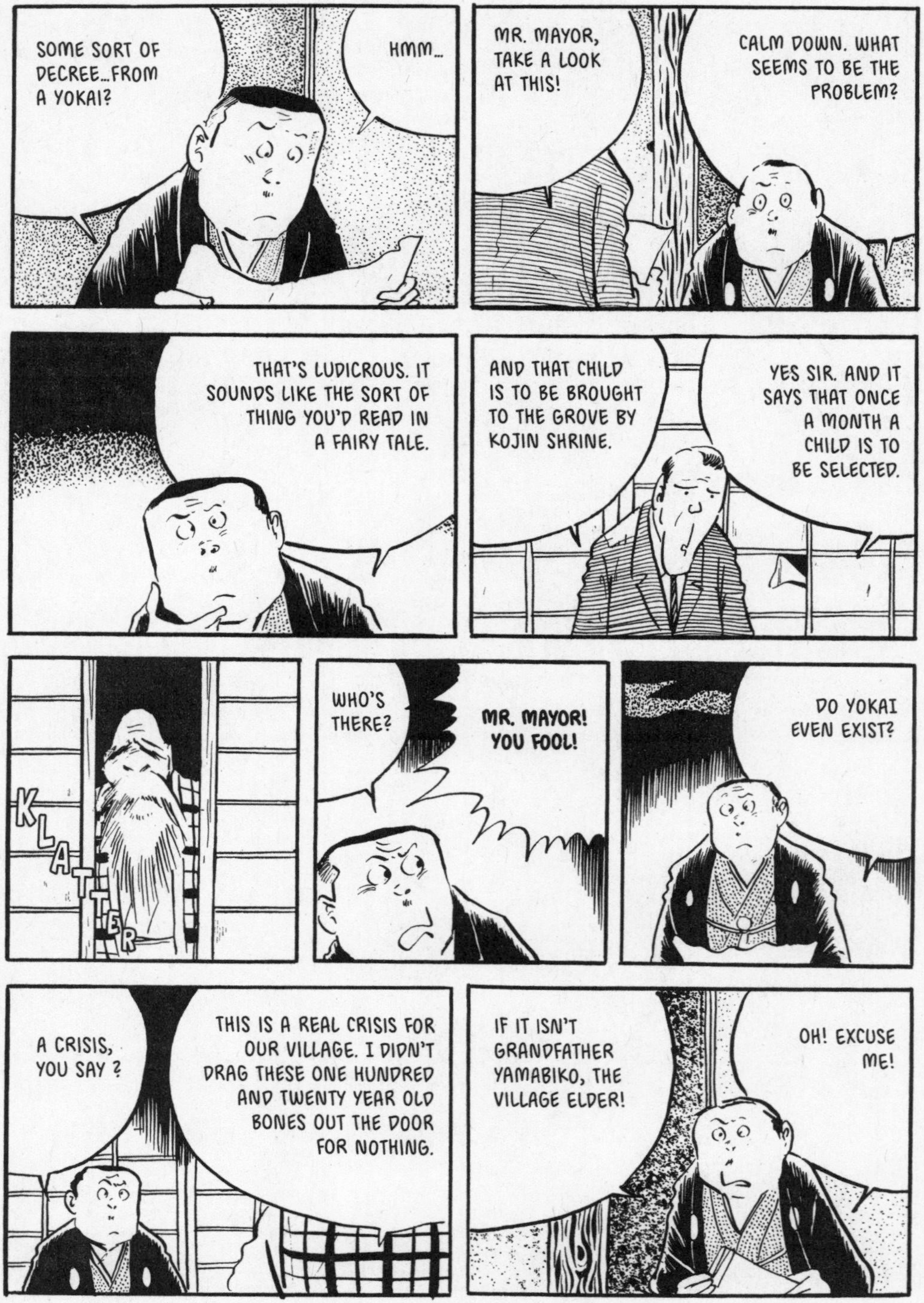
CALM DOWN. WHAT SEEMS TO BE THE PROBLEM?
MR. MAYOR, TAKE A LOOK AT THIS!
HMM...
SOME SORT OF DECREE...FROM A YOKAI?
YES SIR. AND IT SAYS THAT ONCE A MONTH A CHILD IS TO BE SELECTED.
AND THAT CHILD IS TO BE BROUGHT TO THE GROVE BY KOJIN SHRINE.
THAT'S LUDICROUS. IT SOUNDS LIKE THE SORT OF THING YOU'D READ IN A FAIRY TALE.
DO YOKAI EVEN EXIST?
MR. MAYOR! YOU FOOL!
WHO'S THERE?
KLATTER
OH! EXCUSE ME!
IF IT ISN'T GRANDFATHER YAMABIKO, THE VILLAGE ELDER!
THIS IS A REAL CRISIS FOR OUR VILLAGE. I DIDN'T DRAG THESE ONE HUNDRED AND TWENTY YEAR OLD BONES OUT THE DOOR FOR NOTHING.
A CRISIS, YOU SAY?

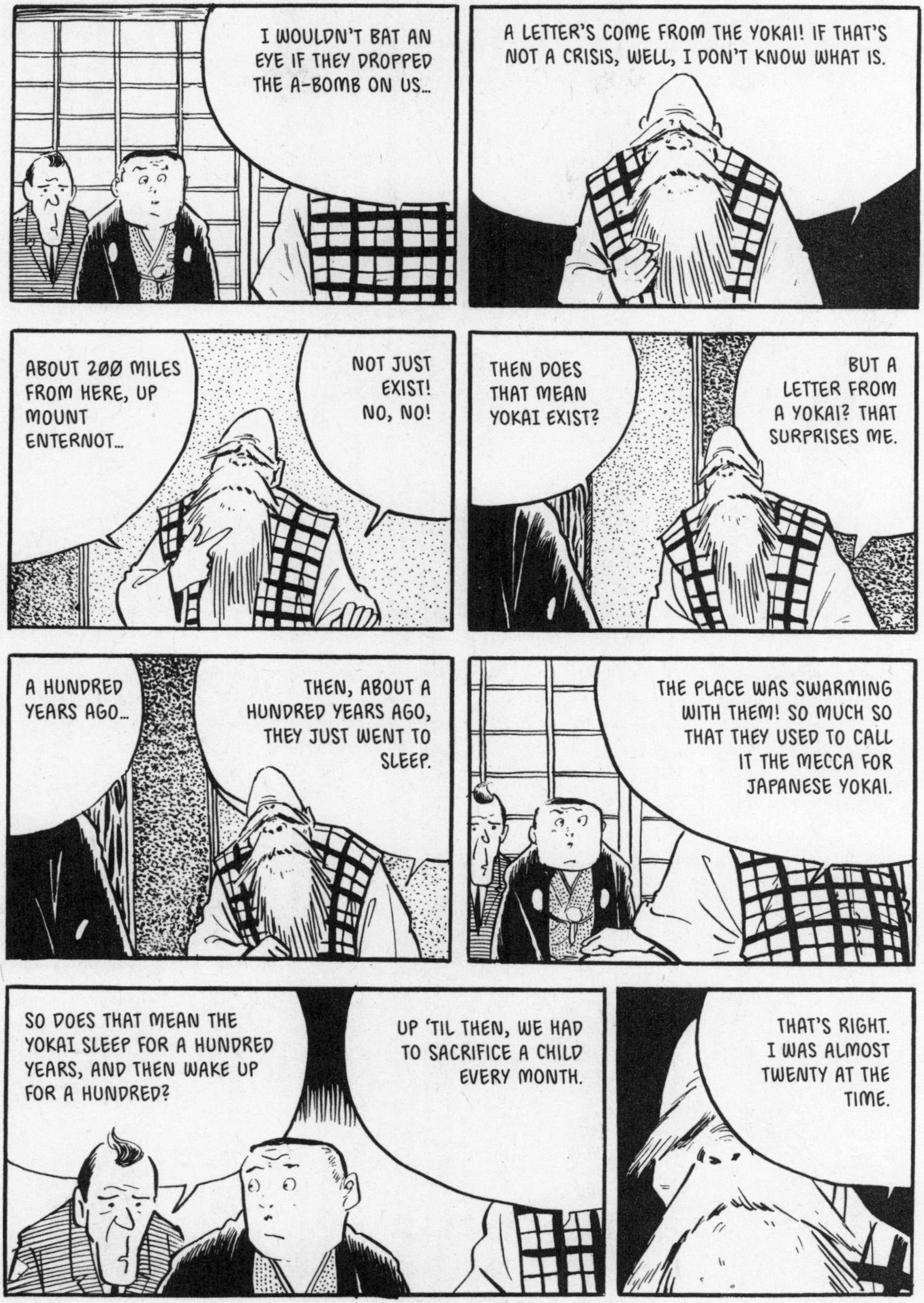
A LETTER'S COME FROM THE YOKAI! IF THAT'S NOT A CRISIS, WELL, I DON'T KNOW WHAT IS.
I WOULDN'T BAT AN EYE IF THEY DROPPED THE A-BOMB ON US...
BUT A LETTER FROM A YOKAI? THAT SURPRISES ME.
THEN DOES THAT MEAN YOKAI EXIST?
NOT JUST EXIST! NO, NO!
ABOUT 200 MILES FROM HERE, UP MOUNT ENTERNOT...
THE PLACE WAS SWARMING WITH THEM! SO MUCH SO THAT THEY USED TO CALL IT THE MECCA FOR JAPANESE YOKAI.
THEN, ABOUT A HUNDRED YEARS AGO, THEY JUST WENT TO SLEEP.
A HUNDRED YEARS AGO...
THAT'S RIGHT. I WAS ALMOST TWENTY AT THE TIME.
UP 'TIL THEN, WE HAD TO SACRIFICE A CHILD EVERY MONTH.
SO DOES THAT MEAN THE YOKAI SLEEP FOR A HUNDRED YEARS, AND THEN WAKE UP FOR A HUNDRED?

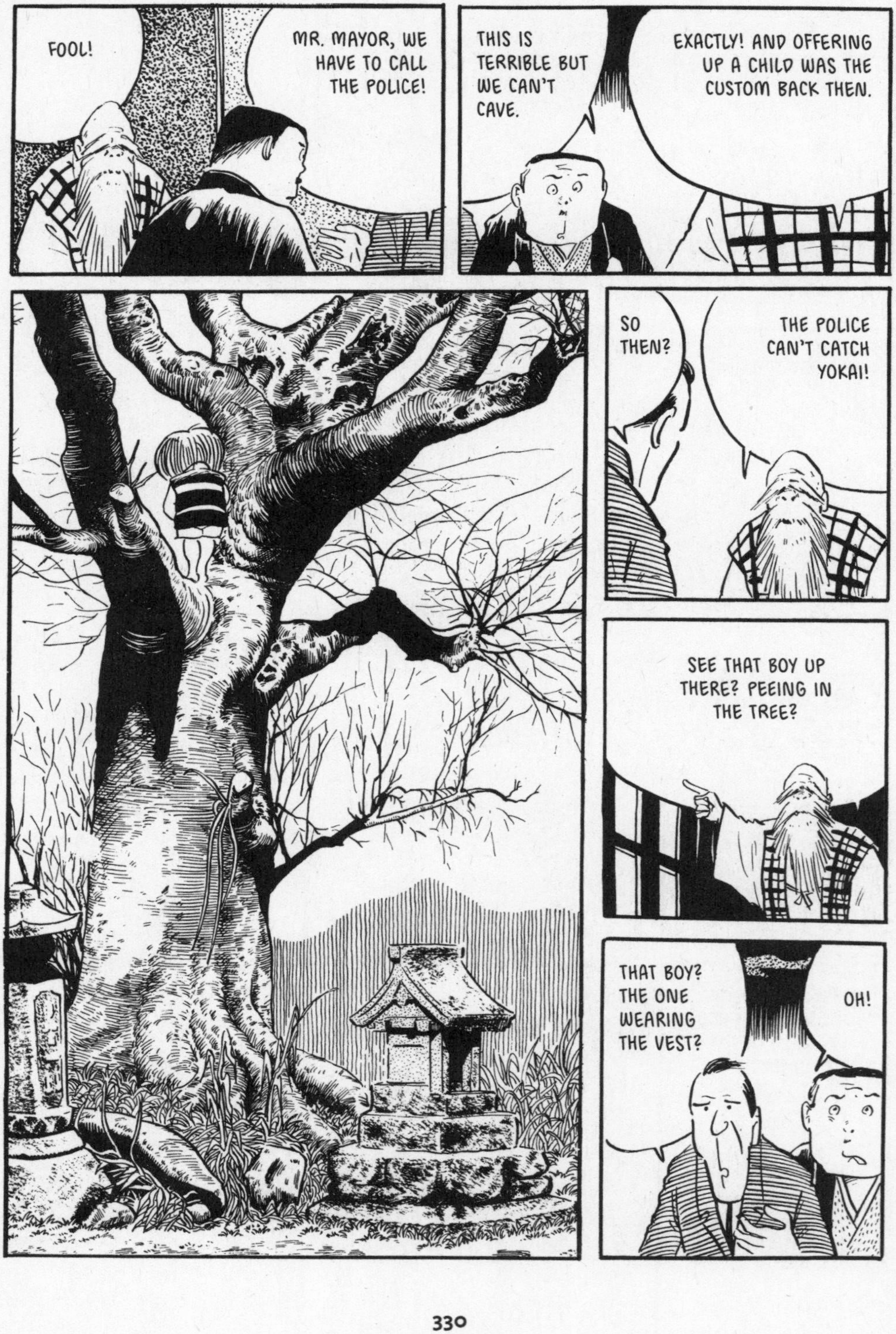
EXACTLY! AND OFFERING UP A CHILD WAS THE CUSTOM BACK THEN.
THIS IS TERRIBLE BUT WE CAN'T CAVE.
MR. MAYOR, WE HAVE TO CALL THE POLICE!
FOOL!
THE POLICE CAN'T CATCH YOKAI!
SO THEN?
SEE THAT BOY UP THERE? PEEING IN THE TREE?
OH!
THAT BOY? THE ONE WEARING THE VEST?

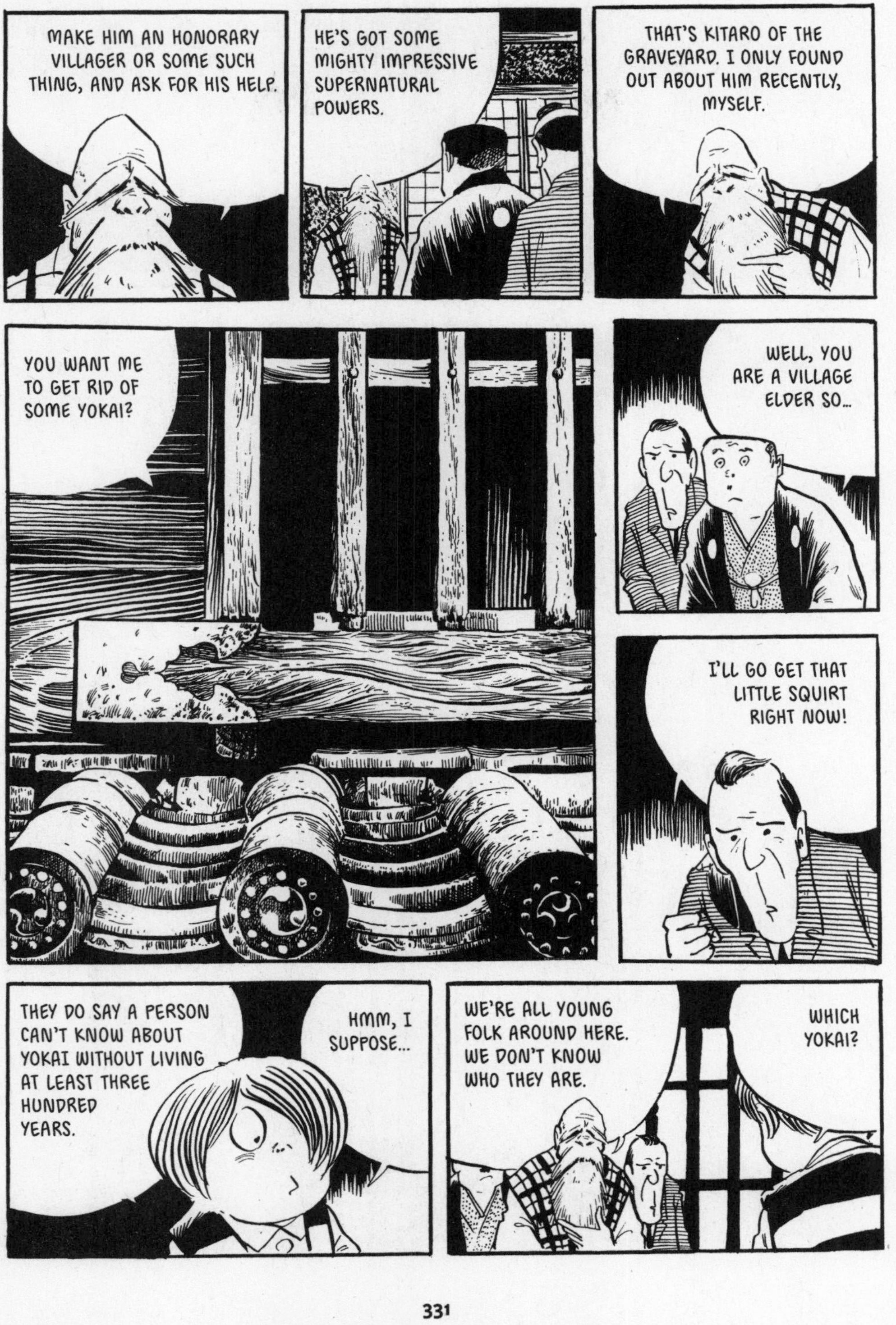
THAT'S KITARO OF THE GRAVEYARD. I ONLY FOUND OUT ABOUT HIM RECENTLY, MYSELF.
HE'S GOT SOME MIGHTY IMPRESSIVE SUPERNATURAL POWERS.
MAKE HIM AN HONORARY VILLAGER OR SOME SUCH THING, AND ASK FOR HIS HELP.
WELL, YOU ARE A VILLAGE ELDER SO...
I'LL GO GET THAT LITTLE SQUIRT RIGHT NOW!
YOU WANT ME TO GET RID OF SOME YOKAI?
WHICH YOKAI?
WE'RE ALL YOUNG FOLK AROUND HERE. WE DON'T KNOW WHO THEY ARE.
HMM, I SUPPOSE...
THEY DO SAY A PERSON CAN'T KNOW ABOUT YOKAI WITHOUT LIVING AT LEAST THREE HUNDRED YEARS.

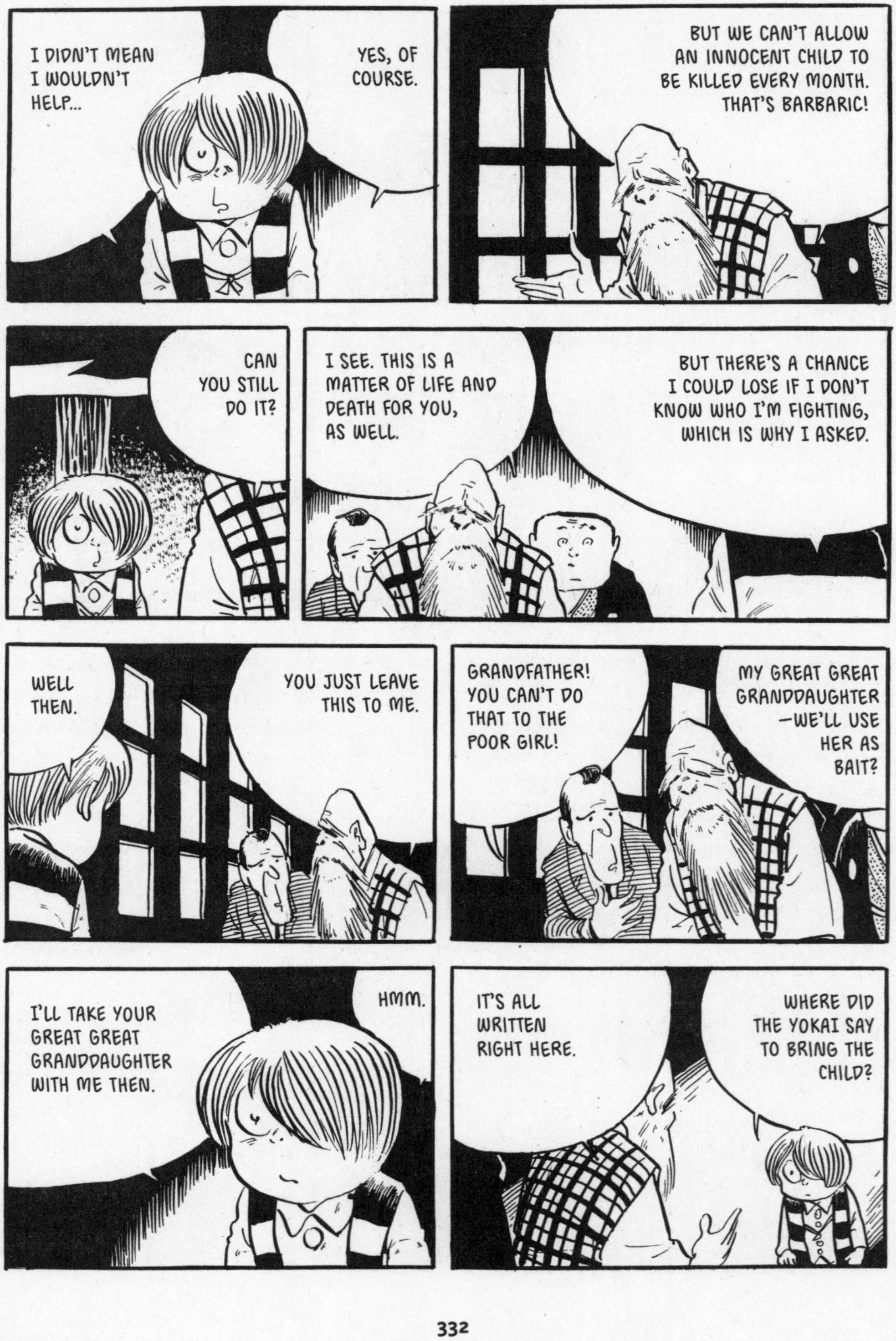
BUT WE CAN'T ALLOW AN INNOCENT CHILD TO BE KILLED EVERY MONTH. THAT'S BARBARIC!
YES, OF COURSE.
I DIDN'T MEAN I WOULDN'T HELP...
BUT THERE'S A CHANCE I COULD LOSE IF I DON'T KNOW WHO I'M FIGHTING, WHICH IS WHY I ASKED.
I SEE. THIS IS A MATTER OF LIFE AND DEATH FOR YOU, AS WELL.
CAN YOU STILL DO IT?
MY GREAT GREAT GRANDDAUGHTER —WE'LL USE HER AS BAIT?
GRANDFATHER! YOU CAN'T DO THAT TO THE POOR GIRL!
YOU JUST LEAVE THIS TO ME.
WELL THEN.
WHERE DID THE YOKAI SAY TO BRING THE CHILD?
IT'S ALL WRITTEN RIGHT HERE.
HMM.
I'LL TAKE YOUR GREAT GREAT GRANDDAUGHTER WITH ME THEN.

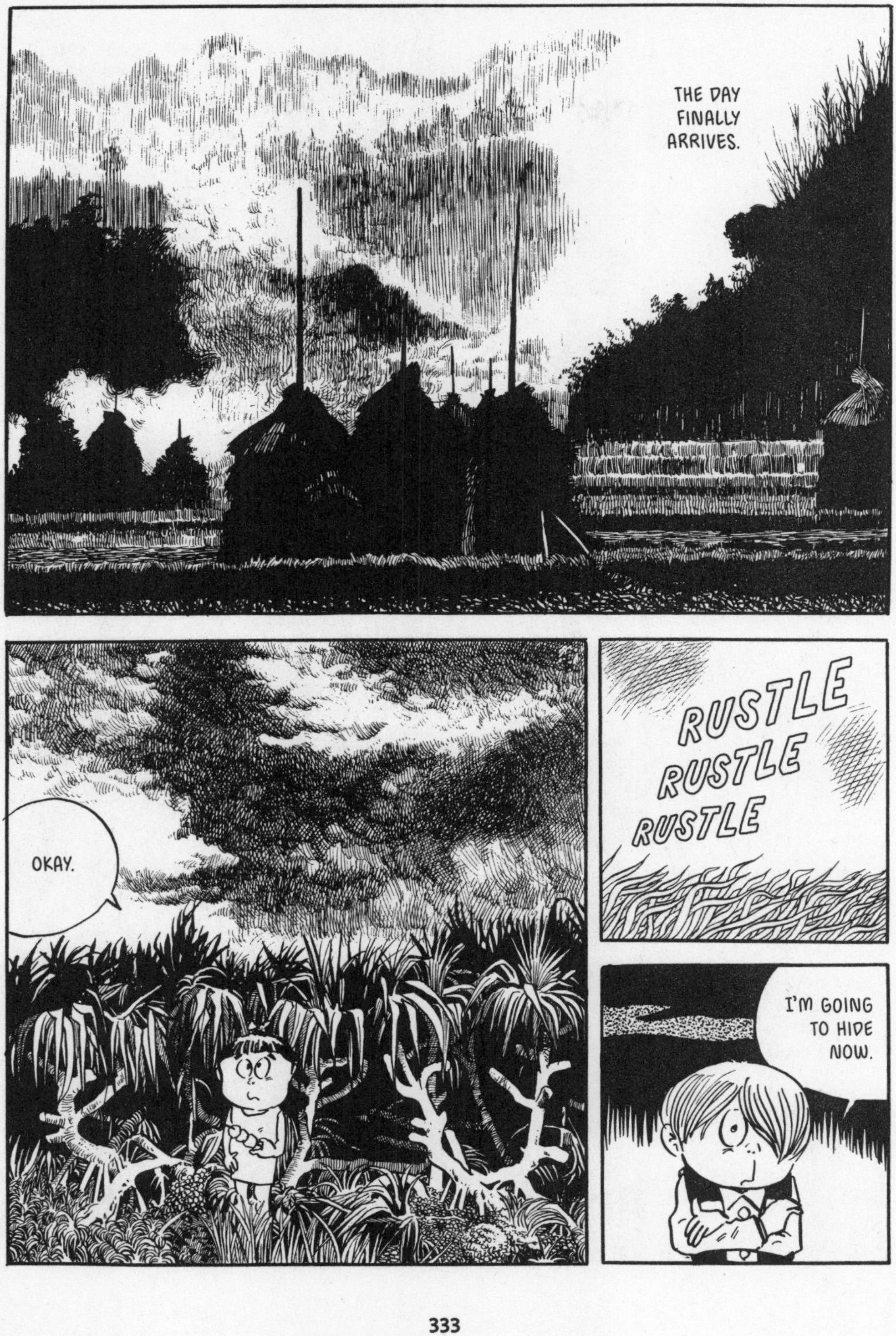
THE DAY FINALLY ARRIVES.
RUSTLE
RUSTLE
RUSTLE
I'M GOING TO HIDE NOW.
OKAY.

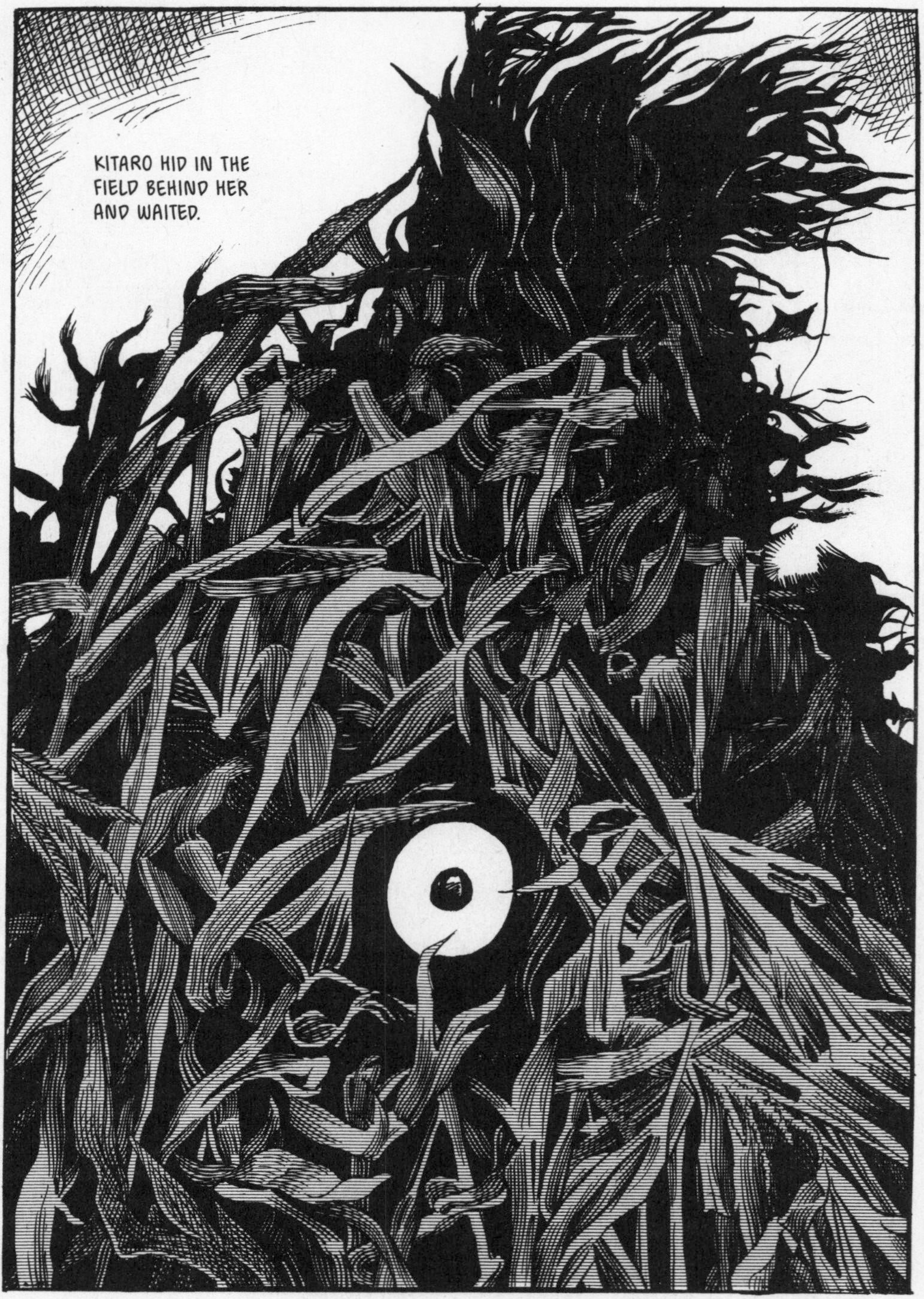
KITARO HID IN THE
FIELD BEHIND HER
AND WAITED.

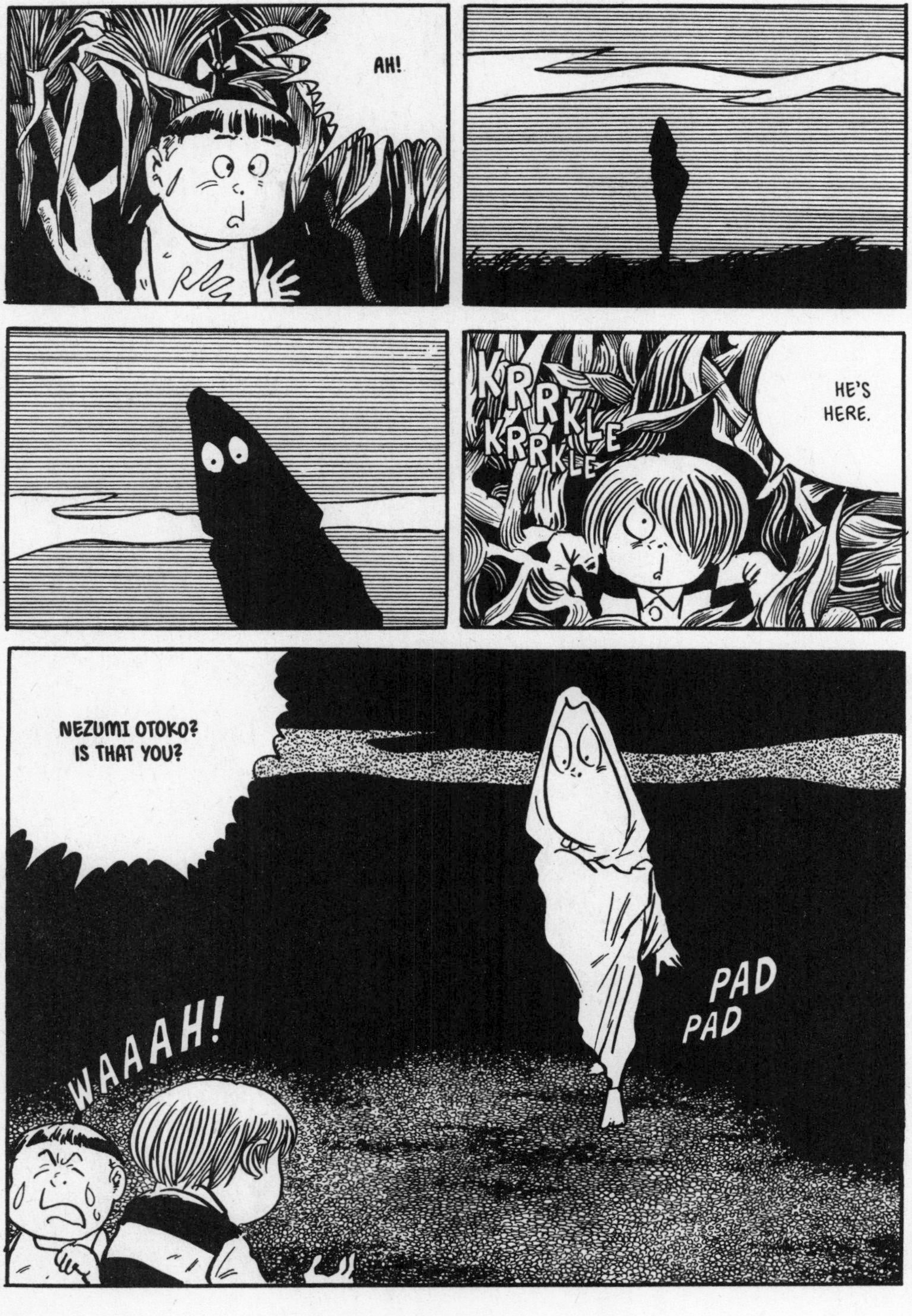
AH!
KRRRKLE
KRRRKLE
HE'S HERE.
NEZUMI OTOKO? IS THAT YOU?
PAD
PAD
WAAAH!

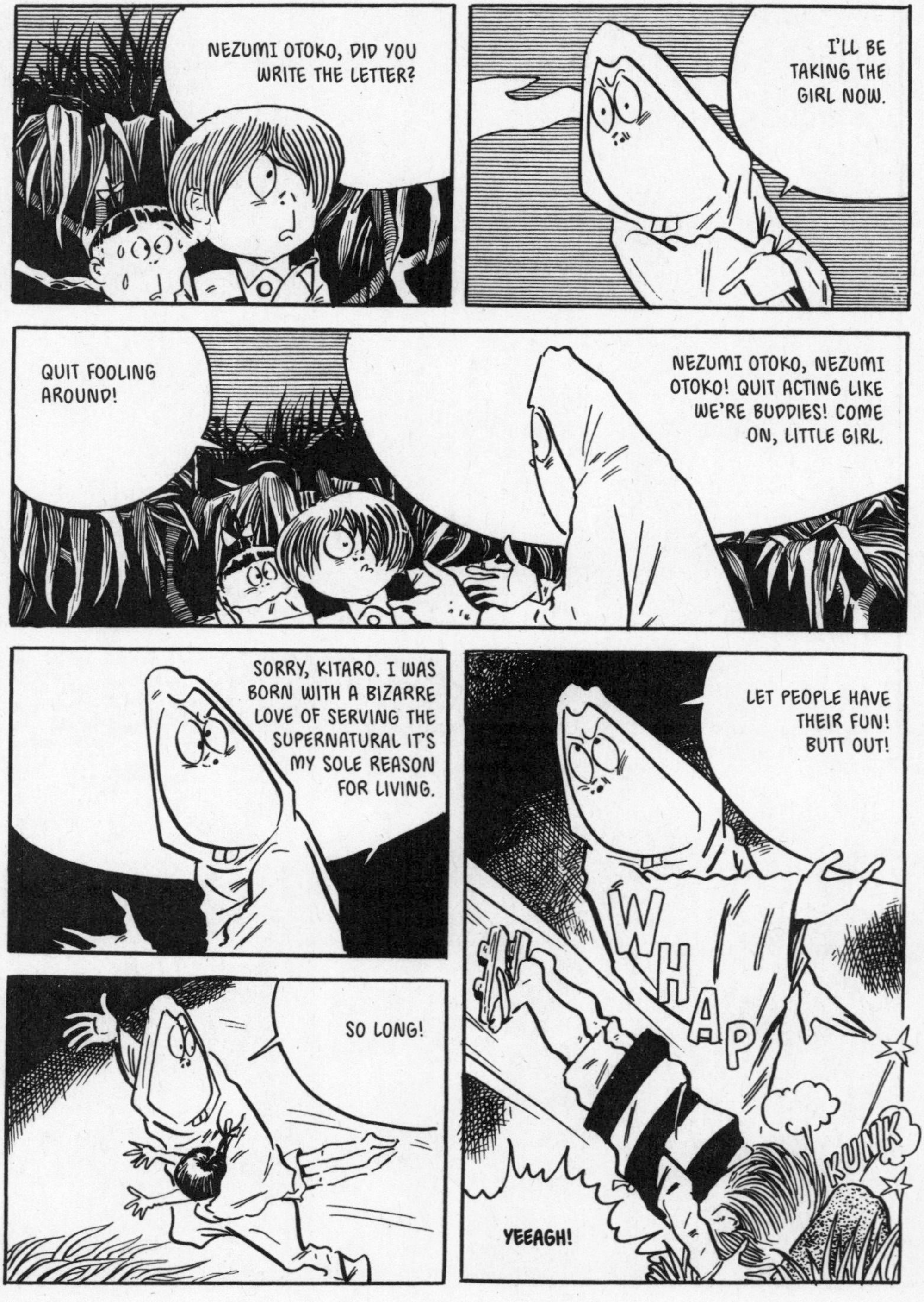
I'LL BE TAKING THE GIRL NOW.
NEZUMI OTOKO, DID YOU WRITE THE LETTER?
NEZUMI OTOKO, NEZUMI OTOKO! QUIT ACTING LIKE WE'RE BUDDIES! COME ON, LITTLE GIRL.
QUIT FOOLING AROUND!
LET PEOPLE HAVE THEIR FUN! BUTT OUT!
WHAP
KUNK
YEEAGH!
SORRY, KITARO. I WAS BORN WITH A BIZARRE LOVE OF SERVING THE SUPERNATURAL IT'S MY SOLE REASON FOR LIVING.
SO LONG!

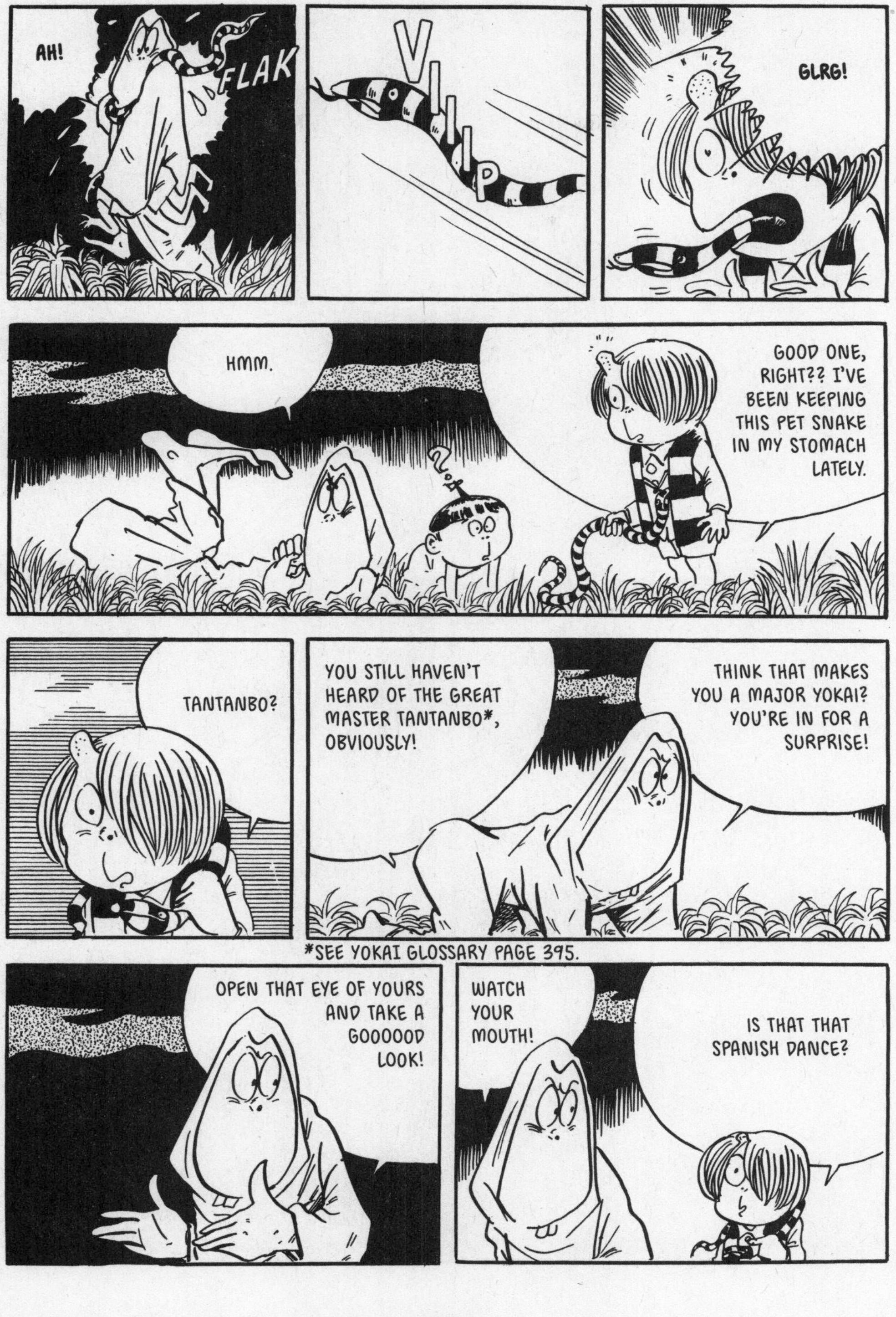
GLRG!
VIIIP
AH!
FLAK
GOOD ONE, RIGHT?? I'VE BEEN KEEPING THIS PET SNAKE IN MY STOMACH LATELY.
HMM.
THINK THAT MAKES YOU A MAJOR YOKAI? YOU'RE IN FOR A SURPRISE!
YOU STILL HAVEN'T HEARD OF THE GREAT MASTER TANTANBO*, OBVIOUSLY!
TANTANBO?
IS THAT THAT SPANISH DANCE?
WATCH YOUR MOUTH!
OPEN THAT EYE OF YOURS AND TAKE A GOOOOOD LOOK!

*SEE YOKAI GLOSSARY PAGE 395.

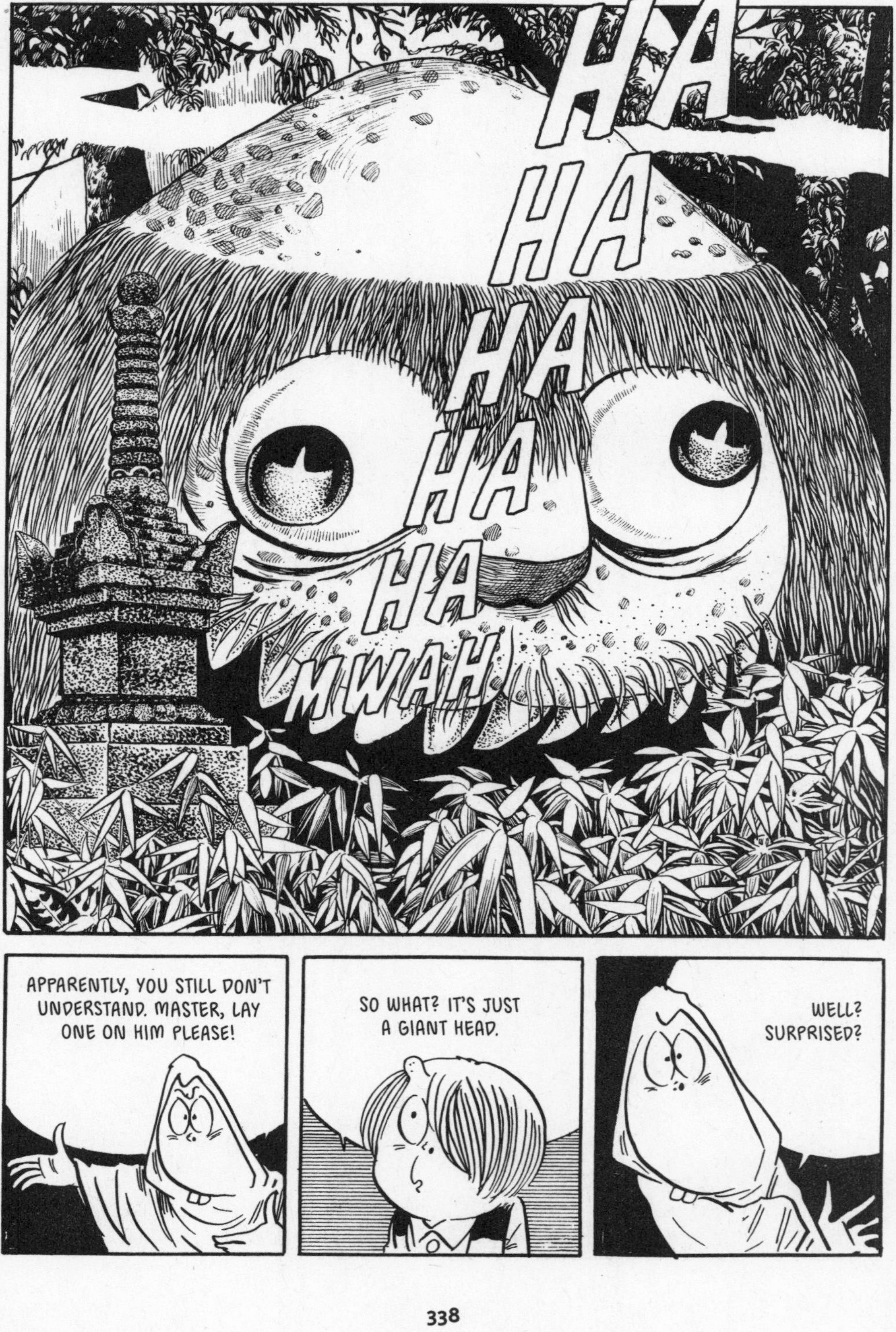
HA
HA
HA
HA
HA
HA
MWAH
WELL? SURPRISED?
SO WHAT? IT'S JUST A GIANT HEAD.
APPARENTLY, YOU STILL DON'T UNDERSTAND. MASTER, LAY ONE ON HIM PLEASE!

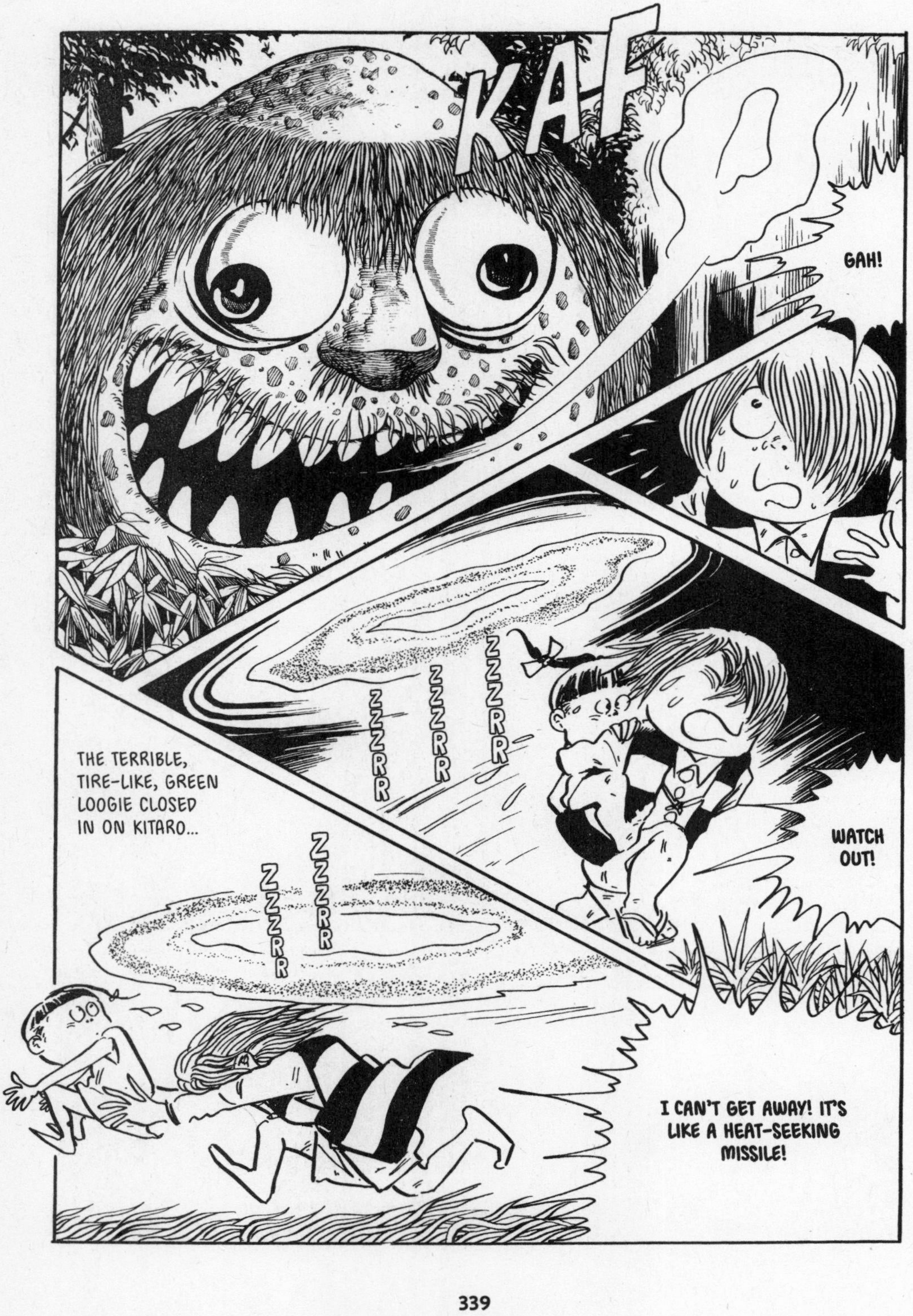
KAF
GAH!
ZZZRR
ZZZRR
ZZZRR
WATCH OUT!
THE TERRIBLE, TIRE-LIKE, GREEN LOOGIE CLOSED IN ON KITARO...
ZZZRR
ZZZRR
I CAN'T GET AWAY! IT'S LIKE A HEAT-SEEKING MISSILE!

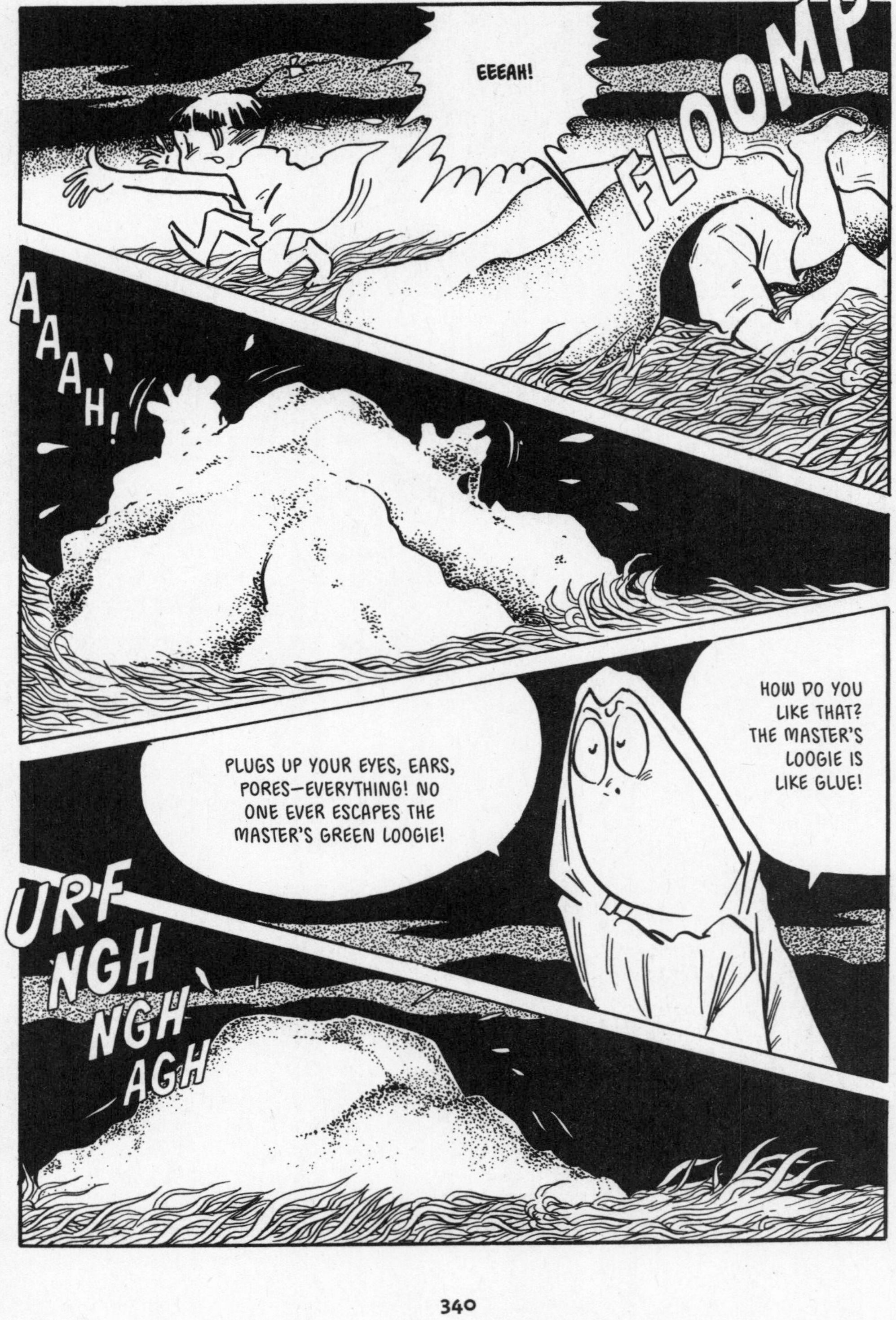
EEEAH!
FLOOMP
AAAAH!
HOW DO YOU LIKE THAT? THE MASTER'S LOOGIE IS LIKE GLUE!
PLUGS UP YOUR EYES, EARS, PORES—EVERYTHING! NO ONE EVER ESCAPES THE MASTER'S GREEN LOOGIE!
URF NGH NGH AGH

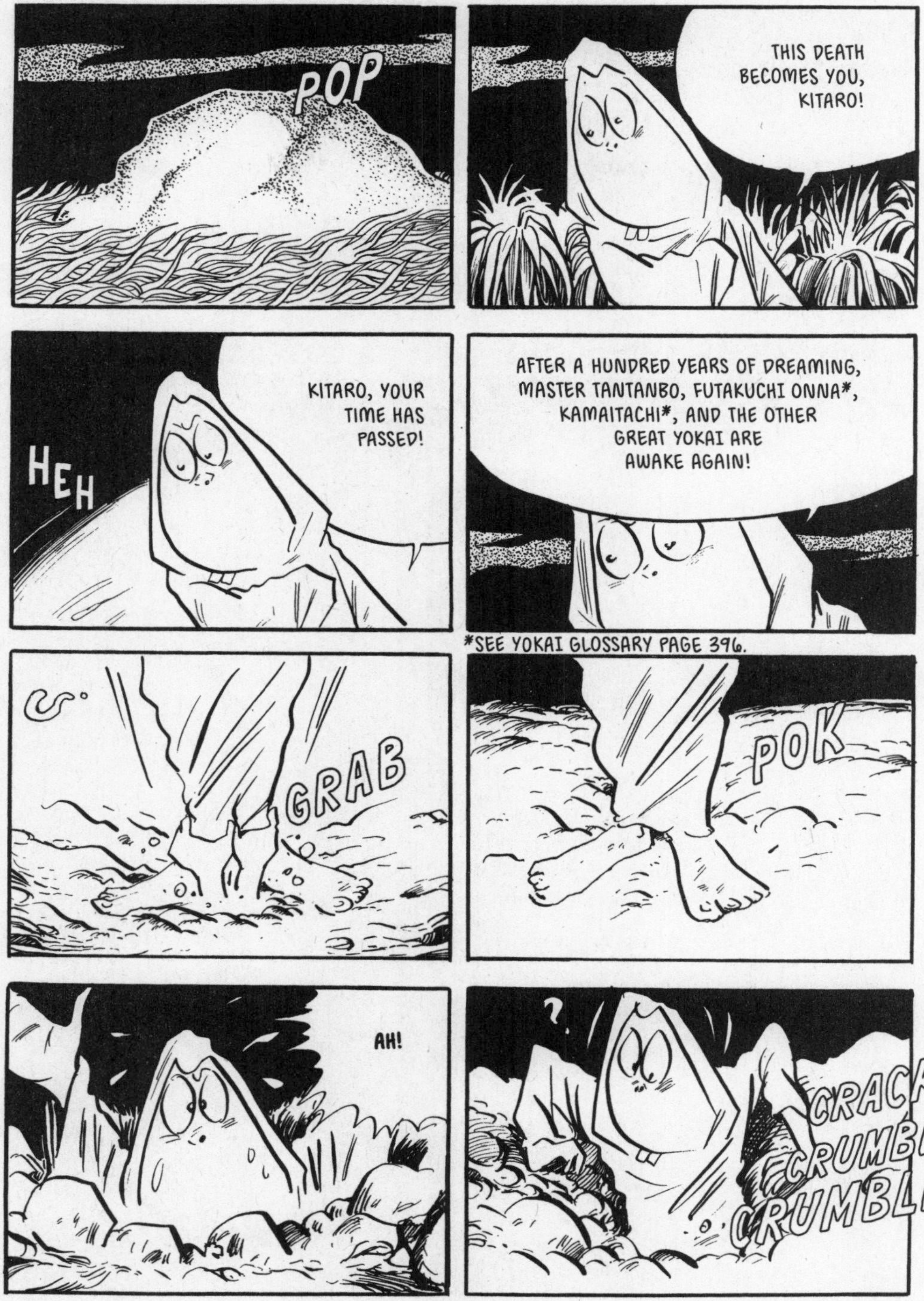
THIS DEATH BECOMES YOU, KITARO!
POP
AFTER A HUNDRED YEARS OF DREAMING, MASTER TANTANBO, FUTAKUCHI ONNA*, KAMAITACHI*, AND THE OTHER GREAT YOKAI ARE AWAKE AGAIN!
KITARO, YOUR TIME HAS PASSED!
HEH
POK
GRAB
?
CRACK
CRUMBLE
CRUMBLE
AH!

*SEE YOKAI GLOSSARY PAGE 396.

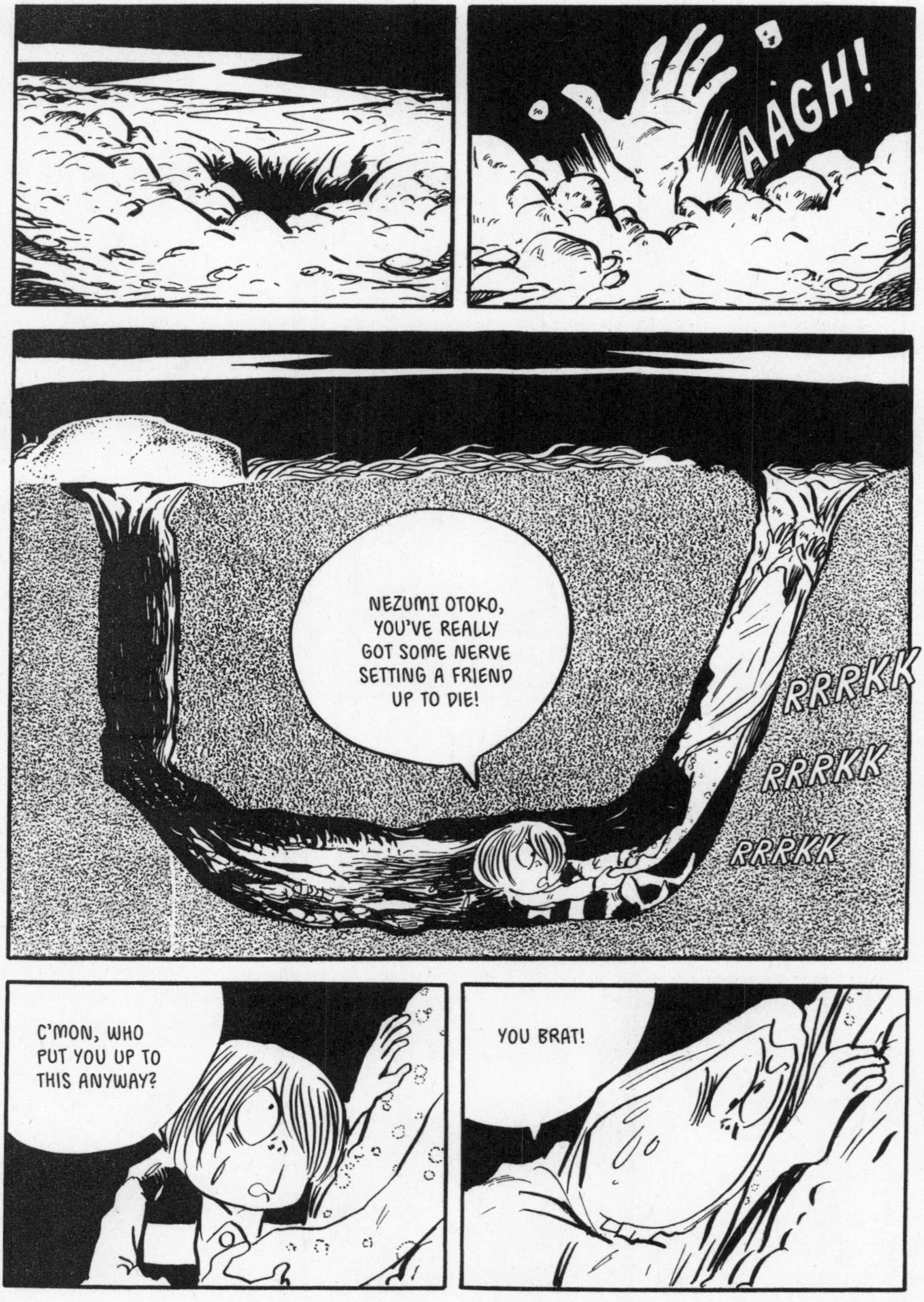
AAGH!
NEZUMI OTOKO, YOU'VE REALLY GOT SOME NERVE SETTING A FRIEND UP TO DIE!
RRRKK
RRRKK
RRRKK
YOU BRAT!
C'MON, WHO PUT YOU UP TO THIS ANYWAY?

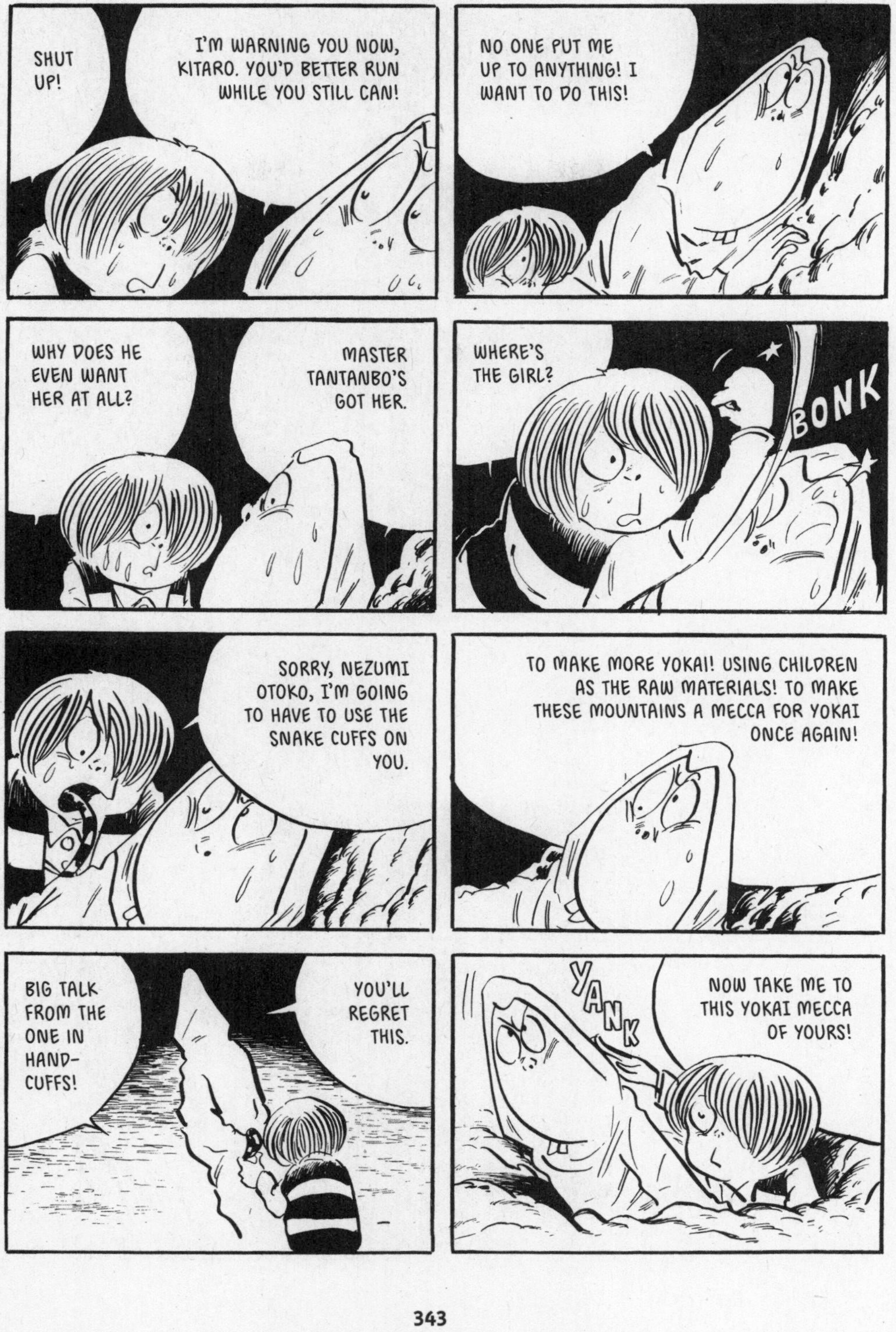
NO ONE PUT ME UP TO ANYTHING! I WANT TO DO THIS!
I'M WARNING YOU NOW, KITARO. YOU'D BETTER RUN WHILE YOU STILL CAN!
SHUT UP!
WHERE'S THE GIRL?
BONK
MASTER TANTANBO'S GOT HER.
WHY DOES HE EVEN WANT HER AT ALL?
TO MAKE MORE YOKAI! USING CHILDREN AS THE RAW MATERIALS! TO MAKE THESE MOUNTAINS A MECCA FOR YOKAI ONCE AGAIN!
SORRY, NEZUMI OTOKO, I'M GOING TO HAVE TO USE THE SNAKE CUFFS ON YOU.
YANK
NOW TAKE ME TO THIS YOKAI MECCA OF YOURS!
YOU'LL REGRET THIS.
BIG TALK FROM THE ONE IN HAND-CUFFS!

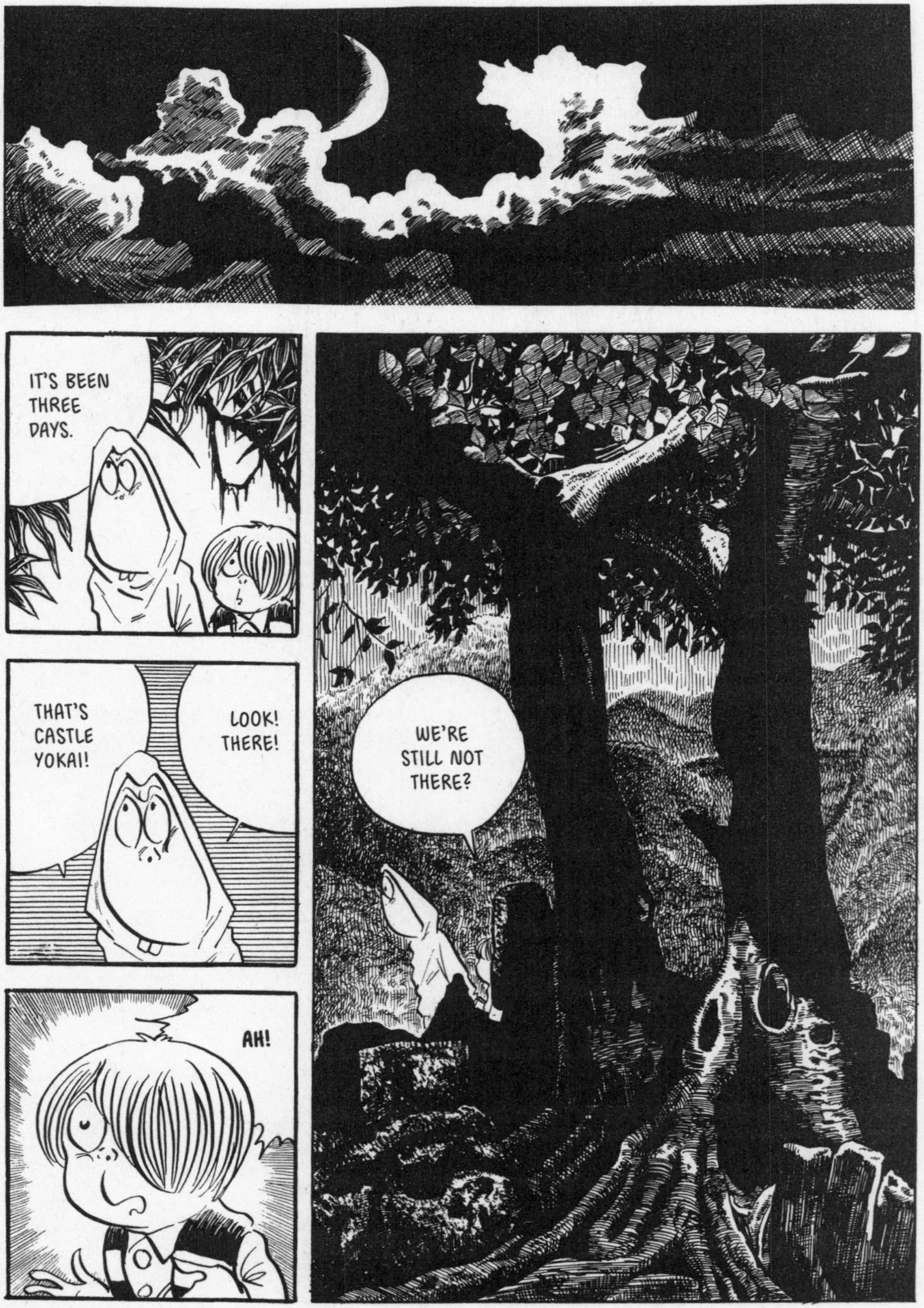
WE'RE STILL NOT THERE?
IT'S BEEN THREE DAYS.
LOOK! THERE!
THAT'S CASTLE YOKAI!
AH!

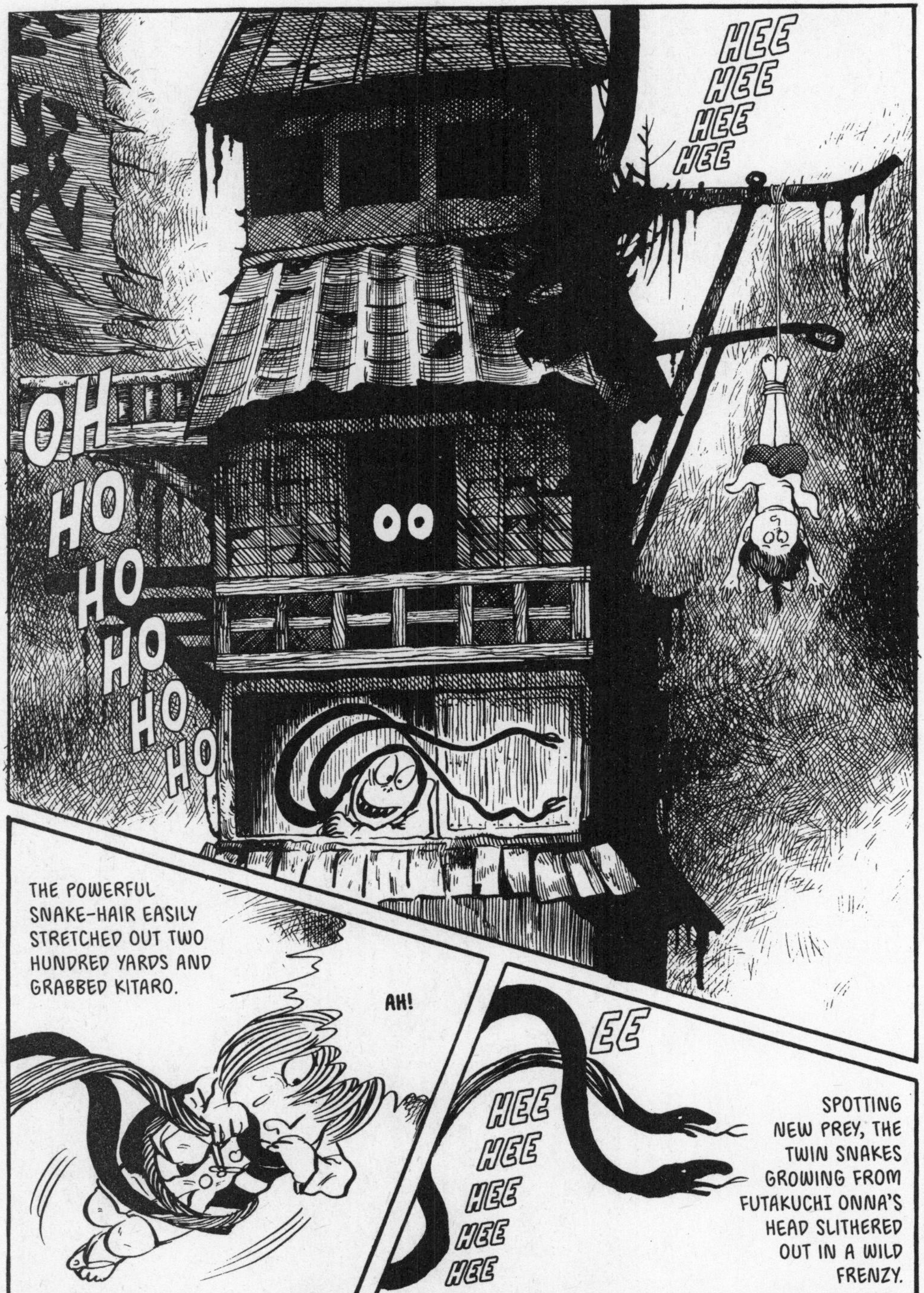
HEE HEE HEE HEE
OH HO HO HO HO HO HO
EE
HEE HEE HEE HEE HEE
SPOTTING NEW PREY, THE TWIN SNAKES GROWING FROM FUTAKUCHI ONNA'S HEAD SLITHERED OUT IN A WILD FRENZY.
THE POWERFUL SNAKE-HAIR EASILY STRETCHED OUT TWO HUNDRED YARDS AND GRABBED KITARO.
AH!

WITH HIS VITAL ORGANS IN A DEATH GRIP, KITARO WAS UNABLE TO USE HIS POWERFUL MAGIC AGAINST FUTAKUCHI ONNA. DESPITE HIS STRUGGLES, HE WAS DRAGGED HELPLESSLY TOWARDS HER.

FOR THE MOMENT, FUTAKUCHI ONNA HAD THE UPPER HAND.

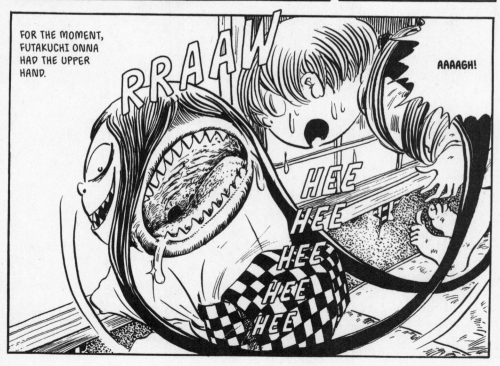

RRAAW

AAAAGH!

HEE HEE HEE HEE HEE

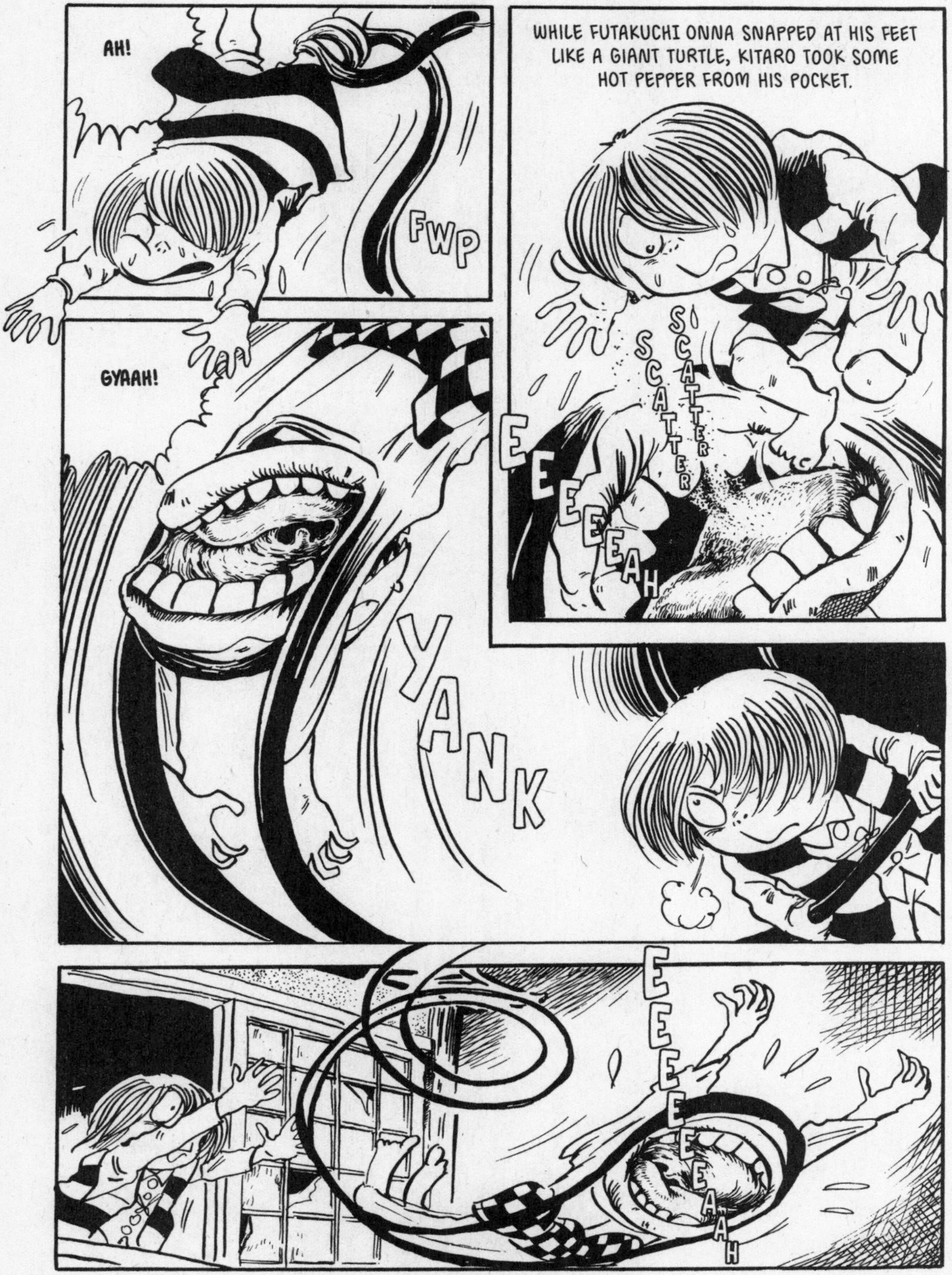
WHILE FUTAKUCHI ONNA SNAPPED AT HIS FEET LIKE A GIANT TURTLE, KITARO TOOK SOME HOT PEPPER FROM HIS POCKET.
SCATTER
SCATTER
EEEEEEAH
AH!
FWP
GYAAH!
YANK
EEEEEEEAH

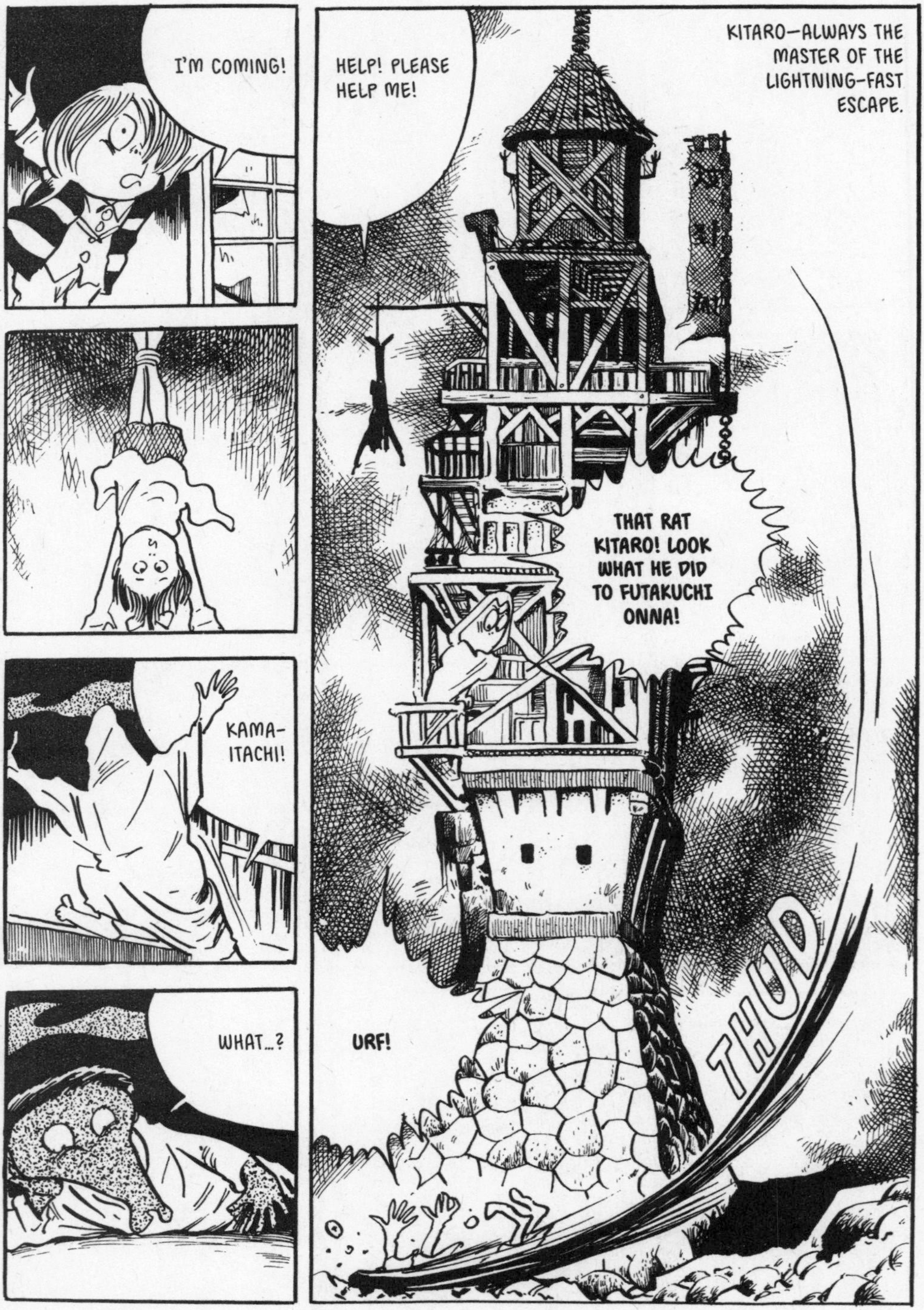
KITARO—ALWAYS THE MASTER OF THE LIGHTNING-FAST ESCAPE.
HELP! PLEASE HELP ME!
THAT RAT KITARO! LOOK WHAT HE DID TO FUTAKUCHI ONNA!
THUD
URF!
I'M COMING!
KAMA-ITACHI!
WHAT...?

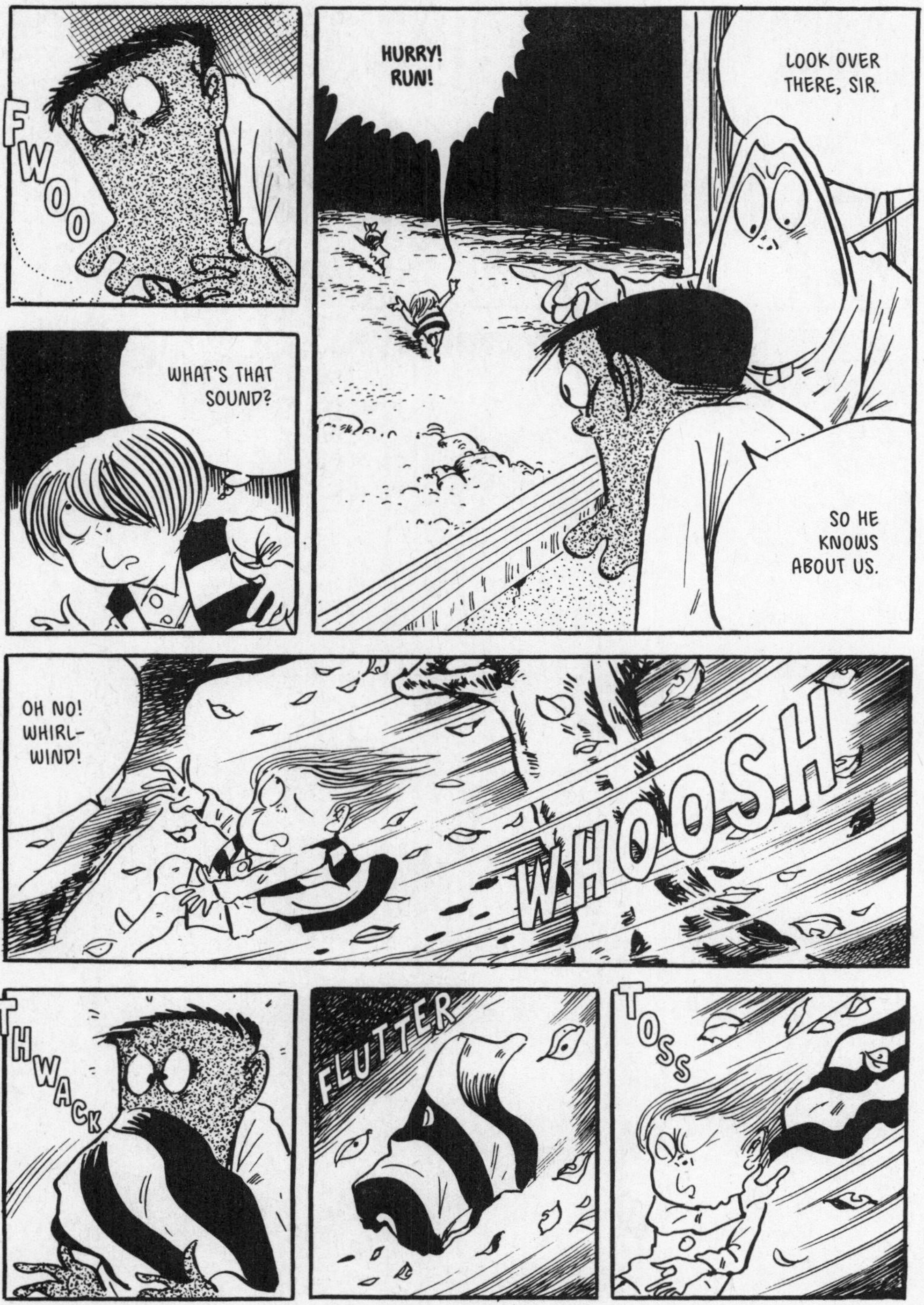
LOOK OVER THERE, SIR.
HURRY! RUN!
SO HE KNOWS ABOUT US.
FWOOO
WHAT'S THAT SOUND?
WHOOSH
OH NO! WHIRL-WIND!
TOSS
FLUTTER
THWACK

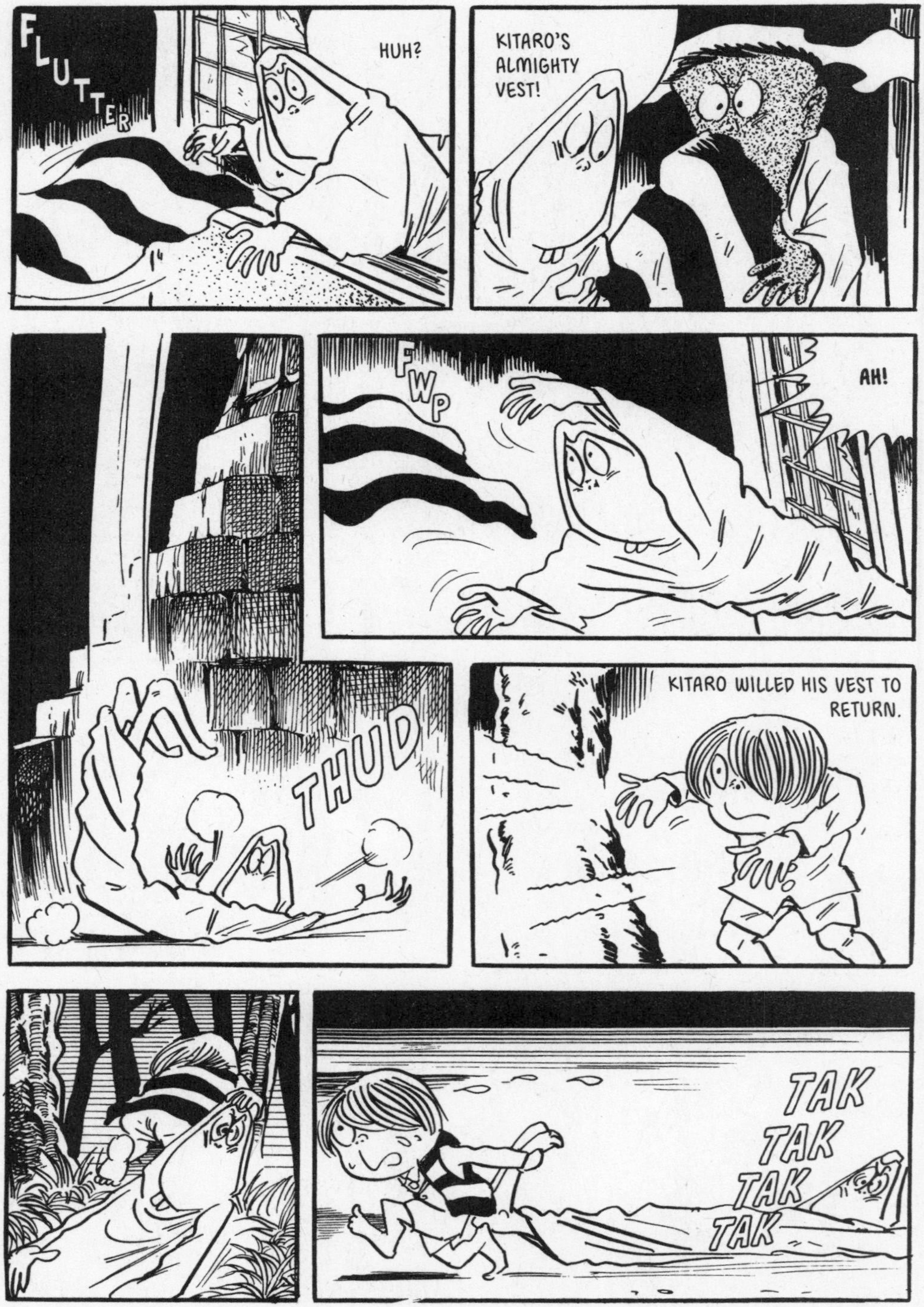
KITARO'S ALMIGHTY VEST!
HUH?
FLUTTER
AH!
FWP
KITARO WILLED HIS VEST TO RETURN.
THUD
TAK
TAK
TAK
TAK

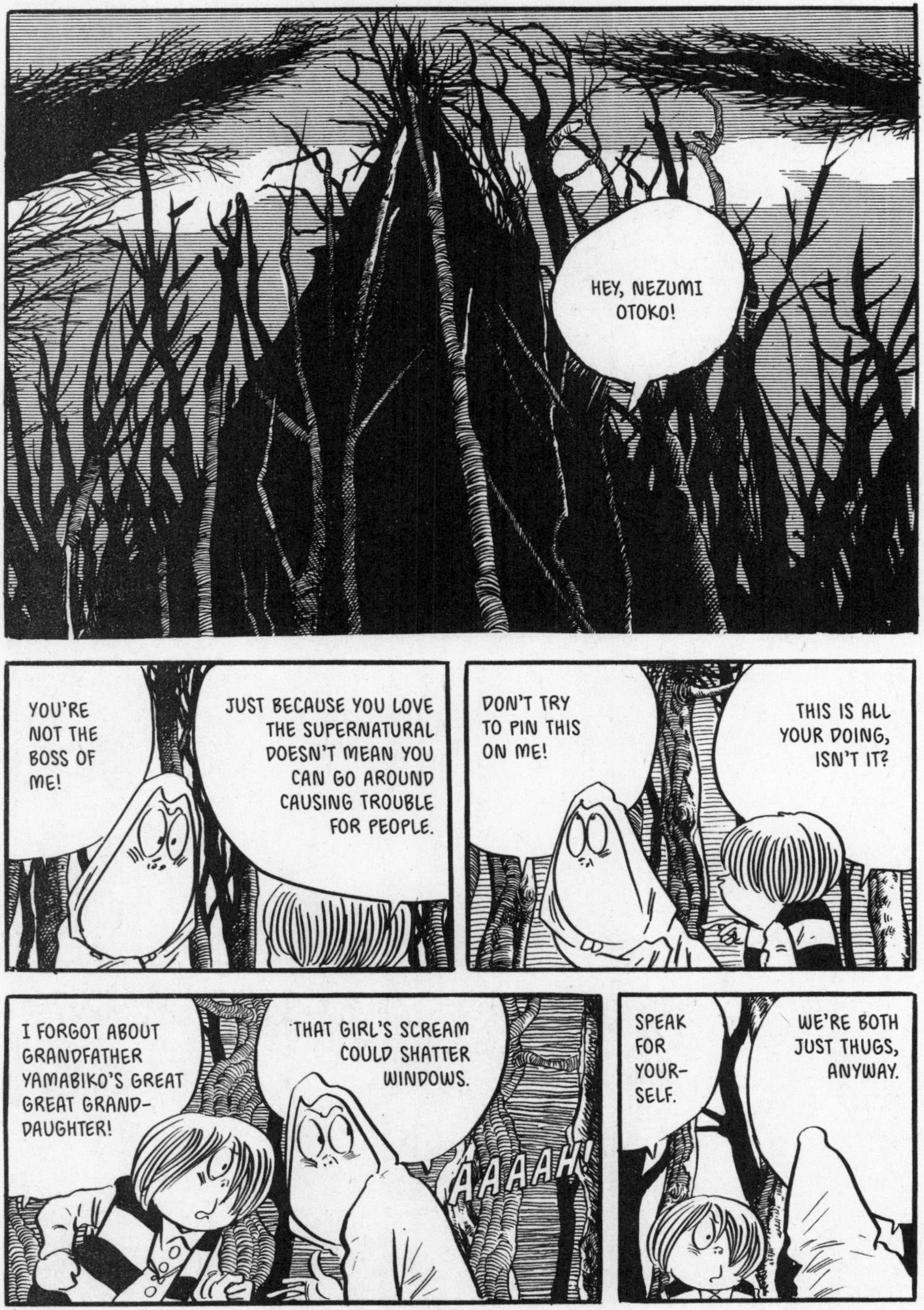
HEY, NEZUMI OTOKO!
THIS IS ALL YOUR DOING, ISN'T IT?
DON'T TRY TO PIN THIS ON ME!
JUST BECAUSE YOU LOVE THE SUPERNATURAL DOESN'T MEAN YOU CAN GO AROUND CAUSING TROUBLE FOR PEOPLE.
YOU'RE NOT THE BOSS OF ME!
WE'RE BOTH JUST THUGS, ANYWAY.
SPEAK FOR YOUR-SELF.
THAT GIRL'S SCREAM COULD SHATTER WINDOWS.
AAAAH!
I FORGOT ABOUT GRANDFATHER YAMABIKO'S GREAT GREAT GRAND-DAUGHTER!

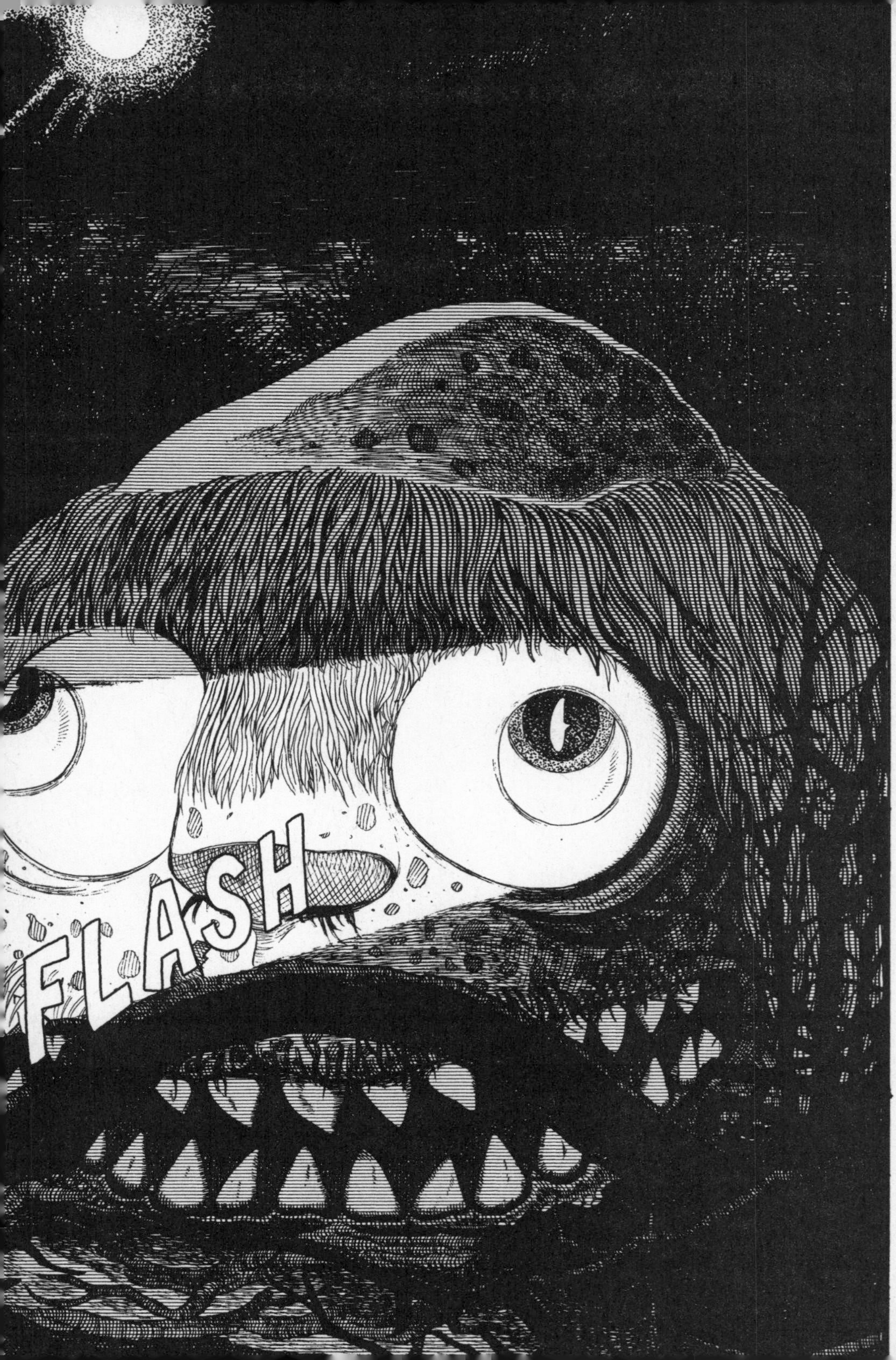
FLASH

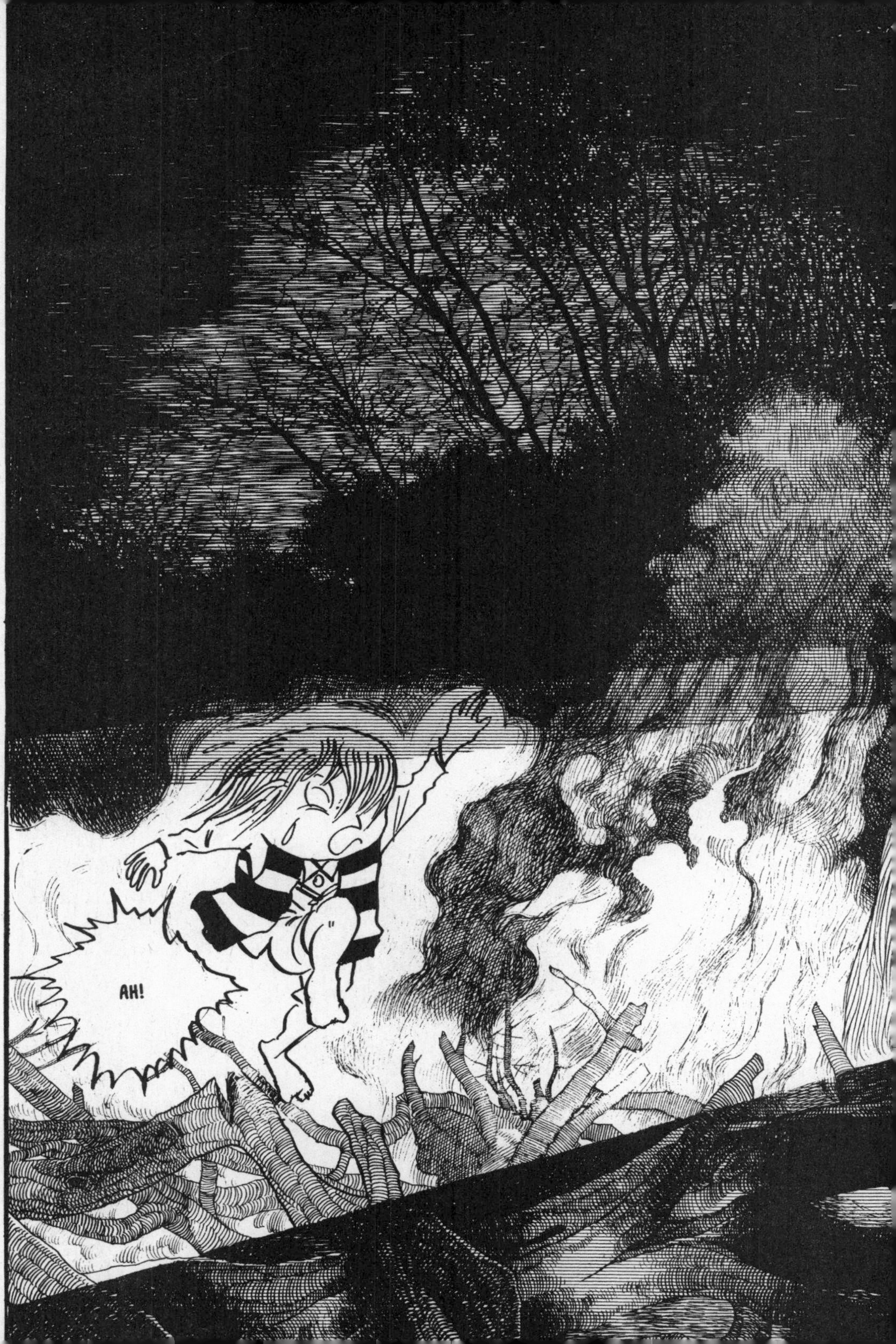
AH!

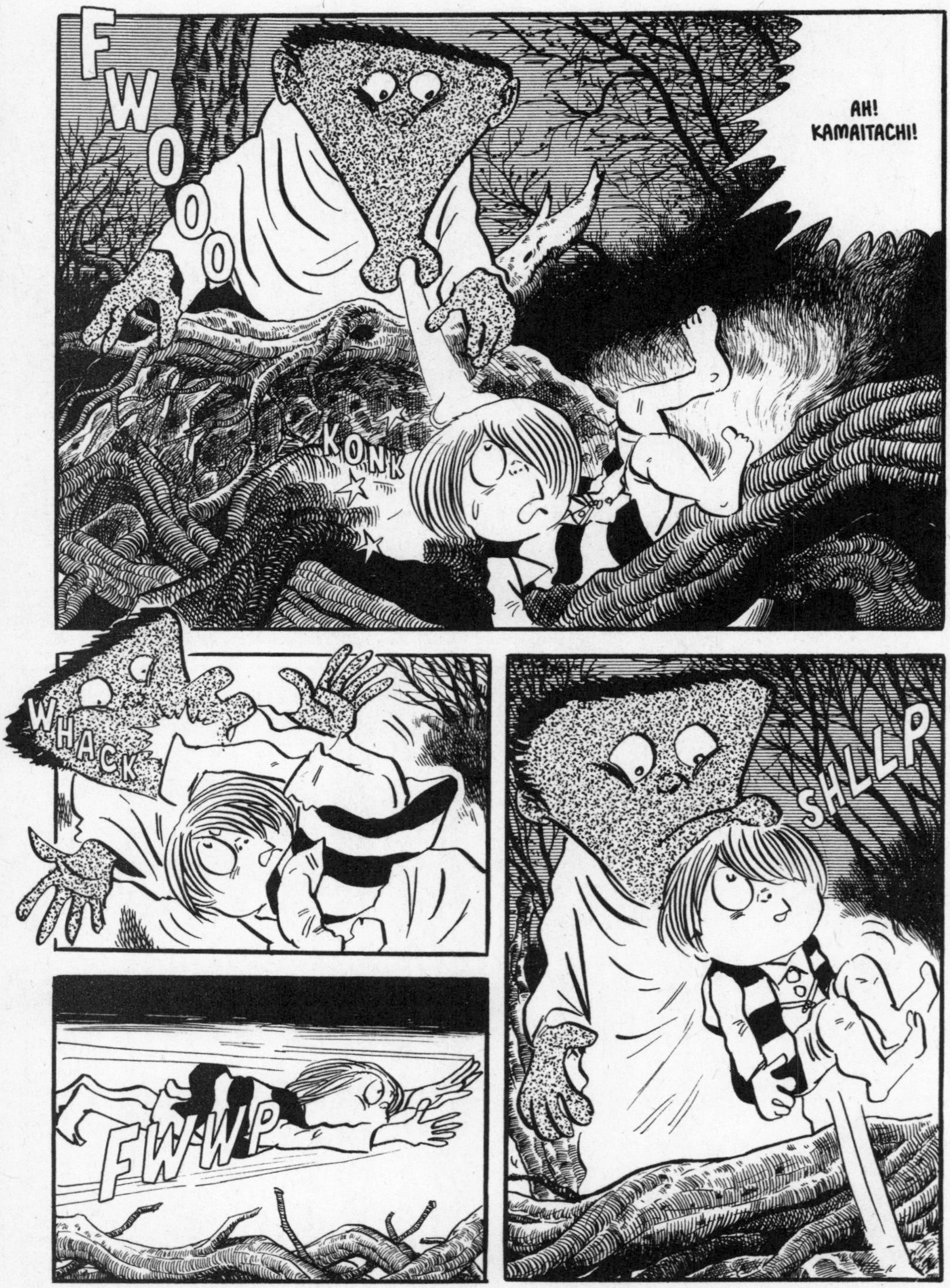
AH! KAMAITACHI!
FWOOO
KONK
SHLLP
WHACK
FWWP

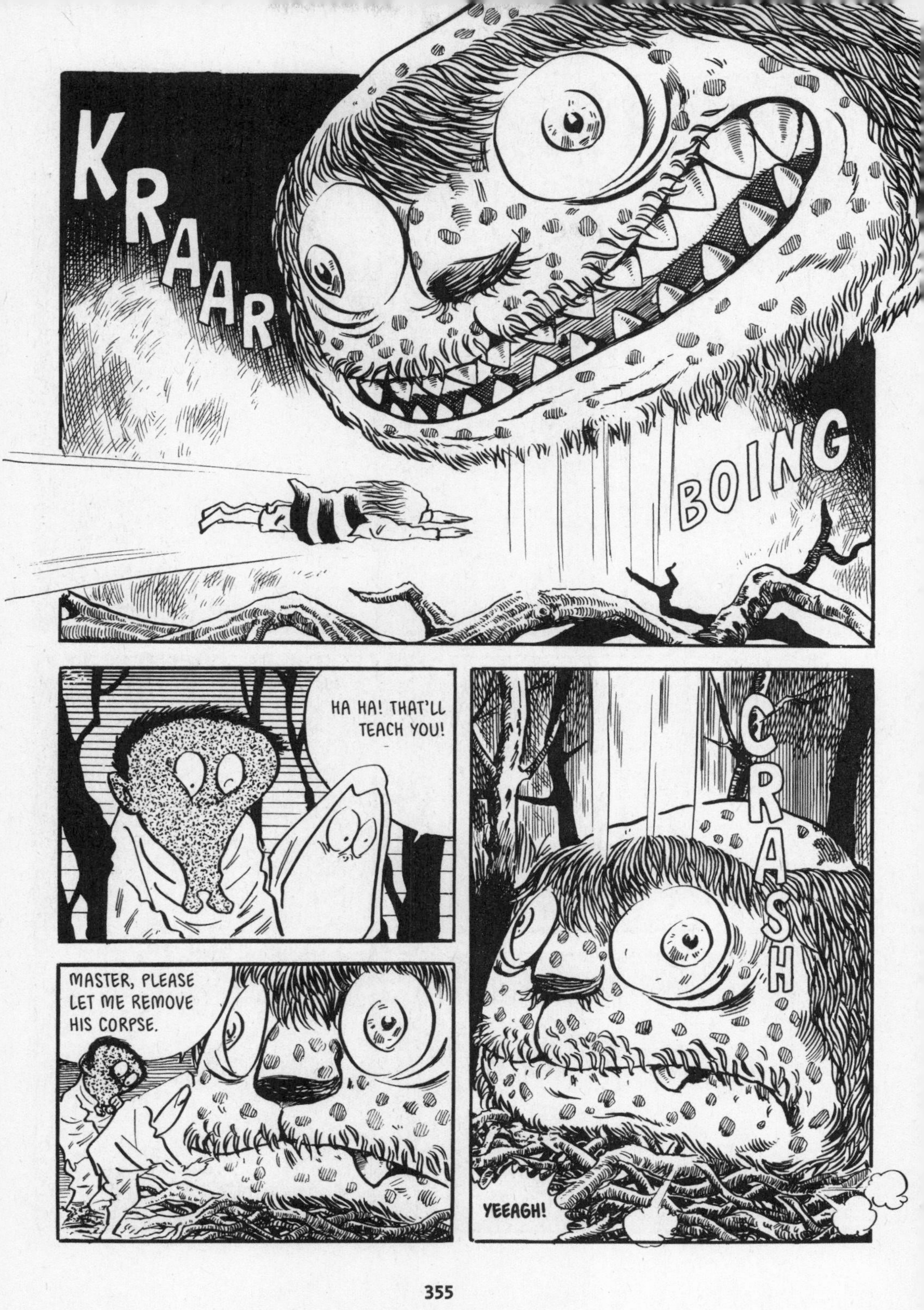
KRAAR
BOING
CRASH
YEEAGH!
HA HA! THAT'LL TEACH YOU!
MASTER, PLEASE LET ME REMOVE HIS CORPSE.

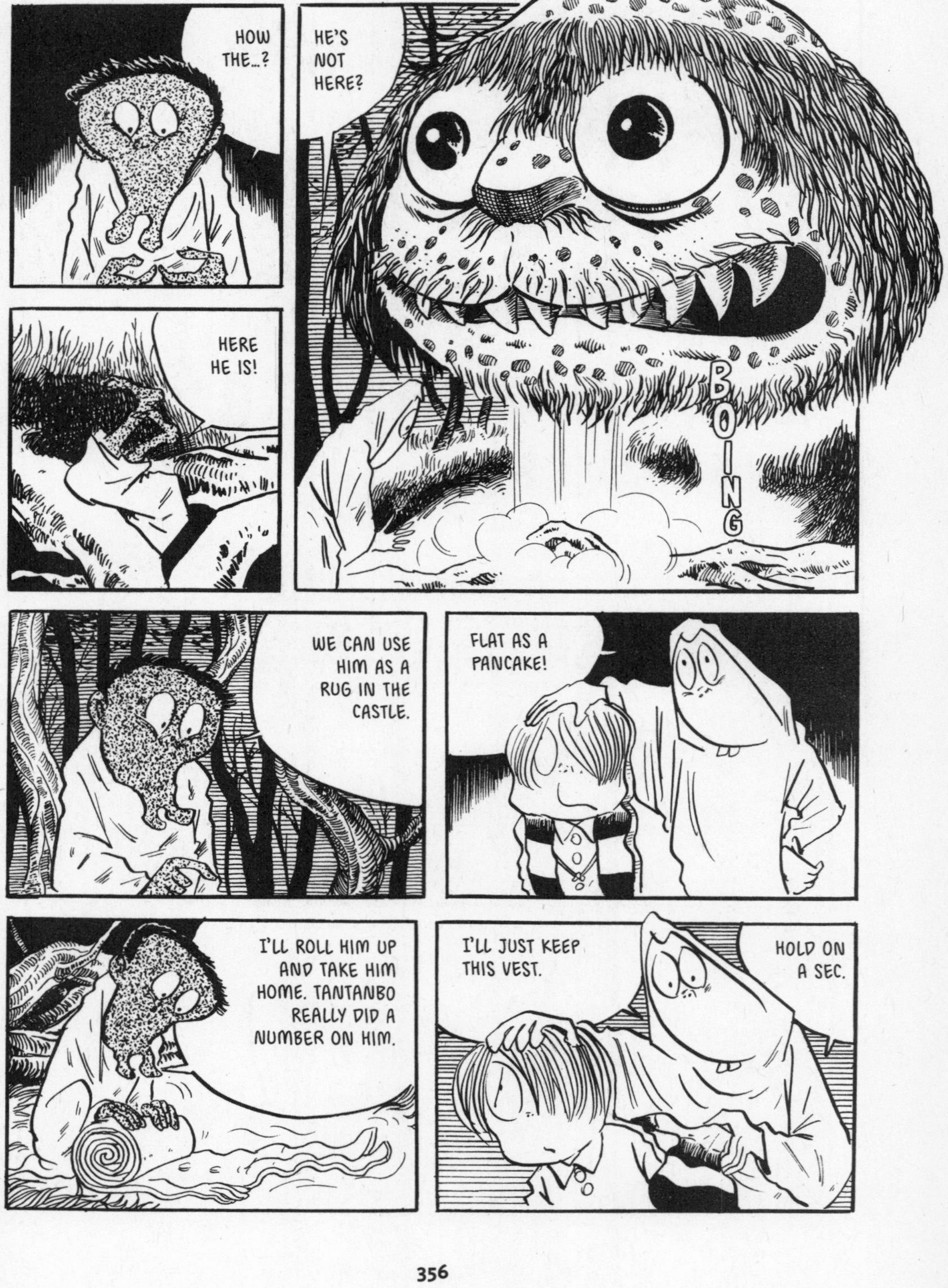
HE'S NOT HERE?
BOING
HOW THE...?
HERE HE IS!
FLAT AS A PANCAKE!
WE CAN USE HIM AS A RUG IN THE CASTLE.
HOLD ON A SEC.
I'LL JUST KEEP THIS VEST.
I'LL ROLL HIM UP AND TAKE HIM HOME. TANTANBO REALLY DID A NUMBER ON HIM.

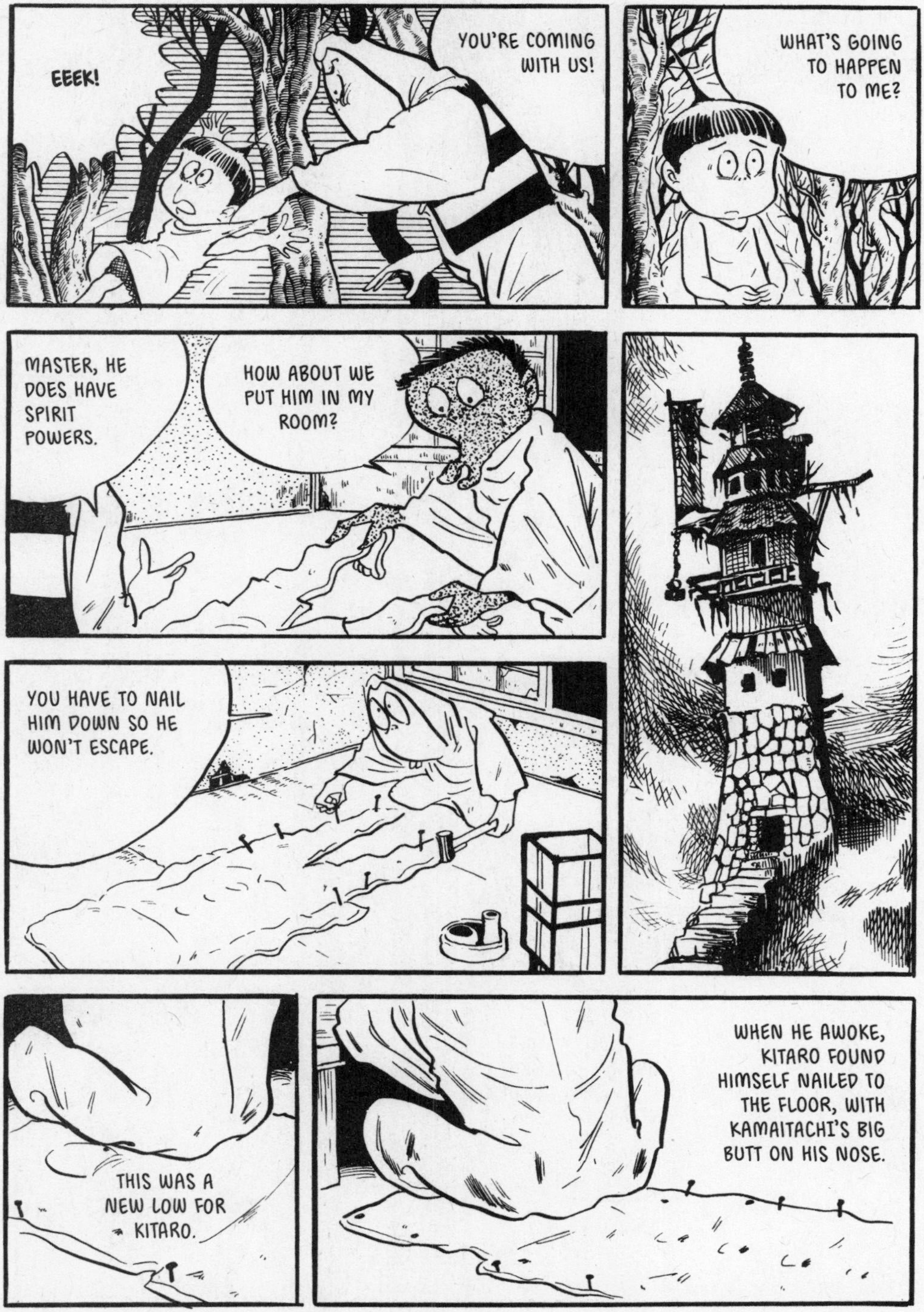
WHAT'S GOING TO HAPPEN TO ME?
YOU'RE COMING WITH US!
EEEK!
HOW ABOUT WE PUT HIM IN MY ROOM?
MASTER, HE DOES HAVE SPIRIT POWERS.
YOU HAVE TO NAIL HIM DOWN SO HE WON'T ESCAPE.
WHEN HE AWOKE, KITARO FOUND HIMSELF NAILED TO THE FLOOR, WITH KAMAITACHI'S BIG BUTT ON HIS NOSE.
THIS WAS A NEW LOW FOR KITARO.

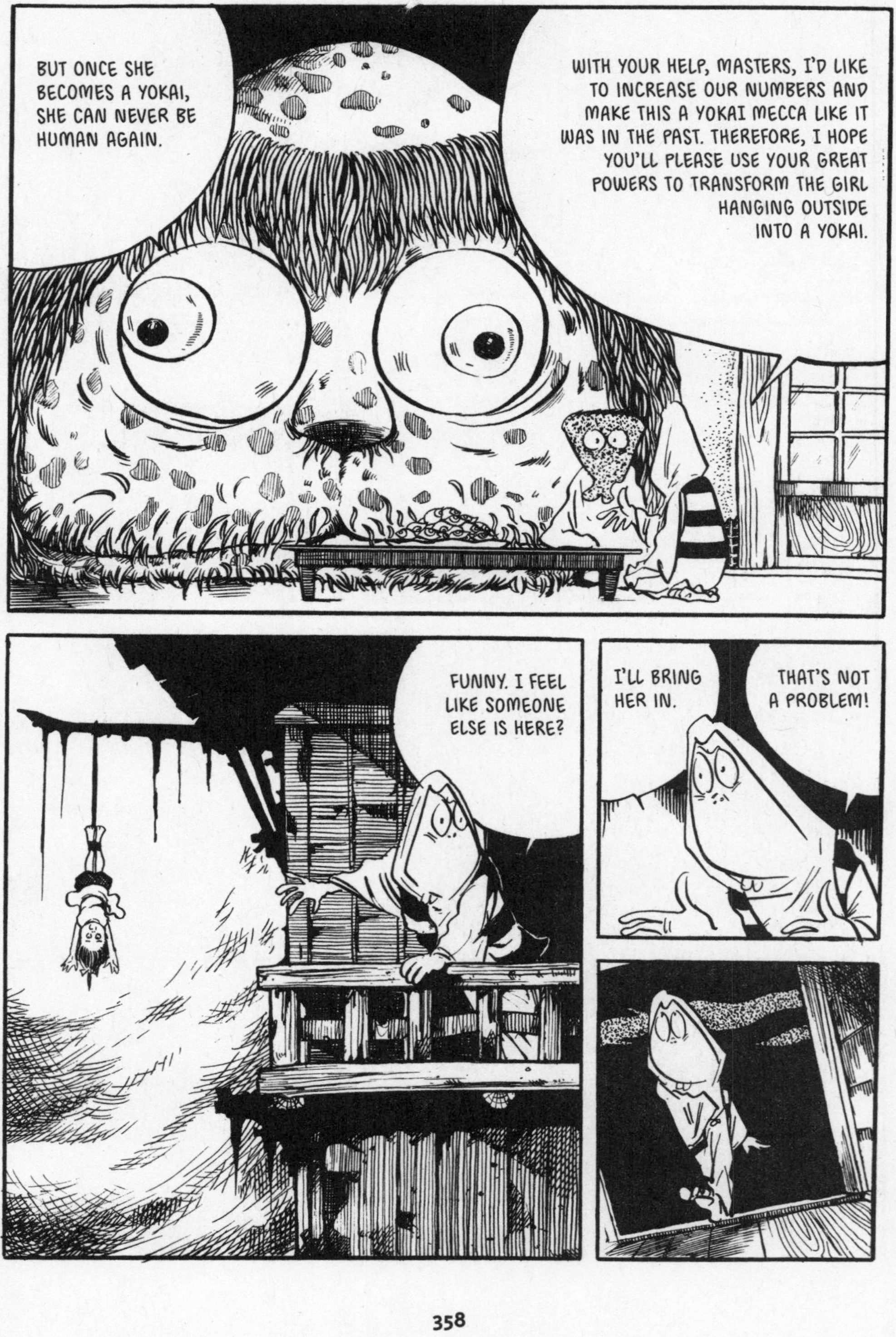
WITH YOUR HELP, MASTERS, I'D LIKE TO INCREASE OUR NUMBERS AND MAKE THIS A YOKAI MECCA LIKE IT WAS IN THE PAST. THEREFORE, I HOPE YOU'LL PLEASE USE YOUR GREAT POWERS TO TRANSFORM THE GIRL HANGING OUTSIDE INTO A YOKAI.
BUT ONCE SHE BECOMES A YOKAI, SHE CAN NEVER BE HUMAN AGAIN.
THAT'S NOT A PROBLEM!
I'LL BRING HER IN.
FUNNY. I FEEL LIKE SOMEONE ELSE IS HERE?

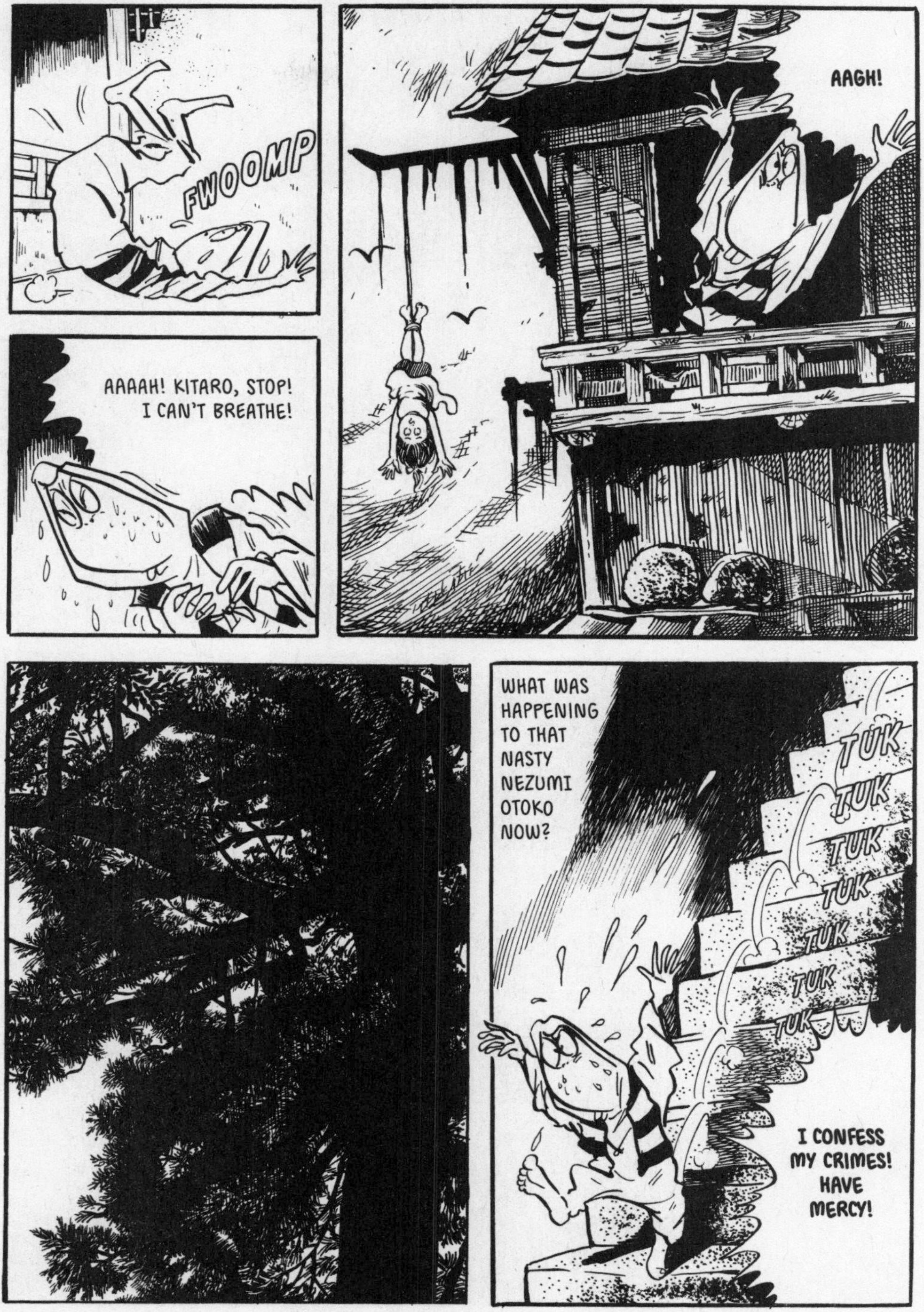
AAGH!
FWOOMP
AAAAH! KITARO, STOP! I CAN'T BREATHE!
WHAT WAS HAPPENING TO THAT NASTY NEZUMI OTOKO NOW?
TUK
TUK
TUK
TUK
TUK
TUK
TUK
I CONFESS MY CRIMES! HAVE MERCY!

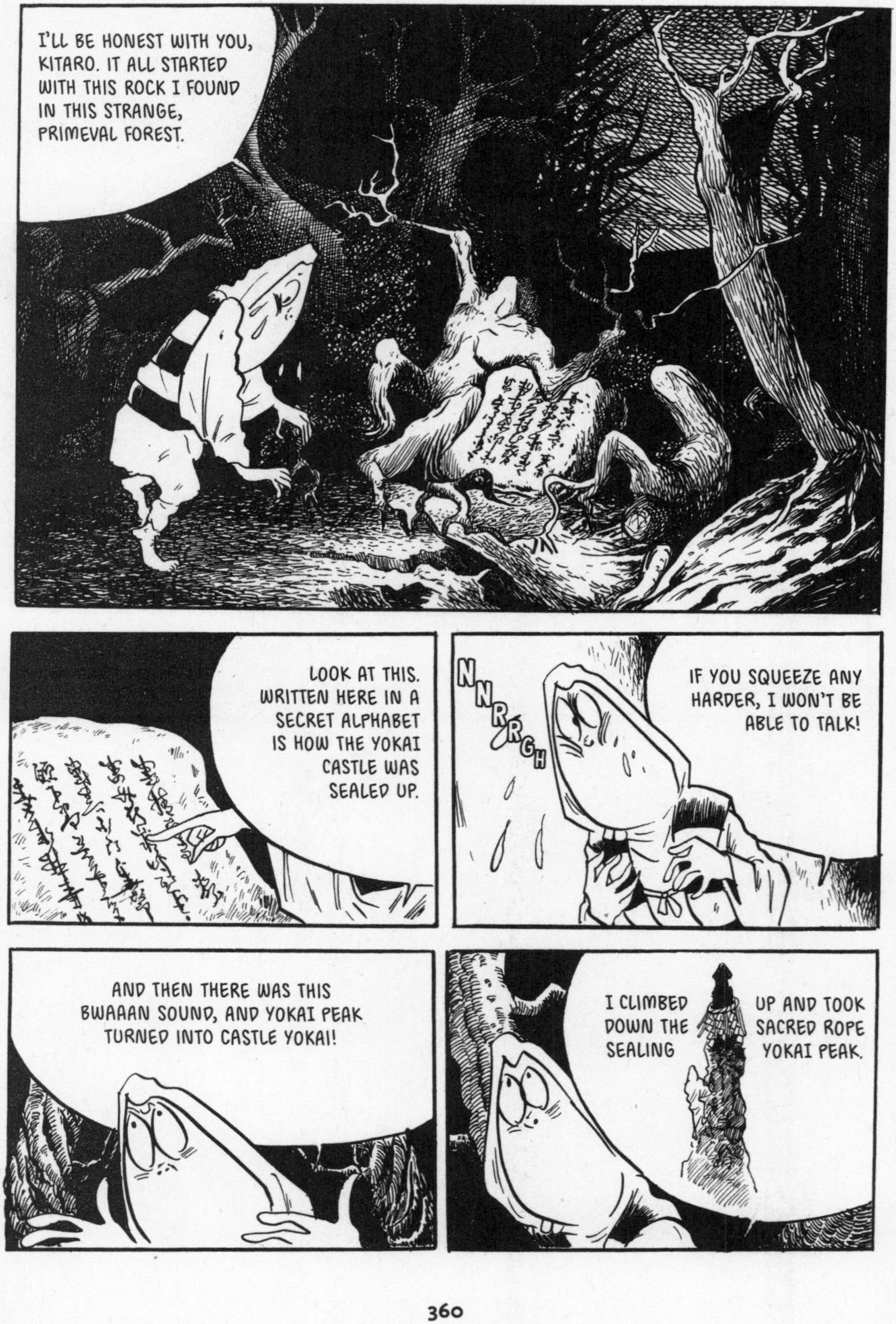
I'LL BE HONEST WITH YOU, KITARO. IT ALL STARTED WITH THIS ROCK I FOUND IN THIS STRANGE, PRIMEVAL FOREST.
IF YOU SQUEEZE ANY HARDER, I WON'T BE ABLE TO TALK!
NNRRGH
LOOK AT THIS. WRITTEN HERE IN A SECRET ALPHABET IS HOW THE YOKAI CASTLE WAS SEALED UP.
I CLIMBED UP AND TOOK DOWN THE SACRED ROPE SEALING YOKAI PEAK.
AND THEN THERE WAS THIS BWAAAN SOUND, AND YOKAI PEAK TURNED INTO CASTLE YOKAI!

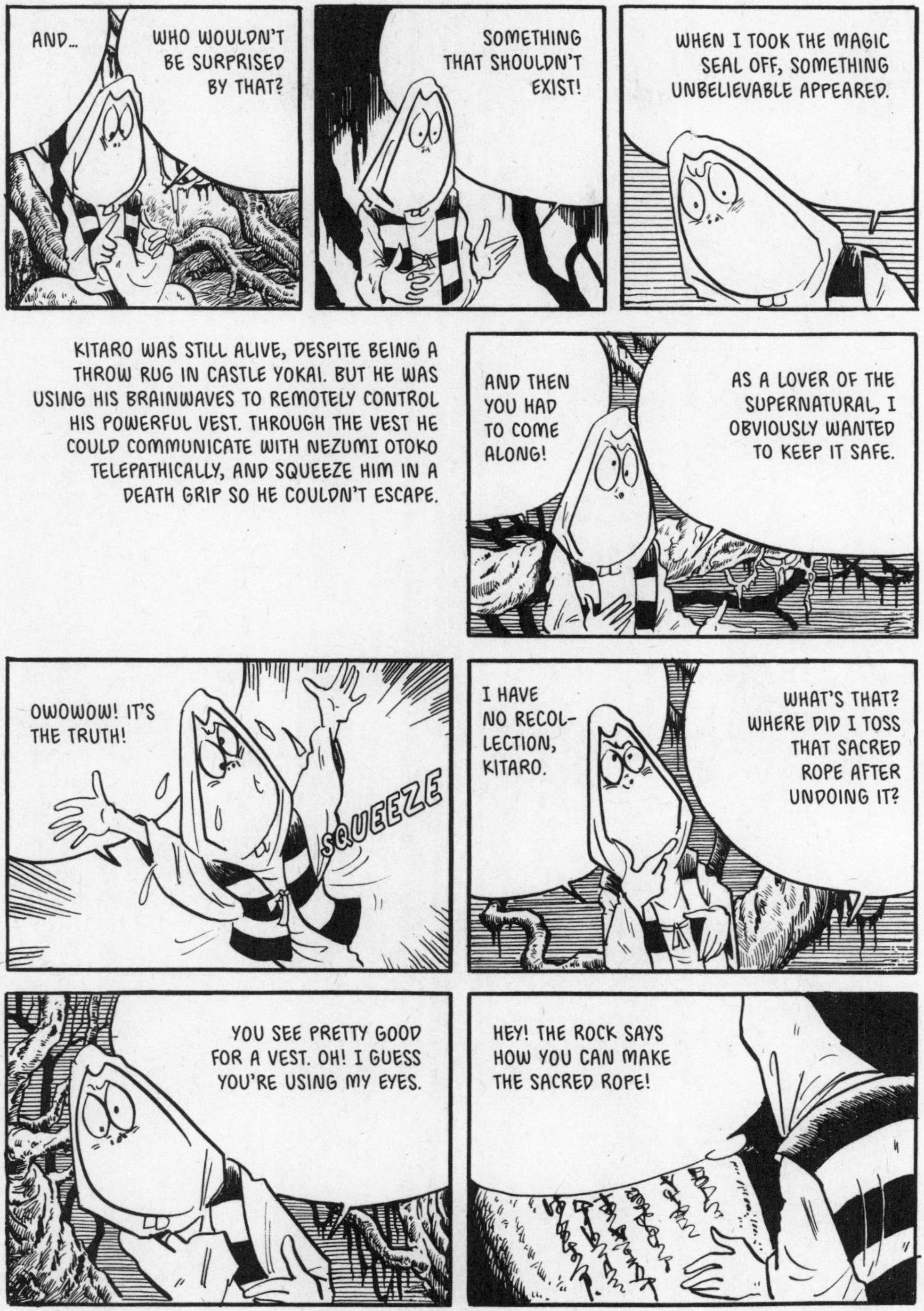
WHEN I TOOK THE MAGIC SEAL OFF, SOMETHING UNBELIEVABLE APPEARED.
SOMETHING THAT SHOULDN'T EXIST!
WHO WOULDN'T BE SURPRISED BY THAT?
AND...
AS A LOVER OF THE SUPERNATURAL, I OBVIOUSLY WANTED TO KEEP IT SAFE.
AND THEN YOU HAD TO COME ALONG!
KITARO WAS STILL ALIVE, DESPITE BEING A THROW RUG IN CASTLE YOKAI. BUT HE WAS USING HIS BRAINWAVES TO REMOTELY CONTROL HIS POWERFUL VEST. THROUGH THE VEST HE COULD COMMUNICATE WITH NEZUMI OTOKO TELEPATHICALLY, AND SQUEEZE HIM IN A DEATH GRIP SO HE COULDN'T ESCAPE.
WHAT'S THAT? WHERE DID I TOSS THAT SACRED ROPE AFTER UNDOING IT?
I HAVE NO RECOLLECTION, KITARO.
SQUEEZE
OWOWOW! IT'S THE TRUTH!
HEY! THE ROCK SAYS HOW YOU CAN MAKE THE SACRED ROPE!
YOU SEE PRETTY GOOD FOR A VEST. OH! I GUESS YOU'RE USING MY EYES.

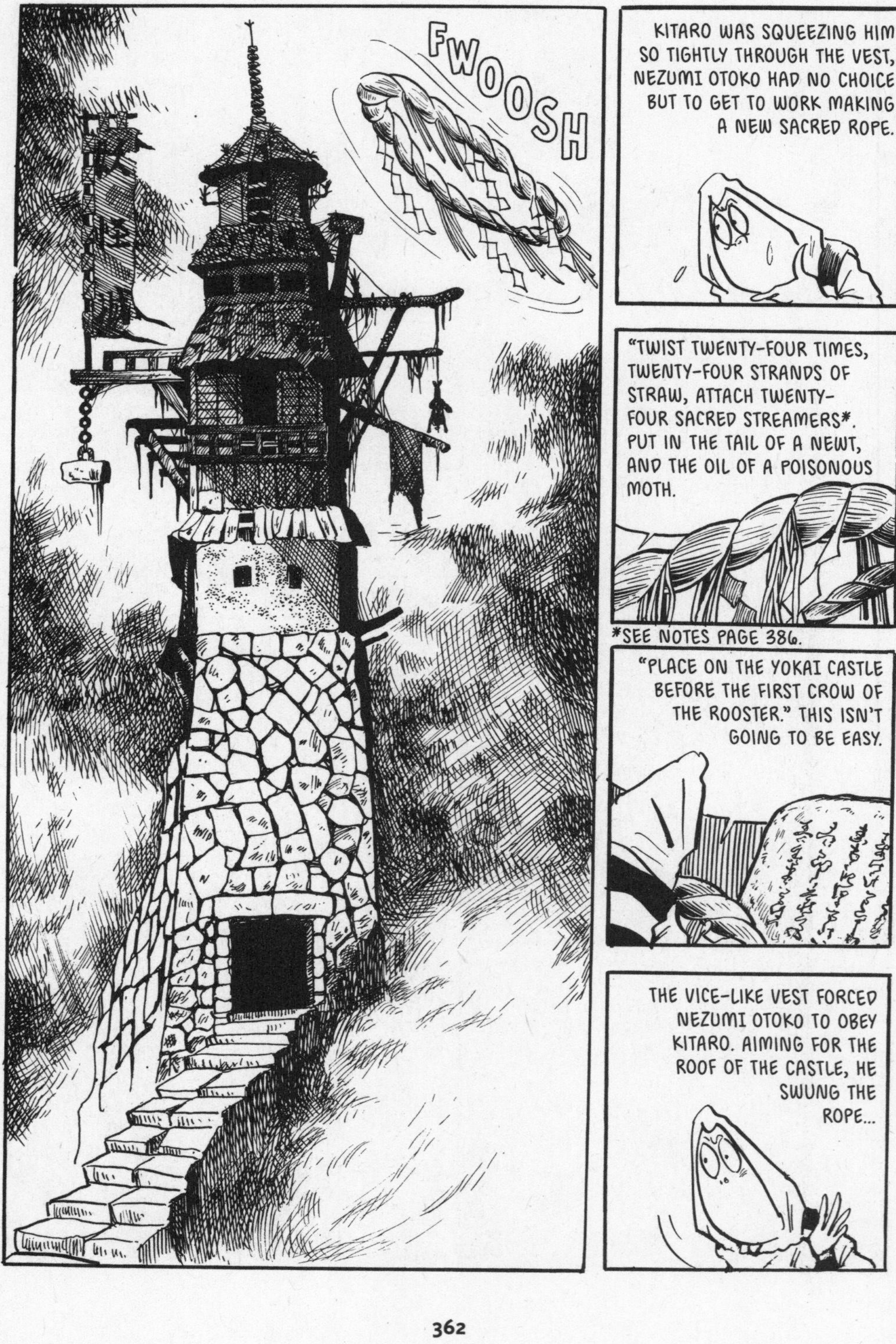
KITARO WAS SQUEEZING HIM SO TIGHTLY THROUGH THE VEST, NEZUMI OTOKO HAD NO CHOICE BUT TO GET TO WORK MAKING A NEW SACRED ROPE.
"TWIST TWENTY-FOUR TIMES, TWENTY-FOUR STRANDS OF STRAW, ATTACH TWENTY-FOUR SACRED STREAMERS*. PUT IN THE TAIL OF A NEWT, AND THE OIL OF A POISONOUS MOTH.
*SEE NOTES PAGE 386.
"PLACE ON THE YOKAI CASTLE BEFORE THE FIRST CROW OF THE ROOSTER." THIS ISN'T GOING TO BE EASY.
THE VICE-LIKE VEST FORCED NEZUMI OTOKO TO OBEY KITARO. AIMING FOR THE ROOF OF THE CASTLE, HE SWUNG THE ROPE...
FWOOSH

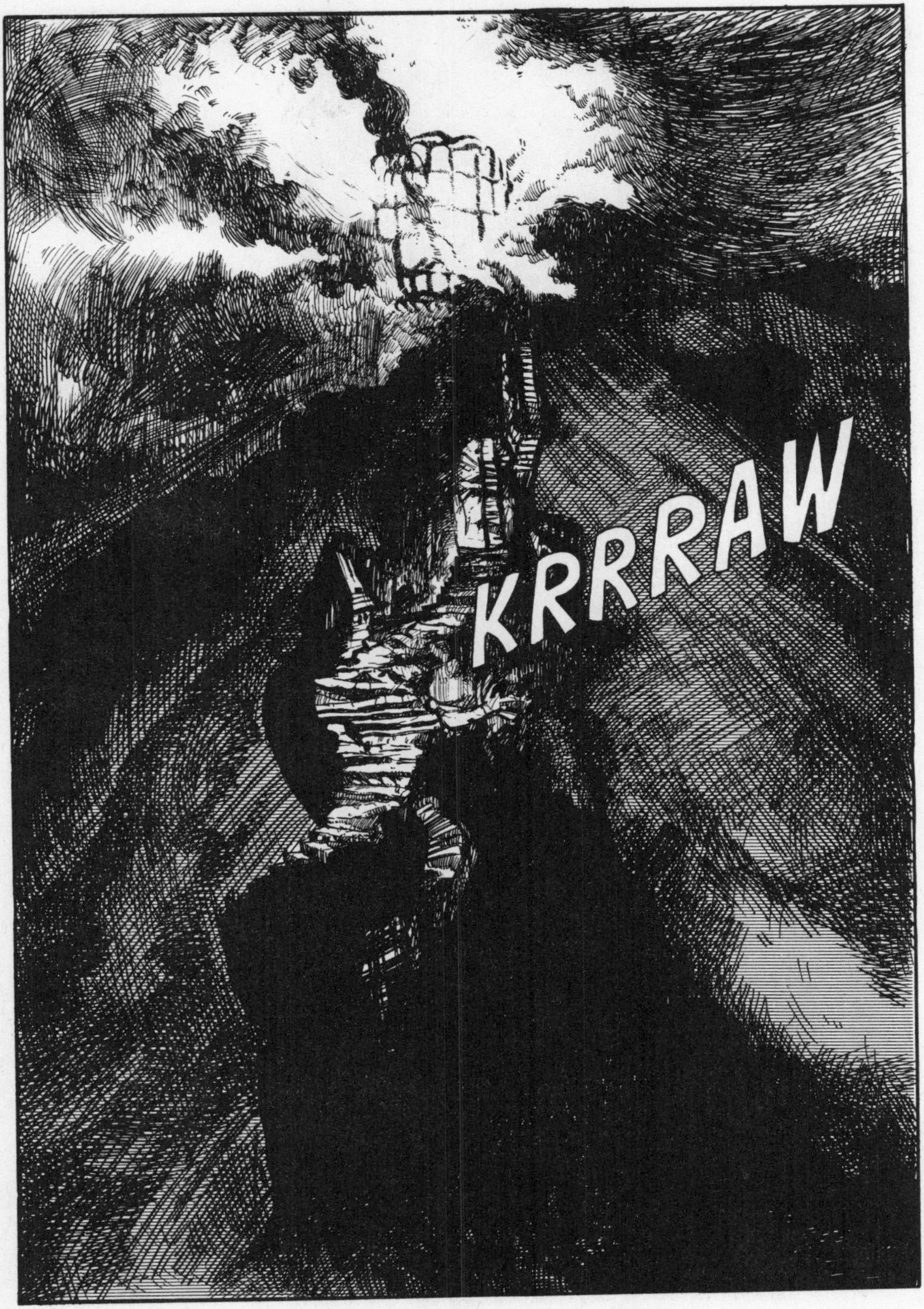
KRRRAW

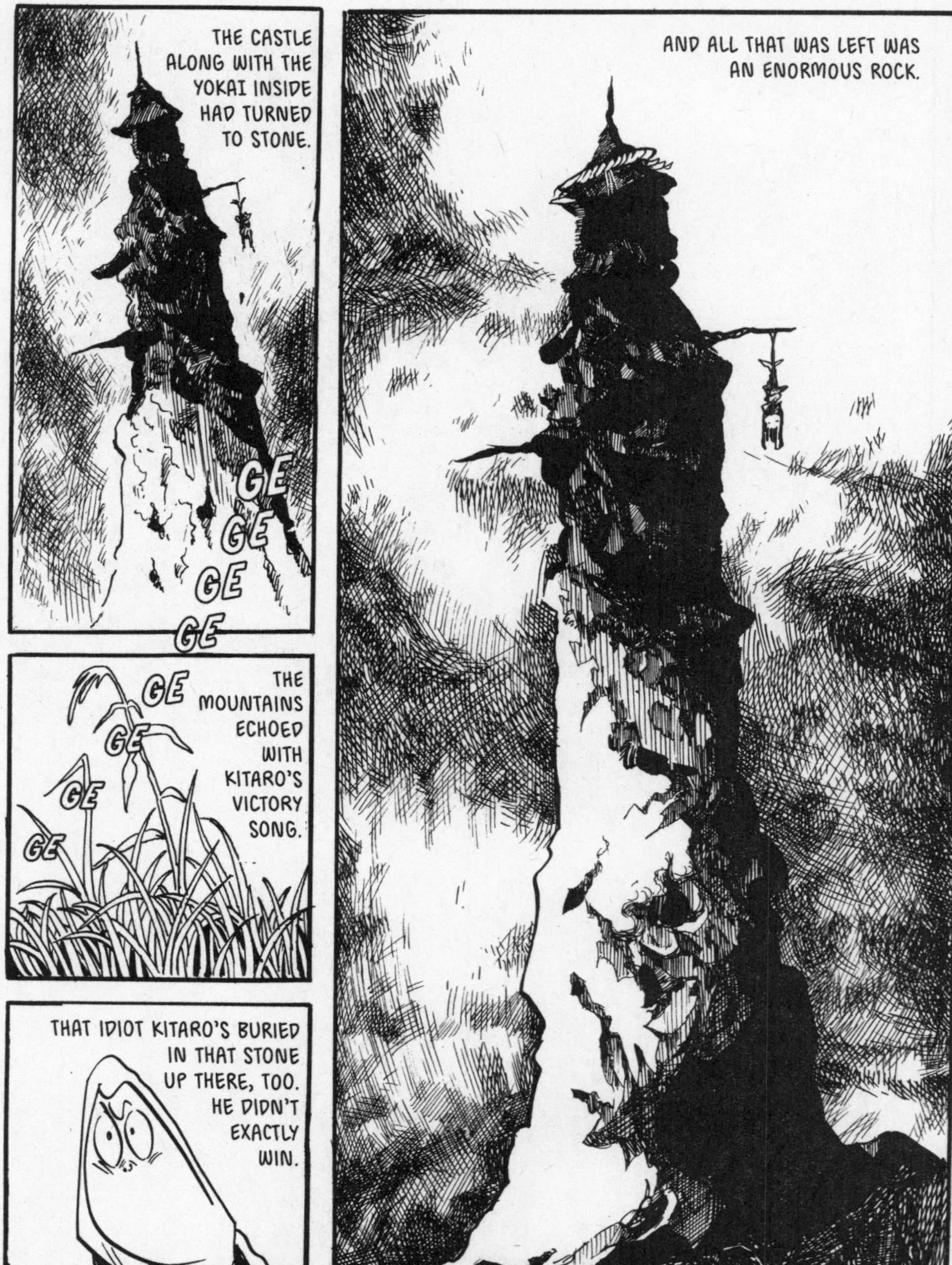
AND ALL THAT WAS LEFT WAS AN ENORMOUS ROCK.
THE CASTLE ALONG WITH THE YOKAI INSIDE HAD TURNED TO STONE.
GE GE GE GE
THE MOUNTAINS ECHOED WITH KITARO'S VICTORY SONG.
GE GE GE GE
THAT IDIOT KITARO'S BURIED IN THAT STONE UP THERE, TOO. HE DIDN'T EXACTLY WIN.

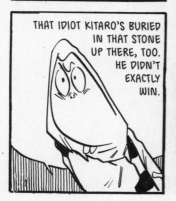

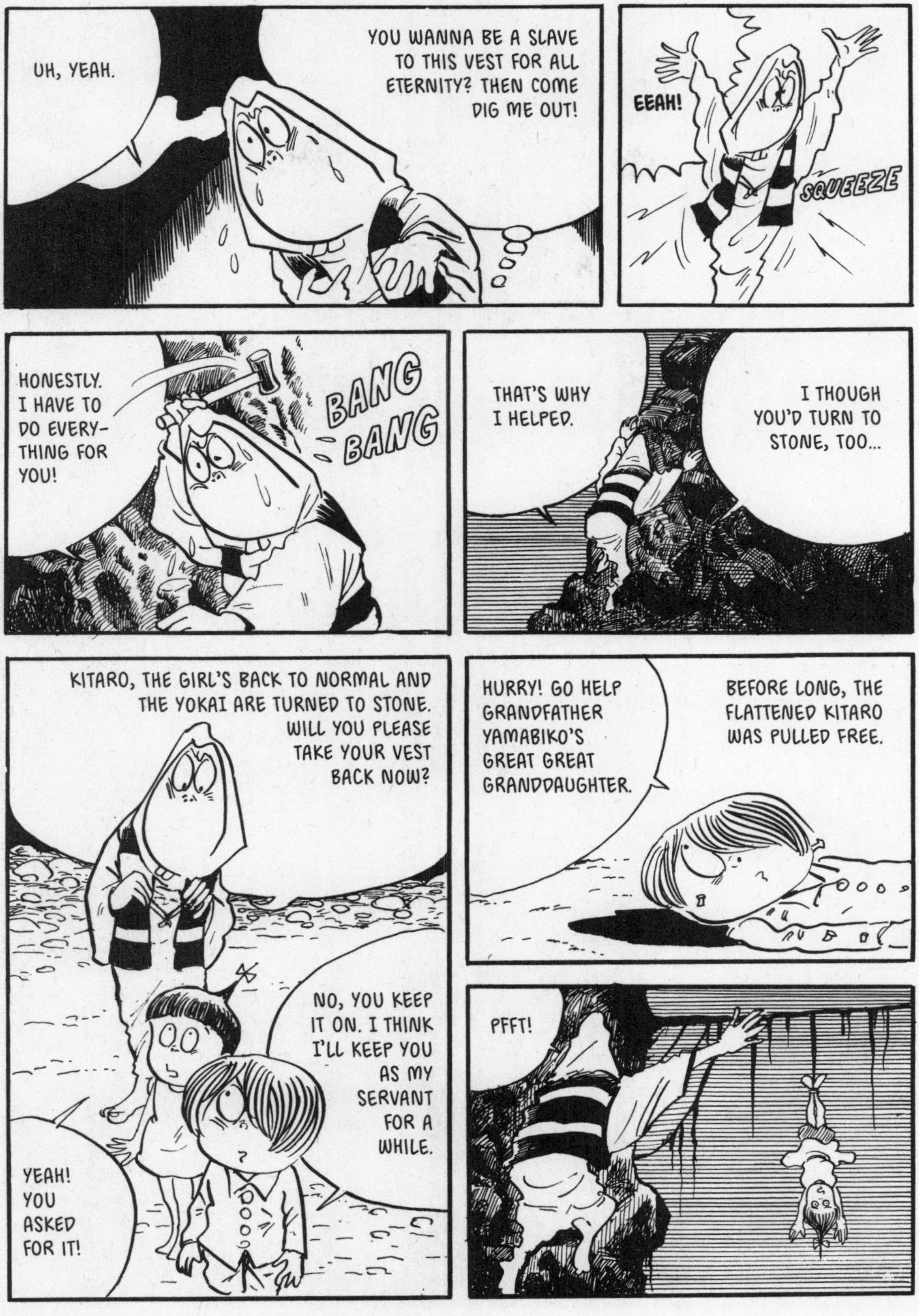
EEAH!
SQUEEZE
YOU WANNA BE A SLAVE TO THIS VEST FOR ALL ETERNITY? THEN COME DIG ME OUT!
UH, YEAH.
I THOUGH YOU'D TURN TO STONE, TOO...
THAT'S WHY I HELPED.
BANG
BANG
HONESTLY. I HAVE TO DO EVERY-THING FOR YOU!
BEFORE LONG, THE FLATTENED KITARO WAS PULLED FREE.
HURRY! GO HELP GRANDFATHER YAMABIKO'S GREAT GREAT GRANDDAUGHTER.
PFFT!
KITARO, THE GIRL'S BACK TO NORMAL AND THE YOKAI ARE TURNED TO STONE. WILL YOU PLEASE TAKE YOUR VEST BACK NOW?
NO, YOU KEEP IT ON. I THINK I'LL KEEP YOU AS MY SERVANT FOR A WHILE.
YEAH! YOU ASKED FOR IT!

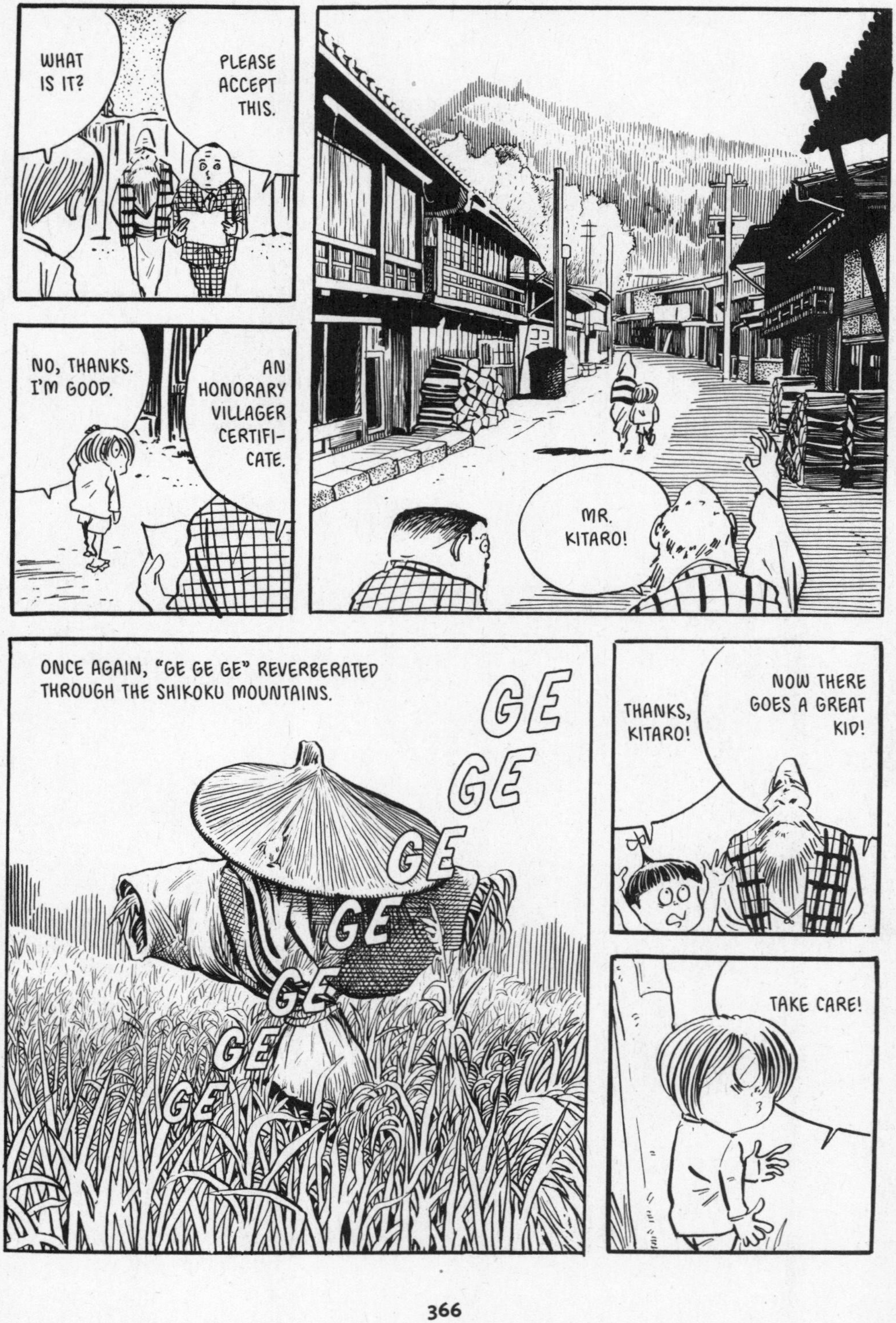
MR. KITARO!
PLEASE ACCEPT THIS.
WHAT IS IT?
AN HONORARY VILLAGER CERTIFICATE.
NO, THANKS. I'M GOOD.
NOW THERE GOES A GREAT KID!
THANKS, KITARO!
TAKE CARE!
ONCE AGAIN, "GE GE GE" REVERBERATED THROUGH THE SHIKOKU MOUNTAINS.
GE GE GE GE GE GE GE

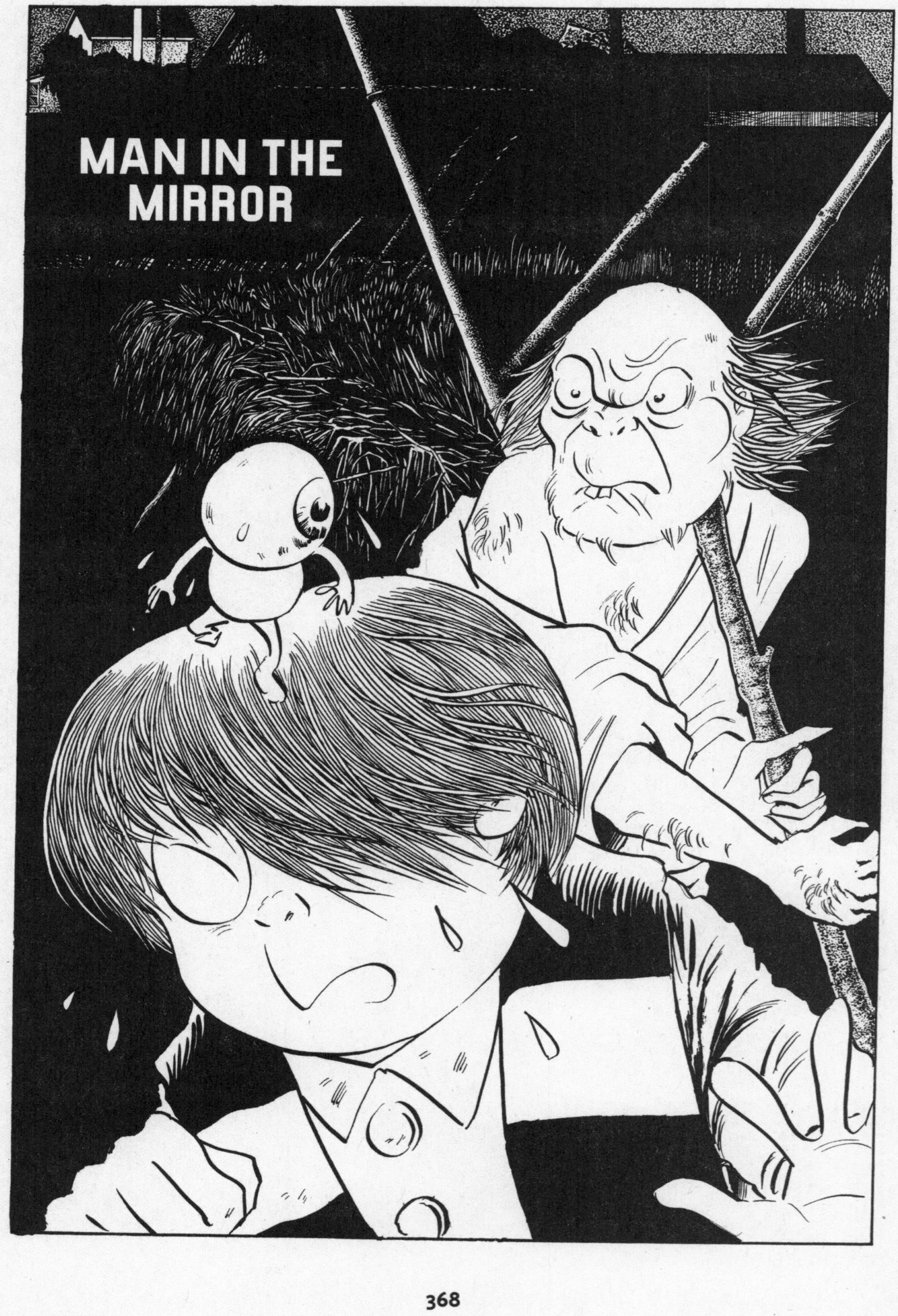
MAN IN THE
MIRROR

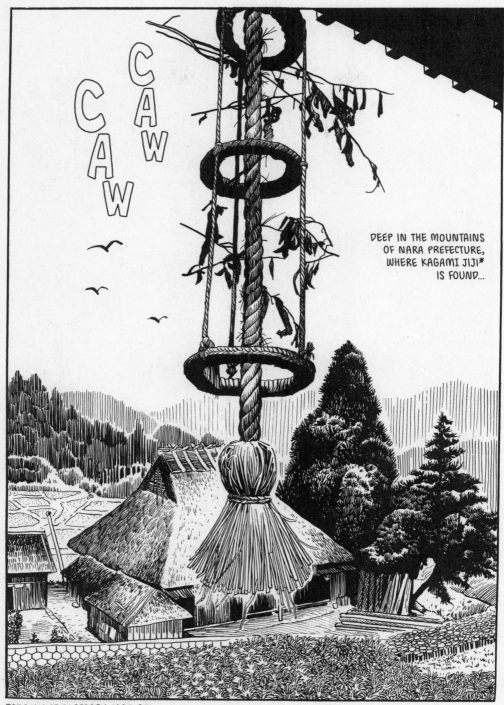

DEEP IN THE MOUNTAINS OF NARA PREFECTURE, WHERE KAGAMI JIJI* IS FOUND...

*SEE YOKAI GLOSSARY PAGE 396.

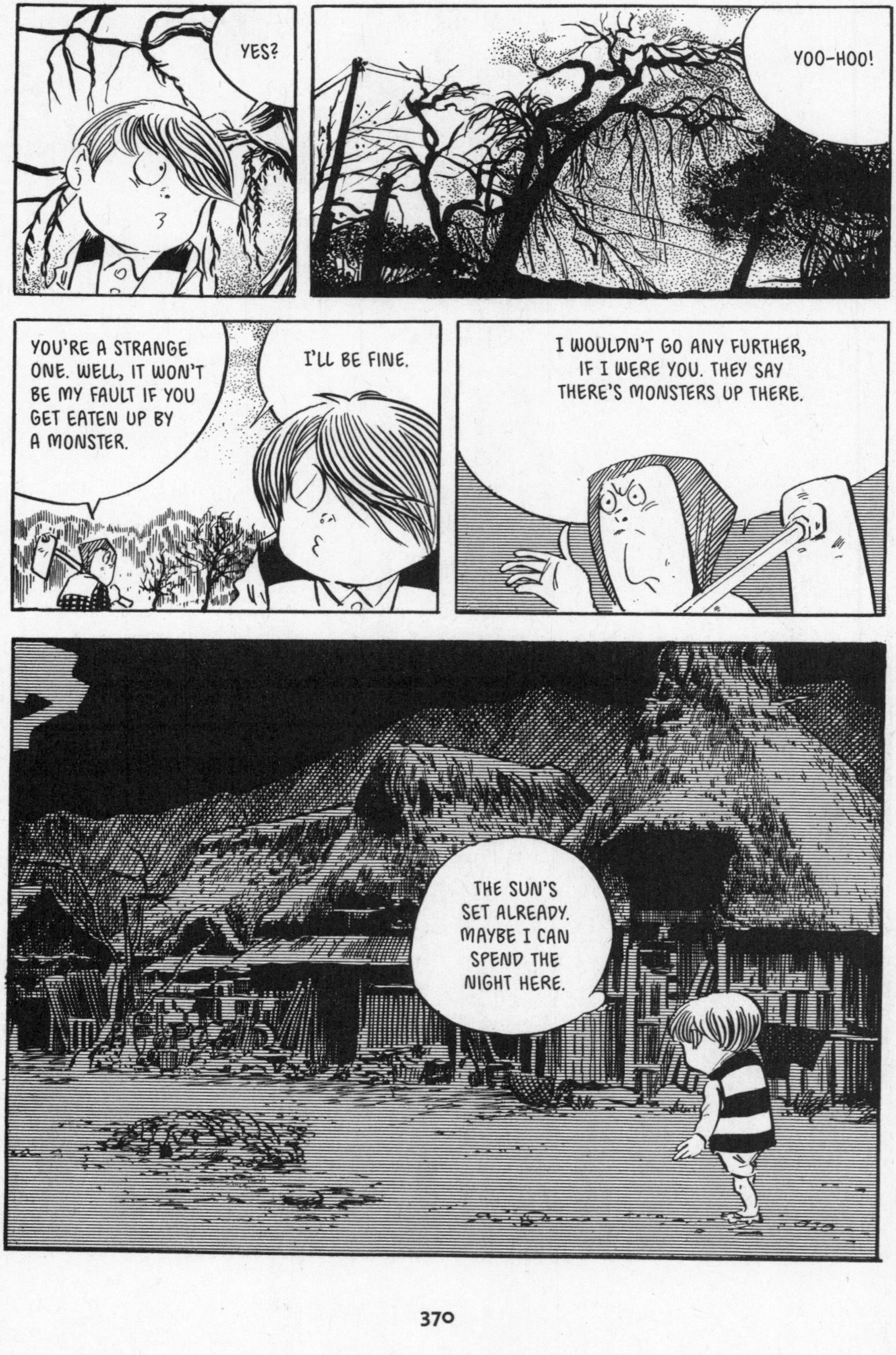
YOO-HOO!
YES?
I WOULDN'T GO ANY FURTHER, IF I WERE YOU. THEY SAY THERE'S MONSTERS UP THERE.
I'LL BE FINE.
YOU'RE A STRANGE ONE. WELL, IT WON'T BE MY FAULT IF YOU GET EATEN UP BY A MONSTER.
THE SUN'S SET ALREADY. MAYBE I CAN SPEND THE NIGHT HERE.

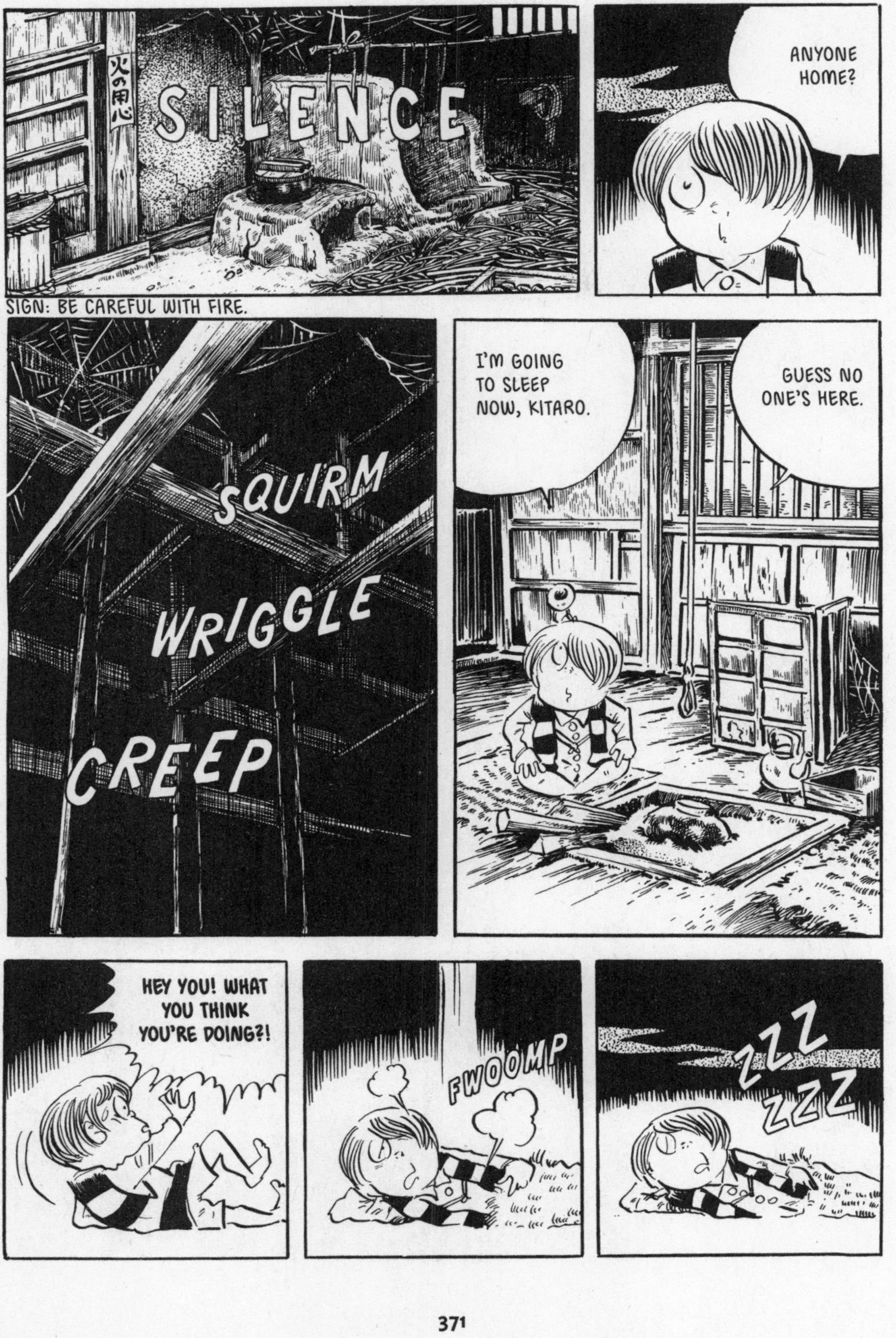
ANYONE HOME?
SILENCE
火の用心
SIGN: BE CAREFUL WITH FIRE.
GUESS NO ONE'S HERE.
I'M GOING TO SLEEP NOW, KITARO.
SQUIRM
WRIGGLE
CREEP
ZZZ
ZZZ
FWOOMP
HEY YOU! WHAT YOU THINK YOU'RE DOING?!

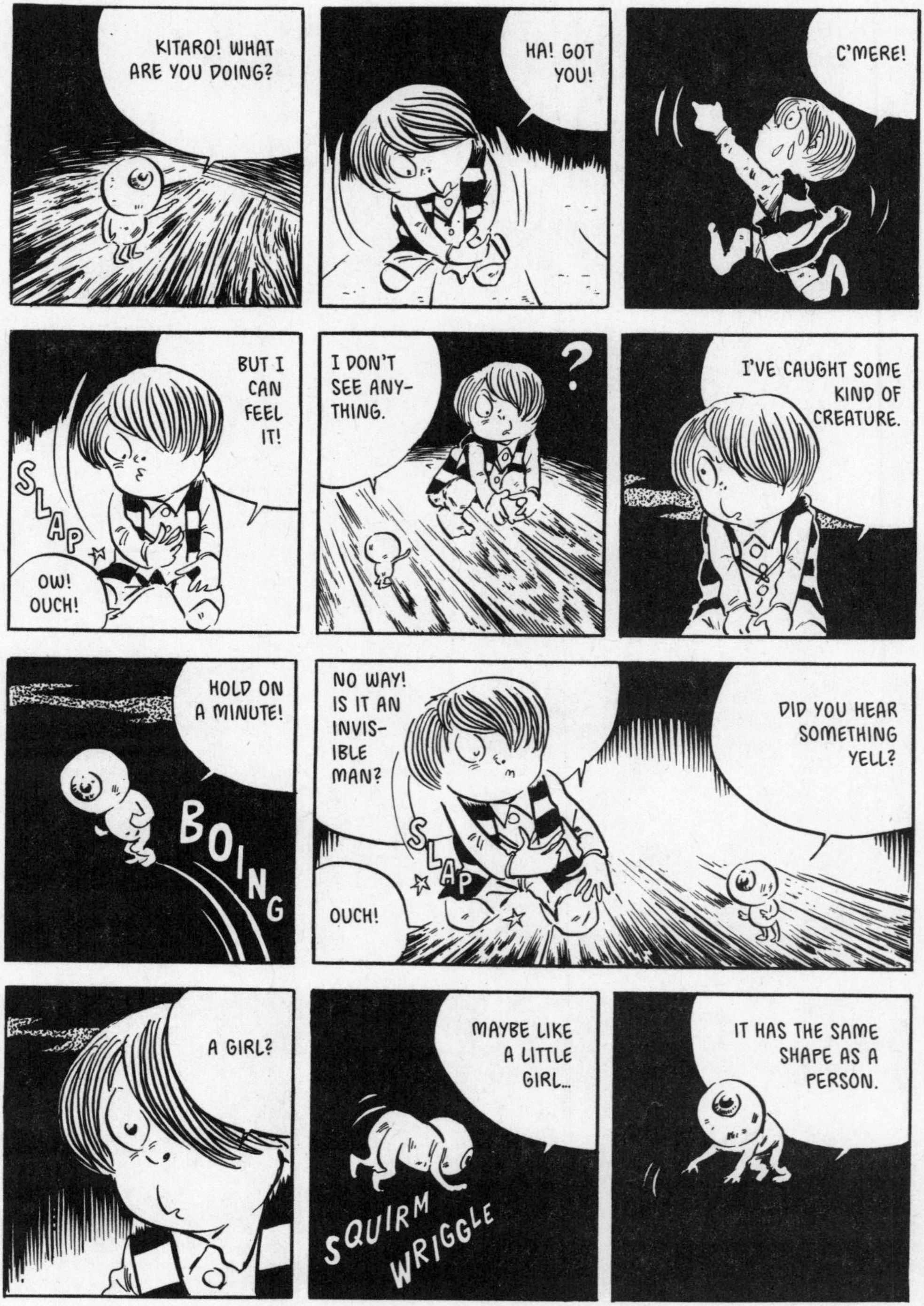
C'MERE!
HA! GOT YOU!
KITARO! WHAT ARE YOU DOING?
I'VE CAUGHT SOME KIND OF CREATURE.
?
I DON'T SEE ANY-THING.
BUT I CAN FEEL IT!
SLAP
OW! OUCH!
DID YOU HEAR SOMETHING YELL?
NO WAY! IS IT AN INVIS-IBLE MAN?
SLAP
OUCH!
HOLD ON A MINUTE!
BOING
IT HAS THE SAME SHAPE AS A PERSON.
MAYBE LIKE A LITTLE GIRL...
SQUIRM
WRIGGLE
A GIRL?

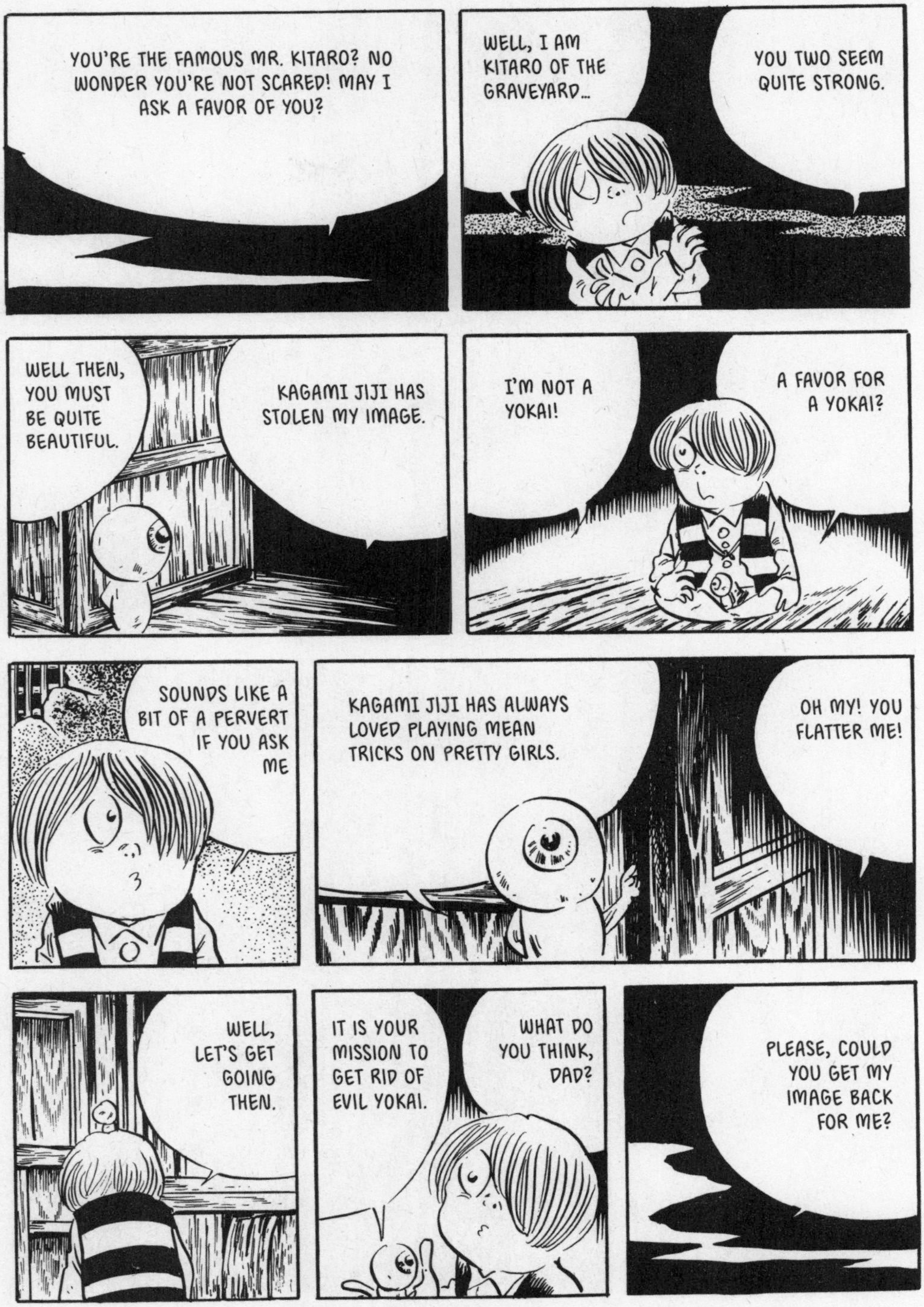
YOU TWO SEEM QUITE STRONG.
WELL, I AM KITARO OF THE GRAVEYARD...
YOU'RE THE FAMOUS MR. KITARO? NO WONDER YOU'RE NOT SCARED! MAY I ASK A FAVOR OF YOU?
A FAVOR FOR A YOKAI?
I'M NOT A YOKAI!
KAGAMI JIJI HAS STOLEN MY IMAGE.
WELL THEN, YOU MUST BE QUITE BEAUTIFUL.
OH MY! YOU FLATTER ME!
KAGAMI JIJI HAS ALWAYS LOVED PLAYING MEAN TRICKS ON PRETTY GIRLS.
SOUNDS LIKE A BIT OF A PERVERT IF YOU ASK ME
PLEASE, COULD YOU GET MY IMAGE BACK FOR ME?
WHAT DO YOU THINK, DAD?
IT IS YOUR MISSION TO GET RID OF EVIL YOKAI.
WELL, LET'S GET GOING THEN.

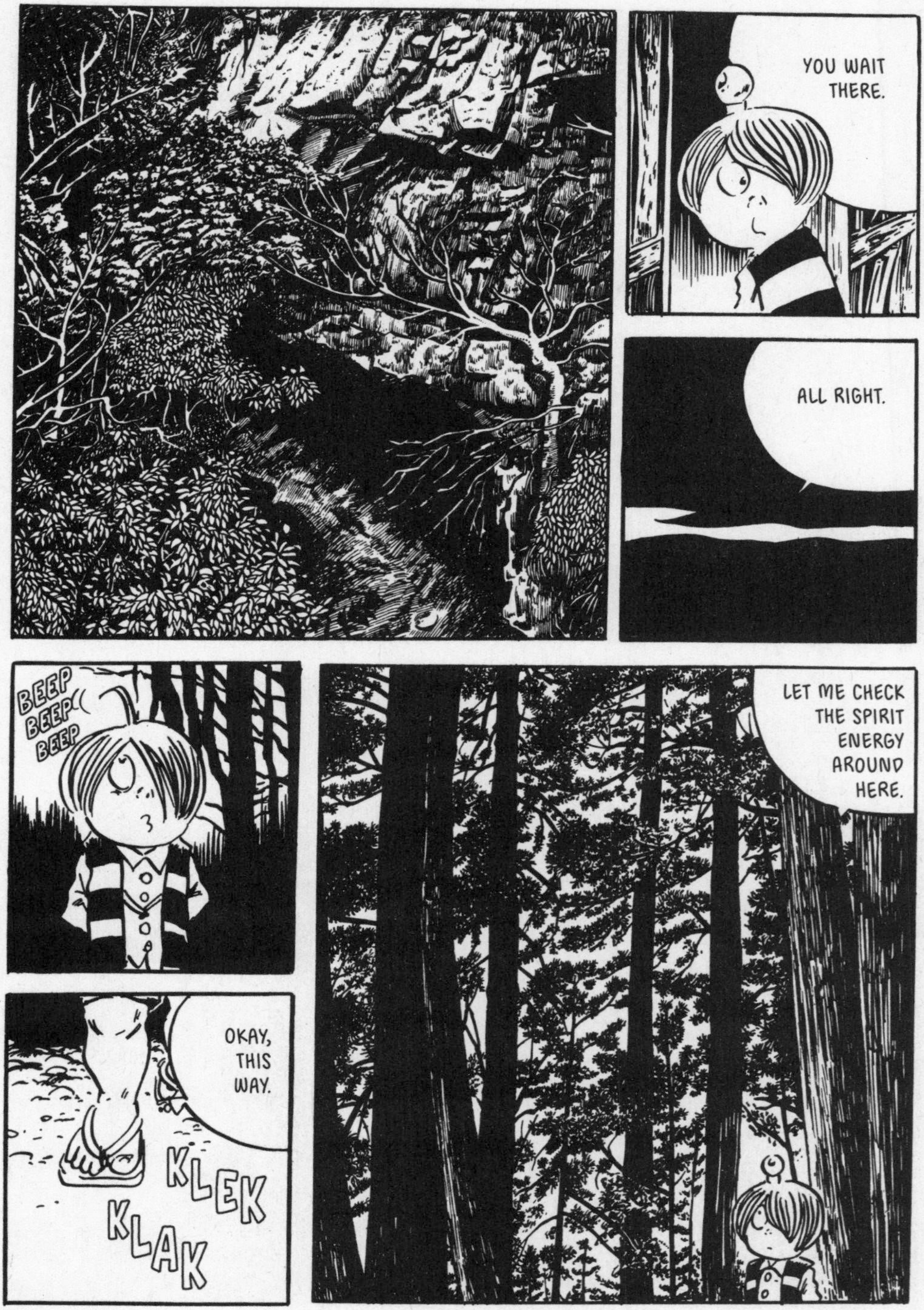
YOU WAIT THERE.
ALL RIGHT.
LET ME CHECK THE SPIRIT ENERGY AROUND HERE.
BEEP BEEP BEEP
OKAY, THIS WAY.
KLEK KLAK

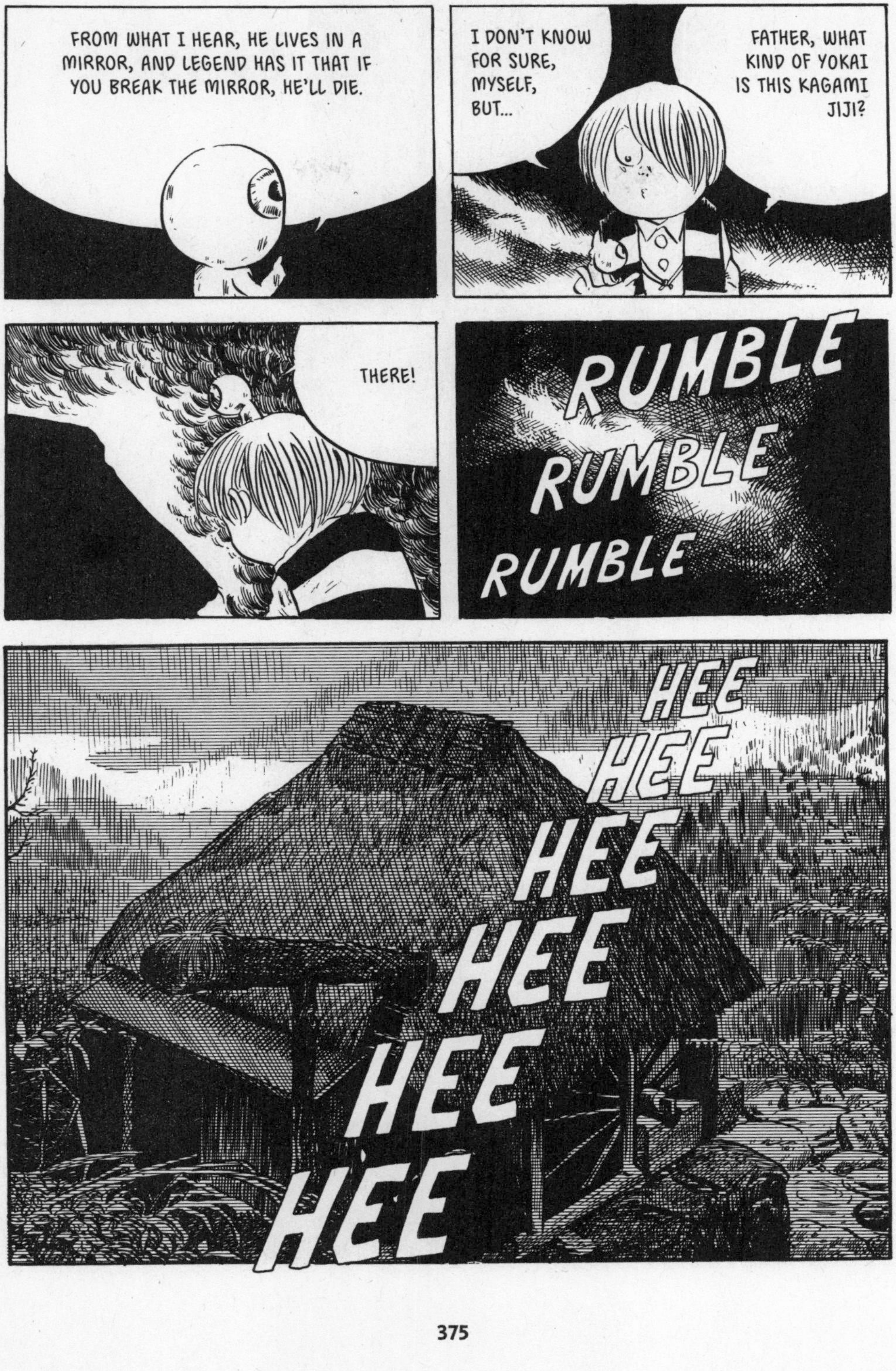
FATHER, WHAT KIND OF YOKAI IS THIS KAGAMI JIJI?
I DON'T KNOW FOR SURE, MYSELF, BUT...
FROM WHAT I HEAR, HE LIVES IN A MIRROR, AND LEGEND HAS IT THAT IF YOU BREAK THE MIRROR, HE'LL DIE.
RUMBLE RUMBLE RUMBLE
THERE!
HEE HEE HEE HEE HEE HEE

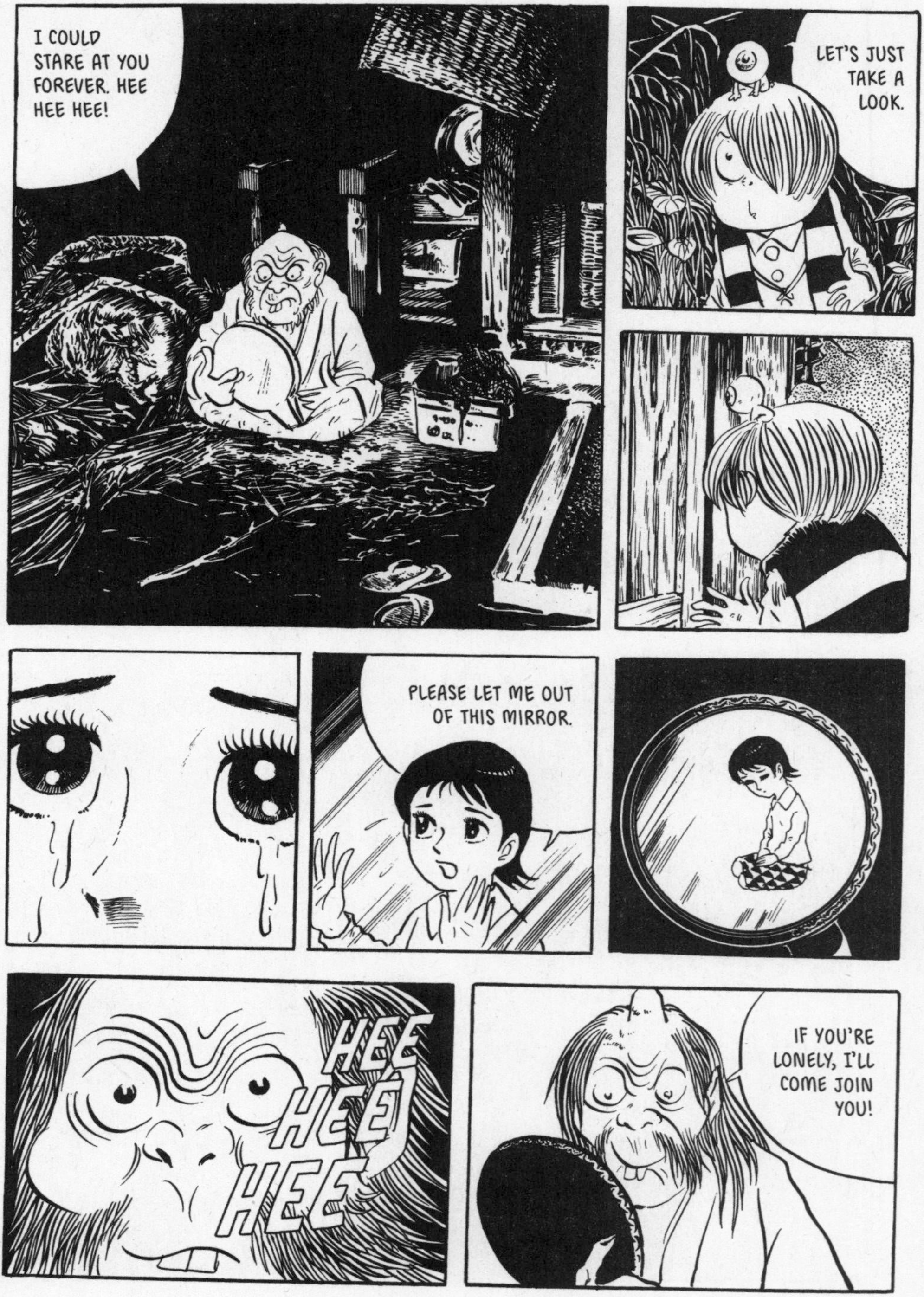
LET'S JUST TAKE A LOOK.
I COULD STARE AT YOU FOREVER. HEE HEE HEE!
PLEASE LET ME OUT OF THIS MIRROR.
IF YOU'RE LONELY, I'LL COME JOIN YOU!
HEE HEE HEE

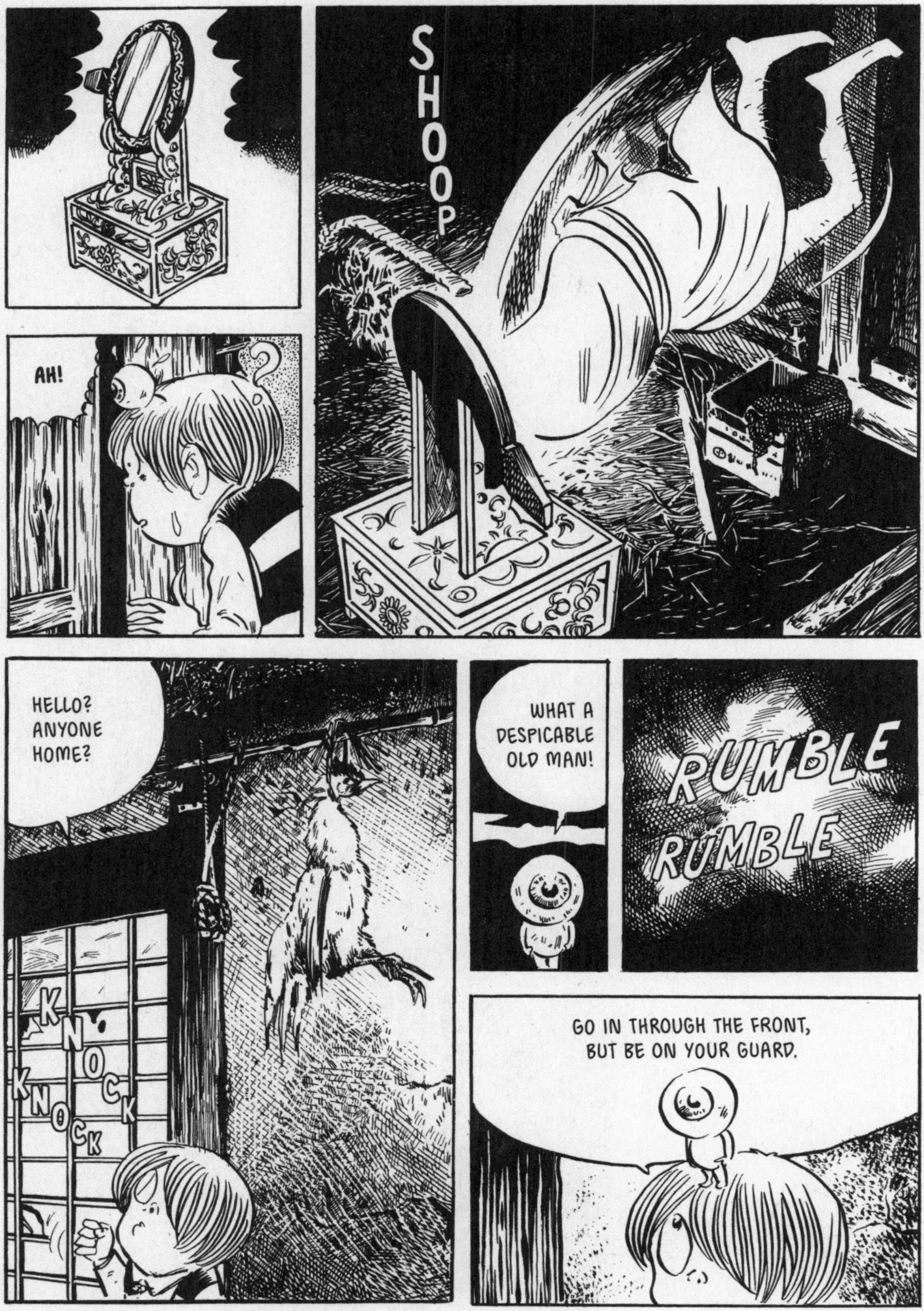
SHOOP
AH!
RUMBLE RUMBLE
WHAT A DESPICABLE OLD MAN!
GO IN THROUGH THE FRONT, BUT BE ON YOUR GUARD.
HELLO? ANYONE HOME?
KNOCK KNOCK

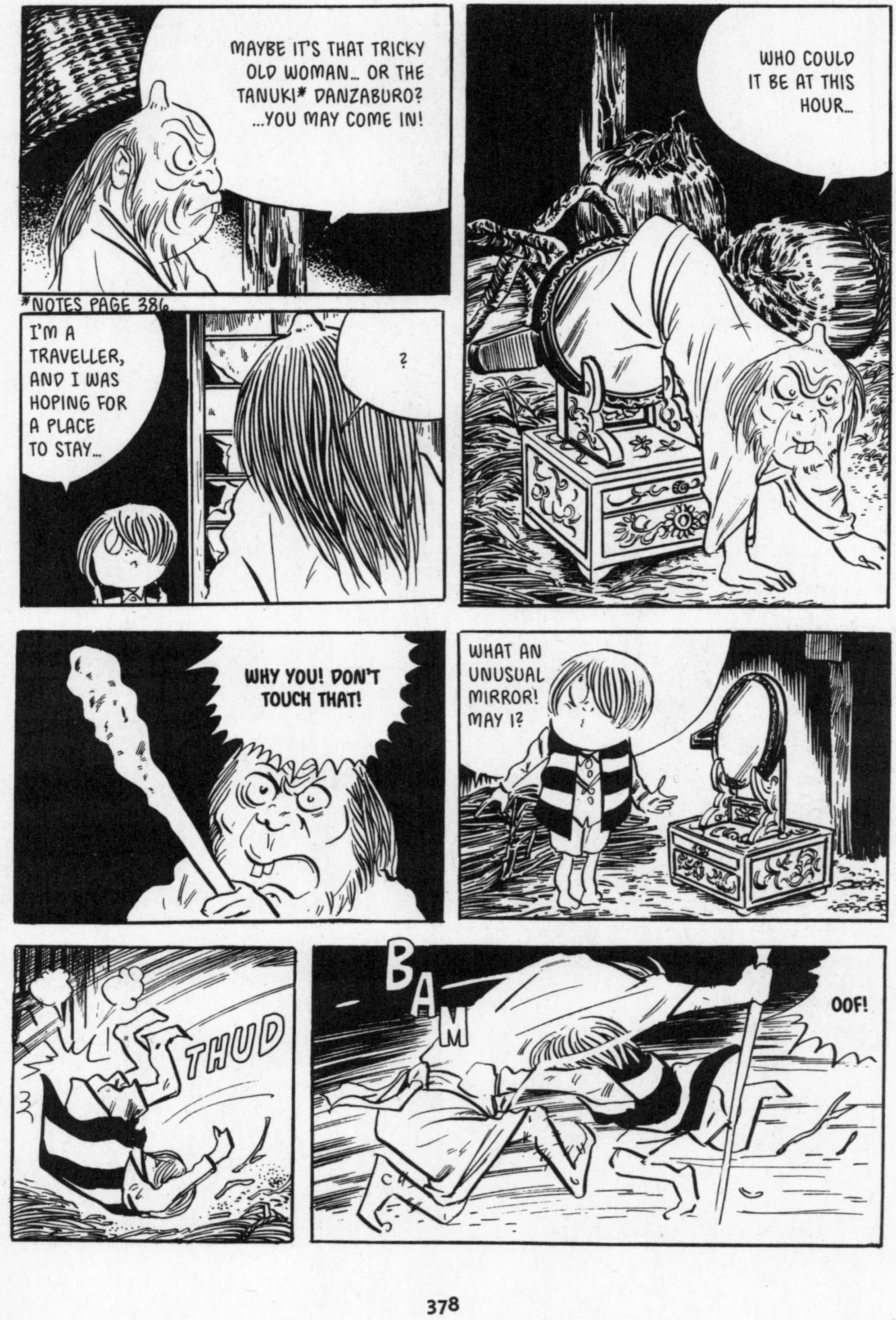
WHO COULD IT BE AT THIS HOUR...
MAYBE IT'S THAT TRICKY OLD WOMAN... OR THE TANUKI* DANZABURO? ...YOU MAY COME IN!
?
I'M A TRAVELLER, AND I WAS HOPING FOR A PLACE TO STAY...
WHAT AN UNUSUAL MIRROR! MAY I?
WHY YOU! DON'T TOUCH THAT!
OOF!
BAM
THUD

*NOTES PAGE 386

FOOL.

KAGAMI JIJI HAS NO SOLID FORM. WHETHER IT WAS KITARO'S FISTS OR HIS SPIRIT POWERS, NOTHING COULD TOUCH HIM.

GET IN THERE.

FWWRRK

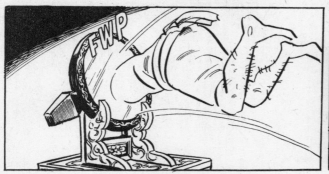

FWP

AH!

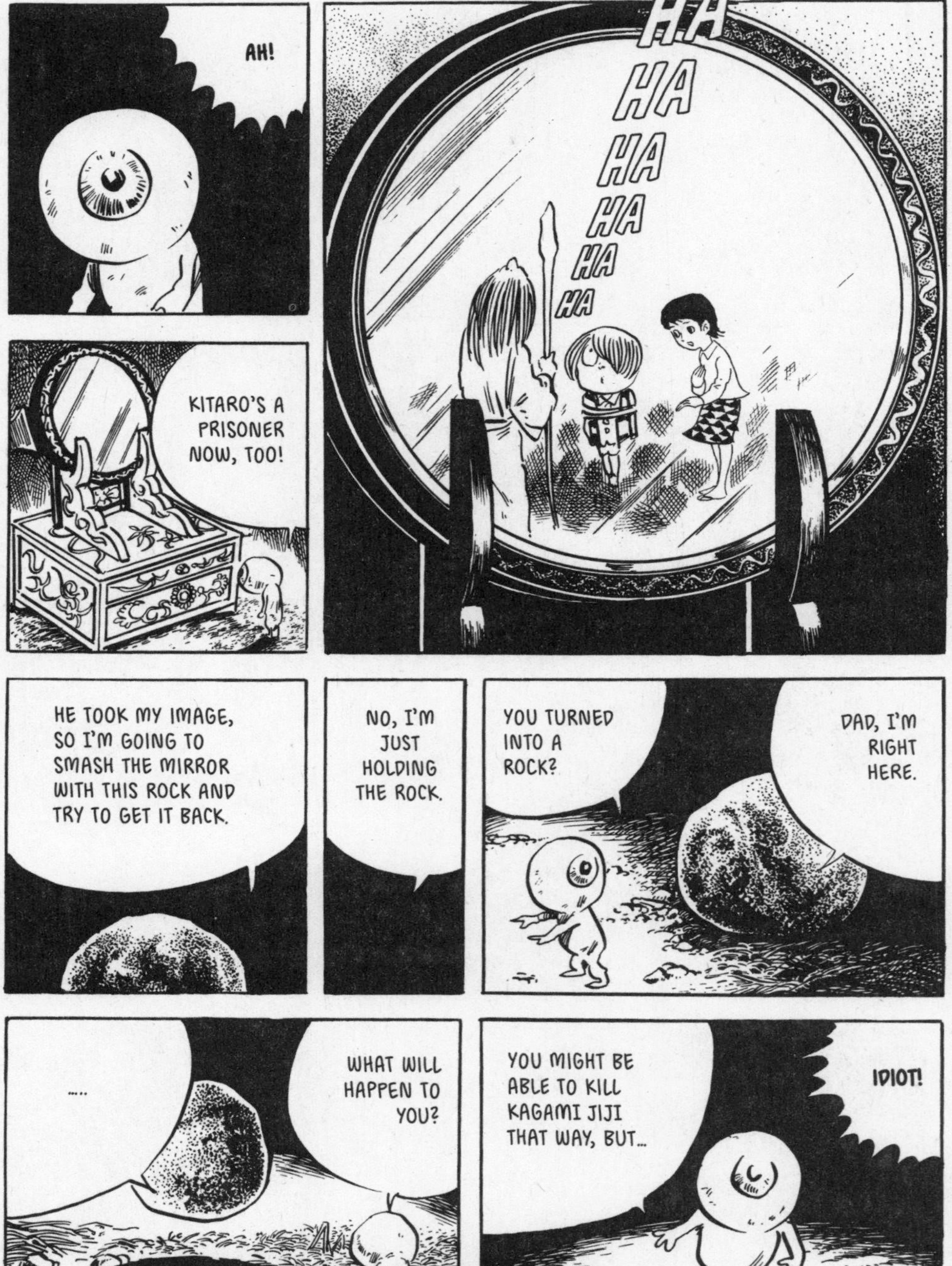
HA
HA
HA
HA
HA
HA
HA
AH!
KITARO'S A PRISONER NOW, TOO!
DAD, I'M RIGHT HERE.
YOU TURNED INTO A ROCK?
NO, I'M JUST HOLDING THE ROCK.
HE TOOK MY IMAGE, SO I'M GOING TO SMASH THE MIRROR WITH THIS ROCK AND TRY TO GET IT BACK.
IDIOT!
YOU MIGHT BE ABLE TO KILL KAGAMI JIJI THAT WAY, BUT...
WHAT WILL HAPPEN TO YOU?
.....

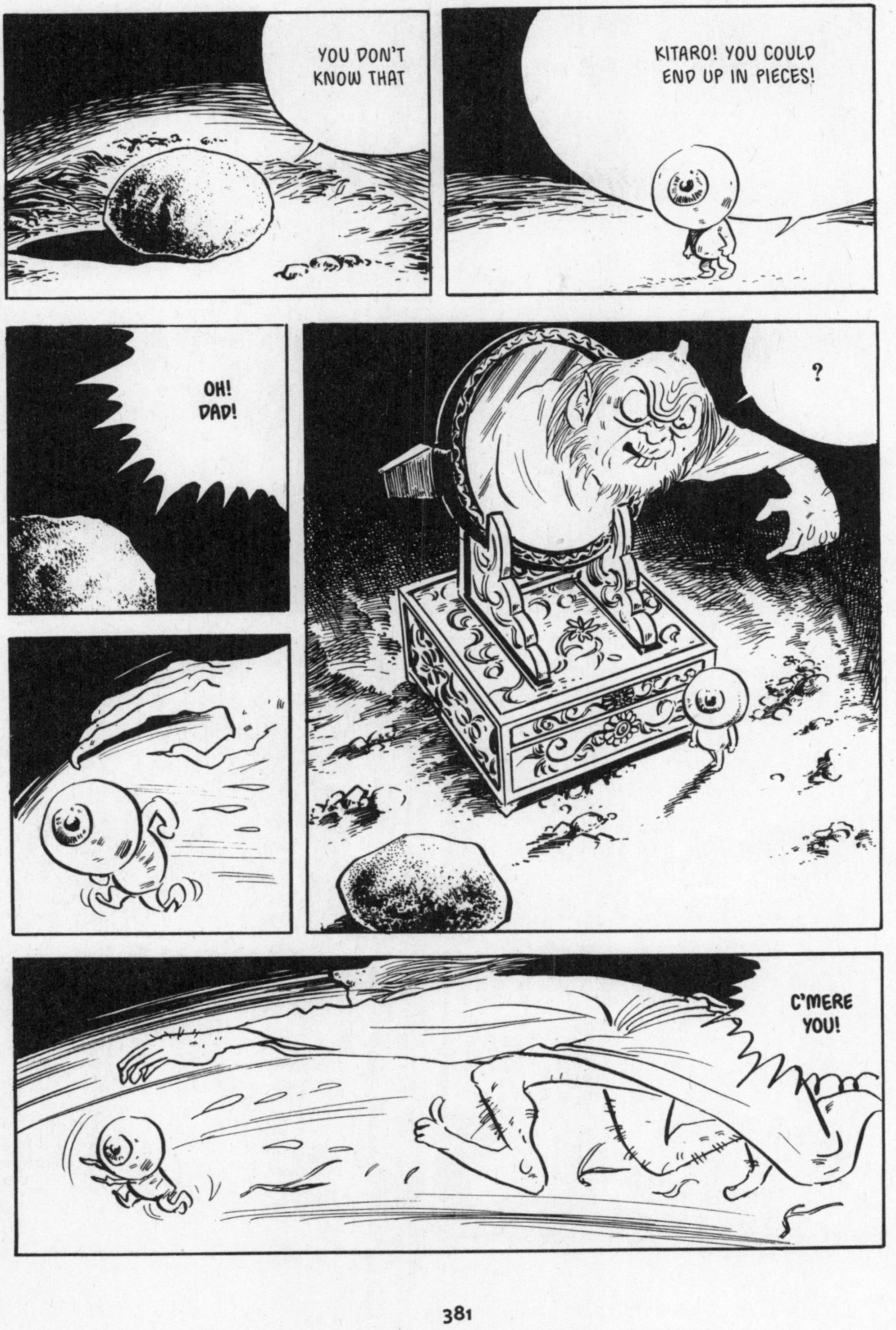
KITARO! YOU COULD END UP IN PIECES!
YOU DON'T KNOW THAT
?
OH! DAD!
C'MERE YOU!

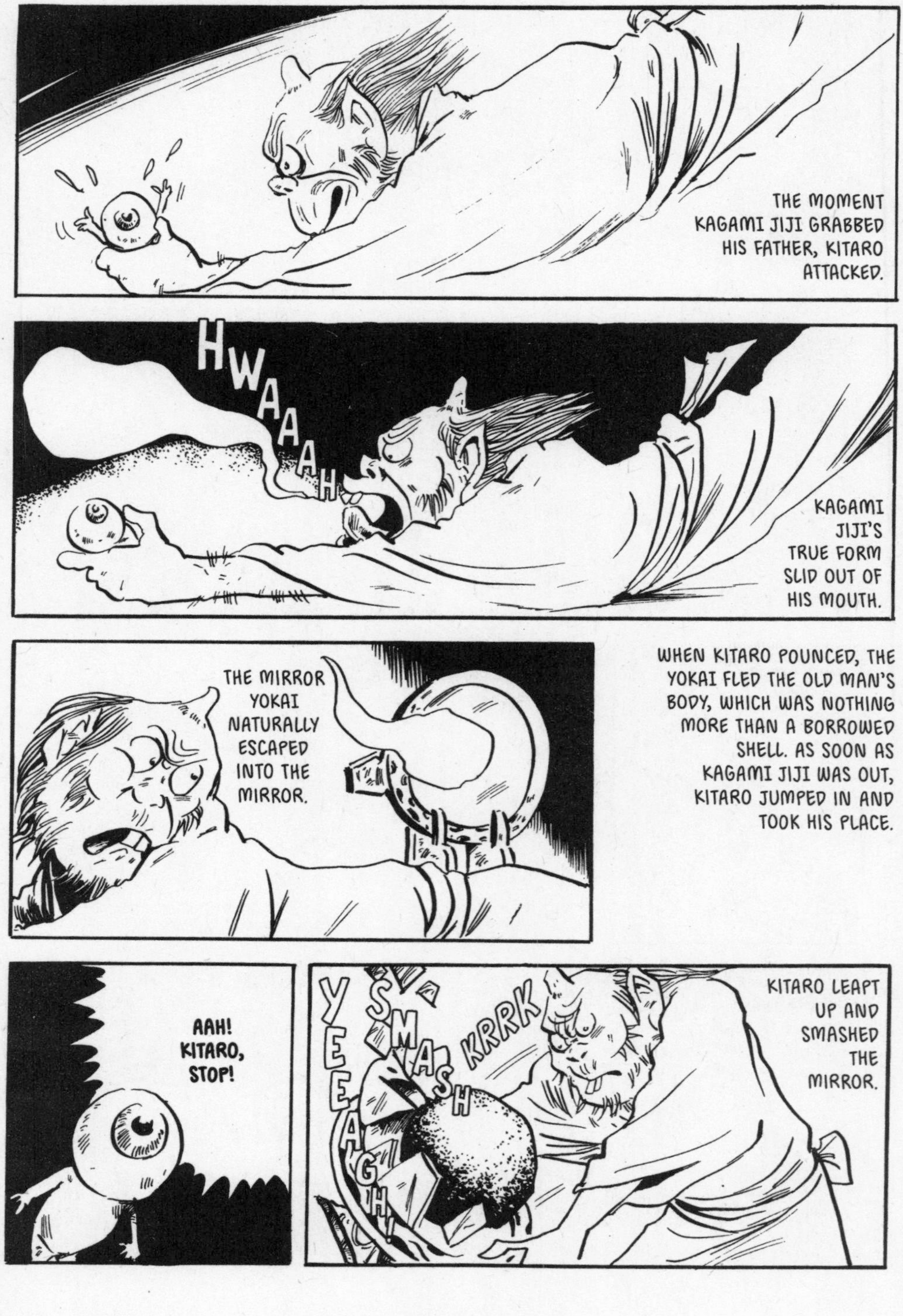
THE MOMENT KAGAMI JIJI GRABBED HIS FATHER, KITARO ATTACKED.
KAGAMI JIJI'S TRUE FORM SLID OUT OF HIS MOUTH.
HWAAAAH
WHEN KITARO POUNCED, THE YOKAI FLED THE OLD MAN'S BODY, WHICH WAS NOTHING MORE THAN A BORROWED SHELL. AS SOON AS KAGAMI JIJI WAS OUT, KITARO JUMPED IN AND TOOK HIS PLACE.
THE MIRROR YOKAI NATURALLY ESCAPED INTO THE MIRROR.
KITARO LEAPT UP AND SMASHED THE MIRROR.
KRRK
SMASH
YEEAAGH!
AAH! KITARO, STOP!

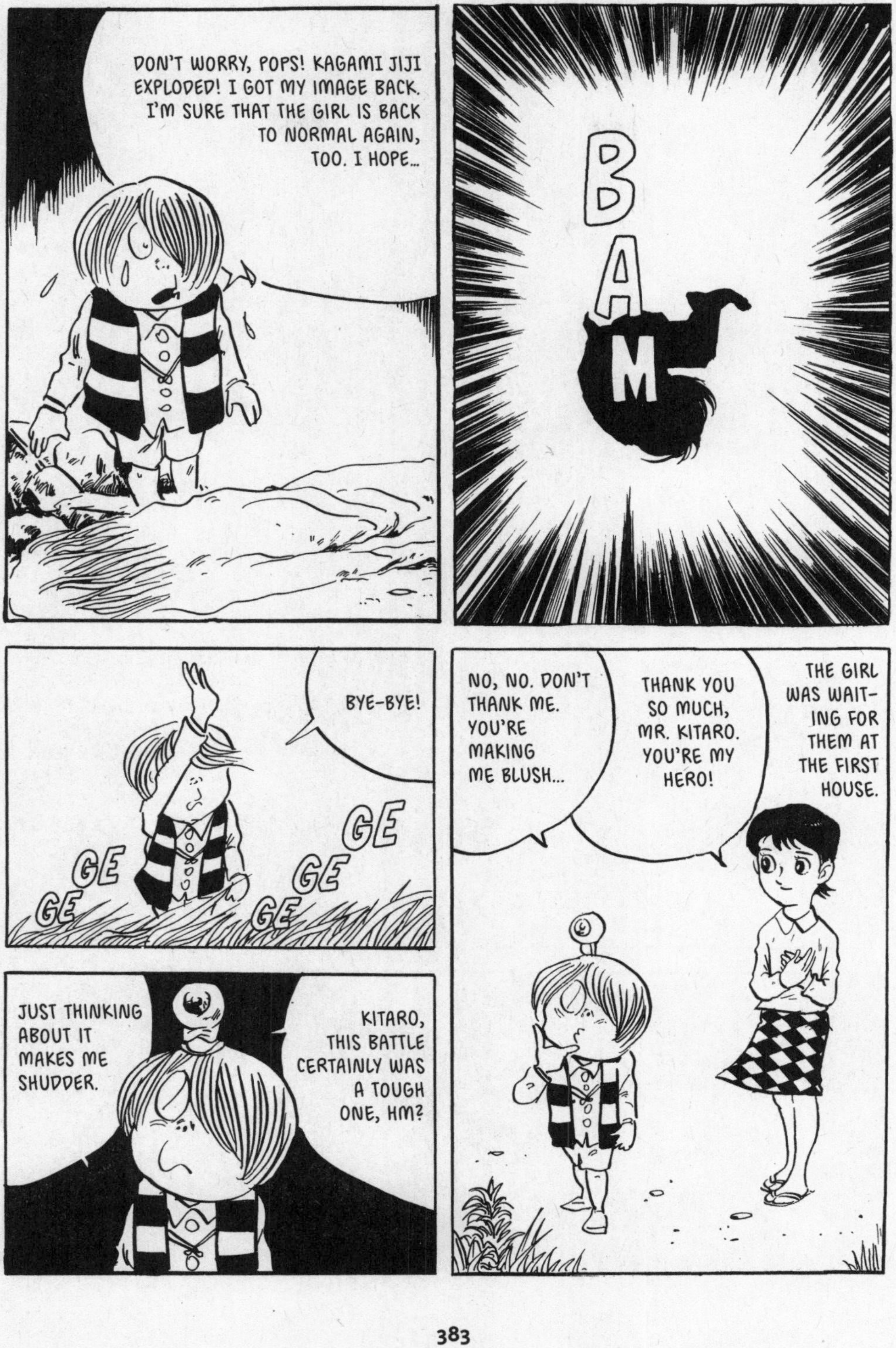
BAM
DON'T WORRY, POPS! KAGAMI JIJI EXPLODED! I GOT MY IMAGE BACK. I'M SURE THAT THE GIRL IS BACK TO NORMAL AGAIN, TOO. I HOPE...
THE GIRL WAS WAITING FOR THEM AT THE FIRST HOUSE.
THANK YOU SO MUCH, MR. KITARO. YOU'RE MY HERO!
NO, NO. DON'T THANK ME. YOU'RE MAKING ME BLUSH...
BYE-BYE!
GE GE GE GE GE
KITARO, THIS BATTLE CERTAINLY WAS A TOUGH ONE, HM?
JUST THINKING ABOUT IT MAKES ME SHUDDER.

NOTES

8 Article: Three more dead. The strange illness spreading through Tokyo is very similar to an outbreak in Paris, France.

20 *Gomoku* (also known as GoBang or Five-In-A-Row) is a game played with black and white stones on a Go board. The object of the game is to get an unbroken row of five stones in any direction.

22 The "ge ge ge" of the song and of Kitaro's Japanese title *Ge Ge Ge no Kitaro* comes from Shigeru Mizuki's own childhood nickname. As a boy, he was unable to pronounce his given name, and ended up calling himself "Gegeru". The name stuck and was generally shortened to "Gege". *Kitaro* was originally called *Kitaro of the Graveyard* with the "ge ge ge" only appearing in the song in praise of Kitaro, but when the manga was turned into an animated TV series in 1968, sponsors thought "Graveyard" was too scary for a kids show, so the program became *Ge Ge Ge no Kitaro*. The title of the manga was changed to *Ge Ge Ge no Kitaro* to match in November 1967 while the show was in production.

61 A *shamisen* is a three-stringed instrument, the cover of which is made out of cat skin (or dog skin for cheaper student instruments).

86 Donpei has placed the bat in the alcove, a space usually reserved for the display of beautiful and valuable objects.

98 The traditional *suiko* is often confused with the *kappa* (water-dwelling yokai known for their love of eating children and cucumbers) due to their similar appearance, but the *suiko* is larger, fiercer and much more likely to take a person's life. However, the *suiko* Mizuki depicts here has little in common with this standard interpretation of the yokai, aside from the shared ability to possess people.

122 The Dragon King's palace (*ryugu-jo*) is the mythical palace of the dragon god at the bottom of the sea, which appears often in Japanese folklore.

131 Momotaro is a hero from a Japanese fairytale often translated as "Peach Boy". Momotaro comes to earth in a giant peach floating down a river where a poor, old childless couple live. When she and her husband open the peach to eat it, they discover the baby boy and adopt him as their son. When Momotaro grows up, he goes off to fight the demons terrorizing a far-off island, teaming up with a dog, a monkey, and a pheasant, who use their various talents to help him defeat the demons. He returns home with the spoils of his victory to provide a comfortable life for his old parents.

142 Nishi Chofu is a station in the Chofu area of western Tokyo, where Mizuki has lived for a number of years.

148 The Sai Riverbed is said to be the head of the underworld's Sanzu River, and is the place where children who die before their parents are punished and tormented for their lack of filial piety.

157 The characters in the Japanese name (*Kikaigashima*) are "Demon", "World" and "Island".

159 Ad: Yokai Wanted, Destination: Kikai Island, Remuneration: One gold piece, Place: Tama Cemetery, Date/Time: April 1, 12:00 a.m.

175 Yamato was a World War II battleship, one of the most powerful ships ever built. Designed to fight the US fleet, it was hit by at least eleven torpedos and sunk south of the Japanese island of Kyushu.

243 Kannon-zaki is a small peninsula in Yokosuka, Kanagawa Prefecture, about eighty kilometers south of Tokyo.

295 The Hedgehog was an anti-submarine munition developed during World War II.

310 A *daruma* is a round doll, usually painted red with a beard and made from papier-maché, that is thought to bring luck and make wishes come true. The daruma usually has unpainted eyes: one is filled in when the owner makes a wish or goal, and the other is filled in when the wish comes true or the goal is met.

312 The character for the number four can be read as *shi*, the same reading as the character for the word "death."

327 Shikoku is the smallest of the four main islands of Japan, south of the main island of Honshu.

362 The sacred rope Nezumi Otoko is making is a *shimenawa*, a braided straw rope used for ritual purification and to mark sacred places in Shintoism. The sacred streamers— *gohei* or *shime*—are pieces of white paper cut into strips and hung from the shimenawa ropes to symbolize purity.

378 The *tanuki* is a raccoon dog famous in Japanese folklore for its mischievousness and its ability to change shape.

YOKAI GLOSSARY ZACH DAVISSON

BRIEF DESCRIPTIONS OF SOME OF THE KEY YOKAI PLAYERS IN THIS VOLUME

MEDAMA OYAJI

Kitaro's father. An eyeball that rolled from his own jellified corpse, Medama Oyaji willed himself back to life so he could keep an eye on his newborn baby Kitaro, the last of the Ghost Tribe. He rides around in Kitaro's empty eye socket and is always ready to lend a hand. Medama Oyaji is a scholar extraordinaire on all things yokai with centuries of experience and contacts in the yokai world. He advises Kitaro on problems that inevitably arise, and pulls the boy out of scrapes when Kitaro has gotten in over his head. Medama Oyaji likes nothing better to kick back and relax, soaking in a teacup bath.

NEZUMI OTOKO

Half yokai. Half human. All scoundrel. Nezumi Otoko is over 360 years old and boasts that he has never seen the inside of a bathtub. His greatest weapon is his stench—his breath alone can knock you out cold. In spite of his tattered appearance, he claims to be a degreed scholar from Yokai University. But I wouldn't trust a word he says. Deceitful. Conniving. Greedy. Nezumi Otoko is also one of Kitaro's best friends—the kind of friend that would sell Kitaro out for the price of a candy bar. But despite Nezumi Otoko's most Machiavellian mechanizations, he always seems to end up on the right side in the end.

LA SEINE

A vampire from France who came to test his powers against the famous Kitaro and sample Japanese blood. La Seine takes his name from the Seine River that flows through Paris.

YASHA

A soul-swallowing night demon, Yasha is more than just a handsome face crowned with fine, flowing hair. His guitar and sweet voice charms the souls right out of children's bodies like a Japanese Pied Piper. If you ever seen the Yasha's true form, watch out. You'll find yourself in a hairy situation.

NEKO SENIN

Neko Senin is a 1,200-year old man who mastered the secret of immortality by separating his soul from his body. To protect his body, he hid it deep inside an ancient burial mound. His soul he placed inside of a cat, moving from cat to cat across the centuries to become a cat immortal.

HYAKUME

In Hyakume's case, the name says it all. "Hyakume" means "one hundred eyes" and that's pretty much what you get with this grotesque yokai. Hyakume only comes out at night. With that many eyes, the sun is blinding and it is hard to find sunglasses that fit.

SUIKO

A sweet tasting water spirit, the suiko tempts children to drink it and then possesses their bodies from the inside. Suiko are as mutable as liquid, and can transform into clouds or mist. But they share the same weakness of all liquids—suiko can be frozen solid. The best way to trap a suiko is inside a clay jar, where it will pass the ages waiting for someone foolish enough to crack the seal and take a sip.

KYUKETSU-KI

Growing deep under the Earth's surface, the vast, blood sucking tree called the kyuketsu-ki sends its spores to the surface to plant seeds in human bodies and feed off their blood. It has something in common with another bloodsucker—the kyuketsu-ki's name is a pun on the Japanese word for vampire. The kyuketsu-ki is originally misidentified as a nobiagari, a type of yokai that stretches when you look at it, but Kitaro soon discovers the truth.

KONNAKI JIJI

The body of a baby. The face of an old man. Konnaki Jiji is one of Kitaro's most bizarre looking allies. And one of the most dangerous. This yokai from Tokushima prefecture hides his withered face and cries like a lost, innocent baby. When a good Samaritan (or a bad guy!) picks him up, he increases his weight to up to two tons, crushing the poor soul with the weight of a boulder. If you see a wailing baby where it shouldn't be, think twice before lending a hand! Or at least check its face to ensure an old man isn't staring back at you.

ITTAMOMEN

This yokai from Kagoshima prefecture is a friend of the wind who flies freely through the air. Its favorite attack is to swoop down, wrap around the necks of enemies, and choke their life out. Watch out for that wisp of white! But Ittamomen is not entirely sinister—it's always there when Kitaro and his gang needs a ride. Ittamomen's body is a single strip of cotton and impervious to most harm. In all the world it fears only fire and scissors.

SUNAKAKE BABA

Deep in the woods of Nara prefecture, the yokai Sunakake Baba lurks to fling sand from her hair on unwitting passers-by. Why does she do this? No one knows. The ways of the yokai are dark and mysterious. Sunakake Baba does more than just irritate people by throwing sand on them. She is one of Kitaro's staunchest allies, and plays a special role in his life. She is the landlord of the Yokai Apartments where Kitaro lives with his father, Medama Oyaji.

WITCH

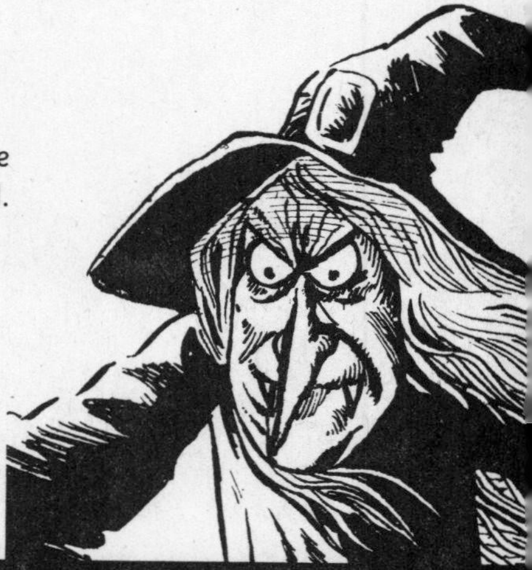

The mistress of maleficium, this is a traditional witch of the oldest school—flying broomstick, pointed hat, warts and all. She fights on the side of the Western yokai.

NURIKABE

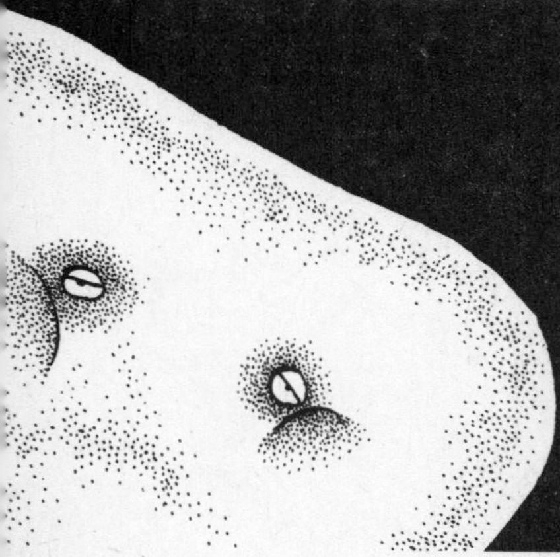

If you are wandering the streets at night, and suddenly find a wall in front of you that wasn't there before—a wall you can't seem to walk around no matter how far you go—you have probably just encountered the yokai Nurikabe. Hailing from Fukuoka prefecture, Nurikabe doesn't say much but is one of Kitaro's biggest supporters. Kitaro brings him in whenever there is sizable work to be done. Nurikabe is both strong and flexible. He looks like rock, but he's actually made of blacktop tar.

DRACULA

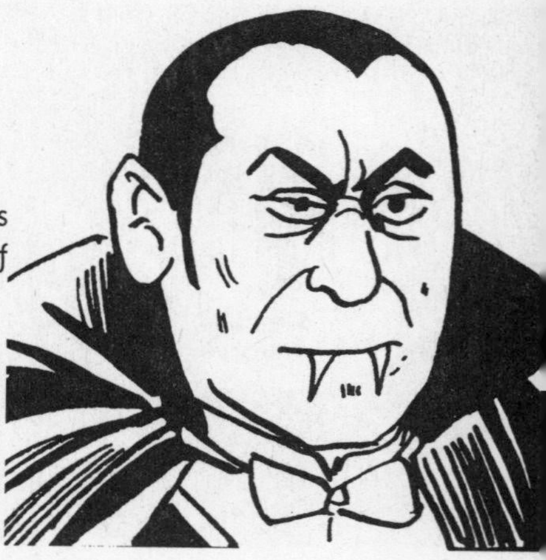

A monster that needs no introduction, this is the famous Transylvanian Count Dracula himself. A bloodsucker of high pedigree.

WEREWOLF

Widespread in European folklore, the werewolf transforms during a full moon to feast on human flesh. Although this werewolf seems more comfortable in a suit and tie than romping through the wilderness.

FRANKENSTEIN'S MONSTER

One of the most famous monsters in the world, but he was never given a name. The Monster was stitched together from corpses by Victor Frankenstein, and then brought to life through a mysterious process.

THE BACKBEARD

An American yokai, Backbeard is a giant eye with a body formed from shadow and smog. His massive bulk and clutching tendrils are only part of his horror. Do not look Backbeard in the eye—he can cause vertigo with a glance. Backbeard is the leader of the Western yokai, and one of Kitaro's most powerful enemies.

ZEUGLODON

With the head of a whale, and the body of a yeti, Zeuglodon (also known as the South Sea Monster) is a legendary monster from New Guinea. Like many mythical yokai, the Zeuglodon's blood is said to grant immortality. However, that immortality comes at a price.

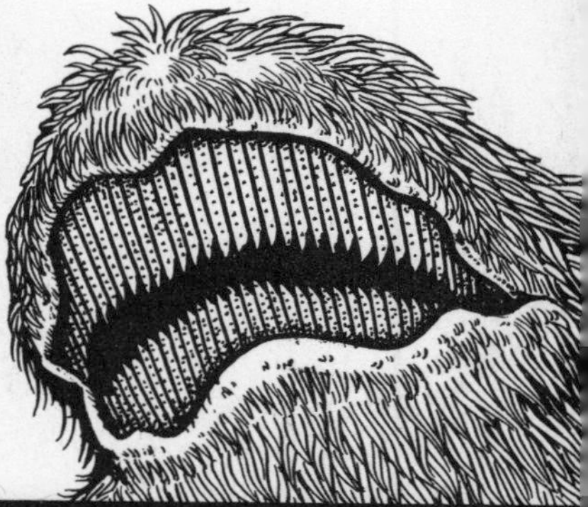

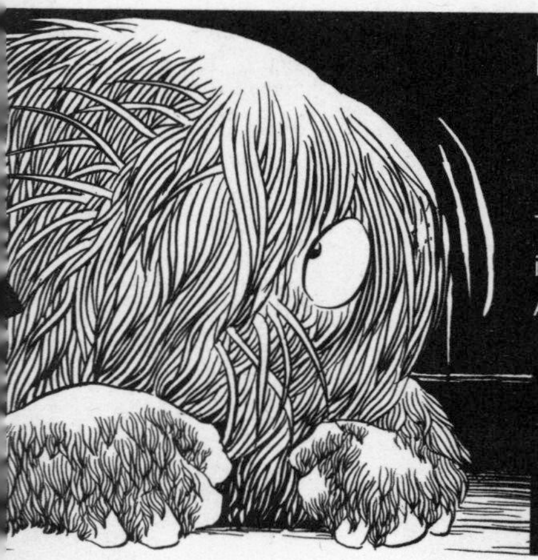

KAIJU KITARO

The blood of the Zeuglodon did not turn Kitaro immortal, just into a brainless, giant monster bent on destroying Tokyo. Almost as good, right?

MECHA ZEUGLODON

In a country attacked by giant monsters as often as Japan, it only makes good sense to build a giant robot for defense. The remote-controlled Mecha Zeuglodon tackles Kaiju Kitaro in one of the first Giant Robot vs. Monster battles in history.

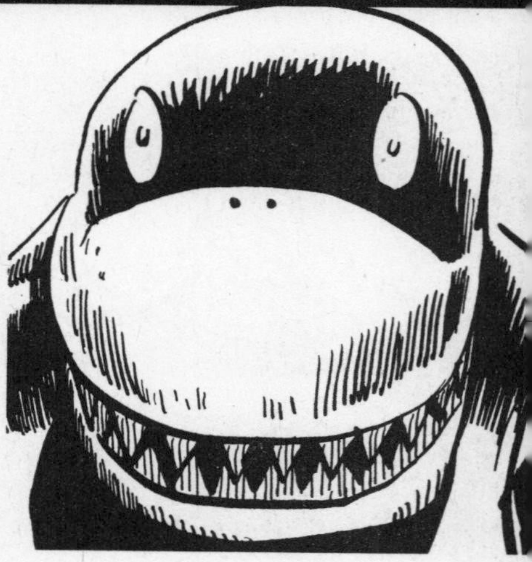

BRIGADOON EFFECT

Named after a folkloric Scottish village that appears for only one day every hundred years, the Brigadoon Effect refers to any location that is unstuck in time.

OBAKE DARUMA

This yokai looks like a traditional roly-poly Daruma doll that sprouted arms and legs, but that is where the resemblance ends. Instead of a wise sage of endurance, the Obake Daruma lives in the hidden 4th floor of buildings and solves problems only a yokai can handle. He does not cause too much trouble, but if you cross him he has a secret attack—a bellyful of little buddies, made from his own organs.

TANTANBO

This giant head is a dangerous cousin of the Tokushima prefecture yokai Okamuro. Whereas Okamuro is content just to poke out of doors and surprise people, Tantanbo is more ambitious. He wants to put his giant mouth to good use. Tantanbo may be just a head, but he has a variety of weapons at his disposal. From his missile spit to his flash beam eyes, Tantanbo is a force to be reckoned with.

FUTAKUCHI ONNA

The Futakuchi Onna has two mouths, and both of them are hungry. While she may look dainty and sweet from the front, hidden behind her luxurious hair is a second gaping maw ready to swallow you whole. Her reach never exceeds her grasp—her serpent-like hair can stretch to over 650 feet and snatch things to feed her ravenous hunger.

KAMAITACHI

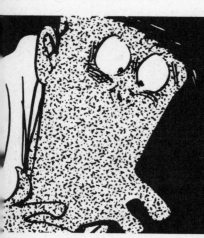

Most commonly depicted as a trio of weasels, this Kamaitachi is just one guy but with an awfully big mouth. The master of the whirlwind, when Kamaitachi puts his lips together to blow it is time for Kitaro to take a spin. The Kamaitachi traditional attack hits you three times in an instant—first knocking you down, then cutting you, then healing you—leaving you undamaged but in terrible pain.

KAGAMI JIJI

Born of ancient temple mirrors that have been abandoned and forgotten, the Kagami Jiji knows the secrets of the land beyond the reflecting glass. Lonely and lustful, he kidnaps pretty, young girls and takes them into his mirror world. The old man of the mirror has no true form, but his soul is tied to the mirror that gave him birth. Shatter the mirror and his captives go free.

This book is presented in the traditional Japanese manner and is meant to be read from right to left. The cover at the opposite end is considered the front of the book.

To begin reading, please flip over and start at the other end, making your way "backward" through the book, starting at the top right corner and reading the panels (and the word balloons) from right to left. Continue on to the next row and repeat.